THE JOY OF THOSE W
THE TEMPLE OF TH

Cry out with jóy to
Sérve the Lórd with
Come befóre him, sí

Know that hé, the Lórd, is God.†
He máde us, we belóng to hím,*
we are his péople, the shéep of his flóck.

Gó within his gátes, giving thánks.†
Enter his córts with sóngs of práise.*
Give thánks to him and bléss his náme.

Indéed, how góod is the Lórd,†
etérnal his mérciful lóve.*
He is fáithful from áge to áge.

Alternative Invitatory Psalm

ALL THE PEOPLES WILL GIVE
PRAISE TO THE LORD   PSALM 66(67)

O Gód, be grácious and bléss us*
and let your fáce shed its líght upón us.
So will your wáys be knówn upón éarth*
and all nátions learn your sáving hélp.

Let the péoples práise you, O Gód;*
let áll the péoples práise you.

Let the nátions be glád and exúlt*
for you rúle the wórld with jústice.
With fáirness you rúle the péoples,*
you guíde the nátions on éarth.

Let the péoples práise you, O Gód;*
let áll the péoples práise you.

The éarth has yíelded its frúit*
for Gód, our Gód, has bléssed us.

May Gód still gíve us his bléssing*
till the énds of the éarth revére him.

Let the péoples práise you, O Gód;*
let áll the péoples práise you.

Alternative Invitatory Psalm

The Lórd's is the éarth and its fúlness,*
the wórld and áll its péoples.
It is hé who sét it on the séas;*
on the wáters he máde it fírm.

Who shall clímb the móuntain of the Lórd?*
Who shall stánd in his hóly pláce?
The mán with clean hánds and pure héart,†
who desíres not wórthless thíngs,*
who has not swórn so as to decéive his néighbour.

He shall recéive bléssings from the Lórd*
and rewárd from the Gód who sáves him.
Súch are the mén who séek him,*
seek the fáce of the Gód of Jácob.

O gátes, lift hígh your héads;†
grow hígher, áncient dóors.*
Let him énter, the kíng of glóry!

Whó is the kíng of glóry?†
The Lórd, the míghty, the váliant,*
the Lórd, the váliant in wár.

O gátes, lift hígh your héads;†
grow hígher, áncient dóors.*
Let him énter, the kíng of glóry!

Who is hé, the kíng of glóry?†
Hé, the Lórd of ármies,*
hé is the kíng of glóry.

MORNING AND
EVENING PRAYER

Morning and Evening Prayer

with Night Prayer

from
The Divine Office

COLLINS   E. J. DWYER   TALBOT

LONDON · GLASGOW   SYDNEY   DUBLIN

Taken from *The Divine Office*, a translation of *Liturgia Horarum*, approved by the Episcopal Conferences of Australia, England and Wales, Ireland, Scotland.

Also approved for use in Gambia, Ghana, India, Kenya, Liberia, Malaysia and Singapore, New Zealand, Nigeria, Zimbabwe, Sierra Leone, Tanzania, Uganda.

Cum originali concordat: John P Dewis
Imprimatur: David Norris
Westminster, 11 May 1976
First printed 1976
Twelfth printing 1993

ISBN 0 00 599565 5
Set in Times Roman 327
Printed in Great Britain by
HarperCollins Manufacturing, Glasgow

CONTENTS

CONTENTS

INTRODUCTION

The New Testament leaves us in no doubt that we should pray regularly. Our Lord taught us by word and example that we should pray continually and never lose heart (Lk 18:1). St Paul and the other writers of the New Testament re-echo Our Lord's teaching that we must 'pray constantly' (Eph 6:18; 1 Thess 5:16).

For this reason the public and communal prayer of the People of God has always been considered among the first duties of the Church. The writer of the Acts of the Apostles tells us that from the very beginning the baptized 'remained faithful to the teaching of the apostles, to the brotherhood, to the breaking of bread and to the prayers' (Acts 2:42). Many times in the Acts of the Apostles and in the Letters of the Apostles we are provided with a picture of the Christian community praying together.

In the course of time a form of worship developed within the local churches under the leadership of the priest as a necessary complement to the sacrifice of the Eucharist, the highest act of worship of God, so that this worship was extended into the different hours of the day. Over the course of many centuries a book of the Divine Office evolved in which the traditional elements of this Christian Prayer were carefully arranged and organized: psalms, hymns and spiritual songs, reflective reading of the Word of God, as well as prayers and intercessions for the needs of the Church and the World. Through the ages all these have made up that Prayer of Christians which is the worship of God throughout the day, the sanctification of the *whole* day, in fact the Liturgy of the Hours. It is that title, *The Liturgy of the Hours,* that has been given to the Divine Office, revised and renewed according to the directives given by the pope together with the whole college of bishops at the Second Vatican Council (1962-5).

In the first two sessions of the Council, major decisions were taken about the whole work of restoring and renewing the worship of the Church. *The Constitution on the Sacred Liturgy* dealt with the matter at a length and in a depth which had never been attempted before in the history of the Church. But, in addition to setting down the principles which would govern the revision of the rites for the

Mass and the Sacraments, the Fathers of the Council also provided a programme for the renewal of the Church's daily prayer. The work was begun almost immediately. It took seven years to complete, and the renewed Divine Office, *The Liturgy of the Hours*, was published in Latin in 1971.

The fact that the Divine Office has been renewed prompts us to ask why it needed renewing. As time went on it had come less and less to fulfil the needs of the vast majority of the ordinary faithful of the Church. It was celebrated in a language they did not understand. It became the preserve of the monastic communities, of the clergy and the religious. It tended to be seen as the purely external worship of the Church and was not understood as expressing the interior worship of the minds and hearts of those who offered it on behalf of the Church. Gradually it became less and less suited to the needs of those who recited it privately, and many who did recite it came to regard it as a burdensome obligation rather than a real nourishment to spiritual growth.

The Fathers of the Council had realized all this when they set down the programme of renewal in 1963. When this work of renewal was almost complete, Pope Paul VI announced the forthcoming publication of the *Liturgia Horarum* (The Liturgy of the Hours) in an Apostolic Constitution, *Laudis canticum* (1 November 1970). In this document the Holy Father made clear that the first aim of the renewal was to ensure that the Divine Office should once again become the prayer of the *whole* church, not merely the prayer of clergy and religious. He went on to outline the way in which the day is to be sanctified: principally by prayer in the Morning and in the Evening, but also by prayer at some time during the day and again just before retiring to bed. In addition, he promised an 'Office of Readings', which would replace Matins, and which is essentially a period for reading and reflecting upon sacred scripture and upon the writings of the Church's greatest spiritual authors.

In order to ensure that *The Liturgy of the Hours* does become once more the prayer of the *whole* Church, in the same Apostolic Constitution Pope Paul laid the responsibility upon local Bishops' Conferences to publish vernacular editions of the Liturgy of the Hours. And so it was in 1971, when representatives of all the Bishops' Conferences were meeting in Synod in Rome, that the

Presidents of the Bishops' Conferences of Australia, England and Wales, and Ireland agreed to appoint a group of people which would co-ordinate the mammoth task of translating and compiling necessary to produce in the English language an edition of the Liturgy of the Hours.

This task was completed in two years and the work was published in three volumes early in 1974, with the title *The Divine Office*. This complete revision of the official prayer of the Church, which takes into account both the oldest traditions of the Church as well as the needs of modern life, was offered to the Catholics of many countries where English is spoken. As Pope Paul VI himself said in the Apostolic Constitution, this was done in the hope that it 'will renew and vivify all Christian prayer and serve to nourish the spiritual life of the People of God'.

The content of Morning and Evening Prayer

Morning and Evening Prayer is a short edition of *The Divine Office*. It contains the kernel of *The Divine Office*. The Fathers of the Council taught us that 'by the venerable tradition of the universal Church, Lauds as morning prayer and Vespers as evening prayer are the two hinges on which the daily office turns; hence they are to be considered as the chief hours and are to be celebrated as such' (*Constitution on the Sacred Liturgy, n.89*). Those who are not able to recite the whole of the Liturgy of the Hours each day, but who wish nonetheless to be united with the whole Church in prayer, can by using this book share at least in the principal Hours of prayer: in the morning and in the evening.

Morning and Evening Prayer for every day of the year, exactly as it is in the complete edition of the Liturgy of the Hours, *The Divine Office*, is available in this book. All the rich variety of texts which occur in the seasons of the Church's year and on the feasts of Our Lord, Our Lady and the saints, is provided without omission. Also included is the Church's own prayer at the end of the day: Night Prayer (Compline), arranged for each day of the week. Those who wish to do so, especially those who have been unable to celebrate any part of the Church's prayer during the day, will welcome the opportunity to unite themselves in prayer with the whole Church at least before retiring to bed.

The purpose of this book

This book is intended primarily for lay people, for those who are preparing for the priesthood and for those religious who are not bound by their rule of life to celebrate the Liturgy of the Hours in its entirety every day. It can be used at the public celebration of Morning, Evening and Night Prayer whenever this takes place in cathedral or parish churches. It can be used for the celebration of these same Hours in common whenever a group is gathered together for a spiritual purpose. It can be used also for the private recitation of these Hours by those who wish to be united in prayer with the whole Church.

Consequently, this book will be most useful in cathedral and parish churches. It will be of special value in communities of religious, in seminaries and in retreat houses. It will become especially dear to all who wish to be united in spirit with the Church at prayer, and who desire, even though they belong to no group or community of Christians, to praise and pray with disciplined regularity. In due time it should become the book which every Catholic society and sodality uses for prayer in common. The General Instruction on the Liturgy of the Hours tells us that 'wherever groups of the laity are gathered and whatever the purpose which has brought them together, such as prayer or the apostolate, they are encouraged to recite the Church's Office by celebrating part of the Liturgy of the Hours' (n.27). The purpose of this book is to make possible that high ideal.

Furthermore, *The Divine Office*, which is the complete edition of the Liturgy of the Hours, *Daily Prayer*, which contains all the day Hours, and this volume, *Morning and Evening Prayer*, form a family of books. All those who use these books, whether priests, religious or laity, will always be able to celebrate Morning, Evening and Night Prayer together. By these means there will resound in one voice throughout the Church in these countries a magnificent hymn of praise to God. 'Let it be united to that hymn of praise sung in the courts of heaven by the angels and saints. May the days of our earthly exile be filled more and more with that praise which throughout the ages is given to the One seated on the throne and to the Lamb' (*Apostolic Constitution, Laudis canticum*).

THE SANCTIFICATION OF THE DAY

The structure of the Celebration

1 The essential structure of each Hour of this Liturgy, whether it is celebrated in common or in private, is a dialogue between God and man. The fundamental pattern of Christian Prayer—Reading from Sacred Scripture, Response, Prayer—is found in each of the Hours. The Word of God always has pride of place; it is the central and most important element of each Hour. We prepare ourselves to listen to the Word by singing or at least reciting a hymn and by chanting or reciting psalms. The Reading is followed by meditative responses. And we conclude by praying for our own needs as well as for the needs of the whole Church and the world. By means of this pattern of prayer, which has behind it centuries of Christian tradition, we can seek God and penetrate ever more deeply into the mystery of Christ.

Celebration in common

2 Whenever the Liturgy of the Hours is celebrated in common, it is shown more clearly to be the Prayer of the Church. The active participation of everyone is encouraged by means of acclamations, dialogues, alternating psalmody and other things of the same kind. Whenever a communal celebration can take place with the active participation of the faithful, this is to be preferred to individual and quasi-private celebration. Obviously, when the Office is celebrated publicly or in common, it should be sung whenever possible.

The Introduction to the Office each day

3 The whole Office is normally begun with an invitatory. This consists in the verse *Lord, open our lips: And we shall praise your name,* and Psalm 94 with its antiphon. This invitatory verse and psalm daily invite the faithful to sing the praises of God, hear his voice and look forward to the 'Rest of the Lord'.[1]

If desired, Ps 99, Ps 66 or Ps 23 may be used in place of Ps 94.

As indicated elsewhere, it is fitting that the invitatory psalm be said in responsorial fashion, that is, with its antiphon said first, repeated, and taken up again after each verse of the psalm.

[1] Cf Heb 3:7—4:16.

4 The Invitatory should begin the sequence of prayer each day. Thus, it can be sung or recited before Morning Prayer.

5 The way of varying the Invitatory antiphon, according to the different liturgical days, is indicated in its proper place.

Morning Prayer (Lauds) and Evening Prayer (Vespers)

6 Morning Prayer is designed and structured to sanctify the morning, as is clear from many of its parts. St Basil the Great excellently described its character in these words: 'Morning Prayer consecrates to God the first movements of our minds and hearts; no other care should engage us before we have been moved with the thought of God, as it is written, "I thought of God and sighed" (Ps 76:4), nor should the body undertake any work before we have done what is said, "I say this prayer to you, Lord, for at daybreak you listen for my voice; and at dawn I hold myself in readiness for you, I watch for you" (Ps 5:4-5).'[2]

This Hour, recited as the light of a new day dawns, recalls the resurrection of the Lord Jesus, the true light, enlightening every man (cf John 1:9), 'the Sun of Justice' (Malachi 4:2), 'arising on high' (Luke 1:78). Thus the remark of Saint Cyprian may be well understood: 'We should pray in the morning to celebrate the resurrection of the Lord with morning prayer.'[3]

7 Evening Prayer is celebrated when the day is drawing to a close, so that 'we may give thanks for what has been given us during the day, or for the things we have done well during it'.[4] We also call to mind our redemption, through the prayer we offer 'like incense in the sight of the Lord', and in which 'the raising up of our hands' becomes 'an evening sacrifice'.[5] This 'evening sacrifice' 'may be more fully understood as that true evening sacrifice which was given in the evening by our Lord and Saviour when he instituted the most holy mysteries of the Church at supper with his apostles; or which on the following day he offered for all time to his Father by the raising up of his hands for the salvation of the whole world.'[6] Placing

[2]St Basil the Great, *Regulae fusius tractatae, Resp.* 37, 3:PG 31, 1014.
[3]St Cyprian, *De oratione dominica*, 35: PL 4, 561.
[4]St Basil the Great, *op cit*, PG 31, 1015.
[5]Cf Ps 140:2.
[6]Cassian, *De institutione coenob.*, lib 3, c. 3: PL 49, 124, 125.

our hope in that Sun which never sets, 'we pray and beg that his light may shine on us again; we pray that Christ may come bringing the grace of eternal light'.[7] Finally, in this Hour, we join with the Eastern Churches and invoke 'blessed Jesus Christ, the Light of our Heavenly Father's sacred and eternal glory; as the sun sets we behold the evening light and sing to God, Father, Son and Holy Spirit . . .'

8 In the prayer of the Christian community, Morning Prayer and Evening Prayer are of the highest importance. Their public and common celebration should be encouraged especially among those who lead a common life. The recitation of these prayers is also recommended for the individual faithful who are not able to participate in a common celebration.

9 Morning Prayer and Evening Prayer begin with the introductory verse *O God, come to our aid: O Lord, make haste to help us.* The *Glory be to the Father* with *Alleluia* follows. The *Alleluia* is omitted during Lent. This form of introduction is not used when the invitatory immediately precedes Lauds.

10 A suitable hymn is then sung or said. The hymn should be chosen so as to express the particular characteristic of each Hour or feast. It makes an easy and pleasant opening to the prayer, especially in celebrations in common.

11 The psalmody follows the hymn, in accordance with the norms of nn.55-7 below.

The psalmody of Morning Prayer consists of one morning psalm, followed by an Old Testament canticle, and a second psalm which traditionally is one of praise.

The psalmody of Evening Prayer consists of two psalms or two sections of longer psalms, well suited to the Hour and to celebration with the people, followed by a canticle from the Epistles or Revelation.

12 There is a short or long reading after the psalmody.

13 A short reading is given according to the liturgical day, season or feast. It is to be read and heard as the true proclamation of the

[7] St Cyprian, *De oratione dominica*, 35: PL 4, 560.

xvi

STRUCTURE OF
MORNING AND EVENING PRAYER

MORNING PRAYER	EVENING PRAYER
INTRODUCTION	
℣ Lord, open our lips.	℣ O God, come to our aid.
℟ And we shall praise your name.	℟ O Lord, make haste to
[Invitatory Psalm (Pss 94, 99, 66	help us
or 23) with its antiphon]	
HYMN	
PSALMODY	
Antiphon 1	Antiphon 1
A 'morning' psalm	A psalm
Antiphon repeated	Antiphon repeated
(*Silent Prayer*)	(*Silent Prayer*)
Antiphon 2	Antiphon 2
Old Testament canticle	A psalm
Antiphon repeated	Antiphon repeated
(*Silent Prayer*)	(*Silent Prayer*)
Antiphon 3	Antiphon 3
A psalm of praise	New Testament canticle
Antiphon repeated	Antiphon repeated
(*Silent Prayer*)	(*Silent prayer*)
SCRIPTURE READING	
(*Silent Prayer*)	
SHORT RESPONSORY	
GOSPEL CANTICLE	
Benedictus antiphon	Magnificat antiphon
Canticle of Zachariah	Canticle of Mary
Antiphon repeated	Antiphon repeated
INTERCESSIONS	
Invocations of praise	Prayers of intercession
	(*final prayer always for the faithful departed*)
(*Silent Prayer*)	
The Lord's Prayer	
CONCLUDING PRAYER	
BLESSING	

word of God; it emphasizes certain short passages which may receive less attention in the continuous reading of the scriptures.

The short readings vary according to the daily arrangement of the psalmody.

14 A long scripture reading may be chosen, especially for celebrations with the people. It may be taken from the passage read at Mass or from the Office of Readings in *The Divine Office*, and especially from those texts of scripture left unread for various reasons.

15 In celebrations with the people, a brief homily may be added to explain the reading.

16 After the reading or homily, there may be a silent pause.

17 In response to the word of God, there may be a responsorial song, or short responsory. This may be omitted if so desired.

Other songs of the same type and for the same purpose may replace the responsory, provided that these are duly approved by the Episcopal Conference.

18 A Gospel canticle is then solemnly recited with its antiphon; at Morning Prayer it is the *Benedictus*, the Canticle of Zechariah; at Evening Prayer the *Magnificat*, the Canticle of the Blessed Virgin Mary. These canticles express praise and thanksgiving for our redemption and have been in popular use for centuries in the Roman Church. The antiphons for the *Benedictus* and the *Magnificat* vary according to the liturgical day, season or feast.

19 After the canticle: at Morning Prayer, intercessions consecrate the day and its work to God; at Evening Prayer there are petitions (cf. nn.81–99).

20 After the intercessions or petitions, the Lord's Prayer is said by all.

21 A concluding prayer follows immediately: for ordinary ferial days it is found in the psalter; for other days in the Proper.

22 If a priest or deacon is present, he dismisses the people as at Mass with the greeting *The Lord be with you*, and a blessing· then follows the invitation *Go in the peace of Christ: Thanks be to God.* Otherwise the celebration is concluded with *The Lord bless us*, etc.

Night Prayer (Compline)

23 Night Prayer (Compline) is the final prayer of the day to be said before going to bed, even if this is after midnight.

STRUCTURE OF NIGHT PRAYER

INTRODUCTION

℣ O God, come to our aid
℟ O Lord, make haste to help us.
(*Examination of conscience   Act of Repentance*)

HYMN

PSALMODY
Antiphon
Psalm
Antiphon

SCRIPTURE READING
(*Silent Prayer*)

SHORT RESPONSORY

GOSPEL CANTICLE
Antiphon
Canticle of Simeon
Antiphon repeated

CONCLUDING PRAYER

BLESSING

ANTHEM TO THE BLESSED VIRGIN

24   Night Prayer, like Morning and Evening Prayer, is begun with the verse *O God, come to our aid*, with the *Glory be to the Father*, and (outside of Lent) the *Alleluia*.

25   It is praiseworthy to follow the introductory verse with an examination of conscience. In common recitation it is made in silence or inserted into one of the penitential acts given in the Roman Missal.

26   A suitable hymn is then sung or said.

27   The psalmody: after Evening Prayer I of Sundays (i.e. on Saturday evening)—Ps 4 and Ps 133; after Evening Prayer II of Sundays (i.e. on Sunday evening)—Ps 90.
    Psalms which evoke confidence in God are chosen for the other days. It is always permissible to substitute the Sunday psalms on weekdays; this is particularly helpful for those who may want to recite Compline from memory.

28   After the psalmody, there is a short reading and then the responsory *Into your hands*. Then follows the Gospel canticle with its antiphon—the culmination of the whole Hour.

29   The concluding prayer is said as in the Psalter.

30   After the prayer, the blessing *The Lord grant us a quiet night* is said even in individual recitation.

31   Finally one of the antiphons of the Blessed Virgin Mary is said. In Eastertide this is always the *Regina caeli* (*Joy fill your heart, O Queen most high*). In addition to the antiphons given in *The Divine Office*, others may be approved by the Episcopal Conference.

How Morning or Evening Prayer can be joined with Mass
32   In special cases, if the circumstances require it, Morning or Evening Prayer celebrated in public or in common may be joined more closely with Mass, provided that they are both of the same Office. This should be done in accordance with the norms which follow. Care should be taken to ensure that this is not pastorally harmful, especially on Sundays.

33   When Morning Prayer, celebrated in choir or in common, immediately precedes Mass, the liturgical function may begin either

with the introductory verse and hymn of Morning Prayer (especially on ferial days), or with the entrance song and procession, and the celebrant's greeting (especially on festive days). When one of these introductory forms is used, the other is omitted.

The psalmody of Morning Prayer is said in the usual way as far as the short reading exclusively. The penitential act of the Mass is omitted, as also the *Kyrie*, if so desired; the *Gloria in excelsis* is then said, if the rubrics require it, and the celebrant says the opening prayer of the Mass. The Liturgy of the Word follows in the usual way.

The Prayer of the Faithful is said at the normal time and in the form customary at Mass. During the morning Mass of a ferial day, however, the intercessions of Morning Prayer may replace the Prayer of the Faithful.

After the communion song, the *Benedictus* is sung with its antiphon, followed by the postcommunion prayer and the remainder of Mass is as normal.

34 Evening Prayer celebrated immediately before Mass is joined with it in the same way as Morning Prayer. First Evening Prayer of solemnities, Sundays and feasts of our Lord occurring on Sundays may not be celebrated until after the Mass of the previous day or the Saturday.

35 When Evening Prayer follows Mass, the Mass is celebrated in the usual way as far as the postcommunion prayer inclusively.

The psalmody begins without an introductory verse immediately after the postcommunion prayer. The *Magnificat* with its antiphon follows immediately after the psalmody—there is no reading, no intercessions and no Lord's Prayer—and then comes the concluding prayer and the blessing of the people.

THE VARIOUS PARTS OF THE LITURGY OF THE HOURS

The Psalms and their Close Relationship with Christian Prayer
36 In the Liturgy of the Hours, the Church for the most part prays with those beautiful songs composed under the inspiration of the Spirit of God by the sacred authors of the Old Testament. From the

beginning they have had the power to raise men's minds to God, to evoke in them holy and wholesome thoughts, to help them to give thanks in time of favour, and to bring consolation and constancy in adversity.

37   The psalms offer only a foretaste of the fulness of time revealed in Christ our Lord and from which the prayer of the Church receives its strength; therefore it is not surprising if, even though all Christians agree in having the highest regard for the psalms, difficulty sometimes arises when a person tries to make these songs his own in prayer.

38   The Holy Spirit, who inspired the psalmists, is always present with his grace to those believing Christians who with good intention sing and recite these songs. It is necessary, however, for each according to his powers, to have 'more intensive biblical instruction, especially with regard to the psalms',[8] and be led to see how and in what way he may be able to recite and pray the psalms properly.

39   The psalms are not readings nor were they specifically composed as prayers, but as poems of praise. Though sometimes they may be proclaimed like a reading, nevertheless, because of their literary character, they are rightly called in Hebrew *Tehillim*, that is, 'songs of praise', and in Greek *Psalmoi*, 'songs to be sung to the sound of the harp'. In all the psalms there is a certain musical quality which determines the correct way of praying them. Therefore, though a psalm may be recited without being sung even by an individual in silence, its musical character should not be overlooked. Whilst certainly offering a text to our mind, the psalm is more concerned with moving the spirits of those singing and listening, and indeed of those accompanying it with music.

40   Whoever sings the psalms properly, meditating as he passes from verse to verse, is always prepared to respond in his heart to the movements of that Spirit who inspired the psalmists and is present to devout men and women ready to accept his grace. Thus the psalmody, though it commands the reverence due to the majesty of God, should be conducted in joy and a spirit of charity, as befits

[8]Second Vatican Council, *Const. on Sacred Liturgy, Sacrosanctum Concilium*, n.90.

the freedom of the children of God, and is in harmony with divinely inspired poetry and song.

41 Often enough the words of the psalm help us to pray easily and fervently: when they express thanksgiving or joyfully bless God, or when they present us with a prayer from the depths of sorrow. On the other hand, especially if the psalm is not addressed to God, we may sometimes find ourselves in difficulties. Because the psalmist is a poet, he often speaks to the people, recalling, for example, the history of Israel; sometimes he addresses others, including those created things which lack the use of reason. He may sometimes write as if God himself and men, and even, as in Ps 2, the enemies of God, are talking to one another. Clearly a psalm has not the same quality of prayer that a prayer or collect composed by the Church may possess. Moreover, since the psalms have a musical and poetic character, they are not necessarily addressed to God, but may be sung before God; St Benedict remarked: 'Let us consider what we should be in the sight of God and angels; we should stand to sing psalms in such a way that our mind is in accord with our voice.'[9]

42 Whoever sings a psalm opens his heart to those emotions which inspired the psalm, each according to its literary type, whether it be a psalm of lament, confidence, thanksgiving or any other type designated by exegetes.

43 The person praying the psalms is conscious of their importance for Christian living by keeping to their literal meaning.

Each psalm was composed in particular circumstances, suggested by the titles which head the psalms in the Hebrew Psalter. But whatever may be said of its historical origin, each psalm has a literal meaning which even in our times cannot be neglected. Though these songs originated many centuries ago in a semitic culture, they express the pain and hope, misery and confidence of men of any age and land, and especially sing of faith in God, his revelation and his redemption.

44 Whoever prays the psalms in the Liturgy of the Hours does not say them in his own name so much as in the name of the whole body of Christ, in fact in the person of Christ himself. If he keeps this in

[9] St Benedict, *Regula monasteriorum*, c.19.

mind, difficulties disappear, even if while saying the psalms his own feelings differ from those expressed by the psalmist: for example, if we find ourselves saying a psalm of jubilation, while we are worried or sad, or saying a psalm of lament when in fact we feel in good spirits. This may easily be avoided in merely private prayer, when a psalm can be chosen to suit our mood. In the Divine Office, however, even someone saying the Hour alone is not praying the psalms privately but recites them in the name of the Church and according to the sequence given in her public prayer. Whoever says them in the name of the Church can always find a reason for joy or sorrow, finding applicable to himself the words of the apostle: 'Rejoice with those who rejoice and be sad with those in sorrow' (Rom 12:15); human weakness and selfishness is thus healed by charity so that the mind and heart may harmonize with the voice.[10]

45   Whoever says the psalms in the name of the Church should pay attention to the full meaning of the psalms, especially that messianic understanding which led the Church to adopt the psalter. The messianic meaning is made completely manifest in the New Testament; it is in fact declared by Christ our Lord himself when he said to the apostles: 'Everything written about me in the Law of Moses, in the prophets and in the psalms, has to be fulfilled' (Luke 24:44). The most notable example of this is the dialogue, in Matthew, about the Messiah; David's Son and Lord is understood, in Ps 109, of the Messiah.

Following this path, the Fathers took the whole psalter and explained it as a prophecy about Christ and his Church; and for this same reason psalms were chosen for the sacred liturgy. Even if certain artificial interpretations were sometimes accepted, generally both the Fathers and the liturgy rightly heard in the psalms Christ calling out to his Father, or the Father speaking to the Son; they even recognized in them the voice of the Church, the apostles and the martyrs. This method of interpretation also flourished in the Middle Ages; in many manuscripts of the psalter written at that time, the christological meaning is explained after the heading of each psalm. This christological interpretation in no way refers only to those psalms which are considered messianic but also extends to

[10]*Ibid.*

many in which without doubt there are mere appropriations. Such appropriations, however, have been commended by the tradition of the Church.

Especially in the psalmody of festive days, the psalms are chosen for some christological reason; very often antiphons taken from the psalms themselves are offered to illustrate this.

The Antiphons and Other Parts which Help in Praying the Psalms
46 In the Latin tradition aids are given which greatly assist us to sing the psalms and to turn them into Christian Prayer: namely, the headings, and especially the antiphons.

47 In the psalter of the Liturgy of the Hours, a heading is put before each psalm to indicate its meaning and importance in Christian life. These headings are given in *Morning and Evening Prayer* merely as an aid for the person saying the psalms. To promote prayer in the light of the new revelation, a phrase from the New Testament or Fathers is added as an invitation to pray in a Christian way.

48 Even when the Liturgy of the Hours is not sung, each psalm has its own antiphon which is also to be said in individual recitation. The antiphons help to illustrate the literary character of the psalm; turn the psalm into personal prayer; place in better light a phrase worthy of attention which may otherwise be missed; give special colour to a psalm in differing circumstances; while excluding arbitrary accommodations, help considerably in the typological and festive interpreting of the psalm; and can make more attractive and varied the recitation of the psalms.

49 The antiphons in the psalter may be repeated after each strophe of their psalm. On the ordinary Sundays and weekdays of the year, if the Office is not sung, the phrases attached to the psalms (from the New Testament or the Fathers) may be used instead of these antiphons, if desired (cf. n.47).

50 When a psalm is long it may be divided into several parts within one and the same Hour. Each part has its own antiphon for the sake of variety, especially in sung celebration. The antiphon also serves to highlight the riches of the psalms. However, one is allowed

to complete the psalm without interruption, using only the first antiphon.

51 Proper antiphons are given for each psalm at Morning Prayer and Evening Prayer: in the Easter Triduum, during the octaves of Easter and Christmas, on Sundays of Advent, Christmas, Lent and Eastertide, and also on the ferial days of Holy Week, Eastertide and December 17-24.

52 At Morning Prayer and Evening Prayer on solemnities, there are proper antiphons, or, if this is not the case, they are taken from the appropriate Common. On many of the feasts there are proper antiphons for Morning and Evening Prayer. In addition, some memorias of saints have proper antiphons.

53 The antiphons at the *Benedictus* and the *Magnificat*, in the Seasonal Office, are taken from the Proper of the Season if there are any, otherwise from the current psalter. On solemnities and feasts, they are taken from the Proper, otherwise from the Common. On memorias which do not have a proper antiphon, the antiphon may be said either from the Common or from the current ferial day.

54 In Eastertide, *Alleluia* is added to every antiphon, unless its addition clashes with the meaning of the antiphon.

The Way of Praying the Psalms
55 The psalms can be chanted or recited in various ways taking into account whether they are said by an individual or a group, or recited in a celebration with the people.

A way should be chosen to enable those who pray the psalms to appreciate more easily their spiritual and literary flavour. Psalms are not used just to make up a certain quantity of prayer; a consideration of variety and the character of each enters into their choice.

56 Psalms are sung or said straight through with alternate verses or strophes sung or recited by two choirs or two parts of the congregation, or in responsorial fashion—the ways tested by tradition and experience.

57 An antiphon is sung or said at the beginning of each psalm (cf.

nn.48-54). The psalm is concluded with *Glory be to the Father*.

Tradition has aptly employed this to attribute to the prayer of the Old Testament a quality of praise and a christological and trinitarian meaning. The antiphon may, if so desired, be repeated after the psalm.

The Way the Psalms are Distributed in the Office

58 The psalms are distributed over a four-week cycle, but the traditionally more important ones are repeated more frequently. Morning Prayer, Evening Prayer and Night Prayer have psalms corresponding with their respective Hour.

59 As Morning Prayer and Evening Prayer are designed for celebration with the people, the psalms more suitable for this purpose are chosen for these Hours.

60 At Night Prayer the norm of n.27 should be observed.

61 On Sundays psalms are chosen which traditionally express the paschal mystery. Penitential psalms or ones relating to the Passion are assigned to Fridays.

62 The psalter's four-week cycle is joined to the liturgical year in such a way that the First Sunday of Advent, the First ordinary Sunday of the year, the First Sunday of Lent and Easter Sunday begin the first week of the cycle. Remaining weeks of the cycle before these Sundays are omitted.

After Pentecost, since the cycle of the psalter follows the sequence of weeks, it is taken up from that week of the psalter which is indicated at the beginning of the respective week in the Proper of the Season. (*See Table on p xxviii.*)

63 At Morning Prayer on solemnities and feasts, the psalms and canticle of Sunday I of the psalter are used. At Evening Prayer I of solemnities, the psalms, following an old custom, are taken from the *Laudate* series. At Evening Prayer II of solemnities and at Evening Prayer of feasts, the psalms and canticle are proper.

64 In all other cases, the psalms are said from the current Psalter, unless there happen to be proper antiphons or proper psalms.

THE CYCLE OF THE FOUR WEEK PSALTER

Each year, begin using Psalter Week 1 on:

First Sunday of Advent
Monday after the Baptism of the Lord
First Sunday of Lent
Easter Sunday

Each year on Monday after Pentecost, examine this TABLE and begin using Psalter of the appropriate week as follows:

YEAR	PSALTER WEEK	YEAR	PSALTER WEEK	YEAR	PSALTER WEEK
1976	2	1984	2	1992	2
1977	1	1985	4	1993	1
1978	2	1986	3	1994	4
1979	1	1987	2	1995	1
1980	4	1988	4	1996	4
1981	2	1989	2	1997	3
1982	1	1990	1	1998	1
1983	4	1991	3	1999	4

The Canticles of the Old and New Testament

65   At Morning Prayer, it is customary to insert a canticle of the Old Testament between the first and second psalm. Besides the series found in ancient Roman tradition, and the second series introduced into the Breviary by Pope Pius X, many other canticles are added to the psalter from various books of the Old Testament, so that each ferial day of the four weeks has its own proper canticle; on Sundays, the two parts of the Canticle of the Three Children are used alternately.

66   At Evening Prayer, after the two psalms, a canticle from the Epistles or Revelation of the New Testament is inserted. There are

seven such canticles, one for each day of the week. On Sundays of Lent, instead of the Alleluia canticle from Revelation, a canticle from the First Letter of St Peter is said. On the Epiphany and on the feast of the Transfiguration, the canticle is from the First Letter to Timothy.

67 The Gospel canticles, the *Benedictus*, the *Magnificat* and the *Nunc dimittis*, should be accorded the same solemnity and dignity as is usual for the hearing of the Gospel.

68 The constant rule of tradition is retained in the arrangement of the psalmody and the readings: first the Old Testament, then the Apostles and finally the proclamation of the Gospel.

The Reading of Sacred Scripture

69 Following ancient tradition, sacred scripture is read publicly in the liturgy not only in the celebration of the Eucharist but also in the Divine Office. This liturgical reading of scripture is of the greatest importance for all Christians because it is offered by the Church herself and not by the decision or whim of a single individual. 'Within the cycle of a year' the mystery of Christ is unfolded by his Bride 'not only from his incarnation and birth until his ascension, but also as reflected in the day of Pentecost, and the expectation of a blessed, hoped-for return of the Lord'.[11] In liturgical celebrations prayer always accompanies the reading of sacred scripture. In this way the reading may bear greater fruit, and conversely prayer, especially through the psalms, may be more fully developed by the reading and encourage more intense devotion.

70 In the Liturgy of the Hours, there may be a longer or a shorter reading of sacred scripture.

71 A longer reading is optional for Morning Prayer and Evening Prayer. This has been mentioned above in n.14.

72 The importance of short readings or 'chapters' in the Liturgy of the Hours has been noted in n.13. They are selected to express briefly and succinctly a biblical phrase, theme or exhortation, and have been chosen with an eye to variety.

[11]Cf Second Vatican Council, *Const. on Sacred Liturgy, Sacrosanctum Concilium*, n.102.

73 A four-week cycle of short readings for the ordinary time of the year has been introduced into the psalter, so as to vary the reading every day for four weeks. For Advent, Christmas, Lent and Easter-tide, the variation is on a single-week basis. There are proper short readings for solemnities, feasts and certain memorias, and a single-week series for Night Prayer.

74 In the selection of short readings, the following have been kept in mind:
  a the Gospels have been excluded, as is traditional;
  b the character of Sunday, Friday and the Hours themselves has been taken into account;
  c the short readings at Evening Prayer are chosen from the New Testament, since they follow a New Testament canticle.

The Short Responsory

75 The Short Responsory at Morning, Evening and Night Prayer (about which see nn.17 and 28 above) is a reply to the reading. This brief response is a kind of acclamation, and enables the Word of God to penetrate more deeply into the mind and heart of the person reciting or listening.

The Hymns and other Non-Biblical Songs

76 Hymns have a place in the Office from very early times, a position they continue to retain.[12] Not only does their lyrical nature make them specially suited to the praise of God, but they constitute a popular part, since nearly always they point more immediately than the other parts of the Office to the individual characteristics of the Hours or of each feast. They help to move the people taking part and draw them into the celebration. Their literary beauty often increases their effectiveness. In the Office, the hymns are the principal poetic part composed by the Church.

77 The hymn is traditionally concluded by a doxology, which is usually addressed to the same divine person as the hymn itself.

78 For the sake of variety in the Office for the Ordinary time of the year, two series of hymns are provided for Morning and Evening

[12]Cf Second Vatican Council, *Const. on Sacred Liturgy, Sacrosanctum Concilium*, n.93.

Prayer; they have been arranged on alternate weeks. On Sundays of ordinary time two hymns have been provided: one more popular and the other with more literary content. For Night Prayer a different hymn is chosen for each night of the week.

79 Provided they suit the spirit of the Hour, season or feast, other hymns may be chosen, especially those approved for use in the Liturgy by the Episcopal Conference. However, popular songs which have no artistic merit are completely unworthy of the Liturgy and should not be permitted.

The Intercessions, the Lord's Prayer and the Concluding Prayer

a THE INTERCESSIONS OR PETITIONS AT MORNING AND EVENING PRAYER

80 The Liturgy of the Hours celebrates the praises of God. However, neither Jewish nor Christian tradition separates praise of God from prayer of petition, petition often being drawn out of praise. The apostle Paul advises that 'there should be prayers offered for everyone—petitions, intercessions and thanksgiving—and especially for kings and others in authority, so that we may be able to live religious and reverent lives in peace and quite. To do this is right, and will please God our Saviour: he wants everyone to be saved and reach full knowledge of the truth' (1 Timothy 2:1-4). This exhortation was frequently interpreted by the Fathers in the sense that intercessions should be made morning and evening.[13]

81 The petitions which have been restored to the Mass of the Roman Rite are also found at Evening Prayer, though, as described below, in a different way.

82 Since traditionally prayer is offered in the morning to commend the whole day to God, invocations are given at Morning Prayer to consecrate the day to him.

83 The name 'Intercessions' is applied both to the petitions made at Evening Prayer, and to the invocations dedicating the day to God made at Morning Prayer.

84 For the sake of variety, but above all that the needs of the

[13]For example, St John Chrysostom, *In Epist ad Tim 1, Homilia* 6: PG 62, 530.

Church and mankind may be better expressed according to the different states, groups, persons, conditions and times, different formulas of intercessions are proposed for each day in the arrangement of the psalter and for the sacred seasons of the liturgical year, as also for certain festive celebrations.

85   As in the Lord's Prayer, petitions should be linked with praise of God or acknowledgment of his glory, or with the recalling of the history of salvation.

86   Since the Liturgy of the Hours is above all the prayer of the whole Church for the whole Church, indeed for the salvation of the whole world,[16] general intentions should always have first place, whether the prayer is for the Church and all her members, for the secular authorities, for those who suffer poverty, disease or sorrow, or for the needs of the whole world, namely, for peace and for other things of this kind.

87   It is permissible to add special intentions at Morning and Evening Prayer. However, in the intercessions at Evening Prayer, the final intention is always for the dead.

88   The intercessions of the Office have a structure adaptable for celebration with the people, for celebration in a small community, or for recitation individually.

89   Intercessions for recitation with the people or in common are introduced with a short invitation by the priest or minister. This introduction also includes a phrase or response which the congregation can then repeat after each of the intentions.

90   The intentions should be addressed to God in such a way that they can accord with common celebration or individual recitation.

91   Each intention consists of two parts, the second of which can be used as a variable response.

92   The different methods of saying the intercessions are thus: the priest or minister says both parts of the intention and the congregation adds the invariable response, or pauses for silence; otherwise

---

[16]Cf Second Vatican Council, *Const. on Sacred Liturgy, Sacrosanctum Concilium*, n.111.

the priest or minister says only the first part and the congregation the second part of the intention.

b THE LORD'S PRAYER

93 The Lord's Prayer is solemnly recited three times a day: at Mass, at Morning Prayer and at Evening Prayer.

94 In accordance with tradition, the Lord's Prayer has the place of honour at the end of the intercessions at Morning Prayer and at Evening Prayer.

95 The Lord's Prayer is said by all, preceded if desired by a brief introduction.

c THE CONCLUDING PRAYER

96 A concluding prayer completes the whole Hour. In public celebration with the people, it traditionally pertains to the priest or deacon.[14]

97 At Morning and Evening Prayer on Sundays, ferial days of Advent, Christmastide, Lent and Eastertide the concluding prayer will be found in the Proper. On solemnities, feasts and memorias the concluding prayer will also be found in the Proper. On ordinary ferial days, however, in order to emphasize the particular character of these Hours, the concluding prayer provided in the psalter is said.

98 At Night Prayer the concluding prayer is provided for each night of the week.

The Sacred Silence

99 Since as a general rule in liturgical functions, care must be taken that 'at the proper times all should observe a reverent silence',[15] opportunity for silence should be given in the recitation of the Liturgy of the Hours.

100 The purpose of this silence is to allow the voice of the Holy Spirit to be heard more fully in our hearts, and to unite our personal

---

[14] See below n.135.
[15] Second Vatican Council, *Const. on Sacred Liturgy, Sacrosanctum Concilium*, n.30.

prayer more closely with the word of God and the public voice of the Church. In introducing silence we must use prudence; periods of silence may be inserted in different ways: after the psalm, once its antiphon has been repeated, as was generally the custom; after the reading, whether it is a short reading or an extended one.

Care should be taken that such a silence neither deforms the structure of the Office, nor upsets or bores the participants.

101 In individual recitation, we have more opportunity to pause and meditate on a text which strikes us. The Office will not lose its public character because of this.

VARIOUS CELEBRATIONS IN THE COURSE OF THE YEAR

The Celebration of the Mysteries of the Lord

a SUNDAYS

102 The Sunday Office begins with Evening Prayer I, in which everything is taken from the psalter, except for those things which are given as proper.

103 When a feast of the Lord is celebrated on a Sunday, it has its own Evening Prayer I.

b THE EASTER TRIDUUM

104 During the Easter Triduum, the Office is celebrated as described in the Proper of the season.

105 Those who attend the celebration of evening Mass on Holy Thursday or the celebration of the Passion of the Lord on Good Friday, do not say Evening Prayer of the respective day.

106 Night Prayer on Holy Saturday is only said by those who are not present at the Easter Vigil.

107 On Easter Sunday Morning Prayer is said by all; it is fitting that Evening Prayer should be celebrated in a more solemn manner to mark the close of this holy day and to commemorate the apparitions in which our Lord showed himself to his disciples.

c EASTERTIDE

108 The Liturgy of the Hours receives its paschal character from the *Alleluia* acclamation with which most antiphons conclude. This quality is also given by the hymns, antiphons, and special intercessions, and finally by the proper readings assigned to each Hour.

d CHRISTMAS

109 Before the Midnight Mass of Christmas it is appropriate that a solemn vigil should be celebrated with the Office of Readings. Night Prayer is not said by those who are present at this vigil.

110 Morning Prayer on Christmas Day is usually said before the Dawn Mass.

e OTHER SOLEMNITIES AND FEASTS OF OUR LORD

111 As regards the arrangement of the Office on solemnities and feasts of our Lord, what is said in nn.120-5 should be observed, with the appropriate changes.

The Celebration of the Saints

112 The celebrations of the saints are arranged in such a way that they do not take precedence over the mysteries of salvation as commemorated on festive days and during the major seasons of the year, and so that they do not continually interfere with the sequence of the psalms and readings, or give rise to unnecessary repetitions. The purpose of this is also to give everyone ample opportunity for legitimate devotion. The reform of the Liturgical Calendar, undertaken by the Second Vatican Council, is based on these principles, as is the manner of celebrating the saints in the Liturgy of the Hours; this will be described in the following articles.

113 Celebrations of the saints are either solemnities, feasts or memorias.

114 The memorias are either obligatory, or, if nothing to the contrary is indicated, optional. The decision whether or not to celebrate with the faithful or in common the Office of an optional memoria should depend on the common good and devotion of the group and not on the person presiding.

115   If several optional memorias occur on the same day, only one is to be celebrated and the others omitted.

116   Only solemnities are transferable, and this is done in accordance with the rubrics.

117   The norms which follow apply both to the saints of the General Roman Calendar, and to those found in particular calendars.

118   If the Propers are not complete, the Commons of the Saints are used for the parts which are lacking.

a   HOW THE OFFICE IS ARRANGED ON SOLEMNITIES
119   Solemnities have Evening Prayer I on the preceding day.

120   At Evening Prayer I and II, the hymn, antiphons, short reading with its responsory and the concluding prayer are all proper; if the proper is not complete, the common is used for the parts that are lacking.
   Both psalms in Evening Prayer I are normally taken from the *Laudate* series (that is, Ps 112, 116, 134, 145, 146, 147), in accordance with ancient tradition. The New Testament canticle is indicated in the appropriate place. In Evening Prayer II the psalms and the canticle are proper. The intercessions are either proper or else from the Common.

121   At Morning Prayer, the hymn, antiphons, short reading with its responsory and the concluding prayer are proper; if the proper is lacking, they are taken from the Common. The psalms, however, are to be taken from Sunday I of the Psalter. The intercessions are either proper or else from the Common.

122   At Night Prayer, everything is from the Sunday, after Evening Prayer I and II respectively.

b   HOW THE OFFICE IS ARRANGED ON FEASTS
123   Feasts do not have Evening Prayer I, unless they are feasts of the Lord occurring on Sundays. At Morning and Evening Prayer, everything is the same as on a solemnity.

124   Night Prayer is said as on ordinary days.

C HOW THE OFFICE IS ARRANGED ON MEMORIAS OF SAINTS

125 There is no difference in the manner of arranging the Office between an obligatory memoria, and, if it is decided to celebrate it, an optional memoria, except when the optional memoria occurs during the privileged seasons.

(i) *Memorias occurring on ordinary days*

126 At Morning and Evening Prayer:

a the psalms with their antiphons are taken from the current ferial day, unless there are proper antiphons or psalms, as will be indicated in each case;

b sometimes the hymn, short reading, antiphons at the *Benedictus* and the *Magnificat*, and the intercessions are proper; if so, they will be found in the Office of the Saint. Otherwise they are taken either from the Common or from the current ferial day;

c the concluding prayer is taken from the Office of the Saint.

127 At Night Prayer nothing is taken from the Office of the saint but everything is taken from the ferial day.

(ii) *Memorias occurring during the privileged seasons*

128 On Sundays, solemnities and feasts, on Ash Wednesday, during Holy Week and during the octave of Easter, no memorias are commemorated should they occur.

129 On the ferial days between 17 and 24 December, during the octave of Christmas and on the ferial days of Lent, no obligatory memorias may be celebrated, not even in particular calendars. The memorias which happen to occur during Lent are considered optional memorias for that year.

130 If anyone wishes to celebrate the Office of a saint whose memoria occurs during these seasons, after the concluding prayer at Morning and Evening Prayer, he may add the antiphon (proper or else from the Common) and the prayer of the saint.

(iii) *Memorias of the Blessed Virgin Mary on Saturdays*

131 On ordinary Saturdays on which optional memorias are permitted, an optional memoria of the Blessed Virgin Mary with its proper reading may be celebrated in the same way.

THE RITES TO BE OBSERVED IN COMMUNAL CELEBRATION

The Various Tasks to be Performed

132 In the celebration of the Liturgy of the Hours as in other liturgical actions 'whether as a minister or as one of the faithful, each person should perform his role by doing solely and totally what the nature of things and liturgical norms require of him'.[16]

133 When the bishop presides, especially in his cathedral church, it is desirable that his priests and ministers should gather round him, together with the full and active attendance of the faithful. In every celebration with the people, a priest or deacon should normally preside, and there should also be ministers present.

134 The priest or deacon who presides at the ceremony may wear a stole over his alb or surplice. The priest can also wear a cope. On the major solemnities there is nothing to prevent several priests wearing copes and the deacons dalmatics.

135 It is the role of the presiding priest or deacon, from the seat, to begin the Office with the introductory verse, to begin the Lord's Prayer, say the concluding prayer, greet, bless and dismiss the people.

136 Either a priest or a minister may say the intercessions.

137 When there is no priest or deacon, the person who presides is only one among equals; he does not enter the sanctuary, nor does he greet or bless the people.

138 The lector should stand in a suitable place to proclaim the readings, whether these are long or short.

139 A cantor or cantors should begin the antiphons, psalms and other songs. With regard to the psalmody, the norms of nn.55-57 should be observed.

140 During the Gospel canticle at Morning Prayer and Evening Prayer, the altar may be incensed, and then also the priest and people.

[16]Second Vatican Council, *Const. Sacred Liturgy, Sacrosanctum Concilium*, n 28.

141 The obligation of choir applies to the community and not to the place of celebration. This need not necessarily be a church, especially if it is a question of those Hours which are recited without solemnity.

142 All taking part stand:
   a during the introduction to the Office and the introductory verse of each Hour:
   b during the hymn;
   c during the Gospel canticle;
   d during the intercessions, Lord's Prayer and concluding prayer.

143 Except during the Gospel, everyone is seated while listening to the readings.

144 While the psalms and other songs with their antiphons are being said, the community sits or stands according to custom.

145 Everyone makes the sign of the cross from the forehead to the breast and from the left shoulder to the right;
   a at the beginning of the Hours, when the *O God, come to our aid* is said;
   b at the beginning of the Gospel canticle, the *Benedictus*, the *Magnificat*, and the *Nunc Dimittis*.
Everyone makes the sign of the cross on the mouth at the beginning of the invitatory, when saying the words *Lord, open our lips.*

Singing in the Office
146 'The sung celebration of the Divine Office is the form which best accords with the nature of this prayer. It expresses its solemnity in a fuller way and expresses a deeper union of hearts in performing the praises of God. That is why, in accordance with the wish of the Constitution on the Liturgy, this sung form is strongly recommended to those who celebrate the Office in choir or in common.'[17]

147 What the Second Vatican Council said with regard to singing in the Liturgy applies to every liturgical action but especially to the

[17]S Congregation of Rites, Instruction *Musicam sacram*, 5 March 1967, n.37: *AAS* 59 (1967), p 310; cf Second Vatican Council, *Const. on Sacred Liturgy, Sacrosanctum Concilium*, n.99.

Liturgy of the Hours.[18] Although each and every part has been so arranged that it can fruitfully be recited even by an individual, many of the parts, especially the psalms, canticles, hymns and responsories, are of a lyrical nature and are given their full expression only when sung.

148   Singing in the Liturgy of the Hours is not to be regarded as something merely ornamental or extrinsic to prayer. It springs from the depths of the person praying and praising God, and fully and perfectly reveals the communal character of Christian worship.

To be commended therefore are those Christian communities—whatever their character—which endeavour as often as possible to use this form of praying the Office. Clerics, religious and faithful should be given proper instruction and practice in the singing of the Office, so that especially on festive days they will be able to enjoy singing the Hours. However difficult it is to sing the whole Office, the praise of the Church is not to be considered either in its origins or of its nature as the preserve of clerics and monks; it belongs to the whole Christian community. Many principles are to be borne in mind if the singing of the Liturgy of the Hours is to be carried out correctly, and if its value and beauty are to be appreciated.

149   It is especially appropriate that singing should be used at least on Sundays and festive days. From this the various degrees of solemnity may be recognized.

150   Not all the Hours are of the same importance. Hence it is fitting that the singing of those Hours which form the two hinges of the Office, namely Morning Prayer and Evening Prayer, should be preferred and solemnized more than the others.

151   Which parts should especially be sung depends on what is the best way of arranging the liturgical celebration. This demands that the meaning and proper nature of each part and of each song be carefully observed; some parts require to be sung by their very nature.[19] These are above all: the acclamations, the responses to the

---

[18]Cf Second Vatican Council, *Const. on Sacred Liturgy, Sacrosanctum Concilium*, n.113.
[19]S Congregation of Rites, Instruction *Musicam sacram*, 5 March 1967, n.6: p 302.

greetings of the priest and ministers and the intercessions of litany form, and also the antiphons and psalms, refrains or repeated responses, hymns and canticles.[20]

152 Jewish and Christian tradition confirms that the psalms are closely connected with music. To understand many of the psalms fully it helps a great deal to sing them or at least to regard them from a poetic and musical point of view. If possible, this form is to be preferred, at least on the more important days and Hours, while respecting the original character of the psalms.

153 The different ways of reciting the psalms are described above, nn.55-7. Variety is introduced not because of external circumstances but on account of the various types of psalms which occur in any one celebration. Thus it may be better to say sapiential and historical psalms, while the hymns and psalms of thanksgiving are best sung. It is very important for us to be concerned with the meaning and spirit of what we are doing. The celebration should not be rigid or artificial, nor should we be merely concerned with formalities. Above all, the thing to be achieved is to instil a desire for the authentic prayer of the Church and a delight in celebrating the praise of God (cf Ps 146).

154 The hymns, provided that they have doctrinal and artistic value, can also be of benefit to the person reciting the Hours. As far as possible, hymns should be sung in community celebrations as their nature demands.

155 The short responsory after the reading at Morning Prayer and at Evening Prayer, cf n 17, is, by its nature, designed to be sung in common.

156 The readings, whether they are long or short, are not of themselves intended to be sung. Great care should be taken to proclaim the readings worthily, clearly and distinctly so that they may be easily heard and understood by all. If therefore they are sung, only a form of music which enables them to be better heard and understood may be used.

[20]Cf *Ibid*, nn.16a, 38: pp 305, 311.

157 It may be fitting for the president to sing the texts which are to be proclaimed by him alone, such as the concluding prayers, especially if these are in Latin. This may be more difficult in certain vernacular languages, unless singing helps everyone to hear the text more clearly.

Anthony B. Boylan
Secretary Liturgy Commission,
Bishops' Conference of England and Wales

TABLE OF LITURGICAL DAYS

For purposes of determining which liturgical day is to be celebrated, precedence is regulated according to the position in the following table.

I

1 The Easter Triduum.

2 The Solemnities of Christmas, the Epiphany, the Ascension and Pentecost.

The Sundays of Advent, Lent and Eastertide.

Ash Wednesday.

Holy Week (from the Monday to Holy Thursday).

The days within the Octave of Easter.

3 The Solemnities of the Lord, the Blessed Virgin Mary and the Saints which occur in the General Calendar.

All Souls Day.

4 Solemnities which occur in particular Calendars, in the following order:

    a   The Principal Patron of a town or city or similar place.

    b   The Dedication and Anniversary of the Dedication of one's own church.

    c   The Titular of one's own church.

    d   The Titular or Holy Founder or Principal Patron of a Religious Order or Congregation.

II

5 Feasts of the Lord which occur in the General Calendar.

6 The Sundays of Christmastide and the Ordinary Sundays of the Year.

7 Feasts of the Blessed Virgin Mary and the Saints which occur in the General Calendar.

8 Feasts which occur in particular Calendars, in the following order:

    a   The Principal Patron of a diocese.

    b   The Anniversary of the Dedication of the cathedral church.

    c   The Principal Patron of a region or province or nation or other large territory.

    d   The Titular or Holy Founder or Principal Patron of a Religious Order or Congregation and of a religious province, except those which are celebrated as Solemnities according to n.4, above.

    e   Other feasts of one's own church.

    f   Other feasts which occur in the particular Calendar of a Diocese or Religious Order or Congregation.

9 The weekdays of Advent from 17 to 24 December inclusive.

The days within the Octave of Christmas.

The weekdays of Lent.

III

10 Obligatory Memorias which occur in the General Calendar.

11 Obligatory Memorias which occur in particular Calendars, in the following order:

    a   The Secondary Patrons of a place, diocese, region, province, nation or larger territory, or of a Religious Order or Congregation, or of a religious province.

    b   Other Obligatory Memorias of one's own church.

    c   Other Obligatory Memorias which occur in the particular Calendar of a Diocese or Religious Order or Congregation.

12 Optional Memorias. According to the directives of the General Introduction (cf nn.238-239, above) those Optional Memorias which occur between 17 and 24 December inclusive, within the Octave of Christmas or during Lent may be celebrated subject to special rules. These same rules apply to those Obligatory Memorias which may occur during Lent, when they can only be celebrated as Optional Memorias.

The weekdays of Advent until 16 December inclusive.

The weekdays of Christmastide from 2 January to the Saturday following the Epiphany.

The weekdays of Eastertide from the Monday following the Octave of Easter until the Saturday before Pentecost inclusive.

The Ordinary Weekdays of the Year.

THE OCCURRENCE AND CONCURRENCE OF LITURGICAL DAYS

When it happens that any of the above liturgical days coincide, the Divine Office is said of that celebration which occurs first in the above table.

But when a Solemnity is displaced by another celebration which is higher in the above table, it is transferred to the nearest day which is free of any of the celebrations under numbers 1-8 in the above table. (As an exception to this rule, however, a Solemnity which is displaced by a Sunday of Advent, Lent or Eastertide is anticipated on the Saturday, cf *Norms for the Liturgical Year*, n.5.)

Other celebrations which are less in rank than a Solemnity are omitted for that year if they are displaced.

If on the following day there occurs a celebration which has the right to Evening Prayer I, the decision as to which Evening Prayer is said depends on the relative positions of the celebrations in the above table. Where, however, both celebrations are of the same rank in the above table, Evening Prayer of the day is said, not the Evening Prayer I of the following day.

Year	Ash Wednesday	Easter	Ascension	Pentecost
1976	3 Mar.	18 Apr.	27 May	6 June
1977	23 Feb.	10 Apr.	19 May	29 May
1978	8 Feb.	26 Mar.	4 May	14 May
1979	28 Feb.	15 Apr.	24 May	3 June
1980	20 Feb.	6 Apr.	15 May	25 May
1981	4 Mar.	19 Apr.	28 May	7 June
1982	24 Feb.	11 Apr.	20 May	30 May
1983	16 Feb.	3 Apr.	12 May	22 May
1984	7 Mar.	22 Apr.	31 May	10 June
1985	20 Feb.	7 Apr.	16 May	26 May
1986	12 Feb.	30 Mar.	8 May	18 May
1987	4 Mar.	19 Apr.	28 May	7 June
1988	17 Feb.	3 Apr.	12 May	22 May
1989	8 Feb.	26 Mar.	4 May	14 May
1990	28 Feb.	15 Apr.	24 May	3 June
1991	13 Feb.	31 Mar.	9 May	19 May
1992	4 Mar.	19 Apr.	28 May	7 June
1993	24 Feb.	11 Apr.	20 May	30 May
1994	16 Feb.	3 Apr.	12 May	22 May
1995	1 Mar.	16 Apr.	25 May	4 June
1996	21 Feb.	7 Apr.	16 May	26 May
1997	12 Feb.	30 Mar.	8 May	18 May
1998	25 Feb.	12 Apr.	21 May	31 May
1999	17 Feb.	4 Apr.	13 May	23 May

LITURGICAL DAYS

| Corpus Christi | Ordinary Weeks of the Year | | | | First Sunday of Advent | Year |
| | Before Lent | | After Pentecost | | | |
	Until	Week	From	Week		
17 June	2 Mar.	8	7 June	10	28 Nov.	1976
9 June	22 Feb.	7	30 May	9	27 Nov.	1977
25 May	7 Feb.	5	15 May	6	3 Dec.	1978
14 June	27 Feb.	8	4 June	9	2 Dec.	1979
5 June	19 Feb.	6	26 May	8	30 Nov.	1980
18 June	3 Mar.	8	8 June	10	29 Nov.	1981
10 June	23 Feb.	7	31 Mar.	9	28 Nov.	1982
2 June	15 Feb.	6	23 May	8	27 Nov.	1983
21 June	6 Mar.	9	11 June	10	2 Dec.	1984
6 June	19 Feb.	6	27 May	8	1 Dec.	1985
29 May	11 Feb.	5	19 May	7	30 Nov.	1986
18 June	3 Mar.	8	8 June	10	29 Nov.	1987
2 June	16 Feb.	6	23 May	8	27 Nov.	1988
25 May	7 Feb.	5	15 May	6	3 Dec.	1989
14 June	27 Feb.	8	4 June	9	2 Dec.	1990
30 May	12 Feb.	5	20 May	7	1 Dec.	1991
18 June	3 Mar.	8	8 June	10	29 Nov.	1992
10 June	23 Feb.	7	31 May	9	28 Nov.	1993
2 June	15 Feb.	6	23 May	8	27 Nov.	1994
15 June	28 Feb.	8	5 June	9	3 Dec.	1995
6 June	20 Feb.	7	27 May	8	1 Dec.	1996
29 May	11 Feb.	5	19 May	7	30 Nov.	1997
11 June	24 Feb.	7	1 June	9	29 Nov.	1998
3 June	16 Feb.	6	24 May	8	28 Nov.	1999

THE GENERAL CALENDAR

JANUARY

1	Octave-day of Christmas: **SOLEMNITY OF MARY, MOTHER OF GOD**	Solemnity
2	Ss Basil the Great and Gregory Nazianzen, Bps, Docts	Memoria
3		
4		
5		
6	THE EPIPHANY OF THE LORD	Solemnity
7	*St Raymond of Penyafort, priest**	
8		
9		
10		
11		
12		
13	*St Hilary, Bp, Doct*	
14		
15		
16		
17	St Antony, Ab	Memoria
18		
19		
20	*St Fabian, Pope, M*	
	St Sebastian, M	
21	St Agnes, V, M	Memoria
22	*St Vincent, deacon, M*	
23		
24	St Francis de Sales, Bp, Doct	Memoria
25	THE CONVERSION OF ST PAUL, AP	Feast
26	Ss Timothy and Titus, Bps	Memoria
27	*St Angela Merici, V*	
28	St Thomas Aquinas, priest, Doct	Memoria
29		
30		
31	St John Bosco, priest	Memoria
Sunday after 6 January: THE BAPTISM OF THE LORD		Feast

*Where no rank of celebration is given and the name of the celebration is printed in italics, the rank is that of Optional Memoria. All Memorias indicated as such in the Calendar are Obligatory Memorias.

FEBRUARY

1		
2	THE PRESENTATION OF THE LORD	Feast
3	*St Blaise, Bp, M*	
	St Ansgar, Bp	
4		
5	St Agatha, V, M	Memoria
6	St Paul Miki and his Companions, Mm	Memoria
7		
8	*St Jerome Emilian*	
9		
10	St Scholastica, V	Memoria
11	*Our Lady of Lourdes*	
12		
13		
14	Ss Cyril, monk, and Methodius, Bp	Memoria
15		
16		
17	*Seven Holy Founders of the Servite Order*	
18		
19		
20		
21	*St Peter Damian, Bp, Doct*	
22	THE SEE OF ST PETER THE APOSTLE	Feast
23	St Polycarp, Bp, M	Memoria
24		
25		
26		
27		
28		

MARCH

1		
2		
3		
4	*St Casimir*	
5		
6		
7	Ss Perpetua and Felicity, Mm	Memoria
8	*St John of God, religious*	
9	*St Francis of Rome, religious*	
10		
11		
12		
13		
14		
15		
16		
17	*St Patrick, Bp*	
18	*St Cyril of Jerusalem, Bp, Doct*	
19	ST JOSEPH, HUSBAND OF THE BLESSED VIRGIN MARY	Solemnity
20		
21		
22		
23	*St Turibius of Mongravejo, Bp*	
24		
25	THE ANNUNCIATION OF THE LORD	Solemnity
26		
27		
28		
29		
30		
31		

APRIL

1		
2	*St Francis of Paola, hermit*	
3		
4	*St Isidore, Bp, Doct*	
5	*St Vincent Ferrer, priest*	
6		
7	St John Baptist de la Salle, priest	Memoria
8		
9		
10		
11	*St Stanislaus, Bp, M*	
12		
13	*St Martin I, Pope, M*	
14		
15		
16		
17		
18		
19		
20		
21	*St Anselm, Bp, Doct*	
22		
23	*St George, M*	
24	*St Fidelis of Sigmaringen, priest, M*	
25	ST MARK, EVANGELIST	Feast
26		
27		
28	*St Peter Chanel, priest, M*	
29	St Catherine of Siena, V, Doct	Memoria
30	*St Pius V, Pope*	

MAY

1	*St Joseph the Worker*	
2	St Athanasius, Bp, Doct	Memoria
3	SS PHILIP AND JAMES, APP	Feast
4		
5		
6		
7		
8		
9		
10		
11		
12	*Ss Nereus and Achilleus, Mm* *St Pancras, M*	
13		
14	ST MATTHIAS, AP	Feast
15		
16		
17		
18	*St John I, Pope, M*	
19		
20	*St Bernardine of Siena, priest*	
21		
22		
23		
24		
25	*St Bede the Venerable, priest, Doct* *St Gregory VII, Pope* *St Mary Magdalen of Pazzi, V*	
26	St Philip Neri, priest	Memoria
27	*St Augustine of Canterbury, Bp*	
28		
29		
30		
31	THE VISITATION OF THE BLESSED VIRGIN MARY	Feast

First Sunday after Pentecost: THE MOST HOLY TRINITY   Solemnity
Thursday after the Most Holy Trinity: THE BODY AND
    BLOOD OF CHRIST   Solemnity
Friday after 2nd Sunday after Pentecost: THE MOST SACRED
   HEART OF JESUS   Solemnity
Saturday after 2nd Sunday after Pentecost: *The Immaculate*
   Heart of Mary

JUNE

1	St Justin, M	Memoria
2	*St Marcellinus and Peter, Mm*	
3	Ss Charles Lwanga and his Companions, Mm	Memoria
4		
5	St Boniface, Bp, M	Memoria
6	*St Norbert, Bp*	
7		
8		
9	*St Ephraem, deacon, Doct*	
10		
11	St Barnabas, Ap	Memoria
12		
13	St Antony of Padua, priest, Doct	Memoria
14		
15		
16		
17		
18		
19	*St Romuald, Ab*	
20		
21	St Aloysius Gonzaga, religious	Memoria
22	*St Paulinus of Nola, Bp*	
	Ss John Fisher, Bp, and Thomas More, Mm	
23		
24	THE BIRTHDAY OF ST JOHN THE BAPTIST	Solemnity
25		
26		
27	*St Cyril of Alexandria, Bp, Doct*	
28	St Irenaeus, Bp, M	Memoria
29	SS PETER AND PAUL, APP	Solemnity
30	*The First Martyrs of the See of Rome*	

JULY

1		
2		
3	St Thomas, ap	Feast
4	*St Elizabeth of Portugal*	
5	*St Antony Mary Zaccaria, priest*	
6	*St Maria Goretti, V, M*	
7		
8		
9		
10		
11	St Benedict, Ab	Memoria
12		
13	*St Henry*	
14	*St Camillus of Lellis, priest*	
15	St Bonaventure, Bp, Doct	Memoria
16	*Our Lady of Mount Carmel*	
17		
18		
19		
20		
21	*St Laurence of Brindisi, priest, Doct*	
22	St Mary Magdalen	Memoria
23	*St Bridget, religious*	
24		
25	St James, ap	Feast
26	St Joachim and St Anne, parents of the Blessed Virgin Mary	Memoria
27		
28		
29	St Martha	Memoria
30	*St Peter Chrysologus, Bp, Doct*	
31	St Ignatius Loyola. priest	Memoria

AUGUST

1	St Alphonsus Mary de Liguori, Bp Doct	Memoria
2	*St Eusebius of Vercelli, Bp*	
3		
4	St John Mary Vianney, priest	Memoria
5	*Dedication of the Basilica of St Mary Major*	
6	THE TRANSFIGURATION OF THE LORD	Feast
7	*Ss Sixtus II, Pope and his Companions, Mm*	
	St Cajetan, priest	
8	St Dominic, priest	Memoria
9		
10	ST LAURENCE, DEACON, M	Feast
11	St Clare, V	Memoria
12		
13	*Ss Pontianus, Pope, and Hippolytus, priest, Mm*	
14		
15	THE ASSUMPTION OF THE BLESSED VIRGIN MARY	Solemnity
16	*St Stephen of Hungary*	
17		
18		
19	*St John Eudes, priest*	
20	St Bernard, Ab, Doct	Memoria
21	St Pius X, Pope	Memoria
22	Our Lady, Mother and Queen	Memoria
23	*St Rose of Lima, V*	
24	ST BARTHOLOMEW, AP	Feast
25	*St Louis*	
	St Joseph of Calasanz, priest	
26		
27	St Monica	Memoria
28	St Augustine, Bp, Doct	Memoria
29	The Beheading of St John the Baptist, M	Memoria
30		
31		

SEPTEMBER

1		
2		
3	St Gregory the Great, Pope, Doct	Memoria
4		
5		
6		
7		
8	THE BIRTHDAY OF THE BLESSED VIRGIN MARY	Feast
9		
10		
11		
12		
13	St John Chrysostom, Bp, Doct	Memoria
14	THE EXALTATION OF THE HOLY CROSS	Feast
15	Our Lady of Sorrows	Memoria
16	Ss Cornelius, Pope, and Cyprian, Bp, Mm	Memoria
17	*St Robert Bellarmine, Bp, Doct*	
18		
19	*St Januarius, Bp, M*	
20		
21	ST MATTHEW, AP, EVANGELIST	Feast
22		
23		
24		
25		
26	*Ss Cosmas and Damian, Mm*	
27	St Vincent de Paul, priest	Memoria
28	*St Wenceslaus, M*	
29	SS MICHAEL, GABRIEL AND RAPHAEL, ARCHANGELS	Feast
30	St Jerome, priest, Doct	Memoria

OCTOBER

1	St Teresa of the Child Jesus, V	Memoria
2	The Guardian Angels	Memoria
3		
4	St Francis of Assisi	Memoria
5		
6	*St Bruno, priest*	
7	Our Lady of the Rosary	Memoria
8		
9	*Ss Denis, Bp, and his Companions, Mm*	
	St John Leonardi, priest	
10		
11		
12		
13		
14	*St Callistus, Pope, M*	
15	St Teresa of Avila, V, Doct	Memoria
16	*St Hedwig, religious*	
	St Margaret Mary Alacoque, V	
17	St Ignatius of Antioch, Bp, M	Memoria
18	ST LUKE, EVANGELIST	Feast
19	*Ss John of Brébeuf and Isaac Jogues,*	
	priests, and their Companions, Mm	
	St Paul of the Cross, priest	
20		
21		
22		
23	*St John of Capestrano, priest*	
24	*St Antony Mary Claret, Bp*	
25		
26		
27		
28	SS SIMON AND JUDE, APP	Feast
29		
30		
31		

NOVEMBER

1	ALL SAINTS	Solemnity
2	ALL SOULS DAY	
3	*St Martin de Porres, religious*	
4	St Charles Borromeo, Bp	Memoria
5		
6		
7		
8		
9	DEDICATION OF THE LATERAN BASILICA	Feast
10	St Leo the Great, Pope, Doct	Memoria
11	St Martin of Tours, Bp	Memoria
12	St Josaphat, Bp, M	Memoria
13		
14		
15	*St Albert the Great, Bp, Doct*	
16	*St Margaret of Scotland* *St Gertrude, V*	
17	St Elizabeth of Hungary, religious	Memoria
18	*Dedication of the Basilicas of Ss Peter and Paul, App*	
19		
20		
21	The Presentation of the Blessed Virgin Mary	Memoria
22	St Cecilia, V, M.	Memoria
23	*St Clement I, Pope, M*	
24	*St Columbanus, Ab*	
25		
26		
27		
28		
29		
30	ST ANDREW, AP	Feast

The last Sunday of the Church's Year:
CHRIST THE KING   Solemnity

DECEMBER

1		
2		
3	St Francis Xavier, priest	Memoria
4	*St John Damascene, priest, Doct*	
5		
6	*St Nicholas, Bp*	
7	St Ambrose, Bp, Doct	Memoria
8	THE IMMACULATE CONCEPTION OF THE BLESSED VIRGIN MARY	Solemnity
9		
10		
11	*St Damasus I, Pope*	
12	*St Jane Frances de Chantal, religious*	
13	St Lucy, V, M	Memoria
14	St John of the Cross, priest, Doct	Memoria
15		
16		
17		
18		
19		
20		
21	*St Peter Canisius, priest, Doct*	
22		
23	*St John of Kenty, priest*	
24		
25	CHRISTMAS DAY	Solemnity
26	ST STEPHEN, THE FIRST MARTYR	Feast
27	ST JOHN, AP, EVANGELIST	Feast
28	THE HOLY INNOCENTS, Mm	Feast
29	*St Thomas Beckett, Bp, M*	
30		
31	*St Silvester I, Pope*	

Sunday within the Octave of Christmas, or, if no
Sunday, 30 December: THE HOLY FAMILY   Feast

THE PROPER OF SEASONS

ADVENT
ORDINARY FOR SUNDAYS

EVENING PRAYER I
THE OFFICE OF VESPERS

The Hour begins with the following
℣ O God, come to our aid.
℟ O Lord, make haste to help us.
Glory be to the Father and to the Son and to the Holy Spirit, as it was in the beginning, is now, and ever shall be, world without end. Amen. Alleluia.

This is followed by the
Hymn, from the appendix, for Advent.

The hymn is followed by the

PSALMODY

The antiphons, psalms and canticle for each Sunday are given in the psalter, beginning with Evening Prayer I of Sunday of Week 1, p 382. Note: the antiphons for the Sundays of Advent, Lent, etc., are proper. (For Evening Prayer I of Sundays Weeks 2, 3 and 4, see the respective weeks in the psalter.)

After the psalmody there follows a
Scripture Reading   *1 Thess 5:23-24*
May the God who gives us peace make you completely his, and keep your whole being, spirit, soul, and body, free from all fault, at the coming of our Lord Jesus Christ. He who calls you will do it, for he is faithful!

¶ *The text of this reading may be varied in accordance with General Instruction nos. 44-46, 247 (Introduction nos. 12-14).*
After a pause the short responsory follows.
¶ *This responsory may be omitted. Other songs of the same type and for the same purpose, duly approved by the Episcopal Conference, may replace the responsory (GI no. 49, Introduction no. 17).*

3

Short Responsory
℟ Show us, Lord, your steadfast love. *Repeat* ℟
℣ And grant us your salvation. ℟ Show us, Lord . . .
Glory be to the Father and to the Son and to the Holy Spirit. ℟
Show us, Lord . . .
The short responsory, if said in common, is always said in this manner.

The Magnificat of our Lady is then said with its antiphon:

Magnificat Antiphon
Sunday 1: See the name of the Lord comes from afar. His splendour
fills the whole world.

Sunday 2: Come, Lord, and bring us peace. Let us rejoice before you
with sincere hearts.

Sunday 3: Before me there was no God nor will there be after me.
Every knee shall bend before me and every tongue shall acknowledge
me.

Sunday 4: as provided among the special antiphons for 17 to 23
December, pp 33 ff.

Magnificat, p 376.
*When the antiphon has been repeated after the Magnificat, the inter-
cessions are said:*

Intercessions: *Sundays 1 & 3*
The Son of God is coming with great power: all mankind shall see
his face and be reborn.—℟ Come, Lord Jesus: do not delay!
You will bring us wisdom, fresh understanding and new vision.—℟
You will bring us good news, and power which will transform our
lives.—℟
You will bring us truth, showing us the way to our Father.—℟
Born of a woman, you will open in our flesh the way to eternal life
and joy.—℟

Sundays 2 & 4
Before time began, the Word was with the Father; in the fulness of
time he came to us through the Virgin Mary.—℟ Come today
through the Church, Lord Jesus.

All that came to be was alive with his life:—may our lives be a light for men. ℟ Come today through the church, Lord Jesus.
The Word dwells with God:—may we dwell with him in the Father's love. ℟
The Word entered his own realm, and his own would not receive him.—By responding to those who demand our care, may we welcome him into our hearts. ℟
The Word came among us, full of grace and truth;—may all the dead be counted as children of God. ℟

¶ *Other intercessions may be added in the same general form.*
The Lord's Prayer is then said aloud by all. It may be introduced in this manner:
Let us now pray in the words our Saviour gave us.
Our Father

The concluding prayer is said immediately after the Lord's Prayer, without Let us pray.

Concluding Prayer
Sunday 1: Grant, almighty Father,
that when Christ comes again
we may go out to meet him,
bearing the harvest of good works
achieved by your grace.
We pray that he will receive us into the company of the saints and
    call us into the kingdom of heaven.
(We make our prayer) through our Lord Jesus Christ your Son,
who lives and reigns with you and the Holy Spirit,
God, for ever and ever. ℟ Amen.

Sunday 2: Almighty and merciful God,
let neither our daily work nor the cares of this life
prevent us from hastening to meet your Son;
enlighten us with your wisdom
and lead us into his company.
(We make our prayer) through our Lord.

5

Sunday 3: Grant, almighty God, that looking forward in
faith to the feast of our Lord's birth,
we may feel all the happiness our Saviour brings,
and celebrate his coming with unfailing joy.
(We make our prayer) through our Lord.

Sunday 4: Lord, open our hearts to your grace.
Through the angel's message to Mary
we have learned to believe
in the incarnation of Christ your Son.
Lead us by his passion and cross
to the glory of his resurrection.
(We make our prayer) through our Lord.

Conclusion of the Hour
*In a communal celebration presided over by a priest or deacon he
dismisses the assembly, saying:*
The Lord be with you.
R7 And also with you.
May almighty God bless you, the Father, and the Son, and the Holy
Spirit. R7 Amen.

¶ *Some other form of blessing as given in the Missal may be used.
Then follows the invitation:*
Go in the peace of Christ.
R7 Thanks be to God.

*When no priest or deacon is present, and in recitation on one's own,
the conclusion is:*
The Lord bless us, and keep us from all evil, and bring us to everlasting life. R7 Amen.

NIGHT PRAYER

THE OFFICE OF COMPLINE

*This prayer is given under Night Prayer which appears after Week 4
of the psalter, pp 689ff.*

INTRODUCTION TO THE DAILY OFFICE

This is used at the beginning of the day.
℣ Lord, open our lips.
℟ And we shall praise your name.

The Invitatory Psalm is then said, ps 94, p 371, with its antiphon. It is preferable to repeat the antiphon at the beginning of the psalm and after each strophe, GI no. 34. In recitation on one's own it suffices to say the antiphon once at the beginning of the psalm. (Introduction no. 3).
¶ *Pss 99, 66 or 23 may be said in place of ps 94. When one of them occurs in the Office which follows, it should be replaced there by ps 94. The antiphon varies according to the Season and the celebration, GI nos. 34-36 (Introduction nos. 3-5).*
¶ *The Invitatory Psalm and its antiphon may be omitted when Morning Prayer is the first Office said in the day.*

Invitatory

1 *Daily from Sunday 1 of Advent to 16 December, inclusive:*
Ant. Let us adore the Lord, the king who is to come.

2 *Daily from 17 to 23 December, inclusive:*
Ant. The Lord is at hand: come, let us adore him.

3 *On 24 December:*
Ant. Know today that the Lord will come: in the morning you will see his glory.

MORNING PRAYER
THE OFFICE OF LAUDS

When the Introduction to the Daily Office is not used, this Office begins as follows:
℣ O God, come to our aid.
℟ O Lord, make haste to help us.
Glory be to the Father and to the Son and to the Holy Spirit, as it was in the beginning, is now, and ever shall be, world without end. Amen. Alleluia.
Hymn, from the appendix, for Advent.

7

PSALMODY

As in the psalter for the respective Sundays. Note proper antiphons.

¶ *If Sunday 4 of Advent falls on 24 December the antiphons proper to the day, p 47, are used with the psalms of Sunday. The scripture reading, short responsory, Benedictus antiphon and intercessions are also taken from 24 December.*

Scripture Reading   *Rom 13:11-12*

It is full time now for you to wake from sleep. For salvation is nearer to us now than when we first believed; the night is far gone, the day is at hand. Let us then cast off the works of darkness and put on the armour of light.

Short Responsory

R̷ Christ, Son of the living God, have mercy on us. *Repeat* R̷
V̷ You are coming into the world. R̷
Glory be to the Father and to the Son and to the Holy Spirit. R̷

Benedictus Antiphon

Sunday 1: The Holy Spirit will come upon you, Mary. Do not be afraid, for you will bear in your womb the Son of God, alleluia.

Sunday 2: Behold, I am sending a herald before you to prepare the way for you.

Sunday 3: John, who was in prison, heard what Christ was doing. He sent two of his disciples to ask him, 'Are you the one who is to come, or are we to expect another?'

On 17 December: Know that the kingdom of God is at hand; be sure that he will not delay.

Sunday 4: as provided among the antiphons for 17 to 23 December, pp 33 ff.

Benedictus, p 374.

The intercessions follow.

8

Intercessions: *Sundays 1 & 3*
Father, you have given us the grace of looking forward to the coming of your Son: R/ Send us your loving kindness.
Bring us to life, Lord:—may we be the servants found watching when the Master returns. R/
Send your Son to those who wait in hope:—let no man search for you in vain. R/
Bless us as we work:—give us faith until the end, when your Son will come in glory. R/
Father, we praise you for the presence of the Spirit in our lives, —making men and women bearers of your message and your purpose. R/
Our Father

Sundays 2 & 4
It is time for us to wake out of our sleep: salvation is nearer to us now than when we first believed. R/ Father of light, we praise you!
Christ is coming, the day is near:—in our eucharist today let us look forward with hope and joy. R/
As today we hear the scriptures, heralding the coming of your Son, —may our minds and hearts be touched by your Word. R/
As we receive the Body and Blood of your Son,—may we be healed and refreshed by your love. R/
United in one body, may we pursue the things that make for peace, —and build up our life together until Christ comes. R/
Our Father

Concluding Prayer
This is said immediately after the Lord's Prayer without Let us pray.

Sunday 1: Grant, almighty Father,
that when Christ comes again
we may go out to meet him,
bearing the harvest of good works
achieved by your grace.
We pray that he will receive us into the company of the saints
and call us into the kingdom of heaven.
(We make our prayer) through our Lord.

Sunday 2: Almighty and merciful God,
let neither our daily work nor the cares of this life
prevent us from hastening to meet your Son.
Enlighten us with your wisdom,
and lead us into his company.
(We make our prayer) through our Lord.

Sunday 3: Grant almighty God, that looking forward in faith
to the feast of our Lord's birth,
we may feel all the happiness our Saviour brings,
and celebrate his coming with unfailing joy.
(We make our prayer) through our Lord.

Sunday 4: Lord, open our hearts to your grace.
Through the angel's message to Mary
we have learned to believe
in the incarnation of Christ your Son.
Lead us by his passion and cross
to the glory of his resurrection.
(We make our prayer) through our Lord.

Conclusion of the Hour
The Hour concludes as at Evening Prayer I, p 6.

EVENING PRAYER II

℣ O God, come to our aid.
℟ O Lord, make haste to help us.
Glory be to the Father and to the Son and to the Holy Spirit, as it
was in the beginning, is now, and ever shall be, world without end.
Amen. Alleluia.

Hymn, from the appendix, for Advent.

PSALMODY

The proper antiphons, the psalms and canticle are from Evening Prayer II of Sunday in the psalter according to the week.

Scripture Reading   *Phil 4:4-5*

Rejoice in the Lord always; again I will say, Rejoice. Let all men know your forbearance. The Lord is at hand.

Short Responsory

Ry Show us, Lord, your steadfast love. *Repeat* Ry

Ꝟ And grant us your salvation. Ry Glory be. Ry

Magnificat Antiphon

Sunday 1: Do not be afraid, Mary, for you have found favour with God. Behold, you will conceive and bear a son, alleluia.

Sunday 2: Blessed are you, Mary, because you had faith: the Lord's promise to you will be fulfilled, alleluia.

Sunday 3: 'Are you the one who is to come, or are we to expect another?' 'Tell John what you hear and see: the blind see again, the lame walk, and the good news is preached to those who are poor in spirit, alleluia.'

On 17 December: O Wisdom, you come forth from the mouth of the Most High. You fill the universe and hold all things together in a strong yet gentle manner. O come to teach us the way of truth.

Sunday 4: as for 17 to 23 December, pp 33 ff.

Intercessions: *Sundays 1 & 3*

We pray to our Lord, who is the way, the truth, and the life.

Ry Come, and remain with us, Lord.

Gabriel announced your coming to the Virgin Mary:—Son of the Most High, come to claim your kingdom. Ry

John the Baptist rejoiced to see your day:—come, bring us your salvation. Ry

Simeon acknowledged you, Light of the World:—bring your light to all men of goodwill. Ry

We look for you as watchmen look for the dawn:—you are the sun that will wake the dead to new life. R7 Come, and remain with us, Lord.
Our Father

Sundays 2 & 4
The voice of John crying in the wilderness is echoed tonight in the voice of the Church: R7 Make our hearts ready, O Lord!
For your coming to us in grace this Advent,—R7
For the work man must do in creating a more just world,—R7
For the understanding we shall need this week for our families and friends,—R7
For our death, for our judgment, for eternal life with you,—R7
Our Father

Concluding Prayer
Sunday 1: Grant, almighty Father,
that when Christ comes again
we may go out to meet him,
bearing the harvest of good works
achieved by your grace.
We pray that he will receive us into the company of the saints
and call us into the kingdom of heaven.
(We make our prayer) through our Lord.

Sunday 2: Almighty and merciful God,
let neither our daily work nor the cares of this life
prevent us from hastening to meet your Son.
Enlighten us with your wisdom
and lead us into his company.
(We make our prayer) through our Lord.

Sunday 3: Grant, almighty God, that looking forward in faith
to the feast of our Lord's birth,
we may feel all the happiness our Saviour brings,
and celebrate his coming with unfailing joy.
(We make our prayer) through our Lord.

Sunday 4: Lord, open our hearts to your grace.
Through the angel's message to Mary
we have learned to believe
in the incarnation of Christ your Son.
Lead us by his passion and cross
to the glory of his resurrection.
(We make our prayer) through our Lord.

Conclusion of the Hour
As at Evening Prayer I, p 6.

NIGHT PRAYER

As in the psalter for After Evening Prayer II of Sundays, p 692 ff.

MONDAYS OF ADVENT
To 16 December

INTRODUCTION TO THE OFFICE

℣ Lord, open our lips.
℟ And we shall praise your name.

Invitatory ant. Let us adore the Lord, the king who is to come.

Ps 94, p 371, or other as indicated on p 368.

MORNING PRAYER

℣ O God, come . . . *(See above, p 7).*
Hymn, from the appendix, for Advent.

PSALMODY

All as in the psalter according to the week.

Scripture Reading   *Is 2:3*
'Come, let us go up to the mountain of the Lord, to the house of the

God of Jacob; that he may teach us his ways and that we may walk in his paths.' For out of Zion shall go forth the law, and the word of the Lord from Jerusalem.

¶ *This reading may be lengthened or varied according to GI nos. 44-46, 247, 251 (Introduction nos. 12-14).*

Short Responsory
R/ The glory of the Lord will shine on you, Jerusalem. Like the sun he will rise over you. *Repeat* R/
V/ His glory will appear in your midst. R/ Glory be. R/

Benedictus Antiphon
Week 1: Lift up your eyes, Jerusalem, and see the power of the king. Behold, the Saviour comes. He will free you from your bonds.

Week 2: Be converted and return to me, says the Lord, for the kingdom of heaven is near!

Week 3 (Before 17 December): The Lord, the ruler of the universe, will come from heaven in great majesty.

Benedictus, p 374.

Intercessions: *Weeks 1 & 3*
As we take up again our daily work, we turn to Christ and ask for his blessing. R/ Come, Lord Jesus!
Christ, you are the Daystar, powerfully dispelling our darkness:
—awaken our faith from sleep. R/
Reveal your presence in the world—through the lives of Christian men and women. R/
Come to create a new world,—where justice and peace may find a home. R/
End the long night of our pride,—and make us humble of heart. R/
Our Father

Week 2
As we pray together in the name of the Church, turn our minds and hearts back to you, Lord. R/ Send us your light and your truth.

As we think and pray about your Son's coming,—help us to grasp its meaning in a way that is personal and profound. ℞

May we never despise any of our fellow-men, since we are all your children.—Help us rather to fight against their hurt or degradation. ℞

Heal the broken bonds of human life:—reconcile us in the sharing of our hope in Christ. ℞

Help us to hear your voice—through the situations in which we work today. ℞

Our Father

Concluding Prayer

Week 1: Give us the grace, Lord,
to be ever on the watch for Christ, your Son.
When he comes and knocks at our door,
let him find us alert in prayer,
joyfully proclaiming his glory.
(We make our prayer) through our Lord.

Week 2: Let our prayer rise like incense before you, Lord,
so that we may come
in humility and purity of heart
to celebrate the great mystery of your Son's incarnation.
(We make our prayer) through our Lord.

Week 3: In your love, Father, listen to our prayer;
may your Son at his coming
dispel by his grace the darkness of our hearts.
(We make our prayer) through our Lord.

Conclusion of the Hour as above, at Evening Prayer I of Sunday, p 6.

EVENING PRAYER

Hymn, from the appendix, for Advent.

PSALMODY

All as in the psalter according to the week.

Scripture Reading   *Phil 3:20b-21*
It is to heaven that we look expectantly for the coming of our Lord
Jesus Christ to save us; he will form this humbled body of ours
anew, moulding it into the image of his glorified body, so effective is
his power to make all things obey him.

Short Responsory
R̷ Come to us and save us, Lord, God almighty. *Repeat* R̷
V̷ Let your face smile on us and we shall be safe. R̷ Glory be. R̷

Magnificat Antiphon
Week 1: The angel of the Lord brought the good news to Mary and
she conceived by the power of the Holy Spirit, alleluia.

Week 2: See, the King, the Lord of the earth is coming. He will take
the burden of captivity from our shoulders.

Week 3: All generations will call me blessed, for God has looked
upon his lowly handmaid. ·

Magnificat, p 376.

Intercessions: *Weeks 1 & 3*
As we make our evening prayer, we acknowledge the times when we
have preferred darkness before true light. R̷ Lord, that we may see!
You came, as man, into this world:—free us from the darkness of
its sin. R̷
Forgive us the hatred and envy that cloud our vision—give us a
generous spirit. R̷
You come to us through those who share our lives—open our hearts
to recognize you. R̷
Lord, do not forget our brothers,—who in all ages have hoped to see
your light. R̷
Our Father

16

Week 2
The Lord who is to come is the Judge of the living and the dead.
R℣ Christ, have mercy.
We thank you for the mercy you have shown us—let your compassion support us in our weakness. R℣
You humbled yourself to wash away our guilt:—forgive us the times when we have been indifferent to your pardon. R℣
Grant us also a spirit of understanding—to forgive as we ourselves are forgiven. R℣
If you should mark the guilt of those who have died,—Lord, who would survive? R℣
Our Father

The concluding prayer as at Morning Prayer, p 15.
Conclusion of the Hour as above, at Evening Prayer I of Sunday, p 6.

NIGHT PRAYER

Of Monday, as in the psalter.

TUESDAYS OF ADVENT
To 16 December

Invitatory ant. Let us adore the Lord, the king who is to come.

MORNING PRAYER

Hymn, from the appendix, for Advent.

Scripture Reading   Gen 49:10
Juda shall not want a branch from his stem, a prince drawn from his stock, until the day when he comes who is to be sent to us, he, the hope of the nations.

Short Responsory
R℣ The glory of the Lord will shine on you, Jerusalem. Like the sun he will rise over you. *Repeat* R℣
℣ His glory will appear in your midst. R℣ Glory be. R℣

Benedictus Antiphon

Week 1: A shoot shall spring from the stock of Jesse: the whole world shall be filled with the glory of the Lord and all flesh shall see the saving power of God.

Week 2: Rejoice and be glad, daughter of Sion. Behold, I am coming to live in your midst, says the Lord.

Week 3: Awake, awake; rise up, Jerusalem; throw away your bonds, captive daughter of Sion.

Intercessions: *Weeks 1 & 3*

It is time for us to wake from our sleep: the day of our salvation is near. ℟ Lord, may your kingdom come!

Help us to show our repentance—by a new way of living. ℟

Prepare us for the coming of your Word—by opening our hearts to receive him. ℟

Help us to overcome our pride,—and raise us from the depths of our weakness. ℟

Throw down the walls of hatred between nations;—clear the way for those who work for peace. ℟

Our Father

Week 2

In a world divided by fear and greed, the Church calls again on her Saviour. ℟ Lord Jesus, come to us in love.

Help us to set our hearts—where they will find fulfilment and not betrayal. ℟

As we proclaim your saving power to others,—let us not ourselves lose hold of your salvation. ℟

May our world be flooded with the grace of your coming:—let us experience the fulness of your joy. ℟

May we live our lives to the full in this world,—and transfigure it with the hope of future glory. ℟

Our Father

Concluding Prayer

Week 1: Take pity on our distress, Lord God:
show us your love.
May the coming of your Son strengthen us
and cleanse us from all trace of sin.
(We make our prayer) through our Lord.

Week 2: Lord God,
all the ends of the earth have seen your salvation.
Give us the grace to await with joy
the glorious day of our Saviour's birth.
(We make our prayer) through our Lord.

Week 3: Father,
through your Son you have made us a new people.
Look on us now as the new creation of your love
and by the coming of your Son
cleanse us from every stain of sin.
(We make our prayer) through our Lord.

EVENING PRAYER

Hymn, from the appendix, for Advent.

Scripture Reading　　　*Cf 1 Cor 1:7b-9*
You wait expectantly for our Lord Jesus Christ to reveal himself.
He will keep you firm to the end, without reproach on the Day of
our Lord Jesus. It is God himself who called you to share in the life
of his Son.

Short Responsory
R℣ Come to us and save us, Lord God almighty. *Repeat* R℣
℣ Let your face smile on us and we shall be safe. R℣ Glory be. R℣

Magnificat Antiphon
Week 1: Seek the Lord while he may be found, call upon him while
he is near, alleluia.

Week 2: A voice cries in the wilderness: Prepare a way for the Lord, make straight his paths.

Week 3: Before they came together Mary was found to be with child through the Holy Spirit, alleluia.

Intercessions: *Weeks 1 & 3*
The Lord God said: 'I shall look for the lost one, bring back the stray, bandage the wounded and make the weak strong.' ℟ Lord our God, come to save us.
Lord God, you made us and sustain us with your love:—help us to recognize that you are in our midst. ℟
You are close to each one of us:—open our hearts to love you. ℟
We pray for those who find their lives a burden too heavy to bear:—Lord, be their strength and their hope. ℟
You are Life, and the enemy of death:—rescue us and all the faithful departed from eternal darkness. ℟
Our Father

Week 2
Let us ask our Father to save us from our sins and send us forward into new life. ℟ Father, may your Son bring us freedom.
The Baptist preached a change of heart:—free us from self-satisfaction. ℟
The Pharisees refused the Baptist's witness to the coming of your Son:—free us from fear of the truth. ℟
The Baptist was glad to make way for him:—free us from pride. ℟
The dead longed for life:—free them from death. ℟
Our Father

The concluding prayer as at Morning Prayer, p 19.

WEDNESDAYS OF ADVENT
To 16 December

Invitatory ant. Let us adore the Lord, the king who is to come.

MORNING PRAYER

Hymn, from the appendix, for Advent.

Scripture Reading   *Is 7:14b-15*
The maiden is with child and will soon give birth to a son whom she
will call Immanuel. On curds and honey will he feed until he knows
how to refuse evil and choose good.

Short Responsory
R̥ The glory of the Lord will shine on you, Jerusalem. Like the sun
he will rise over you. *Repeat* R̥
V̥ His glory will appear in your midst. R̥ Glory be. R̥

Benedictus Antiphon
Week 1: There is one coming who is more powerful than I am. I am
not fit to undo the strap of his sandals.

Week 2: He will sit on the throne of David and he will rule his
kingdom for ever, alleluia.

Week 3: Be comforted, my people, be comforted, says your God.

Intercessions: *Weeks 1 & 3*
The Word of God has chosen to live among us: let us thank him and
give him praise: R̥ Come, Lord Jesus!
Bring justice to those bowed down with suffering:—defend the poor
and the powerless. R̥
Prince of Peace, turn our jealousies into love,—teach us to forgive
rather than give way to anger. R̥
When you come to judge the world,—may we stand before you
without fear. R̥
You stand in our midst unknown:—help us to find you in the poor
and the troubled. R̥
Our Father

Week 2
Let us pray to our Lord Jesus Christ, who in his mercy comes to
visit us. R̥ Come, Lord, do not delay.

21

Lord Jesus Christ, our glory lies in praising you;—come to save us, and we shall bless your name. ℟ Come, Lord, do not delay.

Through faith you have already led us into light;—may our lives be worthy of your call. ℟

Lord Jesus, you entered our world and shared our condition;—bring health to the sick and give the dying a share in your glory. ℟

Let us pray for those who work for their living in the cities or in the countryside;—bless and unite their efforts for a better world. ℟

Our Father

Concluding Prayer

Week 1: Prepare our hearts, Lord,
by the power of your grace.
When Christ comes,
may he find us worthy
to receive from his hand the bread of heaven
at the feast of eternal life.
(We make our prayer) through our Lord.

Week 2: At your bidding, Lord,
we are preparing the way for Christ, your Son.
May we not grow faint on our journey
as we wait for his healing presence.
(We make our prayer) through our Lord

Week 3: Almighty God and Father,
by our celebration of the coming feast of your Son's birth
heal our present ills
and lead us to eternal joy.
(We make our prayer) through our Lord.

EVENING PRAYER

Hymn, from the appendix, for Advent.

Scripture Reading   *1 Cor 4:5*

There must be no passing of premature judgment. Leave that until the Lord comes: he will light up all that is hidden in the dark and reveal the secret intentions of men's hearts. Then will be the time for each one to have whatever praise he deserves, from God.

Short Responsory

R℣ Come to us and save us, Lord God almighty. *Repeat* R℣
℣ Let your face smile on us and we shall be safe. R℣ Glory be. R℣

Magnificat Antiphon

Week 1: The Law will go forth from Sion, and the word of the Lord from Jerusalem.

Week 2: Sion, you will be built anew. Your Holy One will come to you and you will see him.

Week 3: You are the one who is to come, Lord. We look to you to save your people.

Intercessions: *Weeks 1 & 3*

Let us pray to God the Father who is Lord and Ruler of all. R℣ Come and visit your people!
Come as the shepherd to tend your flock;—gather all men into the unity of the Church. R℣
Lord, remember all the sons of Abraham,—all who await your promise in faith. R℣
We pray for those who seek to escape from life;—Lord, give them hope to live by and courage to persevere. R℣
Remember those who have died;—show them the glory your Son has gained for them. R℣
Our Father

Week 2

Christ is coming to free us from the dark night of sin. R℣ Come, Lord Jesus!
Gather the nations together;—Lord, give them the peace which the world cannot give. R℣
Strengthen our faith in the midst of uncertainty and doubt;—vindicate the hope which we place in you. R℣
Teach us to use our gifts for others,—and to fulfil the purpose the Father has for each of his sons. R℣

23

Bring all the dead into the light that no darkness can overpower:—
may we all meet in joy with you. R⁷ Come, Lord Jesus!
Our Father

The concluding prayer as at Morning Prayer, p 22.

THURSDAYS OF ADVENT
To 16 December

Invitatory ant. Let us adore the Lord, the king who is to come.

MORNING PRAYER

Hymn, from the appendix, for Advent.

Scripture Reading   *Is 45:8*
Rain righteousness, you heavens, let the skies above pour down; let
the earth open to receive it, that it may bear the fruit of salvation
with righteousness in blossom at its side.

Short Responsory
R⁷ The glory of the Lord will shine on you, Jerusalem. Like the sun
he will rise over you. *Repeat* R⁷
Y⁷ His glory will appear in your midst. R⁷ Glory be. R⁷

Benedictus Antiphon
Week 1: I will wait for the Lord who saves me. I will hope in him,
for he is coming, alleluia.

Week 2: I will help you, says the Lord; I am your rescuer, the Holy
One of Israel.

Week 3: Arise, arise, Lord, and show us your might.

Intercessions: *Weeks 1 & 3*
Let the heavens open, and the skies rain down the just one; let the
earth bring forth Christ, who is the wisdom and power of God.
R⁷ Be near us, Lord, today.
Lord Jesus Christ, you have called us into your kingdom:—may we

enter in, and live according to your call. R⁷
The world does not know you:—show yourself, in our midst, to all
our brothers. R⁷
We thank you, Lord, for all that we have:—move us to give of our
plenty to those who have little. R⁷
We look for your coming, Lord Jesus:—when you knock, may we
be found watching in prayer and rejoicing in praise. R⁷
Our Father

Week 2
Though the Lord's coming is at hand, we must have patience: for he
will come in his own time, in his own way. R⁷ Lord Jesus, help us to
believe that you are coming.
We live in a world weighed down by unbelief:—Lord, increase our
faith. R⁷
Upon the richness and complexity of man's thought, among the
theories and philosophies of our world today,—let your coming
shed its own glorious light. R⁷
Give us the strong faith of the apostles,—and their fervour in
preaching your word. R⁷
Let us love the Church,—which continues to proclaim to all ages
the reality of your coming. R⁷
Our Father

Concluding Prayer
Week 1: Show forth your power, Lord, and come.
Come in your great strength and help us.
Be merciful and forgiving,
and hasten the salvation which only our sins delay.
(We make our prayer) through our Lord.

Week 2: Clear a pathway, Lord, in our hearts
to make ready for your only Son,
so that when he comes
we may serve you in sincerity of heart.
(We make our prayer) through our Lord.

Week 3: With sorrow, Lord, we confess our sins,
unworthy servants that we are.
Heal us and bring us joy
by the coming of your only Son,
who lives and reigns with you and the Holy Spirit,
God, for ever and ever.

EVENING PRAYER

Hymn, from the appendix, for Advent.

Scripture Reading   *Jas 5:7-8,9b*
Be patient, then, my brothers, until the Lord comes. See how the
farmer is patient as he waits for his land to produce precious crops.
He waits patiently for the autumn and spring rains. And you also
must be patient! Keep your hopes high, for the day of the Lord's
coming is near. The Judge is near, ready to come in!

Short Responsory
℟ Come to us and save us, Lord God almighty. *Repeat* ℟
℣ Let your face smile on us and we shall be safe. ℟ Glory be. ℟

Magnificat Antiphon
Week 1: You are the most blessed of all women, and blessed is the
fruit of your womb.

Week 2: The one who will come after me already existed before I
was born. I am not fit to undo his sandals.

Week 3: Rejoice for ever with Jerusalem and exult for her. all you
who love her.

Intercessions: *Weeks 1 & 3*
Let us pray to Christ, the great light promised by the prophets to
those dwelling in the shadow of death: ℟ Come, Lord Jesus!
You enlighten all men—open the hearts of your people to a wider
world. ℟
Son of God, in you we see the Father—come to reveal to us what
true love means. ℟

Christ Jesus, you come to us as man—may the welcome we give you make us sons of God. R̶

You open the gates of liberty and life—bring the dead into everlasting freedom. R̶

Our Father

Week 2

God is light: if we live and move in light, there is love between us. R̶ Lord Jesus, help us to love one another.

May we who are called Christians,—be known by our love. R̶

Without love the world cannot be at peace;—rid our world of hatred and fear. R̶

Help husbands and wives to find comfort in sorrow and strength in trials;—grant them enduring love. R̶

Lord, keep all the dead in your care:—those we have loved and those no one remembers. R̶

Our Father

The concluding prayer as at Morning Prayer, pp 25–6.

FRIDAYS OF ADVENT
To 16 December

Invitatory ant. Let us adore the Lord, the king who is to come.

MORNING PRAYER

Hymn, from the appendix, for Advent.

Scripture Reading   *Jer 30:21,22*

A ruler shall appear, one of themselves,
a governor shall arise from their own number.
I will myself bring him near and so he shall approach me, says the
    Lord.
So you shall be my people,
and I will be your God.

Short Responsory

R︎ The glory of the Lord will shine on you, Jerusalem. Like the sun he will rise over you. *Repeat* R︎

℣ His glory will appear in your midst. R︎ Glory be. R︎

Benedictus Antiphon

Week 1: Behold the one who is both God and man: He comes forth from the stock of David and sits on the throne, alleluia.

Week 2: Say to the faint-hearted, Be strong and do not fear: behold, the Lord our God will come.

Week 3: Observe what is right, and do what is just: for my salvation will come soon.

Intercessions: *Weeks 1 & 3*

It was the Father's will that men should see him in the face of his beloved Son. R︎ Hallowed be your name!

Christ greeted us with good news:—may the world hear it through us, and find hope. R︎

We praise and thank you, Lord of heaven and earth:—the hope and joy of men in every age. R︎

May Christ's coming transform the Church,—renewing its youth and vigour in the service of men. R︎

We pray for Christians who suffer for their beliefs:—sustain them in their hope. R︎

Our Father

Week 2

It is time for us to wake from our sleep: the day of our salvation is near. R︎ Lord, may your kingdom come!

Help us to show our repentance—by a new way of living. R︎

Prepare us for the coming of your Word—by opening our hearts to receive him. R︎

Help us to overcome our pride,—and raise us from the depths of our weakness. R︎

Throw down the walls of hatred between nations,—clear the way for those who work for peace. R︎

Our Father

Concluding Prayer

Week 1: Call forth your power, Lord;
come and save us from the judgment
that threatens us by reason of our sins.
Come, and set us free.
(We make our prayer) through our Lord.

Week 2: Lord, keep us ever alert and watchful
as we await the coming of your Son,
so that, faithful to his teaching,
we may hasten to meet our Saviour with lamps alight.
(We make our prayer) through our Lord.

Week 3: Let your grace, Lord,
light our pilgrim way to the end.
Support us now and always
as we wait, longing with all our hearts,
for the coming of Christ, your Son,
who lives and reigns with you and the Holy Spirit,
God, for ever and ever.

EVENING PRAYER

Hymn, from the appendix, for Advent.

Scripture Reading   *2 Pet 3:8b-9*

There is no difference in the Lord's sight between one day and a thousand years; to him, the two are the same. The Lord is not slow to do what he has promised, as some think. Instead, he is patient with you, because he does not want anyone to be destroyed, but wants all to turn away from their sins.

Short Responsory

R̲ Come to us and save us, Lord God almighty. *Repeat* R̲
V̲ Let your face smile on us and we shall be safe. R̲ Glory be. R̲

Magnificat Antiphon

Week 1: Out of Egypt I have called my son. He will come and save his people.

Week 2: Joyfully you will draw water from the wells of salvation.

Week 3: This is the testimony of John: The one who is coming after me already existed before I was born.

Intercessions: *Weeks 1 & 3*
As we prepare to celebrate the birth of Christ, we pray that the Church may come to birth again in our times. R̷ Be born in us, Lord.
Lord Jesus, born of Mary,—come again into our world. R̷
Help us to show compassion and respect for the mentally ill,—since we are all children of God. R̷
Through the Church's proclamation of your coming,—bring light to those who search for truth. R̷
You were born to die for our sins:—at our death may we be born into your life. R̷
Our Father

Week 2
The Lord God said: 'I shall look for the lost one, bring back the stray, bandage the wounded and make the weak strong.' R̷ Lord our God, come to save us.
Lord God, you made us and sustain us with your love:—help us to recognize that you are in our midst. R̷
You are close to each one of us:—open our hearts to love you. R̷
We pray for those who find their lives a burden too heavy to bear:—Lord, be their strength and their hope. R̷
You are Life, and the enemy of death:—rescue us and all the faithful departed from eternal darkness. R̷
Our Father

The concluding prayer as at Morning Prayer, p 29.

SATURDAYS OF ADVENT
To 16 December

Invitatory ant. Let us adore the Lord, the king who is to come.

MORNING PRAYER

Hymn, from the appendix, for Advent.

Scripture Reading   *Is 11:1-2*
A shoot shall grow from the stock of Jesse, and a branch shall spring from his roots. The spirit of the Lord shall rest upon him, a spirit of wisdom and understanding, a spirit of counsel and power, a spirit of knowledge and the fear of the Lord.

Short Responsory
R̷ The glory of the Lord will shine on you, Jerusalem. Like the sun he will rise over you. *Repeat* R̷
V̷ His glory will appear in your midst. R̷ Glory be. R̷

Benedictus Antiphon
Week 1: Do not be afraid, Sion: behold, your God will come, alleluia.

Week 2: The Lord will raise a signal for the nations and he will gather together the scattered children of Israel.

Intercessions: *Week 1*
The Lord, our God, is coming: let us put aside fear, and look forward to the future with courage. R̷ Your kingdom come!
Lord, you make all things and renew them:—all creation displays your work. R̷
You have given us dominion over the earth;—may our work have a share of your creative power. R̷
We pray for those who work for the relief of suffering in others;—may they also know comfort and understanding. R̷ Your kingdom come!
As we rest from our work at the end of the week,—restore our strength and give us time to know you. R̷
Our Father

Week 2
Let us pray to Christ, whom the scriptures foretold, and whose coming we await in this holy season: R̷ Come, Jesus, our Saviour!

31

Isaiah foretold that the spirit of the Lord would rest upon you:
—come to us bringing wisdom and understanding. R7 Come, Jesus,
our Saviour!
The spirit of counsel and power is given to you;—move the hearts
of all who govern or rule. R7
The fear of the Lord is the beginning of wisdom;—teach us to know
the Father as he is. R7
As now we live with you in faith and hope,—prepare us to see the
Father face to face. R7
Our Father

Concluding Prayer
Week 1: Lord, to free man from his sinful state
you sent your only Son into this world.
Grant to us who in faith and love wait for his coming
your gift of grace
and the reward of true freedom.
(We make our prayer) through our Lord.

Week 2: Almighty God,
let the splendour of your glory dawn in our hearts.
May the coming of your only Son dispel all darkness
and reveal that we are children of light.
(We make our prayer) through our Lord.

ADVENT
FROM 17 TO 24 DECEMBER

Invitatory ant. The Lord is at hand: come, let us adore him.
24 December. Know today that the Lord will come: in the morning
you will see his glory.

*The proper antiphons for Morning and Evening Prayer of weekdays
are given in the psalter, Weeks 3 and 4, under the directive: 17-23
December.*

17 DECEMBER

Invitatory ant. The Lord is at hand: come, let us adore him.

MORNING PRAYER

Hymn, from the appendix, for Advent II.
Psalms and canticle with proper antiphons as in the psalter, and so daily.

Scripture Reading   *Is 11:1-2*
A shoot shall grow from the stock of Jesse, and a branch shall spring from his roots. The spirit of the Lord shall rest upon him, a spirit of wisdom and understanding, a spirit of counsel and power, a spirit of knowledge and the fear of the Lord.

Short Responsory
R℣ The glory of the Lord will shine on you, Jerusalem. Like the sun he will rise over you. Repeat R℣
℣ His glory will appear in your midst. R℣ Glory be. R℣

Benedictus ant. Know that the kingdom of God is at hand; be sure that he will not delay.

Intercessions
The Lord, our God, is coming: let us put aside fear, and look forward to the future with courage. R℣ Your kingdom come!
Lord, you make all things and renew them:—all creation displays your work. R℣
You have given us dominion over the earth;—may our work have a share of your creative power. R℣
We pray for those who work for the relief of suffering in others;—may they also know comfort and understanding. R℣
Bless us as we work;—give us faith until the end, when our labours will receive their reward. R℣
Our Father

Concluding Prayer
Father,
by your will your Son took upon himself

that human nature which you fashioned and redeemed.
Grant that the Word who took flesh
in the womb of the ever-virgin Mary
and became a man like us,
may share with us his godhead.
(We make our prayer) through our Lord.

EVENING PRAYER

Hymn, from the appendix, for Advent II.
Psalms and canticle with proper antiphons as in the psalter, and so daily.

Scripture Reading   *I Thess 5:23-24*
May the God who gives us peace make you completely his, and keep
your whole being, spirit, soul, and body, free from all fault, at the
coming of our Lord Jesus Christ. He who calls you will do it, for he
is faithful!

Short Responsory
R̢ Come to us and save us, Lord, God almighty. *Repeat* R̢
V̢ Let your face smile on us and we shall be safe. R̢ Glory be. R̢

Magnificat ant. O Wisdom, you come forth from the mouth of the
Most High. You fill the universe and hold all things together in a
strong yet gentle manner. O come to teach us the way of truth.

Intercessions
The Son of God is coming with great power: all mankind shall see
his face and be reborn. R̢ Come, Lord Jesus: do not delay!
You will bring us wisdom, fresh understanding and new vision.—R̢
You will bring us good news, and power which will transform our
lives.—R̢
You will bring us truth, showing us the way to our Father.—R̢
Born of a woman, you will open in our flesh the way to eternal life
and joy.—R̢
Our Father

The concluding prayer as at Morning Prayer, p 33.

18 DECEMBER

Invitatory ant. The Lord is at hand: come, let us adore him.

MORNING PRAYER

Hymn, from the appendix, for Advent II.

Scripture Reading   *Rom 13:11-12*
It is now the hour for you to wake from sleep, for our salvation is
closer than when we first accepted the faith. The night is far spent;
the day draws near. Let us cast off deeds of darkness and put on the
armour of light.

Short Responsory
R/ The glory of the Lord will shine on you, Jerusalem. Like the sun
he will rise over you. *Repeat* R/
V/ His glory will appear in your midst. R/ Glory be. R/

Benedictus ant. Watch! The Lord is near.

Intercessions
It is time for us to wake out of our sleep: salvation is nearer to us
now than when we first believed. R/ Father of light, we praise you!
Christ is coming, the day is near:—in our eucharist today let us look
forward with hope and joy. R/
As today we hear the scriptures, heralding the coming of your Son—
may our minds and hearts be touched by your Word. R/
As we receive the Body and Blood of your Son,—may we be healed
and refreshed by your love. R/
United in one body, may we pursue the things that make for peace,—
and build up our life together until Christ comes. R/
Our Father

Concluding Prayer
By the long-awaited coming of your new-born Son
deliver us, Lord,
from the age-old bondage of sin.
(We make our prayer) through our Lord.

EVENING PRAYER

Hymn, from the appendix, for Advent II.

Scripture Reading   *Phil 4:4-5*
Rejoice in the Lord always; again I will say, Rejoice. Let all men
know your forbearance. The Lord is at hand.

Short Responsory
R℣ Come to us and save us, Lord, God almighty. *Repeat* R℣
℣ Let your face smile on us and we shall be safe. R℣ Glory be. R℣

Magnificat ant. O Adonai and leader of Israel, you appeared to
Moses in a burning bush and you gave him the Law on Sinai. O
come and save us with your mighty power.

Intercessions
The voice of John crying in the wilderness is echoed tonight in the
voice of the Church: R℣ Make our hearts ready, O Lord!
For your coming to us in grace this Advent.—R℣
For the work man must do in creating a more just world.—R℣
For the understanding we will need for our families and our friends.
—R℣
For our death, for our judgment, for eternal life with you.—R℣
Our Father

The concluding prayer as at Morning Prayer, p 35.

19 DECEMBER

Invitatory ant. The Lord is at hand: come, let us adore him.

MORNING PRAYER

Hymn, from the appendix, for Advent II.

Scripture Reading   *Is 2:3*
Come, let us go up to the mountain of the Lord, to the house of the

God of Jacob; that he may teach us his ways and that we may walk in his paths. For out of Sion shall go forth the law, and the word of the Lord from Jerusalem.

Short Responsory

R⁊ The glory of the Lord will shine on you, Jerusalem. Like the sun he will rise over you. *Repeat* R⁊

Ⅴ His glory will appear in your midst. R⁊ Glory be. R⁊

Benedictus ant. The Saviour of the world will rise like the sun: and he will come down into the womb of the Virgin like rain gently falling on the earth.

Intercessions

As we pray together in the name of the Church, turn our minds and hearts back to you, Lord. R⁊ Send us your light and your truth.

As we think and pray about your Son's coming,—help us to grasp its meaning in a way that is personal and profound. R⁊

May we never despise any of our fellow-men, since we are all your children.—Help us rather to fight against their hurt or degradation. R⁊

Heal the broken bonds of human life:—reconcile us in the sharing of our hope in Christ. R⁊

Help us to hear your voice—.hrough the situations in which we work today. R⁊

Our Father

Concluding Prayer

Deepen our faith, Lord God,
as we celebrate the great mystery of the incarnation
by which you revealed to the world
the splendour of your glory
through the Virgin Mary when she gave birth to your Son,
who lives and reigns with you and the Holy Spirit,
God, for ever and ever.

EVENING PRAYER

Hymn, from the appendix, for Advent II.

Scripture Reading   *Phil 3:20b-21*
It is to heaven that we look expectantly for the coming of our Lord
Jesus Christ to save us; he will form this humbled body of ours anew,
moulding it into the image of his glorified body, so effective is his
power to make all things obey him.

Short Responsory
R℣ Come to us and save us, Lord, God almighty. *Repeat* R℣
℣ Let your face smile on us and we shall be safe. R℣ Glory be. R℣

Magnificat ant. O stock of Jesse, you stand as a signal for the nations;
kings fall silent before you whom the peoples acclaim. O come to
deliver us, and do not delay.

Intercessions
The Lord who is to come is the Judge of the living and the dead.
R℣ Christ, have mercy.
We thank you for the mercy you have shown us:—Let your com-
passion support us in our weakness. R℣
You humbled yourself to wash away our guilt:—forgive us the times
when we have been indifferent to your pardon. R℣
Grant us also a spirit of understanding—to forgive as we ourselves
are forgiven. R℣
If you should mark the guilt of those who have died,—Lord, who
would survive? R℣
Our Father

The concluding prayer as at Morning Prayer, p 37.

20 DECEMBER

Invitatory ant. The Lord is at hand: come, let us adore him.

MORNING PRAYER

Hymn, from the appendix, for Advent II.

Scripture Reading　　　*Gen 49:10*
Juda shall not want a branch from his stem, a prince drawn from his stock, until the day when he comes who is to be sent to us, he, the hope of the nations.

Short Responsory
R̷ The glory of the Lord will shine on you, Jerusalem. Like the sun he will rise over you. *Repeat* R̷
V̷ His glory will appear in your midst. R̷ Glory be. R̷

Benedictus ant. The angel Gabriel was sent to the Virgin Mary who was betrothed to Joseph.

Intercessions
It is time for us to wake from our sleep: the day of our salvation is near. R̷ Lord, may your kingdom come!
Help us to show our repentance—by a new way of living. R̷
Prepare us for the coming of your Word—by opening our hearts to receive him. R̷
Help us to overcome our pride,—and raise us from the depths of our weakness. R̷
Throw down the walls of hatred between nations,—clear the way for those who work for peace. R̷
Our Father

Concluding Prayer
Lord, at the angel's message,
Mary, the immaculate Virgin,
became the temple of God,

39

and was filled with the light of the Holy Spirit,
when she received your divine Word.
Grant that, after her example,
we may humbly and steadfastly follow your will.
(We make our prayer) through our Lord.

EVENING PRAYER

Hymn, from the appendix, for Advent II.

Scripture Reading   *Cf 1 Cor 1:7b-9*
You wait expectantly for our Lord Jesus Christ to reveal himself.
He will keep you firm to the end, without reproach on the Day of
our Lord Jesus. It is God himself who called you to share in the life
of his Son.

Short Responsory
R̷ Come to us and save us, Lord, God almighty. *Repeat* R̷
V̷ Let your face smile on us and we shall be safe. R̷ Glory be. R̷

Magnificat ant. O key of David and sceptre of Israel, what you open
no one else can close again; what you close no one can open. O
come to lead the captive from prison; free those who sit in darkness
and in the shadow of death.

Intercessions
The Lord God said: 'I shall look tor the lost and bring back the stray,
bandage the wounded and make the weak strong.' R̷ Lord our God,
come to save us.
Lord God, you made us and sustain us with your love:—help us to
recognize that you are in our midst. R̷
You are close to each one of us:—open our hearts to love you. R̷
We pray for those who find their lives a burden too heavy to bear:
—Lord, be their strength and their hope. R̷
You are Life, and the enemy of death:—rescue us and all the faithful
departed from eternal darkness. R̷
Our Father

The concluding prayer as at Morning Prayer, p 39.

21 DECEMBER

Invitatory ant. The Lord is at hand: come, let us adore him.

MORNING PRAYER

Hymn, from the appendix, for Advent II.

Scripture Reading   *Is 7:14b-15*
The maiden is with child and will soon give birth to a son whom she will call Immanuel. On curds and honey will he feed until he knows how to refuse evil and choose good.

Short Responsory
R/ The glory of the Lord will shine on you, Jerusalem. Like the sun he will rise over you. *Repeat* R/
V His glory will appear in your midst. R/ Glory be. R/

Benedictus ant. Do not be afraid. You will see our Lord on the fifth day.

Intercessions
Let us pray to our Lord Jesus Christ, who in his mercy comes to visit us. R/ Come, Lord, do not delay.
Lord Jesus Christ, our glory lies in praising you;—come to save us and we shall bless your name. R/
Through faith you have already led us into light;—may our lives be worthy of your call. R/
Lord Jesus, you entered our world and shared our condition;—bring health to the sick and give the dying a share in your glory. R/
Let us pray for those who work for their living in the cities or in the countryside;—bless and unite their efforts for a better world. R/
Our Father

Concluding Prayer
In your goodness, Lord,
listen to your people's prayer.

As we rejoice at the coming of your Son
in flesh and blood like ours,
grant that when he comes again in glory
we may receive the gift of eternal life.
(We make our prayer) through our Lord.

EVENING PRAYER

Hymn, from the appendix, for Advent II.

Scripture Reading   *1 Cor 4:5*
There must be no passing of premature judgment. Leave that until
the Lord comes: he will light up all that is hidden in the dark and
reveal the secret intentions of men's hearts. Then will be the time for
each one to have whatever praise he deserves, from God.

Short Responsory
R̸ Come to us and save us, Lord, God almighty. *Repeat* R̸
V̸ Let your face smile on us and we shall be safe. R̸ Glory be. R̸

Magnificat ant. O Rising Sun, you are the splendour of eternal light
and the sun of justice. O come and enlighten those who sit in darkness and in the shadow of death.

Intercessions
Christ is coming to free us from the dark night of sin. R̸ Come, Lord
Jesus!
Gather the nations together;—Lord, give them the peace which the
world cannot give. R̸
Strengthen our faith in the midst of uncertainty and doubt;—vindi-
cate the hope which we place in you. R̸
Teach us to use our gifts for others,—and to fulfil the purpose the
Father has for each of his children. R̸
Bring all the dead into the light that no darkness can quench:—may
we all meet in joy with you. R̸
Our Father

The concluding prayer as at Morning Prayer, p 41.

22 DECEMBER

Invitatory ant. The Lord is at hand: come, let us adore him.

MORNING PRAYER

Hymn, from the appendix, for Advent II.

Scripture Reading   *Is 45:8*
Rain righteousness, you heavens, let the skies above pour down; let
the earth open to receive it, that it may bear the fruit of salvation
with righteousness in blossom at its side.

Short Responsory
R̷ The glory of the Lord will shine on you, Jerusalem. Like the sun
he will rise over you. *Repeat* R̷
y̷ His glory will appear in your midst. R̷ Glory be. R̷

Benedictus ant. When the voice of your greeting came to my ears, the
babe in my womb leaped for joy.

Intercessions
In a world divided by fear and greed, the Church calls again on her
Saviour. R̷ Lord Jesus, come to us in love.
Help us to set our hearts where they will find fulfilment;—and not
betrayal. R̷
As we proclaim your saving power to others,—let us not ourselves
lose hold of your salvation. R̷
May our world be flooded with the grace of your coming:—let us
experience the fulness of your joy. R̷
May we live our lives to the full in this world,—and transfigure it
with the hope of future glory. R̷
Our Father

Concluding Prayer
God and Father,
you looked in pity on fallen man

and redeemed us by the coming of your Son.
Grant that we who profess our firm and humble faith
in the incarnation of our Redeemer,
may have some share in his divine life.
(We make our prayer) through our Lord.

EVENING PRAYER

Hymn, from the appendix, for Advent II.

Scripture Reading   *Jas 5:7-8,9b*
Be patient, my brothers, until the Lord comes. See how the farmer is patient as he waits for his land to produce precious crops. He waits patiently for the autumn and spring rains. And you also must be patient! Keep your hopes high, for the day of the Lord's coming is near. The Judge is near, ready to come in!

Short Responsory
R̰ Come to us and save us, Lord, God almighty. *Repeat* R̰
V̰ Let your face smile on us and we shall be safe. R̰ Glory be. R̰

Magnificat ant. O King whom all the peoples desire, you are the cornerstone which makes all one. O come and save man whom you made from clay.

Intercessions
God is light: if we live and move in light, there is love between us.
R̰ Lord Jesus, help us to love one another.
May we who are called Christians—be known by our love. R̰
Without love the world cannot be at peace:—rid our world of hatred and fear. R̰
Help husbands and wives to find comfort in sorrow and strength in trials;—grant them enduring love. R̰
Lord, keep all the dead in your care:—those we have loved and those no one remembers. R̰
Our Father

The concluding prayer as at Morning Prayer, p 43.

23 DECEMBER

Invitatory ant. The Lord is at hand: come, let us adore him.

MORNING PRAYER

Hymn, from the appendix, for Advent II.

Scripture Reading   *Jer 30:21,22*
A ruler shall appear, one of themselves,
a governor shall arise from their own number.
I will myself bring him near and so he shall approach me, says the
    Lord.
So you shall be my people,
and I will be your God.

Short Responsory
R⁷ The glory of the Lord will shine on you, Jerusalem. Like the sun
he will rise over you. *Repeat* R⁷
℣ His glory will appear in your midst. R⁷ Glory be. R⁷

Benedictus ant. Behold, everything is fulfilled which the angel
promised the Virgin Mary.

Intercessions
Though the Lord's coming is at hand, we must have patience: for he
will come in his own time, in his own way. R⁷ Lord Jesus, help us to
believe that you are coming.
We live in a world weighed down by unbelief:—Lord, increase our
faith. R⁷
Upon the richness and complexity of man's thought, among the
theories and philosophies of our world today,—let your coming shed
its own glorious light. R⁷
Give us the strong faith of the apostles,—and their fervour in preaching your word. R⁷
Let us love the Church,—which continues to proclaim to all ages the
reality of your coming. R⁷
Our Father

Concluding Prayer
Almighty God,
now that the birthday of your Son as man is drawing near,
we pray that your eternal Word,
who took flesh in the womb of the Virgin Mary,
and came to dwell among men,
will show your unworthy people the greatness of his love and mercy,
who lives and reigns with you and the Holy Spirit,
God, for ever and ever.

EVENING PRAYER

Hymn, from the appendix, for Advent II.

Scripture Reading   *2 Pet 3:8b-9*
There is no difference in the Lord's sight between one day and a
thousand years, to him, the two are the same. The Lord is not slow
to do what he has promised, as some think. Instead, he is patient
with you, because he does not want anyone to be destroyed, but
wants all to turn away from their sins.

Short Responsory
R︆ Come to us and save us, Lord, God almighty. *Repeat* R︆
℣ Let your face smile on us and we shall be safe. R︆ Glory be. R︆

Magnificat ant. O Immanuel, you are our king and judge, the One
whom the peoples await and their Saviour. O come and save us,
Lord, our God.

Intercessions
Let us ask our Father to save us from our sins and lead us forward
into new life. R︆ Father, may your Son bring us freedom.
The Baptist preached a change of heart:—free us from self-satisfac-
tion. R︆
The Pharisees refused the Baptist's witness to the coming of your
Son:—free us from fear of the truth. R︆
The Baptist was glad to make way for him:—free us from pride. R︆
The dead longed for life:—free them from death. R︆

Our Father

The concluding prayer as at Morning Prayer, p 46.

24 DECEMBER

Invitatory ant. Know today that the Lord will come: in the morning you will see his glory.

MORNING PRAYER

Hymn, from the appendix, for Advent II.

Psalms and canticle from the psalter, according to the week and day, with the following antiphons:

Ant. 1: You, Bethlehem, will not be least among the towns of Juda: for the leader who will rule my people Israel will come from you.

Ant. 2: Lift up your heads for your redemption is at hand.

Ant. 3: Tomorrow your salvation will be with you, says the Lord, God almighty.

Scripture Reading   *Is 11:1-2*
A shoot shall grow from the stock of Jesse, and a branch shall spring from his roots. The spirit of the Lord shall rest upon him, a spirit of wisdom and understanding, a spirit of counsel and power, a spirit of knowledge and the fear of the Lord.

Short Responsory
R℣ Tomorrow is the day on which the sins of the world will be wiped away. *Repeat* R℣
℣ The Saviour of the world will rule us himself. R℣ Glory be. R℣

Benedictus ant. The time is now at hand for the Virgin Mary to give birth to her firstborn Son.

Intercessions

Let us pray to Christ, whom the scriptures foretold, and whose coming we await in this holy season: R℣ Come, Jesus our Saviour! Isaiah foretold that the spirit of the Lord would rest upon you:— come to us bringing wisdom and understanding. R℣

The spirit of counsel and power is given to you;—move the hearts of all who govern or rule. R℣

The fear of the Lord is the beginning of wisdom;—teach us to know the Father as he is. R℣

As now we live with you in faith and hope,—prepare us to see the Father face to face. R℣

Our Father

Concluding Prayer

Come, Lord Jesus, come soon.
In this time of your coming,
support and console us who trust in your love,
who live and reign with the Father and the Holy Spirit,
God, for ever and ever.

CHRISTMASTIDE

THE NATIVITY OF
OUR LORD JESUS CHRIST

Solemnity

EVENING PRAYER I

Hymn

A noble flow'r of Juda from tender roots has sprung,
A rose from stem of Jesse, as prophets long had sung,
A blossom fair and bright,
That in the midst of winter will change to dawn our night.

The rose of grace and beauty of which Isaiah sings
Is Mary, virgin mother, and Christ the flow'r she brings.
By God's divine decree
She bore our loving Saviour, who died to set us free.

To Mary, dearest Mother, with fervent hearts we pray:
Grant that your tender infant will cast our sins away,
And guide us with his love
That we shall ever serve him, and live with him above.

PSALMODY

Ant. 1: The King of Peace has shown himself in glory: all the peoples desire to see him.

PSALM 112(113)

Práise, O sérvants of the Lórd,*
práise the náme of the Lórd!
May the náme of the Lórd be bléssed*
both nów and for évermóre!
From the rísing of the sún to its sétting*
práised be the náme of the Lórd!

Hígh above all nátions is the Lórd,*
abóve the héavens his glóry.
Whó is like the Lórd, our Gód,*
who has rísen on hígh to his thróne
yet stóops from the héights to look dówn,*
to look dówn upon héaven and éarth?

From the dúst he lífts up the lówly,*
from his mísery he ráises the póor
to sét him in the cómpany of prínces,*
yés, with the prínces of his péople.
To the chíldless wífe he gives a hóme*
and gláddens her héart with chíldren.

Ant. The King of Peace has shown himself in glory: all the peoples
desire to see him.
Ant. 2: He sends out his word to the earth and swiftly runs his
command.

PSALM 147

O práise the Lórd, Jerúsalem!*
Síon, práise your Gód!

He has stréngthened the bárs of your gátes,*
he has bléssed the chíldren withín you.
He estáblished péace on your bórders,*
he féeds you with fínest whéat.

He sénds out his wórd to the éarth*
and swíftly rúns his commánd.
He shówers down snów white as wóol,*
he scátters hóar-frost like áshes.

He húrls down háilstones like crúmbs.*
The wáters are frózen at his tóuch;
he sénds forth his wórd and it mélts them:*
at the bréath of his móuth the waters flów.

He mákes his wórd known to Jácob,*
to Ísrael his láws and decrées.

He has not déalt thus with óther nátions;*
he has not táught them hís decrées.

Ant. He sends out his word to the earth and swiftly runs his command.

Ant. 3: The Word of God, born of the Father before time began, humbled himself today for us and became man.

CANTICLE: PHIL 2:6-11

Though he was in the form of God,*
Jesus did not count equality with God a thing to be grasped.

He emptied himself,†
taking the form of a servant,*
being born in the likeness of men.

And being found in human form,†
he humbled himself and became obedient unto death,*
even death on a cross.

Therefore God has highly exalted him*
and bestowed on him the name which is above every name,

That at the name of Jesus every knee should bow,*
in heaven and on earth and under the earth.

And every tongue confess that Jesus Christ is Lord,*
to the glory of God the Father.

Ant. The Word of God, born of the Father before time began, humbled himself today for us and became man.

Scripture Reading   *Gal 4:4-5*
When the appointed time came, God sent his Son, born of a woman, —born a subject of the Law, to redeem the subjects of the Law and to enable us to be adopted as sons.

Short Responsory
℟ Today you know that the Lord will come. *Repeat* ℟
℣ In the morning you will see his glory. ℟ Glory be. ℟

Magnificat ant. **When the sun rises in the heavens you will see the king of kings. He comes forth from the Father like a bridegroom coming in splendour from his wedding chamber.**

Intercessions
Let us turn in prayer to Christ who emptied himself to assume the condition of a slave. He was tempted in every way that we are, but did not sin. ℟ Save us through your birth.

Coming into our world, Lord Jesus, you open the new age which the prophets foretold.—In every age, may the Church come again to new birth. ℟

You took on our human weakness.—Be the eyes of the blind, the strength of the weak, the friend of the lonely. ℟

Lord, you were born among the poor:—show them your love. ℟

Your birth brings eternal life within man's reach;—comfort the dying with hope of new life in heaven. ℟

Gather the departed to yourself;—and make them radiant in your glory. ℟

Our Father

Concluding Prayer
Fill us with confidence, Lord God,
when your Only-begotten Son comes as our judge.
We welcome him with joy as our redeemer;
year by year renew that joy
as we await the fulfilment of our redemption
by Jesus Christ our Lord, your Son,
who lives and reigns with you and the Holy Spirit,
God, for ever and ever.

¶ *Night Prayer is said only by those who do not attend the Office of Readings and Midnight Mass.*

Invitatory
Ant. Christ has been born for us: come, let us adore him.

¶ *Morning Prayer should not regularly be said immediately after Midnight Mass, but in the morning.*

MORNING PRAYER

Hymn

Afar from where the sun doth rise
To lands beneath the western skies,
Homage to Christ our King we pay,
Born of a Virgin's womb this day.

Blessed Creator, thou didst take
A servant's likeness for our sake,
And didst in flesh our flesh restore
To bid thy creature live once more.

Chaste was the womb where thou didst dwell,
Of heavenly grace the hidden cell;
Nor might the blessed Maid proclaim
Whence her dread Guest in secret came.

Down from on high God came to rest
His glory in a sinless breast;
Obedience at his word believed,
And virgin innocence conceived.

Ere long, that holy Child she bore
By Gabriel's message named before,
Whom, yet unborn, with eager pride,
The swift forerunner prophesied.

Fast doth he sleep, where straw doth spread
A humble manger for his bed;
A Mother's milk that strength renewed
Which gives the birds of heaven their food.

Glory to God, the angels cry;
Earth hears the echo from on high;
Mankind's true Shepherd and its Lord
By shepherd hearts is first adored.

PSALMODY

Ant. 1: Shepherds, tell us whom you have seen. Who has appeared on earth? We have seen the newborn child and we have heard the choirs of angels praising the Lord, alleluia.

Psalms and canticle of Sunday, Week 1, pp 390 ff.

Ant. 2: The angel said to the shepherds, 'I bring you news of great joy. Today the Saviour of the world has been born to you, alleluia.'

Ant. 3: Today a child is born to us. His name will be called 'Mighty God', alleluia.

Scripture Reading   *Heb 1:1-2*
When in former times God spoke to our forefathers, he spoke in fragmentary and varied fashion through the prophets. But in this the final age he has spoken to us in the Son whom he has made heir to the whole universe, and through whom he created all orders of existence.

Short Responsory
R⁊ The Lord has made known our salvation, alleluia, alleluia.
Repeat R⁊
V⁊ He has revealed his saving power. R⁊ Glory be. R⁊

Benedictus ant. Glory be to God on high, and on earth peace among his chosen people, alleluia.

Intercessions
God our Father, this morning we eagerly greet the birth of Jesus, our brother and Saviour. He is the Daystar from on high, the light-bearer who brings the dawn to us, who wait patiently for his coming.
R⁊ Glory to God in the highest, and on earth peace among men.
Father, bless on this holy day the Church all over the world.—May she light afresh in men's hearts the lamps of hope and peace. R⁊
Your Son has come to us in the fulness of time:—let those who wait for him recognize his coming. R⁊
His birth bound heaven to earth in harmony and peace.—Establish that same peace among nations and men of today. R⁊
With Mary and Joseph we rejoice in the birth of Jesus.—May we welcome Christ as they did. R⁊
Our Father

Concluding Prayer
Almighty God,
your incarnate Word fills us
with the new light he brought to men.
Let the light of faith in our hearts
shine through all that we do and say.
(We make our prayer) through our Lord.

EVENING PRAYER II

Hymn

Christ, whose blood for all men streamed,
Light, that shone ere morning beamed,
God and God's eternal Son,
Ever with the Father one;

Splendour of the Father's light,
Star of hope for ever bright,
Hearken to the prayers that flow
From thy servants here below.

Lord, remember that in love
Thou didst leave thy throne above,
Man's frail nature to assume
In the holy Virgin's womb.

Now thy Church, each circling year,
Celebrates that love so dear;
Love that brought thee here alone,
For the guilty to atone.

Let not earth alone rejoice,
Seas and skies unite their voice
In a new song, to the morn
When the Lord of life was born.

Virgin-born, to thee be praise,
Now and through eternal days;
Father, equal praise to thee,
With the Spirit, ever be.

PSALMODY

Ant. 1: All authority and dominion are yours on the day of your strength; you are resplendent in holiness. From the womb before the dawn I begot you.

PSALM 109(110):1-5,7

The Lórd's revelátion to my Máster:†
'Sít on my ríght:*
your fóes I will pút beneath your féet.'

The Lórd will wíeld from Síon†
your scéptre of pówer:*
rúle in the mídst of all your fóes.

A prínce from the dáy of your bírth†
on the hóly móuntains;*
from the wómb before the dáwn I begót you.

The Lórd has sworn an óath he will not chánge.†
'You are a príest for éver,*
a príest like Melchízedek of óld.'

The Máster stánding at your ríght hand*
will shatter kíngs in the dáy of his wráth.

He shall drínk from the stréam by the wáyside*
and thérefore he shall líft up his héad.

Ant. All authority and dominion are yours on the day of your strength; you are resplendent in holiness. From the womb before the dawn I begot you.

Ant. 2: With the Lord there is unfailing love. Great is his power to set men free.

PSALM 129(130)

Out of the dépths I crý to you, O Lórd,*
Lórd, hear my vóice!
O lét your éars be atténtive*
to the vóice of my pléading.

If you, O Lórd, should márk our guílt,*
Lórd, who would survíve?
But with yóu is fóund forgíveness:*
for thís we revére you.

My sóul is wáiting for the Lórd,*
I cóunt on his wórd.
My sóul is lónging for the Lórd*
more than wátchman for dáybreak.
Let the wátchman cóunt on dáybreak*
and Ísrael on the Lórd.

Becáuse with the Lórd there is mércy*
and fúlness of redémption,
Ísrael indéed he will redéem*
from áll its iníquity.

Ant. With the Lord there is unfailing love. Great is his power to set men free.
Ant. 3: The Word was God in the beginning and before all time; today he is born to us, the Saviour of the world.

CANTICLE: COL 1:12-20

Let us give thanks to the Father,†
who has qualified us to share*
in the inheritance of the saints in light.

He has delivered us from the dominion of darkness*
and transferred us to the kingdom of his beloved Son,
in whom we have redemption,*
the forgiveness of sins.

He is the image of the invisible God,*
the first-born of all creation,
for in him all things were created, in heaven and on earth,*
visible and invisible.

All things were created*
through him and for him.
He is before all things,*
and in him all things hold together.

57

He is the head of the body, the Church;*
he is the beginning,
the first-born from the dead,*
that in everything he might be pre-eminent,

For in him all the fulness of God was pleased to dwell,*
and through him to reconcile to himself all things,
whether on earth or in heaven,*
making peace by the blood of his cross.

Ant. The Word was God in the beginning and before all time; today he is born to us, the Saviour of the world.

Scripture Reading   *I Jn I:I-3*
Something which has existed since the beginning,
that we have heard,
and we have seen with our own eyes;
that we have watched
and touched with our hands:
the Word, who is life—
this is our subject.
That life was made visible:
we saw it and we are giving our testimony,
telling you of the eternal life
which was with the Father
and has been made visible to us.
What we have seen and heard
we are telling you
so that you too may be in union with us,
as we are in union
with the Father
and with his Son Jesus Christ.

Short Responsory
R7 The Word became flesh, alleluia, alleluia. *Repeat* R7
V7 And he lived among us. R7 Glory be. R7

Magnificat ant. Today Christ is born, today the Saviour has appeared; today the angels sing on earth, the archangels rejoice; today upright men shout out for joy: Glory be to God on high, alleluia.

Intercessions

Today the angels' message rings through the world. Gathered together in prayer, we rejoice in the birth of our brother, the Saviour of us all. R̷ Lord Jesus, your birth is our peace.

May our lives express what we celebrate at Christmas:—may its mystery enrich your Church this year. R̷

We join the shepherds in adoring you,—we kneel before you, holy child of Bethlehem. R̷

We pray for the shepherds of your Church:—be close to them as they proclaim your birth to mankind. R̷

As we travel on this earthly pilgrimage, may your light shine in our hearts,—and may we see your glory, born in our midst. R̷

Word of the Father, you became man for us and raised us to a new life.—May the dead share with us in the new birth which Christmas proclaims. R̷

Our Father

Concluding Prayer

God, our Father,
our human nature is the wonderful work of your hands,
made still more wonderful by your work of redemption.
Your Son took to himself our manhood,
grant us a share in the godhead of Jesus Christ,
who lives and reigns with you and the Holy Spirit,
God, for ever and ever.

¶ *Throughout the octave of Christmas, Evening Prayer is of the octave, as given below for each day. Solemnities and Sunday of the Holy Family are exceptions to this directive.*

¶ *Throughout the octave of Christmas, either form of Night Prayer for Sunday is used each evening.*

Sunday within the Octave of Christmas
FEAST OF THE HOLY FAMILY
Psalter: Week 1

¶ *When Christmas Day falls on a Sunday, the Feast of the Holy Family is celebrated on 30 December and has no Evening Prayer I.*

EVENING PRAYER I
(Only on a Saturday)

Hymn, from the appendix, for Christmastide I.

Ant. 1: Jacob was the father of Joseph the husband of Mary; Mary was the mother of Jesus who is called Christ.

Psalms and canticle from the Common of the Blessed Virgin Mary, p 982.

Ant. 2: Joseph, son of David, do not be afraid to take Mary as your wife. She has conceived this child by the Holy Spirit.

Ant. 3: The shepherds came quickly and they found Mary and Joseph, and the baby lying in the manger.

Scripture Reading   *2 Cor 8:9*
You know how generous our Lord Jesus Christ has been: he was rich, yet for your sake he became poor, so that through his poverty you might become rich.

Short Responsory
R̕ The Word became flesh, and he lived among us. *Repeat* R̕
V̕ From his fulness we have all received. R̕ Glory be. R̕

Magnificat ant. The boy Jesus stayed behind in Jerusalem without his parents knowing it. They thought he was with the other pilgrims and they sought him among their relations and friends.

Intercessions
Let us adore the Son of the living God, who became son in a human
family. ℟ Lord Jesus, bless our families.
By your obedience to Mary and Joseph,—teach us how to respect
proper authority and order. ℟
By the love that filled your home,—give our families the grace of
loving harmony and peace. ℟
Your first intent was the honour of your Father.—May God be the
heart of all our family life. ℟
Your parents found you teaching in your Father's house.—Help us,
like you, to seek first the Father's will. ℟
By your reunion with Mary and Joseph in the joy of heaven,—
welcome our dead into the family of the saints. ℟
Our Father

Concluding Prayer
God, our Father,
in the Holy Family of Nazareth
you have given us the true model of a Christian home.
Grant that by following Jesus, Mary, and Joseph
in their love for each other and in the example of their family life
we may come to your home of peace and joy.
(We make our prayer) through our Lord.

Invitatory
Ant. Let us adore Christ, the Son of God, who made himself obedient
to Mary and to Joseph.

MORNING PRAYER

Hymn, from the appendix, for Christmastide I.

Ant. 1: Every year the parents of Jesus used to go to Jerusalem for the
feast of the Passover.

Psalms and canticle of Sunday, Week 1, pp 390 ff.

Ant. 2: The child grew and became strong, filled with wisdom; and
God's favour was with him.

Ant. 3: His father and mother were filled with wonder at what was being said about him.

Scripture Reading   *Deut 5:16*

Honour your father and your mother, as the Lord your God has commanded you, so that you may have long life and may prosper in the land that the Lord your God gives you.

Short Responsory

℟ Christ, Son of the Living God, have mercy on us. *Repeat* ℟
℣ You lived in obedience to Mary and Joseph. ℟ Glory be. ℟

Benedictus ant. Lord, let the example of your holy family enlighten our minds; set our feet on the way of peace.

Intercessions

Let us adore the Son of the living God, who became son in a human family. ℟ Lord Jesus, bless our families.
Jesus, eternal Word of the Father, you lived under the authority of Mary and Joseph.—Teach us to walk the path of humility. ℟
Mary kept in her heart all that you said and did:—may we learn in her example the spirit of contemplation. ℟
Christ, yours was the strength that shaped the universe, yet you came to learn the tasks of a carpenter.—Help us to see our work as a sharing in yours. ℟
You advanced in wisdom and in favour with God and men:—may we live to the full in you and build up your body in faith and love. ℟
Our Father

Concluding Prayer

God, our Father,
in the Holy Family of Nazareth
you have given us the true model of a Christian home.
Grant that by following Jesus, Mary, and Joseph
in their love for each other and in the example of their family life
we may come to your home of peace and joy.
(We make our prayer) through our Lord.

EVENING PRAYER II

Hymn, from the appendix, for Christmastide I.

Ant. 1: After three days they found Jesus in the Temple, sitting among the doctors, listening to them and asking them questions.

Psalms and canticle from the Common of the Blessed Virgin Mary, p 992.

Ant. 2: Jesus went down with them to Nazareth and lived under their authority.

Ant. 3: As Jesus grew up, he advanced in wisdom and favour with God and men.

Scripture Reading   *Phil 2:6-7*
In your minds you must be the same as Christ Jesus: His state was divine, yet he did not cling to his equality with God but emptied himself to assume the condition of a slave and become as men are.

Short Responsory
R7 He had to be made like his brothers in every way, so that he might be merciful. *Repeat* R7
V7 He appeared on earth and lived among men. R7 Glory be. R7

Magnificat ant. 'Son, why have you treated us like this? Your father and I have been looking for you anxiously.' 'Why were you looking for me? Did you not know that I was bound to be where my Father is?'

Intercessions
Let us adore the Son of the living God, who became son in a human family. R7 Lord Jesus, bless our families.
By your obedience to Mary and Joseph,—teach us how to respect proper authority and order. R7
By the love that filled your home,—give our families the grace of loving harmony and peace. R7

Your first intent was the honour of your Father.—May God be the heart of all our family life. ℟ Lord Jesus, bless our families.

Your parents found you teaching in your Father's house.—Help us, like you, to seek first the Father's will. ℟

By your reunion with Mary and Joseph in the joy of heaven,—welcome our dead into the family of the saints. ℟

Our Father

The concluding prayer as at Morning Prayer, p 62.

26 DECEMBER

If not a Sunday the Office up to Evening Prayer is that of St Stephen, Martyr (see the Proper of Saints, p 957).

EVENING PRAYER

Hymn, antiphons, psalms and canticle from Evening Prayer II of Christmas Day, pp 55 ff.

Scripture Reading *1 Jn 1:5b-7*

God is light, and in him there is no darkness at all. If we walk in the light as he himself is in the light, then we share together a common life, and we are being cleansed from every sin by the blood of Jesus his Son.

Short Responsory

℟ The Word became flesh, alleluia, alleluia. *Repeat* ℟

℣ And he lived among us. ℟ Glory be. ℟

Magnificat ant. While the midnight silence reigned over all, and the night was now half-spent, your almighty Word, O God, came down from his royal throne in heaven.

Intercessions

We place all our trust in the Word of God who dwells within us and goes before us as our Saviour. ℟ From all evil, Lord, deliver us.

By your coming in our flesh to live always for your Father:—Lord, deliver us. R⁷

By your days filled with work, preaching, and making friends with sinners:—Lord, deliver us. R⁷

By your suffering and crucifixion, by your death and burial:—Lord, deliver us. R⁷

By your resurrection and ascension, by the giving of your Spirit:—Lord, deliver us. R⁷

By your joy in being glorified:—Lord, deliver the faithful departed. R⁷

Our Father

Concluding Prayer
Almighty God and Father,
the human birth of your Only-begotten Son
was the beginning of new life.
May he set us free from the tyranny of sin.
(We make our prayer) through our Lord.

27 DECEMBER

If not a Sunday the Office up to Evening Prayer is that of St John, Apostle and Evangelist (see the Proper of Saints, pp 959 ff).

EVENING PRAYER

Hymn, antiphons, psalms and canticle from Evening Prayer II of Christmas Day, pp 55 ff.

Scripture Reading   *Rom 8:3-4*
God condemned sin in human nature by sending his own Son, who came with a nature like man's sinful nature to do away with sin. God did this so that the righteous demands of the Law might be fully satisfied in us who live according to the Spirit, not according to human nature.

Short Responsory

R℣ The Word became flesh, alleluia, alleluia. *Repeat* R℣
℣ And he lived among us. R℣ Glory be. R℣

Magnificat ant. All that the prophets foretold about Christ has been fulfilled through you, Virgin Mary: you were a virgin when you conceived and remained a virgin after you had given birth.

Intercessions

Let us pray to God the Father, who out of his great love sent us his only Son. R℣ May the grace of your Son be with us, Lord.
Father of our Lord Jesus Christ, you have shown your tender mercy for those who live in darkness:—accept the prayers we offer for the salvation of all men. R℣
Father of those who follow Jesus Christ, bless your Church with all its people,—and let them live in harmony and peace. R℣
Father of all men, turn the hearts of nations to your beloved Son,—that they may overthrow the forces that set man against man. R℣
Father of the world to come, peace came down from heaven when your Son was born on earth:—grant to the faithful departed the eternal peace of Christ. R℣
Our Father

Concluding Prayer

Almighty God,
your incarnate Word fills us
with the new light he brought to men.
Let the light of faith in our hearts
shine through all that we do and say.
(We make our prayer) through our Lord.

28 DECEMBER

If not a Sunday the Office up to Evening Prayer is that of the Holy Innocents (see the Proper of Saints, pp 961 ff).

EVENING PRAYER

Hymn, antiphons, psalms and canticle from Evening Prayer II of Christmas Day, pp 55 ff.

Scripture Reading   *Eph 2:3b-5*
By nature we were as much under God's anger as the rest of the world. But God loved us with so much love that he was generous with his mercy: when we were dead through our sins, he brought us to life with Christ—it is through grace that you have been saved.

Short Responsory
Ry The Word became flesh, alleluia, alleluia. *Repeat* Ry
Ÿ And he lived among us. Ry Glory be. Ry

Magnificat ant. The holy and undefiled virgin gave birth to God; when he took on the form of a helpless infant she fed him at her breasts; let us all adore him who has come to save us.

Intercessions
God sent his Son, born a subject of the Law, that he might redeem the subjects of the Law. Let us pray to him: Ry Father, give us life.
We celebrate the time when your Son became man.—May we grow in faith and thankfulness. Ry
Through your Son, who shared our human weakness,—give hope to the sick, the poor, and the aged. Ry
Remember those in prison, and all who are deprived of their freedom.—Stay with them in their sorrow. Ry
Have mercy on the faithful departed;—may they rest in peace. Ry
Our Father

Concluding Prayer
God, our Father,
our human nature is the wonderful work of your hands,
made still more wonderful by your work of redemption.
Your Son took to himself our manhood,
grant us a share in the godhead of Jesus Christ,
who lives and reigns with you and the Holy Spirit,
God, for ever and ever.

29 DECEMBER
Fifth Day within the Octave of Christmas

Invitatory ant. Christ has been born for us: come, let us adore him.

MORNING PRAYER

Hymn, antiphons, psalms and canticle from Christmas Day, pp 53 ff.

Scripture Reading   *Heb 1:1-2*
When in former times God spoke to our forefathers, he spoke in fragmentary and varied fashion through the prophets. But in this the final age he has spoken to us in the Son whom he has made heir to the whole universe, and through whom he created all orders of existence.

Short Responsory
R̸ The Lord has made known our salvation, alleluia, alleluia.
Repeat R̸
V̸ He has revealed his saving power. R̸ Glory be. R̸

Benedictus ant. The shepherds said to one another, 'Let us go to Bethlehem and see this thing which the Lord has made known to us.'

Intercessions
In his loving kindness, God sent us Christ, the Prince of Peace. Let us therefore trustfully declare: R̸ Peace to men of good will!
Father of our Lord Jesus Christ, accept our praise this Christmas-tide,—as the Church celebrates your saving love. R̸
You promised a Saviour to Abraham and his sons:—this Christmas we welcome his coming into our midst. R̸
May the Messiah bring salvation to the Jews,—who waited for him in faith and in hope. R̸
The birth of your Son was proclaimed by angels, preached by apostles, witnessed to by martyrs, celebrated in the Church:—may the message of peace ring out again in our world. R̸
Our Father

Concluding Prayer
Father, all-powerful and unseen God,
you dispelled the shadows of this world
when Christ, the true Light, dawned upon us.
Look favourably upon us, Lord,
and we will praise and glorify his birth as man,
who lives and reigns with you and the Holy Spirit,
God, for ever and ever.

EVENING PRAYER

Hymn, antiphons, psalms and canticle from Evening Prayer II of Christmas Day, pp 55 ff.

Scripture Reading   *1 Jn 1:1-3*
Something which has existed since the beginning,
that we have heard,
and we have seen with our own eyes;
that we have watched
and touched with our hands:
the Word, who is life—
this is our subject.
That life was made visible:
we saw it and we are giving our testimony,
telling you of the eternal life
which was with the Father and has been made visible to us.
What we have seen and heard
we are telling you
so that you too may be in union with us,
as we are in union
with the Father
and with his Son Jesus Christ.

Short Responsory
R℣ The Word became flesh, alleluia, alleluia. *Repeat* R℣
℣ And he lived among us. R℣ Glory be. R℣

Magnificat ant. The King of heaven was born of the Virgin; he came to recall fallen man to his heavenly kingdom.

Intercessions

Let us pray to our merciful Father who anointed Jesus with the Holy Spirit to proclaim the gospel to the poor. ℞ Lord, in your pity, have mercy on us.

We thank you, Lord, for wanting everyone to be saved:—may the whole world rejoice in the birth of your Son. ℞

You sent your Son to proclaim the age of grace:—may all enjoy peace and true freedom. ℞

You led the wise men to worship the child in a stable:—help us to recognize Christ by faith. ℞

You call all men to share your light:—let us set out to be witnesses of the gospel. ℞

Your light dawned upon the nations when Christ was born in Bethlehem:—may the dead see your face and live in glory for ever. ℞

Our Father

The concluding prayer as at Morning Prayer, p 69.

30 DECEMBER
Sixth Day within the Octave of Christmas

If Christmas Day fell on a Sunday, the Feast of the Holy Family, pp 60 ff, is celebrated today, without Evening Prayer I. Otherwise the Office is as follows.

Invitatory ant. Christ has been born for us: come, let us adore him.

MORNING PRAYER

Hymn, antiphons, psalms and canticle from Christmas Day, pp 53 ff.

Scripture Reading   *Is 9:6*

To us a child is born, to us a son is given; and the government will be upon his shoulder, and his name will be called 'Wonderful Counsellor, Mighty God, Everlasting Father, Prince of Peace.'

Short Responsory

R7 The Lord has made known our salvation, alleluia, alleluia.

Repeat R7

V7 He has revealed his saving power. R7 Glory be. R7

Benedictus ant. At the birth of the Lord the choir of angels chanted:
Praise be to our God, who sits on the throne, and to the Lamb.

Intercessions

Let us pray to Christ in whom all things are restored by the Father's
will. R7 Most loving Son of God, hear our prayer.

Son of God, in the fulness of time you became a man:—share with
us your love for everyone. R7

You emptied yourself to enrich us with your glory:—make us selfless
ministers of your gospel. R7

You brought light into the darkness of our lives:—guide all our
actions in the ways of virtue, justice and peace. R7

May our hearts be disposed to hear your word—and so be able to do
good for ourselves and for our fellow-men. R7

Our Father

Concluding Prayer

Almighty God and Father,
the human birth of your Only-begotten Son
was the beginning of new life.
May he set us free from the tyranny of sin.
(We make our prayer) through our Lord.

EVENING PRAYER

*Hymn, antiphons, psalms and canticle from Evening Prayer II of
Christmas Day, pp 55 ff.*

Scripture Reading   *2 Pet 1:3-4*

By his divine power, Christ has given us all the things that we need
for life and for true devotion, bringing us to know God himself, who
has called us by his own glory and goodness. In making these gifts,
he has given us the guarantee of something very great and wonderful

to come: through them you will be able to share the divine nature and to escape corruption in a world that is sunk in vice.

Short Responsory

R̸ The Word became flesh, alleluia, alleluia. *Repeat* R̸
V̸ And he lived among us. R̸ Glory be. R̸

Magnificat ant. We glorify you, Mother of God; for Christ was born of you. Keep safe from harm all those who honour you.

Intercessions

Let us acclaim Christ with joy, for out of Bethlehem, in the land of Judah, came a leader who guides his holy people. R̸ May your grace be with us, Lord.

Christ, our Saviour, speak to those who have not heard your name;—draw all men to yourself. R̸

Lord, gather all nations into your Church—that the family of man may become the people of God. R̸

King of kings, direct the minds and hearts of rulers;—guide them to work justly for peace on earth. R̸

Give faith to those who live in doubt—and hope to those who live in fear. R̸

Console the sad, comfort those who are in their last agony;—lead them to be refreshed at the spring of your grace. R̸

Our Father

The concluding prayer as at Morning Prayer, p 71.

31 DECEMBER

Seventh Day within the Octave of Christmas

Invitatory ant. Christ has been born for us: come, let us adore him.

MORNING PRAYER

Hymn, antiphons, psalms and canticle from Christmas Day, pp 53 ff.

Scripture Reading   *Is 4:2-3*

On that day the plant that the Lord has grown shall become glorious in its beauty, and the fruit of the land shall be the pride and splendour of the survivors of Israel. Then those who are left in Sion, who remain in Jerusalem, every one enrolled in the book of life, shall be called holy.

Short Responsory

R⁰ The Lord has made known our salvation, alleluia, alleluia.
Repeat R⁰
ꙮ He has revealed his saving power. R⁰ Glory be. R⁰

Benedictus ant. Suddenly there was with the angel a great throng of the heavenly host, praising God and saying: Glory be to God on high, and on earth peace among his chosen people, alleluia.

Intercessions

With humble confidence we turn to Christ the Lord whose grace has been revealed for the salvation of all men. R⁰ Lord, have mercy on us.

Christ, radiance of God's glory, sustaining the universe with your all powerful word,—give us life today through the power of your gospel. R⁰

Christ, Liberator of the whole human race,—give all men the freedom needed to do your will. R⁰

Christ, eternal Son of the Father, yet born for us in the stable at Bethlehem,—help your Church to be ever detached from the unnecessary things of this world. R⁰

Christ, Son of David, fulfilment of the prophecies,—may the Jewish people accept you as their awaited Deliverer. R⁰

Our Father

Concluding Prayer

All-powerful, ever-living God,
we thank you for the human birth of your Son,
which is the source and perfection of our Christian life and worship.
Number us among his people,
for the salvation of all mankind is found in him,

who lives and reigns with you and the Holy Spirit,
God, for ever and ever.

Evening Prayer of the following Solemnity.

1 January
Octave Day of Christmas
SOLEMNITY OF MARY, MOTHER OF GOD

EVENING PRAYER I

Hymn, from the appendix, for the Blessed Virgin Mary.

Ant. 1: O wonderful exchange! The Creator of human nature took
on a human body and was born of the Virgin. He became man without having a human father and has bestowed on us his divine
nature.

*Psalms and canticle from the Common of the Blessed Virgin Mary,
pp 982 ff.*

Ant. 2: You were born of the Virgin in a mysterious manner of
which no man can speak; you fulfilled the scriptures: like rain
falling gently on the earth you came hither to save the human race.
We praise you; you are our God.

Ant. 3: Moses saw the thornbush which was on fire yet was not
burnt up. In it we see a sign of your virginity which all must honour;
Mother of God, pray for us.

Scripture Reading   *Gal 4:4-5*
When the appointed time came, God sent his Son, born of a woman,
born a subject of the Law, to redeem the subjects of the Law and to
enable us to be adopted as sons.

Short Responsory
℟ The Word became flesh, alleluia, alleluia. *Repeat* ℟
℣ And he lived among us. ℟ Glory be. ℟

Magnificat ant. God loved us so much that he sent his own Son in a mortal nature like ours: he was born of a woman, he was born subject to the Law, alleluia.

Intercessions

Blessed be the Lord Jesus, our bond of peace with one another. He came to make the Jews and Gentiles one people. Let us therefore pray: R℣ Lord, give peace to all men.

Lord Jesus, you revealed the meaning of human living;—may we never fail to give thanks for all you have given us. R℣

You made Mary, your Mother, full of grace;—enrich with your blessings the life of every man. R℣

You proclaimed the gospel to the world;—may your word in all its power penetrate into the hearts of men. R℣

You became through Mary the brother of every man;—teach us to love one another. R℣

You came like the dawn of a new day;—show to the dead the radiance of your presence. R℣

Our Father

Concluding Prayer

God, our Father,
since you gave mankind a saviour through blessed Mary,
virgin and mother,
grant that we may feel the power of her intercession
when she pleads for us with Jesus Christ, your Son,
the author of life,
who lives and reigns with you and the Holy Spirit,
God, for ever and ever.

Invitatory

Ant. Let us celebrate the Virgin Mary's motherhood. Let us adore her Son, Christ the Lord.

MORNING PRAYER

Hymn, from the appendix, for the Blessed Virgin Mary.

Ant. 1: A shoot has sprung from the stock of Jesse; a star has risen from Jacob: the Virgin has given birth to the Saviour; we praise you, our God.

Psalms and canticle of Sunday, Week 1, pp 390 ff.

Ant. 2: Mary has given birth to our Saviour; John saw him and cried out: this is the Lamb of God who takes away the sins of the world, alleluia.

Ant. 3: Mary gave birth to the king whose name is eternal; she united the joy of a mother with the honour of a virgin; such as this has never happened before nor will it happen again, alleluia.

Scripture Reading   *Mic 5:3,4,5a*
Therefore only so long as a woman is in labour
shall he give up Israel;
and then those that survive of his race
shall rejoin their brethren.
He shall appear and be their shepherd
in the strength of the Lord,
in the majesty of the name of the Lord his God,
and he shall be a man of peace.

Short Responsory
R7 The Lord has made known our salvation, alleluia, alleluia.
Repeat R7
V7 He has revealed his saving power. R7 Glory be. R7

Benedictus ant. Today a wonderful mystery is announced: something new has taken place; God has become man; he remained what he was and has become that which he was not: and though the two natures remain distinct, he is one.

Intercessions
Let us give glory to Christ, born of the Virgin Mary by the power of the Holy Spirit. R7 Son of the Virgin Mary, have mercy on us.
Son of the Virgin Mary, wondrous child and prince of peace,—may your peace be a reality in the world. R7

Lord Jesus, may your gift of faith grow stronger in us every day—
and find expression in all our ways of living. Ry
You took our human nature to yourself;—help us to grow in your
divine life. Ry
You became a citizen of our world;—make us fellow-citizens of your
heavenly kingdom. Ry
Our Father

Concluding Prayer
God, our Father,
since you gave mankind a saviour through blessed Mary,
virgin and mother,
grant that we may feel the power of her intercession
when she pleads for us with Jesus Christ, your Son,
the author of life,
who lives and reigns with you and the Holy Spirit,
God, for ever and ever.

EVENING PRAYER II

Hymn, from the appendix, for the Blessed Virgin Mary.

Ant. 1: O wonderful exchange! The Creator of human nature took
on a human body and was born of the Virgin. He became man
without having a human father and has bestowed on us his divine
nature.

*Psalms and canticle from the Common of the Blessed Virgin Mary,
pp 992 ff.*

Ant. 2: You were born of the Virgin in a mysterious manner of
which no man can speak; you fulfilled the scriptures: like rain
falling gently on the earth you came hither to save the human race.
We praise you; you are our God.

Ant. 3: Moses saw the thornbush which was on fire yet was not
burnt up. In it we see a sign of your virginity which all must honour;
Mother of God, pray for us.

Scripture Reading   *Gal 4:4-5*
When the appointed time came, God sent his Son, born of a woman,
born a subject of the Law, to redeem the subjects of the Law and to
enable us to be adopted as sons.

Short Responsory
R℣ The Word became flesh, alleluia, alleluia. *Repeat* R℣
℣ And he lived among us. R℣ Glory be. R℣

Magnificat ant. Blessed is the womb that bore you, Christ, and
blessed are the breasts that suckled you, for you are the Lord and
Saviour of the world, alleluia.

Intercessions
Blessed be Christ, Immanuel, whom the Virgin conceived and
brought forth. R℣ Son of the Virgin Mary, hear our prayer.
You gave the Virgin Mary the joys of motherhood;—grant to all
parents joy in their children. R℣
King of peace, your kingdom is one of justice and peace;—grant
that we may seek those things that will further harmony among
men. R℣
You came to build the human race into a holy people;—bind the
nations together in the unity of the Spirit. R℣
You were born into a human family;—strengthen with love the
bonds of family life. R℣
You came to a life of weakness in our world;—grant to the dead the
life of glory in your kingdom. R℣
Our Father

The concluding prayer as at Morning Prayer, p 77.

TIME FROM 2 JANUARY

The manner of celebrating this time depends on the day chosen by the Region for the Solemnity of the Epiphany.
The Offices are set out below according to the two possibilities:
A: indicates Offices for Regions where the Epiphany is celebrated on 6 January.
B: indicates Offices for Regions where the Epiphany is celebrated on the Sunday which falls between 2 and 8 January.
AB: indicates Offices celebrated in all regions.
A(B): indicates Offices which may be celebrated in all regions, but which vary from year to year.

A SECOND SUNDAY AFTER CHRISTMAS

Occurring between 2 and 5 January

Psalter: Week 2

EVENING PRAYER I

Hymn, from the appendix, for Christmastide I.

Ant. 1: Through her word the Virgin conceived; she remained a virgin; as a virgin she gave birth to the King of all kings.

Psalms and canticle of Sunday, Week 2, pp 455 ff.

Ant. 2: Rejoice with Jerusalem; the Lord has sent her happiness like a stream of peace.

Ant. 3: Today God is born from God for us; the light that was in the beginning has appeared to us.

Scripture Reading   *1 Jn 5:20*
We know that the Son of God has come and has given us understanding, to know him who is true; and we are in him who is true, in his Son Jesus Christ. This is the true God and eternal life.

Short Responsory

℞ The Word became flesh, alleluia, alleluia. *Repeat* ℞
℣ And he lived among us. ℞ Glory be. ℞

Magnificat ant. Heavenly power enters the womb of the chaste Mother; the maiden carries within her a secret which she does not understand.

Intercessions

Let us turn in prayer to Christ who emptied himself to assume the condition of a slave. He was tempted in every way that we are, but did not sin. ℞ Save us through your birth.

Coming into our world, Lord Jesus, you open the new age which the prophets foretold.—In every age, may the Church come again to new birth. ℞

You took on our human weakness.—Be the eyes of the blind, the strength of the weak, the friend of the lonely. ℞

Lord, you were born among the poor:—enrich them with your love. ℞

Your birth brings eternal life within man's reach;—comfort the dying with hope of new life in heaven. ℞

Gather the departed to yourself;—and make them radiant in your glory. ℞

Our Father

Concluding Prayer

Almighty, ever-living God, light of every faithful soul,
fill the world with your glory,
and reveal to all nations the splendour of your presence.
(We make our prayer) through our Lord.

Invitatory

Ant. Christ has been born for us: come, let us adore him.

MORNING PRAYER

Hymn, from the appendix, for Christmastide I.

Ant. 1: Light dawns for the just, since the Saviour of all men has been born, alleluia.

Psalms and canticle of Sunday, Week 2, pp 462 ff.

Ant. 2: Let us sing a hymn to the Lord our God.

Ant. 3: The people that sat in darkness has seen a great light.

Scripture Reading   *Heb 1:1-2*
When in former times God spoke to our forefathers, he spoke in fragmentary and varied fashion through the prophets. But in this the final age he has spoken to us in the Son whom he has made heir to the whole universe, and through whom he created all orders of existence.

Short Responsory
Ry You are Christ, Son of the living God, have mercy on us.
Repeat Ry
Vy You were born of the Virgin Mary. Ry Glory be. Ry

Benedictus ant. The Virgin trusted in the Lord; though she gave birth to the Word become man; she remained a virgin always. We praise her and say: Blessed are you among women.

Intercessions
Let us praise the Word who was in the beginning with God and became man for us. Ry Let the earth rejoice, because you have come.
Christ, Eternal Word, your birth brought joy to the world;—bring joy to each of us today through your presence in our hearts by grace. Ry
In your coming you showed us the faithfulness of God;—keep us faithful to the promises of our baptism. Ry
At your birth the angels proclaimed peace to men;—keep us in your peace all our days. Ry
You came to be the true vine, bearing for us the fruit of life;—make us branches of the vine, bearing fruit in you. Ry
Our Father

Concluding Prayer
Almighty, ever-living God, light of every faithful soul,
fill the world with your glory,
and reveal to all nations the splendour of your presence.
(We make our prayer) through our Lord.

EVENING PRAYER II

Hymn, from the appendix, for Christmastide I.

Ant. 1: A new day of redemption has dawned for us. It was prepared from of old and holds the promise of eternal joy.

Psalms and canticle of Sunday, Week 2, pp 469 ff.

Ant. 2: The Lord has sent his mercy; he has shown his faithfulness.

Ant. 3: The Lord, the King of kings, has been born for us on earth: now the salvation of the world, our redemption, has come to us, alleluia.

Scripture Reading   *1 Jn 1:1-3*
Something which has existed since the beginning,
that we have heard,
and we have seen with our own eyes;
that we have watched
and touched with our hands:
the Word, who is life—
this is our subject.
That life was made visible:
we saw it and we are giving our testimony,
telling you of the eternal life
which was with the Father and has been made visible to us.
What we have seen and heard
we are telling you
so that you too may be in union with us,
as we are in union
with the Father
and with his Son Jesus Christ.

Short Responsory

R7 The Word became flesh, alleluia, alleluia. *Repeat* R7
V̸ And he lived among us. R7 Glory be. R7

Magnificat ant. Blessed is the womb that bore the Son of the eternal
Father, and blessed are the breasts that suckled Christ the Lord.

Intercessions

At Christ's birth the angels proclaimed peace to the world. Let us
praise him with joy and ask his favour: R7 Let your birth bring
peace to all men.

Lord, fill your Church with all blessings;—strengthen her by the
mystery of your birth. R7

You came as chief shepherd and guardian of our souls;—keep the
pope and the bishops faithful stewards of your grace in all its forms.
R7

Eternal King, it was your will to experience human limitation and
death;—help us in our weakness and grant us a share in your eternal
kingdom. R7

You were awaited from the ages and you came in the fulness of time;
—show yourself to those who still await you. R7

In coming among us as a man you redeemed our human nature from
the corruption of death;—grant to the dead the fulness of your
redemption. R7

Our Father

The concluding prayer as at Morning Prayer, p 82.

A(B)   2 JANUARY
(B *only if not Sunday of the Epiphany*)

Invitatory ant. Christ has been born for us: come, let us adore him.

MORNING PRAYER

Hymn, from the appendix, for Christmastide I.
Antiphons, psalms and canticle from the psalter.

Scripture Reading   *Is 49:8-9*

I have appointed you as covenant of the people.
I will restore the land
and assign you the estates that lie waste.
I will say to the prisoners, 'Come out',
to those who are in darkness, 'Show yourselves'.

Short Responsory

R̷ The Lord has made known our salvation, alleluia, alleluia.
Repeat R̷
V̷ He has revealed his saving power. R̷ Glory be. R̷

Benedictus ant. He lay in the manger and still shone in heaven; he
came to us, yet remained with the Father.

Intercessions

Let us offer our prayer to Christ, God made man, the new Adam,
who has become for us the source of new life. R̷ Lord, have mercy.
Christ, Sun of Justice, you revealed your glory among us;—may
we live through your light with God. R̷
Simeon and Anna proclaimed you as the Saviour;—grant that the
Jewish people may accept your message so long foretold. R̷
At your birth the angels proclaimed glory in heaven and peace on
earth;—fill our world with the spirit of your peace. R̷
You became the second Adam, renewing all our human ways;—
bring hope to those who live under the oppression of sin. R̷
Our Father

Concluding Prayer

Lord, guard the rock of our faith in your only Son
who was born of the Virgin Mother with a body like ours,
and from all eternity shares your glory.
Free your people from present distress,
and give them the joy that will never end.
(We make our prayer) through our Lord.

EVENING PRAYER

Hymn, from the appendix, for Christmastide I.
Antiphons, psalms and canticle from the psalter.

Scripture Reading   *Col 1:13-15*
God has taken us out of the power of darkness and created a place
for us in the kingdom of the Son that he loves, and in him we gain
our freedom, the forgiveness of our sins. He is the image of the unseen God and the first-born of all creation.

Short Responsory
R℣ The Word became flesh, alleluia, alleluia. Repeat R℣
℣ And he lived among us. R℣ Glory be. R℣

Magnificat ant. O blessed childhood! Through you the life of mankind is renewed. Christ came forth from Mary's womb like a
bridegroom coming in splendour from his wedding canopy.

Intercessions
At various times in the past and in various different ways, God
spoke to our ancestors through the prophets; but in our own time,
the last days, he has spoken to us through his Son. Let us pray:
R℣ Lord, have mercy.
We pray for your holy Church:—may she reveal with faith and
courage the person of Christ. R℣
We pray for missionaries throughout the world:—may they make
known to all peoples the name of their Saviour. R℣
We pray for the sick:—make them well again in the name of Jesus.
R℣
We pray for Christians who suffer persecution:—may they bear their
sufferings patiently out of love of Christ. R℣
We pray for those who have died through the violence of men:—
give them life in the greatness of your love. R℣
Our Father

The concluding prayer as at Morning Prayer, p 84.

A(B)   3 JANUARY
(B *only if not Sunday of the Epiphany or after it*)

Invitatory ant. Christ has been born for us: come, let us adore him.

MORNING PRAYER

Hymn, from the appendix, for Christmastide I.

Scripture Reading   *Is 62:11-12*
Tell the daughter of Zion, Behold, your deliverance has come. His recompense comes with him; he carries his reward before him; and they shall be called a Holy People, the ransomed of the Lord.

Short Responsory
R⁷ The Lord has made known our salvation, alleluia, alleluia.
Repeat R⁷
y⁷ He has revealed his saving power. R⁷ Glory be. R⁷

Benedictus ant. The Word was made flesh, and he lived among us, full of grace and truth. From his fulness we have all received grace upon grace, alleluia.

Intercessions
In joy let us pray to our Redeemer, the Son of God, who became man to renew our human nature. R⁷ Immanuel, be with us now.
Jesus, Splendour of the Father, Son of the Virgin Mary,—brighten this day by your presence among us. R⁷
Jesus, Wonderful Counsellor, Mighty God,—put us on the path to holiness, be our guide. R⁷
Jesus, all-powerful, obedient and humble,—inspire all men to pour out their lives in the service of others. R⁷
Jesus, father of the poor, our way and our life,—grant to your Church the spirit of detachment from earthly things. R⁷
Our Father

Concluding Prayer
Almighty God,
your Son's manhood, born of the Virgin,

was a new creation, untainted by our sinful condition.
Renew us, then, in Christ
and cleanse us from all trace of sin.
(We make our prayer) through our Lord.

EVENING PRAYER

Hymn, from the appendix, for Christmastide I.

Scripture Reading   *1 Jn 1:5b,7*
God is light, and in him there is no darkness at all. If we walk in the
light as he himself is in the light, then we share together a common
life, and we are being cleansed from every sin by the blood of Jesus
his Son.

Short Responsory
R7 The Word became flesh, alleluia, alleluia. *Repeat* R7
V And he lived among us. R7 Glory be. R7

Magnificat ant. Let us rejoice and be glad in the Lord, for the
eternal salvation has appeared in the world, alleluia.

Intercessions
With the birth of Christ, God's holy people blossomed into flower.
Let us pray with gratitude to our Saviour. R7 May your birth give
joy to the world.
Christ, our life, you came to be the head of the Church:—give
growth to your body and build it up in love. R7
We adore you, Christ, as God and Man:—share with us your life
with the Father. R7
Through the incarnation you became our mediator:—unite the
ministers of the Church more closely to yourself and make their
entire lives a ministry of grace. R7
Your birth in our flesh reveals the new plan of salvation:—may all
men come to know the God who lives among them. R7
The power of death was broken when you became man:—free the
faithful departed from all the bonds of sin. R7
Our Father

The concluding prayer as at Morning Prayer, p 86.

A(B)   4 JANUARY
(B *only if not Sunday of the Epiphany or after it*)

Invitatory ant. Christ has been born for us: come, let us adore him.

MORNING PRAYER

Hymn, from the appendix, for Christmastide I.

Scripture Reading   *Is 45:22-24*
Turn back to me, and win deliverance, all you that dwell in the remotest corners of the earth; I am God, there is no other. By my own honour I have sworn it, nor shall it echo in vain, this faithful promise I have made, that every knee shall bow before me, and every tongue swear by my name.

Short Responsory
R̸ The Lord has made known our salvation, alleluia, alleluia.
Repeat R̸
V̸ He has revealed his saving power. R̸ Glory be. R̸

Benedictus ant. Christ, our God, in whom the fulness of the divine nature dwells, took on the frailty of our human nature and was born as the new man, alleluia.

Intercessions
The Word of God was manifested in the flesh, seen by angels and preached among the nations. Let us praise him: R̸ Only Son of God, we adore you.
Redeemer of all men, you came into our lives through the Virgin Mary:—by her prayers grant that we may never be parted from you. R̸
You manifested to us the faithfulness of God:—may you always be the light of our lives. R̸
You let us see the Father's love for us:—may we show to other people the loving care of God. R̸
You came to live among us:—make us worthy to be your friends. R̸
Our Father

Concluding Prayer
Almighty God,
the light of a new star in heaven
heralded your saving love.
Let the light of your salvation dawn in our hearts
and keep them always open to your life-giving grace.
(We make our prayer) through our Lord.

EVENING PRAYER

Hymn, from the appendix, for Christmastide 1.

Scripture Reading   *Rom 8:3-4*
God condemned sin in human nature by sending his own Son, who
came with a nature like man's sinful nature to do away with sin.
God did this so that the righteous demands of the Law might be
fully satisfied in us who live according to the Spirit, not according to
human nature.

Short Responsory
R̸ The Word became flesh, alleluia, alleluia. *Repeat* R̸
V̸ And he lived among us. R̸ Glory be. R̸

Magnificat ant. I have not come from myself, but I have come forth
from God; my Father has sent me.

Intercessions
Christ came to us and sacrificed himself to purify a people so that it
could be his very own and would have no ambition except to do
good. Let us fervently pray: R̸ Lord, have mercy.
We pray for your holy Church:—may all her children be alive in your
life. R̸
We pray for the poor, for captives and exiles:—may they know
through our love that you still care for them. R̸
We pray that our joy may be complete:—may we experience all the
blessings God gave us in your birth. R̸
We pray for the faithful departed:—may they glory in your light
for ever. R̸

Our Father

The concluding prayer as at Morning Prayer, p 89.

A(B)   5 JANUARY
(B *only if not Sunday of the Epiphany or after it*)

Invitatory ant. Christ has been born for us: come, let us adore him.

MORNING PRAYER

Hymn, from the appendix, for Christmastide I.

Scripture Reading   *Wis 7:26-27*
Wisdom is a reflection of the eternal light,
untarnished mirror of God's active power,
image of his goodness.
Although alone, she can do all;
herself unchanging, she makes all things new.
In each generation she passes into holy souls,
she makes them friends of God and prophets.

Short Responsory
R̰ The Lord has made known our salvation, alleluia, alleluia.
Repeat R̰
V̰ He has revealed his saving power. R̰ Glory be. R̰

Benedictus ant. God has visited his people and has brought them redemption.

Intercessions
Let us praise Christ who was sent by God to be for us the One who is Wise, Just and Holy—our Redeemer. R̰ Lord, save us through your birth.
Lord of the universe, the shepherds found you in a manger:—save us from selfishness in the way we live. R̰
You so loved us in all our weakness that you came to be our Saviour;—help us to respect the dignity of every man. R̰
You took our nature but you did not sin;—help us to use your gifts

as we should. ℟
You made the Church your bride without defect or blemish:—grant
that all your faithful may persevere in it to the end. ℟
Our Father

Concluding Prayer
God, our Father,
since through the human birth of your only Son
you began in us the work of redemption,
keep us firm in faith,
and with Christ as the Shepherd of our souls
bring us to the glory you have promised.
(We make our prayer) through our Lord.

A *Where the Solemnity of the Epiphany is celebrated on 6 January,
Evening Prayer will be Evening Prayer 1 of the Epiphany, pp 96 ff.*

B *Where the Solemnity of the Epiphany is celebrated on the Sunday,
when this Sunday is 7 or 8 January, then the Office is as below.*

B   EVENING PRAYER

Hymn, from the appendix, for Christmastide I.

Scripture Reading   *1 Jn 5:20*
We know that the Son of God has come and has given us understanding, to know him who is true; and we are in him who is true, in
his Son Jesus Christ. This is the true God and eternal life.

Short Responsory
℟ The Word became flesh, alleluia, alleluia. *Repeat* ℟
℣ And he lived among us. ℟ Glory be. ℟

Magnificat ant. We have found him of whom Moses and the
prophets wrote: Jesus of Nazareth, the son of Joseph.

Intercessions
Blessed be Christ, Immanuel, whom the Virgin conceived and
brought forth. ℟ Son of the Virgin Mary, hear us.
You gave the Virgin Mary the joys of motherhood;—grant to all

parents joy in their children. ℟ Son of the Virgin Mary, hear us.
You began life among men as a child:—share with all children your
own experience of growing in wisdom and grace. ℟
You came to form the human race into a holy people;—help the
nations of our world to live in peace and friendship. ℟
Your birth gave strength to family life:—let the members of each
family be deeply united and live for one another. ℟
You came to a life of weakness in our world;—grant to the dead the
life of glory in your kingdom. ℟
Our Father

The concluding prayer as at Morning Prayer, p 91.

B　　　　　6 JANUARY

Invitatory ant. Christ has been born for us: come, let us adore him.

MORNING PRAYER

Hymn, from the appendix, for Christmastide I.

Scripture Reading　　　*Is 61:1-2a*
The spirit of the Lord God is upon me because the Lord has anointed
me; he has sent me to bring good news to the humble, to bind up the
broken-hearted, to proclaim liberty to captives and release to those
in prison, to proclaim a year of the Lord's favour.

Short Responsory
℟ The Lord has made known our salvation, alleluia, alleluia.
Repeat ℟
℣ He has revealed his saving power. ℟ Glory be. ℟

Benedictus ant. This is he who has come by water and by blood:
Jesus Christ, our Lord.

Intercessions
Let us praise the Word who was in the beginning with God and
became man for us. ℟ Let the earth rejoice, because you have come.

Christ, Eternal Word, your birth brought joy to the world;—bring joy to each of us today through your presence in our hearts by grace. R̥

In your coming you showed us the faithfulness of God;—keep us faithful to the promises of our baptism. R̥

At your birth the angels proclaimed peace to men;—keep us in your peace all our days. R̥

You came to be the true vine, bearing for us the fruit of life;—make us branches of the vine, bearing fruit in you. R̥

Our Father

Concluding Prayer
Lord, in your goodness
open our eyes to your light,
and so fill our hearts with your glory
that we may always acknowledge Jesus as Saviour,
and hold fast to his word in sincerity and truth.
(We make our prayer) through our Lord.

EVENING PRAYER
When the Sunday is 8 January

Hymn, from the appendix, for Christmastide I.

Scripture Reading   *Acts 10:37-38*
You know of the great event that took place throughout all of Judea, beginning in Galilee, after the baptism that John preached. You know about Jesus of Nazareth, how God poured out on him the Holy Spirit and power. He went everywhere, doing good and healing all who were under the power of the Devil, for God was with him.

Short Responsory
R̥ The Word became flesh, alleluia, alleluia. *Repeat* R̥
y̌ And he lived among us. R̥ Glory be. R̥

Magnificat ant. A voice spoke from heaven, 'This is my beloved Son, with whom I am well pleased.'

Intercessions

At Christ's birth the angels proclaimed peace to the world. Let us praise him with joy and ask his favour: ℟ Let your birth bring peace to all men.

Lord, fill your Church with all blessings;—strengthen her by the mystery of your birth. ℟

You are Lord of human history;—may we learn to see your presence in the daily events and experiences of life. ℟

In you God's promise is fulfilled:—reveal yourself to those who yet await their Saviour. ℟

You came to bring life to the world:—may all men be born of God through the waters of baptism. ℟

By taking mortal flesh you raised it from the dead:—restore the faithful departed to the fulness of your glory. ℟

Our Father

The concluding prayer as at Morning Prayer, p 93.

B ### 7 JANUARY
When the Solemnity of the Epiphany is celebrated on 8 January

Invitatory ant. Christ has been born for us: come, let us adore him.

MORNING PRAYER

Hymn, from the appendix, for Christmastide I.

Scripture Reading   *Is 9:6*

To us a child is born,
to us a son is given;
and the government will be upon his shoulder,
and his name will be called
'Wonderful Counsellor, Mighty God,
Everlasting Father, Prince of Peace.'

Short Responsory

R̷ The Lord has made known our salvation, alleluia, alleluia.
Repeat R̷
V̷ He has revealed his saving power. R̷ Glory be. R̷

Benedictus ant. This is he of whom it is written: Christ is born in Israel, and his kingdom will have no end.

Intercessions

We praise you, Christ. Through you God's salvation reaches to the boundaries of the earth. R̷ Glory to you, Christ the Lord.
Christ, our Redeemer, you have drawn all men to yourself;—break down the walls of prejudice that separate man from man. R̷
You came to live among us:—help us to recognize all the ways you are present in the Church and in the lives of men and women. R̷
In you God stands revealed:—may our belief and good works be consistent with your teaching. R̷
Immanuel, God with men, renew our lives completely;—make us a people you can call your own. R̷
Our Father

Concluding Prayer

All-powerful, ever-living God.
a new day dawned
when your Only-begotten Son came among us,
our brother through his birth from the Virgin Mary.
Grant that we who share in his human nature
may be his brethren in the kingdom of his grace
(We make our prayer) through our Lord.

Evening Prayer of the Epiphany, p 96.

¶ *In the following Office, (Baptism) indicates antiphons for use on the Feast of the Baptism of the Lord.*

Christmastide II: From the Solemnity of the Epiphany

THE EPIPHANY OF THE LORD

A 6 January

B Sunday between 2 and 8 January

Solemnity

EVENING PRAYER I

Hymn

Bethlehem, of noblest cities
None can once with thee compare:
Thou alone the Lord from heaven
Didst for us incarnate bear.

Fairer than the sun at morning
Was the star that told his birth;
To the lands their God announcing,
Seen in human form on earth.

By its peerless beauty guided
See the eastern kings appear;
Bowing low, their gifts they offer,
Gifts of incense, gold and myrrh.

Sacred gifts of mystic meaning:
Incense doth the God disclose,
Gold the King of Kings proclaimeth,
Myrrh a future tomb foreshows.

In thy glory, O Lord Jesus,
To the Gentile world displayed,
With the Father and the Spirit
Endless praise to thee be paid.

PSALMODY

Ant. 1: Begotton before the dawn and before all ages, today the Lord, our Saviour, was born of the Virgin.
(*Baptism:*) John appeared in the wilderness. He baptized and preached a baptism of repentance for the forgiveness of sins.

PSALM 134(135)

I

Práise the náme of the Lórd,*
práise him, sérvants of the Lórd,
who stánd in the hóuse of the Lórd*
in the cóurts of the hóuse of our Gód.

Praise the Lórd for the Lórd is góod.*
Sing a psálm to his náme for he is lóving.
For the Lórd has chosen Jácob for himsélf*
and Ísrael for his ówn posséssion.

For I knów the Lórd is gréat,*
that our Lórd is hígh above all góds.
The Lórd does whatéver he wílls,*
in héaven, on éarth, in the séas.

He summons clóuds from the énds of the éarth;†
makes líghtning prodúce the ráin;*
from his tréasuries he sénds forth the wind.

The first-born of the Egýptians he smóte,*
of mán and béast alíke.
Sígns and wónders he wórked†
in the mídst of your lánd, O Égypt,*
against Pháraoh and áll his sérvants.

Nátions in their gréatness he strúck*
and kíngs in their spléndour he sléw.
Síhon, kíng of the Ámorites,†
Óg, the kíng of Báshan,*
and áll the kíngdoms of Cánaan.

He let Ísrael inhérit their lánd;*
on his péople their lánd be bestówed.

Ant. Begotten before the dawn and before all ages, today the Lord, our Saviour, was born of the Virgin.

(*Baptism:*) John appeared in the wilderness. He baptized and preached a baptism of repentance for the forgiveness of sins.

Ant. 2: The Lord, our God, is greater than all gods.

(*Baptism:*) I baptize you with water, but he will baptize you with the Holy Spirit and with fire.

II

Lórd, your náme stands for éver,*
unforgótten from áge to áge:
for the Lórd does jústice for his péople;*
the Lórd takes píty on his sérvants.

Pagan ídols are sílver and góld,*
the wórk of húman hánds.
They have móuths but they cánnot spéak;*
they have éyes but they cánnot sée.

They have éars but they cánnot héar;*
there is néver a bréath on their líps.
Their mákers will come to bé like thém*
and so will áll who trúst in thém!

Sons of Ísrael, bléss the Lórd!*
Sons of Áaron, bléss the Lórd!
Sons of Lévi, bléss the Lórd!*
You who féar him, bléss the Lórd!

From Síon may the Lórd be bléssed,*
hé who dwélls in Jerúsalem!

Ant. 2: The Lord, our God, is greater than all gods.

(*Baptism*): I baptize you with water, but he will baptize you with the Holy Spirit and with fire.

Ant. 3: This star shines like a flame; it points out God, the King of kings: the Magi saw it and they offered presents to the great King.

(*Baptism*): As soon as Jesus was baptized, he came up from the water and suddenly the heavens opened for him.

CANTICLE: CF I TIM 3:16

R7 O praise the Lord, all you nations!

He was manifested in the flesh,*
vindicated in the Spirit.
R7 O praise the Lord, all you nations!

He was seen by angels,*
preached among the nations.
R7 O praise the Lord, all you nations!

He was believed on in the world,*
taken up in glory.
R7 O praise the Lord, all you nations!

Ant. This star shines like a flame; it points out God, the King of kings: the Magi saw it and they offered presents to the great King. (*Baptism:*) As soon as Jesus was baptized, he came up from the water and suddenly the heavens opened for him.

Scripture Reading   *2 Tim 1:9-10*
It is God who brought us salvation and called us to a dedicated life, not for any merit of ours but of his own purpose and his own grace, which was granted to us in Christ Jesus from all eternity, but has now at length been brought fully into view by the appearance on earth of our Saviour Jesus Christ. For he has broken the power of death and brought life and immortality to light through the gospel.

Short Responsory
R7 All the peoples will be blessed in him. *Repeat* R7
y̆ All nations will praise him. R7 Glory be. R7

Magnificat ant. The Magi saw the star and said to one another: This is the sign of the great King; let us go and seek him; let us offer him gifts: gold, frankincense and myrrh.

Intercessions
Today the Magi knelt before our Saviour. Let us also worship him with great joy, and pray: R7 Lord, save us in our need.

King of nations, the wise men came from the East to worship you;—grant us the true spirit of adoration and submission. R⁷ Lord, save us in our need.

King of glory, your people look to you for judgment:—grant an abundance of peace to our world. R⁷

King of ages, your word is ever powerful;—may it penetrate our hearts and lives today. R⁷

King of justice, show your love for the poor and the powerless;—strengthen those who are suffering. R⁷

King of heaven, hope of all who trust in you;—give to the faithful departed the wonders of your salvation. R⁷

Our Father

Concluding Prayer

On this day, Lord God,
by a guiding star you revealed your Only-begotten Son
to all the peoples of the world.
Lead us from the faith by which we know you now
to the vision of your glory, face to face.
(We make our prayer) through our Lord.

Invitatory

Ant. Christ has appeared to us: come, let us adore him.

MORNING PRAYER

Hymn

Songs of thankfulness and praise,
Jesu, Lord, to thee we raise,
Manifested by the star
To the sages from afar;
Branch of royal David's stem
In thy birth at Bethlehem;
Anthems be to thee addressed,
God in man made manifest.

Manifest at Jordan's stream,
Prophet, priest, and king supreme;

And at Cana wedding-guest
In thy Godhead manifest;
Manifest in power divine,
Changing water into wine;
    Anthems be to thee addressed,
    God in man made manifest.

Grant us grace to see thee, Lord,
Mirrored in thy holy word;
May we imitate thee now,
And be pure, as pure art thou;
That we like to thee may be
At thy great Epiphany.
    And may praise thee, ever blest,
    God in man made manifest.

Ant. 1: The Magi opened their treasures and offered the Lord gifts of gold, frankincense and myrrh, alleluia.

Psalms and canticle from Sunday, Week 1, pp 390 ff.

Ant. 2: Seas and rivers, bless the Lord; springs of water, praise the Lord, alleluia.

Ant. 3: Jerusalem, your light has come, and the glory of the Lord has risen upon you: the peoples will walk in your light, alleluia.

Scripture Reading   *Is 52:7-10*
How beautiful upon the mountains are the feet of him who brings
   good tidings,
who publishes peace, who brings good tidings of good,
who publishes salvation,
who says to Zion, 'Your God reigns.'
Hark, your watchmen lift up their voice,
together they sing for joy;
for eye to eye they see
the return of the Lord to Zion.
Break forth together into singing,
you waste places of Jerusalem;
for the Lord has comforted his people,

he has redeemed Jerusalem.
The Lord has bared his holy arm
before the eyes of all the nations;
and all the ends of the earth shall see
the salvation of our God.

Short Responsory

R̹ All the kings of the earth will adore him. *Repeat* R̹
V̹ All the peoples will serve him. R̹ Glory be. R̹

Benedictus ant. Today the Church has been joined to her heavenly
bridegroom, since Christ has purified her of her sins in the river
Jordan: the Magi hasten to the royal wedding and offer gifts: the
wedding guests rejoice since Christ has changed water into wine,
alleluia.

Intercessions

Today the Magi knelt before our Saviour. Let us also worship him
with great joy. R̹ Light of all light, reveal yourself this day.
Christ, manifested in the flesh:—sanctify us by the word of God and
by prayer. R̹
Christ, vindicated in the Spirit;—free our lives from the spirit of
discord. R̹
Christ, seen by angels;—give us even now a share in the joy of
heaven. R̹
Christ, preached among the nations;—move all hearts by the power
of your Spirit. R̹
Christ, believed in by the world;—renew your disciples' faith. R̹
Christ, taken up in glory:—enkindle in us the desire of your king-
dom. R̹
Our Father

Concluding Prayer

On this day, Lord God,
by a guiding star you revealed your Only-begotten Son
to all the peoples of the world.
Lead us from the faith by which we know you now
to the vision of your glory, face to face.
(We make our prayer) through our Lord.

EVENING PRAYER II

Hymn

Bethlehem, of noblest cities
None can once with thee compare:
Thou alone the Lord from heaven
Didst for us incarnate bear.

Fairer than the sun at morning
Was the star that told his birth;
To the lands their God announcing,
Seen in human form on earth.

By its peerless beauty guided
See the eastern kings appear;
Bowing low, their gifts they offer,
Gifts of incense, gold and myrrh.

Sacred gifts of mystic meaning:
Incense doth the God disclose,
Gold the King of Kings proclaimeth,
Myrrh a future tomb foreshows.

In thy glory, O Lord Jesus,
To the Gentile world displayed,
With the Father and the Spirit
Endless praise to thee be paid. Amen.

PSALMODY

Ant. 1: The King of Peace is more glorious than all the kings of the world.
(*Baptism:*) The voice of the Father was heard from heaven: This is my Son with whom I am well pleased; listen to his word.

PSALM 109(110):1-5,7

The Lórd's revelátion to my Máster:†
'Sít on my ríght:*
your fóes I will pút beneath your féet'.

103

The Lórd will wíeld from Síon†
your scéptre of pówer:*
rúle in the mídst of all your fóes.

A prínce from the dáy of your bírth†
on the hóly móuntains;*
from the wómb before the dáwn I begót you.

The Lórd has sworn an óath he will not chánge.†
'You are a príest for éver,*
a príest like Melchízedek of óld.'

The Máster stánding at your ríght hand*
will shatter kíngs in the dáy of his wráth.

He shall drínk from the stréam by the wáyside*
and thérefore he shall líft up his héad.

Ant. The King of Peace is more glorious than all the kings of the world.
(*Baptism:*) The voice of the Father was heard from heaven: This is my Son with whom I am well pleased; listen to his word.

Ant. 2: A beacon now shines in the darkness for honest men; the Lord is compassionate, merciful, and kind.
(*Baptism:*) The Saviour crushed the head of the serpent in the river Jordan; he released all men from his power.

PSALM 111(112)

Happy the mán who féars the Lórd,*
who tákes delíght in all his commánds.
His sóns will be pówerful on éarth;*
the chíldren of the úpright are bléssed.

Ríches and wéalth are in his hóuse;*
his jústice stands fírm, for éver.
He is a líght in the dárkness for the úpright:*
he is génerous, mérciful and júst.

The góod man takes píty and lénds,*
he condúcts his affáirs with hónour.

The júst man will néver wáver:*
hé will be remémbered for éver.

He has no féar of évil néws;*
with a fírm heart he trústs in the Lórd.
With a stéadfast héart he will not féar;*
he will sée the dównfall of his fóes.

Open-hánded, he gíves to the póor;†
his jústice stands fírm for éver.*
His héad will be ráised in glóry.

The wícked man sées and is ángry,†
grinds his téeth and fádes awáy;*
the desíre of the wícked leads to dóom.

Ant. A beacon now shines in the darkness for honest men; the Lord is compassionate, merciful, and kind.
(*Baptism:*) The Saviour crushed the head of the serpent in the river Jordan; he released all men from his power.

Ant. 3: All peoples, that you have made, will come and adore you, Lord.
(*Baptism:*) Today a great mystery is revealed to us: the creator of all things released us from the bond of our sins in the river Jordan.

CANTICLE: REV 15:3-4

Great and wonderful are your deeds,*
O Lord God the Almighty!
Just and true are your ways,*
O King of the ages!

Who shall not fear and glorify your name, O Lord?*
For you alone are holy.
All nations shall come and worship you,*
for your judgments have been revealed.

Ant. All peoples, that you have made, will come and adore you, Lord.
(*Baptism:*) Today a great mystery is revealed to us: the creator of all

things released us from the bond of our sins in the river Jordan.

Scripture Reading *Tit 3:4-5*
When the kindness and love of God our Saviour appeared, he saved us. It was not because of any good works that we ourselves had done, but because of his own mercy that he saved us through the washing by which the Holy Spirit gives us new birth and new life.

Short Responsory
R̃ All the peoples will be blessed in him. *Repeat* R̃
Ỹ All nations will praise him. R̃ Glory be. R̃

Magnificat ant. Three wonders mark this day we celebrate: today the star led the Magi to the manger; today water was changed into wine at the marriage feast; today Christ desired to be baptized by John in the river Jordan to bring us salvation, alleluia.

Intercessions
Today the Magi knelt before our Saviour. Let us also worship him with great joy, and pray: R̃ Lord, save us in our need.
King of nations, the wise men came from the East to worship you:—grant us the true spirit of adoration and submission. R̃
King of glory, your people look to you for judgment:—grant an abundance of peace to our world. R̃
King of ages, your word is ever powerful:—may it penetrate our hearts and lives today. R̃
King of justice, show your love for the poor and the powerless;—strengthen those who are suffering. R̃
King of heaven, hope of all who trust in you;—give to the faithful departed the wonders of your salvation. R̃
Our Father

The concluding prayer as at Morning Prayer, p 102.

A Where the Epiphany is celebrated on 6 January: *on the days after the Solemnity the Office is celebrated as set out below under the date of the month, but after the Sunday of the Baptism of the Lord the Weekdays of the year begin.*

B Where the Epiphany is celebrated on the Sunday (2 to 6 January): *the Office is celebrated as set out under the days of the week.*

Note: *When the Sunday is the 7 or 8 January, the Feast of the Baptism of the Lord is omitted, the Weekdays of the year are begun immediately after the Epiphany, and the following Offices are omitted.*

A   # 7 JANUARY

or

B   # MONDAY AFTER THE
SUNDAY OF THE EPIPHANY

Psalter: Week 2

Invitatory ant. Christ has appeared to us: come, let us adore him.

MORNING PRAYER

Hymn, from the appendix, for Christmastide II.

Scripture Reading   *Is 9:6*
To us a child is born,
to us a son is given;
and the government will be upon his shoulder,
and his name will be called
'Wonderful Counsellor, Mighty God,
Everlasting Father, Prince of Peace'.

Short Responsory
R All the kings of the earth will adore him. *Repeat* R
V All the peoples will serve him. R Glory be. R

Benedictus ant. The Magi came to Bethlehem from the East to adore the Lord; they opened their treasures and offered him precious gifts: gold for a great king, frankincense for the true God, myrrh for his burial, alleluia.

107

Intercessions

We praise you, Christ. Through you God's salvation reaches to the boundaries of the earth. ℟ Glory to you, Christ the Lord.

Christ, our Redeemer, you have drawn all men to yourself;—break down the walls of prejudice that separate man from man. ℟

You came to live among us:—help us to recognize all the ways you are present in the Church and in the lives of men and women. ℟

In you God stands revealed:—may our belief and good works be consistent with your teaching. ℟

Immanuel, God with men, renew our lives completely;—make us a people you can call your own. ℟

Our Father

Concluding Prayer

Lord, may the radiance of your glory light up our hearts,
and bring us through the shadows of this world
until we reach our homeland of everlasting light.
(We make our prayer) through our Lord.

EVENING PRAYER

Hymn, from the appendix, for Christmastide II.

Scripture Reading   *2 Pet 1:3-4*

By his divine power, he has given us all the things that we need for life and for true devotion, bringing us to know God himself, who has called us by his own glory and goodness. In making these gifts, he has given us the guarantee of something very great and wonderful to come: through them you will be able to share the divine nature and to escape corruption in a world that is sunk in vice.

Short Responsory

℟ All the peoples will be blessed in him. *Repeat* ℟

℣ All nations will praise him. ℟ Glory be. ℟

Magnificat ant. When the Magi saw the star they were filled with great joy; they entered the house and offered the Lord gold, frankincense and myrrh.

Intercessions

Blessed be Christ the Lord, who came to be with us, to give light to those who live in darkness and the shadow of death. R̷ Christ, rising Sun, shed your light on all men.

Christ our Lord, at your coming your body the Church was born:— may it ever grow on earth and build itself up in love. R̷

You hold heaven and earth in your hands:—let all races and nations proclaim you as their Lord. R̷

Through your incarnation you became our eternal High Priest:— renew in all your priests the grace of proclaiming your redemption. R̷

You were born of a virgin mother;—bless all religious women and make them the living sign of the Church which is your bride. R̷

By taking mortal flesh you ended the power of death:—unite the departed with yourself in everlasting life. R̷

Our Father

The concluding prayer as at Morning Prayer, p 108.

A	**8 JANUARY**
	or
B	**TUESDAY AFTER**
	SUNDAY OF THE EPIPHANY

Invitatory ant. Christ has appeared to us: come, let us adore him.

MORNING PRAYER

Hymn, from the appendix, for Christmastide II.

Scripture Reading   *Is 4:2-3*

On that day the plant that the Lord has grown shall become glorious in its beauty, and the fruit of the land shall be the pride and splendour of the survivors of Israel. Then those who are left in Zion, who remain in Jerusalem, every one enrolled in the book of life, shall be called holy.

Short Responsory

℟ All the kings of the earth will adore him. *Repeat* ℟
℣ All the peoples will serve him. ℟ Glory be. ℟

Benedictus ant. The Magi offered the Lord three gifts: gold, frankincense and myrrh. They offered these gifts to the Son of God, to the great King, alleluia.

Intercessions

Christ came that creation might be freed from its slavery to corruption, and so enjoy the freedom of the sons of God. Let us ask him:
℟ From all evil, save us through your birth.
Lord Jesus, you came to bring us new life;—renew us by the mystery of your birth. ℟
Christ, God and man, may your divine life penetrate our humanity;—may we live as sons of God. ℟
Light of the nations, teacher of holiness;—may your word enlighten our path through life. ℟
You were made flesh in Mary's womb;—dwell always in our hearts through faith. ℟
Our Father

Concluding Prayer

God, our Father,
when your Only-begotten Son revealed himself in flesh and blood,
we came to know him as our fellow-man.
May he transform us inwardly until we bear his likeness,
who lives and reigns with you and the Holy Spirit,
God, for ever and ever.

EVENING PRAYER

Hymn, from the appendix, for Christmastide II.

Scripture Reading   *Eph 2:3b-5*

By nature we were as much under God's anger as the rest of the world. But God loved us with so much love that he was generous with his mercy: when we were dead through our sins, he brought us to life with Christ—it is through grace that you have been saved.

Short Responsory

℟ All the peoples will be blessed in him. *Repeat* ℟

℣ All nations will praise him. ℟ Glory be. ℟

Magnificat ant. You came to bring us the eternal light; to you, O Christ, the Magi offer gifts, alleluia.

Intercessions

Let us unite ourselves with all Christians, praising the Father and asking for his protection. ℟ Heavenly Father, hear your children.

Father, help those who search for an unknown God;—and let them discover the light of Christ. ℟

Look in mercy on those who adore you as the one and only God;— show them that you are always close. ℟

Remember all your children throughout the world;—see that they never stray far from you. ℟

Send your angels to protect all men;—save them from a sudden and unprovided death. ℟

Bring the dead to the vision of your glory;—give them eternal happiness in your presence. ℟

Our Father

The concluding prayer as at Morning Prayer, p 110.

A
B
9 JANUARY
or
WEDNESDAY AFTER
SUNDAY OF THE EPIPHANY

Invitatory ant. Christ has appeared to us: come, let us adore him.

MORNING PRAYER

Hymn, from the appendix, for Chrismastide II.

Scripture Reading   *Is 49:8-9*

Thus says the Lord:

At the favourable time I will answer you,

on the day of salvation I will help you.
(I have formed you and have appointed you
as covenant of the people.)
I will restore the land
and assign you the estates that lie waste.
I will say to the prisoners, 'Come out',
to those who are in darkness, 'Show yourselves'.
On every roadway they will graze,
and each bare height shall be their pasture.

Short Responsory
R̸ All the kings of the earth will adore him. *Repeat* R̸
V̸ All the peoples will serve him. R̸ Glory be. R̸

Benedictus ant. We saw his star rising in the East and we have come
with gifts to adore the Lord.

Intercessions
The Word of God, eternally begotten of the Father, became in the
fulness of time a child born for us and a son given to us. Let us praise
him: R̸ Blessed be the Lord.
Lord Jesus, be with us today;—help us to live as men who have
heard the good news of salvation. R̸
Sun of Justice, radiance of God's glory and light of the world;—help
those who live in darkness and find no answer to their problems. R̸
For us you became a child at Bethlehem;—renew the childlike
simplicity of our faith. R̸
You are the living bread, the source of eternal life;—fill our hearts
with joy through the sacrament of your body and blood. R̸
Our Father

Concluding Prayer
God and Father, light of all mankind,
make our hearts radiant with the splendour of that light
which long ago you shed on our fathers in the faith,
and give your people the joy of lasting peace.
(We make our prayer) through our Lord.

EVENING PRAYER

Hymn, from the appendix, for Christmastide II.

Scripture Reading   *Col 1:13-15*
God has taken us out of the power of darkness and created a place
for us in the kingdom of the Son that he loves, and in him, we gain
our freedom, the forgiveness of our sins. He is the image of the unseen God and the first-born of all creation.

Short Responsory
R̶ All the peoples will be blessed in him. *Repeat* R̶
V̶ All nations will praise him. R̶ Glory be. R̶

Magnificat ant. Herod asked the Magi, 'What sign have you seen
regarding this newborn king?' We saw a bright star whose light fills
the whole world.

Intercessions
Full of confidence, we pray to the Word of God who came to drown
all our sins in the ocean of his love. R̶ Lord, have mercy.
Eternal High-Priest, in you the fulness of divine worship is given to
us;—grant all men a share in this worship through your Church. R̶
You came to us as healer of soul and body;—strengthen the sick
and restore them to health. R̶
With you there is mercy and fulness of redemption;—may all men
discover the deep joy of repentance. R̶
Mighty King, you broke the chains that held us;—give strength and
comfort to those in prison. R̶
Lord of life and death, you opened the gate of heaven,—receive the
dead into the glory of your presence. R̶
Our Father

The concluding prayer as at Morning Prayer, p 112.

A # 10 JANUARY
or
B # THURSDAY AFTER
SUNDAY OF THE EPIPHANY

Invitatory ant. Christ has appeared to us: come, let us adore him.

MORNING PRAYER

Hymn, from the appendix, for Christmastide II.

Scripture Reading   *Is 62:11-12*
Tell the daughter of Zion,
Behold, your deliverance has come.
His recompense comes with him;
he carries his reward before him;
and they shall be called a Holy People,
the Ransomed of the Lord.

Short Responsory
R℣ All the kings of the earth will adore him. *Repeat* R℣
℣ All the peoples will serve him. R℣ Glory be. R℣

Benedictus ant. All peoples come from afar; they bear gifts with them, alleluia.

Intercessions
God has given us his own Son to be our consolation. Let us acclaim the wonderful deeds of the Lord. R℣ Glory be to God on high.
With the angels, patriarchs and prophets:—we praise you, O Lord. R℣
With Mary the Virgin Mother of God:—we glorify you, O Lord. R℣
With the apostles and evangelists:—we give you thanks, O Lord. R℣
With all the martyrs in heaven:—we offer our bodies as a living sacrifice. R℣
With all the saints of your Church:—we dedicate our lives to you. R℣
Our Father

Concluding Prayer
Through your Son, Lord God,
you shed your eternal light on all mankind.
Give us grace to acknowledge the full splendour of our Redeemer,
so that, going from glory to glory,
we may come at length to your everlasting light.
(We make our prayer) through our Lord.

EVENING PRAYER

Hymn, from the appendix, for Christmastide II.

Scripture Reading   *1 Jn 1:5b,7*
God is light, and in him there is no darkness at all. If we walk in the
light as he himself is in the light, then we share together a common
life, and we are being cleansed from every sin by the blood of Jesus
his Son.

Short Responsory
R̷ All the peoples will be blessed in him. *Repeat* R̷
y̷ All nations will praise him. R̷ Glory be. R̷

Magnificat ant. All the men of Saba shall come. They will bring gold
and frankincense, alleluia.

Intercessions
United in prayer with all our brothers, let us bless God and call upon
his name. R̷ Lord, show us your mercy.
Holy Father, we pray for those who know you only by the light of
reason;—lead them to the knowledge of the gospel. R̷
Guide all outside the Church who strive for a better world;—let them
find Christ, who is the way, the truth and the life. R̷
Help men of all other religions to live in sincerity of heart;—and
bring them into your own marvellous light. R̷
Cleanse the hearts of your faithful;—that they may know the great
depths of your love. R̷
Show your mercy to the dead;—and endow them with the glory of
your saints. R̷

Our Father

The concluding prayer as at Morning Prayer, p 115.

A   11 JANUARY
                       or
B   FRIDAY AFTER
    SUNDAY OF THE EPIPHANY

Invitatory ant. Christ has appeared to us: come, let us adore him.

MORNING PRAYER

Hymn, from the appendix, for Christmastide II.

Scripture Reading   *Is 45:22-24*
Turn back to me, and win deliverance, all you that dwell in the
remotest corners of the earth; I am God, there is no other. By my
own honour I have sworn it, nor shall it echo in vain, this faithful
promise I have made, that every knee shall bow before me, and every
tongue swear by my name.

Short Responsory
R7 All the kings of the earth will adore him. *Repeat* R7
V7 All the peoples will serve him. R7 Glory be. R7

Benedictus ant. All who despised you shall come and bow down at
your feet.

Intercessions
To Christ be honour and glory. He came to create a new man, reborn
in mind and heart. Let us pray that his saving will may be fulfilled:
R7 May your birth renew our lives.
In your manhood you revealed to us your Godhead;— grant that
we may recognize you in the mysteries of your Church. R7
Through the Immaculate Virgin you came to live with men:—help

us, by her prayers, to attain your life with the Father. ℟
You are the source of eternal life;—come to us today in your word
and in the bread which is your body. ℟
We adore you as the holy child of Bethlehem;—help us to attain the
maturity and full vigour of your life. ℟
Our Father

Concluding Prayer
Almighty God and Father,
by the guidance of a star
you revealed the birth of the Saviour of the world.
Open our minds to that revelation,
and let it bear fruit in our lives.
(We make our prayer) through our Lord.

EVENING PRAYER

Hymn, from the appendix, for Christmastide II.

Scripture Reading   *Rom 8:3-4*
God condemned sin in human nature by sending his own Son, who
came with a nature like man's sinful nature to do away with sin.
God did this so that the righteous demands of the Law might be fully
satisfied in us who live according to the Spirit, not according to
human nature.

Short Responsory
℟ All the peoples will be blessed in him. *Repeat* ℟
℣ All nations will praise him. ℟ Glory be. ℟

Magnificat ant. The Magi were warned in a dream by an angel, so
they returned to their own country by another way.

Intercessions
Let us pray to the Father who appointed Christ as light of the
nations. ℟ Father, hear our prayer.
Eternal Father, may your Church spread to far horizons;—may she
make Christ present in the midst of the world. ℟

You guided wise men from the East to see the new-born Jesus:—
reveal your Son to every man who searches for truth. ℟ Father,
hear our prayer.

Lead all nations into the light of Christ;—may they acknowledge
him as their Lord and Saviour. ℟

Send your missionaries through the world—and let men know that
their time of grace has come. ℟

Grant to the dead the fulness of redemption;—raise them up in
Christ who is the Lord of life. ℟

Our Father

The concluding prayer as at Morning Prayer, p 117.

A ## 12 JANUARY
or
B ## SATURDAY AFTER
SUNDAY OF THE EPIPHANY

Invitatory ant. Christ has appeared to us: come, let us adore him.

MORNING PRAYER

Hymn, from the appendix, for Christmastide II.

Scripture Reading   *Wis 7:26-27*
Wisdom is a reflection of the eternal light,
untarnished mirror of God's active power,
image of his goodness.
Although alone, she can do all;
herself unchanging, she makes all things new.
In each generation she passes into holy souls,
she makes them friends of God and prophets.

Short Responsory
℟ All the kings of the earth will adore him. *Repeat* ℟
℣ All the peoples will serve him. ℟ Glory be. ℟

Benedictus ant. This miracle at Cana in Galilee was the first sign by which Jesus revealed his glory.

Intercessions
Let us give glory to Christ, the image of God, and pray to him with living faith. ℟ Son of God, hear us.
Son of God, in you we see the wisdom of the Father:—make our lives a manifestation of your truth. ℟
Lord of life, you raised men from the dead:—renew us with the fulness of your life. ℟
You were obedient unto death:—may we bear your death in our bodies by a life of self-denial. ℟
Splendour of the Father, may your light shine in our hearts;—radiate the light of the knowledge of God's glory. ℟
Our Father

Concluding Prayer
Almighty, ever-living God,
through Christ your Son you made of us a new creation.
Shape us, then, in his likeness,
since in him our human nature now lives with you.
(We make our prayer) through our Lord.

Evening Prayer of the following.

A(B)   Sunday After 6 January
THE BAPTISM OF THE LORD
Feast

B *If the Sunday is 7 or 8 January, the Feast of the Baptism is omitted.*

EVENING PRAYER I

Hymn
    When Jesus comes to be baptized,
    He leaves the hidden years behind,

The years of safety and of peace,
To bear the sins of all mankind.

The Spirit of the Lord comes down,
Anoints the Christ to suffering,
To preach the word, to free the bound,
And to the mourner comfort bring.

Our everlasting Father, praise,
With Christ, his well-beloved Son,
Who with the Spirit reigns serene,
Untroubled Trinity in One.

Antiphons proper to this Feast are said with the psalms and canticle of Evening Prayer I of the Epiphany, pp 97 ff.

Scripture Reading   *Acts 10:37-38*
You know of the great event that took place throughout all of Judea, beginning in Galilee, after the baptism that John preached. You know about Jesus of Nazareth, how God poured out on him the Holy Spirit and power. He went everywhere, doing good and healing all who were under the power of the Devil, for God was with him.

Short Responsory
R/ Lord our God, hear the cry of your people. *Repeat* R/
V/ Open the spring of living water for them. R/ Glory be. R/

Magnificat ant. The Saviour came to be baptized. He, the second Adam, renewed our corrupted nature by the waters of baptism, and he clothed us with a garment which can never perish.

Intercessions
Let us pray to our Redeemer who humbled himself to receive baptism at the hands of John. R/ Lord, send us your Spirit.
Christ, servant of the Father and pleasing to him,—send forth your Spirit among us. R/
Chosen One of God, you did not break the crushed reed nor quench the wavering flame;—let all men know your compassion for our world of weakness. R/

You were anointed with the Holy Spirit to be our Saviour;—lead all men to believe in you and so come to eternal life. ℟
You are God's light to the nations;—open the eyes of the blind in the baptismal waters of the new covenant. ℟
You are the hope of all peoples;—receive the faithful departed into your heavenly kingdom. ℟
Our Father

Concluding Prayer

Almighty, ever-living God,
when Christ was baptized in the river Jordan
the Holy Spirit came upon him
and your voice proclaimed from heaven 'This is my beloved Son.'
Grant that we,
who by water and the Holy Spirit are your adopted children,
may continue steadfast in your love.
(We make our prayer) through our Lord.

Invitatory

Ant. Let us adore Christ, the Son, the Beloved, in whom the Father is well pleased.

MORNING PRAYER

Hymn, as at Evening Prayer I, p 120.

Ant. 1: The soldier baptizes the king, the slave his Lord, John baptizes the Saviour; the waters of the Jordan are astonished, the dove appears as a sign, the voice of the Father declares: This is my Son.

Psalms and canticle from Sunday, Week 1, pp 390 ff.

Ant. 2: The springs of water were made holy when Christ appeared on earth. Draw water from the wells of the Saviour; Christ our God has made the whole creation holy.

Ant. 3: You destroyed mankind's sin by the Holy Spirit and by fire; we praise you and adore you as God and redeemer.

Scripture Reading   *Is 61:1-2a*
The spirit of the Lord God is upon me because the Lord has anointed me; he has sent me to bring good news to the humble, to bind up the broken-hearted, to proclaim liberty to captives and release to those in prison; to proclaim a year of the Lord's favour.

Short Responsory
R̸ You are Christ, the Son of the living God. Have mercy on us. *Repeat* R̸
V̸ You were revealed today. R̸ Glory be. R̸

Benedictus ant. Christ is baptized and the whole world is made holy; he wipes out the debt of our sins; we will all be purified by water and the Holy Spirit.

Intercessions
Let us pray to our Redeemer who humbled himself to receive baptism at the hands of John. R̸ Lord, have mercy.
Christ, our Lord, you taught us how to live;—open our eyes to the light which is ever ready to enlighten them. R̸
You humbled yourself to receive baptism from your servant:—help us to share in your saving mission and give ourselves for others. R̸
Your baptism has made us children of the Father:—grant the spirit of sonship to all who seek you. R̸
With baptism you have opened the door of repentance:—make us living ministers of your gospel of new life. R̸
Your baptism has revealed to us the persons of the Trinity:—renew the spirit of God's sons in the royal priesthood of all the baptized. R̸
Our Father

Concluding Prayer
Almighty, ever-living God,
when Christ was baptized in the river Jordan
the Holy Spirit came upon him
and your voice proclaimed from heaven 'This is my beloved Son.'

Grant that we,
who by water and the Holy Spirit are your adopted children,
may continue steadfast in your love.
(We make our prayer) through our Lord.

EVENING PRAYER II

*Hymn, as at Evening Prayer I, or from the appendix for Christmas-
tide II.*
*Antiphons proper to the Feast are said with the psalms and canticle of
Evening Prayer II of the Epiphany, pp 103 ff.*

Scripture Reading   *Acts 10:37-38*
You know of the great events that took place throughout all of
Judea, beginning in Galilee, after the baptism that John preached.
You know about Jesus of Nazareth, how God poured out on him
the Holy Spirit and power. He went everywhere, doing good and
healing all who were under the power of the Devil, for God was with
him.

Short Responsory
R/ This is he who has come by water and by blood. *Repeat* R/
V/ This is Jesus Christ, our Lord. R/ Glory be. R/

Magnificat ant. Jesus Christ has loved us and has purified us from
our sins in his blood. He has made us a kingdom and priesthood for
God and his Father. To him be glory and kingly power for ever.

The intercessions and concluding prayer as at Evening Prayer I, p 120.

The end of Christmastide.
*The cycle of Weeks of the Year commences on Monday, Week 1 of the
Psalter, p 402.*

LENT

From the beginning of the Office of Ash Wednesday until the Easter Vigil Alleluia *is omitted.*

SUNDAYS AND WEEKDAYS OF LENT

Invitatory ant. Christ the Lord was tempted and suffered for us. Come, let us adore him.

Alternative, except in Holy Week:
O that today you would listen to his voice: harden not your hearts.

ASH WEDNESDAY

Psalter: Week 4

Invitatory antiphon of Lent.

MORNING PRAYER

Hymn, from the appendix, for Lent nos. 15-19.
Psalms and canticle with the antiphons as in the psalter for Friday of Week 3, pp 591 ff, or for Wednesday of Week 4, pp 644 ff.

Scripture Reading   *Deut 7:6,8-9*
The Lord your God has chosen you to be a people for his own possession, out of all the peoples that are on the face of the earth. It is because the Lord loves you, and is keeping the oath which he swore to your fathers, that the Lord has brought you out with a mighty hand, and redeemed you from the house of bondage, from the hand of Pharaoh king of Egypt. Know therefore that the Lord your God is God, the faithful God who keeps covenant and steadfast love with those who love him and keep his commandments, to a thousand generations.

Short Responsory

R̸ It is he who will free me from the snare of the hunters. *Repeat* R̸
Ɏ And from the evil word. R̸ Glory be. R̸

Benedictus ant. When you fast, do not look dismal, like the hypocrites.

Intercessions

As we begin the season of Lent, we give thanks to God the Father
for this time of grace. Let us ask him to cleanse our hearts and
strengthen us in love through the Holy Spirit. R̸ Give us, Lord, your
Holy Spirit.

Lord, your word is life;—may our lives be nourished and sustained
by every word you speak. R̸

In the life of Jesus you have shown us the way of love;—teach us to
follow this way in the great and small events of life. R̸

Grant us a spirit of self-denial,—and move us to help our brothers
in their need. R̸

Let us bear witness in our bodies to the death of your Son,—for in
his body you have brought us to life. R̸

Our Father

Concluding Prayer

Support us, Lord, as with this Lenten fast
we begin our Christian warfare,
so that in doing battle against the spirit of evil
we may be armed with the weapon of self-denial.
(We make our prayer) through our Lord.

EVENING PRAYER

Hymn, from the appendix, for Lent.
Psalms and canticle with the antiphons as in the psalter for Wednesday
of Week 4, pp 649 ff.

Scripture Reading   *Phil 2:12b-15a*

Keep on working, with fear and trembling, to complete your salvation, for God is always at work in you to make you willing and able to obey his own purpose. Do everything without complaining or arguing, that you may be innocent and pure, as God's perfect children.

Short Responsory
R̷ I said: 'Lord, have mercy on me.' *Repeat* R̷
V̷ 'Heal my soul for I have sinned against you.' R̷ Glory be. R̷

Magnificat ant. When you give alms, do not let your left hand know what your right hand is doing.

Intercessions
To God be honour and glory. He has sealed the new covenant in the blood of Christ and renews it in the sacrament of the altar. In confidence we pray: R̷ Lord, bless your people.
Lord, guide nations and their rulers according to your will—may they work for the common good with one mind and heart. R̷
Renew the spirit of service in those who have left all to follow Christ, —may the holiness of your Church be revealed in their lives. R̷
You have made all men in your likeness;—help them to rid the world of every injustice. R̷
Come with your truth and friendship to those who have lost their way;—teach us how to help them. R̷
Let the dead enter into your glory;—let them praise you for ever. R̷
Our Father

The concluding prayer as at Morning Prayer, p 125.

THURSDAY
AFTER ASH WEDNESDAY

Invitatory antiphon of Lent.

MORNING PRAYER

Hymn, from the appendix, for Lent.
Psalms and canticle with the antiphons as in the psalter for Thursday of Week 4, pp 655 ff.

Scripture Reading   *Cf 1 Kings 8:51-53a*

We are your people, Lord, and your heritage. Let your eyes be open to the supplication of your servant and to the supplication of your people Israel, giving ear to us whenever we call to you. For you separated us from among all the peoples of the earth to be your heritage.

Short Responsory

R℣ It is he who will free me from the snare of the hunters. *Repeat* R℣
℣ And from the evil word. R℣ Glory be. R℣

Benedictus ant. If anyone wishes to be a follower of mine, he must deny himself; he must take up his cross and come with me, says the Lord.

Intercessions

Let us praise God for his loving kindness, which is revealed to us in Jesus Christ. R℣ Remember, Lord, that we are your children.
Lead us more deeply into the life of your Church;—and through us make it a clearer sign of the world's salvation. R℣
Lover of men, help us to play our part in the growth of the human city—and help us to build up your kingdom in every way. R℣
May we come to Christ when we are burdened,—for he is the spring of living water who refreshes all who thirst. R℣
Forgive the harm that we have done;—guide us in the path of justice and truth. R℣
Our Father

Concluding Prayer

Lord, be the beginning and end
of all that we do and say.
Prompt our actions with your grace,
and complete them with your all-powerful help.
(We make our prayer) through our Lord.

EVENING PRAYER

Hymn, from the appendix, for Lent.
Psalms and canticle with the antiphons as in the psalter for Thursday of Week 4, pp 660 ff.

Scripture Reading   *Jas 4:7-8,10*
Be God's true subjects; stand firm against the devil and he will run away from you; come close to God, and he will come close to you. You that are sinners must wash your hands clean, you that are in two minds must purify the intention of your hearts. Humble yourselves before the Lord, and he will exalt you.

Short Responsory
R̷ I said: 'Lord, have mercy on me.' *Repeat* R̷
V̷ 'Heal my soul for I have sinned against you.' R̷ Glory be. R̷

Magnificat ant. If a man will lose himself for my sake, says the Lord, he will find his true self in life eternal.

Intercessions
God enlightens us with the grace of the Holy Spirit that our lives may be filled with justice and faith. Let us proclaim his mercy in our evening prayer. R̷ Lord, give life to the people redeemed by Christ.
Lord, unite bishops, priests and deacons more closely with Christ through the mystery of the eucharist;—renew in them each day the grace of ordination. R̷
Nourish the faithful with the food of Christ's word;—feed them with the bread which is his body. R̷
Grant that we may respect the dignity of every man, redeemed by the precious blood of your Son;—let us never violate his rights or his conscience. R̷
Save men from the blind pursuit of wealth;—make them sensitive to the needs of others. R̷
Be merciful to those who have left our world today;—give them everlasting happiness. R̷
Our Father

The concluding prayer as at Morning Prayer, p 127.

FRIDAY
AFTER ASH WEDNESDAY

Invitatory antiphon of Lent.

MORNING PRAYER

Hymn, from the appendix, for Lent.
Psalms and canticle with the antiphons as in the psalter for Friday of Week 4, pp 665 ff.

Scripture Reading   *Is 53:11b-12*
By his sufferings shall my servant justify many, taking their faults on himself. Hence, I will grant whole hordes for his tribute, he shall divide the spoil with the mighty, for surrendering himself to death, and letting himself be taken for a sinner, while he was bearing the faults of many and praying all the time for sinners.

Short Responsory
R7 It is he who will free me from the snare of the hunters. *Repeat* R7
V And from the evil word. R7 Glory be. R7

Benedictus ant. Clothe the man you see to be naked and do not turn away from your own kin. Then shall your light break forth like the dawn, your integrity shall go before you.

Intercessions
Let us pray earnestly to Christ our Saviour, who redeemed us by his death and resurrection. R7 Lord, have mercy on us.
You went up to Jerusalem to endure the passion and enter into glory;—lead your Church into the paschal feast of eternal life. R7
Your heart was pierced with a lance;—heal the wounds of our human weakness. R7
You made your cross the tree of life;—share your victory with all the baptized. R7
You gave salvation to the repentant thief;—pardon all our sins. R7
Our Father

Concluding Prayer
Give us the grace, Lord,
to continue the works of penitence we have begun:
so that the Lenten observance we have taken upon ourselves
may be accomplished in sincerity of heart.
(We make our prayer) through our Lord.

EVENING PRAYER

Hymn, from the appendix, for Lent.
Psalms and canticle with the antiphons as in the psalter for Friday of Week 4, pp 670 ff.

Scripture Reading   *Jas 5:16,19-20*
Confess your sins to one another, and pray for one another, and then you will be healed. My brothers, if one of your number should stray from the truth and another succeed in bringing him back, be sure of this: any man who brings a sinner back from his crooked ways will be rescuing his soul from death and cancelling innumerable sins.

Short Responsory
R̲̅7 I said: 'Lord, have mercy on me.' *Repeat* R̲̅7
V̅ 'Heal my soul for I have sinned against you.' R̲̅7 Glory be. R̲̅7

Magnificat ant. When the bridegroom is taken away from them the wedding guests will fast.

Intercessions
Let us turn in prayer to the Saviour of all men. By dying he destroyed our death and by rising he restored our life. R̲̅7 Sanctify the people you redeemed by your blood.
Christ, our Redeemer, let us share in your passion by works of penance,—let us attain the glory of your resurrection. R̲̅7
Grant us the protection of your Mother, the comforter of the afflicted,—help us to extend to others the consolation you have given us. R̲̅7
Unite the faithful to your passion in times of trouble and distress—

and let the power of your salvation shine forth in their lives. R̷
You humbled yourself even to accepting death, death on a cross;—
grant to your servants obedience and patience. R̷
Share with the dead your bodily glory;—let us rejoice one day with
them in the fellowship of the saints. R̷
Our Father

The concluding prayer as at Morning Prayer, p 130.

SATURDAY
AFTER ASH WEDNESDAY

Invitatory antiphon of Lent.

MORNING PRAYER

Hymn, from the appendix, for Lent.
Psalms and canticle with the antiphons as in the psalter for Saturday
of Week 4, pp 675 ff.

Scripture Reading   *Is 1:16-18*
Wash, make yourselves clean, take your wrong-doing out of my
sight. Cease to do evil. Learn to do good, search for justice, help
the oppressed, be just to the orphan, plead for the widow. Come
now, let us talk this over, says the Lord: though your sins are like
scarlet, they shall be white as snow; though they are red as crimson,
they shall be like wool.

Short Responsory
R̷ It is he who will free me from the snare of the hunters. *Repeat* R̷
V̷ And from the evil word. R̷ Glory be. R̷

Benedictus ant. Store up treasure for yourselves in heaven, where
there is no moth and no rust to spoil it.

Intercessions
Let us give thanks always to Christ, our Saviour, and pray to him

with confidence. ℟ Lord, help us by your grace.
Lord, may we keep our bodies free from sin;—may the Holy Spirit
dwell within us. ℟
Teach us to offer ourselves this morning for our fellow men,—and
strengthen us to do your will throughout the day. ℟
Grant that we may hunger for the food of eternal life;—give us the
bread of your word and your body. ℟
May your Mother, the refuge of sinners, intercede for us;—through
her prayers forgive us in your mercy. ℟
Our Father

Concluding Prayer
All-powerful, ever-living God,
look with compassion on our frailty,
and for our protection
stretch out to us your strong right hand.
(We make our prayer) through our Lord.

ORDINARY FOR LENT
WEEKS 1 TO 4: SUNDAYS

Sunday 1: Psalter Week 1
Sunday 2: Psalter Week 2
Sunday 3: Psalter Week 3
Sunday 4: Psalter Week 4

EVENING PRAYER I

Hymn, from the appendix, for Lent.

PSALMODY

*Psalms and canticle with proper antiphons as in the psalter for the
relevant week.*

Scripture Reading   *2 Cor 6:1-4a*
We urge this appeal upon you: you have received the grace of God;
do not let it go for nothing. God's own words are: In the hour of my

favour I gave heed to you, on the day of deliverance I came to your aid. The hour of favour has now come; now, I say, has the day of deliverance dawned. In order that our service may not be brought into discredit, we avoid giving offence in anything. As God's servants, we try to recommend ourselves in all circumstances.

Short Responsory

℟ Hear us, Lord, and have mercy, for we have sinned against you. *Repeat* ℟

℣ Listen, Christ, to the prayers of those who cry to you. ℟ Glory be. ℟

Magnificat Antiphon

Sunday 1: Man cannot live on bread alone but by every word that comes from the mouth of God.

Sunday 2: A voice came from the cloud, saying, 'This is my beloved Son, with whom I am well pleased; listen to him.'

Sunday 3: Now that we have been justified by faith, let us be at peace with God, through Jesus Christ our Lord.

Sunday 4: God loved the world so much that he gave his only Son, so that everyone who believes in him may not be lost but may have eternal life.

Intercessions

Sundays 1 and 3
Let us give glory to Christ the Lord. He is our master, our example and our brother. ℟ Lord, give life to your people.
Lord Jesus, you became a man like us in every way, but did not sin;
—may we open our lives to others, share their laughter and tears, and grow day by day in love. ℟
Let us serve you in the hungry and give you to eat;—let us see you in the thirsty and give you to drink. ℟
You raised up Lazarus from the dead;—call sinners from their living death to faith and repentance. ℟
May we live up to the example of Mary and the saints;—may we follow you more perfectly in everything. ℟

Let the dead rise in your glory,—let them rejoice for ever in your love. ℞ Lord, give life to your people.
Our Father

Sundays 2 and 4
Let us proclaim the greatness of God, and pray to him, for he cares for all men. ℞ Give salvation, Lord, to those you have redeemed.
God of all truth, grant every good gift to the college of bishops—and preserve in the faith of the apostles the people you have entrusted to them. ℞
May all who share in the one bread of life be filled with your love; —may they be united more closely in the body of your Son. ℞
Help us to put aside our selfish ways;—let us put on Christ, the new man. ℞
May sinners share in the blessings of Christ's atonement;—may they find repentance and forgiveness. ℞
Let the dead praise your goodness in the peace of heaven;—there we hope to glorify your name for ever. ℞
Our Father

Concluding Prayer
Sunday 1: Through our annual Lenten observance, Lord,
deepen our understanding of the mystery of Christ
and make it a reality in the conduct of our lives.
(We make our prayer) through our Lord.

Sunday 2: God our Father,
you bid us listen to your Son, the well-beloved.
Nourish our hearts on your word,
purify the eyes of our mind,
and fill us with joy at the vision of your glory.
(We make our prayer) through our Lord.

Sunday 3: God our Father
in your infinite love and goodness
you have shown us that
prayer, fasting, and almsgiving
are remedies for sin:

accept the humble admission of our guilt,
and when our conscience weighs us down
let your unfailing mercy raise us up.
(We make our prayer) through our Lord.

Sunday 4: Lord God, in your surpassing wisdom
you reconcile man to yourself through your Word.
Grant that your Christian people may come with eager faith and
    ready will
to celebrate the Easter festival.
(We make our prayer) through our Lord.

Invitatory
Antiphon of Lent.

MORNING PRAYER

Hymn, from the appendix, for Lent.
Psalms and canticle with proper antiphons as in the psalter.

Scripture Reading   *Cf Neh 8:8,10*
This day is holy to the Lord your God; do not mourn or weep. For
this day is holy to our Lord; and do not be grieved, for the joy of the
Lord is your strength.

Short Responsory
R⁷ Christ, Son of the living God, have mercy on us. *Repeat* R⁷
V⁷ You were wounded because of our sins. R⁷ Glory be. R⁷

Benedictus Antiphon
Sunday 1: Jesus was led by the Spirit into the desert, to be tempted
by the devil. He fasted for forty days and forty nights, after which he
was hungry.

Sunday 2: Jesus Christ our Lord brought an end to death; he has
proclaimed life and immortality through his gospel.

Sunday 3: Destroy this temple and in three days I will raise it up
again, says the Lord. But the temple he was speaking of was his own
body.

Sunday 4: Ever since the world began it is unheard of for anyone to open the eyes of a man who was born blind. Only Christ, the Son of God, has done this.

Intercessions
Sundays 1 and 3
Let us bless our Redeemer, who has brought us to this day of salvation. ℞ Lord, create a new spirit within us.
Christ, our life, we were buried with you in baptism to rise from the dead;—lead us this day along the new path of life. ℞
You went everywhere, Lord, doing good for everyone;—help us to care for the common good of all. ℞
Help us to work with other people to build the earthly city;—but never let us lose sight of your heavenly kingdom. ℞
Healer of souls and bodies, mend our broken lives;—let us receive all the blessings of your holiness. ℞
Our Father

Sundays 2 and 4
Let us glorify God for his wealth of goodness and pray to him through Jesus Christ, who is always living to intercede for us.
℞ Inflame our hearts with your love.
God of mercy, help us to enrich this day with deeds of kindness;—let men know by our actions that we are all one family. ℞
At the time of the flood you saved Noah through the ark;—grant salvation through water to those preparing for baptism. ℞
May we never live by bread alone;—give us life by every word you speak. ℞
Help us to avoid all anger and dissension;—let us find joy in your peace and love. ℞
Our Father

Concluding Prayer
Sunday 1: Through our annual Lenten observance, Lord,
deepen our understanding of the mystery of Christ
and make it a reality in the conduct of our lives.
(We make our prayer) through our Lord.

Sunday 2: God our Father,
you bid us listen to your Son, the well-beloved.
Nourish our hearts on your word,
purify the eyes of our mind,
and fill us with joy at the vision of your glory.
(We make our prayer) through our Lord.

Sunday 3: God our Father,
in your infinite love and goodness
you have shown us that
prayer, fasting, and almsgiving
are remedies for sin:
accept the humble admission of our guilt,
and when our conscience weighs us down
let your unfailing mercy raise us up.
(We make our prayer) through our Lord.

Sunday 4: Lord God, in your surpassing wisdom
you reconcile man to yourself through your Word.
Grant that your Christian people may come with eager faith and
    ready will
to celebrate the Easter festival.
(We make our prayer) through our Lord.

EVENING PRAYER II

Hymn, from the appendix, for Lent.
Psalms and canticle with proper antiphons as in the psalter.

Scripture Reading   *1 Cor 9:24-25*
All the runners at the stadium are trying to win, but only one of
them gets the prize. You must run in the same way, meaning to win.
All the fighters at the games go into strict training; they do this just
to win a wreath that will wither away, but we do it for a wreath that
will never wither.

Short Responsory
R̸ Hear us, Lord, and have mercy, for we have sinned against you.
Repeat R̸

137

℣ Listen, Christ, to the prayers of those who cry to you. ℟ Glory be.
℟

Magnificat Antiphon

Sunday 1: Keep watch over us, eternal Saviour. Do not let the cunning tempter overcome us, for you have become our helper at all times.

Sunday 2: Tell no man about the vision which you have seen, until the Son of Man has risen from the dead.

Sunday 3: Whoever drinks the water that I shall give, says the Lord, will never be thirsty again.

Sunday 4: My son, you are with me always and all I have is yours. But it was right that we should celebrate and rejoice, because your brother was dead and has come to life; he was lost and is found.

Intercessions

Sundays 1 and 3

God the Father has chosen for himself a people, who are born again, not from any mortal seed but from his everlasting Word. Let us praise his name and turn to him in prayer. ℟ Lord, have mercy on your people.

Merciful God, hear our prayers for all your people;—may they hunger more for your word than for any human food. ℟

Teach us to love sincerely the people of our nation and of every race on earth;—may we work for their peace and welfare. ℟

Strengthen those who will be reborn in baptism;—make them living stones in the temple of your Spirit. ℟

May the dying go forward in hope to meet Christ, their judge;—may they see your face and be happy for ever. ℟

Our Father

Sundays 2 and 4

We give thanks to Christ, our head and our master. Let us pray to him with trust and humility, for he served all men and was good to everyone. ℟ Lord Jesus, visit your family.

Lord, help the bishops and priests of your Church, who share in your office of head and pastor;—unite them with yourself to lead all men to the Father. R̸

Send your angels to protect those who travel;—keep them from harm and bring them safely home. R̸

Teach us to care for everyone;—make us more like you in serving others. R̸

Help us to form a human community where all men live in friendship;—Lord, unite us in your love. R̸

Show your love for the dead:—let them see the light of your face. R̸

Our Father

The concluding prayer as at Morning Prayer, pp 136–7.

WEEKS 1 TO 4: MONDAYS

Invitatory antiphon of Lent.

MORNING PRAYER

Hymn, from the appendix, for Lent.
Psalms and canticle with the antiphons as in the psalter.

Scripture Reading   *Ex 19:4-6a*
You have seen how I bore you on eagles' wings and brought you to myself. Now therefore, if you will obey my voice and keep my covenant, you shall be my own possession among all peoples; for all the earth is mine, and you shall be to me a kingdom of priests and a holy nation.

Short Responsory
R̸ It is he who will free me from the snare of the hunters. *Repeat* R̸
V̸ And from the evil word. R̸ Glory be. R̸

Benedictus Antiphon
Week 1: Come, you blessed of my Father, inherit the kingdom prepared for you from the foundation of the world.

Week 2: Be compassionate as your Father is compassionate, says the Lord.

Week 3: Truly I tell you, there is no respect for a prophet in his own country.

Week 4: There was a certain official whose son was ill at Capharnaum. When he heard that Jesus had arrived in Galilee, he asked him to come and heal his son.

Intercessions

Mondays 1 and 3

Blessed be Jesus, our Saviour. Through his death he has opened up for us the way of salvation. Let us pray: ℟ Direct your people, Lord, in the path of true life.

Merciful God, in baptism you gave us a life that is new;—may we ever grow in your likeness. ℟

Let us bring joy this day to those who are in need;—and draw us nearer to you through the help we give them. ℟

Help us to do what is right and good;—let us seek you always with all our heart. ℟

Forgive us for the times we have hurt other people, and failed to preserve the unity of your family;—Lord, have mercy on us. ℟

Our Father

Mondays 2 and 4

Blessed be God the Father. On this day of Lent he has given us the grace of offering the sacrifice of praise. Let us pray to him with confidence: ℟ Lord, transform our lives by your divine teaching.

Almighty Father, grant us a spirit of prayer and penance;—grant that we may love you and one another. ℟

Let us work with you to restore all things in Christ,—to renew the world through your justice and peace. ℟

In the name of every creature under heaven we praise you;—teach us to respect all that you have made. ℟

Forgive us for the times we have failed Christ in the poor;—have mercy on us in our weakness. ℟

Our Father

Concluding Prayer

Week 1: Turn our hearts back to you, God our Saviour;

form us by your heavenly teaching,
so that we may truly profit by our Lenten observance.
(We make our prayer) through our Lord.

Week 2: You teach us, Lord,
to discipline the body for the good of the soul:
give us grace to refrain from all sin,
and to set our hearts on fulfilling your precepts.
(We make our prayer) through our Lord.

Week 3: By your unfailing mercy, Lord,
purify and guard your Church,
and since without you she cannot stand fast,
support and guide her always by your grace.
(We make our prayer) through our Lord.

Week 4: Lord God, you give the world new life
by mysteries which are beyond our grasp.
May your Church not be deprived of earthly help
while she makes progress by the strength of these eternal gifts.
(We make our prayer) through our Lord.

EVENING PRAYER

Hymn from the appendix, for Lent.
Psalms and canticle with the antiphons as in the psalter.

Scripture Reading   *Rom 12:1-2*
My brothers, I implore you by God's mercy to offer your very selves
to him: a living sacrifice, dedicated and fit for his acceptance, the
worship offered by mind and heart. Adapt yourselves no longer to
the pattern of this present world, but let your minds be remade and
your whole nature thus transformed. Then you will be able to discern
the will of God, and to know what is good, acceptable, and perfect.

Short Responsory
R̸ I said: 'Lord, have mercy on me.' *Repeat* R̸
V̸ 'Heal my soul for I have sinned against you.' R̸ Glory be. R̸

Magnificat Antiphon

Week 1: Anything you did for the least of these who are mine, you did for me, says the Lord.

Week 2: Do not judge, and you will not be judged, because the judgments you give are the judgments you will receive, says the Lord.

Week 3: Jesus walked straight through them all, and went away.

Week 4: The father knew that was the hour when Jesus had said to him, 'Your son will live'; and he and all his household believed.

Intercessions

Mondays 1 and 3

Let us call on the name of the Lord Jesus, who saves his people from their sins. R℣ Jesus, Son of David, have mercy on us.

Christ our Lord, you gave yourself up for the Church to make her holy;—renew her once more through the spirit of repentance. R℣

Good master, let young people discover that way of life which you have planned for each one of them;—may they be faithful to your grace and fulfil your will for them. R℣

Give hope to the sick and make them well again;—help us to comfort and take care of them. R℣

In baptism you made us sons of the Father;—may we live for you now and always. R℣

Grant to the faithful departed peace and glory;—let us reign with them one day in your heavenly kingdom. R℣

Our Father

Mondays 2 and 4

Let us praise God the Father, who hears the prayers of his children and grants what they ask. R℣ Lord, have mercy on your people.

Lord, on Sinai you gave the law to Moses and completed it through Christ;—write your law in the hearts of men that they may be faithful to your covenant. R℣

Help us to create a community where people care for one another;—let us work together for the good of all. R℣

Strengthen missionaries when their courage fails;—send them helpers to gather in your harvest. R℣

May children grow strong in grace;—may the young advance in

your love. ℟
Remember our brothers who rest in your peace;—make them sharers of eternal life. ℟
Our Father

The concluding prayer as at Morning Prayer, pp 140–1.

WEEKS 1 TO 4: TUESDAYS

Invitatory antiphon of Lent.

MORNING PRAYER

Hymn, from the appendix, for Lent.

Scripture Reading   *Joel 2:12-13*
Come back to me with all your hearts, fasting, weeping, mourning. Let your hearts, be broken not your garments torn; turn to the Lord your God again, for he is all tenderness and compassion, slow to anger, rich in graciousness, and ready to relent.

Short Responsory
℟ It is he who will free me from the snare of the hunters. *Repeat* ℟
℣ And from the evil word. ℟ Glory be. ℟

Benedictus Antiphon
Week 1: Lord, teach us to pray, as John taught his disciples.

Week 2: You have only one Teacher, who is in heaven, Christ the Lord.

Week 3: Peter, I do not tell you to forgive seven times, but seventy times seven, said the Lord.

Week 4: The man who healed me told me, 'Take up your bed and go in peace.'

Intercessions
Tuesdays 1 and 3
Let us bless Christ, who is our bread from heaven. ℟ Christ, bread of life, strengthen us.

Lord, give us a share in the bread of the eucharist,—fill us with the blessings of your paschal sacrifice. ℟ Christ, bread of life, strengthen us.

May we take your word to our hearts in faith and obedience;—yield a harvest in us through our perseverance. ℟

Make us eager to fulfil your plan for the world—that the Church may spread the great message of peace. ℟

We have sinned, Lord, we have sinned;—take away our guilt by your saving grace. ℟

Our Father

Tuesdays 2 and 4
Let us pray to God the Father, who gave his own Son, the Word made flesh, to be our bread of life. ℟ May the message of Christ, in all its richness, live in our hearts.

Father, may we hear your voice this Lent and pass with Christ from death to life;—may we celebrate his Easter feast with great joy and love. ℟

Teach us to live by your Spirit,—and help us to bring faith to those who doubt. ℟

May the knowledge of Christ penetrate our minds and our hearts;—may it find expression in all our ways of living. ℟

Purify your Church in these days of salvation;—make her the living witness of your presence in the world. ℟

Our Father

Concluding Prayer
Week 1: Look with favour on your family, Lord,
and as at this time we restrain the desires of the body
may our hearts burn with love of you.
(We make our prayer) through our Lord.

Week 2: Watch over your Church, Lord, with unfailing compassion,
and since, left to ourselves, we are prone to evil,
by your grace turn us away from all that is harmful
and direct us into the way of salvation.
(We make our prayer) through our Lord.

Week 3: Do not withdraw your grace from us, Lord:
by it alone we can give ourselves wholly to your service
and obtain your help in our every need.
(We make our prayer) through our Lord.

Week 4: By our Lenten prayer and observance, Lord,
prepare our hearts to welcome the mystery of Easter
and to proclaim the good news of salvation.
(We make our prayer) through our Lord.

EVENING PRAYER

Hymn, from the appendix, for Lent.

Scripture Reading *Jas 2:14,17,18b*

What does it profit, my brethren, if a man says he has faith but has
not works? Can his faith save him? So faith by itself, if it has no
works, is dead. Show me your faith apart from your works, and I
by my works will show you my faith.

Short Responsory

R̸ I said: 'Lord, have mercy on me.' *Repeat* R̸

V̸ 'Heal my soul for I have sinned against you.' R̸ Glory be. R̸

Magnificat Antiphon

Week 1: When you pray, go into your room and shut the door and
pray to your Father there.

Week 2: You are all brothers. Do not call any man on earth your
father, since you have only one Father, and he is in heaven. Nor
must you be called teachers, for you have only one Teacher, the
Christ.

Week 3: My heavenly Father will deal the same way with you if you
do not forgive your brother from your heart.

Week 4: Now you are well again: leave your sinful ways, or something worse may happen to you.

Intercessions

Tuesdays 1 and 3

Let us pray earnestly to Christ the Lord. He tells us to watch and pray that we may not fall into temptation. ℟ Hear us, Lord, and have mercy.

Lord Jesus, you promised to be with those who are gathered in your name;—keep us united with you as we pray to the Father in the Holy Spirit. ℟

Cleanse your Church from every stain of sin;—make her alive with hope and the power of the Spirit. ℟

Help us to care for our neighbour and show your love for men;—through us let the light of your salvation shine in the world. ℟

Let your peace spread to the ends of the earth;—let men see in every place the signs of your presence. ℟

Bring the dead to everlasting happiness;—let glory and immortal life be theirs. ℟

Our Father

Tuesdays 2 and 4

When the Lord Jesus was lifted up on the cross, he drew all things to himself. Let us glorify him in our prayer. ℟ Lord, draw all men to yourself.

Lord, may your cross light up the darkness of the world;—may it lead every man to you, the way, the truth and the life. ℟

Give the true and living water to all who thirst for you;—let it well up to eternal life. ℟

Shed the light of your knowledge on scientists and artists;—let their work make men more open to the coming of your kingdom. ℟

Look on those who no longer walk with you because of scandal or sin;—may they return to you and remain in your love. ℟

Grant our dead a place in heaven;—let them share the happiness of Mary and the saints. ℟

Our Father

The concluding prayer as at Morning Prayer, pp 144-5.

WEEKS 1 TO 4: WEDNESDAYS

Invitatory antiphon of Lent.

MORNING PRAYER

Hymn, from the appendix, for Lent.

Scripture Reading   *Deut 7:6,8-9*

The Lord your God has chosen you to be a people for his own possession, out of all the peoples that are on the face of the earth. It is because the Lord loves you, and is keeping the oath which he swore to your fathers, that the Lord has brought you out with a mighty hand, and redeemed you from the house of bondage, from the hand of Pharaoh king of Egypt. Know therefore that the Lord your God is God, the faithful God who keeps covenant and steadfast love with those who love him and keep his commandments, to a thousand generations.

Short Responsory

R⁊ It is he who will free me from the snare of the hunters. *Repeat* R⁊
V⁊ And from the evil word. R⁊ Glory be. R⁊

Benedictus Antiphon

Week 1: A wicked, godless generation asks for a sign; and the only sign that will be given it is the sign of the prophet Jonah.

Week 2: The Son of Man did not come to be served, but to serve, and to give his life as a ransom for many.

Week 3: Do not think that I have come to abolish the Law or the Prophets. I have come not to abolish but to complete them.

Week 4: Whoever listens to my word, and believes in the one who sent me, has eternal life, says the Lord.

Intercessions

Wednesdays 1 and 3

Blessed be Christ our Saviour. In him we become a new creation, the old order passes and all things are renewed. Let us pray in living hope. R⁊ Renew us, Lord, in your Spirit.

You promised us, Lord, a new heaven and a new earth;—renew us in your Spirit, that we may come to the new Jerusalem and rejoice in you for ever. ℟ Renew us, Lord, in your Spirit.

Let us work with you to fill the world with your Spirit;—let us perfect our earthly city in justice, charity and peace. ℟

Grant that we may put aside our apathy;—help us to recognize with joy the power you have given us. ℟

Set us free from all evil;—show us in the confusion of our lives the things that really matter. ℟

Our Father

Wednesdays 2 and 4
Let us give thanks to God the Father, who cleanses our hearts and strengthens us in love through the Holy Spirit. ℟ Give us, Lord, your Holy Spirit.

May we always be grateful for all the goodness you have shown us,—and may we bear our trials with patience. ℟

In the life of Jesus you have shown us the way of love;—teach us to follow this way in the great and small events of life. ℟

Grant us a spirit of self-denial,—and move us to help our brothers in their need. ℟

Let us bear witness in our bodies to the death of your Son,—for in his body you have brought us to life. ℟

Our Father

Concluding Prayer
Week 1: Look with favour on our Lenten observance, Lord,
and while we subdue our bodies by self-denial,
renew our spirit with the grace that prompts us to good works.
(We make our prayer) through our Lord.

Week 2: Protect your family, Lord,
trained as it is by the constant exercise of good works.
Strengthen us with your consoling presence,
and lead us to the joys of heaven.
(We make our prayer) through our Lord.

Week 3: Schooled by our Lenten observance, Lord,
and nourished on your word,

may we give you whole-hearted service through our self-denial,
and through our prayer become one in heart and mind.
(We make our prayer) through our Lord.

Week 4: Lord God, you crown the merits of the saints
and pardon sinners when they repent.
Forgive us our sins, now that we come before you,
humbly confessing our guilt.
(We make our prayer) through our Lord.

EVENING PRAYER

Hymn, from the appendix, for Lent.

Scripture Reading *Phil 2:12b-15a*

Keep on working, with fear and trembling, to complete your salvation, for God is always at work in you to make you willing and able to obey his own purpose. Do everything without complaining or arguing, that you may be innocent and pure, as God's perfect children.

Short Responsory

℟ I said: 'Lord, have mercy on me.' *Repeat* ℟
℣ 'Heal my soul for I have sinned against you.' ℟ Glory be. ℟

Magnificat Antiphon

Week 1: As Jonah spent three days and three nights inside the whale, so will the Son of Man be inside the heart of the earth.

Week 2: The Son of Man will be handed over to the Gentiles to be mocked and scourged and crucified; and on the third day he will rise again.

Week 3: The man who keeps the commandments of God and teaches them to others will be considered great in the kingdom of heaven.

Week 4: I can do nothing by myself; I can judge only as I am told to judge, and my judgment is just, says the Lord.

Intercessions

Wednesdays 1 and 3

God our Father knows all the needs of his people, but he wants us to give first place to his kingdom. Let us proclaim his greatness in our prayer. ℟ May your kingdom come in all its justice.

Holy Father, you gave us Christ as the shepherd of our souls;—may your people always have priests who care for them with his great love. ℟

Grant that Christians will prove brothers to the sick;—show them the features of your Son in the faces of those who suffer. ℟

Help those who do not believe in the gospel to come into your Church;—build it up in love to manifest your goodness everywhere. ℟

Father, we know that we are sinners;—grant us your forgiveness and reconcile us with your Church. ℟

May the dead enter eternal life,—may they abide with you for ever. ℟

Our Father

Wednesdays 2 and 4

To God be honour and glory. He has sealed the new covenant in the blood of Christ and renews it in the sacrament of the altar. In confidence we pray: ℟ Lord, bless your people.

Lord, guide nations and their rulers according to your will;—may they work for the common good with one mind and heart. ℟

Renew the spirit of service in those who have left all to follow Christ; —may the holiness of your Church be revealed in their lives. ℟

You have made all men in your likeness;—help them to rid the world of every injustice. ℟

Come with your truth and friendship to those who have lost their way;—teach us how to help them. ℟

Let the dead enter into your glory;—let them praise you for ever. ℟

Our Father

The concluding prayer as at Morning Prayer, pp 148-9.

WEEKS 1 TO 4: THURSDAYS

Invitatory antiphon of Lent.

MORNING PRAYER

Hymn, from the appendix, for Lent.

Scripture Reading   *Cf 1 Kings 8:51-53a*
We are your people, Lord, and your heritage. Let your eyes be open
to the supplication of your servant and to the supplication of your
people Israel, giving ear to us whenever we call to you. For you
separated us from among all the people of the earth to be your
heritage.

Short Responsory
R̷ It is he who will free me from the snare of the hunters. *Repeat* R̷
V̷ And from the evil word. R̷ Glory be. R̷

Benedictus Antiphon
Week 1: If you, evil though you are, know how to give good gifts
to your children, how much more will your Father who is in heaven
give good things to those who ask him.

Week 2: My son, remember that during your life you received good
things, just as Lazarus received bad things.

Week 3: If it is through the finger of God that I cast out devils,
then know that the kingdom of God has already come upon you,
said the Lord.

Week 4: I do not depend on human testimony, says the Lord, but I
have said this that you may be saved.

Intercessions
Thursdays 1 and 3
We give praise to Christ our Lord, the radiant light of the world.
He guides our steps in a path of light and we no longer live in dark-
ness. Let us turn to him in confident prayer. R̷ May your word light
up our way.
Christ, our Saviour, may we grow today in your likeness,—may we
gain through the second Adam what was lost by the first. R̷
May your word take flesh in our lives and your truth shine forth in
our actions;—may your love burn brightly within us. R̷
Teach us to work for the good of all, whether the time is right or not;
—make your Church a welcome light for the whole human family. R̷
May we always treasure your friendship and come to know its
depth;—may we atone for the sins against your wisdom and love. R̷
Our Father

Thursdays 2 and 4
Let us praise God for his loving kindness, which is revealed to us in Jesus Christ. ℟ Remember, Lord, that we are your children.
Lead us more deeply into the life of your Church;—and through us make it a clearer sign of the world's salvation. ℟
Lover of men, help us to play our part in the growth of the human city—and help us to build up your kingdom in every way. ℟
May we come to Christ when we are burdened,—for he is the spring of living water who refreshes all who thirst. ℟
Forgive the harm that we have done;—guide us in the path of justice and truth. ℟
Our Father

Concluding Prayer
Week 1: In your bounty, Lord,
give us the Spirit
who alone can teach us to think and do what is right,
so that we, who without you cannot exist,
may live in loving obedience to your will.
(We make our prayer) through our Lord.

Week 2: Lord God,
you love innocence of heart,
and when it is lost you alone can restore it.
Turn then our hearts to you,
and kindle in them the fire of your Spirit,
so that we may be steadfast in faith
and unwearied in good works.
(We make our prayer) through our Lord.

Week 3: We approach your throne of grace, Lord,
humbly asking that as the Easter festival draws nearer,
we may prepare with ever greater devotion
to celebrate the paschal mystery.
(We make our prayer) through our Lord.

Week 4: Compassionate Lord, you have chastened us by penance and schooled us in good works;

grant us now a single-hearted perseverance in keeping your
  commandments,
and bring us untouched by sin to the joys of Easter.
(We make our prayer) through our Lord.

EVENING PRAYER

Hymn, from the appendix, for Lent.

Scripture Reading   *Jas 4:7-8,10*
Be God's true subjects; stand firm against the devil, and he will run
away from you; come close to God, and he will come close to you.
You that are sinners must wash your hands clean, you that are in
two minds must purify the intention of your hearts. Humble yourselves before the Lord, and he will exalt you.

Short Responsory
R̷ I said: 'Lord, have mercy on me.' *Repeat* R̷
Ɏ 'Heal my soul for I have sinned against you.' R̷ Glory be. R̷

Magnificat Antiphon
Week 1: Ask, and it will be given to you; seek, and you will find;
knock, and the door will be open to you.

Week 2: The rich man, who would not give a crust of bread to
Lazarus, begged for a drop of water.

Week 3: A woman in the crowd called out, 'Blessed is the womb that
bore, and the breasts that suckled you,' Jesus said to her, 'Blessed,
rather, those who hear the word of God and keep it.'

Week 4: The very works that I do bear witness to me, since the
Father has sent me, says the Lord.

Intercessions
Thursdays 1 and 3
Let us pray to Christ the Lord, who gave us the new commandment
to love one another. R̷ Lord, may your people grow in love.
Good master, teach us to love you in our fellow men,—teach us to
serve you in our brothers. R̷
You interceded with the Father for those who nailed you to the

cross;—help us to love our enemies and pray for those who injure us. ℟ Lord, may your people grow in love.

Through the mystery of your body and blood deepen our courage and faith,—strengthen the weak, comfort the sorrowful and fill the dying with new hope. ℟

Light of the world, you gave sight to the man born blind;—enlighten men in baptism through the washing in water and the word of life. ℟

Grant to the dead your everlasting love;—count us among the chosen of God. ℟

Our Father

Thursdays 2 and 4

God enlightens us with the grace of the Holy Spirit that our lives may be filled with justice and faith. Let us proclaim his mercy in our evening prayer. ℟ Lord, give life to the people redeemed by Christ.

Lord, unite bishops, priests and deacons more closely with Christ through the mystery of the eucharist;—renew in them each day the grace of ordination. ℟

Nourish the faithful with the food of Christ's word;—feed them with the bread which is his body. ℟

Grant that we may respect the dignity of every man, redeemed by the precious blood of your Son;—let us never violate his rights or his conscience. ℟

Save men from the blind pursuit of wealth;—make them sensitive to the needs of others. ℟

Be merciful to those who have left our world today;—give them everlasting happiness. ℟

Our Father

The concluding prayer as at Morning Prayer, pp 152–3.

WEEKS 1 TO 4: FRIDAYS

Invitatory antiphon of Lent.

MORNING PRAYER

Hymn, from the appendix, for Lent.

Scripture Reading *Is 53:11b-12*
By his sufferings shall my servant justify many, taking their faults on himself. Hence, I will grant whole hordes for his tribute, he shall divide the spoil with the mighty, for surrendering himself to death, and letting himself be taken for a sinner, while he was bearing the faults of many and praying all the time for sinners.

Short Responsory
℟ It is he who will free me from the snare of the hunters. *Repeat* ℟
℣ And from the evil word. ℟ Glory be. ℟

Benedictus Antiphon
Week 1: If your virtue does not surpass that of the scribes and Pharisees, you will never enter the kingdom of heaven.

Week 2: He will bring those bad men to a bad end, and hand the vineyard over to other tenants, who will give him the fruits in due season.

Week 3: 'Master, which is the greatest commandment of the Law?' Jesus said, 'You must love the Lord your God with all your heart.'

Week 4: You know me and you know where I came from. Yet I have not come of myself: my Father has sent me, says the Lord.

Intercessions
Fridays 1 and 3
We give thanks to Christ the Lord, who died on the cross that we might live. Let us pray to him with all our heart. ℟ Lord Jesus, may your death bring us to life.
Master and Saviour, you have taught us by your life and renewed us by your passion;—do not allow us to grow used to sin. ℟
You call on us to feed the hungry;—let us deny ourselves some food this day to help our brothers in their need. ℟
May we accept from your hands this day of Lent:—may we make it yours by deeds of love. ℟
End the rebellion within our hearts;—make us generous and willing to share. ℟
Our Father

Fridays 2 and 4
Let us pray earnestly to Christ our Saviour, who redeemed us by his death and resurrection. R̷ Lord, have mercy on us.
You went up to Jerusalem to endure the passion and enter into glory;—lead your Church into the paschal feast of eternal life. R̷
Your heart was pierced with a lance;—heal the wounds of our human weakness. R̷
You made your cross the tree of life;—share your victory with all the baptized. R̷
You gave salvation to the repentant thief;—pardon all our sins. R̷
Our Father

Concluding Prayer
Week 1: Bend our wills, Lord, so that by this Lenten observance we may fit ourselves to celebrate the Easter festival;
and as we have all undertaken to subdue the body,
may we all be renewed in spirit.
(We make our prayer) through our Lord.

Week 2: Purify us, almighty God,
through our whole-hearted endeavour to renew our lives,
so that we may approach the coming festival with single-minded devotion.
(We make our prayer) through our Lord.

Week 3: Lord, open our hearts to your grace.
Restrain us from all human waywardness
and keep us faithful to your commandments.
(We make our prayer) through our Lord.

Week 4: Lord God, you have prepared fitting remedies for our weakness;
grant that we may reach out gladly for your healing grace,
and thereby live in accordance with your will.
(We make our prayer) through our Lord.

EVENING PRAYER

Hymn, from the appendix, for Lent.

Scripture Reading *Jas 5:16,19-20*
Confess your sins to one another, and pray for one another, and
then you will be healed. My brothers, if one of your number should
stray from the truth and another succeed in bringing him back, be
sure of this: any man who brings a sinner back from his crooked
ways will be rescuing his soul from death and cancelling innumerable
sins.

Short Responsory
℟ I said: 'Lord, have mercy on me.' *Repeat* ℟
℣ 'Heal my soul for I have sinned against you.' ℟ Glory be. ℟

Magnificat Antiphon
Week 1: If you are offering your gift at the altar and there remember
that your brother has something against you, leave your offering
there before the altar, go and be reconciled with your brother first,
and then come and present your offering.

Week 2: They wanted to arrest Jesus, but they were afraid of the
people, who looked on him as a prophet.

Week 3: To love your neighbour as yourself is far more important
than any sacrifices.

Week 4: No one laid hands on Jesus, because his hour had not yet
come.

Intercessions
Fridays 1 and 3
Let us pray to the Lord Jesus, who sanctified his people by his own
blood. ℟ Lord, have mercy on your people.
Christ our Redeemer, through your suffering help us to mortify our
bodies and stand firm in every trial;—may we be ready to celebrate
your rising from the dead. ℟
As prophets of God's kingdom may Christians make you known
throughout the world,—and may they confirm their message by lives

of faith, hope and love. ℟ Lord, have mercy on your people.
Lord, give strength to the afflicted;—and give us the will to do everything to help and comfort them. ℟
Teach the faithful to be united with your passion in times of trouble and distress;—let the power of your salvation shine forth in their lives. ℟
Lord, giver of life, remember those who have died;—grant them the glory of your resurrection. ℟
Our Father

Fridays 2 and 4
Let us turn in prayer to the Saviour of all men. By dying he destroyed our death and by rising he restored our life. ℟ Sanctify the people you redeemed by your blood.
Christ, our Redeemer, let us share in your passion by works of penance;—let us attain the glory of your resurrection. ℟
Grant us the protection of your Mother, the comforter of the afflicted;—help us to extend to others the consolation you have given us. ℟
Unite the faithful to your passion in times of trouble and distress—and let the power of your salvation shine forth in their lives. ℟
You humbled yourself even to accepting death, death on a cross;—grant to your servants obedience and patience. ℟
Share with the dead your bodily glory;—let us rejoice one day with them in the fellowship of the saints. ℟
Our Father

The concluding prayer as at Morning Prayer, p 156.

WEEKS 1 TO 4: SATURDAYS

Invitatory antiphon of Lent.

MORNING PRAYER

Hymn, from the appendix, for Lent.

Scripture Reading *Is 1:16-18*

Wash, make yourselves clean, take your wrong-doing out of my sight. Cease to do evil. Learn to do good, search for justice, help the oppressed, be just to the orphan, plead for the widow. Come now, let us talk this over, says the Lord: though your sins are like scarlet, they shall be white as snow; though they are red as crimson, they shall be like wool.

Short Responsory

Ry It is he who will free me from the snare of the hunters. *Repeat* Ry
ỹ And from the evil word. Ry Glory be. Ry

Benedictus Antiphon

Week 1: Pray for those who persecute you and for those who treat you badly; in this way you will be sons of your Father in heaven, says the Lord.

Week 2: Father, I have sinned against heaven and against you; I no longer deserve to be called your son; treat me as one of your paid servants.

Week 3: The tax collector stood afar off and did not dare to raise his eyes to heaven. He beat his breast and said, 'God, be merciful to me, a sinner.'

Week 4: No one has ever spoken like this man.

Intercessions

Saturdays 1 and 3

Christ the Lord has made men into a new creation. He gives them a new birth in the waters of baptism and nourishes them with his word and his body. Let us glorify him in our prayer. Ry Renew us, Lord, by your grace.

Jesus, you are gentle and humble in spirit;—grant us something of your pity, something of your kindness and something of your patience towards all men. Ry

Teach us to be neighbours to the sad and the needy;—let us imitate you, the good Samaritan. Ry

May the Blessed Virgin, your Mother, intercede for religious women;

—through her prayers may they serve you in the Church ever more perfectly. R̷ Renew us, Lord, by your grace.

Grant us the gift of your mercy,—pardon our sins and save us from punishment. R̷

Our Father

Saturdays 2 and 4

Let us give thanks always to Christ, our Saviour, and pray to him with confidence. R̷ Lord, help us by your grace.

Lord, may we keep our bodies free from sin;—may the Holy Spirit dwell within us. R̷

Teach us to offer ourselves this morning for our fellow men,—and strengthen us to do your will throughout the day. R̷

Grant that we may hunger for the food of eternal life;—give us the bread of your word and of your body. R̷

May your Mother, the refuge of sinners, intercede for us;—through her prayers forgive us in your mercy. R̷

Our Father

Concluding Prayer

Week 1: Turn our hearts to yourself, eternal Father,
so that, always seeking the one thing necessary
and devoting ourselves to works of charity,
we may worship you in spirit and in truth.
(We make our prayer) through our Lord.

Week 2: Almighty God, whose healing grace even here on earth
brings us the gifts of heaven,
guide us in this present life
and lead us to that light in which you have your dwelling.
(We make our prayer) through our Lord.

Week 3: As we rejoice in this yearly season of grace,
and ponder the mysteries of Easter:
grant, Lord, that our joy may be completed
by seeing them fulfilled in our lives.
(We make our prayer) through our Lord.

Week 4: In your gentle mercy, Lord,
guide our wayward hearts,
for we know that left to ourselves
we cannot do your will.
(We make our prayer) through our Lord.

WEEK 5: SUNDAY

Psalter: Week 1

EVENING PRAYER I

Hymn, from the appendix, for Lent.
Psalms and canticle with proper antiphons as in the psalter.

Scripture Reading   *1 Pet 1:18-21*
Remember the ransom that was paid to free you from the useless
way of life your ancestors handed down was not paid in anything
corruptible, neither in silver nor gold, but in the precious blood of
a lamb without spot or stain, namely Christ; who, though known
since before the world was made, has been revealed only in our time,
the end of the ages, for your sake. Through him you now have faith
in God, who raised him from the dead and gave him glory for that
very reason—so that you would have faith and hope in God.

Short Responsory
R̸ Hear us, Lord, and have mercy, for we have sinned against you.
Repeat R̸
V̸ Listen, Christ, to the prayers of those who cry to you. R̸ Glory be.
R̸

Magnificat ant. Unless a grain of wheat falls on the ground and dies,
it remains a single grain alone; but if it dies, it yields a rich harvest.

Intercessions
Let us give glory to Christ the Lord. He is our master, our example
and our brother. R̸ Lord, give life to your people.
Lord Jesus, you became a man like us in every way, but did not sin;

—may we open our lives to others, share their laughter and tears, and grow day by day in love. R⁊ Lord, give life to your people.

Let us serve you in the hungry and give you to eat;—let us see you in the thirsty and give you to drink. R⁊

You raised up Lazarus from the dead;—call sinners from their living death to faith and repentance. R⁊

May we live up to the example of Mary and the saints;—may we follow you more perfectly in everything. R⁊

Let the dead rise in your glory,—let them rejoice for ever in your love. R⁊

Our Father

Concluding Prayer
Lord our God, your Son so loved the world
that he gave himself up to death for our sake.
Strengthen us by your grace,
and give us a heart willing to live by that same love.
(We make our prayer) through our Lord

Invitatory
Antiphon of Lent.

MORNING PRAYER

Hymn, from the appendix, for Lent.
Psalms and canticle with proper antiphons as in the psalter.

Scripture Reading   *Lev 23:4-7*
These are the appointed feasts of the Lord, the holy convocations, which you shall proclaim at the time appointed for them. In the first month, on the fourteenth day of the month in the evening is the Lord's passover. And on the fifteenth day of the same month is the feast of unleavened bread to the Lord; seven days you shall eat unleavened bread. On the first day you shall have a holy convocation, you shall do no laborious work.

Short Responsory
R⁊ Christ, Son of the living God, have mercy on us. *Repeat* R⁊
℣ You were wounded because of our sins. R⁊ Glory be. R⁊

Benedictus ant. Our friend Lazarus has fallen asleep, let us go and wake him from sleep.

Intercessions
Let us bless our Redeemer, who has brought us to this day of salvation. R℣ Lord, create a new spirit within us.
Christ, our life, we were buried with you in baptism to rise from the dead;—lead us this day along the new path of life. R℣
You went everywhere, Lord, doing good for everyone;—help us to care for the common good of all. R℣
Help us to work with other people to build the earthly city;—but never let us lose sight of your heavenly kingdom. R℣
Healer of souls and bodies, mend our broken lives;—let us receive all the blessings of your holiness. R℣
Our Father

Concluding Prayer
Lord our God, your Son so loved the world
that he gave himself up to death for our sake.
Strengthen us by your grace,
and give us a heart willing to live by that same love.
(We make our prayer) through our Lord.

EVENING PRAYER II

Hymn, from the appendix, for Lent.
Psalms and canticle with proper antiphons as in the psalter.

Scripture Reading   *Acts 13:26-30a*
My brothers, it is to us that this message of salvation has been sent! For the people who live in Jerusalem and their leaders did not know that he is the Saviour, nor did they understand the words of the prophets that are read every Sabbath day. Yet they made the prophets' words come true by condemning Jesus. And even though they could find no reason to pass the death sentence on him, they asked Pilate to have him put to death. And after they had done everything that the Scriptures say about him, they took him down from the cross and placed him in a grave. But God raised him from the dead.

Short Responsory

R℣ Hear us, Lord, and have mercy, for we have sinned against you. *Repeat* R℣

℣ Listen, Christ, to the prayers of those who cry to you. R℣ Glory be. R℣

Magnificat ant. When I am lifted up from the earth, I shall draw all men to myself.

Intercessions

God the Father has chosen for himself a people, who are born again, not from any mortal seed but from his everlasting Word. Let us praise his name and turn to him in prayer. R℣ Lord, have mercy on your people.

Merciful God, hear our prayers for all your people;—may they hunger more for your word than for any human food. R℣

Teach us to love sincerely the people of our nation and of every race on earth;—may we work for their peace and welfare. R℣

Strengthen those who will be reborn in baptism;—make them living stones in the temple of your Spirit. R℣

May the dying go forward in hope to meet Christ, their judge;—may they see your face and be happy for ever. R℣

Our Father

The concluding prayer as at Morning Prayer, p 163.

LENT: WEEK 5

¶ *On ferial days of this week the hymns given for Holy Week may be used at Morning and Evening Prayer.*

MONDAY

Invitatory antiphon of Lent.

MORNING PRAYER

Hymn, from the appendix, for Lent or Holy Week.

Scripture Reading   *Jer 11:19-20*

I for my part was like a trustful lamb being led to the slaughter-house, not knowing the schemes they were plotting against me, 'Let us destroy the tree in its strength, let us cut him off from the land of the living, so that his name may be quickly forgotten!'
But you, Lord Sabaoth, who pronounce a just sentence,
who probe the loins and heart,
let me see the vengeance you will take on them,
for I have committed my cause to you.

Short Responsory

R⁷ It is he who will free me from the snare of the hunters. *Repeat* R⁷
V⁷ And from the evil word. R⁷ Glory be. R⁷

Benedictus ant. Anyone who follows me will not be walking in the darkness; he will have the light of life, says the Lord.

Intercessions

Blessed be Jesus, our Saviour. Through his death he has opened up for us the way of salvation. Let us pray: R⁷ Direct your people, Lord, in the path of true life.
Merciful God, in baptism you gave us a life that is new;—may we ever grow in your likeness. R⁷
Let us bring joy this day to those who are in need;—and draw us nearer to you through the help we give them. R⁷
Help us to do what is right and good;—let us seek you always with all our heart. R⁷
Forgive us for the times we have hurt other people and failed to preserve the unity of your family;—Lord, have mercy on us. R⁷
Our Father

Concluding Prayer

Lord God, your abounding grace has enriched us with every blessing.
Transform us from our sinful condition to newness of life,
and prepare us for the glory of your kingdom.
(We make our prayer) through our Lord.

EVENING PRAYER

Hymn, from the appendix, for Lent or Holy Week.

Scripture Reading   *Rom 5:8-9*
As if God meant to prove how well he loves us, it was while we were still sinners that Christ, in his own appointed time, died for us. All the more surely, then, now that we have found justification through his blood, shall we be saved, through him, from God's displeasure.

Short Responsory
R̥ I said: 'Lord, have mercy on me.' *Repeat* R̥
V̥ 'Heal my soul for I have sinned against you.' R̥ Glory be. R̥

Magnificat ant. I bear witness to myself, says the Lord; and the Father, who sent me, bears witness to me.

Intercessions
Let us call on the name of the Lord Jesus, who saves his people from their sins. R̥ Jesus, Son of David, have mercy on us.
Christ our Lord, you gave yourself up for the Church to make her holy;—renew her once more through the spirit of repentance. R̥
Good master, let young people discover that way of life which you have planned for each one of them;—may they be faithful to your grace and fulfil your will for them. R̥
Give hope to the sick and make them well again;—help us to comfort and take care of them. R̥
In baptism you made us sons of the Father;—may we live for you now and always. R̥
Grant to the faithful departed peace and glory;—let us reign with them one day in your heavenly kingdom. R̥
Our Father

The concluding prayer as at Morning Prayer, p 165.

TUESDAY

Invitatory antiphon of Lent.

MORNING PRAYER

Hymn, from the appendix, for Lent or Holy Week.

Scripture Reading   *Zech 12:10-11a*
Over the House of David and the citizens of Jerusalem I will pour
out a spirit of kindness and prayer. They will look on the one whom
they have pierced; they will mourn for him as for an only son, and
weep for him as people weep for a first-born child. When that day
comes there will be great mourning in Jerusalem.

Short Responsory
R̷ It is he who will free me from the snare of the hunters. *Repeat* R̷
V̷ And from the evil word. R̷ Glory be. R̷

Benedictus ant. When you have lifted up the Son of Man, then you
will know that I am he, says the Lord.

Intercessions
Let us bless Christ, who is our bread from heaven. R̷ Christ, bread
of life, strengthen us.
Lord, give us a share in the bread of the eucharist;—fill us with the
blessings of your paschal sacrifice. R̷
May we take your word to our hearts in faith and obedience;—
yield a harvest in us through our perseverance. R̷
Make us eager to fulfil your plan for the world—that the Church
may spread the great message of peace. R̷
We have sinned, Lord, we have sinned;—take away our guilt by
your saving grace. R̷
Our Father

Concluding Prayer
May your people, Lord,

persevere in obedience to your will
so that through this obedience
your Church in our time
may grow in grace and increase in numbers.
(We make our prayer) through our Lord.

EVENING PRAYER

Hymn, from the appendix, for Lent or Holy Week.

Scripture Reading   *1 Cor 1:27b-30*
To shame what is strong, God has chosen what the world counts
weakness. He has chosen things low and contemptible, mere
nothings, to overthrow the existing order. And so there is no place
for human pride in the presence of God. You are in Christ Jesus by
God's act, for God has made him our wisdom; he is our righteousness; in him we are consecrated and set free.

Short Responsory
R̸ I said: 'Lord, have mercy on me.' *Repeat* R̸
Ʋ 'Heal my soul for I have sinned against you.' R̸ Glory be. R̸

Magnificat ant. He who sent me is with me, and he has not left me
to myself, for I always do what pleases him.

Intercessions
Let us pray earnestly to Christ the Lord. He tells us to watch and
pray that we may not fall into temptation. R̸ Hear us, Lord, and
have mercy.
Lord Jesus, you promised to be with those who are gathered in your
name;—keep us united with you as we pray to the Father in the
Holy Spirit. R̸
Cleanse your Church from every stain of sin;—make her alive with
hope and the power of the Spirit. R̸
Help us to care for our neighbour and show your love for men;—
through us let the light of your salvation shine in the world. R̸
Let your peace spread to the ends of the earth;—let men see in every
place the signs of your presence. R̸

Bring the dead to everlasting happiness;—let glory and immortal life be theirs. R̥
Our Father

The concluding prayer as at Morning Prayer, p 167.

WEDNESDAY

Invitatory antiphon of Lent.

MORNING PRAYER

Hymn, from the appendix, for Lent or Holy Week.

Scripture Reading   *Is 50:5-7*
The Lord God has opened my ear. For my part, I made no resistance, neither did I turn away. I offered my back to those who struck me, my cheeks to those who tore at my beard; I did not cover my face against insult and spittle. The Lord God comes to my help, so that I am untouched by the insults. So, too, I set my face like flint; I know I shall not be shamed.

Short Responsory
R̥ It is he who will free me from the snare of the hunters. *Repeat* R̥
V̥ And from the evil word. R̥ Glory be. R̥

Benedictus ant. If you remain faithful to my commands you will indeed be my disciples, you will learn the truth and the truth will make you free, says the Lord.

Intercessions
Blessed be Christ our Saviour. In him we become a new creation, the old order passes and all things are renewed. Let us pray in living hope. R̥ Renew us, Lord, in your Spirit.
You promised us, Lord, a new heaven and a new earth;—renew us in your Spirit that we may come to the new Jerusalem and rejoice in you for ever. R̥
Let us work with you to fill the world with your Spirit;—let us perfect

our earthly city in justice, charity and peace. ℟ Renew us, Lord, in your Spirit.

Grant that we may put aside our apathy;—help us to recognize with joy the power you have given us. ℟

Set us free from all evil;—show us in the confusion of our lives the things that really matter. ℟

Our Father

Concluding Prayer

God of mercy, shed your light on hearts that have been purified by penance,

and in your goodness give us a favourable hearing

when you move us to pray.

(We make our prayer) through our Lord.

EVENING PRAYER

Hymn, from the appendix, for Lent or Holy Week.

Scripture Reading   *Eph 4:32-5:2*

Be kind and tender to one another, each of you generous to all, as God in Christ has been generous to you. As God's favoured children, you must be like him. Order your lives in charity, upon the model of that charity which Christ showed to us when he gave himself up on our behalf, a sacrifice breathing out fragrance as he offered it to God.

Short Responsory

℟ I said: 'Lord, have mercy on me.' *Repeat* ℟

℣ 'Heal my soul for I have sinned against you.' ℟ Glory be. ℟

Magnificat ant. Why do you want to kill me when I tell you the truth?

Intercessions

God our Father knows all the needs of his people, but he wants us to give first place to his kingdom. Let us proclaim his greatness in our prayer. ℟ May your kingdom come in all its justice.

Holy Father, you gave us Christ as the shepherd of our souls;—may your people always have priests who care for them with his great

love. R̷
Grant that Christians will prove brothers to the sick;—show them
the features of your Son in the faces of those who suffer. R̷
Help those who do not believe in the gospel to come into your
Church;—build it up in love to manifest your goodness everywhere.
R̷
Father, we know that we are sinners;—grant us your forgiveness
and reconcile us with your Church. R̷
May the dead enter eternal life;—may they abide with you for ever.
R̷
Our Father

The concluding prayer as at Morning Prayer, p 170.

THURSDAY

Invitatory antiphon of Lent.

MORNING PRAYER

Hymn, from the appendix, for Lent or Holy Week.

Scripture Reading   *Heb 2:9b-10*
We see in Jesus one who is now crowned with glory and splendour
because he submitted to death; by God's grace he had to experience
death for all mankind. As it was his purpose to bring a great many
of his sons into glory, it was appropriate that God, for whom everything exists and through whom everything exists, should make
perfect through suffering, the leader who would take them to their
salvation.

Short Responsory
R̷ It is he who will free me from the snare of the hunters. *Repeat* R̷
V̷ And from the evil word. R̷ Glory be. R̷

Benedictus ant. Jesus said to the Jews and to the chief priests, 'He
who is of God hears the words of God; if you do not hear them, it is
because you are not of God.'

Intercessions

We give praise to Christ our Lord, the radiant light of the world. He guides our steps in a path of light and we no longer live in darkness. Let us turn to him in confident prayer: ℟ May your word light up our way.

Christ, our Saviour, may we grow today in your likeness,—may we gain through the second Adam what was lost by the first. ℟

May your word take flesh in our lives and your truth shine forth in our actions;—may your love burn brightly within us. ℟

Teach us to work for the good of all, whether the time is right or not; —make your Church a welcome light for the whole human family. ℟

May we always treasure your friendship and come to know its depth;—may we atone for the sins against your wisdom and love. ℟

Our Father

Concluding Prayer

Stand by your people, Lord, who place all their trust in your mercy. Wash away the stain of our sins,
make us live in your presence our whole life long,
and bring us to the inheritance you have promised.
(We make our prayer) through our Lord.

EVENING PRAYER

Hymn, from the appendix, for Lent or Holy Week.

Scripture Reading   *Heb 13:12-15*

Jesus suffered outside the gate to sanctify the people with his own blood. Let us go to him, then, outside the camp, and share his degradation. For there is no eternal city for us in this life but we look for one in the life to come. Through him let us offer God an unending sacrifice of praise, a verbal sacrifice that is offered every time we acknowledge his name.

Short Responsory

℟ I said: 'Lord, have mercy on me.' *Repeat* ℟

℣ 'Heal my soul for I have sinned against you.' ℟ Glory be. ℟

Magnificat ant. 'You are not yet fifty years old, and you have seen Abraham!' 'I tell you solemnly, before Abraham ever was, I am.'

Intercessions
Let us pray to Christ the Lord, who gave us the new commandment to love one another. R⁄ Lord, may your people grow in love.
Good master, teach us to love you in our fellow men,—teach us to serve you in our brothers. R⁄
You interceded with the Father for those who nailed you to the cross;—help us to love our enemies and pray for those who injure us. R⁄
Through the mystery of your body and blood deepen our courage and faith,—strengthen the weak, comfort the sorrowful and fill the dying with new hope. R⁄
Light of the world, you gave sight to the man born blind;—enlighten men in baptism through the washing in water and the word of life. R⁄
Grant to the dead your everlasting love;—count us among the chosen of God. R⁄
Our Father

The concluding prayer as at Morning Prayer, p 172.

FRIDAY

Invitatory antiphon of Lent.

MORNING PRAYER

Hymn, from the appendix, for Lent or Holy Week.

Scripture Reading   *Is 52:13-15*
See, my servant will prosper, he shall be lifted up, exalted, rise to great heights. As the crowds were appalled on seeing him—so disfigured did he look that he seemed no longer human—so will the crowds be astonished at him and kings stand speechless before him; for they shall see something never told and witness something never heard before.

Short Responsory

R̹ It is he who will free me from the snare of the hunters. *Repeat* R̹
V̹ And from the evil word. R̹ Glory be. R̹

Benedictus ant. I have done many good works for you to see, said
the Lord; for which of these works do you wish to kill me?

Intercessions

We give thanks to Christ the Lord, who died on the cross that we
might live. Let us pray to him with all our heart. R̹ Lord Jesus, may
your death bring us to life.

Master and Saviour, you have taught us by your life and renewed us
by your passion;—do not allow us to grow used to sin. R̹

You call on us to feed the hungry;—let us deny ourselves some food
this day to help our brothers in their need. R̹

May we accept from your hands this day of Lent;—may we make it
yours by deeds of love. R̹

End the rebellion within our hearts;—make us generous and willing
to share. R̹

Our Father

Concluding Prayer

Lord, break the bonds of sin
which our weaknesses have forged to enchain us,
and in your loving mercy forgive your people's guilt.
(We make our prayer) through our Lord.

EVENING PRAYER

Hymn, from the appendix, for Lent or Holy Week.

Scripture Reading   *I Pet 2:21-24*

Christ suffered for you and left an example for you to follow the
way he took. He had not done anything wrong, and there had been
no perjury in his mouth. He was insulted and did not retaliate with
insults; when he was tortured he made no threats but he put his
trust in the righteous judge. He was bearing our faults in his own
body on the cross, so that we might die to our faults and live for

holiness; through his wounds you have been healed.

Short Responsory

R̰ I said: 'Lord, have mercy on me.' *Repeat* R̰

℣ 'Heal my soul for I have sinned against you.' R̰ Glory be. R̰

Magnificat ant. If you refuse to believe in me, believe in the works which I do in my Father's name.

Intercessions

Let us pray to the Lord Jesus, who sanctified his people by his own blood. R̰ Lord, have mercy on your people.

Christ our Redeemer, through your suffering help us to mortify our bodies and stand firm in every trial;—may we be ready to celebrate your rising from the dead. R̰

As prophets of God's kingdom may Christians make you known throughout the world,—and may they confirm their message by lives of faith, hope and love. R̰

Lord, give strength to the afflicted;—and give us the will to do everything to help and comfort them. R̰

Teach the faithful to be united with your passion in times of trouble and distress;—let the power of your salvation shine forth in their lives. R̰

Lord, giver of life, remember those who have died;—grant them the glory of your resurrection. R̰

Our Father

The concluding prayer as at Morning Prayer, p 174.

SATURDAY

Invitatory antiphon of Lent.

MORNING PRAYER

Hymn, from the appendix, for Lent or Holy Week.

Scripture Reading   *Is 65:1b-3a*

I said, I am here, I am here, to a nation that did not invoke my name. Each day I stretched out my hand to a rebellious people that went by evil ways, following their own whims, a people who provoked me to my face incessantly.

Short Responsory

R̷ It is he who will free me from the snare of the hunters. *Repeat* R̷
V̷ And from the evil word. R̷ Glory be. R̷

Benedictus ant. Jesus has died to gather together the children of God, who were scattered.

Intercessions

Christ the Lord has made men into a new creation. He gives them a new birth in the waters of baptism and nourishes them with his word and his body. Let us glorify him in our prayer. R̷ Renew us, Lord, by your grace.

Jesus, you are gentle and humble in spirit;—grant us something of your pity, something of your kindness and something of your patience towards all men. R̷

Teach us to be neighbours to the sad and the needy;—let us imitate you, the good Samaritan. R̷

May the Blessed Virgin, your Mother, intercede for religious women; —through her prayers may they serve you in the Church ever more perfectly. R̷

Grant us the gift of your mercy,—pardon our sins and save us from punishment. R̷

Our Father

Concluding Prayer

Lord God, at all times you are working out the salvation of man, but now more especially you enrich your people with grace.
Look kindly on this people;
keep the seal of baptism inviolate in those who have received it and in those who still await their rebirth in the Spirit.
(We make our prayer) through our Lord.

HOLY WEEK

PALM SUNDAY OF THE
PASSION OF THE LORD

Psalter: Week 2

EVENING PRAYER I

Hymn, from the appendix, for Holy Week.
Psalms and canticle with proper antiphons as in the psalter.

Scripture Reading   *I Pet 1:18-21*
Remember the ransom that was paid to free you from the useless
way of life your ancestors handed down was not paid in anything
corruptible, neither in silver nor gold, but in the precious blood of a
lamb without spot or stain, namely Christ; who, though known
since before the world was made, has been revealed only in our time,
the end of the ages, for your sake. Through him you now have faith
in God, who raised him from the dead and gave him glory for that
very reason—so that you would have faith and hope in God.

Short Responsory
R̸ We worship you, Christ, and we bless you. *Repeat* R̸
℣ By your cross you have redeemed the world. R̸ Glory be. R̸

Magnificat ant. Hail, Son of David, our king and redeemer of the
world! The prophets foretold that you would come and save us.

Intercessions
As his passion drew near, Christ looked on Jerusalem and wept,
because it did not recognize that God's salvation had come. Let us
pray in faith and repentance. R̸ Lord, have mercy on your people.
Lord, you longed to gather the children of Jerusalem as a hen
gathers her chicks under her wings;—help all men to recognize that
their moment of salvation has come. R̸
Do not abandon your faithful, even when they desert you;—restore
us to yourself, Lord Jesus, and we shall be restored. R̸
Through your suffering help us to mortify our bodies—that we may

be ready to celebrate your rising from the dead. ℞ Lord, have mercy on your people.

You are reigning now in the glory of the Father;—remember those who have died today. ℞

Our Father

Concluding Prayer

Almighty, ever-living God,
you gave our Saviour the command
to become man and undergo the cross,
as an example of humility for all men to follow.
We have the lessons of his sufferings:
give us also the fellowship of his resurrection.
(We make our prayer) through our Lord.

Invitatory

Ant. Christ the Lord was tempted and suffered for us. Come, let us adore him.

MORNING PRAYER

Hymn, from the appendix, for Holy Week.
Psalms and canticle with proper antiphons as in the psalter.

Scripture Reading   Zech 9:9

Rejoice, rejoice, daughter of Zion, shout aloud, daughter of Jerusalem; for see, your king is coming to you, his cause won, his victory gained.

Short Responsory

℞ You have redeemed us, Lord, by your blood. *Repeat* ℞
℣ From every tribe and tongue and people and nation. ℞ Glory be. ℞

Benedictus ant. With waving palm branches let us adore the Lord as he comes; let us go to meet him with hymns and songs, rejoicing and singing: Blessed be the Lord.

Intercessions
Let us adore Christ the Lord. When he entered Jerusalem, the crowds proclaimed him Messiah and king. R⁷ Blessed is he who comes in the name of the Lord.
Hosanna to you, the Son of David, the king of ages;—hosanna to you in your triumph over death and hell. R⁷
You went up to Jerusalem to endure the passion and enter into glory;—lead your Church into the paschal feast of eternal life. R⁷
You made your cross the tree of life;—share your victory with all the baptized. R⁷
You came to save sinners;—bring into your kingdom all who believe, hope and love. R⁷
Our Father

Concluding Prayer
Almighty, ever-living God,
you gave our Saviour the command
to become man and undergo the cross,
as an example of humility for all men to follow.
We have the lessons of his sufferings:
give us also the fellowship of his resurrection.
(We make our prayer), through our Lord.

EVENING PRAYER II

Hymn, from the appendix, for Holy Week.
Psalms and canticle with proper antiphons as in the psalter.

Scripture Reading   *Acts 13:26-30a*
My brothers, it is to us that this message of salvation has been sent! For the people who live in Jerusalem and their leaders did not know that he is the Saviour, nor did they understand the words of the prophets that are read every Sabbath day. Yet they made the prophets' words come true by condemning Jesus. And even though they could find no reason to pass the death sentence on him, they asked Pilate to have him put to death. And after they had done everything that the Scriptures say about him, they took him down from the cross and placed him in a grave. But God raised him from the dead.

Short Responsory

℟ We worship you, Christ, and we bless you. *Repeat* ℟
℣ By your cross you have redeemed the world. ℟ Glory be. ℟

Magnificat ant. It is written: 'I will strike the shepherd down and the sheep of his flock will be scattered.' But after my resurrection I will go before you into Galilee; there you will see me, said the Lord.

Intercessions

Let us pray humbly to the Saviour of all men. He went up to Jerusalem to endure the passion and enter into his glory. ℟ Sanctify the people you redeemed by your blood.

Christ our Redeemer, let us share in your passion by works of penance;—let us attain the glory of your resurrection. ℟

Grant us the protection of your Mother, the comforter of the afflicted;—help us to extend to others the consolation you have given us. ℟

Take care of those we have discouraged and those we have wronged; —help us to learn from our sufferings so that justice and love may prevail in the end. ℟

You humbled yourself even to accepting death, death on a cross; —grant to your servants obedience and patience. ℟

Share with the dead your bodily glory;—let us rejoice one day with them in the fellowship of the saints. ℟

Our Father

The concluding prayer as at Morning Prayer, p 179.

MONDAY

Invitatory ant. Christ the Lord was tempted and suffered for us Come, let us adore him.

MORNING PRAYER

Hymn, from the appendix, for Holy Week.
Psalms and canticle with proper antiphons as in the psalter.

Scripture Reading   *Jer II:19-20*

I for my part was like a trustful lamb being led to the slaughter-house, not knowing the schemes they were plotting against me, 'Let us destroy the tree in its strength, let us cut him off from the land of the living, so that his name may be quickly forgotten!'
But you, Lord Sabaoth, who pronounce a just sentence,
who probe the loins and heart,
let me see the vengeance you will take on them,
for I have committed my cause to you.

Short Responsory

R⁷ You have redeemed us, Lord, by your blood. *Repeat* R⁷
V⁷ From every tribe and tongue and people and nation. R⁷ Glory be.
R⁷

Benedictus ant. Father, Righteous One, the world has not known you, but I have known you because it was you that sent me.

Intercessions

Let us pray earnestly to Christ our Saviour, who redeemed us by his death and resurrection. R⁷ Lord, have mercy on us.
You went up to Jerusalem to endure the passion and enter into glory;—lead your Church into the paschal feast of eternal life. R⁷
Your heart was pierced with a lance;—heal the wounds of our human weakness. R⁷
You made your cross the tree of life;—share your victory with all the baptized. R⁷
You gave salvation to the repentant thief;—pardon all our sins. R⁷
Our Father

Concluding Prayer

Almighty God, grant that we who are constantly betrayed by our own weakness,
may draw the breath of new life
from the passion and death of your Only-begotten Son,
who lives and reigns with you and the Holy Spirit,
God, for ever and ever.

EVENING PRAYER

Hymn, from the appendix, for Holy Week.
Psalms and canticle with proper antiphons as in the psalter.

Scripture Reading   *Rom 5:8-9*
As if God meant to prove how well he loves us, it was while we were still sinners that Christ, in his own appointed time, died for us. All the more surely, then, now that we have found justification through his blood, shall we be saved, through him, from God's displeasure.

Short Responsory
R̷ We worship you, Christ, and we bless you. *Repeat* R̷
V̷ By your cross you have redeemed the world. R̷ Glory be. R̷

Magnificat ant. As Moses lifted up the serpent in the desert, so must the Son of Man be lifted up, so that everyone who believes in him may have eternal life.

Intercessions
Let us turn in prayer to the Saviour of all men. By dying he destroyed our death and by rising he restored our life. R̷ Sanctify the people you redeemed by your blood.
Christ, our Redeemer, let us share in your passion by works of penance;—let us attain the glory of your resurrection. R̷
Grant us the protection of your Mother, the comforter of the afflicted;—help us to extend to others the consolation you have given us. R̷
Unite the faithful to your passion in times of trouble and distress—and let the power of your salvation shine forth in their lives. R̷
You humbled yourself even to accepting death, death on a cross;—grant to your servants obedience and patience. R̷
Share with the dead your bodily glory;—let us rejoice one day with them in the fellowship of the saints. R̷
Our Father

The concluding prayer as at Morning Prayer, p 181.

TUESDAY

Invitatory ant. Christ the Lord was tempted and suffered for us. Come, let us adore him.

MORNING PRAYER

Hymn, from the appendix, for Holy Week.
Psalms and canticle with proper antiphons as in the psalter.

Scripture Reading   *Zech 12:10-11a*
Over the House of David and the citizens of Jerusalem I will pour out a spirit of kindness and prayer. They will look on the one whom they have pierced; they will mourn for him as for an only son, and weep for him as people weep for a first-born child. When that day comes there will be great mourning in Jerusalem.

Short Responsory
R̸ You have redeemed us, Lord, by your blood. *Repeat* R̸
V̸ From every tribe and tongue and people and nation. R̸ Glory be. R̸

Benedictus ant. Father, glorify me in your own presence with the glory which I had with you before the world began.

Intercessions
Let us pray earnestly to Christ our Saviour, who redeemed us by his death and resurrection. R̸ Lord, have mercy on us.
You went up to Jerusalem to endure the passion and enter into glory;—lead your Church into the paschal feast of eternal life. R̸
Your heart was pierced with a lance;—heal the wounds of our human weakness. R̸
You made your cross the tree of life;—share your victory with all the baptized. R̸
You gave salvation to the repentant thief;—pardon all our sins. R̸
Our Father

Concluding Prayer
All-powerful, ever-living God,
may our sacramental celebration of the Lord's passion
bring us your forgiveness.
(We make our prayer) through our Lord.

EVENING PRAYER

Hymn, from the appendix, for Holy Week.
Psalms and canticle with proper antiphons as in the psalter.

Scripture Reading   *1 Cor 1:27b-30*
To shame what is strong, God has chosen what the world counts weakness. He has chosen things low and contemptible, mere nothings, to overthrow the existing order. And so there is no place for human pride in the presence of God. You are in Christ Jesus by God's act, for God has made him our wisdom; he is our righteousness; in him we are consecrated and set free.

Short Responsory
R̷ We worship you, Christ, and we bless you. *Repeat* R̷
℣ By your cross you have redeemed the world. R̷ Glory be. R̷

Magnificat ant. I have the right to lay down my life, and I have the right to take it up again.

Intercessions
Let us pray to the Saviour of all men. By dying he destroyed our death and by rising he restored our life. R̷ Sanctify the people whom you redeemed by your blood.
Christ, our Redeemer, let us share in your passion by works of penance;—let us attain the glory of your resurrection. R̷ Sanctify the people whom you redeemed by your blood.
Grant us the protection of your Mother, the comforter of the afflicted;—may we bring to others the consolation you have given us. R̷
Unite the faithful to your passion in times of trouble and distress;—let the power of your salvation shine forth in their lives. R̷

You humbled yourself even to accepting death, death on a cross;—
grant to your servants obedience and patience. R̦
Share with the dead your bodily glory;—let us rejoice one day with
them in the fellowship of the saints. R̦
Our Father

The concluding prayer as at Morning Prayer, p 184.

WEDNESDAY

Invitatory ant. Christ the Lord was tempted and suffered for us.
Come, let us adore him.

MORNING PRAYER

Hymn, from the appendix, for Holy Week.
Psalms and canticle with proper antiphons as in the psalter.

Scripture Reading   *Is 50:5-7*
The Lord God has opened my ear. For my part, I made no resistance, neither did I turn away. I offered my back to those who struck
me, my cheeks to those who tore at my beard; I did not cover my
face against insult and spittle. The Lord God comes to my help, so
that I am untouched by the insults. So, too, I set my face like flint;
I know I shall not be shamed.

Short Responsory
R̦ You have redeemed us, Lord, by your blood. *Repeat* R̦
V̦ From every tribe and tongue and people and nation. R̦ Glory be.
R̦

Benedictus ant. May the blood of Christ, who offered himself as the
perfect sacrifice to God through the Holy Spirit, purify our inner
self from dead actions so that we may serve the living God.

Intercessions
Let us pray earnestly to Christ our Saviour, who redeemed us by his
death and resurrection. R̦ Lord, have mercy on us.

You went up to Jerusalem to endure the passion and enter into glory;—lead your Church into the paschal feast of eternal life.
Ry Lord, have mercy on us.
Your heart was pierced with a lance;—heal the wounds of our human weakness. Ry
You made your cross the tree of life;—share your victory with all the baptized. Ry
You gave salvation to the repentant thief;—pardon all our sins. Ry
Our Father

Concluding Prayer
By your will, Lord God,
your Son underwent the agony of the cross
to break the power of Satan over man.
Give your people grace to rise again with Christ,
who lives and reigns with you and the Holy Spirit,
God, for ever and ever.

EVENING PRAYER

Hymn, from the appendix, for Holy Week.
Psalms and canticle with proper antiphons as in the psalter.

Scripture Reading   *Eph 4:32-5:2*
Be kind and tender to one another, each of you generous to all, as God in Christ has been generous to you. As God's favoured children, you must be like him. Order your lives in charity, upon the model of that charity which Christ showed to us when he gave himself up on our behalf, a sacrifice breathing out fragrance as he offered it to God.

Short Responsory
Ry We worship you, Christ, and we bless you. *Repeat* Ry
Ỹ By your cross you have redeemed the world. Ry Glory be. Ry

Magnificat ant. The Master says: My time is near. It is at your house that I am keeping the Passover with my disciples.

Intercessions
Let us pray to the Saviour of all men. By dying he destroyed our

death and by rising he restored our life. R⁷ Sanctify the people whom you redeemed by your blood.

Christ, our Redeemer, let us share in your passion by works of penance;—let us attain the glory of your resurrection. R⁷

Grant us the protection of your Mother, the comforter of the afflicted;—may we bring to others the consolation you have given us. R⁷

Unite the faithful to your passion in times of trouble and distress;—let the power of your salvation shine forth in their lives. R⁷

You humbled yourself even to accepting death, death on a cross;—grant to your servants obedience and patience. R⁷

Share with the dead your bodily glory;—let us rejoice one day with them in the fellowship of the saints. R⁷

Our Father

The concluding prayer as at Morning Prayer, p 186.

THURSDAY

Invitatory ant. Christ the Lord was tempted and suffered for us. Come, let us adore him.

MORNING PRAYER

Hymn from the appendix for Holy Week.
Psalms and canticle with proper antiphons as in the psalter.

Scripture Reading   *Heb 2:9b-10*
We see in Jesus one who is now crowned with glory and splendour because he submitted to death; by God's grace he had to experience death for all mankind. As it was his purpose to bring a great many of his sons into glory, it was appropriate that God, for whom everything exists and through whom everything exists, should make perfect through suffering, the leader who would take them to their salvation.

Short Responsory

℟ You have redeemed us, Lord, by your blood. *Repeat* ℟
℣ From every tribe and tongue and people and nation. ℟ Glory be.
℟

Benedictus ant. I have longed to eat this Passover with you before I suffer.

Intercessions

Let us humbly pray to Christ, the eternal priest, whom the Father anointed with the Holy Spirit to proclaim release for captives.
℟ Lord, have mercy on us.
You went up to Jerusalem to endure the passion and enter into glory;—lead your Church into the paschal feast of eternal life. ℟
Your heart was pierced with a lance;—heal the wounds of our human weakness. ℟
You made your cross the tree of life;—share your victory with all the baptized. ℟
You gave salvation to the repentant thief;—pardon all our sins. ℟
Our Father

Concluding Prayer

Love of you with our whole heart, Lord God, is holiness.
Increase then your gifts of divine grace in us,
so that, as in your Son's death,
you made us hope for what we believe,
you may likewise, in his resurrection,
make us come to you, our final end.
(We make our prayer) through our Lord.

EASTER TRIDUUM

HOLY THURSDAY

EVENING PRAYER

Evening Prayer is said only by those who do not attend the Evening Mass of the Lord's Supper.

Hymn, from the appendix, for Holy Week.
Psalms and canticle with proper antiphons as in the psalter, pp 513 ff.

Scripture Reading   *Heb 13:12-13*
Jesus suffered outside the gate to sanctify the people with his own blood. Let us go to him, then, outside the camp, and share his degradation. For there is no eternal city for us in this life but we look for one in the life to come. Through him let us offer God an unending sacrifice of praise, a verbal sacrifice that is offered every time we acknowledge his name.

In place of the short responsory the following antiphon is said:
Ant. Christ humbled himself for us, and, in obedience, accepted death.

Magnificat ant. As they were eating, Jesus took bread, and when he had said the blessing he broke it and gave it to his disciples.

Intercessions
Let us adore our Saviour, who at the Last Supper, on the night he was betrayed, entrusted to the Church the memorial of his death and resurrection to be celebrated throughout the ages. Confident that he will hear us, we pray: ℟ Sanctify the people whom you redeemed by your blood.
Christ, our Redeemer, let us share in your passion by works of penance;—let us attain the glory of your resurrection. ℟
Grant us the protection of your Mother, the comforter of the afflicted;—may we bring to others the consolation you have given us. ℟

Unite the faithful to your passion in times of trouble and distress;
—let the power of your salvation shine forth in their lives. ℞ Sanctify
the people whom you redeemed by your blood.
You humbled yourself even to accepting death, death on a cross;—
grant to your servants obedience and patience. ℞
Share with the dead your bodily glory;—let us rejoice one day
with them in the fellowship of the saints. ℞
Our Father

Concluding Prayer
Lord God,
since for your glory and our salvation,
you willed Christ your Son to be the eternal High Priest:
grant that the people he gained for you by his blood,
may be strengthened by his cross and resurrection
when they take part in his memorial sacrifice.
(We make our prayer) through our Lord.

¶ *Night Prayer as given for After Evening Prayer II of Sundays,
pp 692 ff. In place of the short responsory the following antiphon is
said:*

Ant. Christ humbled himself for us, and, in obedience, accepted
death.

GOOD FRIDAY

Invitatory ant. Christ, the Son of God, redeemed us with his blood.
Come, let us adore him.
Psalm, p 371.

MORNING PRAYER

Hymn
　　Gall he drinks; his strength subduing,
　　Reed and thorn and nail and spear
　　Plot his gentle frame's undoing;
　　Blood and water thence appear,

With their cleansing tide renewing
Earth and sea and starry sphere.

Hail, true cross, of beauty rarest,
King of all the forest trees;
Leaf and flower and fruit thou bearest
Medicine for a world's disease;
Fairest wood, and iron fairest—
Yet more fair, who hung on these.

Bend thy branches down to meet him,
Bend that stubborn heart of thine;
Let thy native force, to greet him,
All its ruggedness resign;
Gently let thy wood entreat him,
Royal sufferer, and divine.

Victim of our race, he deignéd
On thy arms to lay his head;
Thou the ark, whose refuge gainéd,
Sinful man no more may dread;
Ark, whose planks are deeply stainéd
With the blood the Lamb hath shed.

Honour, glory, might and merit
To the eternal Trinity,
Father, Son and Holy Spirit,
Throned in heaven co-equally;
All that doth the world inherit,
Praise one God in Persons three.

PSALMODY

Ant. 1: God did not spare his own Son, but gave him up for us all.

PSALM 50(51)

Have mércy on me, Gód, in your kíndness.*
In your compássion blot óut my offénce.
O wásh me more and móre from my guílt*
and cléanse me fróm my sín.

My offénces trúly I knów them;*
my sín is álways befóre me.
Against yóu, you alóne, have I sínned;*
what is évil in your síght I have dóne.

That you may be jústified whén you give séntence*
and be withóut repróach when you júdge,
O sée, in guílt I was bórn,*
a sínner was Í concéived.

Indéed you love trúth in the héart;*
then in the sécret of my héart teach me wísdom.
O púrify me, thén I shall be cléan;*
O wásh me, I shall be whíter than snów.

Make me héar rejóicing and gládness,*
that the bónes you have crúshed may revíve.
From my síns turn awáy your fáce*
and blót out áll my guílt.

A púre heart creáte for me, O Gód,*
put a stéadfast spírit withín me.
Do not cást me awáy from your présence,*
nor depríve me of your hóly spírit.

Give me agáin the jóy of your hélp;*
with a spírit of férvour sustáin me,
that I may téach transgréssors your wáys*
and sínners may retúrn to yóu.

O réscue me, Gód, my hélper,*
and my tóngue shall ríng out your góodness.
O Lórd, ópen my líps*
and my móuth shall decláre your práise.

For in sácrifice you táke no delíght,*
burnt óffering from mé you would refúse,
my sácrifice, a cóntrite spírit.*
A húmbled, contrite héart you will not spúrn.

In your góodness, show fávour to Síon:*
rebuíld the wálls of Jerúsalem.

Thén you will be pléased with lawful sácrifice,*
hólocausts óffered on your áltar.

Ant. God did not spare his own Son, but gave him up for us all.
Ant. 2: Jesus Christ showed his love for us and freed us from our
sins with his life's blood.

CANTICLE: HAB 3:2-4,13A,16-19

Lord, I have heard of your fame,*
I stand in awe at your deeds.
Do them again in our days,†
in our days make them known!*
In spite of your anger, have compassion.

God comes forth from Teman,*
the Holy One comes from Mount Paran.
His splendour covers the sky*
and his glory fills the earth.
His brilliance is like the light,†
rays flash from his hands;*
there his power is hidden.

You march out to save your people,*
to save the one you have anointed.
You make a path for your horses in the sea,*
in the raging of the mighty waters.

This I heard and I tremble with terror,
my lips quiver at the sound.
Weakness invades my bones,*
my steps fail beneath me,
yet I calmly wait for the doom*
that will fall upon the people who assail us.

For even though the fig does not blossom,*
nor fruit grow on the vine,
even though the olive crop fail,*
and fields produce no harvest,
even though flocks vanish from the folds*
and stalls stand empty of cattle,

Yet I will rejoice in the Lord*
and exult in God my saviour.
The Lord my God is my strength.†
He makes me leap like the deer,*
he guides me to the high places.

Ant. Jesus Christ showed his love for us and freed us from our sins
with his life's blood.
Ant. 3: We venerate your cross, Lord; we praise and glorify your
holy resurrection: because of the tree joy has come into the whole
world.

PSALM 147

O práise the Lórd, Jerúsalem!*
Síon, práise your Gód!

He has stréngthened the bárs of your gátes,*
he has bléssed the chíldren withín you.
He estáblished péace on your bórders,*
he féeds you with fínest whéat.

He sénds out his wórd to the éarth*
and swíftly rúns his commánd.
He shówers down snów white as wóol,*
he scátters hóar-frost like áshes.

He húrls down háilstones like crúmbs.*
The wáters are frózen at his tóuch;
he sénds forth his wórd and it mélts them:*
at the bréath of his móuth the waters flów.

He mákes his wórd known to Jácob,*
to Ísrael his láws and decrées.
He has not déalt thus with óther nátions;*
he has not táught them hís decrées.

Ant. We venerate your cross, Lord; we praise and glorify your holy
resurrection: because of the tree joy has come into the whole world.

Scripture Reading   *Is 52:13-15*
See, my servant will prosper, he shall be lifted up, exalted, rise to
great heights. As the crowds were appalled on seeing him—so disfigured did he look that he seemed no longer human—so will the
crowds be astonished at him and kings stand speechless before him;
for they shall see something never told and witness something never
heard before.

In place of the short responsory the following antiphon is said:
Ant. Christ humbled himself for us, and, in obedience, accepted
death, even death on a cross.

Benedictus ant. Over his head was placed the charge against him:
'This is Jesus, the Nazarene, the King of the Jews.'

Intercessions
Let us pray to our Redeemer, who suffered for us, was buried, and
rose from the dead. ℞ Lord, have mercy on us.
Lord and master, for us you became obedient even to death;—keep
us faithful to God's will in the darkness of our lives. ℞
Jesus, our life, by dying on the cross you destroyed hell and death;—
grant that we may die with you and rise with you in glory. ℞
Christ, our king, you were the scorn of the people, a worm not a
man;—teach us to tread your path of humility. ℞
Jesus, our Saviour, you laid down your life for your friends;—let us
love one another as you have loved us. ℞
Jesus, our hope, you stretched out your hands on the cross to
embrace all ages of men;—gather all God's scattered children into
the kingdom of salvation. ℞
Our Father

Concluding Prayer
Be mindful, Lord, of this your family,
for whose sake our Lord Jesus Christ, when betrayed,
did not hesitate to yield himself into his enemies' hands,
and undergo the agony of the cross:
he who lives and reigns with you and the Holy Spirit,
God, for ever and ever.

EVENING PRAYER

Evening Prayer is said only by those who do not attend the Afternoon Liturgical Action of the Passion.
Hymn, from the appendix, for Holy Week.

PSALMODY

Ant. 1: Look, all you peoples, and see my grief.

PSALM 115(116)

I trústed, éven when I sáid:*
'I am sórely afflícted,'
and whén I sáid in my alárm:*
'No mán can be trústed.'

How cán I repáy the Lórd*
for his góodness to mé?
The cúp of salvátion I will ráise;*
I will cáll on the Lórd's name.

My vóws to the Lórd I will fulfíl*
befóre all his péople.
O précious in the éyes of the Lórd*
i⸱ the déath of his fáithful.

Your sérvant, Lord, your sérvant am Í;*
you have lóosened my bónds.
A thánksgiving sácrifice I máke:*
I will cáll on the Lórd's name.

My vóws to the Lórd I will fulfíl*
befóre all his péople,
in the córts of the hóuse of the Lórd,*
in your mídst, O Jerúsalem.

Ant. Look, all you peoples, and see my grief.
Ant. 2: My spirit fails; my heart is numb within me.

PSALM 142(143):1-11

Lórd, lísten to my práyer:†
túrn your éar to my appéal.*

You are fáithful, you are júst; give ánswer.
Do not cáll your sérvant to júdgment*
for nó one is júst in your síght.

The énemy pursúes my sóul;*
he has crúshed my lífe to the gróund;
he has máde me dwéll in dárkness*
like the déad, lóng forgótten.
Thérefore my spírit fáils;*
my héart is númb withín me.

I remémber the dáys that are pást:*
I pónder áll your wórks.
I múse on what your hánd has wróught†
and to yóu I strétch out my hánds.*
Like a párched land my sóul thirsts for yóu.

Lórd, make háste and ánswer;*
for my spírit fáils withín me.
Dó not híde your fáce*
lest I becóme like thóse in the gráve.

In the mórning let me knów your lóve*
for I pút my trúst in yóu.
Make me knów the wáy I should wálk:*
to yóu I líft up my sóul.

Réscue me, Lórd, from my énemies;*
I have fléd to yóu for réfuge.
Téach me to dó your wíll*
for yóu, O Lórd, are my Gód.
Let yóur good spírit guíde me*
in wáys that are lével and smóoth.

For your náme's sake Lórd, save my lífe;*
in your jústice save my sóul from distréss.

Ant. My spirit fails; my heart is numb within me.
Ant. 3: After Jesus had taken the vinegar he said, 'It is accomplished'; and bowing his head he gave up his spirit.

Though he was in the form of God,*
Jesus did not count equality with God a thing to be grasped.

He emptied himself,†
taking the form of a servant,*
being born in the likeness of men.

And being found in human form,†
he humbled himself and became obedient unto death,*
even death on a cross.

Therefore God has highly exalted him*
and bestowed on him the name which is above every name,

That at the name of Jesus every knee should bow,*
in heaven and on earth and under the earth,

And every tongue confess that Jesus Christ is Lord,*
to the glory of God the Father.

Ant. After Jesus had taken the vinegar he said, 'It is accomplished';
and bowing his head he gave up his spirit.

Scripture Reading   *1 Pet 2:21-24*
Christ suffered for you and left an example for you to follow the
way he took. He had not done anything wrong, and there had been
no perjury in his mouth. He was insulted and did not retaliate with
insults; when he was tortured he made no threats but he put his
trust in the righteous judge. He was bearing our faults in his own
body on the cross, so that we might die to our faults and live for
holiness; through his wounds you have been healed.

In place of the short responsory the following antiphon is said:
Ant. Christ humbled himself for us, and, in obedience, accepted
death, even death on a cross.

Magnificat ant. When we were still God's enemies, we were reconciled to him through the death of his Son.

198

Intercessions

The universal prayer given in the missal for today is recommended for use at this Office. One is free, however, to use the intercessions given below, or silent prayer may be made for the intentions specified.

As we recall Christ's saving death, let us pray to God the Father.
  Ry Through the death of your Son, Lord hear us.
Lord, unite your Church throughout the world. Ry
Keep Pope N in your loving care. Ry
Sanctify by your Spirit the entire people of God. Ry
Deepen the faith and understanding of those preparing for baptism.
Ry
Gather all Christians into unity. Ry
Bring the Jewish people to the fulness of redemption. Ry
Shed your light on those who do not believe in Christ. Ry
Show the signs of your love to those who deny your existence. Ry
Guide the minds and hearts of governments and rulers. Ry
Comfort those who live in sorrow. Ry
Grant to the dead eternal rest. Ry
Our Father

The concluding prayer as at Morning Prayer, p 195.

¶ *Night Prayer as given for After Evening Prayer II of Sundays, pp 692 ff. In place of the short responsory the following antiphon is said:*
Ant. Christ humbled himself for us, and, in obedience, accepted death, even death on a cross.

HOLY SATURDAY

Invitatory ant. Christ the Lord suffered for us and was buried.
Come, let us adore him.

MORNING PRAYER

Hymn
  O loving wisdom of our God!
  When all was sin and shame,

A second Adam to the fight
And to the rescue came.

O generous love! that he who smote
In man for man the foe,
The double agony in man
For man should undergo;

And in the garden secretly,
And on the cross on high,
Should teach his brethren, and inspire
To suffer and to die.

Praise to the Holiest in the height,
And in the depth be praise,
In all his words most wonderful,
Most sure in all his ways.

PSALMODY

Ant. 1: They will mourn for him as for an only son, since it is the innocent one of the Lord who has been slain.

PSALM 63(64)

Hear my vóice, O Gód, as I compláin,*
guard my life from dréad of the fóe.
Híde me from the bánd of the wícked,*
from the thróng of thóse who do évil.

They shárpen their tóngues like swórds;*
they áim bitter wórds like árrows
to shóot at the ínnocent from ámbush,*
shóoting súddenly and récklessly.

They schéme their évil cóurse;*
They conspíre to lay sécret snáres.
They sáy: 'Whó will sée us?*
Whó can séarch out our crímes?'

He will séarch who séarches the mínd*
and knóws the dépths of the héart.
Gód has shót them with his árrow*

and déalt them súdden wóunds.
Their ówn tongue has bróught them to rúin*
and áll who sée them móck.

Thén will áll men féar;†
they will téll what Gód has dóne.*
They will únderstánd God's déeds.
The júst will rejóice in the Lórd†
and flý to hím for réfuge.*
All the úpright héarts will glóry.

Ant. They will mourn for him as for an only son, since it is the
innocent one of the Lord who has been slain.
Ant. 2: Save my soul from the gates of hell, Lord.

CANTICLE: IS 38:10-14,17-20

I said, In the noontide of my days I must depart;†
I am consigned to the gates of Sheol*
for the rest of my years.

I said, I shall not see the Lord*
in the land of the living;
I shall look upon man no more*
among the inhabitants of the world.

My dwelling is plucked up and removed from me*
like a shepherd's tent;
like a weaver I have rolled up my life;*
he cuts me off from the loom;

From day to night you bring me to an end;*
I cry for help until morning;
like a lion he breaks all my bones;*
from day to night you bring me to an end.

Like a swallow or a crane I clamour,*
I moan like a dove.
My eyes are weary with looking upward.*
O Lord, I am oppressed; be my security.

Lo, it was for my welfare*
that I had great bitterness;
but you have held back my life*
from the pit of destruction,
for you have cast all my sins*
behind your back.

For Sheol cannot thank you,*
death cannot praise you;
those who go down to the pit*
cannot hope for your faithfulness.

The living, the living, he thanks you†
as I do this day;*
the father makes known to the children your
faithfulness.

The Lord will save me,*
and we will sing to stringed instruments
all the days of our life,*
at the house of the Lord.

Ant. Save my soul from the gates of hell, Lord.
Ant. 3: I was dead and now I am to live for ever and ever, and I hold
the keys of death and of hell.

PSALM 150

Práise Gód in his hóly pláce,*
práise him in his míghty héavens.
Práise him for his pówerful déeds,*
práise his surpássing gréatness.

O práise him with sóund of trúmpet,*
práise him with lúte and hárp.
Práise him with tímbrel and dánce,*
práise him with stríngs and pípes.

O práise him with resóunding cýmbals,*
práise him with cláshing of cýmbals.
Let éverything that líves and that bréathes*
give práise to the Lórd.

Ant. I was dead and now I am to live for ever and ever, and I hold the keys of death and of hell.

Scripture Reading   *Hos 6:1-3a*
Come, let us return to the Lord. He has torn us to pieces, but he will heal us; he has struck us down, but he will bandage our wounds; after a day or two he will bring us back to life, on the third day he will raise us and we shall live in his presence.

In place of the short responsory the following antiphon is said:
Ant. Christ humbled himself for us, and, in obedience, accepted death, even death on a cross. Therefore God raised him to the heights and gave him the name which is above all other names.

Benedictus ant. Save us, Saviour of the world. By the cross and the shedding of your blood you have redeemed us. Come to help us, Lord, our God.

Intercessions
Let us pray to our Redeemer, who suffered for us, was buried, and rose from the dead. ℟ Lord, have mercy on us.
Christ, our Lord, you saw your mother standing by the cross;—may we share your saving passion in our time of suffering. ℟
Christ, our Saviour, you died like a grain of wheat falling into the ground;—gather us to yourself in the harvest of redemption. ℟
Christ, our shepherd, lying in the tomb you were hidden from men; —teach us to love our real life, which is hidden with you in God. ℟
Christ, the new Adam, you went down into the world of the dead to free the just;—may those who are dead in sin hear your voice and live. ℟
Son of the living God, we were buried with you in baptism;—let us rise with you, alive to God for ever. ℟
Our Father

Concluding Prayer
Almighty, ever-living God,
whose Only-begotten Son descended to the realm of the dead,
and rose from there to glory,

grant that your faithful people,
who were buried with him in baptism,
may, by his resurrection, obtain eternal life.
(We make our prayer) through our Lord.

EVENING PRAYER

Hymn

My God, I love thee—though there were
No heaven for me to win,
No hell to punish those who dare
Against thy love to sin.

Upon the cross, thy wide embrace
Made me, dear Lord, thy own;
The nails, the spear, the long disgrace
For me should all atone.

That night of fear, those hours of pain,
Those bitter griefs of thine,
That death itself was borne, to gain
A sinner's love—'twas mine.

And shall the fear of hell below
Or hope of heaven above
Be all the reason heart can know
This loving Lord to love?

The love that asks not anything,
Love like thy own love free,
Jesus, I give, who art my King,
Who art my God, to thee.

PSALMODY

Ant. 1: O Death, I will be your death; Sheol, I will be your destruction.

PSALM 115(116)

I trústed, éven when I sáid:*
'I am sórely afflícted,'

and whén I sáid in my alárm:*
'No mán can be trústed'.

How cán I repáy the Lórd*
for his góodness to mé?
The cúp of salvátion I will ráise;*
I will cáll on the Lórd's name.

My vóws to the Lórd I will fulfíl*
befóre all his péople.
O précious in the éyes of the Lórd*
is the déath of his fáithful.

Your sérvant, Lord, your sérvant am Í;*
you have lóosened my bónds.
A thánksgiving sácrifice I máke:*
I will cáll on the Lórd's name.

My vóws to the Lórd I will fulfíl*
befóre all his péople,
in the córts of the hóuse of the Lórd,*
in your mídst, O Jerúsalem.

Ant. O Death, I will be your death; Sheol, I will be your destruction.
Ant. 2: As Jonah was inside the whale for three days and three nights,
so will the Son of Man be held in the heart of the earth.

PSALM 142(143):1-11

Lórd, lísten to my práyer:†
túrn your éar to my appéal.*
You are fáithful, you are júst; give ánswer.
Do not cáll your sérvant to júdgment*
for nó one is júst in your síght.

The énemy pursúes my sóul;*
he has crúshed my lífe to the gróund;
he has máde me dwéll in dárkness*
like the déad, lóng forgótten.
Thérefore my spírit fáils;*
my héart is númb withín me.

205

I remémber the dáys that are pást:*
I pónder áll your wórks.
I múse on what your hánd has wróught†
and to yóu I strétch out my hánds.*
Like a párched land my sóul thirsts for yóu.

Lórd, make háste and ánswer;*
for my spírit fáils withín me.
Dó not híde your fáce*
lest I becóme like thóse in the gráve.

In the mórning let me knów your lóve*
for I pút my trúst in yóu.
Make me knów the wáy I should wálk:*
to yóu I líft up my sóul.

Réscue me, Lórd, from my énemies;*
I have fléd to yóu for réfuge.
Téach me to dó your wíll*
for yóu, O Lórd, are my Gód.
Let yóur good spírit guíde me*
in wáys that are lével and smóoth.

For your náme's sake, Lórd, save my lífe;*
in your jústice save my sóul from distréss.

Ant. As Jonah was inside the whale for three days and three nights,
so will the Son of Man be held in the heart of the earth.
Ant. 3: 'Destroy this Temple, and in three days I will raise it up,'
said the Lord. He said this of the temple that was his own body.

CANTICLE: PHIL 2:6-11

Though he was in the form of God,*
Jesus did not count equality with God a thing to be grasped.

He emptied himself,†
taking the form of a servant,*
being born in the likeness of men.

And being found in human form,†
he humbled himself and became obedient unto death,*

even death on a cross.

Therefore God has highly exalted him*
and bestowed on him the name which is above every name,

That at the name of Jesus every knee should bow,*
in heaven and on earth and under the earth,

And every tongue confess that Jesus Christ is Lord,*
to the glory of God the Father.

Ant. 'Destroy this Temple, and in three days I will raise it up,' said
the Lord. He said this of the temple that was his own body.

Scripture Reading *I Pet I:18-21*
Remember, the ransom that was paid to free you from the useless
way of life your ancestors handed down was not paid in anything
corruptible, neither in silver nor gold, but in the precious blood of a
lamb without spot or stain, namely Christ; who, though known since
before the world was made, has been revealed only in our time, the
end of the ages, for your sake. Through him you now have faith in
God, who raised him from the dead and gave him glory for that
very reason—so that you would have faith and hope in God.

In place of the short responsory the following antiphon is said:
Ant. Christ humbled himself for us, and, in obedience, accepted
death, even death on a cross. Therefore God raised him to the
heights and gave him the name which is above all other names.

Magnificat ant. Now the Son of Man has been glorified, and in him
God has been glorified, and God will glorify him now and forever.

Intercessions
Let us pray to our Redeemer, who suffered for us, was buried, and
rose from the dead. R̂ Lord, have mercy on us.
Lord Jesus, from your opened side you poured out blood and water,
the wonderful sign of the Church;—bring your bride to life through
your death, burial and resurrection. R̂
You remembered those who had forgotten your promise of rising
from the dead;—give new hope to men when life has lost its meaning.
R̂

Lamb of God, you became our paschal sacrifice;—draw all men to yourself. R̸ Lord, have mercy on us.

Lord of the universe, you were enclosed in the walls of a tomb;—deliver men from hell and grant them the glory of immortal life. R̸

Son of the living God, you gave paradise to a thief on the cross;—look on your brothers who have died and share with them your resurrection. R̸

Our Father

The concluding prayer as at Morning Prayer, p 203.

¶ *Night Prayer as given for After Evening Prayer II of Sundays, pp 692 ff. It is only said, however, by those who do not attend the Easter Vigil. In place of the short responsory, the following antiphon is said:*

Ant. Christ humbled himself for us, and, in obedience, accepted death, even death on a cross. Therefore God raised him to the heights and gave him the name which is above all other names.

EASTER SUNDAY
Eastertide Begins

MORNING PRAYER

Today the Invitatory is always said at the beginning of Morning Prayer.
Invitatory ant. The Lord has truly risen, alleluia.
Psalm, p 371.

Hymn
Bring, all ye dear-bought nations, bring, alleluia,
Your richest praises to your King, alleluia,
That spotless Lamb, who more than due, alleluia,
Paid for his sheep, and those sheep you, alleluia.
Alleluia, alleluia, alleluia.

That guiltless Son, who bought your peace, alleluia,
And made his Father's anger cease, alleluia.
Then, Life and Death together fought, alleluia,
Each to a strange extreme were brought, alleluia.
Alleluia, alleluia, alleluia.

We, Lord, with faithful hearts and voice, alleluia,
On this thy rising day rejoice, alleluia.
O thou, whose power o'ercame the grave, alleluia,
By grace and love us sinners save, alleluia.
Alleluia, alleluia, alleluia.

Ant. 1: Christ has risen; he is the light of his people, whom he has redeemed with his blood, alleluia.

Psalms and canticle of Sunday, Week 1, pp 390 ff.

Ant. 2: Christ, our Redeemer, has risen from the tomb: let us sing a hymn to the Lord, our God, alleluia.

Ant. 3: Alleluia, the Lord has risen as he promised, alleluia.

Scripture Reading   *Acts 10:40-43*

God raised Jesus from death on the third day and caused him to
appear. He was not seen by all the people, but only by us who are the
witnesses that God had already chosen. We ate and drank with him
after God raised him from death. And he commanded us to preach
the gospel to the people, and to testify that he is the one whom God
has appointed Judge of the living and the dead. All the prophets
spoke about him, saying that everyone who believes in him will have
his sins forgiven through the power of his name.

In place of the short responsory the following antiphon is said:
Ant. This is the day which was made by the Lord: let us rejoice and
be glad, alleluia.

Benedictus ant. Very early on the Sunday morning, just after the
sun had risen, they came to the tomb, alleluia.

Intercessions

Let us pray to Christ, the author of life. God raised him from the
dead, and he himself will raise us to life by his own power. ℟ Christ,
our life, save us.

Christ, you are the light that drives out darkness and draws men to
holiness;—let us make this day a living hymn of praise. ℟

Lord, you followed the way of suffering, even to the cross;—grant
that we may die with you and come to life with you. ℟

Our master and our brother, you have made us a kingdom of
priests to serve God our Father;—let us offer you with joy the
sacrifice of praise. ℟

King of glory, we look forward to the day of your coming,—then
we shall see your face and share in your splendour. ℟

Our Father

Concluding Prayer

On this day, Lord God,
you opened for us the way to eternal life
through your only Son's victory over death.
Grant that as we celebrate the feast of his resurrection
we may be renewed by your Holy Spirit

and rise again in the light of life.
(We make our prayer) through our Lord.

The concluding invitation: Go in the peace of Christ, alleluia, alleluia.
R̷ Thanks be to God, alleluia, alleluia.

¶ *This concluding invitation is used at Morning and Evening Prayer
for the whole Easter Octave.*

EVENING PRAYER

Hymn no. 25 from the appendix.

PSALMODY

Ant. 1: Mary Magdalen came with the other Mary to see the tomb
where the Lord had been laid, alleluia.

PSALM 109(110):1-5,7

The Lórd's revelátion to my Máster:†
'Sít on my ríght:*
your foes I will pút beneath your féet.'

The Lórd will wíeld from Síon†
your scéptre of pówer:*
rúle in the mídst of all your fóes.

A prínce from the dáy of your bírth†
on the hóly móuntains;*
from the wómb before the dáwn I begót you.

The Lórd has sworn an óath he will not chánge.†
'You are a príest for éver,*
a príest like Melchízedek of óld.'

The Máster stánding at your ríght hand*
will shatter kíngs in the dáy of his wráth.

He shall drínk from the stréam by the wáyside*
and thérefore he shall líft up his héad.   Glory be.

211

Ant. Mary Magdalen came with the other Mary to see the tomb where the Lord had been laid, alleluia.
Ant. 2: Come and see where the Lord was laid, alleluia.

PSALM 113A(114)

When Ísrael came fórth from Égypt,*
Jacob's sóns from an álien péople,
Júdah becáme the Lord's témple,*
Ísrael becáme his kíngdom.

The séa fléd at the síght:*
the Jórdan turned báck on its cóurse,
the móuntains léapt like ráms*
and the hílls like yéarling shéep.

Whý was it, séa, that you fléd,*
that you túrned back, Jórdan, on your cóurse?
Móuntains, that you léapt like ráms,*
hílls, like yéarling shéep?

Trémble, O éarth, before the Lórd,*
in the présence of the Gód of Jácob,
who túrns the róck into a póol*
and flínt into a spríng of wáter.

Ant. Come and see where the Lord was laid, alleluia.
Ant. 3: Jesus said, 'Go, and tell my brothers that they are to leave for Galilee; they will see me there.' Alleluia.

When chanted, this canticle is sung with Alleluia *as set out below; when recited it suffices to say* Alleluia *at the beginning and end of each strophe.*

CANTICLE: REV 19:1,5-7

Alleluia.
Salvation and glory and power belong to our God,*
(℞ Alleluia.)
His judgments are true and just.
℞ Alleluia (alleluia).

212

Alleluia.
Praise our God, all you his servants,*
(R̦ Alleluia.)
you who fear him, small and great.
R̦ Alleluia (alleluia).

Alleluia.
The Lord our God, the Almighty, reigns.*
(R̦ Alleluia.)
Let us rejoice and exult and give him the glory.
R̦ Alleluia (alleluia).

Alleluia.
The marriage of the Lamb has come,*
(R̦ Alleluia.)
and his bride has made herself ready.
R̦ Alleluia (alleluia).

Ant. Jesus said, 'Go, and tell my brothers that they are to leave for Galilee; they will see me there.' Alleluia.

Scripture Reading   *Heb 10:12-14*
Christ has offered one single sacrifice for sins, and then taken his place for ever at the right hand of God, where he is now waiting until his enemies are made into a footstool for him. By virtue of that one single offering he has achieved the eternal perfection of all whom he is sanctifying.

In place of the short responsory the following antiphon is said:
Ant. This is the day which was made by the Lord: let us rejoice and be glad, alleluia.

Magnificat ant. On the evening of that Sunday, when the disciples were gathered behind locked doors, Jesus came and stood among them. He said to them, 'Peace be with you, alleluia.'

Intercessions
Let us pray with joy to Christ the Lord. He rose from the dead and is living now to intercede for us. R̦ Victorious king, hear us.
Christ, you are the light of the world and the salvation of nations;

—set us on fire with your Spirit as we proclaim the wonder of your resurrection. ℟ Victorious king, hear us.

Let Israel recognize in you the Messiah it has longed for;—fill all men with the knowledge of your glory. ℟

Keep us united in the communion of saints;—may we find rest with them, when life's work is done. ℟

You have overcome death, the last enemy of man;—destroy everything in us that is at enmity with God. ℟

Christ, our Saviour, you became obedient to death, but God raised you to the heights;—receive our brothers into the kingdom of your glory. ℟

Our Father

Concluding Prayer

On this day, Lord God,
you opened for us the way to eternal life
through your only Son's victory over death.
Grant that as we celebrate the feast of his resurrection
we may be renewed by your Holy Spirit
and rise again in the light of life.
(We make our prayer) through our Lord.

Concluding invitation: Go in the peace of Christ, alleluia, alleluia.
℟ Thanks be to God, alleluia, alleluia.

The end of the Easter Triduum.

NIGHT PRAYER

During Eastertide, psalms are said or sung under the following single antiphon:
Ant. Alleluia, alleluia, alleluia.

During the Easter Octave either form of Night Prayer for Sundays, pp 689 ff, or pp 692 ff, is used daily, and in place of the short responsory, the following antiphon is said:

Ant. This is the day which was made by the Lord: let us rejoice and be glad, alleluia.

EASTER OCTAVE

Invitatory
Ant. The Lord has truly risen, alleluia.

MONDAY

MORNING PRAYER

Hymn, antiphons, psalms and canticle as on Easter Sunday, pp 209 ff.

Scripture Reading   *Rom 10:8b-10*
It is on your lips, it is in your heart, meaning by that the message of faith which we preach. You can find salvation, if you will use your lips to confess that Jesus is the Lord, and your heart to believe that God has raised him up from the dead. The heart has only to believe, if we are to be justified; the lips have only to make confession, if we are to be saved.

In place of the short responsory the following antiphon is said:
Ant. This is the day which was made by the Lord: let us rejoice and be glad, alleluia.

Benedictus ant. Go quickly and tell the disciples that the Lord has risen, alleluia.

Intercessions
The Father has glorified Jesus and handed over to him the whole of creation. Let us praise him in our morning prayer. ℟ Lord, save us through your victory.
Lord Jesus, you have broken the power of hell, destroying sin and death;—do not let us be defeated in our struggle with temptation. ℟
You have ended death for ever and given us new life;—guide our steps today along the path that leads to God. ℟
You rose from the dead to renew all men;—grant eternal life to everyone we meet. ℟
The disciples rejoiced, when you came back from the grave;—fill the hearts of your servants with overflowing joy. ℟

Our Father

Concluding Prayer
Lord God,
you increase day by day
the number of your Church's children
born in the waters of baptism.
Grant that your people may hold fast in life
to the mystery of new birth,
which they received by faith.
(We make our prayer) through our Lord.

EVENING PRAYER

Hymn, antiphons, psalms and canticle as on Easter Sunday, pp 211 ff.

Scripture Reading   *Heb 8:1b-3a*
This high priest of ours is one who has taken his seat in heaven, on
the right hand of that throne where God sits in majesty, ministering
now in the sanctuary, in that true tabernacle which the Lord, not
man, has set up. After all, it is the very function of a priest to offer
gift and sacrifice.

In place of the short responsory the following antiphon is said:
Ant. This is the day which was made by the Lord: let us rejoice and
be glad, alleluia.

Magnificat ant. Jesus met the women and gave them his greeting.
But they came up to him and grasped hold of his feet, alleluia.

Intercessions
Let us pray to Christ, who was raised up by the Holy Spirit in his
living and life-giving body. R/ Lord, renew the whole of your
creation.
Christ, Saviour of the world, king of the new creation, you are
enthroned at God's right hand;—set our hearts on the things that
are of heaven. R/
Lord, you are living always in your Church:—lead her through the

Holy Spirit into the fulness of your truth. R̷
Have pity on the sick, the distressed and the dying;—strengthen,
comfort and sustain them. R̷
Christ, unfailing light, accept our devotion at the close of this day;—
shed the radiance of your glory on the faithful departed. R̷
Our Father

The concluding prayer as at Morning Prayer, p 216.

TUESDAY

Invitatory ant. The Lord has truly risen, alleluia.

MORNING PRAYER

Hymn, antiphons, psalms and canticle as on Easter Sunday, pp 209 ff.

Scripture Reading   *Acts 13:30-33*
God raised Jesus from the dead and for many days he was seen by
those who had travelled with him from Galilee to Jerusalem. They
are now witnesses for him to the people of Israel. And we are here
to bring the Good News to you: what God promised our ancestors
he would do, he has now done for us, who are their descendants, by
raising Jesus to life. As it is written: You are my son, Today I have
become your Father.

In place of the short responsory the following antiphon is said:
Ant. This is the day which was made by the Lord: let us rejoice and
be glad, alleluia.

Benedictus ant. Jesus said, 'Mary!' She turned to him and said,
'Master'. He said to her, 'Do not hold on to me; I have not yet
ascended to my Father, alleluia.'

Intercessions
By his own power Christ rebuilt the temple of his body, when it was

217

torn down by death. Let us pray to him with joy. ℟ Lord, grant us the blessings of your resurrection.

Lord Jesus, in your risen body you brought the good news of salvation to the women and the apostles;—let us be your witnesses in this present age. ℟

You gave all men the promise of rising from the dead;—make us heralds of your gospel, bringing men new hope. ℟

You appeared to the apostles and breathed the Holy Spirit upon them;—pour out on us the Spirit who creates and renews. ℟

You promised to be with your disciples to the end of time;—stay with us throughout this day and remain with us for ever. ℟

Our Father

Concluding Prayer
Lord God,
you brought us healing through the Easter mysteries.
Continue to be bountiful to your people:
lead us to the perfect freedom,
by which the joy that gladdens our way on earth
will be fulfilled in heaven.
(We make our prayer) through our Lord.

EVENING PRAYER

Hymn, antiphons, psalms and canticle as on Easter Sunday, pp 211 ff.

Scripture Reading   *1 Pet 2:4-5*
He is the living stone, rejected by men, but chosen by God and precious to him; set yourselves close to him so that you too, the holy priesthood that offers the spiritual sacrifices which Jesus Christ has made acceptable to God, may be living stones making a spiritual house.

In place of the short responsory the following antiphon is said:
Ant. This is the day which was made by the Lord: let us rejoice and be glad, alleluia.

Magnificat ant. While I was weeping at the tomb, I saw the Lord, alleluia.

Intercessions

Rejoicing, let us pray to Christ who was buried in the heart of the earth to awake in the light of glory. ℞ King of glory, hear us.

We pray for bishops, priests and deacons: may they be dedicated to their ministry;—grant that they may present to you a people ready for every kind of good work. ℞

We pray for those who serve the Church as teachers of the faith:—may they always seek your truth with sincerity of heart. ℞

We pray for all the faithful: may they run the great race, finish the course;—let them receive the crown of victory in the kingdom of heaven. ℞

Lord, you cancelled on the cross our sentence of damnation;—free us from the darkness of our sins. ℞

You descended into hell and opened wide its gates;—receive the faithful departed into your Father's house. ℞

Our Father

The concluding prayer as at Morning Prayer, p 218.

WEDNESDAY

Invitatory ant. The Lord has truly risen, alleluia.

MORNING PRAYER

Hymn, antiphons, psalms and canticle as on Easter Sunday, pp 209 ff.

Scripture Reading   *Rom 6:8-11*

If we have died with Christ, we have faith to believe that we shall share his life. We know that Christ, now he has risen from the dead, cannot die any more; death has no more power over him; the death he died was a death, once for all, to sin; the life he now lives is a life that looks towards God. And you, too, must think of yourselves as dead to sin, and alive with a life that looks towards God, through Christ Jesus our Lord.

In place of the short responsory the following antiphon is said:
Ant. This is the day which was made by the Lord: let us rejoice and be glad, alleluia.

Benedictus ant. He began with Moses and the prophets, and explained to them everything that was written in the scriptures about himself, alleluia.

Intercessions
Let us pray to Christ, who was put to death for our sins and rose to life for our justification. R⁷ Lord, save us by your victory.
Christ our Saviour, you have overcome death to give us joy and have risen to lift us to the heights;—awaken our hearts and make us holy this day by the gift of the Spirit. R⁷
Angels in heaven praise you, men on earth adore you;—in this Easter season let us worship you in spirit and in truth. R⁷
Lord Jesus, look with kindness on your people who hope for the resurrection;—have mercy on us today and keep us from all evil. R⁷
Christ, our life, we look forward to the day of your coming;—let us appear with you and share in your glory. R⁷
Our Father

Concluding Prayer
God our Father,
you give us the joy
of celebrating our Lord's resurrection,
each passing year.
Let this yearly feast
bring us to eternal joy.
(We make our prayer) through our Lord.

EVENING PRAYER

Hymn, antiphons, psalms and canticle as on Easter Sunday, pp 211 ff.

Scripture Reading　　　*Heb 7:24-27*
Jesus, because he remains for ever, can never lose his priesthood. It follows, then, that his power to save is utterly certain, since he is

living for ever to intercede for all who come to God through him. To suit us, the ideal high priest would have to be holy, innocent and uncontaminated, beyond the influence of sinners, and raised up above the heavens; one who would not need to offer sacrifices every day, as the other high priests do for their own sins and then for those of the people, because he has done this once and for all by offering himself.

In place of the short responsory the following antiphon is said:
Ant. This is the day which was made by the Lord: let us rejoice and be glad, alleluia.

Magnificat ant. He went in to stay with them, and while they were sitting at table, he took the bread and said the blessing; then he broke it and handed it to them, alleluia.

Intercessions
Let us pray to Christ, who rose from the dead and is seated at the right hand of the Father. ℟ Ever-living Christ, hear us.
Lord, remember those who are consecrated to your service;—may they set before your holy people the example of their lives. ℟
Grant to those who rule us your spirit of justice and peace;—may men be united, heart and soul. ℟
Make our daily life a pilgrimage of salvation;—let the earth be rich and plentiful to meet the needs of the poor. ℟
Christ, our Saviour, light of the world, you have called all mortal men to imperishable life;—shed eternal light on our departed brothers. ℟
Our Father

The concluding prayer as at Morning Prayer, p 220.

THURSDAY

Invitatory ant. The Lord has truly risen, alleluia.

MORNING PRAYER
Hymn, antiphons, psalms and canticle as on Easter Sunday, pp 209 ff.

Scripture Reading   *Rom 8:10-11*

If Christ lives in you, then although the body be a dead thing in virtue of our guilt, the spirit is a living thing, by virtue of our justification. And if the Spirit of him who raised up Jesus from the dead dwells in you, he who raised up Jesus Christ from the dead will give life to your perishable bodies too, for the sake of his Spirit who dwells in you.

In place of the short responsory the following antiphon is said:
Ant. This is the day which was made by the Lord: let us rejoice and be glad, alleluia.

Benedictus ant. Jesus stood among the disciples and he said to them, 'Peace be with you, alleluia.'

Intercessions

Let us offer our prayer to Christ, who rose from the dead and is living always in his Church. ℟ Lord, stay always with us.

Lord, you triumphed over sin and death;—be present in our midst with your eternal life. ℟

Come to us with your untiring strength;—and reveal in our lives the loving-kindness of God. ℟

You alone can reconcile men and create a new spirit within them;—end the conflicts which divide our world. ℟

Deepen our faith in your final victory;—let us find strength in the hope of your coming. ℟

Our Father

Concluding Prayer

Lord God,
you have made one people
out of many different races and nations,
united through confessing the glory of your name.
They were born to new life in baptism:
let there be one faith in their hearts,
one love in their Christian way of life.
(We make our prayer) through our Lord.

EVENING PRAYER

Hymn, antiphons, psalms and canticle as on Easter Sunday, pp 211 ff.

Scripture Reading   *1 Pet 3:18-22*

Christ himself, innocent though he was, died once for sins, died for the guilty, to lead us to God. In the body, he was put to death, in the spirit he was raised to life. He has entered heaven and is at God's right hand, now that he has made the angels and Dominations and Powers his subjects.

In place of the short responsory the following antiphon is said:
Ant. This is the day which was made by the Lord: let us rejoice and be glad, alleluia.

Magnificat ant. Look at my hands and feet, and know that I am truly here, alleluia.

Intercessions

Christ has risen from the dead, the first-fruits of all who have fallen asleep. Let us praise him in our prayer. ℟ Risen Lord, hear us.

Lord, remember the Church you built on the apostles;—bless all those who believe in you. ℟

You are the healer of body and soul;—come to us with your salvation. ℟

Comfort the sick and renew their strength;—deliver them from all pain and distress. ℟

Help the anguished and the oppressed;—in your love uphold the needy. ℟

Through your cross and resurrection you have won immortal life; —grant to our dead the joys of your kingdom. ℟

Our Father

The concluding prayer as at Morning Prayer, p 222.

FRIDAY

Invitatory ant. The Lord has truly risen, alleluia.

MORNING PRAYER

Hymn, antiphons, psalms and canticle as on Easter Sunday, pp 209 ff.

Scripture Reading   *Acts 5:30-32*

The God of our fathers raised Jesus from death, after you had killed him by nailing him to a cross. And God raised him to his right side as Leader and Saviour, to give to the people of Israel the opportunity to repent and have their sins forgiven. We are witnesses to these things—we and the Holy Spirit, who is God's gift to those who obey him.

In place of the short responsory the following antiphon is said:
Ant. This is the day which was made by the Lord: let us rejoice and be glad, alleluia.

Benedictus ant. This was the third time that Jesus showed himself to his disciples after rising from the dead, alleluia.

Intercessions

Let us pray to God the Father, who has given us new life through the resurrection of Christ. ℟ Make us radiant with Christ's glory.
Almighty God, creator of the world, you revealed the old covenant by your mighty deeds and were faithful to men down through the ages;—loving Father, hear the prayer of your children. ℟
Cleanse our hearts by your truth and guide our lives by your holiness;—may we do what is right and pleasing to you. ℟
Let the light of your face shine upon us;—free us from sin and fill us with your goodness. ℟
Peace was your Son's parting gift to the apostles;—grant your peace to us and to people everywhere. ℟
Our Father

Concluding Prayer

Almighty, ever-living God,
you offer the covenant of reconciliation to mankind
in the mystery of Easter.

Grant that what we celebrate in worship,
we may carry out in our lives.
(We make our prayer) through our Lord.

EVENING PRAYER

Hymns, antiphons, psalms and canticle as on Easter Sunday, pp 211 ff.

Scripture Reading   *Heb 5:8-10*
Although he was Son, Christ learnt to obey through suffering; but
having been made perfect, he became for all who obey him the
source of eternal salvation and was acclaimed by God with the title
of high priest of the order of Melchizedek.

In place of the short responsory the following antiphon is said:
Ant. This is the day which was made by the Lord: let us rejoice and
be glad, alleluia.

Magnificat ant. That disciple whom Jesus loved said, 'It is the Lord,'
alleluia.

Intercessions
Let us pray to Christ, the way, the truth and the life. R⁄ Son of the
living God, bless your people.
We pray for all the ministers of your Church:—may they be nourish-
ed and sustained as they break for their brothers the bread of life.
R⁄
We pray for the whole Christian people:—may they be faithful to
their calling and hold fast in bonds of peace the unity of the spirit. R⁄
We pray for those who govern our country that they may exercise
their office with justice and compassion;—help them to promote the
peace of the world. R⁄
Make us worthy to adore you in the communion of saints;—grant
eternal joy to the faithful departed, whom we entrust to your care. R⁄
Our Father

The concluding prayer as at Morning Prayer, p 224.

SATURDAY

Invitatory ant. The Lord has truly risen, alleluia.

MORNING PRAYER

Hymn, antiphons, psalms and canticle as on Easter Sunday, pp 209 ff.

Scripture Reading   *Rom 14:7-9*
None of us lives for himself only, none of us dies for himself only; if we live, it is for the Lord that we live, and if we die, it is for the Lord that we die. Whether we live or die, then, we belong to the Lord. For Christ died and rose to life in order to be the Lord of the living and of the dead.

In place of the short responsory the following antiphon is said:
Ant. This is the day which was made by the Lord: let us rejoice and be glad, alleluia.

Benedictus ant. When Jesus had risen from the dead early on the Sunday morning, he appeared first to Mary Magdalen, from whom he had cast out seven devils; alleluia.

Intercessions
Christ is the bread of life and he will raise up on the last day those who are nourished by his word and his body. ℟ Lord, give us peace and joy.
Son of God, risen from the dead, you are the Lord of life;—bless all our brothers and make us holy. ℟
You are the peace and joy of all who believe in you;—help us to live as children of light, rejoicing in your victory. ℟
May your pilgrim Church grow in faith;—strengthen us to bear witness before the world to your resurrection. ℟
You underwent great sufferings to enter the Father's glory;—wipe away all tears and turn sorrow into joy. ℟
Our Father

Concluding Prayer
Lord God,
you increase and multiply your faithful
by your abundant gift of grace.
Look now on your chosen people,
and clothe for ever in the garment of eternal life
all those who have been reborn in baptism.
(We make our prayer) through our Lord.

LOW SUNDAY
THE OCTAVE DAY OF EASTER
Sunday 2 of Eastertide

EVENING PRAYER I

Hymn, antiphons, psalms and canticle as on Easter Sunday, pp 211 ff.

Scripture Reading   *I Pet 2:9-10*
You are a chosen race, a royal priesthood, a consecrated nation, a
people set apart to sing the praises of God who called you out of
darkness into his wonderful light. Once you were not a people at all,
and now you are the people of God; once you were outside the mercy
and now you have been given mercy.

In place of the short responsory the following antiphon is said:
Ant. This is the day which was made by the Lord: let us rejoice and
be glad, alleluia.

Magnificat ant. Eight days later, though the doors were locked,
Jesus entered and said to them, 'Peace be with you, alleluia.'

Intercessions
Let us pray to Christ, who rose from the dead to restore our life.
℟ Ever-living Christ, hear us.
Jesus, you are the stone rejected by the builders but you have proved

227

to be the keystone of God's house;—make us living stones in the temple of your Church. R̷ Ever-living Christ, hear us.

You are the faithful and true witness, the first-born from the dead; —may the Church never cease to proclaim you to the world. R̷

Through your death and resurrection you took the Church to yourself as a bride:—cherish her, and keep her faithful, and prepare her for the day of your coming. R̷

You are the first and the last, you were dead and now you are alive; —may all the baptized be faithful unto death and gain the crown of glory. R̷

You are the light and joy of the city of God;—shine on the faithful departed that they may reign for ever. R̷

Our Father

Concluding Prayer

God of eternal compassion,
each Easter you rekindle the faith of your consecrated people.
Give them still greater grace,
so that all may truly understand
the waters in which they were cleansed,
the Spirit by which they were reborn,
the blood by which they were redeemed.
(We make our prayer) through our Lord.

Invitatory

Ant. The Lord has truly risen, alleluia.

MORNING PRAYER

Hymn, antiphons, psalms and canticle as on Easter Sunday, pp 209 ff.

Scripture Reading   *Acts 10:40-43*

God raised Jesus from death on the third day and caused him to appear. He was not seen by all the people, but only by us who are the witnesses that God had already chosen. We ate and drank with him after God raised him from death. And he commanded us to preach the gospel to the people, and to testify that he is the one whom God has appointed Judge of the living and the dead. All the prophets spoke about him, saying that everyone who believes in him will have his sins forgiven through the power of his name.

In place of the short responsory the following antiphon is said:
Ant. This is the day which was made by the Lord: let us rejoice and be glad, alleluia.

Benedictus ant. Put your hand here and see the mark of the nails; doubt no longer but believe, alleluia.

Intercessions
Let us pray to the Father, the all-powerful God, who raised up Jesus, our prince and our Saviour. R̸ Glorify us, Lord, with the glory of Christ.
Father, you brought your beloved Son from the darkness of death to the light of glory;—let us enter into the regions of your own wonderful light. R̸
You saved us through faith in Jesus Christ;—help us to live today in the grace of our baptism. R̸
You have told us to seek the things that are in heaven;—enable us to resist the attraction of sin. R̸
Reveal the riches of our hidden life in Christ—that men may see the signs of the new heaven and the new earth. R̸
Our Father

Concluding Prayer
God of eternal compassion,
each Easter you rekindle the faith of your consecrated people.
Give them still greater grace,
so that all may truly understand
the waters in which they were cleansed,
the Spirit by which they were reborn,
the blood by which they were redeemed.
(We make our prayer) through our Lord.

EVENING PRAYER II

Hymn, antiphons, psalms and canticle as on Easter Sunday, pp 211 ff.

Scripture Reading   *Heb 10:12-14*

Christ has offered one single sacrifice for sins, and then taken his place for ever at the right hand of God, where he is now waiting until his enemies are made into a footstool for him. By virtue of that one single offering he has achieved the eternal perfection of all whom he is sanctifying.

In place of the short responsory the following antiphon is said:
Ant. This is the day which was made by the Lord: let us rejoice and be glad, alleluia.

Magnificat ant. You believe because you have seen me, Thomas. Blessed are those who have never seen me and yet believe.

Intercessions

Let us pray to God the Father, who raised Jesus to life and exalted him at his own right hand. ℟ Lord, protect your people through the glory of Christ.

Father, through the victory of the cross you have lifted up Jesus from the earth;—may he draw all men to himself. ℟

Through the exaltation of Christ send your Spirit into the Church; —make her the sign of unity for the whole human family. ℟

You have become the Father of men through water and the Spirit; —keep them faithful to their baptism until they enter eternal life. ℟

Through the exaltation of your Son raise up the sorrowful, set prisoners free, heal the sick;—may the whole world rejoice in your wonderful gifts. ℟

You nourished the faithful departed with Christ's body and blood; —let them share in his glory on the day of resurrection. ℟

Our Father

The concluding prayer as at Morning Prayer, p 229.

Concluding invitation: Go in the peace of Christ, alleluia, alleluia.
℟ Thanks be to God, alleluia, alleluia.

The end of the Easter Octave.

¶ *The Ordinary for Weeks 2 to 6 of Eastertide will be found on pp 238ff, immediately after the Ordinary for Sundays 3 to 6.*

Ordinary for Eastertide 1: to the Ascension
WEEKS 3 TO 6: SUNDAYS

Sunday 3: Psalter Week 3
Sunday 4: Psalter Week 4
Sunday 5: Psalter Week 1
Sunday 6: Psalter Week 2

EVENING PRAYER I

Hymn, from the appendix, for Eastertide.
Psalms and canticle with proper antiphons as in the psalter.

Scripture Reading   *1 Pet 2:9-10*
You are a chosen race, a royal priesthood, a consecrated nation, a people set apart to sing the praises of God who called you out of darkness into his wonderful light. Once you were not a people at all, and now you are the people of God; once you were outside the mercy and now you have been given mercy.

Short Responsory
℟ The disciples rejoiced, alleluia, alleluia. *Repeat* ℟
℣ They saw the Lord. ℟ Glory be. ℟

Magnificat Antiphon
Sunday 3: Stay with us, Lord, for evening is approaching and the day is almost over, alleluia.

Sunday 4: I am the door, says the Lord. Anyone who enters through me shall be safe and he will find a place of pasture, alleluia.

Sunday 5: I am the Way, the Truth, and the Life. No one can come to the Father except through me, alleluia.

Sunday 6: I shall ask the Father, and he will give you another Advocate, to be with you for ever, alleluia.

Intercessions

Sundays 3 and 5

Let us pray to Christ, our life and our resurrection. ℟ Son of the living God, protect your people.

We pray for your Catholic Church;—may she reveal among the nations your kingdom of justice and holiness. ℟

We pray for the sick, the sorrowful, captives and exiles:—show them your power and compassion. ℟

We pray for those who have lost you in the maze of life:—let them know once more the joy of coming home. ℟

Crucified and risen Saviour, you will come again in judgment:—be merciful to us sinners. ℟

We pray for all the living,—and for those who have left this world in the hope of the resurrection. ℟

Our Father

Sundays 4 and 6

Let us pray to Christ, who rose from the dead to restore our life. ℟ Ever-living Christ, hear our prayer.

Jesus, you are the stone rejected by the builders but you have proved to be the keystone of God's house;—make us living stones in the temple of your Church. ℟

You are the faithful and true witness, the first-born from the dead; —may the Church never cease to proclaim you to the world. ℟

Through your death and resurrection you took the Church to yourself as a bride;—cherish her, and keep her faithful, and prepare her for the day of your coming. ℟

You are the first and the last, you were dead and now you are alive; —may all the baptized be faithful unto death and gain the crown of eternal life. ℟

You are the light and joy of the city of God;—shine on the faithful departed that they may reign for ever. ℟

Our Father

Concluding Prayer

Sunday 3: Lord God,
grant your people constant joy
in the renewed vigour of their souls.
They rejoice because you have restored them
to the glory of your adopted children:
let them look forward gladly
in the certain hope of resurrection.
(We make our prayer) through our Lord.

Sunday 4: Almighty, ever-living God,
bring us to the joy of your heavenly city:
so that we, your little flock,
may follow where Christ, our Good Shepherd,
has gone before us by the power of his resurrection.
(We make our prayer) through our Lord.

Sunday 5: Since it is from you, God our Father,
that redemption comes to us, your adopted children:
look with favour on the family you love,
give true freedom to us and to all who believe in Christ,
and bring us all alike to our eternal heritage.
(We make our prayer) through our Lord.

Sunday 6: Almighty God,
give us the grace of an attentive love
to celebrate these days of joy
devoted to the honour of the Risen Lord.
Teach us to hold fast in our actions
to the mystery we recall in worship.
(We make our prayer) through our Lord.

Invitatory

Ant. The Lord has truly risen, alleluia.

233

MORNING PRAYER

Hymn, from the appendix, for Eastertide.
Psalms and canticle with proper antiphons as in the psalter.

Scripture Reading   *Acts 10:40-43*

God raised Jesus from death on the third day and caused him to appear. He was not seen by all the people, but only by us who are the witnesses that God had already chosen. We ate and drank with him after God raised him from death. And he commanded us to preach the gospel to the people, and to testify that he is the one whom God has appointed Judge of the living and the dead. All the prophets spoke about him, saying that everyone who believes in him will have his sins forgiven through the power of his name.

Short Responsory

R7 Have mercy on us, Christ, Son of the living God, alleluia, alleluia.
Repeat R7
V7 You have risen from the dead. R7 Glory be. R7

Benedictus Antiphon

Sunday 3: It was necessary that Christ should suffer and on the third day rise from the dead, alleluia.

Sunday 4: I am the shepherd of the flock; I am the way, the truth and the life; I am the good shepherd; I know my own and mine know me, alleluia.

Sunday 5: Whoever remains in me, and I in him, bears fruit in plenty, says the Lord, alleluia.

Sunday 6: As the Father has loved me, so I have loved you. Remain in my love, alleluia.

Intercessions

Sundays 3 and 5

Let us pray to Christ, the author of life. God raised him from the dead, and he himself will raise us to life by his own power. R7 Christ, our life, save us.
Christ, you are the light that drives out darkness and draws men to

holiness;—let us make this day a living hymn of praise. ℟
Lord, you followed the way of suffering, even to the cross;—grant
that we may die with you and come to life with you. ℟
Our master and our brother, you have made us a kingdom of priests
to serve God our Father;—let us offer to you with joy the sacrifice of
praise. ℟
King of glory, we look forward to the day of your coming;—grant
that we may see your face and share in your splendour. ℟
Our Father

Sundays 4 and 6
Let us pray to the Father, the all-powerful God, who raised up
Jesus, our prince and our Saviour. ℟ Glorify us, Lord, with the
glory of Christ.
Father, you brought your beloved Son from the darkness of death
to the light of glory;—let us enter into the regions of your own
wonderful light. ℟
You saved us through faith in Jesus Christ;—help us to live today
in the grace of our baptism. ℟
You have told us to seek the things that are in heaven,—grant that
we may resist the attraction of sin. ℟
Reveal the riches of our hidden life in Christ;—enable men to see
the signs of the new heaven and the new earth. ℟
Our Father

Concluding Prayer
Sunday 3: Lord God,
grant your people constant joy
in the renewed vigour of their souls.
They rejoice because you have restored them
to the glory of your adopted children:
let them look forward gladly
in the certain hope of resurrection.
(We make our prayer) through our Lord.

Sunday 4: Almighty, ever-living God,
bring us to the joy of your heavenly city:
so that we, your little flock,

may follow where Christ, our Good Shepherd,
has gone before us by the power of his resurrection.
(We make our prayer) through our Lord.

Sunday 5: Since it is from you, God our Father,
that redemption comes to us, your adopted children:
look with favour on the family you love,
give true freedom to us and to all who believe in Christ,
and bring us all alike to our eternal heritage.
(We make our prayer) through our Lord.

Sunday 6: Almighty God,
give us the grace of an attentive love
to celebrate these days of joy
devoted to the honour of the Risen Lord.
Teach us to hold fast in our actions
to the mystery we recall in worship.
(We make our prayer) through our Lord.

EVENING PRAYER II

Hymn, from the appendix, for Eastertide.
Psalms and canticle with proper antiphons as in the psalter.

Scripture Reading   *Heb 10:12-14*
Christ has offered one single sacrifice for sins, and then taken his
place for ever at the right hand of God, where he is now waiting
until his enemies are made into a footstool for him. By virtue of
that one single offering he has achieved the eternal perfection of all
whom he is sanctifying.

Short Responsory
R̸ The Lord has truly risen, alleluia, alleluia. *Repeat* R̸
V̸ He has appeared to Simon. R̸ Glory be. R̸

Magnificat Antiphon
Sunday 3: Jesus said to his disciples, 'Bring some of the fish you
have just caught.' Simon Peter went aboard and dragged the net to
the shore, full of fish, alleluia.

Sunday 4: The sheep that belong to me listen to my voice; and I, the Lord, know them, alleluia.

Sunday 5: I give you a new commandment: love one another, as I have loved you, says the Lord, alleluia.

Sunday 6: If anyone loves me he will keep my word, and my Father will love him, and we shall come to him and make our home with him, alleluia.

Intercessions
Sundays 3 and 5
Let us pray with joy to Christ the Lord. He rose from the dead and is living now to intercede for us. R⁷ Victorious king, hear us.
Christ, you are the light of the world and the salvation of nations; —set us on fire with your Spirit as we proclaim the wonder of your resurrection. R⁷
Let Israel recognize in you the Messiah they have longed for:—fill all men with the knowledge of your glory. R⁷
Keep us united in the communion of saints;—may we find rest with them, when life's work is done. R⁷
You have overcome death, the last enemy of man;—destroy everything in us that is at enmity with God. R⁷
Christ, our Saviour, you became obedient to death, but God raised you to the heights;—receive our brothers into the kingdom of your glory. R⁷
Our Father

Sundays 4 and 6
Let us pray to God the Father, who raised Jesus to life and exalted him at his own right hand. R⁷ Lord, protect your people through the glory of Christ.
Father, through the victory of the cross you have lifted up Jesus from the earth;—may he draw all men to himself. R⁷
Through the exaltation of Christ send your Spirit into the Church; —make her the sign of unity for the whole human family. R⁷
You have become the Father of men through water and the Spirit; —keep them faithful to their baptism until they enter eternal life. R⁷
Through the exaltation of your Son raise up the sorrowful, set prisoners free, heal the sick;—may the whole world rejoice in your

wonderful gifts. ℟ Lord, protect your people through the glory of Christ.

You nourished the faithful departed with Christ's body and blood; —let them share in his glory on the day of resurrection. ℟

Our Father

The concluding prayer as at Morning Prayer, pp 235–6.

Ordinary for Eastertide 1: to the Ascension

WEEKS 2 TO 6: MONDAYS

Weeks 2 and 6: Psalter, Week 2
Week 3: Psalter, Week 3
Week 4: Psalter, Week 4
Week 5: Psalter, Week 1

Invitatory ant. The Lord has truly risen, alleluia.

MORNING PRAYER

Hymn, from the appendix, for Eastertide.
Psalms and canticle with the antiphons for Eastertide as in the psalter.

Scripture Reading   *Rom 10:8b–10*

It is on your lips, it is in your heart, meaning by that the message of faith which we preach. You can find salvation, if you will use your lips to confess that Jesus is the Lord, and your heart to believe that God has raised him up from the dead. The heart has only to believe, if we are to be justified; the lips have only to make confession, if we are to be saved.

Short Responsory

℟ The Lord has risen from the dead, alleluia, alleluia. *Repeat* ℟

℣ For our sake he died on the cross. ℟ Glory be. ℟

Benedictus Antiphon

Week 2: I tell you solemnly, unless a man is born again he cannot see the kingdom of God, alleluia.

238

Week 3: Work not for the food that cannot last, but work for food that endures to eternal life, alleluia.

Week 4: I am the good shepherd: I feed my sheep, and I lay down my life for them, alleluia.

Week 5: Anyone who loves me will be loved by my Father, and I shall love him and show myself to him, alleluia.

Week 6: God gave us new birth as his sons and daughters, by raising Jesus Christ from the dead, so that we have a sure hope and the promise of an inheritance that will never perish, alleluia.

Intercessions
Weeks 2, 4 and 6
Let us pray to the Father, whose glory was displayed in the death and resurrection of his Son. R℣ Lord, enlighten our minds and hearts.
God, Father of light, you have illumined the world with the glory of Christ;—may the light of faith shine in our lives today. R℣
Through the resurrection of your Son you have opened man's way to everlasting life;—may all our work today be filled with the hope of your kingdom. R℣
Through your risen Son you sent the Holy Spirit into the world;—set our hearts on fire with his divine love. R℣
By hanging on the cross, your Son won our lasting freedom;—may he stay with us today as our Saviour and Redeemer. R℣
Our Father

Weeks 3 and 5
The Father has glorified Jesus and handed over to him the whole of creation. Let us praise him in our morning prayer. R℣ Lord, save us through your victory.
Lord Jesus, you have broken the power of hell, destroying sin and death;—do not let us be defeated in our struggle with temptation. R℣
You have ended death for ever and given us new life;—guide our steps today along the path that leads to God. R℣
You rose from the dead to renew all men;—grant eternal life to everyone we meet. R℣
The disciples rejoiced, when you came back from the grave;—fill the

hearts of your servants with overflowing joy. ℟ Lord, save us through your victory.
Our Father

Concluding Prayer

Week 2: Almighty, ever-living God,
we confidently call you Father as well as Lord.
Renew your Spirit in our hearts,
make us ever more perfectly your children,
so that we may enter upon the inheritance you have promised us.
(We make our prayer) through our Lord.

Week 3: God and Father,
to those who go astray you reveal the light of your truth
and enable them to return to the right path:
grant that all who have received the grace of baptism
may strive to be worthy of their Christian calling,
and reject everything opposed to it.
(We make our prayer) through our Lord.

Week 4: Almighty God and Father,
through your Son's self-abasement
you raised up the world when it lay prostrate.
You have rescued your faithful from enslavement to sin:
fill them with a holy joy,
and give them happiness for ever.
(We make our prayer) through our Lord.

Week 5: Lord, by your grace we are made one in mind and heart.
Give us a love for what you command
and a longing for what you promise,
so that, amid this world's changes,
our hearts may be set on the world of lasting joy.
(We make our prayer) through our Lord.

Week 6: God of mercy,
let the mystery we celebrate at Eastertide
bear fruit for us in every season.
(We make our prayer) through our Lord.

EVENING PRAYER

Hymn, from the appendix, for Eastertide.
Psalms and canticle with antiphons for Eastertide as in the psalter.

Scripture Reading   *Heb 8:1b-3a*
This high priest of ours is one who has taken his seat in heaven, on the right hand of that throne where God sits in majesty, ministering now in the sanctuary, in that true tabernacle which the Lord, not man, has set up. After all, it is the very function of a priest to offer gift and sacrifice.

Short Responsory
R̥ The disciples rejoiced, alleluia, alleluia. *Repeat* R̥
y̥ They saw the Lord. R̥ Glory be. R̥

Magnificat Antiphon
Week 2: What is born of the flesh is flesh; what is born of the Spirit is spirit, alleluia.

Week 3: This is the work that God requires: believe in the one whom he has sent, alleluia.

Week 4: I have other sheep that are not of this fold, and these I must also lead. They too will listen to my voice, and there will be only one flock, and one shepherd, alleluia.

Week 5: The Holy Spirit, the Advocate, whom the Father will send in my name, will teach you everything and remind you of all I have said to you, alleluia.

Week 6: The Spirit of truth who comes from the Father will be my witness. And you also will be my witnesses, alleluia.

Intercessions
Weeks 2, 4 and 6
Rejoicing, let us pray to Christ the Lord, who sheds glory on the universe through his resurrection. R̥ Christ, our life, hear us.
Lord Jesus, you joined your disciples on the way to Emmaus;—accompany your Church on her journey through life. R̥

241

May we, your faithful, not be slow to believe;—give us the courage to proclaim your victory over death. ℞ Christ, our life, hear us.

Look upon those who have not recognized your presence in their lives;—let their hearts rejoice in the knowledge of their Saviour. ℞ You are the judge of the living and the dead;—grant to the faithful departed forgiveness of their sins. ℞

Our Father

Weeks 3 and 5

Let us pray to Christ, who was raised up by the Holy Spirit in his living and life-giving body. ℞ Lord, renew the whole of your creation.

Christ, Saviour of the world, king of the new creation, you are enthroned at God's right hand;—set our hearts on the things that are in heaven. ℞

Lord, you are living always in your Church:—lead her through the Holy Spirit into the fulness of your truth. ℞

Have pity on the sick, the distressed and the dying;—strengthen, comfort and sustain them. ℞

Christ, unfailing light, accept our devotion at the close of this day; —shed the radiance of your glory on the faithful departed. ℞

Our Father

The concluding prayer as at Morning Prayer, p 240.

WEEKS 2 TO 6: TUESDAYS

Invitatory ant. The Lord has truly risen, alleluia.

MORNING PRAYER

Hymn, from the appendix, for Eastertide.

Scripture Reading   *Acts 13:30-33*

God raised Jesus from the dead and for many days he was seen by those who had travelled with him from Galilee to Jerusalem. They are now witnesses for him to the people of Israel. And we are here to bring the Good News to you: what God promised our ancestors he would do, he has now done for us, who are their descendants, by raising Jesus to life. As it is written: You are my son, Today I have become your Father.

Short Responsory
℟ The Lord has risen from the dead, alleluia, alleluia. *Repeat* ℟
℣ For our sake he died on the cross. ℟ Glory be. ℟

Benedictus Antiphon
Week 2: I am the Alpha and the Omega, the beginning and the end; I am of the house and family of David, the bright star of the morning, alleluia.

Week 3: I tell you solemnly, Moses did not give you bread from heaven; it is my Father who gives you the true bread from heaven, alleluia.

Week 4: The works I do in my Father's name are my witness, alleluia.

Week 5: Peace I leave you, alleluia; it is my own peace I give you, alleluia.

Week 6: In a short time the world will no longer see me; but you will see me, because I live and you will live, alleluia.

Intercessions
Weeks 2, 4 and 6
Let us pray to God the Father, whose Son became the Lamb without blemish to take away the sins of the world. ℟ God of life, save us.
Father, be mindful of your Son, who died on the cross and was raised again to life;—hear him interceding for us now. ℟
Let us cast out the leaven of corruption and malice;—let us celebrate Christ's passover in purity and truth. ℟
May we overcome today all envy and dissension;—help us to take care of our brothers in their every need. ℟
Place deep in our hearts the spirit of the gospel;—may it inspire us to keep your commandments today and always. ℟
Our Father

Weeks 3 and 5

By his own power Christ rebuilt the temple of his body, when it was torn down by death. Let us pray to him with joy. R̹ Lord, grant us the blessings of your resurrection.

Lord Jesus, in your risen body you brought the good news of salvation to the women and the apostles;—let us be your witnesses in this present age. R̹

You gave all men the promise of rising from the dead;—make us heralds of your gospel, bringing men new hope. R̹

You appeared to the apostles and breathed the Holy Spirit upon them;—pour out on us the Spirit who creates and renews. R̹

You promised to be with your disciples to the end of time;—stay with us throughout this day and remain with us for ever. R̹

Our Father

Concluding Prayer

Week 2: Almighty God,
give your Church the grace
to proclaim the power of Jesus, our Risen Lord.
We have received the first fruits of his grace:
prepare us for the full revelation of his gifts.
(We make our prayer) through our Lord.

Week 3: God our Father,
you open the gates of the kingdom of heaven
to those who are born again of water and the Holy Spirit.
Increase the grace you have given,
so that the people who have purified from all sin
may not forfeit the promised blessings of your love.
(We make our prayer) through our Lord.

Week 4: Grant, we pray, almighty God,
that we who celebrate the mystery of our Lord's resurrection,
may enter upon the joy of our redemption.
(We make our prayer) through our Lord.

Week 5: Lord our God,
in the resurrection of Christ

you create us anew for eternal life.
Grant your people firmness in faith and constancy in hope.
Let us never doubt that you will fulfil
what we know you have promised.
(We make our prayer) through our Lord.

Week 6: Lord God,
grant your people constant joy
in the renewed vigour of their souls.
They rejoice because you have restored them
to the glory of your adopted children:
let them look forward gladly
in the certain hope of resurrection.
(We make our prayer) through our Lord.

EVENING PRAYER

Hymn, from the appendix, for Eastertide.

Scripture Reading   *1 Pet 2:4-5*
He is the living stone, rejected by men, but chosen by God and
precious to him; set yourselves close to him so that you too, the
holy priesthood that offers the spiritual sacrifices which Jesus Christ
has made acceptable to God, may be living stones making a spiritual
house.

Short Responsory
R̸ The disciples rejoiced, alleluia, alleluia. *Repeat* R̸
V̸ They saw the Lord. R̸ Glory be. R̸

Magnificat Antiphon
Week 2: Did not our hearts burn within us as Jesus talked to us
on the road, alleluia.

Week 3: The bread of God is that which came down from heaven
and gives life to the world, alleluia.

Week 4: I know my sheep and they follow me. I give them eternal
life, alleluia.

245

Week 5: If you loved me you would be glad that I am going to the Father, alleluia.

Week 6: I tell you the truth: it is for your good that I am going because unless I go, the Advocate will not come, alleluia.

Intercessions
Weeks 2, 4 and 6
Let us pray to Christ, who by his resurrection strengthens his people in hope. ℟ Ever-living Christ, hear us.
Lord Jesus, from your opened side there poured out blood and water;—cleanse the Church, your bride, from every stain of sin. ℟
Good shepherd, risen from the dead, you gave to the apostle Peter the care of your flock;—may Pope N. be ever strengthened in charity and zeal. ℟
Beside the lake of Galilee, you directed your disciples to a great catch of fish;—direct the work of your disciples today, and give them your abundant blessing. ℟
On the shore of the lake you prepared food for your disciples;—help us to find your joy in caring for others. ℟
Jesus, the last Adam, life-giving Spirit, conform the dead to your likeness;—make their joy complete. ℟
Our Father

Weeks 3 and 5
Rejoicing, let us pray to Christ who was buried in the heart of the earth to awake in the light of glory. ℟ King of glory, hear us.
We pray for bishops, priests and deacons: may they be dedicated to their ministry;—grant that they may present to you a people ready for every kind of good work. ℟
We pray for those who serve the Church as teachers of the faith;—may they always seek your truth with sincerity of heart. ℟
We pray for all the faithful: may they run the great race, finish the course;—let them receive the crown of victory in the kingdom of heaven. ℟
Lord, you cancelled on the cross our sentence of damnation;—free us from the darkness of our sins. ℟
You descended into hell and opened wide its gates;—receive the

faithful departed into your Father's house. R℞
Our Father

The concluding prayer as at Morning Prayer, pp 244–5.

WEEKS 2 TO 6: WEDNESDAYS

Invitatory ant. The Lord has truly risen, alleluia.

MORNING PRAYER

Hymn, from the appendix, for Eastertide.

Scripture Reading   *Rom 6:8-11*
If we have died with Christ, we have faith to believe that we shall
share his life. We know that Christ, now he has risen from the dead,
cannot die any more; death has no more power over him; the death
he died was a death, once for all, to sin; the life he now lives is a life
that looks towards God. And you, too, must think of yourselves as
dead to sin, and alive with a life that looks towards God, through
Christ Jesus our Lord.

Short Responsory
R℞ The Lord has risen from the dead, alleluia, alleluia. *Repeat* R℞
℣ For our sake he died on the cross. R℞ Glory be. R℞

Benedictus Antiphon
Week 2: God loved the world so much that he gave his only Son,
so that everyone who believes in him may not be lost but may have
eternal life, alleluia.

Week 3: Anyone who sees the Son and believes in him has eternal
life, and I will raise him up on the last day, alleluia.

Week 4: I, the Light, have come into the world, so that whoever
believes in me will stay in the darkness no more, alleluia.

Week 5: I am the true vine, alleluia; you are the branches, alleluia.

Week 6: I still have many things to say to you but they would be too much for you now. When the Spirit of truth comes he will lead you to the complete truth, alleluia.

Intercessions
Weeks 2, 4 and 6
Let us pray to God, who manifested to the apostles the glory of the risen Christ. ℟ Glorify us. Lord, with the glory of Christ.
Father, we praise you today with grateful hearts, because you have called us into your own marvellous light;—help us always to see your loving-kindness. ℟
Through your Holy Spirit strengthen and purify men;—give them new heart in their struggle to improve the quality of life. ℟
May we pour out our lives in the service of men:—bless our efforts, that the whole of humanity may become a sacrifice acceptable to you. ℟
At the start of the day fill our hearts with your love;—let the praise of your glory be the joy of our lives. ℟
Our Father

Weeks 3 and 5
Let us pray to Christ, who was put to death for our sins and rose to life for our justification. ℟ Lord, save us by your victory.
Christ our Saviour, you have overcome death to give us joy and have risen to lift us to the heights;—awaken our hearts and make us holy this day by the gift of the Spirit. ℟
Angels in heaven praise you, men on earth adore you;—in this Easter season let us worship you in spirit and in truth. ℟
Lord Jesus, look with kindness on your people who hope for the resurrection;—have mercy on us today and keep us from all evil. ℟
Christ, our life, we look forward to the day of your coming;—let us appear with you and share in your glory. ℟
Our Father

Concluding Prayer
Week 2: Year by year, Lord,
we recall the mystery of Easter,
the mystery which restored mankind to its lost dignity

and brought the hope of resurrection.
Grant that we may possess eternally in love
what we now worship in faith.
(We make our prayer) through our Lord.

Week 3: Lord God,
stand by your people
on whom you have bestowed the gift of faith.
Grant them their eternal heritage
in the resurrection of your only Son.
(We make our prayer) through our Lord.

Week 4: Lord God, life of those who believe in you,
glory of the humble and happiness of the saints,
listen kindly to our prayer.
We long for what you promise;
fill us from your abundance.
(We make our prayer) through our Lord.

Week 5: Lord our God,
you love innocence of heart,
you restore it when we have lost it.
Lead the hearts of your devoted people to yourself,
so that freed from the blindness of unbelief,
they may never abandon the light of your truth.
(We make our prayer) through our Lord.

Week 6: God and Father,
we honour the yearly feast of your Son's resurrection
by celebrating it in the sacramental mystery.
Give us likewise the grace
to rejoice with all the saints
when he comes in glory.
(We make our prayer) through our Lord.

Week 6

A *Where the Solemnity of the Ascension is celebrated on the Thursday of Week 6: Evening Prayer as on pp 263 ff.*

B *Where the Solemnity of the Ascension is celebrated on Sunday 7 of Eastertide the Office is said as follows:*

EVENING PRAYER

Hymn, from the appendix, for Eastertide.

Scripture Reading   *Heb 7:24-27*

Jesus, because he remains for ever, can never lose his priesthood. It follows, then, that his power to save is utterly certain, since he is living for ever to intercede for all who come to God through him. To suit us, the ideal high priest would have to be holy, innocent and uncontaminated, beyond the influence of sinners, and raised up above the heavens; one who would not need to offer sacrifices every day, as the other high priests do for their own sins and then for those of the people, because he has done this once and for all by offering himself.

Short Responsory

R̷ The disciples rejoiced, alleluia, alleluia. *Repeat* R̷
У They saw the Lord. R̷ Glory be. R̷

Magnificat Antiphon

Week 2: The man who lives by the truth comes into the light, so that it may be plainly seen that what he does is done in God, alleluia.

Week 3: All that the Father gives me will come to me, and whoever comes to me I shall not turn away, alleluia.

Week 4: God sent his Son into the world not to condemn the world, but so that the world might be saved through him, alleluia.

Week 5: If you remain in me and my words remain in you, you may ask for what you will and you shall have it, alleluia.

Week 6B: The Spirit will glorify me, since all he tells you will be taken from what is mine, alleluia.

Intercessions

Weeks 2, 4 and 6B

In Christ, who was raised from the dead, the Father has opened for us the way to eternal life. Let us pray to him: R̦ Save your people through the victory of Christ.

God of our fathers, in the resurrection you glorified your Son;—grant us true repentance that we may walk in newness of life. R̦

You have brought us to Christ, the shepherd and guardian of our souls;—keep us faithful to him, under the guidance of our pastors. R̦

From the Jewish people you chose Christ's first disciples;—show the children of Israel that your promises are fulfilled. R̦

Remember the orphans, the widows and the homeless of our world;—your Son has reconciled men with God, do not abandon them now. R̦

You called Stephen to yourself as he bore witness to Jesus;—welcome the faithful departed who have loved and desired you. R̦

Our Father

Weeks 3 and 5

Let us pray to Christ, who rose from the dead and is seated at the right hand of the Father. R̦ Ever-living Christ, hear us.

Lord, remember those who are consecrated to your service;—may they set before your holy people the example of their lives. R̦

Grant to those who rule us your spirit of justice and peace;—may men be united, heart and soul. R̦

Make our daily life a pilgrimage of salvation;—let the earth be rich and plentiful to meet the needs of the poor. R̦

Christ, our Saviour, light of the world, you have called all mortal men to imperishable life;—shed eternal light on our departed brothers. R̦

Our Father

The concluding prayer as at Morning Prayer, pp 248–9.

WEEKS 2 TO 5, AND 6B: THURSDAYS

Invitatory ant. The Lord has truly risen, alleluia.

MORNING PRAYER

Hymn, from the appendix, for Eastertide.

Scripture Reading   *Rom 8:10-11*
If Christ lives in you, then although the body be a dead thing in virtue of our guilt, the spirit is a living thing, by virtue of our justification. And if the Spirit of him who raised up Jesus from the dead dwells in you, he who raised up Jesus Christ from the dead will give life to your perishable bodies too, for the sake of his Spirit who dwells in you.

Short Responsory
R/ The Lord has risen from the dead, alleluia, alleluia. *Repeat* R/
V/ For our sake he died on the cross. R/ Glory be. R/

Benedictus Antiphon
Week 2: The Father loves the Son, and has entrusted everything to him, alleluia.

Week 3: I tell you solemnly, everyone who believes in me has eternal life, alleluia.

Week 4: The disciple is not above his master; but the fully trained disciple will be like his master, alleluia.

Week 5: If you keep my commandments you will remain in my love, alleluia.

Week 6B: In a short time you will no longer see me, says the Lord; and then a short time later you will see me again, since I am going to the Father, alleluia.

Intercessions
Weeks 2, 4 and 6B
Let us pray with confidence to God our Father. In Christ he has given all his children the pledge of resurrection. ℞ May the Lord Jesus be our life.
Father, by a pillar of fire you led your people through the desert; —may the risen Christ be the light of our lives. ℞
Through the voice of Moses you spoke on the mountain;—may the risen Christ be our word of life. ℞
With the gift of manna you fed your wandering people;—may the risen Christ be our bread from heaven. ℞
You drew water from the rock to save your children;—may the risen Christ fill us with his Spirit. ℞
Our Father

Weeks 3 and 5
Let us offer our prayer to Christ, who rose from the dead and is living always in his Church. ℞ Lord, stay always with us.
Lord, you triumphed over sin and death;—be present in our midst with your eternal life. ℞
Come to us with your untiring strength;—and reveal in our lives the loving-kindness of God. ℞
You alone can reconcile men and create a new spirit within them; —end the conflicts which divide our world. ℞
Deepen our faith in your final victory;—let us find strength in the hope of your coming. ℞
Our Father

Concluding Prayer
Week 2: God of mercy,
let the mystery we celebrate at Eastertide
bear fruit for us in every season.
(We make our prayer) through our Lord.

Week 3: Almighty, ever-living God,
make our hearts more open to your love
in these days of Eastertide,
when you have made known to us

the depth of that love.
You have rescued us from the darkness of error:
make us adhere more firmly to the teachings of your truth.
(We make our prayer) through our Lord.

Week 4: Lord God,
you restore our human nature
to a dignity higher than you gave it at creation.
Look with favour on the mystery of your love;
keep your gifts of grace intact
in those whose life you have renewed in baptism,
the sacrament of new birth.
(We make our prayer) through our Lord.

Week 5: Lord God,
we were sinners and your grace made us holy,
we were without hope and you filled us with joy.
Stand by us in your saving work,
and stay with us in your gifts of grace.
May we never fail to persevere
in the holiness that comes from faith.
(We make our prayer) through our Lord.

Week 6B: God our Father,
you have given a saviour to your people:
fill our hearts with constant thanks and praise
that Christ the Lord is risen from the dead.
(We make our prayer) through our Lord.

EVENING PRAYER

Hymn, from the appendix, for Eastertide.

Scripture Reading   *1 Pet 3:18,22*
Christ himself, innocent though he was, died once for sins, died for
the guilty, to lead us to God. In the body, he was put to death, in
the spirit he was raised to life. He has entered heaven and is at God's
right hand, now that he has made the angels and Dominations and
Powers his subjects.

Short Responsory

℟ The disciples rejoiced, alleluia, alleluia. *Repeat* ℟

℣ They saw the Lord. ℟ Glory be. ℟

Magnificat Antiphon

Week 2: Anyone who believes in the Son has eternal life, alleluia.

Week 3: I am the bread of life that has come down from heaven. Anyone who eats this bread will live for ever: and the bread that I shall give is my flesh, for the life of the world, alleluia.

Week 4: I am the shepherd of the flock; I have come so that they may have life, and have it in all its fulness, alleluia.

Week 5: I have told you these things so that my own joy may be in you and your joy be complete, alleluia.

Week 6 B: Your sorrow will be turned into joy, and that joy no one will take from you, alleluia.

Intercessions

Weeks 2, 4 and 6B

Let us pray to Christ, who is our living hope of rising from the dead.

℟ King of glory, hear us.

Lord Jesus, by shedding your blood and rising from death you entered into your glory;—let us go with you into the presence of your Father. ℟

You sent your disciples into the world, their faith made strong by the resurrection;—grant that bishops and priests may be faithful ministers of your gospel. ℟

Through your resurrection you united the faithful in one hope and love;—may we share in your ministry of peace and reconciliation. ℟

Through your resurrection you healed the cripple who begged at the entrance to the temple;—look with pity on the sick and display in them your glory. ℟

You are the first to rise from the dead, the first of many brothers;—share your glory with those who have hoped in you. ℟

Our Father

Weeks 3 and 5

Christ has risen from the dead, the first-fruits of all who have fallen asleep. Let us praise him in our prayer. ℟ Risen Lord, hear us.

Lord, remember the Church you built on the apostles;—bless all those who believe in you. ℟

You are the healer of body and soul;—come to us with your salvation. ℟

Comfort the sick and renew their strength;—deliver them from all pain and distress. ℟

Help the anguished and the oppressed;—in your love uphold the needy. ℟

Through your cross and resurrection you have won immortal life; —grant to our dead the joys of your kingdom. ℟

Our Father

The concluding prayer as at Morning Prayer, p 253–4.

WEEKS 2 TO 5, AND 6B: FRIDAYS

Invitatory ant. The Lord has truly risen, alleluia.

MORNING PRAYER

Hymn, from the appendix, for Eastertide.

Scripture Reading *Acts 5:30-32*

The God of our fathers raised Jesus from death, after you had killed him by nailing him to a cross. And God raised him to his right side as Leader and Saviour, to give to the people of Israel the opportunity to repent and have their sins forgiven. We are witnesses to these things—we and the Holy Spirit, who is God's gift to those who obey him.

Short Responsory

℟ The Lord has risen from the dead, alleluia, alleluia. *Repeat* ℟
℣ For our sake he died on the cross. ℟ Glory be. ℟

256

Benedictus Antiphon
Week 2: Jesus took the loaves, gave thanks and distributed them to the people as they sat there, alleluia.

Week 3: He who eats my flesh and drinks my blood lives in me and I in him, alleluia.

Week 4: I am going now to prepare a place for you, and I shall return to take you with me; so that where I am you also may be, alleluia.

Week 5: This is my commandment: love one another, as I have loved you, alleluia.

Week 6 B: In Jesus we see one who is crowned now with glory and honour because he suffered death, alleluia.

Intercessions
Weeks 2, 4 and 6B
Through his Spirit God raised Jesus from the dead and he will give life to our own mortal bodies. Let us pray to him, saying: R̹ Lord, give us life through your Holy Spirit.
Father, you accepted the sacrifice of your Son, raising him from the dead;—receive our morning offering and lead us to eternal life. R̹
Reveal your presence in our work this day;—may we do everything for your glory and for the sanctification of our world. R̹
Do not allow our work to come to nothing;—let it serve our fellow men and bring us to your kingdom. R̹
Open our eyes to see our brother's need;—warm our hearts that we may offer him our love. R̹
Our Father

Weeks 3 and 5
Let us pray to God the Father, who has given us new life through the resurrection of Christ. R̹ Make us radiant with Christ's glory.
Almighty God, creator of the world, you revealed the old covenant by your mighty deeds and were faithful to men down through the ages;—loving Father, hear the prayer of your children. R̹
Cleanse our hearts by your truth and guide our lives by your holiness;—may we do what is right and pleasing to you. R̹

Let the light of your face shine upon us;—free us from sin and fill us with your goodness. R̸

Peace was your Son's parting gift to the apostles;—grant your peace to us and to people everywhere. R̸

Our Father

Concluding Prayer

Week 2: By your will, Lord God,
your Son underwent the agony of the cross
to break the power of Satan over man.
Give your people grace to rise again with Christ,
who lives and reigns with you and the Holy Spirit,
God, for ever and ever.

Week 3: Almighty God,
we have come to know the grace of our Lord's resurrection.
Grant that through the love of your Spirit
we may rise to new life.
(We make our prayer) through our Lord.

Week 4: Lord God, source of our freedom and salvation,
listen to our humble prayer.
You redeemed us by the shedding of your Son's blood:
enable us to live by your grace,
and grant us at all times
the joy of your safe keeping.
(We make our prayer) through our Lord.

Week 5: Lord God,
grant that the Easter mystery may shape our lives,
so that what we celebrate with joy
may be our constant defence and salvation.
(We make our prayer) through our Lord.

Week 6B: Lord, hear our prayer.
Send out on all mankind
the Spirit who makes us your sons,
as foretold by Christ, the witness of your truth:

and so bring to completion through the gospel,
the sanctification promised by your Word.
(We make our prayer) through our Lord.

EVENING PRAYER

Hymn, from the appendix, for Eastertide.

Scripture Reading   *Heb 5:8-10*
Although he was Son, Christ learnt to obey through suffering; but
having been made perfect, he became for all who obey him the
source of eternal salvation and was acclaimed by God with the title
of high priest of the order of Melchizedek.

Short Responsory
R/ The disciples rejoiced, alleluia, alleluia. *Repeat* R/
V/ They saw the Lord. R/ Glory be. R/

Magnificat Antiphon
Week 2: By submitting to death on the cross he destroyed the power
of hell; he has covered himself in glory by rising on the third day,
alleluia.

Week 3: Christ died on the cross and rose again from the dead to
redeem us, alleluia.

Week 4: The good shepherd lays down his life for his sheep, alleluia.

Week 5: A man can have no greater love than to lay down his life
for his friends, alleluia.

Week 6B: Your heavenly Father will give the Holy Spirit to those
who ask him, alleluia.

Intercessions
Weeks 2, 4 and 6B
Let us pray to Christ, the fount of life and the source of virtue.
R/ Lord, restore your kingdom in the world.
Jesus, our Saviour, in the body you were put to death, in the Spirit
you were raised to life;—grant that we may die to sin, and live in the

power of your resurrection. ℟ Lord, restore your kingdom in the world.

You sent your disciples to proclaim throughout the world the gospel of salvation;—may all who preach your word be alive with the Holy Spirit. ℟

You received all power in heaven and on earth to bear witness to the truth;—guide in the spirit of truth the plans of governments and rulers. ℟

Keep our eyes fixed on the new heaven and the new earth;—make us care more deeply for our world and its future. ℟

You descended into hell to bring the dead good news;—let the faithful departed come to you, their joy, their hope, their glory. ℟

Our Father

Weeks 3 and 5

Let us pray to Christ, the way, the truth and the life. ℟ Son of the living God, bless your people.

We pray for all the ministers of your Church:—may they be nourished and sustained as they break for their brothers the bread of life. ℟

We pray for the whole Christian people:—may they be faithful to their calling and hold fast in bonds of peace the unity of the spirit. ℟

We pray for those who govern our country that they may exercise their office with justice and compassion;—help them to promote the peace of the world. ℟

Make us worthy to adore you in the communion of saints;—grant eternal joy to the faithful departed, whom we entrust to your care. ℟

Our Father

The concluding prayer as at Morning Prayer, p 258.

WEEKS 2 TO 5, AND 6B: SATURDAYS

Invitatory ant. The Lord has truly risen, alleluia.

MORNING PRAYER

Hymn, from the appendix, for Eastertide.

Scripture Reading   *Rom 14:7-9*
None of us lives for himself only, none of us dies for himself only; if we live, it is for the Lord that we live, and if we die, it is for the Lord that we die. Whether we live or die, then, we belong to the Lord. For Christ died and rose to life in order to be the Lord of the living and of the dead.

Short Responsory
R/ The Lord has risen from the dead, alleluia, alleluia. *Repeat* R/
V/ For our sake he died on the cross. R/ Glory be. R/

Benedictus Antiphon
Week 2: Peace be with you, it is I, alleluia; do not be afraid, alleluia.

Week 3: Simon Peter said, 'Lord, to whom shall we go? You have the words of eternal life, and we believe; we know that you are the Christ, the Son of God', alleluia.

Week 4: When the chief shepherd appears, you will be given the crown of unfading glory, alleluia.

Week 5: Christ died and came to life again to establish his dominion over the living and the dead, alleluia.

Week 6B: I tell you solemnly, anything you ask from the Father in my name, he will grant it to you, alleluia.

Intercessions
Weeks 2, 4 and 6B
Let us pray to Christ, who has revealed to us the knowledge of everlasting life. R/ Lord, may your resurrection enrich us with your grace.
Eternal Shepherd, strengthen us for the coming day with the bread of your word;—nourish us with the bread of the eucharist. R/
May your voice find a response in our hearts;—do not let your word be silenced by rejection or indifference. R/

You are at work in those who spread the gospel, confirming the truth of their message;—help us to manifest your resurrection by our way of living. ℟ Lord, may your resurrection enrich us with your grace.

You yourself are the joy that can never be taken away;—may we leave behind the sadness of sin and experience eternal life. ℟

Our Father

Weeks 3 and 5

Christ is the bread of life and he will raise up on the last day those who are nourished by his word and his body. ℟ Lord, give us peace and joy.

Son of God, risen from the dead, you are the Lord of life;—bless all our brothers and make us holy. ℟

You are the peace and joy of all who believe in you;—help us to live as children of light, rejoicing in your victory. ℟

May your pilgrim Church grow in faith;—strengthen us to bear witness before the world to your resurrection. ℟

You underwent great sufferings to enter the Father's glory;—wipe away all tears and turn sorrow into joy. ℟

Our Father

Concluding Prayer

Week 2: Since it is from you, God our Father,
that redemption comes to us, your adopted children:
look with favour on the family you love,
give true freedom to us and to all who believe in Christ,
and bring us all alike to our eternal heritage.
(We make our prayer) through our Lord.

Week 3: God our Father,
by the waters of baptism
you have given new life
to those who believe in you.
Protect these new-born members of Christ,
help them to resist all false beliefs,
and so keep intact the grace of your blessing.
(We make our prayer) through our Lord.

Week 4: All-powerful, ever-living God,
keep the mystery of Easter alive in us always.
You gave us a new birth in holy baptism:
give us grace to bear much fruit,
and bring us to the joys of eternal life.
(We make our prayer) through our Lord.

Week 5: Almighty, ever-living God,
you gave us the life of heaven
by the new birth of baptism;
you implanted in us the seed of eternity
by your gift of grace.
Lead us, in your providence, to the fulness of glory.
(We make our prayer) through our Lord.

Week 6B: Mould our minds, we pray you, Lord,
by the works of your law.
Always striving after what is best,
may we make our lives
a constant sharing in Christ's death and resurrection.
(We make our prayer) through our Lord.

Weeks 2 to 5: Evening Prayer of the following Sunday, see pp 276 ff.
Week 6B: Evening Prayer I of the Ascension, see below.

Eastertide II: from the Ascension
THE ASCENSION OF THE LORD
Solemnity

A *Thursday of Week 6 of Eastertide*
B *Sunday 7 of Eastertide*

EVENING PRAYER I

Hymn
The Lord goes up with shouts of joy,
While trumpets all his triumph tell;

With him humanity is raised
Above angelic worlds to dwell.

He sits with God, at his right hand,
Who is the Lord of everything;
The Father's glory is his own:
Christ Jesus, all creations' king.

And when he comes again in might,
To raise us on that splendid day,
We shall be gathered up to him,
And every tear be wiped away.

O God, our Father, hear our prayer:
With Christ, our Lord, your only Son,
Send forth the Spirit of your love
To live in us and make us one.

PSALMODY

Ant. 1: I came from the Father and have come into the world and now I leave the world to go to the Father, alleluia.

PSALM 112(113)

Práise, O sérvants of the Lórd,*
práise the náme of the Lórd!
May the náme of the Lórd be bléssed*
both nów and for évermóre!
From the rísing of the sún to its sétting*
práised be the náme of the Lórd!

Hígh above all nátions is the Lórd,*
abóve the héavens his glóry.
Whó is like the Lórd, our Gód,*
who has rísen on hígh to his thróne
yet stóops from the héights to look dówn,*
to look dówn upon héaven and éarth?

From the dúst he lifts up the lówly,*
from his mísery he ráises the póor
to sét him in the cómpany of prínces,*

yés, with the prínces of his péople.
To the chíldless wífe he gives a hóme*
and gláddens her héart with chíldren.

Ant. I came from the Father and have come into the world and now I leave the world to go to the Father, alleluia.

Ant. 2: After he had spoken to his disciples, the Lord Jesus ascended to heaven where he is seated at the right hand of the Father, alleluia.

PSALM 116(117)

O práise the Lórd, all you nátions,*
accláim him all you péoples!

Stróng is his lóve for ús;*
he is fáithful for éver.

Ant. After he had spoken to his disciples, the Lord Jesus ascended to heaven where he is seated at the right hand of the Father, alleluia.

Ant. 3: No one has gone up to heaven except the one who first came down from heaven, the Son of Man who is in heaven, alleluia.

CANTICLE
REV 11:17-18;12:10B-12A

We give thanks to you, Lord God Almighty,*
who are and who were,
that you have taken your great power*
and begun to reign.

The nations raged,*
but your wrath came,
and the time for the dead to be judged,*
for rewarding your servants, the prophets and saints,
and those who fear your name,*
both small and great.

Now the salvation and the power†
and the kingdom of our God*
and the authority of his Christ have come,
for the accuser of our brethren has been thrown down,*
who accuses them day and night before our God.

265

And they have conquered him*
by the blood of the Lamb
and by the word of their testimony,*
for they loved not their lives even unto death.
Rejoice, then, O heaven,*
and you that dwell therein!

Ant. No one has gone up to heaven except the one who first came down from heaven, the Son of Man who is in heaven, alleluia.

Scripture Reading   *Eph 2:4-6*
God's mercy is so abundant, and his love for us is so great, that while we were spiritually dead in our disobedience he brought us to life with Christ; it is by God's grace that you have been saved. In our union with Christ Jesus he raised us up with him to rule with him in the heavenly world.

Short Responsory
R̸ God ascends with shouts of joy, alleluia, alleluia. *Repeat* R̸
V̸ The Lord goes up with trumpet blast. R̸ Glory be. R̸

Magnificat ant. Father, I have made your name known to the men you gave me; now I pray for them, not for the world, since I am coming to you, alleluia.

Intercessions
Rejoicing, let us pray to Christ who is seated at the right hand of the Father. R̸ You, Christ, are the king of glory.
King of glory, in you our mortal flesh has been lifted to the heights;
—deliver us from the corruption of sin and restore us to immortal life. R̸
Following the path of love, you came down to us from heaven;—let us follow that same path in our ascent to you. R̸
You promised to draw all men to yourself;—do not let any of us be separated from your body. R̸
You have ascended into heaven;—let us be there with you in our minds and hearts. R̸
We await your coming in majesty on the great day of judgment;—

may we then gaze upon your glory, with all the faithful departed. ℟
Our Father

Concluding Prayer
Almighty God,
fill us with a holy joy,
teach us how to thank you with reverence and love
on account of the ascension of Christ your Son.
You have raised us up with him:
where he, the head, has preceded us in glory,
there we, the body, are called in hope.
(We make our prayer) through our Lord.

Invitatory
Ant. Alleluia, Christ ascends into heaven as Lord. Come, let us
adore him, alleluia.
Psalm, p 371.

MORNING PRAYER

Hymn
  Sower and seed of man's reprieving,
  Jesus, the longing heart's repose,
  Thy own creation's fault retrieving,
  Pure light thy lover only knows;

  What sovereign pity earthward drew thee,
  Our load of sins thy charge to make,
  Slain, that the guilty race that slew thee
  Life from thy guiltless death might take?

  Now hell is harrowed, now is stricken
  From captive hands the age-long chain;
  Thronged by the souls thy life doth quicken,
  Thou at thy Father's side dost reign.

  Be thou the end of our wayfaring,
  As thou the guide, as thou the way,
  Our friend, these earthly shadows sharing,
  Our crown of life in perfect day.

Ant. 1: Men of Galilee, why do you stand there looking up into the sky? This Jesus, who has been taken away from you up to heaven, will come in the same way as you have seen him go, alleluia.

Psalms and canticle of Sunday, Week 1, pp 390 ff.

Ant. 2: Exalt the king of kings; sing praise to God, alleluia.

Ant. 3: As they watched, he was lifted up, and a cloud removed him from their sight into heaven, alleluia.

Scripture Reading   *Heb 10:12-14*
Christ has offered one single sacrifice for sins, and then taken his place for ever at the right hand of God, where he is now waiting until his enemies are made into a footstool for him. By virtue of that one single offering he has achieved the eternal perfection of all whom he is sanctifying.

Short Responsory
R7 Christ ascended on high, alleluia, alleluia. *Repeat* R7
V7 He led captivity captive. R7 Glory be. R7

Benedictus ant. I am ascending to my Father and your Father, to my God and your God, alleluia.

Intercessions
Let us pray to the Lord who is now lifted up from the earth, drawing all things to himself. R7 You, Christ, are the king of glory.
Lord Jesus, you offered one sacrifice for sin and then ascended in victory to the Father;—achieve the eternal perfection of those whom you are sanctifying. R7
Eternal priest, minister of the new covenant, you are alive and interceding for us;—save your people who turn to you in prayer. R7
After your passion, you appeared to your disciples, and they knew you to be alive:—strengthen our belief that you are with us today. R7
On this day you promised the Holy Spirit to the apostles, for the spreading of your gospel to the ends of the earth;—strengthen us by the power of the Spirit in bearing witness before the world. R7
Our Father

Concluding Prayer
Almighty God,
fill us with a holy joy,
teach us how to thank you with reverence and love
on account of the ascension of Christ your Son.
You have raised us up with him;
where he, the head, has preceded us in glory,
there we, the body, are called in hope.
(We make our prayer) through our Lord.

EVENING PRAYER II

Hymn as at Evening Prayer I, p 263.

PSALMODY

Ant. 1: He ascended to heaven and is seated at the right hand of the
Father, alleluia.

PSALM 109(110):1-5,7

The Lórd's revelátion to my Máster:†
'Sít on my ríght:*
your fóes I will pút beneath your féet.'

The Lórd will wíeld from Síon†
your scéptre of pówer:*
rúle in the mídst of all your fóes.

A prínce from the dáy of your bírth†
on the hóly móuntains;*
from the wómb before the dáwn I begót you.

The Lórd has sworn an óath he will not chánge.†
'You are a príest for ever,*
a príest like Melchízedek of óld.'

The Máster stánding at your ríght hand*
will shatter kíngs in the dáy of his wráth.

He shall drínk from the stréam by the wáyside*
and thérefore he shall líft up his héad.   Glory be.

Ant. He ascended to heaven and is seated at the right hand of the Father, alleluia.

Ant. 2: God goes up with shouts of joy; the Lord ascends with trumpet blast, alleluia.

PSALM 46(47)

All péoples, cláp your hánds,*
cry to Gód with shóuts of jóy!
For the Lórd, the Most Hígh, we must féar,*
great kíng over áll the éarth.

He subdúes péoples únder us*
and nátions únder our féet.
Our inhéritance, our glóry, is from hím,*
gíven to Jácob out of lóve.

God goes úp with shóuts of jóy;*
the Lord ascénds with trúmpet blást.
Sing práise for Gód, sing práise,*
sing práise to our kíng, sing práise.

God is kíng of áll the éarth,*
Sing práise with áll your skíll.
God is kíng óver the nátions;*
God réigns on his hóly thróne.

The prínces of the péoples are assémbled*
with the péople of Ábraham's Gód.
The rúlers of the éarth belong to Gód,*
to Gód who réigns over áll.

Ant. God goes up with shouts of joy; the Lord ascends with trumpet blast, alleluia.

Ant 3: Now the Son of Man has been glorified, and in him God has been glorified, alleluia.

CANTICLE
REV 11:17-18;12:10B-12A

We give thanks to you, Lord God Almighty,*
who are and who were,

that you have taken your great power,*
and begun to reign.

The nations raged,*
but your wrath came,
and the time for the dead to be judged,*
for rewarding your servants, the prophets and saints,
and those who fear your name,*
both small and great.

Now the salvation and the power†
and the kingdom of our God*
and the authority of his Christ have come,
for the accuser of our brethren has been thrown down,*
who accuses them day and night before our God.

And they have conquered him*
by the blood of the Lamb
and by the word of their testimony,*
for they loved not their lives even unto death.
Rejoice, then, O heaven,*
and you that dwell therein!

Ant. Now the Son of Man has been glorified, and in him God has been glorified, alleluia.

Scripture Reading   *1 Pet 3:18-22*
Christ himself, innocent though he was, died once for sins, died for the guilty, to lead us to God. In the body, he was put to death, in the spirit he was raised to life. He has entered heaven and is at God's right hand, now that he has made the angels and Dominations and Powers his subjects.

Short Responsory
R̸ I am ascending to my Father and your Father, alleluia, alleluia.
Repeat R̸
V̸ I go to my God and your God. R̸ Glory be. R̸

Magnificat ant. King of Glory, Lord Almighty, today you have

271

ascended victoriously above the heavens; do not leave us as orphans without a guide, but send the one whom you promised, the gift of the Father, the Spirit of Truth, alleluia.

Intercessions
Let us pray to the Lord who is now lifted up from the earth, drawing all things to himself. ℟ You, Christ, are the king of glory.
Lord Jesus, you offered one sacrifice for sin and then ascended in victory to the Father;—achieve the eternal perfection of those whom you are sanctifying. ℟
Eternal priest, minister of the new covenant, you are alive and interceding for us;—save your people who turn to you in prayer. ℟
After your passion, you appeared to your disciples, and they knew you to be alive:—strengthen our belief that you are with us today. ℟
On this day you promised the Holy Spirit to the apostles, for the spreading of your gospel to the ends of the earth;—strengthen us by the power of the Spirit in bearing witness before the world. ℟
Our Father

The concluding prayer as at Morning Prayer, p 269.

FRIDAY AFTER THE ASCENSION

Invitatory ant. Christ the Lord has promised us the Holy Spirit: come, let us adore him, alleluia.

MORNING PRAYER

Hymn, from the appendix, for Eastertide II.

Scripture Reading   *Acts 5:30-32*
The God of our fathers raised Jesus from death, after you had killed him by nailing him to a cross. And God raised him to his right side as Leader and Saviour, to give to the people of Israel the opportunity to repent and have their sins forgiven. We are witnesses to

these things—we and the Holy Spirit, who is God's gift to those who obey him.

Short Responsory

R︦ The Lord has risen from the dead, alleluia, alleluia. *Repeat* R︦
V︦ For our sake he died on the cross. R︦ Glory be. R︦

Benedictus ant. In Jesus we see one who is crowned now with glory and honour because he suffered death, alleluia.

Intercessions

Let us pray to Christ, who ascended into heaven to send the Holy Spirit to the apostles. R︦ Send your Spirit upon us.
Lord, pour on us the Holy Spirit, the promise of the Father;—clothe us with power from on high. R︦
You wanted your disciples to be wise as serpents and yet simple as doves:—teach us by your Spirit wisdom and simplicity. R︦
You are now seated at the right hand of the Father;—intercede for us now, as we look to you, our Eternal Priest. R︦
Let us suffer with you in our time of sorrow;—may we rise with you in glory. R︦
Our Father

Concluding Prayer

Lord God,
you restore us to eternal life by our Saviour's resurrection.
Place us at your right hand
where he is enthroned with you.
You gave us a new birth in baptism:
clothe us in the garment of eternal happiness
when Christ comes in his glory.
(We make our prayer) through our Lord.

EVENING PRAYER

Hymn, from the appendix, for Eastertide II.

Scripture Reading   *Heb 5:8-10*
Although he was Son, Christ learnt to obey through suffering; but

having been made perfect, he became for all who obey him the source of eternal salvation and was acclaimed by God with the title of high priest of the order of Melchizedek.

Short Responsory
℟ The Holy Spirit is the Advocate, alleluia, alleluia. *Repeat* ℟
℣ He will teach you everything. ℟ Glory be. ℟

Magnificat ant. Your heavenly Father will give the Holy Spirit to those who ask him, alleluia.

Intercessions
Let us pray to Christ, who was anointed with the Holy Spirit.
℟ Exalted Christ, intercede for us.
Lord Jesus, look upon Christians all over the world;—gather them into unity through your Holy Spirit. ℟
Give your light to all who suffer persecution for your name;—grant that they may know what to say to those who persecute them. ℟
Let all men know you, the one true vine;—make them your branches, bearing the fruit of the Spirit. ℟
King of the universe, you ascended into heaven to the joy of angels and men;—reign over our world and rule all the nations. ℟
You have made the baptized sharers in your death and resurrection;—at the hour of death let them pass with you into eternal life. ℟
Our Father

The concluding prayer as at Morning Prayer, p 273.

SATURDAY
AFTER THE ASCENSION

Invitatory ant. Christ the Lord has promised us the Holy Spirit: come, let us adore him, alleluia.

MORNING PRAYER

Hymn, from the appendix, for Eastertide II.

Scripture Reading   *Rom 14:7-9*

None of us lives for himself only, none of us dies for himself only; if we live, it is for the Lord that we live, and if we die, it is for the Lord that we die. Whether we live or die, then, we belong to the Lord. For Christ died and rose to life in order to be the Lord of the living and of the dead.

Short Responsory

R̠ The Lord has risen from the dead, alleluia, alleluia. *Repeat* R̠
V̠ For our sake he died on the cross. R̠ Glory be. R̠

Benedictus ant. I tell you solemnly, anything you ask from the Father in my name, he will grant it to you, alleluia.

Intercessions

To Christ be praise and glory! He promised the apostles that the power of the Holy Spirit would come upon them. R̠ Send forth your light and your truth.

You are the Word of truth, the wisdom and splendour of the Father;—let us be your witnesses today, in word and in deed. R̠

May we recognize the things of the Spirit and set our hearts on them; —where our hearts are, there will our treasure be. R̠

Grant that the Holy Spirit may come to help us in our weakness— and teach us how we ought to pray. R̠

Let us be filled with all knowledge and love;—enable us to counsel one another in truth and charity. R̠

Our Father

Concluding Prayer

God and Father,
your Son, at his ascension,
promised the Holy Spirit to the apostles.
They received abundant graces of wisdom from heaven:
grant us also, we pray, the gifts of your Spirit.
(We make our prayer) through our Lord.

EASTERTIDE: WEEK 7
SUNDAY

Psalter: Week 3

B*: In regions where the Ascension of the Lord is celebrated today the Office is given on pp 263 ff.*
A*: Elsewhere the Office of the Sunday is as follows:*

EVENING PRAYER I

Hymn, from the appendix, for Eastertide II.
Psalms and canticle with proper antiphons as in the psalter.

Scripture Reading　　*1 Pet 2:9-10*
You are a chosen race, a royal priesthood, a consecrated nation, a people set apart to sing the praises of God who called you out of darkness into his wonderful light. Once you were not a people at all, and now you are the people of God; once you were outside the mercy and now you have been given mercy.

Short Responsory
R⁷ The Holy Spirit is the Advocate, alleluia, alleluia. *Repeat* R⁷
V⁷ He will teach you everything. R⁷ Glory be. R⁷

Magnificat ant. I will not leave you desolate like orphans: I am going now, but I will return to you and then your hearts will be filled with joy, alleluia.

Intercessions
Blessed be Christ, the Son of God. At the Jordan the Holy Spirit descended on him in the form of a dove. Let us confirm our prayer to him by saying: R⁷ Amen. Amen.
Lord Jesus, send forth your Holy Spirit to renew the life of the Church—and make her radiant with hope. R⁷
May all the nations praise you as their king and Lord;—make Israel the people whom you call your own. R⁷

Make us generous, make us humble;—let us forget our own needs in the service of others. R̷

At Pentecost you reversed the disaster of Babel, which divided and confused the family of man;—through your Holy Spirit let all men speak the same language of faith and love. R̷

May your Holy Spirit dwell within us—to give life to our mortal bodies. R̷

Our Father

Concluding Prayer
Lord God,
we believe that the Saviour of mankind
is enthroned with you in majesty.
Listen to our prayer,
and, according to his promise,
let us feel his presence among us
until the end of time.
(We make our prayer) through our Lord.

Invitatory
Ant. Christ the Lord has promised us the Holy Spirit: come, let us adore him, alleluia.
Psalm, p 371.

MORNING PRAYER

Hymn, from the appendix, for Eastertide II.
Psalms and canticle with proper antiphons as in the psalter.

Scripture Reading   *Acts 10:40-43*
God raised Jesus from death on the third day and caused him to appear. He was not seen by all the people, but only by us who are the witnesses that God had already chosen. We ate and drank with him after God raised him from death. And he commanded us to preach the gospel to the people, and to testify that he is the one whom God has appointed Judge of the living and the dead. All the prophets spoke about him, saying that everyone who believes in him will have his sins forgiven through the power of his name.

Short Responsory

℟ Have mercy on us, Christ, Son of the living God, alleluia, alleluia. *Repeat* ℟

℣ You have risen from the dead. ℟ Glory be. ℟

Benedictus ant. Father, I have glorified you on earth: I have accomplished the work that you gave me to do, alleluia.

Intercessions

Let us be united in prayer with all who are justified in the Spirit of God, and let us say to Christ, our Lord: ℟ May your Spirit come to our aid.

Lord Jesus, help us to live by your Spirit;—and show us that we are God's children. ℟

Through your Holy Spirit intercede for us with the Father;—make us worthy of your promises. ℟

Make us generous, warm-hearted and unselfish;—help us always to think of the needs of others. ℟

Through the Holy Spirit grant us the desire to seek God's kingdom and his justice;—strengthen our resolve to know you and the Father. ℟

Our Father

Concluding Prayer

Lord God,
we believe that the Saviour of mankind
is enthroned with you in majesty.
Listen to our prayer,
and, according to his promise,
let us feel his presence among us
until the end of time.
(We make our prayer) through our Lord.

EVENING PRAYER II

Hymn, from the appendix, for Eastertide II.
Psalms and canticle with proper antiphons as in the psalter.

Scripture Reading   *Heb 10:12-14*

Christ has offered one single sacrifice for sins, and then taken his place for ever at the right hand of God, where he is now waiting until his enemies are made into a footstool for him. By virtue of that one single offering he has achieved the eternal perfection of all whom he is sanctifying.

Short Responsory

R̸ The Holy Spirit is the Advocate, alleluia, alleluia. *Repeat* R̸
V̸ He will teach you everything. R̸ Glory be. R̸

Magnificat ant. I will send you the Advocate, the Spirit of truth who comes from the Father. He will be my witness, alleluia.

Intercessions

Christ our Lord urged us to pray and the Holy Spirit came to fill our hearts and minds. R̸ May the Holy Spirit plead for us.
Eternal shepherd, give to the pastors of your Church wisdom and understanding;—may they lead your faithful people in the way of salvation. R̸
Heavenly Christ, you are rich in mercy and compassion;—do not forget the poor and the needy you have left behind on earth. R̸
By the power of the Holy Spirit you were conceived of the Virgin Mary;—preserve in religious women the spirit of loving service. R̸
Christ, our priest, you give glory to the Father in the Holy Spirit; —unite all men together in your hymn of praise. R̸
Grant to the dead the glorious freedom of God's sons—and the completion of bodily redemption. R̸
Our Father

The concluding prayer as at Morning Prayer, p 278.

WEEK 7: MONDAY

Invitatory ant. Christ the Lord has promised us the Holy Spirit: come, let us adore him, alleluia.
Psalm, p 371.

MORNING PRAYER

Hymn, from the appendix, for Eastertide II.

Scripture Reading   *Rom 10:8b-10*

It is on your lips, it is in your heart, meaning by that the message of
faith which we preach. You can find salvation, if you will use your
lips to confess that Jesus is the Lord, and your heart to believe that
God has raised him up from the dead. The heart has only to believe,
if we are to be justified; the lips have only to make confession, if we
are to be saved.

Short Responsory

℟ The Lord has risen from the dead, alleluia, alleluia. *Repeat* ℟
℣ For our sake he died on the cross. ℟ Glory be. ℟

Benedictus ant. In the world you have suffering. But have courage: I
have conquered the world, alleluia.

Intercessions

Let us pray to Christ, who promised that the Father would send the
Paraclete in his name. ℟ Give us your Holy Spirit.
We thank you, Christ our Lord, and through you we give thanks to
the Father in the Holy Spirit;—let everything we do this day speak
your name. ℟
May your Holy Spirit dwell within us;—may he make us living
members of your body. ℟
Do not allow us to judge or despise our brothers;—make us
remember that one day we shall all stand before your judgment seat.
℟
Fill us with all joy and peace in believing;—by the power of the
Holy Spirit enlarge the horizons of our hope. ℟
Our Father

Concluding Prayer

Lord God,
let the grace of the Holy Spirit come upon us,
so that we may hold fast to your will with fidelity,

and show it forth in a holy life.
(We make our prayer) through our Lord.

EVENING PRAYER

Hymn, from the appendix, for Eastertide II.

Scripture Reading   *Rom 8:14-17*
Those who follow the leading of God's Spirit are all God's sons; the
Spirit you have now received is not, as of old, a spirit of slavery to
govern you by fear; it is the spirit of adoption, which makes us cry
out Abba, Father. The Spirit himself thus assures our spirit that we
are children of God; and if we are his children, then we are his heirs
too; heirs of God, sharing the inheritance of Christ; only we must
share his sufferings, if we are to share his glory.

Short Responsory
R⁊ The Holy Spirit is the Advocate, alleluia, alleluia. *Repeat* R⁊
℣ He will teach you everything. R⁊ Glory be. R⁊

Magnificat ant. The Holy Spirit, the Advocate, will remain among
you and he will dwell within you, alleluia.

Intercessions
Christ filled the apostles and the whole Church with the comfort of
the Holy Spirit. In our evening prayer let us give thanks to him.
R⁊ Lord, comfort your Church and make us grateful.
Mediator of God and men, you have chosen priests to be your
fellow workers;—through their saving ministry bring all men to the
Father. R⁊
Be present in the hearts of the rich and the lives of the poor;—inspire
men to care for one another, whatever their needs. R⁊
Reveal your gospel to all the nations—and restore the broken unity
of the human family. R⁊
Send your Holy Spirit to dry the tears of the world;—may the
Comforter turn sorrow into joy. R⁊
Cleanse the dead from sin;—take them up to heaven into the
company of the saints. R⁊

Our Father

The concluding prayer as at Morning Prayer, p 280.

WEEK 7: TUESDAY

Invitatory ant. Christ the Lord has promised us the Holy Spirit: come, let us adore him, alleluia.

MORNING PRAYER

Hymn, from the appendix, for Eastertide II.

Scripture Reading   *Acts 13:30-33*
God raised Jesus from the dead and for many days he was seen by those who had travelled with him from Galilee to Jerusalem. They are now witnesses for him to the people of Israel. And we are here to bring the Good News to you: what God promised our ancestors he would do, he has now done for us, who are their descendants, by raising Jesus to life. As it is written: You are my son, Today I have become your Father.

Short Responsory
R̷ The Lord has risen from the dead, alleluia, alleluia. *Repeat* R̷
V̷ For our sake he died on the cross. R̷ Glory be. R̷

Benedictus ant. The Lord has risen from the dead, as he promised; let us all rejoice and be glad; he is king for ever and ever, alleluia.

Intercessions
Christ the Lord has promised us the Holy Spirit, whom he sends from the Father. Let us give glory to him, saying: R̷ Christ, our Lord, give us your Spirit.
Lord Jesus, may your word in all its richness dwell within us;—let us sing psalms and hymns and spiritual songs with thankfulness to you. R̷
Through the Holy Spirit you have made us sons of God;—at all times let us pray through the Spirit to you and the Father. R̷
Guide our actions by your wisdom;—in the events of daily living let us tell of God's glory. R̷

You are long suffering and full of compassion;—help us to live at peace with everyone. ℟
Our Father

Concluding Prayer
God of power and mercy,
grant that when the Holy Spirit comes,
he may dwell in us,
and make of us a temple
filled with his glory.
(We make our prayer) through our Lord.

EVENING PRAYER

Hymn, from the appendix, for Eastertide II.

Scripture Reading   *Rom 8:26-27*
The Spirit comes to the aid of our weakness; when we do not know what prayer to offer, to pray as we ought, the Spirit himself intercedes for us, with groans beyond all utterance; and God, who can read our hearts, knows well what the Spirit's intent is; for indeed it is according to the mind of God that he makes intercession for the saints.

Short Responsory
℟ The Holy Spirit is the Advocate, alleluia, alleluia. *Repeat* ℟
℣ He will teach you everything. ℟ Glory be. ℟

Magnificat ant. The power of the Holy Spirit will come into you; you will be my witnesses to the very ends of the earth, alleluia.

Intercessions
To Christ be honour and glory. He has made his people sharers of the Holy Spirit. ℟ Christ, hear us.
Send from the Father the Holy Spirit into the Church;—may he purify, strengthen and perfect it. ℟
Guide rulers and governments by your Holy Spirit;—give them the gifts of wisdom and courage. ℟

Send your Holy Spirit to the poor;—help and support all those who are in need. ℟

We pray for your servants who are stewards of God's mysteries;—keep them always faithful to their ministry of grace. ℟

Grant to the bodies and souls of the dead the fulness of redemption; —strengthen us in your passion, resurrection and ascension. ℟

Our Father

The concluding prayer as at Morning Prayer, p 283.

WEEK 7: WEDNESDAY

Invitatory ant. Christ the Lord has promised us the Holy Spirit: come, let us adore him, alleluia.

MORNING PRAYER

Hymn, from the appendix, for Eastertide II.

Scripture Reading   *Rom 6:8-11*

If we have died with Christ, we have faith to believe that we shall share his life. We know that Christ, now he has risen from the dead, cannot die any more; death has no more power over him; the death he died was a death, once for all, to sin; the life he now lives is a life that looks towards God. And you, too, must think of yourselves as dead to sin, and alive with a life that looks towards God, through Christ Jesus our Lord.

Short Responsory

℟ The Lord has risen from the dead, alleluia, alleluia. *Repeat* ℟

℣ For our sake he died on the cross. ℟ Glory be. ℟

Benedictus ant. Let us thank God who has given us victory through our Lord Jesus Christ, alleluia.

Intercessions

The Holy Spirit joins with our spirit in bearing witness that we are

children of God. Let us give thanks to our heavenly Father.
R̶̷ Father, hear your children.

God of patience and encouragement, grant that we may agree with one another by following the example of Christ;—united in mind and voice, let us glorify you. R̶̷

Let each of us think of his brother's good and strive to please him; —enable us to strengthen his faith. R̶̷

Do not allow us to be led astray by the power of the Evil One;—fill us instead with the Spirit who comes from you. R̶̷

Lord, you know everything that is in our hearts;—lead us in the ways of sincerity and truth. R̶̷

Our Father

Concluding Prayer
God of mercy,
you have gathered your Church together by the Holy Spirit.
Keep us devoted to your service,
and united among ourselves.
(We make our prayer) through our Lord.

EVENING PRAYER

Hymn, from the appendix, for Eastertide II.

Scripture Reading   *I Cor 2:9-10*
The things that no eye has seen and no ear has heard, things beyond the mind of man, all that God has prepared for those who love him: these are the very things that God has revealed to us through the Spirit, for the Spirit reaches the depths of everything, even the depths of God.

Short Responsory
R̶̷ The Holy Spirit is the Advocate, alleluia, alleluia. *Repeat* R̶̷
V̶̷ He will teach you everything. R̶̷ Glory be. R̶̷

Magnificat ant. Christ will baptize you with the Holy Spirit and with fire, alleluia.

Intercessions
With the apostles and with all who have received the pledge of the

Spirit we praise and call on God. R℟ Lord, hear us.

God of power and might, you have taken up Christ into the glory of heaven;—help all men to see that he is living in his Church. R℟

Father, you said of Christ, 'This is my Son, the beloved, Listen to him.'—Make the voice of your Son resound in men's hearts and bring them to salvation. R℟

May your Holy Spirit come to dwell in the hearts of your faithful,—and renew the face of the earth. R℟

Into your hands we commend our dead;—confirm our hope in the resurrection to come. R℟

Our Father

The concluding prayer as at Morning Prayer, p 285.

WEEK 7: THURSDAY

Invitatory ant. Christ the Lord has promised us the Holy Spirit: come, let us adore him, alleluia.

MORNING PRAYER

Hymn, from the appendix, for Eastertide II.

Scripture Reading   *Rom 8:10-11*

If Christ lives in you, then although the body be a dead thing in virtue of our guilt, the spirit is a living thing, by virtue of our justification. And if the Spirit of him who raised up Jesus from the dead dwells in you, he who raised up Jesus Christ from the dead will give life to your perishable bodies too, for the sake of his Spirit who dwells in you.

Short Responsory

R℟ The Lord has risen from the dead, alleluia, alleluia. *Repeat* R℟

V℣ For our sake he died on the cross. R℟ Glory be. R℟

Benedictus ant. Go into the world and teach all people; baptize them in the name of the Father, and of the Son, and of the Holy Spirit, alleluia.

Intercessions
Blessed be Christ the Lord. It is through him that we have access
to the Father in the Holy Spirit. R̷ Christ, hear us.
Send your Holy Spirit, the welcome guest of the heart;—do not
allow us to grieve him by the harshness of our words. R̷
Lord Jesus, ascended to the Father, we turn to you in the night of
our anxiety and the day of our over-confidence;—plead for us with
the Father. R̷
May your Spirit make us one with you;—let us never be separated
from your love by distress, persecution or danger. R̷
As our brother, you accepted us;—teach us to glorify God and to
accept one another. R̷
Our Father

Concluding Prayer
Lord God,
let your Spirit come upon us in power
and fill us with his gifts,
to render our minds pleasing to you,
and make us docile to your will.
(We make our prayer) through our Lord.

EVENING PRAYER

Hymn, from the appendix, for Eastertide II.

Scripture Reading   *1 Cor 6:19-20*
Your body, you know, is the temple of the Holy Spirit, who is in you
since you received him from God. You are not your own property;
you have been bought and paid for. That is why you should use your
body for the glory of God.

Short Responsory
R̷ The Holy Spirit is the Advocate, alleluia, alleluia. *Repeat* R̷
V̷ He will teach you everything. R̷ Glory be. R̷

Magnificat ant. When the Spirit of truth comes he will teach you the
whole truth; he will reveal to you things that are to come, alleluia.

Intercessions

Let us pray to Christ, who is blessed for ever. Let us ask him to send the Holy Spirit to those he has redeemed. ℟ Lord, protect those you have redeemed.

Send the Spirit of unity into your Church;—take away from us anger and dissension. ℟

You freed men who were possessed by devils;—heal the sickness of our world. ℟

By praying through the Holy Spirit, you found the inspiration for your ministry;—may priests discover through prayer how to follow the Holy Spirit and fulfil their life of service. ℟

May your Spirit guide the rulers of all nations;—let them see your vision of peace and make it a reality. ℟

You are living now in the glory of the Father;—call the faithful departed to share in your splendour. ℟

Our Father

The concluding prayer as at Morning Prayer, p 287.

WEEK 7: FRIDAY

Invitatory ant. Christ the Lord has promised us the Holy Spirit: come, let us adore him, alleluia.

MORNING PRAYER

Hymn, from the appendix, for Eastertide II.

Scripture Reading   *Acts 5:30-32*

The God of our fathers raised Jesus from death, after you had killed him by nailing him to a cross. And God raised him to his right side as Leader and Saviour, to give to the people of Israel the opportunity to repent and have their sins forgiven. We are witnesses to these things—we and the Holy Spirit, who is God's gift to those who obey him.

Short Responsory

R/ The Lord has risen from the dead, alleluia, alleluia. *Repeat* R/
V/ For our sake he died on the cross. R/ Glory be. R/

Benedictus ant. Jesus Christ died and has risen from the dead; he sits at the right hand of God where he lives for ever, making intercession for us, alleluia.

Intercessions

To God be honour and glory for ever. May he fill us with hope and with the power of the Holy Spirit. R/ Lord, you are our help and our salvation.

Almighty Father, send your Holy Spirit to turn our words into prayers and our seeking into finding;—Lord, you are our help and our salvation.

Send your Holy Spirit to turn our darkness into light and our falseness into truth;—Lord, you are our help and our salvation.

Send your Holy Spirit to bring order out of chaos and love out of hatred;—Lord, you are our help and our salvation.

Send your Holy Spirit to change contempt for the weak into reverence for your children;—Lord, you are our help and our salvation.

Our Father

Concluding Prayer

Lord God,
you opened for us the way to eternal life
when Christ your Son was taken up to glory,
and your Holy Spirit came to enlighten your Church.
Grant that, as we share in so great a gift,
our faith may grow ever stronger,
our service ever more loyal.
(We make our prayer) through our Lord.

EVENING PRAYER

Hymn, from the appendix, for Eastertide II.

Scripture Reading   *Gal 5:16,22a,25*
Learn to live and move in the Spirit; then there is no danger of your giving way to the impulses of corrupt nature. The Spirit yields a harvest of love, joy, peace, patience, kindness, generosity, forbearance, gentleness, faith, courtesy, temperateness, purity. Since we live by the Spirit, let the Spirit be our rule of life.

Short Responsory
R℟ The Holy Spirit is the Advocate, alleluia, alleluia. *Repeat* R℟
℣ He will teach you everything. R℟ Glory be. R℟

Magnificat ant. They all persevered together in prayer with Mary, the mother of Jesus, alleluia.

Intercessions
Let us bless the Father, who has poured on the nations the grace of the Spirit. R℟ May the grace of the Spirit spread through the world.
Father, you gave your beloved Son as a light for all peoples;—open the eyes of a blind world to see Christ as the future of humanity. R℟
You anointed Christ with the power of the Spirit for his ministry of salvation;—may he pass once more among us, healing the sick and doing good for everyone. R℟
Send your Holy Spirit to give rest to the weary and to strengthen our faith;—give life and joy to broken hearts. R℟
Fulfil the hope of the faithful departed;—raise them up in glory when Christ comes again. R℟
Our Father

The concluding prayer as at Morning Prayer, p 289.

WEEK 7: SATURDAY

Invitatory ant. Christ the Lord has promised us the Holy Spirit: come, let us adore him, alleluia.

MORNING PRAYER

Hymn, from the appendix, for Eastertide II.

Scripture Reading   *Rom 14:7-9*
None of us lives for himself only, none of us dies for himself only; if we live, it is for the Lord that we live, and if we die, it is for the Lord that we die. Whether we live or die, then, we belong to the Lord. For Christ died and rose to life in order to be the Lord of the living and of the dead.

Short Responsory
R҃ The Lord has risen from the dead, alleluia, alleluia. *Repeat* R҃
V҃ For our sake he died on the cross. R҃ Glory be. R҃

Benedictus ant. Behold, I am with you all days, even till the end of the world, alleluia.

Intercessions
Strengthened by the Holy Spirit, let us join with all the baptized in giving glory to the Lord. R҃ Lord Jesus, make us holy by your Spirit.
Send your Holy Spirit into our minds and hearts;—let us proclaim before men that you are king and Lord. R҃
Grant us a love that is genuine;—give us respect and a real affection for one another. R҃
Renew the hearts of the faithful by your life-giving grace;—move them to respond gladly to the gifts of the Spirit. R҃
Grant us the power of your Spirit to repair our damaged lives;—may he turn decay into growth. R҃
Our Father

Concluding Prayer
Give us grace, almighty God,

291

to hold fast in life and conduct
to the mystery we have celebrated at Easter.
(We make our prayer) through our Lord.

PENTECOST SUNDAY

Solemnity

EVENING PRAYER I

Hymn no. 32 or no. 33 from the appendix.

PSALMODY

Ant. 1: On the day of Pentecost they were all together in one place, alleluia.

PSALM 112(113)

Práise, O sérvants of the Lórd,*
práise the náme of the Lórd!
May the náme of the Lórd be bléssed*
both nów and for évermóre!
From the rísing of the sún to its sétting*
práised be the náme of the Lórd!

Hígh above all nátions is the Lórd,*
abóve the héavens his glóry.
Whó is like the Lórd, our Gód,*
who has rísen on hígh to his thróne
yet stóops from the héights to look dówn,*
to look dówn upon héaven and éarth?

From the dúst he lífts up the lówly,*
from his mísery he ráises the póor
to sét him in the cómpany of prínces,*
yés, with the prínces of his péople.
To the chíldless wífe he gives a hóme*
and gláddens her héart with chíldren.

Ant. On the day of Pentecost they were all together in one place, alleluia.

Ant. 2: There appeared to the apostles what seemed like tongues of fire, and the Holy Spirit came upon each of them, alleluia.

PSALM 146(147)

Praise the Lórd for hé is góod;†
sing to our Gód for hé is lóving:*
to hím our práise is dúe.

The Lórd buílds up Jerúsalem*
and bríngs back Ísrael's éxiles,
he héals the bróken-héarted,*
he bínds up áll their wóunds.
He fíxes the númber of the stárs;*
he cálls each óne by its náme.

Our Lórd is gréat and almíghty;*
his wísdom can néver be méasured.
The Lórd ráises the lówly;*
he húmbles the wícked to the dúst.
O síng to the Lórd, giving thánks;*
sing psálms to our Gód with the hárp.

He cóvers the héavens with clóuds;*
he prepáres the ráin for the éarth,
making móuntains spróut with gráss*
and with plánts to sérve man's néeds.
He provídes the béasts with their fóod*
and young rávens that cáll upón him.

His delíght is nót in hórses*
nor his pléasure in wárriors' stréngth.
The Lórd delights in thóse who revére him,*
in thóse who wáit for his lóve.

Ant. There appeared to the apostles what seemed like tongues of fire, and the Holy Spirit came upon each of them, alleluia.

Ant. 3: The Holy Spirit, who comes from the Father, will glorify me, alleluia.

CANTICLE: REV 15:3-4

Great and wonderful are your deeds,*
O Lord God the Almighty!
Just and true are your ways,*
O King of the ages!

Who shall not fear and glorify your name, O Lord?*
For you alone are holy.
All nations shall come and worship you,*
for your judgments have been revealed.

Ant. The Holy Spirit, who comes from the Father, will glorify me, alleluia.

Scripture Reading   *Rom 8:11*
If the Spirit of God who raised up Jesus from the dead dwells in you, he who raised up Jesus Christ from the dead will give life to your perishable bodies too, for the sake of his Spirit who dwells in you.

Short Responsory
R̸ The Holy Spirit is the Advocate, alleluia, alleluia. *Repeat* R̸
V̸ He will teach you everything. R̸ Glory be. R̸

Magnificat ant. Come, Holy Spirit, fill the hearts of your faithful, and enkindle in them the fire of your love; though the peoples spoke different tongues you united them in proclaiming the same faith, alleluia.

Intercessions
The apostles waited and prayed for the coming of the Spirit. Gathered together in their company, we pray for his coming tonight, and joyfully proclaim the greatness of God. R̸ Father, send us your Spirit.
In Christ you restored the universe which you made;—through your Spirit renew the faith of the earth. R̸
You breathed into Adam the breath of life:—breathe your Spirit into the Church, that the world may find life in her. R̸
May your Spirit bring light to our darkness;—turn hatred into love,

sorrow into joy, and doubt into hope. ℟

Cleanse and refresh us in the waters of the Spirit;—where there is anguish and sin, bring healing and rebirth. ℟

Through the Holy Spirit you bring men to life and glory:—may the dead enter their home in heaven to enjoy your love forever. ℟

Our Father

Concluding Prayer

Almighty, ever-living God,
you ordained that the paschal mystery
be completed by the mystery of Pentecost.
Gather together, by your gift of grace,
the scattered nations and divided tongues
to one faith in your Name.
(We make our prayer) through our Lord.

Invitatory

Ant. Alleluia, the Spirit of the Lord has filled the whole world. Come, let us adore him, alleluia.

MORNING PRAYER

Hymn

A mighty wind invades the world,
So strong and free on beating wing:
It is the Spirit of the Lord
From whom all truth and freedom spring.

The Spirit is a fountain clear
For ever leaping to the sky,
Whose waters give unending life,
Whose timeless source is never dry.

The Spirit comes in tongues of flame,
With love and wisdom burning bright,
The wind, the fountain and the fire
Combine in this great feast of light.

O tranquil Spirit, bring us peace,
With God the Father and the Son.

We praise you, blessed Trinity,
Unchanging, and for ever One.

Ant. 1: How good and how kind, Lord, is your Spirit in us, alleluia.

Psalms and canticle from Sunday: Week1, pp 390 ff.

Ant. 2: Let every spring of water bless the Lord; let everything that lives in water sing a hymn to God, alleluia.

Ant. 3: The apostles spoke in different tongues and proclaimed the wonderful deeds of God, alleluia.

Scripture Reading   *Acts 5:30-32*
The God of our fathers raised Jesus from death, after you had killed him by nailing him to a cross. And God raised him to his right side as Leader and Saviour, to give to the people of Israel the opportunity to repent and have their sins forgiven. We are witnesses to these things—we and the Holy Spirit, who is God's gift to those who obey him.

Short Responsory
R̷ They were all filled with the Holy Spirit, alleluia, alleluia.
Repeat R̷
V̷ They began to speak. R̷ Glory be. R̷

Benedictus ant. Receive the Holy Spirit. Those whose sins you forgive will be forgiven them, alleluia.

Intercessions
On this day of Pentecost, the Church is filled with joy. Strengthened with measureless hope, we pray to Christ, who is calling his Church together in the Holy Spirit. R̷ Lord, renew the face of the earth.
Lord Jesus, raised on the cross, you poured out the water of rebirth for the life of the world.—Quicken the life of all men with the gift of the Spirit. R̷
Raised up to God's right hand, you bestowed on the apostles the Father's Gift;—your Church now waits for the same Gift, the same hope. R̷

You breathed your Spirit upon the apostles, and gave them the power of forgiveness:—set all men free today from the prison of sin. ℟ You promised to send us the Spirit of truth, that we might become your heralds throughout the world.—Through his presence in the Church may we bear faithful witness to you. ℟

Our Father

Concluding Prayer
Lord God,
you sanctify your Church in every race and nation
by the mystery we celebrate on this day.
Pour out the gifts of the Holy Spirit on all mankind,
and fulfil now in the hearts of your faithful
what you accomplished
when the Gospel was first preached on earth.
(We make our prayer) through our Lord.

EVENING PRAYER II

Hymn no. 32 or no. 33 from the appendix.

PSALMODY
Ant. 1: The Spirit of the Lord has filled the whole world, alleluia.

PSALM 109(110):1-5,7

The Lórd's revelátion to my Máster:†
'Sít on my ríght:*
your fóes I will pút beneath your féet.'

The Lórd will wíeld from Síon†
your scéptre of pówer:*
rúle in the mídst of all your fóes.

A prínce from the dáy of your bírth†
on the hóly móuntains,*
from the wómb before the dáwn I begót you.

The Lórd has sworn an óath he will not chánge.†
'You are a príest for éver,*
a príest like Melchízedek of óld.'

The Máster stánding at your ríght hand*
will shatter kíngs in the dáy of his wráth.

He shall drínk from the stréam by the wáyside*
and thérefore he shall líft up his héad.

Ant. The Spirit of the Lord has filled the whole world, alleluia.
Ant. 2: Send forth your power, Lord, from your holy temple in
Jerusalem, and bring to perfection your work among us, alleluia.

PSALM 113A(114)

When Ísrael came fórth from Égypt,*
Jacob's sóns from an álien péople,
Júdah becáme the Lord's témple,*
Ísrael becáme his kíngdom.

The séa fléd at the síght:*
the Jórdan turned báck on its cóurse,
the móuntains léapt like ráms*
and the hílls like yéarling shéep.

Whý was it, séa, that you fléd,*
that you túrned back, Jórdan, on your cóurse?
Móuntains, that you léapt like ráms,*
hílls, like yéarling shéep?

Trémble, O éarth, before the Lórd,*
in the présence of the Gód of Jácob,
who túrns the róck into a póol*
and flínt into a spríng of wáter.

Ant. Send forth your power, Lord, from your holy temple in
Jerusalem, and bring to perfection your work among us, alleluia.
Ant. 3: They were all filled with the Holy Spirit and began to speak,
alleluia.

When chanted this canticle is sung with Alleluia *as set out below.*
When recited it suffices to say Alleluia *at the beginning and end of each*
strophe.

CANTICLE: REV 19:1,2,5-7

Alleluia.
Salvation and glory and power belong to our God,*
(R⁊ Alleluia.)
His judgments are true and just.
R⁊ Alleluia (alleluia).

Alleluia.
Praise our God, all you his servants,*
(R⁊ Alleluia.)
You who fear him, small and great.
R⁊ Alleluia (alleluia).

Alleluia.
The Lord our God, the Almighty, reigns,*
(R⁊ Alleluia.)
Let us rejoice and exult and give him the glory.
R⁊ Alleluia (alleluia).

Alleluia.
The marriage of the Lamb has come,*
(R⁊ Alleluia.)
And his bride has made herself ready.
R⁊ Alleluia (alleluia).

Ant. They were all filled with the Holy Spirit and began to speak,
alleluia.

Scripture Reading   *Eph 4:3-6*
Do your best to preserve the unity which the Spirit gives, by the
peace that binds you together. There is one Body and one Spirit,
just as there is one hope to which God has called you. There is one
Lord, one faith, one baptism; there is one God and Father of all
men, who is Lord of all, works through all, and is in all.

Short Responsory
R⁊ The Spirit of the Lord has filled the whole world, alleluia, alleluia.
Repeat R⁊
℣ It is he who holds all things in being and understands every word
that is spoken. R⁊ Glory be. R⁊

Magnificat ant. This is the day of Pentecost, alleluia; today the Holy Spirit appeared to the disciples in the form of fire and gave to them his special gifts; he sent them into the world to proclaim that whoever believes and is baptized will be saved alleluia.

Intercessions

We know that the Father is with us because of the Spirit he has given us. With this confidence we turn to you in prayer: ℟ Father, send your Spirit into the Church!

Father, you want to unite all men by baptism in the Spirit;—draw all believers together in mind and heart. ℟

You sent the Spirit to fill the earth with your love;—let men build the human city in justice and peace. ℟

Lord God, Father of all men, bring to your scattered children unity of faith:—make the world alive with the power of your Spirit. ℟

By the work of the Spirit you create all minds afresh:—heal the sick, comfort the afflicted, and bring all men to salvation. ℟

Through the Holy Spirit you raised your Son from the dead.—Raise us by the power of your Spirit when we come to your kingdom. ℟

Our Father

Concluding Prayer

Lord God,
you sanctify your Church in every race and nation
by the mystery we celebrate on this day.
Pour out the gifts of the Holy Spirit on all mankind,
and fulfil now in the hearts of your faithful
what you accomplished
when the Gospel was first preached on earth.
(We make our prayer) through our Lord.

The invitation to leave is:
Go in the peace of Christ, alleluia, alleluia.
℟ Thanks be to God, alleluia, alleluia.

So Eastertide ends.

THE MOST HOLY TRINITY

Solemnity

EVENING PRAYER I

Hymn no. 37 from the appendix.

Ant. 1: All glory belongs to you, Holy Trinity, one God, before all ages, now and for ever.

PSALM 112(113)

Práise, O sérvants of the Lórd,*
práise the náme of the Lórd!
May the náme of the Lórd be bléssed*
both nów and for évermóre!
From the rísing of the sún to its sétting*
práised be the náme of the Lórd!

Hígh above all nátions is the Lórd,*
abóve the héavens his glóry.
Whó is like the Lórd, our Gód,*
who has rísen on hígh to his thróne
yet stóops from the héights to look dówn,*
to look dówn upon héaven and éarth?

From the dúst he lífts up the lówly,*
from his mísery he ráises the póor
to sét him in the cómpany of prínces,*
yés, with the prínces of his péople.
To the chíldless wífe he gives a hóme*
and gláddens her héart with chíldren.

Ant. All glory belongs to you, Holy Trinity, one God, before all ages, now and for ever.

Ant. 2: Blessed be the Holy Trinity and undivided Unity; let us give praise to him, for he has shown mercy to us.

O práise the Lórd, Jerúsalem!*
Síon, práise your Gód!

He has stréngthened the bárs of your gátes,*
he has bléssed the chíldren withín you.
He estáblished péace on your bórders,*
he féeds you with fínest whéat.

He sénds out his wórd to the éarth*
and swíftly rúns his commánd.
He shówers down snów white as wóol,*
he scátters hóar-frost like áshes.

He húrls down háilstones like crúmbs.*
The wáters are frózen at his tóuch;
he sénds forth his wórd and it mélts them:*
at the bréath of his móuth the waters flów.

He mákes his wórd known to Jácob,*
to Ísrael his láws and decrées.
He has not déalt thus with óther nátions;*
he has not táught them hís decrées.

Ant. Blessed be the Holy Trinity and undivided Unity; let us give
praise to him, for he has shown mercy to us.
Ant. 3: Glory and honour be to God in the unity of the Trinity; to
the Father and to the Son with the Holy Spirit, for ever and ever.

Blessed be the God and Father*
of our Lord Jesus Christ,
who has blessed us in Christ*
with every spiritual blessing in the heavenly places.

He chose us in him*
before the foundation of the world,
that we should be holy*
and blameless before him.

He destined us in love*

to be his sons through Jesus Christ,
according to the purpose of his will,†
to the praise of his glorious grace*
which he freely bestowed on us in the Beloved.

In him we have redemption through his blood,*
the forgiveness of our trespasses,
according to the riches of his grace*
which he lavished upon us.

He has made known to us†
in all wisdom and insight*
the mystery of his will,
according to his purpose*
which he set forth in Christ.

His purpose he set forth in Christ,*
as a plan for the fulness of time,
to unite all things in him,*
things in heaven and things on earth.

Ant. Glory and honour be to God in the unity of the Trinity; to the Father and to the Son with the Holy Spirit, for ever and ever.

Scripture Reading   *Rom 11:33-36*
How rich are the depths of God—how deep his wisdom and knowledge—and how impossible to penetrate his motives or understand his methods! Who could ever know the mind of the Lord? Who could ever be his counsellor? Who could ever give him anything or lend him anything? All that exists comes from him; all is by him and for him. To him be glory for ever! Amen.

Short Responsory
R̸ Let us bless the Father and the Son with the Holy Spirit. Let us praise him for ever. *Repeat* R̸
V̸ To God alone be all honour and glory. R̸ Glory be. R̸

Magnificat ant. We give you thanks, O God; we give thanks to you the one and true Trinity, the one and highest God, the one and all-holy Unity.

303

Intercessions

Father, through your Holy Spirit you gave Christ your Son to us in the flesh, so that we might have life through him. Filled now with that life, we raise our hearts in praise of the Holy Trinity, saying:

℟ Glory be to the Father and to the Son and to the Holy Spirit.

Father almighty, eternal God, in the name of your Son send your Holy Spirit upon the Church:—may the Comforter preserve us in unity, harmony and the fulness of truth. ℟

Lord, send your labourers into the harvest to teach all nations and baptize them in the name of the Father and of the Son and of the Holy Spirit:—strengthen them all in the faith. ℟

Lord, support all those who suffer persecution on account of their faith in your Son:—give them the Spirit of truth who will, according to his promise, speak through them. ℟

Father almighty, all acknowledge that you, the Word and the Spirit are one:—as we believe in one God, so may we hope in you and love you. ℟

Father of the living, bring those who have died to share your glory:—with your Son and the Holy Spirit may they reign eternally with you in heaven. ℟

Our Father

Concluding Prayer

God our Father,
you revealed the great mystery of your godhead to men
when you sent into the world
the Word who is Truth
and the Spirit who makes us holy.
Help us to believe in you and worship you,
as the true faith teaches:
three Persons, eternal in glory,
one God, infinite in majesty.
(We make our prayer) through our Lord.

Invitatory

Ant. The true God is one in Trinity and a Trinity in One: come, let us adore him.

Psalm, p 371.

MORNING PRAYER

Hymn

Father most holy, gracious and forgiving,
Christ, high exalted, prince of our salvation,
Spirit of counsel, nourishing creation,
God ever-living.

Trinity blessèd, Unity unshaken,
Only true Godhead, sea of bounty endless,
Light of the angels, succour thou the friendless,
Shield the forsaken.

All things thou madest—nothing doth but preach thee,
Serving thee ever in its course ordainèd;
We too would hymn thee; this our prayer unfeignèd
Hear, we beseech thee.

Boundless thy praise be, whom no limit boundeth,
God in three Persons, high in heaven living,
Where adoration, homage and thanksgiving
Ever resoundeth.

PSALMODY

Ant. 1: All majesty and power, glory and honour, praise and adoration belongs to you, O blessed Trinity, for ever and ever.

Psalms and canticle of Sunday, Week 1, pp 390 ff.

Ant. 2: All your creatures rightly give you praise, worship and honour, O blessed Trinity.

Ant. 3: From him, through him, and in him are all things: to him be glory for ever.

Scripture Reading   *1 Cor 12:4-6*

There is a variety of gifts but always the same Spirit; there are all sorts of service to be done, but always to the same Lord; working in all sorts of different ways in different people, it is the same God who is working in all of them.

Short Responsory

R̷ To you be praise and glory, O blessed Trinity. *Repeat* R̷
V̷ To you be thanksgiving for ever and ever. R̷ Glory be. R̷

Benedictus ant. Blessed be the creator and ruler of all things, the holy and undivided Trinity, both now and for ever and for ages unending.

Intercessions

Full of joy on this morning, we adore and glorify the Father, Son and Holy Spirit, saying: R̷ Glory be to the Father and to the Son and to the Holy Spirit.

Holy Father, of ourselves we are nothing. We beg you to give us the Holy Spirit:—may he strengthen us in our weakness and intercede for us before your face. R̷

Son of God, you asked the Father to send the Comforter to your Church:—may he, the Spirit of truth, remain with us always. R̷

Come, Holy Spirit, and give us an abundance of your fruits. Make us loving, joyful, peaceful, patient and kind:—give us integrity, forbearance, gentleness, faith, modesty, temperance and chastity. R̷

Father almighty, you sent the Spirit of your Son into our hearts:—fill us with your Spirit, that we may be your heirs and co-heirs with Christ. R̷

Lord Jesus Christ, you sent the Paraclete from the Father's side to be your witness:—make us also your witnesses before men. R̷

Our Father

Concluding Prayer

God our Father,
you revealed the great mystery of your godhead to men
when you sent into the world
the Word who is Truth
and the Spirit who makes us holy.
Help us to believe in you and worship you,
as the true faith teaches:
three Persons, eternal in glory,
one God, infinite in majesty.
(We make our prayer) through our Lord.

EVENING PRAYER II

Hymn no. 37 from the appendix.

PSALMODY

Ant. 1: O true, highest and everlasting Trinity, Father, Son and Holy Spirit.

PSALM 109(110):1-5,7

The Lórd's revelátion to my Máster:†
'Sít on my ríght:*
your fóes I will pút beneath your féet.'

The Lórd will wíeld from Síon†
your scéptre of pówer:*
rúle in the mídst of all your fóes.

A prínce from the dáy of your bírth†
on the hóly móuntains;*
from the wómb before the dáwn I begót you.

The Lórd has sworn an óath he will not chánge.†
'You are a príest for éver,*
a príest like Melchízedek of óld.'

The Máster stánding at your ríght hand*
will shatter kíngs i n the dáy of his wráth.

He shall drínk from the stréam by the wáyside*
and thérefore he shall líft up his héad.

Ant. O true, highest and everlasting Trinity, Father, Son and Holy Spirit.
Ant. 2: Give us freedom, salvation and life, O blessed Trinity.

PSALM 113A(114):1-8

When Ísrael came fórth from Égypt,*
Jacob's sóns from an álien péople,
Júdah becáme the Lord's témple,*
Ísrael becáme his kíngdom.

307

The séa fléd at the síght:*
the Jórdan turned báck on its cóurse,
the móuntains léapt like ráms*
and the hílls like yéarling shéep.

Whý was it, séa, that you fléd,*
that you túrned back, Jórdan, on your cóurse?
Móuntains, that you léapt like ráms,*
hílls, like yéarling shéep?

Trémble, O éarth, before the Lórd,*
in the présence of the Gód of Jácob,
who túrns the róck into a póol*
and flínt into a spríng of wáter.

Ant. Give us freedom, salvation and life, O blessed Trinity.
Ant. 3: Holy, holy, holy is the Lord God almighty, who was, who is, and who is to come.

When chanted, this canticle is sung with Alleluia *as set out below. When recited it suffices to say* Alleluia *at the beginning and end of each strophe.*

CANTICLE: REV 19:1-2,5-7

Alleluia.
Salvation and glory and power belong to our God,*
(R∕ Alleluia.)
His judgments are true and just.
R∕ Alleluia (alleluia).

Alleluia.
Praise our God, all you his servants,*
(R∕ Alleluia.)
You who fear him, small and great.
R∕ Alleluia (alleluia).

Alleluia.
The Lord our God, the Almighty, reigns,*
(R∕ Alleluia.)
Let us rejoice and exult and give him the glory.
R∕ Alleluia (alleluia).

Alleluia.
The marriage of the Lamb has come,*
(R̷ Alleluia.)
And his bride has made herself ready.
R̷ Alleluia (alleluia).

Ant. Holy, holy, holy is the Lord God almighty, who was, who is, and who is to come.

Scripture Reading   *Eph 4:3-6*
Do your best to preserve the unity which the Spirit gives, by the peace that binds you together. There is one body and one Spirit, just as there is one hope to which God has called you. There is one Lord, one faith, one baptism; there is one God and Father of all men, who is Lord of all, works through all and is in all.

Short Responsory
R̷ Let us bless the Father and the Son with the Holy Spirit. Let us praise him for ever. *Repeat* R̷
V̷ To God alone be all honour and glory. R̷ Glory be. R̷

Magnificat ant. With our heart and lips we praise you, we worship you and we bless you, God the Father unbegotten, only-begotten Son, and Holy Spirit Paraclete: all glory is yours for ever.

Intercessions
Father, through your Holy Spirit you gave Christ your Son to us in the flesh, so that we might have life through him. Filled now with that life, we raise our hearts in praise of the Holy Trinity, saying:
R̷ Glory be to the Father and to the Son and to the Holy Spirit.
Father almighty, eternal God, in the name of your Son send your Holy Spirit upon the Church:—may the Comforter preserve us in unity, harmony and the fulness of truth. R̷
Lord, send your labourers into the harvest to teach all nations and baptize them in the name of the Father and of the Son and of the Holy Spirit:—strengthen them all in the faith. R̷
Lord, support all those who suffer persecution on account of their faith in your Son:—give them the Spirit of truth who will, according

to his promise, speak through them. ℞ Glory be to the Father
and to the Son and to the Holy Spirit.

Father almighty, all acknowledge that you, the Word and the Spirit
are one:—as we believe in one God, so may we hope in you and
love you. ℞

Father of the living, bring those who have died to share your glory:
—with your Son and the Holy Spirit may they reign eternally with
you in heaven. ℞

Our Father

The concluding prayer as at Morning Prayer, p 306.

Thursday after Holy Trinity

THE BODY AND BLOOD
OF CHRIST

Solemnity

*Where the Solemnity of the Body and Blood of Christ is not a holyday
of obligation, it is assigned to the Sunday following Holy Trinity as its
proper day.*

EVENING PRAYER I

Hymn

Hail our Saviour's glorious Body,
Which his Virgin Mother bore;
Hail the Blood which, shed for sinners,
Did a broken world restore;
Hail the sacrament most holy,
Flesh and Blood of Christ adore!

To the Virgin, for man's healing,
His own Son the Father sends;
From the Father's love proceeding
Sower, seed and Word descends;
Wondrous life of Word incarnate
With his greatest wonder ends!

On that paschal evening see him
With the chosen twelve recline,

To the old law still obedient
In its feast of love divine;
Love divine, the new law giving,
Gives himself as Bread and Wine!

By his word the Word almighty
Makes of bread his flesh indeed;
Wine becomes his very life-blood:
Faith God's living Word must heed!
Faith alone may safely guide us
Where the senses cannot lead!

Come, adore this wondrous presence;
Bow to Christ, the source of grace!
Here is kept the ancient promise
Of God's earthly dwelling-place!
Sight is blind before God's glory,
Faith alone may see his face!

Glory be to God the Father,
Praise to his co-equal Son,
Adoration to the Spirit,
Bond of love, in Godhead one!
Blest be God by all creation
Joyously while ages run!

PSALMODY

Ant. 1: The Lord is merciful; he gives food to those who fear him to make them remember his wonders.

PSALM 110(111)

I will thánk the Lórd with all my héart*
in the méeting of the júst and their assémbly.
Gréat are the wórks of the Lórd;*
to be póndered by áll who lóve them.

Majéstic and glórious his wórk,*
his jústice stands fírm for éver.
He mákes us remémber his wónders.*
The Lórd is compássion and lóve.

He gives fóod to thóse who féar him;*
keeps his cóvenant éver in mínd.
He has shówn his míght to his péople*
by gíving them the lánds of the nátions.

His wórks are jústice and trúth:*
his précepts are áll of them súre,
standing fírm for éver and éver:*
they are máde in úprightness and trúth.

He has sént delíverance to his péople*
and estáblished his cóvenant for éver.*
Hóly his náme, to be féared.

To fear the Lórd is the fírst stage of wísdom;*
all who dó so próve themselves wíse.*
His práise shall lást for éver!

Ant. The Lord is merciful; he gives food to those who fear him to
make them remember his wonders.
Ant. 2: The Lord has established peace for his Church, he feeds us
with finest wheat.

PSALM 147

O práise the Lórd, Jerúsalem!*
Síon, práise your Gód!

He has stréngthened the bárs of your gátes,*
he has bléssed the chíldren withín you.
He estáblished péace on your bórders,*
he féeds you with fínest whéat.

He sénds out his wórd to the éarth*
and swiftly rúns his commánd.
He shówers down snów white as wóol,*
he scátters hóar-frost like áshes.

He húrls down háilstones like crúmbs.*
The wáters are frózen at his tóuch;
he sénds forth his wórd and it mélts them:*
at the bréath of his móuth the waters flów.

He mákes his wórd known to Jácob,*
to Ísrael his láws and decrées.
He has not déalt thus with óther nátions;*
he has not táught them hís decrées.

Ant. The Lord has established peace for his Church, he feeds us with finest wheat.
Ant. 3: Truly I say to you, it was not Moses who gave you bread from heaven, it is my Father who gives you the true bread from heaven, alleluia.

CANTICLE: REV 11:17-18;12:10B-12A

We give thanks to you, Lord God Almighty,*
who are and who were,
that you have taken your great power*
and begun to reign.

The nations raged,*
but your wrath came,
and the time for the dead to be judged,*
for rewarding your servants, the prophets and saints,
and those who fear your name,*
both small and great.

Now the salvation and the power†
and the kingdom of our God*
and the authority of his Christ have come,
for the accuser of our brethren has been thrown down,*
who accuses them day and night before our God.

And they have conquered him*
by the blood of the Lamb
and by the word of their testimony,*
for they loved not their lives even unto death.
Rejoice, then, O heaven,*
and you that dwell therein.

Ant. Truly I say to you, it was not Moses who gave you bread from

313

heaven, it is my Father who gives you the true bread from heaven, alleluia.

Scripture Reading   *1 Cor 10:16-17*

The cup of blessing which we bless, is it not a participation in the blood of Christ? The bread which we break, is it not a participation in the body of Christ? Because there is one bread, we who are many are one body, for we all partake of the one bread.

Short Responsory

R̷ He gave them the bread of heaven to eat, alleluia, alleluia. *Repeat* R̷
V̷ Man has tasted the food of angels. R̷ Glory be. R̷

Magnificat ant. Lord, how good you are and how gentle is your spirit. When you wished to show your goodness to your sons you gave them bread from heaven, filling the hungry with good things and sending the rich away empty.

Intercessions

At the supper to which all are invited, Christ gives his body and blood for the life of the world. Earnestly we beseech him, saying:
R̷ Lord Jesus Christ, give us the bread of eternal life.
Lord Jesus Christ, Son of the living God, you have commanded us to celebrate the eucharistic meal in remembrance of you:—enrich your Church with the worthy celebration of these mysteries. R̷
Lord Jesus Christ, eternal high priest, you have committed to your priests the ministration of your sacraments:—help them to do their part in your work with the unfailing gladness of genuine charity. R̷
Lord Jesus Christ, manna from heaven, you make into one all who share the one bread:—grant peace and concord to all who believe in you. R̷
Lord Jesus Christ, heavenly physician, you give an eternal remedy and a pledge of resurrection to those who eat your bread:—grant health to the ailing and a real hope to sinners. R̷
Lord Jesus Christ, king, who is to come, we know that whenever we celebrate these mysteries, we proclaim your death until you come

again:—bring all those who have died in you to share your resurrection. R̥

Our Father

Concluding Prayer

Lord Jesus Christ,
you gave to your Church an admirable sacrament
as the abiding memorial of your passion.
Teach us so to worship
the sacred mystery of your Body and Blood,
that its redeeming power
may sanctify us always.
Who live and reign with the Father and the Holy Spirit,
God, for ever and ever.

Invitatory

Ant. Christ the Lord is the bread of life: come, let us adore him.
Psalm, p 371.

MORNING PRAYER

Hymn

Forth from on high the Father sends
His Son, who yet stays by his side.
The Word made man for man then spends
His life till life's last eventide.

While Judas plans the traitor's sign,
The mocking kiss that Love betrays,
Jesus in form of bread and wine
His loving sacrifice displays.

He gives himself that faith may see
The heavenly Food on which men feed,
That flesh and blood of man may be
Fed by his Flesh and Blood indeed.

By birth he makes himself man's kin;
As Food before his guests he lies;

To death he bears man's cross of sin;
In heaven he reigns as man's blest prize.

O Priest and Victim, Lord of Life,
Throw wide the gates of Paradise!
We face our foes in mortal strife;
Thou art our strength! O heed our cries!

To Father, Son and Spirit blest,
One only God, be ceaseless praise!
May he in goodness grant us rest
In heaven, our home, for endless days!

PSALMODY

Ant. 1: Your people eat the food of angels, you give them bread from heaven, alleluia.

Psalms and canticle of Sunday, Week 1, pp 390 ff.

Ant. 2: Priests are set apart to offer incense and bread to God, alleluia.

Ant. 3: To the one who overcomes I will give the hidden manna and a new name, alleluia.

Scripture Reading   *Mal 1:11*
From farthest east to farthest west my name is honoured among the nations and everywhere a sacrifice of incense is offered to my name, and a pure offering too, since my name is honoured among the nations, says the Lord of Hosts.

Short Responsory
R̦ You bring forth bread from the earth, alleluia, alleluia. *Repeat* R̦
V̦ Your wine gives joy to man's heart. R̦ Glory be. R̦

Benedictus ant. I am the living bread which came down from heaven; whoever eats this bread will live for ever, alleluia.

Intercessions

Joyfully we make our prayer to Jesus Christ, the bread of life, and we say: ℟ Happy are those who are called to your supper, Lord.

Lord Jesus Christ, high priest of the new and eternal covenant, on the altar of the cross you offered a perfect sacrifice to the Father:— teach us how to offer it with you. ℟

Lord Jesus Christ, king of peace and justice, you consecrated bread and wine as a sign of your self-giving:—unite us as victims to yourself. ℟

Lord Jesus Christ, obedient always to your Father's will, throughout the world the Church renews your offering from the rising of the sun to its setting:—unite in one body those who share the one bread. ℟

Lord Jesus Christ, as the manna came from the heavens, you nourish your Church with your body and blood:—in the strength of your food we will walk in your paths. ℟

Lord Jesus Christ, unseen guest at our banquet, you stand at our door and knock:—come to us, fill our hearts with your truth and stay with us. ℟

Our Father

Concluding Prayer

Lord Jesus Christ,
you gave your Church an admirable sacrament
as the abiding memorial of your passion.
Teach us so to worship
the sacred mystery of your Body and Blood,
that its redeeming power
may sanctify us always.
Who live and reign with the Father and the Holy Spirit,
God, for ever and ever.

EVENING PRAYER II

Hymn as at Evening Prayer I, p 310.

PSALMODY

Ant. 1: Christ the Lord is a priest for ever. Like Melchizedek he made an offering of bread and wine.

PSALM 109(110):1-5,7

The Lórd's revelátion to my Máster:†
'Sít on my ríght:*
your fóes I will pút beneath your féet.'

The Lórd will wíeld from Síon†
your scéptre of pówer:*
rúle in the mídst of all your fóes.

A prínce from the dáy of your bírth†
on the hóly móuntains;*
from the wómb before the dáwn I begót you.

The Lórd has sworn an óath he will not chánge.†
'You are a príest for éver,*
a príest like Melchízedek of óld.'

The Máster stánding at your ríght hand*
will shatter kíngs in the dáy of his wráth.

He shall drínk from the stréam by the wáyside*
and thérefore he shall líft up his héad.

Ant. Christ the Lord is a priest for ever. Like Melchizedek he made
an offering of bread and wine.
Ant. 2: I will take the chalice of salvation and I will offer a thanksgiving sacrifice.

PSALM 115(116)

I trústed, éven when I sáid:*
'I am sórely afflícted,'
and whén I sáid in my alárm:*
'No mán can be trústed.'

How cán I repáy the Lórd*
for his góodness to mé?
The cúp of salvátion I will ráise;*
I will cáll on the Lórd's name.

My vóws to the Lórd I will fulfíl*
befóre all his péople.

O précious in the éyes of the Lórd*
is the déath of his fáithful.

Your sérvant, Lord, your sérvant am Í;*
you have lóosened my bónds.
A thánksgiving sácrifice I máke:*
I will cáll on the Lórd's name.

My vóws to the Lórd I will fulfíl*
befóre all his péople,
in the cóurts of the hóuse of the Lórd,*
in your mídst, O Jerúsalem.

Ant. I will take the chalice of salvation and I will offer a thanksgiving sacrifice.
Ant. 3: You are the Way, you are the Truth, you, O Lord, are the Life of the world.

When chanted, this canticle is sung with Alleluia *as set out below. When recited, it suffices to say* Alleluia *at the beginning and end of each strophe.*

CANTICLE: REV 19:1-2,5-7

Alleluia.
Salvation and glory and power belong to our God,*
(R⁷ Alleluia.)
His judgments are true and just.
R⁷ Alleluia (alleluia).

Alleluia.
Praise our God, all you his servants,*
(R⁷ Alleluia.)
You who fear him, small and great.
R⁷ Alleluia (alleluia).

Alleluia.
The Lord our God, the Almighty, reigns,*
(R⁷ Alleluia.)
Let us rejoice and exult and give him the glory.
R⁷ Alleluia (alleluia).

Alleluia.
The marriage of the Lamb has come,*
(R Alleluia.)
And his bride has made herself ready.
R Alleluia (alleluia).

Ant. You are the Way, you are the Truth, you, O Lord, are the Life of the world.

Scripture Reading   *I Cor 11:23-25*

This is what I received from the Lord, and in turn passed on to you: that on the same night that he was betrayed, the Lord Jesus took some bread, and thanked God for it and broke it, and he said: 'This is my body which is for you; do this as a memorial of me.' In the same way he took the cup after supper, and said: 'This cup is the new covenant in my blood. Whenever you drink it, do this as a memorial of me.'

Short Responsory

R He gave them the bread of heaven to eat, alleluia, alleluia.
Repeat R
V Man has tasted the food of angels. R Glory be. R

Magnificat ant. O sacred feast in which we partake of Christ: his sufferings are remembered, our minds are filled with his grace and we receive a pledge of the glory that is to be ours, alleluia.

Intercessions

At the supper to which all are invited, Christ gives his body and blood for the life of the world. Earnestly we beseech him, saying:
R Lord Jesus Christ, give us the bread of eternal life.
Lord Jesus Christ, Son of the living God, you have commanded us to celebrate the eucharistic meal in remembrance of you:—enrich your Church with the worthy celebration of these mysteries. R
Lord Jesus Christ, eternal high priest, you have committed to your priests the ministration of your sacraments:—help them to do their part in your work with the unfailing gladness of genuine charity. R
Lord Jesus Christ, manna from heaven, you make into one all who share the one bread:—grant peace and concord to all who believe

in you. R̷
Lord Jesus Christ, heavenly physician, you give an eternal remedy
and a pledge of resurrection to those who eat your bread:—grant
health to the ailing and a real hope to sinners. R̷
Lord Jesus Christ, king who is to come, we know that whenever we
celebrate these mysteries, we proclaim your death until you come
again:—bring all those who have died in you to share your resurrection. R̷
Our Father

The concluding prayer as at Morning Prayer, p 317.

Friday after the Second Sunday after Pentecost
THE MOST SACRED HEART
OF JESUS
Solemnity

EVENING PRAYER I

Hymn
As at Morning Prayer, p 325, or

All ye who seek a comfort sure
In trouble and distress,
Whatever sorrows vex the mind,
Or guilt the soul oppress:

Jesus, who gave himself for you
Upon the Cross to die,
Opens to you his sacred heart,—
Oh, to that heart draw nigh.

Ye hear how kindly he invites;
Ye hear his words so blest,
'All ye that labour, come to me,
And I will give you rest.'

What meeker than the Saviour's heart?
As on the Cross he lay,
It did his murderers forgive,
And for their pardon pray.

PSALMODY

Ant. 1: God has loved us with an everlasting love; therefore, when he was raised up from the earth he showed us his mercy and drew us to love his sacred heart.

PSALM 112(113)

Práise, O sérvants of the Lórd,*
práise the náme of the Lórd!
May the náme of the Lórd be bléssed*
both nów and for évermóre!
From the rísing of the sún to its sétting*
práised be the náme of the Lórd!

Hígh above all nátions is the Lórd,*
abóve the héavens his glóry.
Whó is like the Lórd, our Gód,*
who has rísen on hígh to his thróne
yet stóops from the héights to look dówn,*
to look dówn upon héaven and éarth?

From the dúst he lífts up the lówly,*
from his mísery he ráises the póor
to sét him in the cómpany of prínces,*
yés, with the prínces of his people.
To the chíldless wífe he gives a hóme*
and gláddens her héart with chíldren.

Ant. God has loved us with an everlasting love; therefore, when he was raised up from the earth he showed us his mercy and drew us to love his sacred heart.

Ant. 2: Learn from me, for I am meek and humble of heart, and you will find rest for your souls.

PSALM 145(146)

My sóul, give práise to the Lórd;†
I will práise the Lórd all my dáys,*
make músic to my Gód while I líve.

Pút no trúst in prínces,*
in mortal mén in whóm there is no hélp.
Take their bréath, they retúrn to cláy*
and their pláns that dáy come to nóthing.

He is háppy who is hélped by Jacob's Gód,*
whose hópe is in the Lórd his Gód,
who alóne made héaven and éarth,*
the séas and áll they contáin.

It is hé who keeps fáith for éver,*
who is júst to thóse who are oppréssed.
It is hé who gives bréad to the húngry,*
the Lórd, who sets prísoners frée,

the Lórd who gives síght to the blínd,*
who ráises up thóse who are bowed dówn,
the Lórd, who protécts the stránger*
and uphólds the wídow and órphan.

It is the Lórd who lóves the júst*
but thwárts the páth of the wícked.
The Lórd will réign for éver,*
Sion's Gód, from áge to áge.

Ant. Learn from me, for I am meek and humble of heart, and you
will find rest for your souls.
Ant. 3: I am the good shepherd who leads his sheep to good pastures,
and I lay down my life for my sheep.

CANTICLE: REV 4:11;5:9,10,12

Worthy are you, our Lord and God,*
to receive glory and honour and power,
for you created all things,*
and by your will they existed and were created.

Worthy are you, O Lord,*
to take the scroll and to open its seals,
for you were slain,†
and by your blood you ransomed men for God*
from every tribe and tongue and people and nation.

You have made us a kingdom and priests to our God,*
and we shall reign on earth.

Worthy is the Lamb who was slain,*
to receive power and wealth,
and wisdom and might,*
and honour and glory and blessing.

Ant. I am the good shepherd who leads his sheep to good pastures,
and I lay down my life for my sheep.

Scripture Reading   *Eph 5:25b-27*
Christ loved the Church and sacrificed himself for her to make her
holy. He made her clean by washing her in water with a form of
words, so that when he took her to himself she would be glorious,
with no speck or wrinkle or anything like that, but holy and faultless.

Short Responsory
R̸ Christ loved us and washed away our sins with his blood.
Repeat R̸
V̸ He made us a kingdom and priests to serve his God and Father. R̸
Glory be. R̸

Magnificat ant. I have come to spread fire on earth, and how I wish
it were blazing already.

Intercessions
We make our prayers to Jesus, in whom we find rest for our souls,
and we say to him: R̸ Beloved Lord, have mercy on us.
Jesus, your heart was pierced by the lance and from it flowed blood
and water so that your bride, the Church, might be born:—keep
her in holiness without spot or wrinkle. R̸

Jesus, holy temple of God, you were condemned by men and raised up by the Father:—make the Church the tabernacle of the Most High. ℟

Jesus, king and centre of all hearts, in your loving mercy you never cease to draw us to yourself:—keep alive your covenant with us all. ℟

Jesus, our peace and reconciliation, from the cross you forgave your enemies and you bring all men together in peace:—show us how to reach the Father. ℟

Jesus, our life and resurrection, you lighten our burden and give rest to our souls:—draw all sinners to yourself. ℟

Jesus, because of your infinite love you were obedient even unto death on a cross:—bring to life all those who are sleeping in peace. ℟

Our Father

Concluding Prayer
Almighty God and Father,
we glory in the Sacred Heart of Jesus, your beloved Son,
as we call to mind the great things his love has done for us.
Fill us with the grace that flows in abundance
from the Heart of Jesus, the source of heaven's gifts.
(We make our prayer) through our Lord.

Invitatory
Ant. The heart of Jesus was wounded for love of us: come, let us adore him.
Psalm, p 371.

MORNING PRAYER

Hymn
The love of God was shown to man
In Christ our Saviour's wounded heart;
He asks us now to share his Cross
And in his passion take our part.

We are the Father's gift to Christ
Who loved his own until the end,
Whose burden light we bear with joy,
And gladly to his yoke we bend.

Where love and loving-kindness are,
The God of love will always be;
He binds us with a weightless chain
That leaves the willing captive free.

Praise Father, Son and Spirit blest,
Eternal Trinity sublime,
Who make their home in humble hearts,
Indwelling to the end of time.

PSALMODY

Ant. 1: Jesus stood and cried out, 'If any man thirsts, let him come to me and drink.'

Psalms and canticle of Sunday, Week 1, pp 390 ff.

Ant. 2: Come to me, all you who labour and are burdened, and I will give you rest.

Ant. 3: My son, let your heart attend to me, keep your eyes fixed on my advice.

Scripture Reading   *Jer 31:33*
This is the covenant which I will make with Israel after those days, says the Lord; I will set my law within them and write it on their hearts; I will become their God and they shall become my people.

Short Responsory
R℣ Take my yoke upon you and learn from me. *Repeat* R℣
℣ I am meek and humble of heart. R℣ Glory be. R℣

Benedictus ant. In his tender mercy God has visited us; he has redeemed his people, alleluia.

Intercessions

We make our prayers to Jesus, who is meek and humble of heart, and we say to him: R⁷ Beloved Lord, have mercy on us.

Jesus, in you abides the fulness of godhead:—let us share in your divine nature. R⁷

Jesus, in you are found all the treasures of wisdom and knowledge:—through your Church reveal to us the manifold wisdom of God. R⁷

Jesus, in you the Father was well pleased:—make us persevere in following your teaching. R⁷

Jesus, of your fulness we have all received:—pour out upon us in abundance the grace and truth of the Father. R⁷

Jesus, you are the source of life and holiness:—make us holy and perfect in charity. R⁷

Our Father

Concluding Prayer

Almighty God and Father,
we glory in the Sacred Heart of Jesus, your beloved Son,
as we call to mind the great things his love has done for us.
Fill us with the grace that flows in abundance
from the Heart of Jesus, the source of heaven's gifts.
(We make our prayer) through our Lord.

EVENING PRAYER II

Hymn as at Evening Prayer I, p 321, or Morning Prayer, p 325.

PSALMODY

Ant. 1: With your gentle yoke, Lord, rule in the midst of your foes.

PSALM 109(110):1-5,7

The Lórd's revelátion to my Máster:†
'Sít on my ríght:*
your fóes I will pút beneath your féet.'

The Lórd will wíeld from Síon†
your scéptre of pówer:*
rúle in the mídst of all your fóes.

A prínce from the dáy of your bírth†
on the hóly móuntains;*
from the wómb before the dáwn I begót you.

The Lórd has sworn an óath he will not chánge.†
'You are a príest for éver,*
a príest like Melchízedek of óld.'

The Máster stánding at your ríght hand*
will shatter kíngs in the dáy of his wráth.

He shall drínk from the stréam by the wáyside*
and thérefore he shall líft up his héad.

Ant. With your gentle yoke, Lord, rule in the midst of your foes.
Ant. 2: The Lord is compassion and love: he gives food to those who
fear him.

PSALM 110(111)

I will thánk the Lórd with all my héart*
in the méeting of the júst and their assémbly.
Gréat are the wórks of the Lórd;*
to be póndered by áll who lóve them.

Majéstic and glórious his wórk,*
his jústice stands fírm for éver.
He mákes us remémber his wónders.*
The Lórd is compássion and lóve.

He gives fóod to thóse who féar him;*
keeps his cóvenant éver in mínd.
He has shówn his míght to his péople*
by gíving them the lánds of the nátions.

His wórks are jústice and trúth:*
his précepts are áll of them súre,
standing fírm for éver and éver:*
they are máde in úprightness and trúth.

He has sént delíverance to his péople†
and estáblished his cóvenant for éver.*
Hóly his náme, to be féared.

To fear the Lórd is the fírst stage of wísdom;†
all who dó so próve themselves wíse.*
His práise shall lást for éver!

Ant. The Lord is compassion and love: he gives food to those who
fear him.
Ant. 3: This is the Lamb of God, this is he who takes away the sins
of the world.

CANTICLE: PHIL 2:6-11

Though he was in the form of God,*
Jesus did not count equality with God a thing to be grasped.

He emptied himself †
taking the form of a servant,*
being born in the likeness of men.

And being found in human form,†
he humbled himself and became obedient unto death,*
even death on a cross.

Therefore God has highly exalted him*
and bestowed on him the name which is above every name,

That at the name of Jesus every knee should bow,*
in heaven and on earth and under the earth,

And every tongue confess that Jesus Christ is Lord,*
to the glory of God the Father.

Ant. This is the Lamb of God, this is he who takes away the sins of
the world.

Scripture Reading   *Eph 2:4-7*
God's mercy is so abundant, and his love for us is so great, that
while we were spiritually dead in our disobedience, he brought us to
life with Christ; it is by God's grace that you have been saved. In our
union with Christ Jesus, he raised us up with him to rule with him in
the heavenly world. He did this to demonstrate for all time to come
the abundant riches of his grace in the love he showed us in Christ
Jesus.

Short Responsory

R̷ Christ loved us and washed away our sins and his blood.
Repeat R̷

V̷ He made us a kingdom and priests to serve his God and Father.
R̷ Glory be. R̷

Magnificat ant. The Lord has received us into his own self, into his heart, remembering his mercy, alleluia.

Intercessions

We make our prayers to Jesus, in whom we find rest for our souls, and we say to him: R̷ Beloved Lord, have mercy on us.

Jesus, your heart was pierced by the lance and from it flowed blood and water so that your bride, the Church, might be born:—keep her in holiness without spot or wrinkle. R̷

Jesus, holy temple of God, you were condemned by men and raised up by the Father:—make the Church the tabernacle of the Most High. R̷

Jesus, king and centre of all hearts, in your loving mercy you never cease to draw us to yourself:—keep alive your covenant with us all. R̷

Jesus, our peace and reconciliation, from the cross you forgave your enemies and you bring all men together in peace:—show us how to reach the Father. R̷

Jesus, our life and resurrection, you lighten our burden and give rest to our souls:—draw all sinners to yourself. R̷

Jesus, because of your infinite love you were obedient even unto death on a cross:—bring to life all those who are sleeping in peace. R̷

Our Father

The concluding prayer as at Morning Prayer, p 327.

THE ORDINARY SUNDAYS
OF THE YEAR

WEEK 1

Psalter: Week 1

The Feast of the Baptism of the Lord takes the place of the Sunday.

SUNDAY 2

Psalter: Week 2

EVENING PRAYER I

Magnificat ant. Behold the Lamb of God who takes away the sins of the world, alleluia.

The concluding prayer as at Morning Prayer.

MORNING PRAYER

Benedictus ant. The disciples went and saw where Jesus was staying, and they spent the rest of the day with him.

Concluding Prayer
Almighty God,
ruler of all things in heaven and on earth,
listen favourably to the prayer of your people,
and grant us your peace in our day.
(We make our prayer) through our Lord.

EVENING PRAYER II

Magnificat ant. There was a wedding at Cana in Galilee, and Jesus was there with Mary his mother.

The concluding prayer as at Morning Prayer.

SUNDAY 3

EVENING PRAYER I

Magnificat ant. Jesus preached the gospel of the kingdom of God, and cured those who were in need of healing.

The concluding prayer as at Morning Prayer.

MORNING PRAYER

Benedictus ant. Come, follow me, and the Lord; I will make you fishers of men.

Concluding Prayer
All-powerful, ever-living God,
direct our steps in the way of your love,
so that our whole life may be fragrant
with all we do in the name of Jesus, your beloved Son,
who lives and reigns with you and the Holy Spirit,
God, for ever and ever.

EVENING PRAYER II

Magnificat ant. The spirit of the Lord rests upon me; he has sent me to preach his gospel to the poor.

The concluding prayer as at Morning Prayer.

SUNDAY 4

EVENING PRAYER I

Magnificat ant. When Jesus saw the crowds he went up the mountain; his disciples came and gathered round him and he began to teach them.

The concluding prayer as at Morning Prayer.

MORNING PRAYER

Benedictus ant. The people were astounded at his teaching because he taught them with authority.

Concluding Prayer
Lord our God,
make us love you above all things,
and all our fellow-men
with a love that is worthy of you.
(We make our prayer) through our Lord.

EVENING PRAYER II

Magnificat ant. Everyone was astonished at the words that came from the mouth of God.

The concluding prayer as at Morning Prayer.

SUNDAY 5

Psalter: Week 1

EVENING PRAYER I

Magnificat ant. You are the light of the world. Let your light shine before men; let them see your good works and give honour to your Father in heaven.

The concluding prayer as at Morning Prayer.

MORNING PRAYER

Benedictus ant. Jesus got up early in the morning and left the house. He went to a deserted place and prayed there.

Concluding Prayer
Guard your family, Lord, with constant loving care,
for in your divine grace we place our only hope.
(We make our prayer) through our Lord.

EVENING PRAYER II

Magnificat ant. Master, we have worked hard all night and have caught nothing; but if you say so, I will let down the nets.

The concluding prayer as at Morning Prayer

SUNDAY 6

Psalter: Week 2

EVENING PRAYER I

Magnificat ant. If you are offering your gift at the altar and there remember that your brother has something against you, leave your offering there before the altar, go and be reconciled with your brother first, and then come and present your offering, alleluia.

The concluding prayer as at Morning Prayer.

MORNING PRAYER

Benedictus ant. Lord, if it is your will, you can make me clean. Jesus answered: It is my will, may you be clean.

Concluding Prayer
To those who love you, Lord,
you promise to come with your Son
and make your home within them.
Come then with your purifying grace
and make our hearts a place where you can dwell.
(We make our prayer) through our Lord.

EVENING PRAYER II

Magnificat ant. Blessed are you who are in need; the kingdom of God is yours. Blessed are you who hunger now; you shall be satisfied.

The concluding prayer as at Morning Prayer.

SUNDAY 7

EVENING PRAYER I

Magnificat ant. Pray for those who persecute you and for those who treat you badly; in this way you will be sons of your Father in heaven, says the Lord.

The concluding prayer as at Morning Prayer

MORNING PRAYER

Benedictus ant. The paralytic took up the bed on which he was lying and gave praise to God. When the people saw this they also praised God.

Concluding Prayer
Grant, almighty God,
that with our thoughts always on the things of the Spirit
we may please you in all that we say and do.
(We make our prayer) through our Lord.

EVENING PRAYER II

Magnificat ant. Do not judge, and you will not be judged, says the Lord; as you judge others, so you also will be judged.

The concluding prayer as at Morning Prayer.

SUNDAY 8

EVENING PRAYER I

Magnificat ant. Set your hearts first on the kingdom of God, and on keeping his commandments, and then all these other things will be given you as well, alleluia.

The concluding prayer as at Morning Prayer.

MORNING PRAYER

Benedictus ant. No man puts new wine into old wineskins; new wine must be kept in new skins.

Concluding Prayer
In your mercy, Lord, direct the affairs of men so peaceably
that your Church may serve you in tranquillity and joy.
(We make our prayer) through our Lord.

EVENING PRAYER II

Magnificat ant. A good tree cannot bear bad fruit; a bad tree cannot bring forth good fruit.

The concluding prayer as at Morning Prayer.

SUNDAY 9

Psalter: Week I

EVENING PRAYER I

Magnificat ant. It is not the man who says to me, 'Lord, Lord', who will enter the kingdom of heaven: but the man who does the will of my Father will enter the kingdom of heaven.

The concluding prayer as at Morning Prayer.

MORNING PRAYER

Benedictus ant. The sabbath day was made for man, not man for the sabbath.

Concluding Prayer
Lord God, by whom our lives are governed with unfailing
    wisdom and love,
take away from us all that is harmful

and give us all that will be for our good.
(We make our prayer) through our Lord.

EVENING PRAYER II

Magnificat ant. Lord, I am not worthy to have you under my roof;
only say the word and my servant will be healed.

The concluding prayer as at Morning Prayer.

SUNDAY 10

Psalter: Week 2

EVENING PRAYER I

Magnificat ant. Mercy is what I want, not sacrifice. For I did not
come to call the virtuous, but sinners.

The concluding prayer as at Morning Prayer.

MORNING PRAYER

Benedictus ant. Whoever does the will of God is my brother, and my
sister, and my mother.

Concluding Prayer
Lord God, source of all good,
hear our prayer:
inspire us with good intentions,
and help us to fulfil them.
(We make our prayer) through our Lord.

EVENING PRAYER II

Magnificat ant. A great prophet has risen up among us and God has
come to visit his people.

The concluding prayer as at Morning Prayer.

SUNDAY 11

EVENING PRAYER I

Magnificat ant. Go, preach the gospel of the kingdom; you received without cost, you must give without charge, alleluia.

The concluding prayer as at Morning Prayer.

MORNING PRAYER

Benedictus ant. The kingdom of heaven is like a mustard seed which is the smallest of all seeds; yet it grows into the biggest shrub of all.

Concluding Prayer
Lord God, strength of those who hope in you,
support us in our prayer:
because we are weak and can do nothing without you,
give us always the help of your grace
so that, in fulfilling your commandments,
we may please you in all we desire and do.
(We make our prayer) through our Lord.

EVENING PRAYER II

Magnificat ant. Jesus said to the woman, 'Your faith has saved you. Go in peace.'

The concluding prayer as at Morning Prayer.

SUNDAY 12

EVENING PRAYER I

Magnificat ant. If any man bears witness to me before men, I also will bear witness to him in the presence of my Father.

The concluding prayer as at Morning Prayer.

MORNING PRAYER

Benedictus ant. Save us, Lord, we are in danger; O God, give the command, and there will be peace.

Concluding Prayer
Lord God,
teach us at all times to fear and love your holy name,
for you never withdraw your guiding hand
from those you establish in your love.
(We make our prayer) through our Lord.

EVENING PRAYER II

Magnificat ant. If any man wishes to come after me, he must deny himself and take up his cross, and in that way he must follow me.

The concluding prayer as at Morning Prayer.

SUNDAY 13

Psalter: Week I

EVENING PRAYER I

Magnificat ant. Whoever receives you, receives me; and whoever receives me, receives the one who sent me, says the Lord.

The concluding prayer as at Morning Prayer.

MORNING PRAYER

Benedictus ant. Jesus turned round and saw the woman. He said, 'Take courage, daughter: your faith has saved you, alleluia.'

Concluding Prayer
Lord God,
since by the adoption of grace,
you have made us children of light:

339

do not let false doctrine darken our minds,
but grant that your light may shine within us
and we may always live in the brightness of truth.
(We make our prayer) through our Lord.

EVENING PRAYER II

Magnificat ant. The Son of Man came not to destroy souls but to save them.

The concluding prayer as at Morning Prayer.

SUNDAY 14

Psalter: Week 2

EVENING PRAYER

Magnificat ant. My yoke is easy and my burden is light, says the Lord.

The concluding prayer as at Morning Prayer.

MORNING PRAYER

Benedictus ant. Many were astonished when they heard the teaching of Jesus. They said, 'How is it that all this has come to him? Surely this is the carpenter, the son of Mary?'

Concluding Prayer
Lord God,
when our world lay in ruins
you raised it up again
on the foundation of your Son's passion and death;
give us grace to rejoice in the freedom from sin
which he gained for us,
and bring us to everlasting joy.
(We make our prayer) through our Lord.

EVENING PRAYER II

Magnificat ant. The harvest is great, but the labourers are few. Pray to the Lord of the harvest that he may send labourers into his harvest.

The concluding prayer as at Morning Prayer.

SUNDAY 15

Psalter: Week 3

EVENING PRAYER I

Magnificat ant. The seed is the word of God and Christ is the sower; whoever listens to this word will live for ever.

The concluding prayer as at Morning Prayer.

MORNING PRAYER

Benedictus ant. The disciples set out to preach repentance; and they anointed many sick people with oil and cured them.

Concluding Prayer
God and Father,
to those who go astray you reveal the light of your truth
and enable them to return to the right path:
grant that all who have received the grace of baptism
may strive to be worthy of their Christian calling,
and reject everything opposed to it.
(We make our prayer) through our Lord.

EVENING PRAYER II

Magnificat ant. 'Master, what is the greatest commandment in the Law?' Jesus said to him, 'You must love the Lord your God with all your heart, alleluia.'

The concluding prayer as at Morning Prayer.

SUNDAY 16

Psalter: Week 4

EVENING PRAYER I

Magnificat ant. The kingdom is like the yeast a woman took and mixed in with three measures of flour till it was leavened all through.

The concluding prayer as at Morning Prayer.

MORNING PRAYER

Benedictus ant. Jesus saw the great multitude and he was moved to compassion for them because they were like a flock of sheep with no shepherd.

Concluding Prayer
Be gracious, Lord, to us who serve you,
and in your kindness increase your gifts of grace within us:
so that fervent in faith, hope and love
we may be ever on the watch
and persevere in doing what you command.
(We make our prayer) through our Lord.

EVENING PRAYER II

Magnificat ant. Mary has chosen the better part and it will never be taken from her.

The concluding prayer as at Morning Prayer.

SUNDAY 17

Psalter: Week 1

EVENING PRAYER I

Magnificat ant. The kingdom of heaven is like a merchant seeking good pearls; when he has found one of great value he sells everything else and buys it.

The concluding prayer as at Morning Prayer.

MORNING PRAYER

Benedictus ant. When those men saw the sign that Jesus had given, they said, 'This really is the Prophet who is to come into the world.'

Concluding Prayer
Lord God, protector of those who hope in you,
without whom nothing is strong, nothing holy,
support us always with your love.
Guide us so to use the good things of this world,
that even now we may hold fast to what endures for ever.
(We make our prayer) through our Lord.

EVENING PRAYER II

Magnificat ant. Ask, and you will receive; seek and you will find; knock, and the door will be opened to you, alleluia.

The concluding prayer as at Morning Prayer.

SUNDAY 18

Psalter: Week 2

EVENING PRAYER I

Magnificat ant. A great crowd had gathered about Jesus, and they had nothing to eat. He called his disciples and said to them, 'I feel compassion for all these people.'

The concluding prayer as at Morning Prayer.

MORNING PRAYER

Benedictus ant. Do not work for food that cannot last, but work for food that endures to eternal life.

Concluding Prayer
We recognize with joy
that you, Lord, created us,
and that you guide us by your providence.
In your unfailing kindness
support us in our prayer:
renew your life within us,
guard it and make it bear fruit for eternity.
(We make our prayer) through our Lord.

EVENING PRAYER II

Magnificat ant. If you wish to be truly rich, my brothers, then seek true riches.

The concluding prayer as at Morning Prayer.

SUNDAY 19

Psalter: Week 3

EVENING PRAYER I

Magnificat ant. 'Lord, bid me to come to you on the waters.' Jesus reached out his hand and took hold of Peter. He said, 'Man of little faith, why did you doubt?'

The concluding prayer as at Morning Prayer.

MORNING PRAYER

Benedictus ant. Truly I say to you, 'Whoever has faith in me has eternal life, alleluia.'

Concluding Prayer
Almighty, ever-living God,
we confidently call you Father as well as Lord.
Renew your Spirit in our hearts,

make us ever more perfectly your children,
so that we may enter upon the inheritance you have promised us.
(We make our prayer) through our Lord.

EVENING PRAYER II

Magnificat ant. Wherever your treasure is, there also will your heart
be, says the Lord.

The concluding prayer as at Morning Prayer.

SUNDAY 20

Psalter: Week 4

EVENING PRAYER I

Magnificat ant. Woman, your faith is great; let it be done for you
as you have asked.

The concluding prayer as at Morning Prayer.

MORNING PRAYER

Benedictus ant. I am the living bread which has come down from
heaven. If any man eats of this bread he will live for ever, alleluia.

Concluding Prayer
Lord God,
you have prepared for those who love you
what no eye has seen, no ear has heard.
Fill our hearts with your love,
so that loving you above all and in all,
we may attain your promises
which the heart of man has not conceived.
(We make our prayer) through our Lord.

EVENING PRAYER II

Magnificat ant. I have come to spread a fire on earth, and how I wish it were blazing already.

The concluding prayer as at Morning Prayer.

SUNDAY 21

Psalter: Week I

EVENING PRAYER I

Magnificat ant. 'You are the Christ, the Son of the living God.' 'Blessed are you, Simon, Bar Jona.'

The concluding prayer as at Morning Prayer.

MORNING PRAYER

Benedictus ant. To whom shall we go, Lord? You have the words of eternal life. We believe and we know that you are the Christ, the Son of God, alleluia.

Concluding Prayer
Lord, by your grace we are made one in mind and heart.
Give us a love for what you command
and a longing for what you promise,
so that, amid this world's changes,
our hearts may be set on the world of lasting joy.
(We make our prayer) through our Lord.

EVENING PRAYER II

Magnificat ant. Many will come from the east and from the west to take their places with Abraham and Isaac and Jacob in the kingdom of heaven.

The concluding prayer as at Morning Prayer.

SUNDAY 22

Psalter: Week 2

EVENING PRAYER I

Magnificat ant. What does it profit a man if he gains the whole world, but suffers the loss of his own soul?

The concluding prayer as at Morning Prayer.

MORNING PRAYER

Benedictus ant. Listen, and understand these traditions which the Lord has given to you.

Concluding Prayer
Father of might and power,
every good and perfect gift
comes down to us from you.
Implant in our hearts the love of your name,
increase our zeal for your service,
nourish what is good in us
and tend it with watchful care.
(We make our prayer) through our Lord.

EVENING PRAYER II

Magnificat ant. When you are invited to a marriage feast sit in the lowest place, so that the one who invited you can say to you, 'Friend, take a higher place.' Then everyone with you at table will see you honoured, alleluia.

The concluding prayer as at Morning Prayer.

SUNDAY 23

Psalter: Week 3

EVENING PRAYER I

Magnificat ant. Where two or three are gathered together in my name, I am there in their midst, says the Lord.

The concluding prayer as at Morning Prayer.

MORNING PRAYER

Benedictus ant. He has done all things well: he made the deaf hear and the dumb speak, alleluia.

Concluding Prayer
Since it is from you, God our Father,
that redemption comes to us, your adopted children:
look with favour on the family you love,
give true freedom to us and to all who believe in Christ,
and bring us all alike to our eternal heritage.
(We make our prayer) through our Lord.

EVENING PRAYER II

Magnificat ant. Whoever does not take up his cross and follow me, cannot be my disciple, says the Lord.

The concluding prayer as at Morning Prayer.

SUNDAY 24

Psalter: Week 4

EVENING PRAYER I

Magnificant ant. Jesus said to Peter, 'I do not say to you that you should forgive seven times, but rather seventy-seven times.'

The concluding prayer as at Morning Prayer.

MORNING PRAYER

Benedictus ant. Whoever loses his life for my sake and for the sake of the gospel, will save it, says the Lord.

Concluding Prayer
Look upon us, Lord, creator and ruler of the whole world:
give us grace to serve you with all our heart
that we may come to know the power of your forgiveness and love.
(We make our prayer) through our Lord.

EVENING PRAYER II

Magnificat ant. I say to you that there is great joy among the angels when one sinner repents.

The concluding prayer as at Morning Prayer.

SUNDAY 25

Psalter: Week 1

EVENING PRAYER I

Magnificat ant. You also must go into my vineyard; and I will pay you what is just.

The concluding prayer as at Morning Prayer.

MORNING PRAYER

Benedictus ant. The greatest among you must be your servant, says the Lord. Anyone who humbles himself will be exalted, alleluia.

Concluding Prayer
Father,
you summed up the whole law
as love of you and of our neighbour.
Grant that by keeping this commandment of love,

349

we may come to eternal life.
(We make our prayer) through our Lord.

EVENING PRAYER II

Magnificat ant. No man can serve two masters. You cannot serve both God and money.

The concluding prayer as at Morning Prayer.

SUNDAY 26

Psalter: Week 2

EVENING PRAYER I

Magnificat ant. It is not the man who says to me, 'Lord, Lord,' who will enter the kingdom of heaven, but the man who does the will of my Father, alleluia.

The concluding prayer as at Morning Prayer.

MORNING PRAYER

Benedictus ant. Whoever gives you a drink of water in my name, because you follow Christ, will not lose his reward, says the Lord.

Concluding Prayer
Lord,
you reveal your mighty power
most of all by your forgiveness and compassion:
fill us constantly with your grace
as we hasten to share the joys you have promised us in heaven.
(We make our prayer) through our Lord.

EVENING PRAYER II

Magnificat ant. My son, remember that you received good things during your life, just as Lazarus received bad things.

The concluding prayer as at Morning Prayer.

SUNDAY 27

EVENING PRAYER I

Magnificat ant. He will bring those wretched men to a wretched end and lease the vineyard to other tenants who will deliver the fruits to him at the proper season.

The concluding prayer as at Morning Prayer.

MORNING PRAYER

Benedictus ant. Let the little children come to me; for the kingdom of heaven belongs to such as these.

Concluding Prayer
Almighty, ever-living God,
whose love surpasses all that we ask or deserve,
open up for us the treasures of your mercy.
Forgive us all that weighs on our conscience,
and grant us more even than we dare to ask.
(We make our prayer) through our Lord.

EVENING PRAYER II

Magnificat ant. Say to yourselves, 'We are useless servants, we only did what we had to do.'

The concluding prayer as at Morning Prayer.

SUNDAY 28

EVENING PRAYER I

Magnificat ant. A certain man prepared a great feast and invited many guests. When everything was ready and the time for the feast had come he sent his servant to call those who had been invited, alleluia.

The concluding prayer as at Morning Prayer

MORNING PRAYER

Benedictus ant. You, who have left everything and have come after me, will receive a hundredfold in return and will possess eternal life.

Concluding Prayer
Lord God,
open our hearts to your grace.
Let it go before us and be with us,
that we may always be intent upon doing your will.
(We make our prayer) through our Lord.

EVENING PRAYER II

Magnificat ant. When one of them saw that he had been made clean, he went back and gave praise to God with a loud voice, alleluia.

The concluding prayer as at Morning Prayer.

SUNDAY 29

Psalter: Week 1

EVENING PRAYER I

Magnificat ant. Give to Caesar the things that belong to Caesar, and to God the things that belong to God, alleluia.

The concluding prayer as at Morning Prayer.

MORNING PRAYER

Benedictus ant. The Son of Man did not come to be served but to serve, and to give up his life to redeem many.

Concluding Prayer
Almighty, ever-living God,
make us ever obey you willingly and promptly.
Teach us how to serve you
with sincere and upright hearts
in every sphere of life.
(We make our prayer) through our Lord.

EVENING PRAYER II

Magnificat ant. When the Son of Man comes, do you think he will find faith on earth?

The concluding prayer as at Morning Prayer.

SUNDAY 30

Psalter: Week 2

EVENING PRAYER I

Magnificat ant. 'Master, what is the greatest commandment in the Law?' Jesus said to him, 'You must love the Lord your God with all your heart, alleluia.'

The concluding prayer as at Morning Prayer.

MORNING PRAYER

Benedictus ant. 'Have mercy on me, Son of David,' 'What do you wish me to do for you?' 'Lord, that I may see.'

Concluding Prayer
Lord God, deepen our faith,
strengthen our hope,
enkindle our love:
and so that we may obtain what your promise

make us love what you command.
(We make our prayer) through our Lord.

EVENING PRAYER II

Magnificat ant. The publican went home justified, for everyone who exalts himself will be humbled, but the man who humbles himself will be exalted.

The concluding prayer as at Morning Prayer.

SUNDAY 31

Psalter: Week 3

EVENING PRAYER I

Magnificat ant. You have only one master and he is in heaven: Christ, the Lord.

The concluding prayer as at Morning Prayer.

MORNING PRAYER

Benedictus ant. You must love the Lord your God with all your heart. You must love your fellow man as yourself. There is no other commandment that is more important than these.

Concluding Prayer
God of power and mercy,
by whose grace your people give you praise and worthy service:
save us from faltering on our way
to the joys you have promised.
(We make our prayer) through our Lord.

EVENING PRAYER II

Magnificat ant. The Son of Man came to seek out and to save that which was lost.

The concluding prayer as at Morning Prayer.

SUNDAY 32

Psalter: Week 4

EVENING PRAYER I

Magnificat ant. At midnight a cry was raised: 'Behold, the bridegroom is coming, go out and meet him.'

The concluding prayer as at Morning Prayer.

MORNING PRAYER

Benedictus ant. That poor widow gave more than all the others, for in her poverty she gave all she had.

Concluding Prayer
Defend us, Lord, against every distress
so that unencumbered in body and soul,
we may devote ourselves to your service in freedom and joy.
(We make our prayer) through our Lord.

EVENING PRAYER II

Magnificat ant. He is God, not of the dead, but of the living: because for him all things are alive, alleluia.

The concluding prayer as at Morning Prayer.

SUNDAY 33

Psalter: Week 1

(*If this is the last Sunday of the Year the solemnity of Christ the King, pp 357 ff, is celebrated.*)

EVENING PRAYER I

Magnificat ant. Well done, my good servant, you have proved yourself faithful in small things. Enter into the joy of your Lord.

The concluding prayer as at Morning Prayer.

MORNING PRAYER

Benedictus ant. They will see the Son of Man coming on the clouds of heaven with great power and glory.

Concluding Prayer
Lord our God,
give us grace to serve you always with joy,
because our full and lasting happiness
is to make of our lives
a constant service to the Author of all that is good.
(We make our prayer) through our Lord.

EVENING PRAYER II

Magnificat ant. Your endurance will win you your lives, says the Lord.

The concluding prayer as at Morning Prayer.

CHRIST THE KING

Solemnity

EVENING PRAYER I

Hymn
As at Morning Prayer, p 361, or

Hail Redeemer, King divine!
Priest and Lamb, the throne is thine,
King, whose reign shall never cease,
Prince of everlasting peace.
  Angels, saints and nations sing
  'Praised be Jesus Christ, our King;
  Lord of life, earth, sky and sea,
  King of love on Calvary.'

King, whose name creation thrills,
Rule our minds, our hearts, our wills,
Till in peace each nation rings
With thy praises, King of kings.
  Angels, etc.

King most holy, King of truth,
Guide the lowly, guide the youth;
Christ, thou King of glory bright,
Be to us eternal light.
  Angels, etc.

Shepherd-King o'er mountains steep
Homeward bring the wandering sheep;
Shelter in one royal fold
States and kingdoms, new and old.
  Angels, etc.

PSALMODY

Ant. 1: He will be called the 'Peacemaker', and his throne will stand
for ever.

PSALM 112(113)

Práise, O sérvants of the Lórd,*
práise the náme of the Lórd!
May the náme of the Lórd be bléssed*
both nów and for évermóre!
From the rísing of the sún to its sétting*
práised be the náme of the Lórd!

Hígh above all nátions is the Lórd,*
abóve the héavens his glóry.
Whó is like the Lórd, our Gód,*
who has rísen on hígh to his thróne
yet stóops from the héights to look dówn,*
to look dówn upon héaven and éarth?

From the dúst he lífts up the lówly,*
from his mísery he ráises the póor
to sét him in the cómpany of prínces,*
yés, with the prínces of his péople.
To the chíldless wífe he gives a hóme*
and gláddens her héart with chíldren.

Ant. He will be called the 'Peacemaker', and his throne will stand
firm for ever.
Ant. 2: His kingdom is an everlasting kingdom; all kings will serve
him and obey him.

PS 116(117)

O práise the Lórd, all you nátions,*
accláim him all you péoples!

Stróng is his lóve for ús;*
he is fáithful for éver.

Ant. His kingdom is an everlasting kingdom; all kings will serve him
and obey him.
Ant. 3: Christ has received the authority and glory of a king; every
people, tribe and nation will serve him for ever.

CANTICLE: REV 4:11;5:9,10,12

Worthy are you, our Lord and God,*
to receive glory and honour and power,
for you created all things,*
and by your will they existed and were created.

Worthy are you, O Lord,*
to take the scroll and to open its seals,
for you were slain,†
and by your blood you ransomed men for God*
from every tribe and tongue and people and nation.

You have made us a kingdom and priests to our God,*
and we shall reign on earth.

Worthy is the Lamb who was slain,*
to receive power and wealth,
and wisdom and might,*
and honour and glory and blessing.

Ant. Christ has received the authority and glory of a king; every people, tribe and nation will serve him for ever.

Scripture Reading   *Cf Eph 1:20-23*
God raised Christ from the dead, and enthroned him at his right hand in the heavenly realms, far above all government and authority, all power and dominion, and any title of sovereignty that can be named, not only in this age but in the age to come. He put everything in subjection beneath his feet, and appointed him as supreme head to the church, which is his body and as such holds within it the fulness of him who himself receives the entire fulness of God.

Short Responsory
R7 Yours are majesty and power; yours, Lord, is the sovereignty.
Repeat R7
V7 You are ruler of all. R7 Glory be. R7

Magnificat ant. The Lord God will give him the throne of David, his ancestor; he will reign in the house of Jacob for ever and his kingdom will know no end, alleluia.

Intercessions

To Christ our King, who is first in all things and in whom all things exist, let us confidently pray: R̷ Lord, may your kingdom come.

Lord Jesus Christ, our king and our shepherd, gather your flock from every corner of the earth:—protect it in your fresh and fertile pastures. R̷

Jesus, our leader and Saviour, make all people your own; heal the sick, seek out the lost, preserve the strong:—bring back the strayed, reunite those who are scattered and give new hope to the down-hearted. R̷

Jesus, eternal judge, when you hand over your kingdom to your Father, remember us, your faithful people:—let us take possession of the kingdom prepared for us since the foundation of the world. R̷

Jesus, prince of peace, remove from men's hearts the greed that leads to war:—speak words of peace to your people. R̷

Jesus, heir of all nations, bring all mankind to the kingdom of your Church, entrusted to you by the Father:—move all men to acknowledge you as the Head in the unity of the Holy Spirit. R̷

Jesus, first-born of all creation and first to be born from the dead:—bring all the departed to the glory of your resurrection. R̷

Our Father

Concluding Prayer

Almighty, ever-living God,
it is your will
to unite the entire universe
under your beloved Son,
Jesus Christ, the King of heaven and earth.
Grant freedom to the whole of creation,
and let it praise and serve your majesty for ever.
(We make our prayer) through our Lord.

Invitatory

Ant. Jesus Christ is the king of kings: come, let us adore him.
Psalm, p 371.

MORNING PRAYER

Hymn

To Christ the Lord of worlds we sing,
The nations' universal King.
Hail, conquering Christ, whose reign alone
Over our hearts and souls we own.

Christ, who art known the prince of peace,
Bid all rebellious tumults cease;
Call home thy straying sheep, and hold
For ever in one faithful fold.

For this, thine arms, on Calvary,
Were stretched across th' empurpled tree,
And the sharp spear that through thee ran
Laid bare the heart that burned for man.

For this, in forms of bread and wine
Lies hid the plenitude divine,
And from thy wounded body runs
The stream of life to all thy sons.

PSALMODY

Ant. 1: Behold a man whose name is 'The Rising Sun'; he will sit on the throne and rule over all; he will speak of peace to the peoples.

Psalms and canticle of Sunday, Week 1, pp 390 ff.

Ant. 2: He will receive glory throughout the earth, he himself will be peace.

Ant. 3: The Lord has given him power and honour and kingdom; every people, tribe and nation will serve him.

Scripture Reading   *Eph 4:15-16*

By speaking the truth in a spirit of love, we must grow up in every way to Christ, who is the head. Under his control all the different parts of the body fit together, and the whole body is held together by every joint with which it is provided. So when each separate part works as it should, the whole body grows and builds itself up through love.

Short Responsory
℟ O Lord, your saints will tell of the glory of your kingdom. *Repeat* ℟
℣ They will speak of your power. ℟ Glory be. ℟

Benedictus ant. He made us a kingdom for his God and Father; he is the firstborn from the dead, the leader of the kings of the earth, alleluia.

Intercessions
To Christ our King, who is first in all things and in whom all things exist, let us confidently pray: ℟ Lord, may your kingdom come.
Lord Jesus Christ, our God and Saviour, you are our king and our shepherd:—lead your people through all the troubles of life. ℟
Jesus, the Good Shepherd, you laid down your life for your sheep:
—guide us to make the most of our opportunities for good. ℟
Jesus, our Redeemer, you are the king of the whole universe:—restore all things in yourself. ℟
Jesus, king of all men, you came into the world to bear witness to the truth:—make men aware of your primacy in all things. ℟
Jesus, our master and model, you have brought us into your kingdom:—help us to give an example which is innocent, holy and worthy of you. ℟
Our Father

Concluding Prayer
Almighty, ever-living God,
it is your will
to unite the entire universe
under your beloved Son,
Jesus Christ, the King of heaven and earth.
Grant freedom to the whole of creation,
and let it praise and serve your majesty for ever.
(We make our prayer) through our Lord.

EVENING PRAYER II

Hymn as at Evening Prayer I, p 357, or Morning Prayer, p 361.

PSALMODY

Ant. 1: He will sit on the throne of David and will rule his kingdom for ever, alleluia.

PSALM 109(110):1-5,7

The Lórd's revelátion to my Máster:†
'Sít on my ríght:*
your fóes I will pút beneath your féet.'

The Lórd will wíeld from Síon†
your scéptre of pówer:*
rúle in the mídst of all your fóes.

A prínce from the dáy of your bírth†
on the hóly móuntains;*
from the wómb before the dáwn I begót you.

The Lórd has sworn an óath he will not chánge.†
'You are a príest for éver,*
a príest like Melchízedek of óld.'

The Máster stánding at your ríght hand*
will shatter kíngs in the dáy of his wráth.

He shall drínk from the stréam by the wáyside*
and thérefore he shall líft up his héad.

Ant. He will sit on the throne of David and will rule his kingdom for ever, alleluia.

Ant. 2: Yours is an everlasting kingdom; Lord, your rule lasts from age to age.

PSALM 144(145):1-13

I will give you glóry, O Gód my Kíng,*
I will bléss your náme for éver.

I will bléss you dáy after dáy*

363

and práise your náme for éver.
The Lord is gréat, híghly to be práised,*
his gréatness cánnot be méasured.

Age to áge shall procláim your wórks,*
shall decláre your míghty déeds,
shall spéak of your spléndour and glóry,*
tell the tále of your wónderful wórks.

They will spéak of your térrible déeds,*
recóunt your gréatness and míght.
They will recáll your abúndant góodness;*
age to áge shall ríng out your jústice.

The Lord is kínd and fúll of compássion,*
slow to ánger, abóunding in lóve.
How góod is the Lórd to áll,*
compássionate to áll his créatures.

All your créatures shall thánk you, O Lórd,*
and your fríends shall repéat their bléssing.
They shall spéak of the glóry of your réign*
and decláre your míght, O Gód,

to make knówn to mén your mighty déeds*
and the glórious spléndour of your réign.
Yóurs is an éverlasting kíngdom;*
your rúle lasts from áge to áge.

Ant. Yours is an everlasting kingdom; Lord, your rule lasts from age to age.
Ant. 3: On his cloak and on his thigh there was a name written: The King of kings and the Lord of lords. To him be glory and honour for ever and ever.

When chanted, this canticle is sung with Alleluia *as set out below. When recited, it suffices to say* Alleluia *at the beginning and end of each strophe.*

Alleluia.
Salvation and glory and power belong to our God,*
(R⁷ Alleluia.)
His judgments are true and just.
R⁷ Alleluia (alleluia).

Alleluia.
Praise our God, all you his servants,*
(R⁷ Alleluia.)
You who fear him, small and great.
R⁷ Alleluia (alleluia).

Alleluia.
The Lord our God, the Almighty, reigns,*
(R⁷ Alleluia.)
Let us rejoice and exult and give him the glory.
R⁷ Alleluia (alleluia).

Alleluia.
The marriage of the Lamb has come,*
(R⁷ Alleluia.)
And his bride has made herself ready.
R⁷ Alleluia (alleluia).

Ant. On his cloak and on his thigh there was a name written: The King of kings and the Lord of lords. To him be glory and honour for ever and ever.

Scripture Reading   *1 Cor 15:25-28*
He must be king until he has put all his enemies under his feet, and the last of the enemies to be destroyed is death, for everything is to be put under his feet. Though when it is said that everything is subjected, this clearly cannot include the One who subjected everything to him. And when everything is subjected to him, then the Son himself will be subject in his turn to the One who subjected all things to him, so that God may be all in all.

Short Responsory

℟ Your throne, O God, shall stand for ever and ever. *Repeat* ℟
℣ The sceptre of your kingdom is a sceptre of justice. ℟ Glory be. ℟

Magnificat ant. All authority in heaven and on earth has been given to me, says the Lord.

Intercessions and concluding prayer as at Evening Prayer I, p 360.

FREQUENTLY RECURRING
TEXTS

FREQUENTLY RECURRING
TEXTS

INTRODUCTION TO THE DAILY OFFICE

This is used at the beginning of the day, but may be omitted, together with the invitatory psalm.

℣ Lord, open our lips.
℟ And we shall praise your name.

The invitatory psalm is then said, ps 94, p 371, with its antiphon. It is preferable to repeat the antiphon at the beginning of the psalm and after each strophe, GI no. 34 (Introduction no. 3). In recitation on one's own it suffices to say the antiphon once at the beginning of the psalm.

¶ *Pss 99, 66 or 23 may be said in place of ps 94. When one of them occurs in the Office which follows it should be replaced there by ps 94. For the ordinary Sundays and Weekdays of the Year the invitatory antiphon is given in the psalter at the beginning of each day.*
For the Proper of Seasons it is given in the respective proper.

For convenience, the antiphons for the seasons, which are used on more than one occasion, and the series from the psalter are, as well, printed below with ps 94.
For Solemnities and Feasts the antiphon is given either in the appropriate Proper or Common.
On Memorias, unless the antiphon is proper, it may be taken from the appropriate Common or the Weekday or the Season.

Invitatory Antiphon

The Proper of Seasons

ADVENT

I (*to 16 Dec.*): Let us adore the Lord, the king who is to come.
II (*17–23 Dec.*): The Lord is at hand: come, let us adore him.

CHRISTMASTIDE

I (*before Epiphany*): Christ has been born for us: come, let us adore him.
II (*after Epiphany*): Christ has appeared to us: come, let us adore him.

LENT

I (*including Holy Week*): Christ the Lord was tempted and suffered for us: come, let us adore him.
II (*alternative, except in Holy Week*): O that today you would listen to his voice: harden not your hearts.†

EASTERTIDE

I (*to the Ascension*): The Lord has truly risen, alleluia.
II (*Ascension to Pentecost*): Christ the Lord has promised us the Holy Spirit: come, let us adore him, alleluia.

Invitatory Antiphon

Through the Year

WEEKS I AND 3

Sunday: Come, ring out our joy to the Lord; hail the God who saves us, alleluia.†

Monday: Let us come before the Lord, giving thanks.

Tuesday: The Lord is a great king: come, let us adore him.

Wednesday: Let us adore the Lord, for it is he who made us.

Thursday: Come, let us adore the Lord, for he is our God.

Friday: Give thanks to the Lord, for his great love is without end.

Saturday: The Lord's is the earth and its fulness: come, let us adore him.

WEEKS 2 AND 4

Sunday: We are the people of the Lord, the flock that is led by his hand: come, let us adore him, alleluia.

Monday: Let us rejoice in the Lord; with songs let us praise him.

Tuesday: A mighty God is the Lord: come, let us adore him.

Wednesday: Cry out with joy to God, all the earth: serve the Lord with gladness.

Thursday: Come before the Lord, singing for joy.

Friday: Indeed, how good is the Lord; bless his holy name.

Saturday: Let us listen for the voice of the Lord and enter into his peace.

Invitatory Psalm

A CALL TO PRAISE GOD   PSALM 94(95)

Every day, as long as this 'today' lasts, keep encouraging one another
(Heb 3:13)

Come, ríng out our jóy to the Lórd;
háil the Gód who sáves us.
†Let us cóme before him, gíving thánks,
with sóngs let us háil the Lórd. (*Antiphon*)

A míghty Gód is the Lórd,
a gréat king abóve all góds.
In his hánd are the dépths of the éarth;
the héights of the móuntains are hís.
To hím belongs the séa, for he máde it,
and the drý land sháped by his hánds. (*Antiphon*)

Come ín; let us bów and bend lów;
let us knéel before the Gód who máde us
for hé is our Gód and wé
the péople who belóng to his pásture,
the flóck that is léd by his hánd. (*Antiphon*)

O that todáy you would lísten to his vóice!
'Hárden not your héarts† as at Meríbah,
as on that dáy at Mássah in the désert
when your fáthers pút me to the tést;
when they tríed me, thóugh they saw my wórk. (*Antiphon*)

For forty yéars I was wéaried of these péople
and I said: "Their héarts are astráy,
these péople do not knów my wáys."
Thén I took an óath in my ánger:
"Néver shall they énter my rést." ' (*Antiphon*)

Glory be to the Father and to the Son and to the
  Holy Spirit.
As it was in the beginning, is now, and ever shall be,
  world without end. Amen. (*Antiphon*)

Alternative Invitatory Psalms

THE JOY OF THOSE WHO ENTER   PSALM 99(100)
   THE TEMPLE OF THE LORD

The Lord calls all those he has redeemed to sing a hymn of victory (St Athanasius)

> Cry out with jóy to the Lórd, all the éarth.†
> Sérve the Lórd with gládness.*
> Come befóre him, sínging for jóy.

> Know that hé, the Lórd, is Gód.†
> He máde us, we belóng to hím,*
> we are his péople, the shéep of his flóck.

> Gó within his gátes, giving thánks.†
> Enter his cóurts with sóngs of praíse.*
> Give thánks to him and bléss his náme.

> Indéed, how góod is the Lórd,†
> etérnal his mérciful lóve.*
> He is fáithful from áge to áge.

ALL THE PEOPLES WILL GIVE PRAISE TO THE LORD   PSALM 66(67)
Let it be known to you that this salvation from God has been sent to all peoples (Acts 28:28)

> O Gód, be grácious and bléss us*
> and let your fáce shed its líght upón us.
> So will your wáys be knówn upon éarth*
> and all nátions learn your sáving hélp.

> Let the péoples praíse you, O Gód;*
> let áll the péoples praíse you.

> Let the nátions be glád and exúlt*
> for you rúle the wórld with jústice.
> With fáirness you rúle the péoples,*
> you guíde the nátions on éarth.

> Let the péoples praíse you, O Gód;*
> let áll the péoples praíse you.

> The éarth has yíelded its frúit*
> for Gód, our Gód, has bléssed us.

May Gód still gíve us his bléssing*
till the énds of the éarth revére him.

Let the péoples práise you, O Gód;*
let áll the péoples práise you.

THE LORD COMES TO HIS TEMPLE PSALM 23(24)
*The gates of heaven were opened to Christ because he was lifted up in
the flesh* (St Irenaeus)

The Lórd's is the éarth and its fúlness,*
the wórld and áll its péoples.
It is hé who sét it on the séas;*
on the wáters he máde it fírm.

Who shall clímb the móuntain of the Lórd?*
Who shall stánd in his hóly pláce?
The mán with clean hánds and pure héart,†
who desíres not wórthless thíngs,*
who has not swórn so as to decéive his néighbour.

He shall recéive bléssings from the Lórd*
and rewárd from the Gód who sáves him.
Súch are the mén who séek him,*
seek the fáce of the Gód of Jácob.

O gátes, lift hígh your héads;†
grow hígher, áncient dóors.*
Let him énter, the kíng of glóry!

Whó is the kíng of glóry?†
The Lórd, the míghty, the váliant,*
the Lórd, the váliant in wár.

O gátes, lift hígh your héads;†
grow hígher, áncient dóors.*
Let him énter, the kíng of glóry!

Who is hé, the kíng of glóry?†
Hé, the Lórd of ármies,*
hé is the kíng of glóry.

INTRODUCTION TO EACH HOUR

℣ O God, come to our aid.
℟ O Lord, make haste to help us.
Glory be to the Father and to the Son and to the Holy Spirit, as it was in the beginning, is now, and ever shall be, world without end. Amen. Alleluia.

This introduction is omitted a) when the Invitatory is used, and b) when the Hour follows immediately on another Hour. Alleluia *is omitted during Lent.*

THE GOSPEL CANTICLES

The following canticles are used daily in the Divine Office

THE BENEDICTUS
The Canticle of Zechariah

LK 1:68-79

The Messiah and the one who was sent before him

Blessed be the Lord, the God of Israel!*
He has visited his people and redeemed them.

He has raised up for us a mighty saviour*
in the house of David his servant,
as he promised by the lips of holy men,*
those who were his prophets from of old.

A saviour who would free us from our foes,*
from the hands of all who hate us.
So his love for our fathers is fulfilled*
and his holy covenant remembered.

He swore to Abraham our father to grant us,*
that free from fear, and saved from the hands of our foes,
we might serve him in holiness and justice*
all the days of our life in his presence.

As for you, little child,*
you shall be called a prophet of God, the Most High.
You shall go ahead of the Lord*
to prepare his ways before him,

To make known to his people their salvation*
through forgiveness of all their sins,
the loving-kindness of the heart of our God*
who visits us like the dawn from on high.

He will give light to those in darkness,†
those who dwell in the shadow of death,*
and guide us into the way of peace.

Glory be to the Father and to the Son and to the Holy Spirit.*
As it was in the beginning, is now, and ever shall be,
    world without end. Amen.

This is said at Morning Prayer with its antiphon.

*On Sundays and during Advent, Christmastide, Lent and Eastertide
the antiphon each day is proper.*
*On the celebrations of Saints the antiphon, if no proper one is given,
is taken from the Commons.*
*On ordinary Weekdays of the Year the antiphon is taken from the
psalter. These weekday antiphons may also be used in place of
antiphons from the Commons on the Memorias of Saints.*

*The Glory be to the Father is said after every canticle unless ex-
pressly noted to the contrary.*

THE MAGNIFICAT
The Canticle of Mary.

LK 1:46-55

My soul rejoices in the Lord

My soul glorifies the Lord,*
my spirit rejoices in God, my Saviour.
He looks on his servant in her lowliness;*
henceforth all ages will call me blessed.

The Almighty works marvels for me.*
Holy his name!
His mercy is from age to age,*
on those who fear him.

He puts forth his arm in strength*
and scatters the proud-hearted.
He casts the mighty from their thrones*
and raises the lowly.

He fills the starving with good things,*
sends the rich away empty.

He protects Israel, his servant,*
remembering his mercy,
the mercy promised to our fathers,*
to Abraham and his sons for ever.

This is said at Evening Prayer with its antiphon. The choice of antiphon is determined in the same way as is that of the Benedictus antiphon.

THE NUNC DIMITTIS
The Canticle of Simeon

LK 2:29-32

Christ is the light of the nations and the glory of Israel

At last, all-powerful Master,†
you give leave to your servant*
to go in peace, according to your promise.

For my eyes have seen your salvation*
which you have prepared for all nations,
the light to enlighten the Gentiles*
and give glory to Israel, your people.

This canticle is said at Night Prayer with its antiphon.

¶ *The ICET text of these canticles is at the end of this book.*

THE LORD'S PRAYER

The Lord's Prayer is said by all at Morning and Evening Prayer after the intercessions and before the concluding prayer. It may be introduced in this manner:

Let us now pray in the words our Saviour gave us: *Our Father ...*

or by some similar formula, e.g.

I

Let us now pray to the Father, in the words our Saviour gave us: *Our Father ...*

2

As we look to the coming of God's kingdom, let us say: *Our Father ...*

3

Let us sum up our praise and petitions in the words of Christ, saying: *Our Father ...*

4

Let us give a sure foundation to our praise and petitions by the Lord's Prayer: *Our Father ...*

5

Let us, once more, praise the Father and pray to him in the words of Christ himself, saying: *Our Father ...*

6

(*Addressed to Christ*) Lord, remember us in your kingdom, as following your teaching we say: *Our Father ...*

7

Following our Lord's teaching, let us say with faith and trust: *Our Father ...*

8

Let us fulfil our Lord's instruction, and say: *Our Father ...*

9

Let us now together say those words which the Lord gave us as the pattern of all prayer: *Our Father ...*

Our Father, who art in heaven,
hallowed be thy name.
Thy kingdom come.
Thy will be done on earth, as it is in heaven.
Give us this day our daily bread,
and forgive us our trespasses,
as we forgive those who trespass against us
and lead us not into temptation,
but deliver us from evil.

THE CONCLUDING PRAYER

The concluding prayer is prefixed with Let us pray *when said at Night Prayer. At Morning and Evening Prayer it is said after the Lord's Prayer, without this introduction.*

Conclusion of this prayer at Morning and Evening Prayer:

(We make our prayer) through our Lord Jesus Christ, your Son,
who lives and reigns with you and the Holy Spirit,
God, for ever and ever.
R/ Amen.

The lead words only are usually given in the text.
If a different conclusion is to be used it is set out in full in the text.

At Night Prayer the following short conclusions are said:

1 When the prayer is addressed to the Father:
    Through Christ our Lord.

2 When the prayer is addressed to the Father, but ends with a mention of the Son:
    Who lives and reigns for ever and ever.

3 When the prayer is addressed to the Son:
    Who live and reign for ever and ever.

During Advent, Christmastide, Lent and Eastertide the prayer proper to each day concludes all the Hours of the Divine Office except Night Prayer.
On ordinary Sundays of the Year the same rule holds; but on week-days, prayers are given in the psalter for all the Hours.
On the Solemnities and Feasts of Saints the prayer of the celebration is used at all the Hours of the Divine Office except Night Prayer.
On the Memorias of Saints the prayer of the Saint is used at Morning and Evening Prayer only.

CONCLUSION OF THE HOURS

Morning and Evening Prayer
¶ *When a priest or deacon presides over the Office and no other Hour follows:*
The Lord be with you.
R̷ And also with you.
May almighty God bless you, the Father, and the Son, and the Holy Spirit. R̷ Amen.
Another form of blessing may be used as in the Missal.

The people are then invited to leave:
Go in the peace of Christ.
R̷ Thanks be to God.

¶ *When no priest or deacon is present, or in recitation on one's own, the conclusion is as follows:*
The Lord bless us, and keep us from all evil, and bring us to ever-lasting life. R̷ Amen.

Night Prayer
Night Prayer concludes with a blessing:
The Lord grant us a quiet night and a perfect end. R̷ Amen.

Then, at Night Prayer, one of the final anthems to the Blessed Virgin is said or sung.

THE FOUR WEEK PSALTER

WEEK 1: SUNDAY

EVENING PRAYER I

℣ O God, come to our aid.
℟ O Lord, make haste to help us.
Glory be to the Father and to the Son and to the Holy Spirit, as it was in the beginning, is now, and ever shall be, world without end. Amen. Alleluia.

Hymn, from the appendix, for the Season.

THROUGH THE YEAR
O Light serene of God the Father's glory,
To you, O Christ, we sing,
And with the evening star, at hour of sunset,
Our worship bring.

To Father, Son and God's most Holy Spirit,
Eternal praise is due.
O Christ, who gave your life, the world gives glory
And thanks to you.

PSALMODY

ANTIPHON I
Advent: Proclaim it, say to the peoples: Behold, God will come and save us.
Lent, Sunday 1: Accept us, Lord, since we come with contrite heart and humbled spirit. Let our sacrifice be pleasing to you today, Lord God.
Lent, Sunday 5: I will put my law into their hearts; I will be their God and they shall be my people.
Eastertide: Let the raising of my hands in prayer please you like the evening oblation, alleluia.

Through the Year: Lord, let my prayer rise before you like incense.

382

PRAYER IN TIME OF DANGER   PSALM 140(141):1-9
*The smoke of incense rose before God with the prayers of the saints
from the hand of the angel* (Rev 8:4)

I have cálled to you, Lórd; hásten to hélp me!*
Héar my vóice when I crý to yóu.
Let my práyer aríse befóre you like íncense,*
the ráising of my hánds like an évening oblátion.

Sét, O Lórd, a guard óver my móuth;*
keep wátch, O Lórd, at the dóor of my líps!
Do not túrn my héart to thíngs that are wróng,†
to évil déeds with mén who are sínners.*

Néver allów me to sháre in their féasting.
If a góod man stríkes or repróves me it is kíndness;†
but let the óil of the wícked not anóint my héad.*
Let my práyer be éver agáinst their málice.

Their prínces were thrown dówn by the síde of the róck:*
thén they understóod that my wórds were kínd.
As a míllstone is sháttered to píeces on the gróund,*
so their bónes were stréwn at the móuth of the gráve.

To yóu, Lord Gód, my éyes are túrned:*
in yóu I take réfuge; spáre my sóul!
From the tráp they have láid for me kéep me sáfe:*
kéep me from the snáres of thóse who do évil.

Glory be to the Father and to the Son and to the Holy Spirit,*
As it was in the beginning, is now, and ever shall be, world without
    end. Amen.

*This doxology is said after each psalm and canticle unless otherwise
noted.*

Ant. Through the Year: Lord, let my prayer rise before you like
incense.

Ant. Advent: Proclaim it, say to the peoples: Behold, God will
come and save us.

Advent, Ant. 2: Behold the Lord will come, and all his holy ones with him. On that day a great light will appear, alleluia.

Ant. Lent, Sunday 1: Accept us, Lord, since we come with contrite heart and humbled spirit. Let our sacrifice be pleasing to you today, Lord God.
Ant. 2: If you call, the Lord will hear you; if you cry to him, he will say, 'Here I am.'

Ant. Lent, Sunday 5: I will put my law into their hearts: I will be their God and they shall be my people.
Ant. 2: I count everything as loss because of the surpassing worth of knowing my Lord Jesus Christ.

Ant. Eastertide: Let the raising of my hands in prayer please you like the evening oblation, alleluia.
Ant. 2: You have brought me out from prison to give praise to your name, alleluia.

Ant. 2: Through the Year: You are my refuge, Lord; my heritage in the land of the living.

YOU ARE MY REFUGE   PSALM 141(142)
All these things were fulfilled by the Lord at the time of his passion
(St Hilary)

With all my vóice I crý to the Lórd,†
with all my vóice I entréat the Lórd.*
I póur out my tróuble befóre him;
I téll him áll my distréss†
while my spírit fáints withín me.*
But yóu, O Lórd, know my páth.

On the wáy where Í shall wálk*
they have hídden a snáre to entráp me.
Lóok on my ríght and sée:*
there is nó one who tákes my párt.
I have nó meáns of escápe,*
not óne who cáres for my sóul.

I crý to yóu, O Lórd.†
I have sáid: 'Yóu are my réfuge,*
all I háve in the lánd of the líving.'
Lísten, thén, to my crý*
for Í am in the dépths of distréss.

Réscue me from thóse who pursúe me*
for théy are strónger than Í.
Bríng my sóul out of this príson*
and thén I shall práise your náme.
Aróund me the júst will assémble*
becáuse of your góodness to mé.

Ant. Through the Year: You are my refuge, Lord; my heritage in the land of the living.

Ant. Advent: Behold the Lord will come, and all his holy ones with him. On that day a great light will appear, alleluia.
Ant 3: The Lord will come with great might and all flesh will see him.

Ant. Lent, Sunday 1: If you call, the Lord will hear you; if you cry to him, he will say, 'Here I am.'
Ant. 3: Christ suffered for our sins. Innocent though he was, he suffered for the guilty, to lead us to God. In the body he was put to death; in the spirit he was raised to life.

Ant. Lent, Sunday 5: I count everything as loss because of the surpassing worth of knowing my Lord Jesus Christ.
Ant. 3: Although he was the Son of God, he learned to obey through suffering.

Ant. Eastertide: You have brought me out from prison to give praise to your name, alleluia.
Ant. 3: The Son of God learned to obey through suffering, and he became the source of eternal salvation for all those who obey him, alleluia.

Ant. 3, Through the Year: The Lord Jesus humbled himself; therefore God has highly exalted him for ever.

CHRIST, THE SERVANT OF GOD   CANTICLE: PHIL 2:6-11

Though he was in the form of God,*
Jesus did not count equality with God a thing to be grasped.

He emptied himself,†
taking the form of a servant,*
being born in the likeness of men.

And being found in human form,†
he humbled himself and became obedient unto death,*
even death on a cross.

Therefore God has highly exalted him*
and bestowed on him the name which is above every name.

That at the name of Jesus every knee should bow,*
in heaven and on earth and under the earth,

And every tongue confess that Jesus Christ is Lord,*
to the glory of God the Father.

Ant. Through the Year: The Lord Jesus humbled himself; therefore God has highly exalted him for ever.

Ant. Advent: The Lord will come with great might and all flesh will see him.

Lent, Sunday 1: Christ suffered for our sins. Innocent though he was, he suffered for the guilty, to lead us to God. In the body he was put to death; in the spirit he was raised to life.

Lent, Sunday 5: Although he was the Son of God, he learned to obey through suffering.

Eastertide: The Son of God learned to obey through suffering, and he became the source of eternal salvation for all those who obey him, alleluia.

¶ *In Advent, Christmastide, Lent and Eastertide all from the Scripture Reading, inclusive, is from the Proper of Seasons.*

Scripture Reading   *Rom 11:33-36*
How great are God's riches! How deep are his wisdom and knowledge! Who can explain his decisions? Who can understand his
ways? As the scripture says, 'Who knows the mind of the Lord?
Who is able to give him advice? Who has ever given him anything,
so that he had to pay it back?' For all things were created by him,
and all things exist through him and for him. To God be glory
forever! Amen.

Short Responsory
Cantor: How great are your works, O Lord.
All: How great are your works, O Lord.
Cantor: In wisdom you have made them all.
All: How great are our works, O Lord.
Cantor: Glory be to the Father and to the Son and to the Holy
Spirit.
All: How great are your works, O Lord.

Magnificat antiphon from the Proper of Seasons.

Intercessions
Glory be to the one God, Father, Son, and Holy Spirit as we
humbly pray: ℟ Lord, be with your people.
Almighty Father, bring justice to our world,—that your people may
live in the joy of your peace. ℟
Bring all peoples into your kingdom,—that all mankind may be
saved. ℟
Give to married people the strength of your peace, the guidance of
your will,—and the grace to live together in constant love. ℟
Be the reward of all who have given us their help,—and grant them
eternal life. ℟
Have mercy on those who have lost their lives through warfare or
violence,—and receive them into your rest. ℟
Our Father

The concluding prayer from the Proper of Seasons.
Conclusion of the Hour as above, pp 379.

¶ *In the Offices which follow, all texts not otherwise designated are those of the time: Through the Year.*
Night Prayer pp 689 ff.

Invitatory

℣ Lord, open our lips.
℟ And we shall praise your name.

Ant. Through the Year: Come, ring out our joy to the Lord; hail the God who saves us, alleluia.†

Invitatory Psalm, p 371.

MORNING PRAYER

℣ O God, come to our aid.
℟ O Lord, make haste to help us.
Glory be to the Father and to the Son and to the Holy Spirit, as it was in the beginning, is now, and ever shall be, world without end. Amen. Alleluia.

This versicle is omitted when the Invitatory immediately precedes this Hour.

Hymn, from the appendix, for the Season.

THROUGH THE YEAR

Transcendent God in whom we live,
The Resurrection and the Light,
We sing for you a morning hymn
To end the silence of the night.

When early cock begins to crow
And everything from sleep awakes,
New life and hope spring up again
While out of darkness colour breaks.

Creator of all things that are,
The measure and the end of all,

388

Forgiving God, forget our sins,
And hear our prayer before we call.

Praise Father, Son and Holy Ghost,
Blest Trinity and source of grace,
Who call us out of nothingness
To find in you our resting-place.

Alternative hymn

Christ is the world's redeemer,
The lover of the pure,
The font of heavenly wisdom,
Our trust and hope secure,
The armour of his soldiers,
The Lord of earth and sky,
Our health while we are living,
Our life when we shall die.

Down in the realm of darkness,
He lay a captive bound,
But at the hour appointed
He rose a victor crowned.
And now, to heaven ascended,
He sits upon a throne,
Whence he had ne'er departed,
His Father's and his own.

All glory to the Father,
The unbegotten One,
All honour be to Jesus,
His sole-begotten Son;
And to the Holy Spirit,
The perfect Trinity,
Let all the worlds give answer,
Amen—so let it be.

PSALMODY

ANTIPHON I

Advent: On that day the mountains will run with sweet wine. The hills will flow with milk and honey.

Lent, Sunday 1: I will bless you all my life, Lord; in your name I will lift up my hands.

Lent, Sunday 5: You, my God, have become my help.

Eastertide: Let anyone who is thirsty come and drink the water of life, a free gift for those who desire it, alleluia.

Through the Year: To you, O God, I keep vigil at dawn, to look upon your power, alleluia.

A SOUL THIRSTING FOR GOD   PSALM 62(63):2-9
Let the man who has put away the deeds of the night watch for God

O Gód, you are my Gód, for you I lóng;*
for yóu my sóul is thírsting,
My bódy pínes for yóu*
like a drý, weary lánd without wáter.
So I gáze on yóu in the sánctuary*
to sée your stréngth and your glóry.

For your lóve is bétter than lífe,*
my líps will spéak your práise.
So I will bléss you áll my lífe,*
in your náme I will líft up my hánds.
My sóul shall be fílled as with a bánquet,*
my móuth shall práise you with jóy.

On my béd I remémber yóu.*
On yóu I múse through the níght
for yóu have béen my hélp;*
in the shádow of your wíngs I rejóice.
My sóul clíngs to yóu;*
your ríght hand hólds me fást.

Ant. To you, O God, I keep vigil at dawn, to look upon your power, alleluia.

390

Ant. Advent: On that day the mountains will run with sweet wine. The hills will flow with milk and honey.
Ant. 2: The mountains and hills will sing praise to God, and all the trees of the countryside will clap their hands, for the Lord will come and he will reign for ever, alleluia.

Ant. Lent, Sunday 1: I will bless you all my life, Lord; in your name I will lift up my hands.
Ant. 2: Sing and praise God for ever.

Ant. Lent, Sunday 5: You, my God, have become my help.
Ant. 2: Deliver us by your wonderful works; save us from the power of death.

Ant. Eastertide: Let anyone who is thirsty come and drink the water of life, a free gift for those who desire it, alleluia.
Ant. 2: Worship the maker of heaven and earth and the sea and every spring of water, alleluia.

Ant. 2: The three sang with one voice in the heart of the fire: Blessed be God, alleluia.

LET EVERY CREATURE PRAISE THE LORD   CANTICLE
DAN 3:57-88, 56

Praise our God, all you his servants (Rev 19:5)

O all you works of the Lord, O bless the Lord.*
To him be highest glory and praise for ever.
And you, angels of the Lord, O bless the Lord.*
To him be highest glory and praise for ever.

And you, the heavens of the Lord, O bless the Lord.*
And you, clouds of the sky, O bless the Lord.
And you, all armies of the Lord, O bless the Lord.*
To him be highest glory and praise for ever.

And you, sun and moon, O bless the Lord.*
And you, the stars of the heav'ns, O bless the Lord.
And you, showers and rain, O bless the Lord.*
To him be highest glory and praise for ever.

And you, all you breezes and winds, O bless the Lord.*
And you, fire and heat, O bless the Lord.
And you, cold and heat, O bless the Lord.*
To him be highest glory and praise for ever.

And you, showers and dew, O bless the Lord.*
And you, frosts and cold, O bless the Lord.
And you, frost and snow, O bless the Lord.*
To him be highest glory and praise for ever.

And you, night-time and day, O bless the Lord.*
And you, darkness and light, O bless the Lord.
And you, lightning and clouds, O bless the Lord.*
To him be highest glory and praise for ever.

O let the earth bless the Lord.*
To him be highest glory and praise for ever.

And you, mountains and hills, O bless the Lord.*
And you, all plants of the earth, O bless the Lord.
And you, fountains and springs, O bless the Lord.*
To him be highest glory and praise for ever.

And you, rivers and seas, O bless the Lord.*
And you, creatures of the sea, O bless the Lord.
And you, every bird in the sky, O bless the Lord.†
And you, wild beasts and tame, O bless the Lord.*
To him be highest glory and praise for ever.

And you, children of men, O bless the Lord.*
To him be highest glory and praise for ever.

O Israel, bless the Lord. O bless the Lord.*
And you, priests of the Lord, O bless the Lord.
And you, servants of the Lord, O bless the Lord.*
To him be highest glory and praise for ever.

And you, spirits and souls of the just, O bless the Lord.*
And you, holy and humble of heart, O bless the Lord.
Ananias, Azarias, Mizael, O bless the Lord.*
To him be highest glory and praise for ever.

Let us praise the Father, the Son, and Holy Spirit:*
To you be highest glory and praise for ever.
May you be blessed, O Lord, in the heavens.*
To you be highest glory and praise for ever.

The Glory be *is not said after this Canticle, as it contains a doxology.*

Ant. The three sang with one voice in the heart of the fire: Blessed
be God, alleluia.

Ant. Advent: The mountains and hills will sing praise to God, and
all the trees of the countryside will clap their hands, for the Lord
will come and he will reign for ever, alleluia.
Ant. 3: Behold, a great Prophet will come and he will renew
Jerusalem, alleluia.

Ant. Lent, Sunday 1: Sing and praise God for ever.
Ant. 3: The Lord takes delight in his people. He crowns the poor
with salvation.

Ant. Lent, Sunday 5: Deliver us by your wonderful works; save us
from the power of death.
Ant. 3: Now the hour has come for the Son of Man to be glorified.

Ant. Eastertide: Worship the maker of heaven and earth and the
sea and every spring of water, alleluia.
Ant. 3: Let the saints rejoice in glory, alleluia.

Ant. 3: Let Sion's sons exult in their king, alleluia.

THE SONG OF JOY OF THE SAINTS   PSALM 149
*The members of the Church, God's new people, will rejoice in their
king, who is Christ* (Hesychius)

Síng a new sóng to the Lórd,*
his práise in the assémbly of the fáithful.
Let Ísrael rejóice in its Máker,*
let Síon's sons exúlt in their kíng.
Let them práise his náme with dáncing*
and make músic with tímbrel and hárp.

For the Lórd takes delíght in his péople.*
He crówns the póor with salvátion.

393

Let the fáithful rejóice in their glóry,*
shout for jóy and táke their rést.
Let the práise of Gód be on their líps*
and a twó-edged swórd in their hánd,

to déal out véngeance to the nátions*
and púnishment on áll the péoples;
to bínd their kíngs in cháins*
and their nóbles in fétters of íron;
to cárry out the séntence pre-ordáined:*
this hónour is for áll his fáithful.

Ant. Let Sion's sons exult in their king, alleluia.

Ant. Advent: Behold, a great Prophet will come and he will renew Jerusalem, alleluia.

Lent, Sunday 1: The Lord takes delight in his people. He crowns the poor with salvation.

Lent, Sunday 5: Now the hour has come for the Son of Man to be glorified.

Eastertide: Let the saints rejoice in glory, alleluia.

THROUGH THE YEAR

Scripture Reading   *Rev 7:10,12*

Victory to our God, who sits on the throne, and to the Lamb! Praise and glory and wisdom and thanksgiving and honour and power and strength to our God for ever and ever. Amen.

Short Responsory

Cantor: You are the Christ, the Son of the living God. Have mercy on us.

All: You are the Christ, the Son of the living God. Have mercy on us.

Cantor: You are seated at the right hand of the Father.

All: You are the Christ, the Son of the living God. Have mercy on us.

Cantor: Glory be to the Father and to the Son and to the Holy Spirit.

All: You are the Christ, the Son of the living God. Have mercy on us.

Benedictus antiphon from the Proper of Seasons.

Intercessions

Let us pray to Christ the Lord, the sun who enlightens all men,
whose light will never fail us: R/ Lord our Saviour, give us life!

Lord of the sun and the stars, we thank you for the gift of a new
day;—and we celebrate the day of resurrection. R/

Lead us by your Spirit to do your will;—guide and protect us by
your wisdom. R/

Bring us to share with joy this Sunday's eucharist;—nourish us by
your word, and by your body. R/

Lord, grant us your gifts, though we are unworthy;—with all our
hearts we thank you. R/

Our Father

The concluding prayer from the Proper of Seasons.
Conclusion of the Hour as on p 379.

EVENING PRAYER II

V/ O God, come to our aid.

R/ O Lord, make haste to help us.

Glory be to the Father and to the Son and to the Holy Spirit, as it
was in the beginning, is now, and ever shall be, world without end.
Amen. Alleluia.

Hymn, from the appendix, for the Season.

THROUGH THE YEAR

Praise to the holiest in the height,
And in the depth be praise,
In all his words most wonderful,
Most sure in all his ways.

O loving wisdom of our God!
When all was sin and shame,
A second Adam to the fight
And to the rescue came.

O wisest love! that flesh and blood
Which did in Adam fail,
Should strive afresh against their foe,
Should strive and should prevail.

And that a higher gift than grace
Should flesh and blood refine,
God's presence and his very self,
And essence all divine.

O generous love! that he who smote
In man for man the foe,
The double agony in man
For man should undergo.

And in the garden secretly,
And on the cross on high,
Should teach his brethren, and inspire
To suffer and to die.

Praise to the holiest in the height,
And in the depth be praise,
In all his words most wonderful,
Most sure in all his ways.

Alternative hymn

In the beginning God created heaven,
The dark and empty earth;
His Spirit moved across the sombre waters
And stirred them with his breath.

Then God created light, and with its coming
The dark was swept away;
The morning came, and then the quiet evening:
The end of God's first day.

To God the Father of the world give glory,
With Christ his only Son,
Who with the Spirit govern all creation:
Blest Trinity in One.

PSALMODY

ANTIPHON I

Advent: Rejoice greatly, daughter of Sion, shout with gladness, daughter of Jerusalem, alleluia.

Lent, Sunday 1: You must worship the Lord, your God, and serve him alone.

Lent, Sunday 5: As Moses lifted up the serpent in the desert, so the Son of Man must be lifted up.

Eastertide: The Lord has risen and sits at the right hand of God, alleluia.

Through the Year: The Lord will send his mighty sceptre from Sion, and he will rule for ever, alleluia.

THE MESSIAH IS KING AND PRIEST   PSALM 109(110):1-5,7
He must be king so that he may put all his enemies under his feet
(1 Cor 15:25)

The Lórd's revelátion to my Máster:†
'Sít on my ríght:*
your fóes I will pút beneath your féet.'

The Lórd will wíeld from Síon†
your scéptre of pówer:*
rúle in the mídst of all your fóes.

A prínce from the dáy of your bírth†
on the hóly móuntains;*
from the wómb before the dáwn I begót you.

The Lórd has sworn an óath he will not chánge.†
'You are a príest for éver,*
a príest like Melchízedek of óld.'

The Máster stánding at your ríght hand*
will shatter kíngs in the dáy of his wráth.

He shall drínk from the stréam by the wáyside*
and thérefore he shall líft up his héad.

397

Ant. The Lord will send his mighty sceptre from Sion, and he will rule for ever, alleluia.

Ant. Advent: Rejoice greatly, daughter of Sion, shout with gladness, daughter of Jerusalem, alleluia.
Ant. 2: Christ our King will come. He is the Lamb that John announced.

Ant. Lent, Sunday 1: You must worship the Lord, your God, and serve him alone.
Ant. 2: Now is the favourable time; this is the day of salvation.

Ant. Lent, Sunday 5: As Moses lifted up the serpent in the desert, so the Son of Man must be lifted up.
Ant. 2: The Lord of hosts protects and rescues; he spares and he saves.

Ant. Eastertide: The Lord has risen and sits at the right hand of God, alleluia.
Ant. 2: He has freed us from the power of darkness and has given us a place in the kingdom of his Son, alleluia.

Ant. 2: The earth trembled before the Lord, alleluia.

ISRAEL IS FREED FROM EGYPT   PSALM 113A(114):1-8
You, who have renounced this world, have also been led forth from Egypt (St Augustine)

When Ísrael came fórth from Égypt,*
Jacob's sóns from an álien péople,
Júdah becáme the Lord's témple,*
Ísrael becáme his kíngdom.

The séa fléd at the síght:*
the Jórdan turned báck on its cóurse,
the móuntains léapt like ráms*
and the hílls like yéarling shéep.

Whý was it, séa, that you fléd,*
that you túrned back, Jórdan, on your cóurse?

Móuntains, that you léapt like ráms,*
hílls, like yéarling shéep?

Trémble, O éarth, before the Lórd,*
in the présence of the Gód of Jácob,
who túrns the róck into a póol*
and flínt into a spríng of wáter.

Ant. The earth trembled before the Lord, alleluia.

OUTSIDE LENT

Ant. Advent: Christ our King will come. He is the Lamb that
John announced.
Ant. 3: Behold I am coming soon to reward every man according to
his deeds, says the Lord.

Ant. Eastertide: He has freed us from the power of darkness and has
given us a place in the kingdom of his Son, alleluia.
Ant. 3: Alleluia, the Lord, our God, is King; let us rejoice and give
glory to him, alleluia.

Ant. 3: The Lord is King, our God, the Almighty! alleluia.

When chanted, this canticle is sung with Alleluia *as set out below.
When recited, it suffices to say* Alleluia *at the beginning and end of
each strophe.*

THE MARRIAGE FEAST OF THE LAMB   CANTICLE: REV 19:1,2,5-7
    Alleluia.
    Salvation and glory and power belong to our God,*
    (R̷ Alleluia.)
    His judgments are true and just.
    R̷ Alleluia (alleluia).

    Alleluia.
    Praise our God, all you his servants,
    (R̷ Alleluia.)
    You who fear him, small and gréat.
    R̷ Alleluia (alleluia).

Alleluia.
The Lord our God, the Almighty, reigns,*
(R℣ Alleluia.)
Let us rejoice and exult and give him the glory.
R℣ Alleluia (alleluia).

Alleluia.
The marriage of the Lamb has come,*
(R℣ Alleluia.)
And his bride has made herself ready.
R℣ Alleluia (alleluia).

Ant. The Lord is King, our God, the Almighty! alleluia.

Ant. Advent: Behold I am coming soon to reward every man according to his deeds, says the Lord.
Eastertide: Alleluia, the Lord, our God, is King; let us rejoice and give glory to him, alleluia.

LENT

Ant. Lent, Sunday 1: Now is the favourable time; this is the day of salvation.
Ant. 3: Now we are going up to Jerusalem, and everything that is written about the Son of Man will come true.

Ant. Lent, Sunday 5: The Lord of hosts protects and rescues; he spares and he saves.
Ant. 3: He was wounded for our faults, he was bruised for our sins. Through his wounds we are healed.

CHRIST, THE SERVANT OF GOD,	CANTICLE
FREELY ACCEPTS HIS PASSION	I PET 2:21-24

Christ suffered for you,†
leaving you an example*
that you should follow in his steps.

He committed no sin;*
no guile was found on his lips.

When he was reviled,*
he did not revile in return.

When he suffered,*
he did not threaten;
but he trusted to him*
who judges justly.

He himself bore our sins*
in his body on the tree,
that we might die to sin*
and live to righteousness.

By his wounds you have been healed.

Ant. Sunday 1: Now we are going up to Jerusalem, and everything that is written about the Son of Man will come true.
Sunday 5: He was wounded for our faults, he was bruised for our sins. Through his wounds we are healed.

THROUGH THE YEAR

Scripture Reading   *2 Cor 1:3-4*
Let us give thanks to the God and Father of our Lord Jesus Christ, the merciful Father, the God from whom all help comes! He helps us in all our troubles, so that we are able to help those who have all kinds of troubles, using the same help that we ourselves have received from God.

Short Responsory
Cantor: Blessed are you in the vault of heaven.
All: Blessed are you in the vault of heaven.
Cantor: You are exalted and glorified above all else for ever.
All: Blessed are you in the vault of heaven.
Cantor: Glory be to the Father and to the Son and to the Holy Spirit.
All: Blessed are you in the vault of heaven.

Magnificat antiphon from the Proper of Seasons.

Intercessions

Christ is the Head of his body, the Church, and we are the members of that body; gathered this evening to pray in his name, we say:
℟ Your kingdom come!

May your Church be a light to the nations, the sign and source of your power to unite all men:—may she lead mankind to the mystery of your love. ℟

Guide the Pope and all the bishops of your Church:—grant them the gifts of unity, of love, and of peace. ℟

Lord, give peace to our troubled world—and give to your children security of mind and freedom from anxiety. ℟

Help us to bring your compassion to the poor, the sick, the lonely, the unloved;—lead us to find you in the coming week. ℟

Awaken the dead to a glorious resurrection:—may we be united with them at the end of time. ℟

Our Father

The concluding prayer from the Proper of Seasons.
Conclusion of the Hour as on p 379.

WEEK 1: MONDAY

Invitatory ant. Let us come before the Lord, giving thanks.
Psalm, p 371.

MORNING PRAYER

Hymn, from the appendix, for the Season.

THROUGH THE YEAR

The day is filled with splendour
When God brings light from light,
And all renewed creation
Rejoices in his sight.

The Father gives his children
The wonder of the world

402

In which his power and glory
Like banners are unfurled.

With every living creature,
Awaking with the day,
We turn to God our Father,
Lift up our hearts and pray:

O Father, Son and Spirit,
Your grace and mercy send,
That we may live to praise you
Today and to the end.

PSALMODY

The first antiphon given with each psalm is used Through the Year and, except for Eastertide, during the other seasons unless otherwise noted.

Ant. 1: It is you whom I invoke, O Lord. In the morning you hear me.
Eastertide: In you they rejoice, those who love your name, alleluia.

MORNING PRAYER FOR HELP   PSALM 5:2-10,12-13
Those who have received the Word of God which dwells within will rejoice for ever.

To my wórds give éar, O Lórd,*
give héed to my gróaning.
Atténd to the sóund of my críes,*
my Kíng and my Gód.

It is yóu whom I invóke, O Lórd.*
In the mórning you héar me;
in the mórning I óffer you my práyer,*
wátching and wáiting.

Yóu are no Gód who loves évil;*
no sínner is your guést.
The bóastful shall not stánd their gróund*
befóre your fáce.

You háte áll who do évil:*
you destróy all who líe.
The decéitful and blóodthirsty mán*
the Lórd detésts.

But Í through the gréatness of your lóve*
have áccess to your hóuse.
I bów down befóre your holy témple,*
fílled with áwe.

Léad me, Lórd, in your jústice,†
because of thóse who lie in wáit;*
make cléar your way befóre me.

No trúth can be fóund in their móuths,*
their héart is all míschief,
their thróat a wíde-open gráve,*
all hóney their spéech.

All thóse you protéct shall be glád*
and ríng out their jóy.
You shélter them; in yóu they rejóice,*
those who lóve your náme.

It is yóu who bless the júst man, Lórd:*
you surróund him with fávour as with a shíeld.

Ant. It is you whom I invoke, O Lord. In the morning you hear me.
Eastertide: In you they rejoice, those who love your name, alleluia.

Ant. 2: Lord our God, we praise the splendour of your name.
Eastertide: Yours is the kingdom, O Lord, and you are exalted as
head above all, alleluia.

TO GOD ALONE BE HONOUR AND GLORY   CANTICLE
                                              I CHRON 29:10-13
Blessed be the God and Father of our Lord Jesus Christ (Eph 1:3)

Blessed are you, O Lord,†
the God of Israel our father,*
for ever and ever.

Yours, O Lord, is the greatness, and the power,†
and the glory, and the victory, and the majesty;*
for all that is in the heavens and in the earth is yours;

Yours is the kingdom, O Lord,*
and you are exalted as head above all.

Both riches and honour come from you,*
and you rule over all.
In your hand are power and might;*
and in your hand it is to make great and to give strength to all.

And now we thank you, our God,*
and praise your glorious name.

Ant. Lord our God, we praise the splendour of your name.
Eastertide: Yours is the kingdom, O Lord, and you are exalted as
head above all, alleluia.

Ant. 3: Adore the Lord in his holy court.
Eastertide: The Lord is enthroned as king for ever, alleluia.

PUBLIC PRAISE OF THE WORD OF GOD   PSALM 28(29)
A voice was heard from heaven, saying, 'This is my beloved Son'
(Mt 3:17)

O give the Lórd you sóns of Gód,*
give the Lórd glóry and pówer;
give the Lórd the glóry of his náme.*
Adore the Lórd in his hóly court.

The Lord's vóice resóunding on the wáters,*
the Lórd on the imménsity of wáters;
the vóice of the Lórd, full of pówer,*
the vóice of the Lórd, full of spléndour.

The Lord's vóice sháttering the cédars,*
the Lord shátters the cédars of Lébanon;
he makes Lébanon léap like a cálf*
and Sírion like a yóung wild-óx.

405

⎧ The Lord's vóice fláshes flames of fíre.†

⎩ The Lord's vóice sháking the wílderness,*
the Lord shákes the wílderness of Kádesh;
the Lord's voíce rénding the óak tree*
and strípping the fórest báre.

The Gód of glóry thúnders.*
In his témple they áll cry: 'Glóry!'
The Lórd sat enthróned over the flóod;*
the Lórd sits as kíng for éver.

The Lórd will give stréngth to his péople,*
the Lórd will bless his péople with péace.

Ant. Adore the Lord in his holy court.
Eastertide: The Lord is enthroned as king for ever, alleluia.

THROUGH THE YEAR

Scripture Reading   *2 Thess 3:10b-13*
We gave you a rule when we were with you: not to let anyone have
any food if he refused to do any work. Now we hear that there are
some of you who are living in idleness, doing no work themselves
but interfering with everyone else's. In the Lord Jesus Christ, we
order and call on people of this kind to go on quietly working and
earning the food that they eat. My brothers, never grow tired of
doing what is right.

Short Responsory
℞ Blessed be the Lord from age to age. *Repeat* ℞
℣ He alone has wrought marvellous works. ℞ Glory be. ℞

Benedictus ant. Blessed be the Lord, our God.

Intercessions
As the new day begins let us praise Christ, in whom is the fulness of
grace and the Spirit of God. ℞ Lord, give us your Spirit.
We praise you, Lord,—and we thank you for all your blessings. ℞
Give us peace of mind and generosity of heart;—grant us health
and strength to do your will. ℞

May your love be with us during the day;—guide us in our work. ℟
Be with all those who have asked our prayers,—and grant them all
their needs. ℟
Our Father

Concluding Prayer
Lord, be the beginning and end
of all that we do and say.
Prompt our actions with your grace,
and complete them with your all-powerful help.
(We make our prayer) through our Lord.

Conclusion of the Hour as on p 379.

EVENING PRAYER

Hymn, from the appendix, for the Season.

THROUGH THE YEAR
Come, praise the Lord, the Almighty, the King of all nations!
Tell forth his fame, O ye peoples, with loud acclamations!
His love is sure;
Faithful his word shall endure,
Steadfast through all generations!

Praise to the Father most gracious, the Lord of creation!
Praise to his Son, the Redeemer who wrought our salvation!
O heav'nly Dove,
Praise to thee, fruit of their love,
Giver of all consolation.

PSALMODY

Ant. 1: The Lord cares for the weak and oppressed.
Eastertide: Courage! The victory is mine; I have conquered the
world, alleluia.

THE LORD HAS GIVEN SECURITY PSALM 10(11)
TO THE UPRIGHT MAN

Blessed are those who hunger and thirst for what is right: they shall be satisfied (Mt 5:6)

In the Lórd I have táken my réfuge.†
Hów can you sáy to my sóul:*
'Flý like a bírd to its móuntain.

See the wícked brácing their bów;†
they are fíxing their árrows on the stríng*
to shóot upright mén in the dárk.
Foundátions once destróyed,* what can the júst do?'

The Lórd is in his hóly témple,*
the Lórd, whose thróne is in héaven.
His éyes look dówn on the wórld;*
his gáze tests mórtal mén.

The Lórd tests the júst and the wícked:*
the lóver of víolence he hátes.
He sends fíre and brímstone on the wícked;*
he sends a scórching wínd as their lót.

The Lórd is júst and loves jústice:*
the úpright shall sée his fáce.

Ant. The Lord cares for the weak and oppressed.
Eastertide: Courage! The victory is mine; I have conquered the world, alleluia.

Ant. 2: Blessed are the pure in heart: they shall see God.
Eastertide: He shall live in your tabernacle; he shall dwell on your holy mountain, alleluia.

WHO SHALL BE WORTHY TO STAND PSALM 14(15)
BEFORE THE LORD?

You have come to Mount Sion to the city of the living God (Heb 12:22)

Lord, whó shall be admítted to your tént*
and dwéll on your hóly móuntain?

Hé who wálks without fáult;*
hé who ácts with jústice
and spéaks the trúth from his héart;*
hé who does not slánder with his tóngue;

hé who does no wróng to his bróther,*
who cásts no slúr on his néighbour,
who hólds the gódless in disdáin,*
but hónours those who féar the Lórd;

hé who keeps his plédge, come what máy;†
who tákes no ínterest on a lóan*
and accépts no bríbes against the ínnocent.
Such a mán will stand fírm for éver.

Ant. Blessed are the pure in heart: they shall see God.
Eastertide: He shall live in your tabernacle; he shall dwell on your
holy mountain, alleluia.

Ant. 3: God chose us in his Son and made us his adopted sons.
Eastertide: When I am lifted up from the earth, I shall draw all
men to myself, alleluia.

GOD, THE SAVIOUR   CANTICLE: EPH 1:3-10
Blessed be the God and Father*
of our Lord Jesus Christ,
who has blessed us in Christ*
with every spiritual blessing in the heavenly places.

He chose us in him*
before the foundation of the world,
that we should be holy*
and blameless before him.

He destined us in love*
to be his sons through Jesus Christ,
according to the purpose of his will,†
to the praise of his glorious grace*
which he freely bestowed on us in the Beloved.

In him we have redemption through his blood,*
the forgiveness of our trespasses,
according to the riches of his grace*
which he lavished upon us.

He has made known to us†
in all wisdom and insight*
the mystery of his will,
according to his purpose*
which he set forth in Christ.

His purpose he set forth in Christ,*
as a plan for the fulness of time,
to unite all things in him,*
things in heaven and things on earth.

Ant. God chose us in his Son and made us his adopted sons.
Eastertide: When I am lifted up from the earth, I shall draw all men
to myself, alleluia.

THROUGH THE YEAR

Scripture Reading   *Col 1:9b-11*
We ask God to fill you with the knowledge of his will, with all the
wisdom and understanding that his Spirit gives. Then you will be
able to live as the Lords wants, and always do what pleases him.
Your lives will be fruitful in all kinds of good works, and you will
grow in your knowledge of God. May you be made strong with all
the strength which comes from his glorious might, so that you may
be able to endure everything with patience.

Short Responsory
Ȓ Heal my soul for I have sinned against you. *Repeat* Ȓ
V̑ I said: 'Lord, have mercy on me.' Ȓ Glory be. Ȓ

Magnificat ant. My soul magnifies the Lord, since God has had
regard for my humble state.

Intercessions
God our Father has bound himself to us in an everlasting covenant.

In thankfulness and faith, we pray to him: R7 Lord, bless your people!
In Christ you have given a new covenant to men:—may they know the greatness which they have inherited. R7
Gather into one all who bear the name of Christian,—that the world may believe in the Christ you have sent. R7
Pour out your love on our friends, and on all whom we know;—may they carry with them the gentleness of Christ. R7
Comfort the dying;—may they know your saving love. R7
Show your mercy to the dead;—may they find their rest in Christ. R7
Our Father

Concluding Prayer
Let our worship give you glory, Lord,
who for our salvation looked upon
the lowliness of Mary your handmaid:
raise us up to share with her
the fulness of redemption.
(We make our prayer) through our Lord.

Conclusion of the Hour on p 379.
Night Prayer, see pp 689 ff.

WEEK 1: TUESDAY

Invitatory ant. The Lord is a great king: come, let us adore him.
Psalm, p 371.

MORNING PRAYER

Hymn, from the appendix, for the Season.

THROUGH THE YEAR
O Christ, the Light of heaven
And of the world true Light,
You come in all your radiance
To cleave the web of night.

May what is false within us
Before your truth give way,
That we may live untroubled,
With quiet hearts this day.

May steadfast faith sustain us,
And hope made firm in you;
The love that we have wasted,
O God of love, renew.

Blest Trinity we praise you
In whom our quest will cease;
Keep us with you for ever
In happiness and peace.

PSALMODY

Ant. 1: The man with clean hands and pure heart will climb the mountain of the Lord.
Eastertide: He who came down is he who has now risen higher than all the heavens, alleluia.

When the following psalm has been used at the Invitatory, ps 94, p 371, is said here in place of it.

THE LORD COMES TO HIS TEMPLE   PSALM 23(24)
The gates of heaven were opened to Christ because he was lifted up in the flesh (St Irenaeus)

The Lórd's is the éarth and its fúlness,*
the wórld and áll its péoples.
It is hé who sét it on the séas;*
on the wáters he máde it fírm.

Who shall clímb the móuntain of the Lórd?*
Who shall stánd in his hóly pláce?
The mán with clean hánds and pure héart,†
who desíres not wórthless thíngs,*
who has not swórn so as to decéive his néighbour.

He shall recéive bléssings from the Lórd*
and rewárd from the Gód who sáves him.
Súch are the mén who séek him,*
seek the fáce of the Gód of Jácob.

O gátes, lift hígh your héads;†
grow hígher, áncient dóors.*
Let him énter, the kíng of glóry!

Whó is the kíng of glóry?†
The Lórd, the míghty, the váliant,*
the Lórd, the váliant in wár.

O gátes, lift hígh your héads;†
grow hígher, áncient dóors.*
Let him énter, the kíng of glóry!

Who is hé, the kíng of glóry?†
Hé, the Lórd of ármies,*
hé is the kíng of glóry.

Ant. The man with clean hands and pure heart will climb the mountain of the Lord.
Eastertide: He who came down is he who has now risen higher than all the heavens, alleluia.

Ant. 2: Praise the king of the ages in all your deeds.
Eastertide: Keep these days with joy and give glory to the Lord, alleluia.

GOD PUNISHES AND ALSO SAVES   CANTICLE: TOB 13:1-5B,7-8
Blessed be the God and Father of our Lord Jesus Christ! Because of his great love we have been born anew (1 Pet 1:3)

Blessed is God who lives for ever,*
and blessed is his kingdom.
For he afflicts, and he shows mercy;†
he leads down to Hades, and brings up again,*
and there is no one who can escape his hand.

413

Acknowledge him before the nations, O sons of Israel;*
for he has scattered us among them.
Make his greatness known there,*
and exalt him in the presence of all the living;
because he is our Lord and God,*
he is our Father for ever.

He will afflict us for our iniquities;*
and again he will show mercy,
but see what he will do with you;*
give thanks to him with your full voice.
Praise the Lord of righteousness,*
and exalt the King of the ages.

I give him thanks in the land of my captivity,*
and I show his power and majesty to a nation of sinners.
Turn back, you sinners, and do right before him;*
who knows if he will accept you and have mercy on you?

I exalt my God;†
my soul exalts the King of heaven,*
and will rejoice in his majesty.
Let all men speak,*
and give him thanks in Jerusalem.

Ant. Praise the king of the ages in all your deeds.
Eastertide: Keep these days with joy, and give glory to the Lord,
alleluia.

Ant. 3: Praise is fitting for loyal hearts.
Eastertide: The Lord fills the earth with his love, alleluia.

PRAISE OF THE PROVIDENCE OF THE LORD   PSALM 32(33)
All things were made through him (Jn 1:3)

Ring out your jóy to the Lórd, O you júst;*
for praise is fítting for loyal héarts.

Give thánks to the Lórd upon the lýre*
with a tén-stringed hárp sing him sóngs.

414

O síng him a sóng that is néw,*
play lóudly, with áll your skíll.

For the wórd of the Lórd is fáithful*
and áll his wórks to be trústed.
The Lórd loves jústice and ríght*
and fílls the éarth with his lóve.

By his wórd the héavens were máde,*
by the bréath of his móuth all the stárs.
He collécts the wáves of the ócean;*
he stóres up the dépths of the séa.

Let all the éarth féar the Lórd,*
all who líve in the wórld revére him.
He spóke; and it cáme to bé.*
He commánded; it spráng into béing.

He frustrátes the desígns of the nátions,*
he deféats the pláns of the péoples.
His ówn designs shall stánd for éver,*
the pláns of his héart from age to áge.

They are háppy, whose Gód is the Lórd,*
the péople he has chósen as his ówn.
From the héavens the Lórd looks fórth,*
he sées all the chíldren of mén.

From the pláce where he dwélls he gázes*
on áll the dwéllers on the éarth,
he who shápes the héarts of them áll*
and consíders áll their déeds.

A kíng is not sáved by his ármy,*
nor a wárrior presérved by his stréngth.
A váin hope for sáfety is the hórse;*
despíte its pówer it cannot sáve.

The Lórd looks on thóse who revére him,*
on thóse who hópe in his lóve,
to réscue their sóuls from déath,*
to kéep them alíve in fámine.

415

Our sóul is wáiting for the Lórd.*
The Lórd is our hélp and our shíeld.
In hím do our héarts find jóy.*
We trúst in his hóly náme.

May your lóve be upón us, O Lórd,*
as we pláce all our hópe in yóu.

Ant. Praise is fitting for loyal hearts.
Eastertide: The Lord fills the earth with his love, alleluia.

THROUGH THE YEAR

Scripture Reading   *Rom 13:11b,12-13a*
You know what hour it is, how it is full time now for you to wake
from sleep. The night is far gone, the day is at hand. Let us then
cast off the works of darkness and put on the armour of light; let us
conduct ourselves becomingly as in the day.

Short Responsory
R̥ My helper is my God; I will place my trust in him. *Repeat* R̥
V̥ He is my refuge; he sets me free. R̥ Glory be. R̥

Benedictus ant. The Lord has raised up a mighty saviour for us, as
he promised through the lips of his prophets.

Intercessions
As Christians called to share the life of God, let us praise the Lord
Jesus, the high priest of our faith. R̥ You are our Saviour and our
God.
Almighty King, you have baptized us, and made us a royal priest-
hood:—may we offer you a constant sacrifice of praise. R̥
Help us to keep your commandments;—so that through your Holy
Spirit we may dwell in you, and you in us. R̥
Everlasting Wisdom, come to us:—dwell with us and work in us
today. R̥
Help us to be considerate and kind;—grant that we may bring joy,
not pain, to those we meet. R̥
Our Father

Concluding Prayer
Look with favour on our morning prayer, Lord,
and in your saving love
let your light penetrate the hidden places of our hearts.
May no sordid desires darken our minds,
renewed and enlightened as we are by your heavenly grace.
(We make our prayer) through our Lord.

EVENING PRAYER

Hymn, from the appendix, for the Season.

THROUGH THE YEAR
O Strength and Stay upholding all creation,
Who ever dost thyself unmoved abide,
Yet day by day the light in due gradation
From hour to hour in all its changes guide,

Grant to life's day a calm unclouded ending,
An eve untouched by shadows of decay,
The brightness of a holy death-bed blending
With dawning glories of the eternal day.

Hear us, O Father, gracious and forgiving,
Through Jesus Christ thy co-eternal Word,
Who, with the Holy Ghost, by all things living
Now and to endless ages art adored.

PSALMODY

Ant. 1: The Lord will give victory to his anointed one.
Eastertide: Now our God reigns, and power belongs to Christ, his
anointed, alleluia.

PRAYER FOR A KING BEFORE BATTLE   PSALM 19(20)
Whoever calls upon the name of the Lord will be saved (Acts 2:21)

May the Lord ánswer in tíme of tríal;*
may the náme of Jacob's Gód protéct you.

May he sénd you hélp from his shríne*
and gíve you suppórt from Síon.
May he remémber áll your ófferings*
and recéive your sácrifice with fávour.

May he gíve you your héart's desíre*
and fulfíl every óne of your pláns.
May we ríng out our jóy at your víctory†
and rejóice in the náme of our Gód.*
May the Lórd gránt all your práyers.

I am súre nów that the Lórd*
will give víctory tó his anóinted,
will replý from his hóly héaven*
with the míghty víctory of his hánd.

Sóme trust in cháriots or hórses,*
but wé in the náme of the Lórd.
Théy will collápse and fáll,*
but wé shall hóld and stand fírm.

Give víctory to the kíng, O Lórd,*
give ánswer on the dáy we cáll.

Ant. The Lord will give victory to his anointed one.
Eastertide: Now our God reigns, and power belongs to Christ, his
anointed, alleluia.

Ant. 2: We shall sing and praise your power.
Eastertide: You have assumed your great power, you have begun
your reign, alleluia.

THANKSGIVING FOR A KING'S VICTORY   PSALM 20(21):2-8,14
*He accepted human life, so that he could rise from the dead and live
for ever and ever* (St Irenaeus)

O Lórd, your stréngth gives jóy to the kíng;*
hów your sáving hélp makes him glád!
You have gránted hím his héart's desíre;*
you háve not refúsed the práyer of his líps.

You cáme to méet him with the bléssings of succéss,*
you have sét on his héad a crówn of pure góld.
He ásked you for lífe and thís you have gíven,*
dáys that will lást from áge to áge.

Your sáving hélp has gíven him glóry.*
You have láid upón him májesty and spléndour,
you have gránted your bléssings to hím for éver.*
You have máde him rejóice with the jóy of your présence.

The kíng has pút his trúst in the Lórd:*
through the mércy of the Most Hígh hé shall stand fírm.
O Lórd, aríse in your stréngth;*
we shall síng and práise your pówer.

Ant. We shall sing and praise your power.
Eastertide: You have assumed your great power, you have begun
your reign, alleluia.

Ant. 3: Lord, you made us a kingdom and priests to serve our God.
Eastertide: May your whole creation serve you, for you spoke and
they came into being, alleluia.

HYMN OF THE REDEEMED   CANTICLE: REV 4:11;5:9,10,12

Worthy are you, our Lord and God,*
to receive glory and honour and power,
for you created all things,*
and by your will they existed and were created.

Worthy are you, O Lord,*
to take the scroll and to open its seals,
for you were slain,†
and by your blood you ransomed men for God*
from every tribe and tongue and people and nation.

You have made us a kingdom and priests to our God,*
and we shall reign on earth.

Worthy is the Lamb who was slain,*

to receive power and wealth,
and wisdom and might,*
and honour and glory and blessing.

Ant. Lord, you made us a kingdom and priests to serve our God.
Eastertide: May your whole creation serve you, for you spoke and
they came into being, alleluia.

THROUGH THE YEAR

Scripture Reading   *I Jn 3:1a,2*
Think of the love that the Father has lavished on us,
by letting us be called God's children;
and that is what we are.
My dear people, we are already the children of God
but what we are to be in the future has not yet been revealed;
we shall be like him
because we shall see him as he really is.

Short Responsory
R̹ Your word, O Lord, will endure for ever. *Repeat* R̹
V̹ Your truth will last from age to age. R̹ Glory be. R̹

Magnificat ant. My spirit exults in the Lord God, my saviour.

Intercessions
Through Christ we are sons of God; in him we see what we shall be
when we come to the Father. With confidence we pray: R̹ Lord, in
your mercy, hear our prayer.
Guide leaders and governments:—give them wisdom and integrity.
R̹
You are the Lord and source of our freedom:—bring those in
captivity of mind or body to the freedom of the children of God. R̹
Give courage and strength to the young.—Help them to choose their
work, and make the right decisions for their way of life. R̹
Give patient tolerance to all who are no longer young;—open the
hearts of the young to accept from them understanding and love. R̹
Receive the departed into your eternal kingdom;—sustain our hope
to reign with you for ever. R̹
Our Father

Concluding Prayer
We give you thanks, Lord God Almighty,
for bringing us safely to the evening of this day;
we humbly ask that the prayer we make with uplifted hands
may be an offering pleasing in your sight.
(We make our prayer) through our Lord.

WEEK 1: WEDNESDAY

Invitatory ant. Let us adore the Lord, for it is he who made us.
Psalm, p 371.

MORNING PRAYER

Hymn, from the appendix, for the Season.

THROUGH THE YEAR
Lord God, your light which dims the stars
Awakes all things,
And all that springs to life in you
Your glory sings.

Your peaceful presence, giving strength,
Is everywhere,
And fallen men may rise again
On wings of prayer.

You are the God whose mercy rests
On all you made;
You gave us Christ, whose love through death
Our ransom paid.

We praise you, Father, with your Son
And Spirit blest,
In whom creation lives and moves,
And finds its rest.

PSALMODY

Ant. 1: In your light, God, we see light.
Eastertide: In you, Lord, is the source of life, alleluia.

THE EVIL OF THE SINNER;   PSALM 35(36)
 THE GOODNESS OF THE LORD

*The man who follows me will not walk in darkness, but he will have
the light of life for his guide* (Jn 8:12)

Sín spéaks to the sínner*
in the dépths of his héart.
There ís no féar of Gód*
befóre his éyes.

He so flátters himsélf in his mínd*
that he knóws not his guílt.
In his móuth are míschief and decéit.*
All wísdom is góne.

He plóts the deféat of góodness*
as he líes on his béd.
He has sét his fóot on evil wáys,*
he clíngs to what is évil.

Your lóve, Lord, réaches to héaven;*
your trúth to the skíes.
Your jústice is líke God's móuntain,*
your júdgments like the déep.

To both mán and béast you give protéction.*
O Lórd, how précious is your lóve.
My Gód, the sóns of mén*
find réfuge in the shélter of your wíngs.

They féast on the ríches of your hóuse;*
they drínk from the stréam of your delíght.
In yóu is the sóurce of lífe*
and ín your líght we see líght.

Keep on lóving thóse who knów you,*
doing jústice for úpright héarts.

Let the fóot of the próud not crúsh me*
nor the hánd of the wícked cast me óut.

Sée how the évil-doers fáll!*
Flung dówn, they shall néver aríse.

Ant. In your light, God, we see light.
Eastertide: In you, Lord, is the source of life, alleluia.

Ant. 2: Lord, you are great, you are glorious, you are wonderfully strong.
Eastertide: You sent forth your Spirit, and they were created, alleluia.

THE LORD, CREATOR OF THE WORLD,   CANTICLE
    PROTECTS HIS PEOPLE   JUD 16:2-3A,13-15
They began to sing a new song (Rev 5:9)

Begin a song to my God with tambourines,*
sing to my Lord with cymbals.
Raise to him a new psalm;†
exalt him and call upon his name.*
For God is the Lord who crushes wars.

I will sing to my God a new song:†
O Lord, you are great and glorious,*
wonderful in strength, invincible.

Let all your creatures serve you,*
for you spoke, and they were made.
You sent forth your Spirit, and it formed them;*
there is none that can resist your voice.

For the mountains shall be shaken to their foundations with
    the waters;*
at your presence the rocks shall melt like wax,
but to those who fear you*
you will continue to show mercy.

Ant. Lord, you are great, you are glorious, you are wonderfully strong.

Eastertide: You sent forth your Spirit, and they were created, alleluia.

Ant. 3: Cry to God with shouts of joy.

Eastertide: God is king of all the earth; sing praise with all your skill, alleluia.

THE LORD IS THE KING OF ALL   PSALM 46(47)

He is seated at the right hand of the Father, and his kingdom will have no end.

All péoples, cláp your hánds,*
cry to Gód with shóuts of jóy!
For the Lórd, the Most Hígh, we must féar,*
great kíng over áll the éarth.

He subdúes péoples únder us*
and nátions únder our féet.
Our inhéritance, our glóry, is from hím,*
gíven to Jácob out of lóve.

God goes úp with shóuts of jóy;*
the Lord ascénds with trúmpet blást.
Sing práise for Gód, sing práise,*
sing práise to our kíng, sing práise.

God is kíng of áll the éarth,*
Sing práise with áll your skíll.
God is kíng óver the nátions;*
God réigns on his hóly thróne.

The prínces of the péoples are assémbled*
with the péople of Ábraham's Gód.
The rúlers of the éarth belong to Gód,*
to Gód who réigns over áll.

Ant. Cry to God with shouts of joy.

Eastertide: God is king of all the earth; sing praise with all your skill, alleluia.

THROUGH THE YEAR

Scripture Reading   *Tob 4:16-17,19-20*

Do to no one what you would not want done to you. Give your bread to those who are hungry, and your clothes to those who are naked. Ask advice of every wise person. Bless the Lord God in everything; beg him to guide your ways and bring your paths and purposes to their end.

Short Responsory

℟ Bend my heart to your will, O God. *Repeat* ℟
℣ By your word, give me life. ℟ Glory be. ℟

Benedictus ant. Show us your mercy, O Lord; remember your holy covenant.

Intercessions

We give thanks to Christ and we praise him because he was not ashamed to call us his brothers. ℟ Lord Jesus, we are your brothers.
Help us to live the new life of Easter,—so that men may know through us the power of your love. ℟
Every day is a proof of your love:—As you bring us to this new day, make us new in mind and in heart. ℟
Teach us to see you present in all men;—help us to recognize you most of all in those who suffer. ℟
May our lives today be filled with your compassion;—give us the spirit of forgiveness and a generous heart. ℟
Our Father

Concluding Prayer

God our Saviour,
through the grace of baptism
you made us children of light.
Hear our prayer that we may always walk in that light
and work for truth, as your witnesses before men.
(We make our prayer) through our Lord.

EVENING PRAYER

Hymn, from the appendix, for the Season.

THROUGH THE YEAR

Christ be near at either hand,
Christ behind, before me stand,
Christ with me where'er I go,
Christ around, above, below.

Christ be in my heart and mind,
Christ within my soul enshrined,
Christ control my wayward heart;
Christ abide and ne'er depart.

Christ my life and only way,
Christ my lantern night and day;
Christ be my unchanging friend,
Guide and shepherd to the end.

PSALMODY

Ant. 1: The Lord is my light and my help; whom shall I fear?†
Eastertide: God has exalted him at his own right hand as leader and
Saviour, alleluia.

TRUST IN TIME OF AFFLICTION   PSALM 26(27)
Behold, the place where God dwells among men (Rev 21:3)

I

The Lórd is my líght and my hélp;*
whóm shall I féar?
†The Lórd is the strónghold of my lífe;*
before whóm shall I shrínk?

When évil-dóers draw néar*
to devóur my flésh,
it is théy, my énemies and fóes,*
who stúmble and fáll.

Though an ármy encámp agáinst me*
my héart would not féar.
Though wár break óut agáinst me*
even thén would I trúst.

There is óne thing I ásk of the Lórd,*
for thís I lóng,
to líve in the hóuse of the Lórd,*
all the dáys of my lífe,
to sávour the swéetness of the Lórd,*
to behóld his témple.

For thére he keeps me sáfe in his tént*
in the dáy of évil.
He hídes me in the shélter of his tént,*
on a róck he sets me sáfe.

And nów my héad shall be ráised*
above my fóes who surróund me
and I shall óffer withín his tént†
a sácrifice of jóy.*
I will síng and make músic for the Lórd.

Ant. The Lord is my light and my help; whom shall I fear?
Eastertide: God has exalted him at his own right hand as leader and
Saviour, alleluia.

Ant. 2: It is your face, O Lord, that I seek; hide not your face.
Eastertide: I am sure I shall see the Lord's goodness in the land of the
living, alleluia.

Some stood up and submitted false evidence against Jesus (Mk 14:57)

II

O Lórd, hear my vóice when I cáll;*
have mércy and ánswer.
Of yóu my héart has spóken:*
'Séek his fáce.'

It is your fáce, O Lórd, that I séek;*
híde not your fáce.
Dismíss not your sérvant in ánger;*
yóu have been my hélp.

Dó not abándon or forsáke me,*
O Gód my hélp!
Though fáther and móther forsáke me,*
The Lórd will recéive me.

Instrúct me, Lórd, in your wáy;*
on an éven path léad me.
When they líe in ámbush protéct me*
from my énemy's gréed.
False wítnesses ríse agáinst me,*
bréathing out fúry.

I am súre I shall sée the Lord's góodness*
in the lánd of the líving.
Hope in hím, hold fírm and take héart.*
Hópe in the Lórd!

Ant. It is your face, O Lord, that I seek; hide not your face.
Eastertide: I am sure I shall see the Lord's goodness in the land of
the living, alleluia.

Ant. 3: He is the firstborn of all creation; he is supreme over all
creatures.
Eastertide: From him, through him and in him are all things that
exist: to him be glory for ever, alleluia.

CHRIST IS THE FIRSTBORN OF ALL CREATION,   CANTICLE
   THE FIRSTBORN FROM THE DEAD   COL I:12-20

Let us give thanks to the Father,†
who has qualified us to share*
in the inheritance of the saints in light.

He has delivered us from the dominion of darkness*
and transferred us to the kingdom of his beloved Son,

in whom we have redemption,*
the forgiveness of sins.

He is the image of the invisible God,*
the firstborn of all creation,
for in him all things were created, in heaven and on earth,*
visible and invisible.

All things were created*
through him and for him.
He is before all things,*
and in him all things hold together.

He is the head of the body, the Church;*
he is the beginning,
the firstborn from the dead,*
that in everything he might be pre-eminent.

For in him all the fulness of God was pleased to dwell,*
and through him to reconcile to himself all things,
whether on earth or in heaven,*
making peace by the blood of his cross.

Ant. He is the firstborn of all creation; he is supreme over all creatures.
Eastertide: From him, through him and in him are all things that exist: to him be glory for ever, alleluia.

THROUGH THE YEAR

Scripture Reading   *Jas 1:22,25*
You must do what the word tells you, and not just listen to it and deceive yourselves. But the man who looks steadily at the perfect law of freedom and makes that his habit—not listening and then forgetting, but actively putting it into practice—will be happy in all that he does.

Short Responsory
R̷ Redeem me, Lord, and show me your mercy. *Repeat* R̷
V̷ Do not cast me away with sinners. R̷ Glory be. R̷

Magnificat ant. The Almighty has done great things for me; holy is his name.

Intercessions

The world is ablaze with the glory of God, who cares for his chosen people with infinite love. In the name of the Church we pray:
R℣ Lord, show your love to all men.

Be mindful of your Church:—keep her free from evil and make her perfect in your love. R℣

Let all peoples acknowledge that you alone are God, and that Jesus Christ is your Son;—give them the light of faith. R℣

Grant to those around us all that they need,—so that they may know thankfulness and live in peace. R℣

Keep us mindful of those whose work is hard and unrewarded:—may we give every man the respect which is his right. R℣

Give peace to those who have died today;—grant them eternal rest. R℣

Our Father

Concluding Prayer

Lord, support us as we pray,
protect us day and night,
so that we who under your guiding hand
live in a world of change,
may always draw strength from you,
with whom there is no shadow of alteration.
(We make our prayer) through our Lord.

WEEK 1: THURSDAY

Invitatory ant. Come, let us adore the Lord, for he is our God.
Psalm, p 371.

MORNING PRAYER

Hymn, from the appendix, for the Season.

THROUGH THE YEAR

The Father's glory, Christ our light,
With love and mercy comes to span

The vast abyss of sin between
The God of holiness and man.

Christ yesterday and Christ today,
For all eternity the same,
The image of our hidden God;
Eternal Wisdom is his name.

He keeps his word from age to age,
Is with us to the end of days,
A cloud by day, a flame by night,
To go before us on his ways.

We bless you, Father, fount of light,
And Christ, your well-beloved Son,
Who with the Spirit dwell in us:
Immortal Trinity in One.

PSALMODY

Ant. 1: Awake, lyre and harp, I will awake the dawn.
Eastertide: O God, arise above the heavens, alleluia.

MORNING PRAYER IN TIME OF AFFLICTION   PSALM 56(57)
This psalm celebrates the passion of Christ (St Augustine)

Have mércy on me, Gód, have mércy*
for in yóu my sóul has taken réfuge.
In the shádow of your wíngs I take réfuge*
till the stórms of destrúction pass bý.

I cáll to Gód the Most Hígh,*
to Gód who has álways been my hélp.
May he sénd from héaven and sáve me†
and sháme thóse who assáil me.*
May Gód send his trúth and his lóve.

My sóul lies dówn among líons,*
who would devóur the sóns of mén.
Their téeth are spéars and árrows,*
their tóngue a shárpened swórd.

431

O Gód, aríse above the héavens;*
may your glóry shine on eárth!

They láid a snáre for my stéps,*
my sóul was bowed dówn.
They dúg a pít in my páth*
but féll in it themsélves.

My héart is réady, O Gód,†
my héart is réady.*
I will síng, I will síng your práise.

Awáke my sóul,†
awáke lýre and hárp,*
I will awáke the dáwn.

I will thánk you Lórd among the péoples,*
among the nátions I will práise you
for your lóve réaches to the héavens*
and your trúth to the skíes.

O Gód, aríse above the héavens;*
may your glóry shine on eárth!

Ant. Awake, lyre and harp, I will awake the dawn.
Eastertide: O God, arise above the heavens, alleluia.

Ant. 2: Thus says the Lord: my people shall be filled with my good things.
Eastertide: The Lord has ransomed his people, alleluia.

THE JOY OF A LIBERATED PEOPLE   CANTICLE: JER 31:10-14
Jesus had to die to reunite the children of God who had been scattered
(Jn 11:51,52)

O nations, hear the word of the Lord,*
proclaim it to the far-off coasts.
Say: 'He who scattered Israel will gather him*
and guard him as a shepherd guards his flock.'
For the Lord has ransomed Jacob,*
has saved him from an overpowering hand.

They will come and shout for joy on Mount Sion,*
they will stream to the blessings of the Lord,
to the corn, the new wine and the oil,*
to the flocks of sheep and the herds.
Their life will be like a watered garden.*
They will never be weary again.

Then the young girls will rejoice and will dance,*
the men, young and old, will be glad.
I will turn their mourning into joy,*
I will console them, give gladness for grief.
The priests I will again feed with plenty,*
and my people shall be filled with my blessings.

Ant. Thus says the Lord: my people shall be filled with my good things.
Eastertide: The Lord has ransomed his people, alleluia.

Ant. 3: The Lord is great and worthy to be praised in the city of our God.†
Eastertide: God is here, our God for ever and ever, alleluia.

THANKSGIVING FOR THE SALVATION PSALM 47(48)
OF GOD'S PEOPLE
He took me to the top of a great mountain, and showed me the holy city of Jerusalem (Rev 21:10)

The Lord is gréat and wórthy to be práised*
in the cíty of our Gód.
†His holy móuntain ríses in béauty,*
the jóy of all the éarth.

Mount Síon, true póle of the éarth,*
the Gréat King's cíty!
Gód, in the mídst of its cítadels,*
has shówn himself its strónghold.

For the kíngs assémbled togéther,*
togéther they advánced.

433

They sáw; at ónce they were astóunded;*
dismáyed, they fled in féar.

A trémbling séized them thére,*
like the pángs of bírth,
By the éast wind yóu have destróyed*
the shíps of Thársis.

As we have héard, só we have séen*
in the cíty of our Gód,
in the cíty of the Lórd of hósts*
which Gód upholds for éver.

O Gód, we pónder your lóve*
withín your témple.
Your práise, O Gód, like your náme*
reaches the énds of the éarth.

With jústice your ríght hand is fílled.*
Mount Síon rejóices;
the péople of Júdah rejóice*
at the síght of your júdgments.

Walk through Síon, wálk all róund it;*
count the númber of its tówers.
Review áll its rámparts,*
exámine its cástles,

that you may téll the néxt generátion*
that súch is our Gód,
our Gód for éver and álways.*
It is hé who léads us.

Ant. The Lord is great and worthy to be praised in the city of our God.

Eastertide: God is here, our God for ever and ever, alleluia.

THROUGH THE YEAR

Scripture Reading   *Is 66:1-2*
Thus says the Lord:
With heaven my throne

434

and earth my footstool,
what house could you build me,
what place could you make for my rest?
All of this was made by my hand
and all of this is mine—it is the Lord who speaks.
But my eyes are drawn to the man
of humbled and contrite spirit,
who trembles at my word.

Short Responsory

R̶/ I called with all my heart; Lord, hear me. *Repeat* R̶/
V̶/ I will keep your commandments. R̶/ Glory be. R̶/

Benedictus ant. Let us serve the Lord in holiness, and he will deliver us from the hands of our enemies.

Intercessions

Let us begin this new day with Christ, thanking him for all he has brought to us, and asking him to bless us. R̶/ Lord accept and bless our work today.
You offered yourself to the Father on our behalf:—join our offering with yours. R̶/
You are gentle and humble of heart:—teach us to receive others as you did. R̶/
As each day begins, may your light rise in our hearts;—may it shine forth in charity to the world. R̶/
Show your mercy to those who are sick:—may each new day increase their trust in you. R̶/
Our Father

Concluding Prayer

Almighty ever-living God,
we make our prayer to you at morning, noon and evening:
dispel from our hearts the darkness of sin,
and bring us to the true light, Christ your Son,
who lives and reigns with you and the Holy Spirit,
God, for ever and ever.

EVENING PRAYER

Hymn, from the appendix, for the Season.

THROUGH THE YEAR

When God had filled the earth with life
And blessed it, to increase,
Then cattle dwelt with creeping things,
And lion with lamb, at peace.

He gave them vast, untrodden lands,
With plants to be their food;
Then God saw all that he had made
And found it very good.

Praise God the Father of all life,
His Son and Spirit blest,
By whom creation lives and moves,
In whom it comes to rest.

PSALMODY

Ant. 1: O Lord, I cried to you for help and you have healed me. I
will thank you for ever.
Eastertide: You changed my sorrow into joy, alleluia.

THANKSGIVING FOR LIBERATION FROM DEATH   PSALM 29(30)
Christ gives thanks to his Father after his glorious resurrection
(Cassian)

I will práise you, Lórd, yóu have réscued me*
and have nót let my énemies rejóice óver me.

O Lórd, I críed to you for hélp*
and yóu, my Gód, have héaled me.
O Lórd, you have ráised my sóul from the déad,*
restóred me to lífe from those who sínk into the gráve.

Sing psálms to the Lórd, you who lóve him,*
give thánks to his hóly náme.
His ánger lasts a móment; his fávour all through lífe.*
At níght there are téars, but jóy comes with dáwn.

436

I sáid to mysélf in my good fórtune:*
'Nóthing will éver distúrb me.'
Your fávour had sét me on a móuntain fástness,*
then you híd your fáce and I was pút to confúsion.

To yóu, Lórd, I críed,*
to my Gód I máde appéal:
'What prófit would my déath be, my góing to the gráve?*
Can dúst give you práise or procláim your trúth?'

The Lórd lístened and had píty.*
The Lórd cáme to my hélp.
For mé you have chánged my móurning into dáncing,*
you remóved my sáckcloth and clóthed me with jóy.
So my sóul sings psálms to you uncéasingly.*
O Lord my Gód, I will thánk you for éver.

Ant. O Lord, I cried to you for help and you have healed me. I will
thank you for ever.
Eastertide: You changed my sorrow into joy, alleluia.

Ant. 2: Happy the man to whom the Lord imputes no guilt.
Eastertide: We are reconciled to God by the death of his Son,
alleluia.

HAPPY IS THE MAN WHOSE OFFENCE IS FORGIVEN   PSALM 31(32)
*David says that a man is blessed if God considers him righteous,
irrespective of good deeds* (Rom 4:6)

Happy the mán whose offénce is forgíven,*
whose sín is remítted.
O háppy the mán to whom the Lórd†
impútes no guílt,*
in whose spírit is no guíle.

I kept it sécret and my fráme was wásted.*
I gróaned all day lóng
for níght and dáy your hánd*
was héavy upón me.

437

Indéed, my stréngth was dried úp*
as by the súmmer's héat.

But nów I have acknówledged my síns;*
my guílt I did not híde.
I saíd: 'Í will conféss*
my offénce to the Lórd.'
And yóu, Lórd, have forgíven*
the guílt of my sín.

So let évery good mán pray to yóu*
in the tíme of néed.
The flóods of wáter may reach hígh*
but hím they shall not réach.
Yóu are my híding place, O Lórd;†
you sáve me from distréss.*
You surróund me with críes of delíverance.

Í will instrúct you and téach you*
the wáy you should gó;
Í will gíve you cóunsel*
with my éye upón you.

Be not like hórse and múle, unintélligent,†
needing brídle and bít,*
élse they wíll not appróach you.
Many sórrows has the wícked†
but hé who trústs in the Lórd,*
loving mércy surróunds him.

Rejóice, rejóice in the Lórd,*
exúlt, you júst!
O cóme, ríng out your jóy,*
all you úpright of héart.

Ant. Happy the man to whom the Lord imputes no guilt.
Eastertide: We are reconciled to God by the death of his Son,
alleluia.

Ant. 3: The Lord has given him power and honour and empire, and all peoples will serve him.
Eastertide: Lord, who is your like, majestic in strength and holiness? alleluia.

THE JUDGMENT OF GOD	CANTICLE
	REV 11:17-18;12:10B-12A

We give thanks to you, Lord God Almighty,*
who are and who were,
that you have taken your great power*
and begun to reign.

The nations raged,*
but your wrath came,
and the time for the dead to be judged,*
for rewarding your servants, the prophets and saints,
and those who fear your name,*
both small and great.

Now the salvation and the power†
and the kingdom of our God*
and the authority of his Christ have come,
for the accuser of our brethren has been thrown down,*
who accuses them day and night before our God.

And they have conquered him*
by the blood of the Lamb
and by the word of their testimony,*
for they loved not their lives even unto death.
Rejoice, then, O heaven,*
and you that dwell therein.

Ant. The Lord has given him power and honour and empire, and all peoples will serve him.
Eastertide: Lord, who is your like, majestic in strength and holiness? alleluia.

THROUGH THE YEAR

Scripture Reading   *1 Pet 1:6-9*

This is a cause of great joy for you, even though you may for a short
time have to bear being plagued by all sorts of trials; so that, when
Jesus Christ is revealed, your faith will have been tested and proved
like gold—only it is more precious than gold, which is corruptible
even though it bears testing by fire—and then you will have praise
and glory and honour. You did not see him, yet you love him; and
still without seeing him, you are already filled with a joy so glorious
that it cannot be described, because you believe; and you are sure
of the end to which your faith looks forward, that is, the salvation
of your souls.

Short Responsory

℟ The Lord fed us with finest wheat. *Repeat* ℟
℣ He filled us with honey from the rock. ℟ Glory be. ℟

Magnificat ant. The Lord brought down the mighty from their seats,
and raised up the lowly.

Intercessions

Let us make our prayer to the God of our salvation because all our
hope rests in him. ℟ Father, our trust is in you.

Father, you established a covenant with men:—we trust in you,
for you are faithful to your word. ℟

Send workers into the harvest,—and bring the world to the knowledge and love of you. ℟

May the unity of the Church be formed by love and understanding;
—gather us together through the gifts of your Holy Spirit. ℟

Help men to create a community where justice and peace may
flourish:—be with us, lest we labour in vain. ℟

Be mindful of the dead, especially those we have known;—have
mercy on those who have given us their help. ℟

Our Father

Concluding Prayer

Lord God,
you give the moon to illumine the night,
and to dispel the darkness you bring in the light of day:
grant that during this night

we may elude the grasp of Satan
and in the morning rise to give you praise.
(We make our prayer) through our Lord.

WEEK 1: FRIDAY

Invitatory ant. Give thanks to the Lord, for his great love is without
end.
Psalm, p 371.

MORNING PRAYER

Hymn, from the appendix, for the Season.

THROUGH THE YEAR

We bless you, Father, Lord of Life,
To whom all living beings tend,
The source of holiness and grace,
Our first beginning and our end.

We give you thanks, Redeeming Christ,
Who bore our weight of sin and shame;
In dark defeat you conquered sin,
And death by dying, overcame.

Come, Holy Spirit, searching fire,
Whose flame all evil burns away.
Come down to us with light and love,
In silence and in peace to stay.

We praise you, Trinity in One,
Sublime in majesty and might,
Who reign for ever, Lord of all,
In splendour and unending light.

PSALMODY

Ant. 1: Lord, you will be pleased with lawful sacrifice offered on
your altar.

441

Eastertide: Remember me, Lord God, when you come into your kingdom, alleluia.

HAVE MERCY ON ME, GOD   PSALM 50(51)
You must be made new in mind and spirit, and put on the new nature of God's creating (Eph 4:23,24)

Have mércy on me, Gód, in your kíndness.*
In your compássion blot óut my offénce.
O wásh me more and móre from my guílt*
and cléanse me fróm my sín.

My offénces trúly I knów them;*
my sín is álways befóre me.
Against yóu, you alóne, have I sínned;*
what is évil in your síght I have dóne.

That you may be jústified whén you give séntence*
and be withóut repróach when you júdge,
O sée, in guílt I was bórn,*
a sínner was Í concéived.

Indéed you love trúth in the héart;*
then in the sécret of my héart teach me wísdom.
O púrify me, thén I shall be cléan;*
O wásh me, I shall be whíter than snów.

Make me héar rejóicing and gládness,*
that the bónes you have crúshed may revíve.
From my síns turn awáy your fáce*
and blót out áll my guílt.

A púre heart creáte for me, O Gód,*
put a stéadfast spírit withín me.
Do not cást me awáy from your présence,*
nor depríve me of your hóly spírit.

Give me agáin the jóy of your hélp;*
with a spírit of férvour sustáin me,
that I may téach transgréssors your wáys*
and sínners may retúrn to yóu.

O réscue me, Gód, my hélper,*
and my tóngue shall ríng out your góodness.
O Lórd, ópen my líps*
and my móuth shall decláre your práise.

For in sácrifice you táke no delíght,*
burnt óffering from mé you would refúse,
my sácrifice a cóntrite spírit.*
A húmbled, contrite héart you will not spúrn.

In your góodness, show fávour to Síon:*
rebuíld the wálls of Jerúsalem.
Thén you will be pléased with lawful sácrifice,*
hólocausts óffered on your áltar.

Ant. Lord, you will be pleased with lawful sacrifice offered on your
altar.
Eastertide: Remember me, Lord God, when you come into your
kingdom, alleluia.

Ant. 2: All the descendants of Israel shall glory in victory through
the Lord.
Eastertide: Truly, God of Israel, the Saviour, you are a God who
lies hidden, alleluia.†

ALL THE PEOPLES WILL TURN TO THE LORD   CANTICLE
IS 45:15-26

Every knee must bow at the name of Jesus (Phil 2:10)

Truly, God of Israel, the Saviour,*
you are a God who lies hidden.
†They will be put to shame and disgraced,*
all who resist you.
They will take themselves off in dismay,*
the makers of idols.

But Israel is saved by the Lord,*
saved for evermore.
You will never be ashamed or disgraced*
through endless ages.

For this is the word of the Lord,*
the creator of heaven,
the God who made earth and shaped it,*
he who made it firm.
He did not create it in vain,*
he made it to be lived in.

'I am the Lord, there is no other.*
I have not spoken in secret, in some dark place,
I have not said to Jacob's sons*
"Search for me in vain."

I am the Lord, I speak the truth,
I proclaim what is right.
Assemble, all of you, draw near*
you who have escaped from the nations.

They know nothing, who carry around*
their idols made of wood
and keep on praying to a god*
that cannot save them.

State your case and bring your proofs,*
consult among yourselves.
Who proclaimed this beforehand,*
who foretold it long ago?

Was it not I, the Lord?*
There is no god but me,
a God of justice, a saviour.*
There is none but me.

Turn to me and be saved,*
all the ends of the earth!
For I am God, there is no other;*
by myself I swear it.

It is truth that goes forth from my mouth,*
a word beyond recall.
To me every knee shall bow,*
every tongue shall swear.

They will say: "In the Lord alone*
are victory and power.
And to him will come in dismay*
all who have resisted.
Through the Lord will come victory and glory*
for all Israel's sons." '

Ant. All the descendants of Israel shall glory in victory through the Lord.
Eastertide: Truly, God of Israel, the Saviour, you are a God who lies hidden, alleluia.

Ant. 3: Come before the Lord, singing for joy.
Eastertide: Serve the Lord with joy, alleluia.

When the following psalm has been used at the Invitatory, ps 94, p 371, is said here in place of it.

THE JOY OF THOSE WHO ENTER   PSALM 99(100)
   THE TEMPLE OF THE LORD
The Lord calls all those he has redeemed to sing a hymn of victory
(St Athanasius)

Cry out with jóy to the Lórd, all the éarth.†
Sérve the Lórd with gládness.*
Come befóre him, sínging for jóy.

Know that hé, the Lórd, is Gód.†
He máde us, we belóng to hím,*
we are his péople, the shéep of his flóck.

Gó within his gátes, giving thánks.†
Enter his cóurts with sóngs of práise.*
Give thánks to him and bléss his náme.

Indéed, how góod is the Lórd,†
etérnal his mérciful lóve.*
He is fáithful from áge to áge.   Glory be.

445

Ant. Come before the Lord, singing for joy.
Eastertide: Serve the Lord with joy, alleluia.

THROUGH THE YEAR

Scripture Reading   *Eph 4:29-32*
Do not use harmful words in talking. Use only helpful words, the kind that build up and provide what is needed, so that what you say will do good to those who hear you. And do not make God's Holy Spirit sad; for the Spirit is God's mark of ownership on you, a guarantee that the Day will come when God will set you free. Get rid of all bitterness, passion, and anger. No more shouting or insults. No more hateful feelings of any sort. Instead, be kind and tender-hearted to one another, and forgive one another, as God has forgiven you in Christ.

Short Responsory
R⁊ In the morning let me know your love. *Repeat* R⁊
V⁊ Make me know the way I should walk. R⁊ Glory be. R⁊

Benedictus ant. The Lord has visited his people, he has come to redeem them.

Intercessions
Lord Jesus Christ, we thank you. Through your cross and resurrection you offer freedom and hope to those ready to receive them. R⁊ Lord, show us your loving-kindness.
We are children of the day:—help us to live in the light of your presence. R⁊
Guide our thoughts, our words, our actions:—so that what we do today may be pleasing to you. R⁊
Help us to avoid wrongdoing:—show us your mercy and love. R⁊
Through your passion and death you have won life for us:—give us the strength of your Holy Spirit. R⁊
Our Father

Concluding Prayer
Lord God,
you hold out the light of your Word

446

to those who do not know you.
Strengthen in our hearts the faith you have given us,
so that no trials may quench the fire
your Spirit has kindled within us.
(We make our prayer) through our Lord.

EVENING PRAYER

Hymn, from the appendix, for the Season.

THROUGH THE YEAR
When God made man, he gave him all the earth,
All growing things, with every bird and beast;
Then Adam named them at the Lord's command,
Subdued the greatest of them, and the least.

In his own image God created man,
And when from dust he fashioned Adam's face,
The likeness of his only Son was formed:
His Word incarnate, filled with truth and grace.

To God the Father and to Christ his Son
And blessed Spirit heaven and earth give praise.
Creation with tremendous voice cries out:
All holy is the mighty Lord of days.

PSALMODY

Ant. 1: Lord, heal my soul for I have sinned against you.
Eastertide: Christ made himself poor for our enrichment, alleluia.

PRAYER IN SICKNESS   PSALM 40(41)
One of you will betray me—one who is eating with me (Mk 14:18)

Happy the mán who consíders the póor and the wéak.*
The Lórd will sáve him in the dáy of évil,
will guárd him, give him lífe, make him háppy in the lánd*
and will nót give him úp to the wíll of his fóes.
The Lórd will hélp him on his béd of páin,*
he will bríng him báck from síckness to héalth.

447

As for mé, I said: 'Lórd, have mércy on mé,*
heal my sóul for Í have sínned agáinst you.'
My fóes are spéaking évil agáinst me.*
'How lóng before he díes and his náme be forgótten?'
They cóme to vísit me and spéak empty wórds,*
their héarts full of málice, they spréad it abróad.

My énemies whísper togéther agáinst me.*
They áll weigh úp the évil which is ón me:
'Some déadly thíng has fástened upón him,*
he will nót rise agáin from whére he líes.'
Thus éven my fríend, in whóm I trústed,*
who áte my bréad, has túrned agáinst me.

But yóu, O Lórd, have mércy on mé.*
Let me ríse once móre and Í will repáy them.
By thís I shall knów that yóu are my fríend,*
if my fóes do not shóut in tríumph óver me.
If yóu uphóld me Í shall be unhármed*
and sét in your présence for évermóre.

Bléssed be the Lórd, the Gód of Ísrael*
from áge to áge. Amén. Amén.

Ant. Lord, heal my soul for I have sinned against you.
Eastertide: Christ made himself poor for our enrichment, alleluia.

Ant. 2: The Lord of hosts is with us: the God of Jacob is our stronghold.
Eastertide: The waters of a river give joy to God's city, alleluia.

GOD IS OUR REFUGE AND STRENGTH   PSALM 45(46)
They will call his name 'Immanuel' which means 'God with us'
(Mt 1:23)

Gód is for ús a réfuge and stréngth,*
a hélper close at hánd, in tíme of distréss:
so wé shall not féar though the éarth should róck,*
though the móuntains fáll into the dépths of the séa,
even thóugh its wáters ráge and fóam,*
even thóugh the móuntains be sháken by its wáves.

The Lórd of hósts is wíth us:*
the Gód of Jácob is our strónghold.

The wáters of a ríver give jóy to God's cíty,*
the hóly pláce where the Móst High dwélls.
Gód is withín, it cánnot be sháken;*
Gód will hélp it at the dáwning of the dáy.
Nátions are in túmult, kíngdoms are sháken:*
he lífts his vóice, the éarth shrinks awáy.

The Lórd of hósts is wíth us:*
the Gód of Jácob is our strónghold.

Cóme, consíder the wórks of the Lórd*
the redóubtable déeds he has dóne on the éarth.
He puts an énd to wárs over áll the éarth;†
the bów he bréaks, the spéar he snáps.*
He búrns the shíelds with fíre.
'Be stíll and knów that Í am Gód,*
supréme among the nátions, supréme on the éarth!'

The Lórd of hósts is wíth us:*
the Gód of Jácob is our strónghold.

Ant. The Lord of hosts is with us: the God of Jacob is our stronghold.
Eastertide: The waters of a river give joy to God's city, alleluia.

Ant. 3: All the peoples will come and adore you, Lord.
Eastertide: Let us sing to the Lord, great is his triumph, alleluia.

HYMN OF ADORATION   CANTICLE: REV 15:3-4

Great and wonderful are your deeds,*
O Lord God the Almighty!
Just and true are your ways,*
O King of the ages!

Who shall not fear and glorify your name, O Lord?*
For you alone are holy.

All nations shall come and worship you,*
for your judgments have been revealed.

Ant. All the peoples will come and adore you, Lord.
Eastertide: Let us sing to the Lord; great is his triumph, alleluia.

THROUGH THE YEAR

Scripture Reading   *Rom 15:1-3*
We who are strong ought to bear with the failings of the weak, and
not to please ourselves; let each of us please his neighbour for his
good, to edify him. For Christ did not please himself; but as it is
written, The reproaches of those who reproached you fell on me.

Short Responsory
R℣ Christ loved us and has washed away our sins with his blood.
Repeat R℣
℣ He made us a line of kings, priests to serve God. R℣ Glory be. R℣

Magnificat ant. The Lord has come to help us, his servants; he has
remembered his mercy.

Intercessions
God is our loving Father, who cares for us and knows all our needs.
With confidence we pray: R℣ Father, may we find rest in your love.
Christ, your Son, suffered and died for the Church:—be with all
Christians who are suffering tonight. R℣
Bring to the sick your comfort and healing;—strengthen them
through the victory of Calvary. R℣
Be near to us, almighty Father,—for you alone can save us from the
evils that threaten us. R℣
Strengthen us in the hour of death:—let us know your peace. R℣
Bring the dead into your light:—comfort them with your presence. R℣
Our Father

Concluding Prayer
Lord God,
teach us the lessons of your Son's Passion,
and so enable us, your people,

to bear the yoke he makes light for us.
(We make our prayer) through our Lord.

WEEK 1: SATURDAY

Invitatory ant. The Lord's is the earth and its fulness: come, let us
adore him.
Psalm, p 371.

MORNING PRAYER

Hymn, from the appendix, for the Season.

THROUGH THE YEAR
It were my soul's desire
To see the face of God;
It were my soul's desire
To rest in his abode.

Grant, Lord, my soul's desire,
Deep waves of cleansing sighs,
Grant, Lord, my soul's desire,
From earthly cares to rise.

It were my soul's desire
To imitate my King,
It were my soul's desire
His endless praise to sing.

It were my soul's desire,
When heaven's gate is won,
To find my soul's desire,
Clear shining like the sun.

This still my soul's desire,
Whatever life afford,
To gain my soul's desire
And see thy face, O Lord.

PSALMODY

Ant. 1: My eyes watch for you before dawn.
Eastertide: In your love, give me life, O Lord, alleluia.

PSALM 118(119):145-152 XIX (KOPH)

I cáll with all my héart; Lord, héar me,*
I will kéep your commánds.
I cáll upón you, sáve me*
and Í will do your wíll.

I ríse before dáwn and cry for hélp,*
I hópe in your wórd.
My éyes wátch through the níght*
to pónder your prómise.

In your lóve hear my vóice, O Lórd;*
give me lífe by your decrées.
Those who hárm me unjústly draw néar:*
they are fár from your láw.

But yóu, O Lórd, are clóse:*
your commánds are trúth.
Lóng have I knówn that your wíll*
is estáblished for éver.

Ant. My eyes watch for you before dawn.
Eastertide: In your love, give me life, O Lord, alleluia.

Ant. 2: The Lord is my strength, I will sing his praise; he is my salvation.
Eastertide: For the victors, theirs is the song of God's servant Moses, theirs is the song of the Lamb, alleluia.

HYMN OF VICTORY AFTER CROSSING   CANTICLE
   THE RED SEA   EX 15:1-4A,8-13,17-18
*Those who overcame the beast sang the hymn of Moses, the Servant
of God* (cf Rev 15:2-3)

I will sing to the Lord, glorious his triumph!*
Horse and rider he has thrown into the sea!

The Lord is my strength, my song, my salvation.†
This is my God and I extol him,*
my father's God and I give him praise.
The Lord is a warrior!* The Lord is his name.

The chariots of Pharaoh he hurled into the sea.*
At the breath of your anger the waters piled high;
the moving waters stood up like a dam.*
The deeps turned solid in the midst of the sea.

The enemy said: 'I will pursue and overtake them,†
I will divide the plunder, I shall have my will.*
I will draw my sword, my hand shall destroy them.'

You blew with your breath, the sea closed over them.*
They went down like lead into the mighty waters.
Who is like you among the gods, O Lord,†
who is like you, so glorious in holiness,*
spreading fear through your deeds, you who do marvels?

You stretched forth your hand,*
the earth engulfed them;
your love has guided the people you redeemed,*
your power has led them to your holy dwelling-place.

You will lead them and plant them on your mountain,†
the place, O Lord, where you have made your home,*
the sanctuary, Lord, which your hands have made.
The Lord will reign* for ever and ever.

Ant. The Lord is my strength, I will sing his praise; he is my salvation.
Eastertide: For the victors, theirs is the song of God's servant Moses, theirs is the song of the Lamb, alleluia.

Ant. 3: O praise the Lord, all you nations.†
Eastertide: Strong is his love for us, alleluia.

PRAISE TO THE GOD OF MERCY   PSALM 116(117)
I ask the nations to give praise to God for his mercy (Rom 15:8-9)

O práise the Lórd, all you nátions,*

†accláim him all you péoples!

Stróng is his lóve for ús;*
he is fáithful for éver.

Ant. O praise the Lord, all you nations.
Eastertide: Strong is his love for us, alleluia.

THROUGH THE YEAR

Scripture Reading   *2 Pet 1:10-11*
Brothers, you have been called and chosen: work all the harder to
justify it by good deeds. If you do all these things there is no danger
that you will ever fall away. In this way you will be granted ad-
mittance into the eternal kingdom of our Lord and saviour Jesus
Christ.

Short Responsory
R̷ I called to you, Lord, you are my refuge. *Repeat* R̷
V̷ You are all I have in the land of the living. R̷ Glory be. R̷

Benedictus ant. Give your light, Lord, to those who sit in darkness
and in the shadow of death.

Intercessions
Christ became man to make us sons of God and he intercedes for
us before God our Father. Let us thank him for his loving mercy,
and pray: R̷ Open to us the treasures of your love.
You have enlightened us in baptism:—we consecrate our day to
you. R̷
Fill us with praise of you today:—may we take your word with us
wherever we may go. R̷
Teach us to respond to your word like Mary our Mother:—may
your word be fruitful in us. R̷
Give us courage when things go wrong:—strengthen us with faith
in you, with hope in your promises and with love of your will. R̷
Our Father

Concluding Prayer
Let the splendour of the resurrection,

light up our hearts and minds, Lord,
scattering the shadows of death,
and bringing us to the radiance of eternity.
(We make our prayer) through our Lord.

WEEK 2: SUNDAY

EVENING PRAYER I

Hymn, from the appendix, for the Season.

THROUGH THE YEAR
Bless'd be the Lord our God!
With joy let heaven ring;
Before his presence let all earth
Its songs of homage bring!
His mighty deeds be told;
His majesty be praised;
To God, enthroned in heav'nly light,
Let every voice be raised!

All that has life and breath,
Give thanks with heartfelt songs!
To him let all creation sing
To whom all praise belongs!
Acclaim the Father's love,
Who gave us God his Son;
Praise too the Spirit, giv'n by both,
With both for ever one!

PSALMODY

ANTIPHON I
Advent: Rejoice and be glad, new Sion. See now how humbly your King, our Saviour, will come to you.
Lent, Sunday 2: Jesus took Peter, James and John the brother of James, and led them up a high mountain where they were alone; and in their presence he was transfigured.

Lent, Palm Sunday: I sat teaching in the Temple day after day and you never laid hands on me. Now you have scourged me and lead me to be crucified.

Eastertide: The man who lives by the truth comes into the light, alleluia.

Through the Year: Your word is a lamp for my steps, Lord, alleluia.†

MEDITATION ON THE WORD OF GOD IN THE LAW

PSALM 118(119):105-112 XIV (NUN)
This is my commandment, that you love each other (Jn 15:12)

Your wórd is a lámp for my stéps*
†and a líght for my páth.
I have swórn and have máde up my mínd*
to obéy your decrées.

Lórd, I am déeply afflícted:*
by your wórd give me lífe.
Accépt, Lord, the hómage of my líps*
and téach me your decrées.

Though I cárry my lífe in my hánds,*
I remémber your láw.
Though the wícked trý to ensnáre me*
I do not stráy from your précepts.

Your wíll is my héritage for éver,*
the jóy of my héart.
I sét myself to cárry out your wíll*
in fúlness, for éver.

Ant. Your word is a lamp for my steps, Lord, alleluia.

Ant. Advent: Rejoice and be glad, new Sion. See now how humbly your King, our Saviour, will come to you.
Ant. 2: Strengthen the weary hands: be strong and say, 'Behold. our God will come and he will save us, alleluia.'

Ant. Lent, Sunday 2: Jesus took Peter, James, and John the brother of James, and led them up a high mountain where they were alone; and in their presence he was transfigured.
Ant. 2: His face shone like the sun and his clothes became as white as snow.

Ant. Palm Sunday: I sat teaching in the Temple day after day and you never laid hands on me. Now you have scourged me and lead me to be crucified.
Ant. 2: The Lord God helps me; no insult can wound me.

Ant. Eastertide: The man who lives by the truth comes into the light, alleluia.
Ant. 2: Freed from the pangs of death, the Lord arose from the grave, alleluia.

Ant. 2: O Lord, you will show me the fulness of joy in your presence, alleluia.

THE LORD IS MY PORTION   PSALM 15(16)
God raised up Jesus, freeing him from the pains of death (Acts 2:24)

Presérve me, Gód, I take réfuge in yóu.†
I sáy to the Lórd: 'Yóu are my Gód.*
My háppiness líes in yóu alóne.'

He has pút into my héart a márvellous lóve*
for the fáithful ónes who dwéll in his lánd.
Those who chóose other góds incréase their sórrows.†
Néver will I óffer their ófferings of blóod.*
Néver will I táke their náme upon my líps.

O Lórd, it is yóu who are my pórtion and cúp;*
it is yóu yoursélf who áre my príze.
The lót marked óut for me is mý delíght:*
welcome indéed the héritage that fálls to mé!

I will bléss the Lórd who gíves me cóunsel,*
who éven at níght dirécts my héart.
I kéep the Lórd ever ín my síght:*
since hé is at my ríght hand, Í shall stand fírm.

457

And so my héart rejóices, my sóul is glád;*
éven my bódy shall rést in sáfety.
For yóu will not léave my sóul among the déad,*
nor lét your belóved knów decáy.

You will shów me the páth of lífe,†
the fúlness of jóy in your présence,*
at your ríght hand háppiness for éver.

Ant. O Lord, you will show me the fulness of joy in your presence, alleluia.

Ant. Advent: Strengthen the weary hands: be strong and say, 'Behold, our God will come and he will save us, alleluia.'
Ant. 3: The Law was given through Moses, grace and truth have come through Jesus Christ.

Ant. Lent, Sunday 2: His face shone like the sun and his clothes became as white as snow.
Ant. 3: Moses and Elijah were speaking of his passion and death, and all he was to fulfil in Jerusalem.

Ant. Lent, Palm Sunday: The Lord God helps me; no insult can wound me.
Ant. 3: The Lord Jesus humbled himself and, in obedience, accepted death, even death on a cross.

Ant. Eastertide: Freed from the pangs of death, the Lord arose from the grave, alleluia.
Ant. 3: Was it not necessary that Christ should suffer thus and so enter into his glory, alleluia?

Ant. 3: Let every creature, in heaven and on earth, bend the knee at the name of Jesus, alleluia.

CHRIST, THE SERVANT OF GOD   CANTICLE: PHIL 2:6-11

Though he was in the form of God,*
Jesus did not count equality with God a thing to be grasped.

He emptied himself,†

taking the form of a servant,*
being born in the likeness of men.

And being found in human form,†
he humbled himself and became obedient unto death,*
even death on a cross.

Therefore God has highly exalted him.*
and bestowed on him the name which is above every name,

That at the name of Jesus every knee should bow,*
in heaven and on earth and under the earth,

And every tongue confess that Jesus Christ is Lord,*
to the glory of God the Father.

Ant. Let every creature, in heaven and on earth, bend the knee at
the name of Jesus, alleluia.

Ant. Advent: The Law was given through Moses, grace and truth
have come through Jesus Christ.
Lent, Sunday 2: Moses and Elijah were speaking of his passion and
death, and all he was to fulfil in Jerusalem.
Lent, Palm Sunday: The Lord Jesus humbled himself and, in
obedience, accepted death, even death on a cross.
Eastertide: Was it not necessary that Christ should suffer thus and
so enter into his glory, alleluia?

THROUGH THE YEAR

Scripture Reading   *Col 1:3-6a*
May God our Father and the Lord Jesus Christ give you grace and
peace. We always give thanks to God, the Father of our Lord
Jesus Christ, when we pray for you. For we have heard of your faith
in Christ Jesus, and of your love for all God's people. When the
true message, the Good News, first came to you, you heard of the
hope it offers. So your faith and love are based on what you hope
for, which is kept safe for you in heaven. The gospel is bringing
blessings and spreading through the whole world, just as it has
among you.

Short Responsory

℟ From the rising of the sun to its setting, great is the name of the Lord. *Repeat* ℟

℣ High above the heavens is his glory. ℟ Glory be. ℟

Magnificat antiphon from the Proper of Seasons.

Intercessions

God our Father leads us forward with great love towards the joyful day when we enter his rest. ℟ Our hope is all in you, Lord God.

Father, we pray for N., our Pope, and N., our bishop:—guide them and bless them in their work. ℟

Help the sick to share their sufferings with Christ:—may they know in him the fulness of life and love. ℟

Lord, you found nowhere to lay your head:—make us aware of the needs of the homeless today. ℟

Bless those who work on the land:—may we receive the fruits of the earth with thankfulness. ℟

Father, have mercy on those who have died in the peace of Christ:— receive them into the home you have prepared for them. ℟

Our Father

The concluding prayer from the Proper of Seasons.

Invitatory

Ant. We are the people of the Lord, the flock that is led by his hand: come, let us adore him, alleluia.

Psalm, p 371.

MORNING PRAYER

Hymn, from the appendix, for the Season.

THROUGH THE YEAR

   I bind unto myself today
   The strong name of the Trinity,
   By invocation of the same,
   The Three in One, and One in Three.

I bind unto myself today
The power of God to hold and lead,
His eye to watch, his might to stay,
His ear to hearken to my need,

The wisdom of my God to teach,
His hand to guide, his shield to ward;
The word of God to give me speech,
His heavenly host to be my guard.

I bind unto myself the name,
The strong name of the Trinity;
By invocation of the same,
The Three in One, and One in Three,

Of whom all nature hath creation;
Eternal Father, Spirit, Word:
Praise to the Lord of my salvation:
Salvation is of Christ the Lord.

Alternative hymn
All people that on earth do dwell,
Sing to the Lord with cheerful voice;
Him serve with mirth, his praise forth tell,
Come ye before him, and rejoice.

The Lord, ye know, is God indeed;
Without our aid he did us make;
We are his folk, he doth us feed;
And for his sheep he doth us take.

For why, the Lord our God is good:
His mercy is for ever sure;
His truth at all times firmly stood,
And shall from age to age endure.

To Father, Son and Holy Ghost,
The God whom heaven and earth adore,
From men and from the angel-host
Be praise and glory evermore.

461

PSALMODY

ANTIPHON I

Advent: We have a strong city. The Saviour will set up wall and rampart to guard it. Open the gates, for God is with us, alleluia.

Lent, Sunday 2: The Lord's right hand has triumphed; his right hand raised me up.

Lent, Palm Sunday: The crowds of people, who had gathered for the feastday, called out to the Lord, 'Blessed is he who comes in the name of the Lord. Hosanna in the highest.'

Eastertide: This is the day which was made by the Lord, alleluia.

Through the Year: Blessed is he who comes in the name of the Lord, alleluia.

SONG OF REJOICING IN SALVATION   PSALM 117(118)
This is the stone which was rejected by you builders, but which has become the corner stone (Acts 4:11).

Give thánks to the Lórd for he is góod,*
for his lóve endures for éver.

Let the sóns of Ísrael sáy:*
'His lóve endures for éver.'
Let the sóns of Áaron sáy:*
'His lóve endures for éver.'
Let thóse who fear the Lórd sáy:*
'His lóve endures for éver.'

I cálled to the Lórd in my distréss;*
he ánswered and fréed me.
The Lórd is at my síde; I do not féar.*
What can mán do agáinst me?
The Lórd is at my síde as my hélper:*
I shall look dówn on my fóes.

It is bétter to take réfuge in the Lórd*
than to trúst in mén:
it is bétter to take réfuge in the Lórd*
than to trúst in prínces.

462

The nátions áll encómpassed me;*
in the Lórd's name I crúshed them.
They cómpassed me, cómpassed me abóut;*
in the Lórd's name I crúshed them.
They cómpassed me abóut like bées;†
they blázed like a fíre among thórns.*
In the Lórd's name I crúshed them.

I was hárd-préssed and was fálling*
but the Lórd came to hélp me.
The Lórd is my stréngth and my sóng;*
hé is my sáviour.
There are shóuts of jóy and víctory*
in the ténts of the júst.

The Lórd's right hánd has tríumphed;*
his ríght hand ráised me.
The Lórd's right hánd has tríumphed;†
I shall not díe, I shall líve*
and recóunt his déeds.
I was púnished, I was púnished by the Lórd,*
but nót doomed to díe.

Ópen to mé the gates of hóliness:*
I will énter and give thánks.
Thís is the Lórd's own gáte*
where the júst may énter.
I will thánk you for yóu have ánswered*
and yóu are my sáviour.

The stóne which the buílders rejécted*
has becóme the córner stone.
This is the wórk of the Lórd,*
a márvel in our éyes.
Thís day was máde by the Lórd;*
we rejóice and are glád.

O Lórd, gránt us salvátion;*
O Lórd, grant succéss.

Bléssed in the náme of the Lórd*
is hé who cómes.
We bléss you from the hóuse of the Lórd;*
the Lord Gód is our líght.

Go fórward in procéssion with bránches*
éven to the áltar.
Yóu are my Gód, I thánk you.*
My Gód, I práise you.
Give thánks to the Lórd for he is góod;*
for his lóve endures for éver.

Ant. Blessed is he who comes in the name of the Lord, alleluia.

Ant. Advent: We have a strong city. The Saviour will set up wall and rampart to guard it. Open the gates, for God is with us, alleluia.
Ant. 2: Come to the water all you who thirst: seek the Lord while he may be found, alleluia.

Ant. Lent, Sunday 2: The Lord's right hand has triumphed; his right hand raised me up.
Ant. 2: Let us sing the hymn of the three young men, which they sang in the blazing furnace, blessing the Lord.

Ant. Palm Sunday: The crowds of people, who had gathered for the feastday, called out to the Lord, 'Blessed is he who comes in the name of the Lord. Hosanna in the highest.'
Ant. 2: May we be counted among the faithful, with the angels and with the children. Triumphant over death, we sing with them, 'Hosanna in the highest.'

Ant. Eastertide: This is the day which was made by the Lord, alleluia.
Ant. 2: O Lord, our God, you are blessed in the firmament of heaven, and worthy of praise, alleluia.

Ant. 2: Let us sing a hymn to our God, alleluia.

LET EVERY CREATURE PRAISE THE LORD

CANTICLE
DAN 3:52-57

The Creator is blessed for ever (Rom 1:25)

You are blest, Lord God of our fathers.*
To you glory and praise for evermore.

Blest your glorious holy name.*
To you glory and praise for evermore.

You are blest in the temple of your glory.*
To you glory and praise for evermore.

You are blest who gaze into the depths.*
To you glory and praise for evermore.

You are blest in the firmament of heaven.*
To you glory and praise for evermore.

You who walk on the wings of the wind:*
To you glory and praise for evermore.

May they bless you, the saints and the angels.*
To you glory and praise for evermore

From the heavens, the earth and the sea,*
To you glory and praise for evermore.

You are blest, Lord God of our fathers.*
To you glory and praise for evermore.

Ant. Let us sing a hymn to our God, alleluia.

Ant. Advent: Come to the water all you who thirst: seek the Lord while he may be found, alleluia.
Ant. 3: Behold, our Lord will come in strength and he will give light to the eyes of his servants, alleluia.

Ant. Lent, Sunday 2: Let us sing the hymn of the three young men, which they sang in the blazing furnace, blessing the Lord.
Ant. 3: Praise the Lord in his mighty heavens.

465

Ant. Lent, Palm Sunday: May we be counted among the faithful, with the angels and with the children. Triumphant over death, we sing with them, 'Hosanna in the highest.'
Ant. 3: Blessed is he who comes in the name of the Lord; peace in heaven; glory in the highest heavens.

Ant. Eastertide: O Lord, our God, you are blessed in the firmament of heaven, and worthy of praise, alleluia.
Ant. 3: Praise God who sits on the throne; saying 'Amen, Alleluia.'

Ant. 3: Praise the Lord for his surpassing greatness, alleluia.

PRAISE THE LORD   PSALM 150
Sing praise in your spirit, sing praise with your soul, that is: give glory to God in both your soul and your body (Hesychius).

Práise Gód in his hóly pláce,*
práise him in his míghty héavens.
Práise him for his pówerful déeds,*
práise his surpássing gréatness.

O práise him with sóund of trúmpet,*
práise him with lúte and hárp.
Práise him with tímbrel and dánce,*
práise him with stríngs and pípes.

O práise him with resóunding cýmbals,*
práise him with cláshing of cýmbals.
Let éverything that líves and that bréathes*
give práise to the Lórd.

Ant. Praise the Lord for his surpassing greatness, alleluia.

Ant. Advent: Behold, our Lord will come in strength and he will give light to the eyes of his servants, alleluia.
Lent, Sunday 2: Praise the Lord in his mighty heavens.
Lent, Palm Sunday: Blessed is he who comes in the name of the Lord; peace in heaven; glory in the highest heavens.
Eastertide: Praise God who sits on the throne; saying, 'Amen, alleluia.'

THROUGH THE YEAR

Scripture Reading   *Ezek 36:25-27*
I shall pour clean water over you and you will be cleansed; I shall cleanse you of all your defilement and all your idols. I shall give you a new heart, and put a new spirit in you; I shall remove the heart of stone from your bodies and give you a heart of flesh instead. I shall put my spirit in you, and make you keep my laws and sincerely respect my observances.

Short Responsory
R7 We give thanks to you, O God, and call upon your name.
Repeat R7
V7 We recount your wonderful deeds. R7 Glory be. R7

Benedictus antiphon from the Proper of Seasons.

Intercessions
Let us thank our Saviour, who came into this world that God might be with us. R7 We praise you, O Lord, and we thank you.
We welcome you with praise, you are the Daystar, the first fruits from the dead:—let us rise with you to walk in the light of Easter. R7
Help us on this day of rest to see goodness in all your creatures:—open our eyes and our hearts to your love in the world. R7
Lord, we meet around your table as your family:—help us to see that our bitterness is forgotten, our discord is resolved, and our sins are forgiven. R7
We pray for all Christian families:—may your Spirit deepen their unity in faith and love. R7
Our Father

The concluding prayer from the Proper of Seasons.

EVENING PRAYER II

Hymn, from the appendix, for the Season.

THROUGH THE YEAR

Holy God, we praise thy name;
Lord of all, we bow before thee!
All on earth thy sceptre own,
All in heaven above adore thee.
Infinite thy vast domain,
Everlasting is thy reign.

Hark! the loud celestial hymn,
Angel choirs above are raising;
Cherubim and seraphim,
In unceasing chorus praising,
Fill the heavens with sweet accord:
Holy, holy, holy, Lord.

Holy Father, holy Son,
Holy Spirit, three we name thee.
While in essence only one
Undivided God we claim thee;
And adoring bend the knee,
While we own the mystery.

Spare thy people, Lord, we pray,
By a thousand snares surrounded;
Keep us without sin today;
Never let us be confounded.
Lo, I put my trust in thee;
Never, Lord, abandon me.

Alternative hymn

Praise, my soul, the King of heaven;
To his feet your tribute bring;
Ransomed, healed, restored, forgiven,
Who like me his praise should sing?
Praise him! Praise him!
Praise him! Praise him!
Praise the everlasting King.

Praise him for his grace and favour,
To our fathers in distress;

Praise him still the same for ever,
Slow to chide and swift to bless,
Praise him! Praise him!
Praise him! Praise him!
Glorious in his faithfulness.

Fatherlike, he tends and spares us;
Well our feeble frame he knows;
In his hand he gently bears us,
Rescues us from all our foes.
Praise him! Praise him!
Praise him! Praise him!
Widely as his mercy flows.

Angels, help us to adore him;
Ye behold him face to face;
Sun and moon bow down before him,
Dwellers all in time and space.
Praise him! Praise him!
Praise him! Praise him!
Praise with us the God of grace.

PSALMODY

ANTIPHON I

Advent: Behold, the Lord will come on the clouds of heaven with great strength, alleluia.

Lent, Sunday 2: The Lord will send forth your sceptre of power with the splendour of the saints.

Lent, Palm Sunday: He was wounded and humbled, but God has raised him up with his own right hand.

Eastertide: He raised Christ from the dead and placed him at his own right hand, in heaven, alleluia.

Through the Year: Christ the Lord is a priest for ever according to the order of Melchizedek, alleluia.

THE MESSIAH IS KING AND PRIEST   PSALM 109(110):1-5,7
He must be king so that he will put all his enemies under his feet (1 Cor 15:25)

The Lórd's revelátion to my Máster:†
'Sít on my ríght:*
your fóes I will pút beneath your féet.'

The Lórd will wíeld from Síon†
your scéptre of pówer:*
rúle in the mídst of all your fóes.

A prínce from the dáy of your bírth†
on the hóly móuntains;*
from the wómb before the dáwn I begót you.

The Lórd has sworn an óath he will not chánge.†
'You are a príest for éver,*
a príest like Melchízedek of óld.'

The Máster stánding at your ríght hand*
will shatter kíngs in the dáy of his wráth.

He shall drínk from the stréam by the wáyside*
and thérefore he shall líft up his héad.

Ant. Christ the Lord is a priest for ever according to the order of Melchizedek, alleluia.

Ant. Advent: Behold, the Lord will come on the clouds of heaven with great strength, alleluia.
Ant. 2: The Lord will come and will not disappoint us. Wait for him if he seems to delay, for he will surely come, alleluia.

Ant. Lent, Sunday 2: The Lord will send forth your sceptre of power with the splendour of the saints.
Ant. 2: We worship the one God, who made heaven and earth.

Ant. Palm Sunday: He was wounded and humbled, but God has raised him up with his own right hand.
Ant. 2: The blood of Christ purifies us to serve the living God.

Ant. Eastertide: He raised Christ from the dead and placed him at his own right hand, in heaven, alleluia.
Ant. 2: You have been converted from idolatry to the living God, alleluia.

Ant. 2: Our God is in heaven: he has power to do whatever he will, alleluia.

PRAISE OF THE GOD OF TRUTH   PSALM 113B(115)
Turn away from idols and worship the living and true God (1 Thess 1:9)

Not to ús, Lórd, not to ús,*
but to yóur náme give the glóry
for the sáke of your lóve and your trúth,*
lest the héathen say: 'Whére is their Gód?'

But our Gód is ín the héavens;*
he dóes whatéver he wílls.
Their ídols are sílver and góld,*
the wórk of húman hánds.

They have móuths but they cánnot spéak;*
they have éyes but they cánnot sée;
they have éars but they cánnot héar;*
they have nóstrils but they cánnot sméll.

With their hánds they cánnot féel;†
with their féet they cánnot wálk.*
No sóund cómes from their thróats.
Their mákers will cóme to be líke them*
and so will áll who trúst in thém.

Sons of Ísrael, trúst in the Lórd;*
hé is their hélp and their shíeld.
Sons of Áaron, trúst in the Lórd;*
hé is their hélp and their shíeld.

You who féar him, trúst in the Lórd;*
hé is their hélp and their shíeld.
He remémbers us, and hé will bléss us:†
he will bléss the sóns of Ísrael.*
He will bléss the sóns of Áaron.

The Lord will bléss thóse who féar him,*
the líttle no léss than the gréat:
to yóu may the Lórd grant íncrease,*
to yóu and áll your chíldren.

May yóu be bléssed by the Lórd,*
the máker of héaven and éarth.
The héavens belóng to the Lórd*
but the éarth he has gíven to mén.

The déad shall not práise the Lórd,*
nor thóse who go dówn into the sílence.
But wé who líve bless the Lórd*
nów and for éver. Amén.

Ant. Our God is in heaven; he has power to do whatever he will, alleluia.

OUTSIDE LENT
Ant. Advent: The Lord will come and will not disappoint us. Wait for him if he seems to delay, for he will surely come, alleluia.
Ant. 3: The Lord is our judge, the Lord is our King. He will come and make us whole.

Ant. Eastertide: You have been converted from idolatry to the living God, alleluia.
Ant. 3: Alleluia, victory and glory and power belong to our God, alleluia.

Ant. 3: Praise God, all you his servants, both great and small, alleluia.

When chanted, this canticle is sung with Alleluia *as set out below. When recited, it suffices to say* Alleluia *at the beginning and end of each strophe.*

THE MARRIAGE FEAST OF THE LAMB

CANTICLE
CF REV 19:1-2,5-7

Alleluia.

Salvation and glory and power belong to our God,*
(R⁊ Alleluia.)
His judgments are true and just.
R⁊ Alleluia (alleluia).

Alleluia.
Praise our God, all you his servants,*
(R⁊ Alleluia.)
You who fear him, small and great.
R⁊ Alleluia (alleluia).

Alleluia.
The Lord our God, the Almighty, reigns,*
(R⁊ Alleluia.)
Let us rejoice and exult and give him the glory.
R⁊ Alleluia (alleluia).

Alleluia.
The marriage of the Lamb has come,*
(R⁊ Alleluia.)
And his bride has made herself ready.
R⁊ Alleluia (alleluia).

Ant. Praise God, all you his servants, both great and small, alleluia.

Ant. Advent: The Lord is our judge, the Lord is our King. He will come and make us whole.
Eastertide: Alleluia, victory and glory and power belong to our God, alleluia.

LENT

Ant. Lent, Sunday 2: We worship the one God, who made heaven and earth.
Ant. 3: God did not spare his own Son but gave him up for us all.

Ant. Palm Sunday: The blood of Christ purifies us to serve the living God.
Ant. 3: He carried our sins in his own body on the cross, so that we might die to sin and live for holiness.

473

CHRIST, THE SERVANT OF GOD,
FREELY ACCEPTS HIS PASSION

CANTICLE
I PET 2:21-24

Christ suffered for you,†
leaving you an example*
that you should follow in his steps.

He committed no sin;*
no guile was found on his lips.
When he was reviled,*
he did not revile in return.

When he suffered,*
he did not threaten;
but he trusted to him*
who judges justly.

He himself bore our sins*
in his body on the tree,
that we might die to sin*
and live to righteousness.

By his wounds you have been healed.

Ant. Lent, Sunday 2: God did not spare his own Son but gave him
up for us all.
Palm Sunday: He carried our sins in his own body on the cross, so
that we might die to sin and live for holiness.

THROUGH THE YEAR

Scripture Reading   *2 Thess 2:13-14*
We feel that we must be continually thanking God for you, brothers
whom the Lord loves, because God chose you as first fruits to be
saved by the sanctifying Spirit and by faith in the truth. Through
the Good News that we brought he called you to this so that you
should share the glory of our Lord Jesus Christ.

Short Responsory
R7 Great is our Lord; great is his might. *Repeat* R7

℣ His wisdom can never be measured. ℟ Glory be. ℟

Magnificat antiphon from the Proper of Seasons.

Intercessions
Through the gospel, the Lord Jesus calls us to share in his glory. Let us make our prayer with him to our heavenly Father. ℟ Lord, in your mercy hear our prayer.
We pray for all nations:—that they may seek the way that leads to peace; that human rights and freedom may be everywhere respected, and that the world's resources may be generously shared. ℟
We pray for the Church:—that her leaders may be faithful ministers of your word, that all her members may be strong in faith and hope and that you may be recognized in the love she bears to all. ℟
We pray for our families, and the community in which we live:— that we may find you in them. ℟
We pray for ourselves:—that in the coming week we may serve others in our work, and find peace when we rest. ℟
We pray for the faithful departed:—that through your mercy they may rest in peace. ℟
Our Father

The concluding prayer from the Proper of Seasons.

WEEK 2: MONDAY

Invitatory ant. Let us rejoice in the Lord; with songs let us praise him.
Psalm, p 371.

MORNING PRAYER

Hymn, from the appendix, for the Season.

THROUGH THE YEAR
    Come, O Creator Spirit, come,
    and make within our hearts your home;

to us your grace eternal give,
who of your breathing move and live.

Our senses with your light inflame,
our hearts to heavenly love reclaim;
our bodies' poor infirmity
with strength perpetual fortify.

Our earthly foe afar repel,
grant us henceforth in peace to dwell;
and so to us, with you for guide,
no ill shall come, no harm betide.

May we by you the Father learn,
and know the Son, and you discern,
who are of both; and thus adore
in perfect faith for evermore.

PSALMODY

Ant. 1: When can I enter and see the face of God?
Holy Week: Jesus said, 'My soul is sorrowful to the point of death.
Wait here and keep awake with me.'
Eastertide: My soul is yearning for you, my God, like a deer that
seeks running streams, alleluia.

THE EXILE'S NOSTALGIA FOR THE LORD'S TEMPLE   PSALM 41(42)
*Let all who are thirsty come; all who want it may have the water of
life* (Rev 22:17)

Líke the déer that yéarns*
for rúnning stréams,
só my sóul is yéarning*
for yóu, my Gód.

My sóul is thírsting for Gód,*
the Gód of my lífe;
whén can I énter and sée*
the fáce of Gód?

My téars have becóme my bréad,*
by níght, by dáy,
as I héar it sáid all the day lóng:*
'Whére is your Gód?'

Thése things will Í remémber*
as I póur out my sóul:
how I would léad the rejóicing crówd*
into the hóuse of Gód,
amid críes of gládness and thanksgíving,*
the thróng wild with jóy.

Whý are you cast dówn, my sóul,*
why gróan withín me?
Hope in Gód; I will práise him stíll,*
my sáviour and my Gód.

My sóul is cast dówn withín me*
as I thínk of yóu,
from the cóuntry of Jórdan and Mount Hérmon,*
from the Híll of Mízar.

Déep is cálling on déep,*
in the róar of wáters:
your tórrents and áll your wáves*
swept óver mé.

By dáy the Lórd will sénd*
his lóving kíndness;
by níght I will síng to hím,*
praise the Gód of my lífe.

I will sáy to Gód, my róck:*
'Whý have you forgótten me?
Whý do Í go móurning*
oppréssed by the fóe?'

With críes that píerce me to the héart,*
my énemies revíle me,
sáying to me áll the day lóng:*
'Whére is your Gód?'

Whý are you cast dówn, my sóul,*
why gróan withín me?
Hope in Gód; I will práise him stíll,*
my sáviour and my Gód.

Ant. When can I enter and see the face of God?
Holy Week: Jesus said, 'My soul is sorrowful to the point of death.
Wait here and keep awake with me.'
Eastertide: My soul is yearning for you, my God, like a deer that
seeks running streams, alleluia.

Ant. 2: Show us, Lord, the light of your mercy.
Holy Week: Now sentence is being passed on this world; now the
prince of this world is to be overthrown.
Eastertide: Fill Sion with songs of your praise, Lord, and let the
stories of your great deeds be told, alleluia.

PRAYER FOR THE HOLY CITY OF JERUSALEM   CANTICLE
SIR 36:1-7,13-16

*This is eternal life; to know you the one true God, and Jesus Christ
whom you have sent* (Jn 17:3)

Save us, God of all things,*
strike all the nations with terror;
raise your hand against foreign nations*
that they may see the greatness of your might.

Our sufferings proved your holiness to them;*
let their downfall prove your glory to us.
Let them know, as we ourselves know,*
that there is no other God but you.

Give us signs again, work further wonders,*
clothe your hand, your right arm in glory.

Assemble all the tribes of Jacob,*
as when they first received their inheritance.
Pity the poor people called by your name,*
pity Israel, chosen as your first-born.

478

Have compassion on the holy city,*
Jerusalem, the place of your rest.
Let Sion ring with your praises,*
let your temple be filled with your glory.

Ant. Show us, Lord, the light of your mercy.
Holy Week: Now sentence is being passed on this world; now the prince of this world is to be overthrown.
Eastertide: Fill Sion with songs of your praise, Lord, and let the stories of your great deeds be told, alleluia.

Ant. 3: Blessed are you, Lord, in the vault of heaven.
Holy Week: Jesus leads us in our faith and brings it to perfection; he endured the cross, disregarding the shamefulness of it, and has taken his seat at God's right hand.
Eastertide: The glory of God will illumine the city; the Lamb will be its light, alleluia.

PRAISE FOR THE LORD, CREATOR OF ALL THINGS   PSALM 18(19)A
The Rising Sun has come to visit us to guide our feet in the way of peace (Lk 1:78, 79)

The héavens procláim the glóry of Gód*
and the fírmament shows fórth the wórk of his hánds.
Dáy unto dáy tákes up the stóry*
and níght unto níght makes knówn the méssage.

No spéech, no wórd, no vóice is héard†
yet their spán exténds through áll the eárth,*
their wórds to the útmost bóunds of the wórld.

Thére he has pláced a tént for the sún;†
it comes fórth like a brídegroom cóming from his tént,*
rejóices like a chámpion to rún its cóurse.

At the énd of the ský is the rísing of the sún;†
to the fúrthest énd of the ský is its cóurse.*
There is nóthing concéaled from its búrning héat.

Ant. Blessed are you, Lord, in the vault of heaven.

Holy Week: Jesus leads us in our faith and brings it to perfection; he endured the cross, disregarding the shamefulness of it, and has taken his seat at God's right hand.

Eastertide: The glory of God will illumine the city; the Lamb will be its light, alleluia.

THROUGH THE YEAR

Scripture Reading   *Jer 15:16*

When your words came, I devoured them:
your word was my delight
and the joy of my heart;
for I was called by your name,
Lord, God of Sabaoth.

Short Responsory

R̸ Rejoice in the Lord, O you just; for praise is fitting for loyal hearts. *Repeat* R̸

V̸ Sing to him a new song. R̸ Glory be. R̸

Benedictus ant. Blessed be the Lord, for he has visited us and freed us.

Intercessions

Christ has given us all a share in his priesthood. We offer our prayers and ourselves in union with him. R̸ Lord, accept our love and service.

Jesus Christ, you are the eternal priest:—make this morning's offering acceptable to the Father. R̸

Lord, you are love itself:—grant that we may love you. R̸

Give us today the fruits of the Holy Spirit:—make us patient, kind and gentle. R̸

Give us the discernment to know the needs of our neighbours,—and give us the courage to love them as brothers. R̸

Our Father

Concluding Prayer

Almighty Lord and God,

protect us by your power throughout the course of this day,
even as you have enabled us to begin it:
do not let us turn aside to any sin,
but let our every thought, word and deed
aim at doing what is pleasing in your sight.
(We make our prayer) through our Lord.

EVENING PRAYER

Hymn, from the appendix, for the Season.

THROUGH THE YEAR

O Strength and Stay upholding all creation,
Who ever dost thyself unmoved abide,
Yet day by day the light in due gradation
From hour to hour in all its changes guide,

Grant to life's day a calm unclouded ending,
An eve untouched by shadows of decay.
The brightness of a holy death-bed blending
With dawning glories of the eternal day.

Hear us, O Father, gracious and forgiving,
Through Jesus Christ thy co-eternal Word,
Who, with the Holy Ghost, by all things living
Now and to endless ages art adored.

PSALMODY

Ant. 1: You are the fairest of the children of men and graciousness
is poured upon your lips.
Holy Week: He had no beauty, no majesty to draw our eyes, no
grace to make us delight in him.
Easteride: Blessed is he who comes in the name of the Lord, alleluia.

ROYAL WEDDING SONG   PSALM 44(45)
Behold, the bridegroom is coming; go out to meet him (Mt 25:6)

I

My héart overflóws with nóble wórds.†
To the kíng I must spéak the sóng I have máde,*

my tóngue as nímble as the pén of a scríbe.

Yóu are the fáirest of the chíldren of mén†
and gráciousness is póured upón your líps:*
because Gód has bléssed you for évermóre.

O míghty one, gírd your swórd upon your thígh;†
in spléndour and státe, ríde on in tríumph*
for the cáuse of trúth and góodness and ríght.

Take aím with your bów in your dréad right hánd.†
Your árrows are shárp: peóples fall benéath you.*
The fóes of the kíng fall dówn and lose héart.

Your thróne, O Gód, shall endúre for éver.†
A scéptre of jústice is the scéptre of your kíngdom.*
Your lóve is for jústice; your hátred for évil.

Therefore Gód, your Gód, has anóinted yóu†
with the óil of gládness abóve other kíngs:*
your róbes are frágrant with áloes and mýrrh.

From the ívory pálace you are gréeted with músic.†
The dáughters of kíngs are amóng your lóved ones.*
On your ríght stands the quéen in góld of Óphir.

Ant. You are the fairest of the children of men and graciousness is poured upon your lips.
Holy Week: He had no beauty, no majesty to draw our eyes, no grace to make us delight in him.
Eastertide: Blessed is he who comes in the name of the Lord, alleluia.

Ant. 2: Behold, the bridgeroom is coming; go out and meet him.
Holy Week: I will grant him very many people as his own, for surrendering himself to death.
Eastertide: Blessed are those who are called to the wedding feast of the Lamb, alleluia.

II
Lísten, O dáughter, give éar to my wórds:*

forgét your own péople and your fáther's hóuse.
Só will the kíng desíre your béauty:*
Hé is your lórd, pay hómage to hím.

And the péople of Týre shall cóme with gifts,*
the ríchest of the péople shall séek your fávour.
The dáughter of the kíng is clóthed with spléndour,*
her róbes embróidered with péarls set in góld.

She is léd to the kíng with her máiden compánions.†
Théy are escórted amid gládness and jóy;*
they páss withín the pálace of the kíng.

Sóns shall be yóurs in pláce of your fáthers:*
you will máke them prínces over áll the éarth.
May this sóng make your náme for éver remémbered.*
May the péoples práise you from áge to áge.

Ant. Behold, the bridegroom is coming; go out and meet him.
Holy Week: I will grant him very many people as his own, for surrendering himself to death.
Eastertide: Blessed are those who are called to the wedding feast of the Lamb, alleluia.

Ant. 3: God planned to bring all things together under Christ when the fulness of time had come.
Holy Week: God has given freely of his goodness to us in his beloved Son, in whom we gain our freedom through the shedding of his blood.
Eastertide: From his fulness we have all received, grace upon grace, alleluia.

GOD, THE SAVIOUR   CANTICLE: EPH 1:3-10
Blessed be the God and Father*
of our Lord Jesus Christ,
who has blessed us in Christ*
with every spiritual blessing in the heavenly places.

He chose us in him*
before the foundation of the world,

that we should be holy*
and blameless before him.

He destined us in love*
to be his sons through Jesus Christ,
according to the purpose of his will,†
to the praise of his glorious grace*
which he freely bestowed on us in the Beloved.

In him we have redemption through his blood,*
the forgiveness of our trespasses,
according to the riches of his grace
which he lavished upon us.

He has made known to us†
in all wisdom and insight*
the mystery of his will,
according to his purpose*
which he set forth in Christ.

His purpose he set forth in Christ,*
as a plan for the fulness of time,
to unite all things in him,*
things in heaven and things on earth.

Ant. God planned to bring all things together under Christ when
the fulness of time had come.
Holy Week: God has given freely of his goodness to us in his
beloved Son, in whom we gain our freedom through the shedding
of his blood.
Eastertide: From his fulness we have all received, grace upon grace,
alleluia.

THROUGH THE YEAR

Scripture Reading   *I Thess 2:13*
Another reason why we constantly thank God for you is that as
soon as you heard the message that we brought you as God's
message, you accepted it for what it really is, God's message and not
some human thinking; and it is still a living power among you who
believe it.

Short Responsory

R̷ Let my prayer come before you, O Lord. *Repeat* R̷
V̷ Let it rise in your presence like incense. R̷ Glory be. R̷

Magnificat ant. Let my soul proclaim your greatness for ever, O my God.

Intercessions

Let us give thanks to Christ our Lord who loves and cherishes his Church. R̷ Be near us, Lord, this evening.
Lord Jesus grant that all men may be saved,—and come to knowledge of the truth. R̷
Protect Pope N. and N., our Bishop:—help them, Lord, in your strength and mercy. R̷
Support those who meet with difficulty and disappointment:—renew their confidence and sense of purpose. R̷
Christ our loving Lord, in your kindness be with the sick and the poor, the weak and the dying:—bring them your comfort. R̷
We commend to you all those who, in their lifetime, shared in the sacred ministry:—let them praise you for ever in heaven. R̷
Our Father

Concluding Prayer

All-powerful God,
since you have given us, your unworthy servants,
the strength to work throughout this day:
accept this evening sacrifice of praise
as we thank you for your gifts.
(We make our prayer) through our Lord.

WEEK 2: TUESDAY

Invitatory ant. A mighty God is the Lord: come, let us adore him.
Psalm, p 371.

485

MORNING PRAYER

Hymn, from the appendix, for the Season.

THROUGH THE YEAR

Father, we praise you, now the night is over,
active and watchful, stand we all before you;
singing, we offer prayer and meditation: thus we adore you.

Monarch of all things, fit us for your mansions;
banish our weakness, health and wholeness sending;
bring us to heaven, where your saints united joy without ending.

All-holy Father, Son and equal Spirit,
Trinity blessed, send us your salvation;
yours is the glory, gleaming and resounding through all Creation.

PSALMODY

Ant. 1: Lord, send forth your light and your truth.
Holy Week: Lord, plead my cause; from deceitful and cunning men rescue me.
Eastertide: You have come to Mount Sion, and the city of the living God, alleluia.

DESIRE FOR GOD'S TEMPLE   PSALM 42(43)
I, the light, have come into the world (Jn 12:46)

Defénd me, O Gód, and plead my cáuse*
against a gódless nátion.
From decéitful and cúnning mén*
réscue me, O Gód.

Since yóu, O Gód, are my strónghold,*
whý have you rejécted me?
Whý do Í go móurning*
oppréssed by the fóe?

O sénd forth your líght and your trúth;*
let thése be my guíde.

Let them bríng me to your hóly móuntain*
to the pláce where you dwéll.

And I will cóme to the áltar of Gód,*
the Gód of my jóy.
My redéemer, I will thánk you on the hárp,*
O Gód, my Gód.

Whý are you cast dówn, my sóul,*
why gróan withín me?
Hope in Gód; I will práise him stíll,*
my sáviour and my Gód.

Ant. Lord, send forth your light and your truth.
Holy Week: Lord, plead my cause; from deceitful and cunning men rescue me.
Eastertide: You have come to Mount Sion, and the city of the living God, alleluia.

Ant. 2: Lord, come to our help all the days of our life.
Holy Week: Lord, you have defended the cause of my soul; you have redeemed my life, Lord my God.
Eastertide: Lord, you have kept my soul from destruction, alleluia.

THE ANGUISH OF SICKNESS;   CANTICLE
   THE JOY OF HEALTH   IS 38:10-14,17-20
I was dead, and behold, I am alive and I hold the keys of death (Rev
1:17-18)

I said, In the noontide of my days I must depart;†
I am consigned to the gates of Sheol*
for the rest of my years.

I said, I shall not see the Lord*
in the land of the living;
I shall look upon man no more*
among the inhabitants of the world.

My dwelling is plucked up and removed from me*
like a shepherd's tent;

487

like a weaver I have rolled up my life;*
he cuts me off from the loom.

From day to night you bring me to an end;*
I cry for help until morning;
like a lion he breaks all my bones;*
from day to night you bring me to an end.

Like a swallow or a crane I clamour,*
I moan like a dove.
My eyes are weary with looking upward.*
O Lord, I am oppressed; be my security.

Lo, it was for my welfare*
that I had great bitterness;
but you have held back my life*
from the pit of destruction,
for you have cast all my sins*
behind your back.

For Sheol cannot thank you,*
death cannot praise you;
those who go down to the pit*
cannot hope for your faithfulness.

The living, the living, he thanks you,†
as I do this day;*
the father makes known to the children your faithfulness.

The Lord will save me,*
and we will sing to stringed instruments
all the days of our life,*
at the house of the Lord.

Ant. Lord, come to our help all the days of our life.
Holy Week: Lord, you have defended the cause of my soul; you
have redeemed my life, Lord my God.
Eastertide: Lord, you have kept my soul from destruction, alleluia.

Ant. 3: To you our praise is due in Sion, O God.†
Holy Week: My servant, the Just One, will justify many; he will

take their faults on himself.
Eastertide: You care for the earth, you give it water, alleluia.

SOLEMN THANKSGIVING   PSALM 64(65)
Sion is to be understood as the heavenly city (Origen)

To yóu our práise is dúe*
in Síon, O Gód.
†To yóu we páy our vóws,*
you who héar our práyer.

To yóu all flésh will cóme*
with its búrden of sín.
Too héavy for ús, our offénces,*
but you wípe them awáy.

Blessed is hé whom you chóose and cáll*
to dwéll in your cóurts.
We are fílled with the bléssings of your hóuse,*
of your hóly témple.

You kéep your plédge with wónders,*
O Gód our sáviour,
the hópe of áll the éarth*
and of fár distant ísles.

You uphóld the móuntains with your stréngth,*
you are gírded with pówer.
You stíll the róaring of the séas,†
the róaring of their wáves*
and the túmult of the péoples.

The énds of the éarth stand in áwe*
at the síght of your wónders.
The lánds of súnrise and súnset*
you fíll with your jóy.

You cáre for the éarth, give it wáter,*
you fíll it with ríches.
Your ríver in héaven brims óver†

⎧ to províde its gráin.*

⎩ And thús you províde for the éarth;
You drénch its fúrrows,†
you lével it, sóften it with shówers,*
you bléss its grówth.

You crówn the yéar with your góodness.†
Abúndance flóws in your stéps,*
in the pástures of the wílderness it flóws.

The hílls are gírded with jóy,*
the méadows cóvered with flócks,
the válleys are décked with whéat.*
They shoút for jóy, yes, they síng.

Ant. To you our praise is due in Sion, O God.
Holy Week: My servant, the Just One, will justify many; he will take their faults on himself.
Eastertide: You care for the earth, you give it water, alleluia.

THROUGH THE YEAR

Scripture Reading   *1 Thess 5:4-5*
It is not as if you live in the dark, my brothers, for that Day to overtake you like a thief. No, you are all sons of light and sons of the day: we do not belong to the night or to darkness.

Short Responsory
R︎ Hear my cry, Lord, for I hope in your word. *Repeat* R︎
V︎ I rise before dawn and call for help. R︎ Glory be. R︎

Benedictus ant. Lord, save us from the hands of all who hate us.

Intercessions
Let us bless our Saviour, who by his rising to new life has freed the world from fear. R︎ Lord, lead us to the truth.
Lord Jesus, as this day begins we remember that you are risen,—
and therefore we look to the future with confidence. R︎

We offer you our prayer this morning,—take to yourself our cares, our hopes, and our needs. R̷

Deepen in us our love for you today,—so that in all things we may find our good, and the good of others. R̷

Lord Jesus, we pray that through our own troubles, we may learn to feel the sufferings of others;—help us to show them your compassion. R̷

Our Father

Concluding Prayer
True Light of the world, Lord Jesus Christ,
as you enlighten all men for their salvation,
give us grace, we pray,
to herald your coming
by preparing the ways of justice and of peace.
Who live and reign with the Father and the Holy Spirit,
God, for ever and ever.

EVENING PRAYER

Hymn, from the appendix, for the Season.

THROUGH THE YEAR

Before we end our day, O Lord,
We make this prayer to you:
That you continue in your love
To guard your people here.

Give us this night untroubled rest
And build our strength anew:
Your Splendour driving far away
All darkness of the foe.

Our hearts' desire to love you, Lord,
Watch over while we sleep,
That when the new day dawns on high
We may your praises sing.

All glory be to you, O Christ,
Who saved mankind from death—

491

To share with you the Father's love
And in the Spirit live.

PSALMODY

Ant. 1: You cannot serve both God and wealth.
Holy Week: Insult and terror have been my lot, but the Lord is at my side, a mighty hero.
Eastertide: Look for the things of heaven, not for the things which are upon this earth, alleluia.

THE USELESSNESS OF RICHES   PSALM 48(49)
The rich man will find it very hard to enter the kingdom of heaven (Mt 19:23)

I

Héar this, áll you péoples,*
give héed, all who dwéll in the wórld,
mén both lów and high,*
rích and póor alíke!

My líps will speak wórds of wísdom.*
My héart is fúll of ínsight.
I will túrn my mínd to a párable,*
with the hárp I will sólve my próblem.

Whý should I féar in evil dáys*
the málice of the fóes who surróund me,
mén who trúst in their wéalth,*
and bóast of the vástness of their ríches?

For nó man can búy his own ránsom,*
or pay a príce to Gód for his life.
The ránsom of his sóul is beyónd him.†
He cánnot buy lífe without énd,*
nor avóid cóming to the gráve.

He knows that wíse men and fóols must both pérish*
and léave their wéalth to óthers.
Their gráves are their hómes for éver,†
their dwélling place from áge to áge,*

though their námes spread wíde through the lánd.

In his ríches, mán lacks wísdom:*
hé is like the béasts that are destróyed.

Ant. You cannot serve both God and wealth.
Holy Week: Insult and terror have been my lot, but the Lord is at my side, a mighty hero.
Eastertide: Look for the things of heaven, not for the things which are upon this earth, alleluia.

Ant. 2: Store up treasure for yourselves in heaven, says the Lord.
Holy Week: Deliver me, Lord, and set me close to you; let who will raise his hand against me.
Eastertide: The Lord saved my soul from the power of death, alleluia.

II

This is the lót of those who trúst in themsélves,*
who have óthers at their béck and cáll.
Like shéep they are dríven to the gráve,†
where déath shall bé their shépherd*
and the júst shall becóme their rúlers.

With the mórning their óutward show vánishes*
and the gráve becómes their hóme.
But Gód will ránsom me from déath*
and táke my sóul to himsélf.

Then do not féar when a mán grows rích,*
when the glóry of his hóuse incréases.
He takes nóthing wíth him when he díes,*
his glóry does not fóllow him belów.

Though he fláttered himsélf while he líved:*
'Men will práise me for áll my succéss,'
yet he will gó to jóin his fáthers,*
who will néver see the líght any móre.

In his ríches, mán lacks wísdom:*
hé is like the béasts that are destróyed.

Ant. Store up treasure for yourselves in heaven, says the Lord.
Holy Week: Deliver me, Lord, and set me close to you; let who will raise his hand against me.
Eastertide: The Lord saved my soul from the power of death, alleluia.

Ant. 3: Worthy is the Lamb that was slain, to receive glory and honour.
Holy Week: You were slain, Lord, and with your blood you bought us for God.
Eastertide: Yours, Lord, is the greatness and the power, the glory and the victory, alleluia.

HYMN OF THE REDEEMED   CANTICLE: REV 4:11;5:9,10,12

Worthy are you, our Lord and God,*
to receive glory and honour and power,
for you created all things,*
and by your will they existed and were created.

Worthy are you, O Lord,*
to take the scroll and to open its seals,
for you were slain,†
and by your blood you ransomed men for God*
from every tribe and tongue and people and nation.

You have made us a kingdom and priests to our God,*
and we shall reign on earth.
Worthy is the Lamb who was slain,*
to receive power and wealth,
and wisdom and might.*
and honour and glory and blessing.

Ant. Worthy is the Lamb that was slain, to receive glory and honour.
Holy Week: You were slain, Lord, and with your blood you bought us for God.
Eastertide: Yours, Lord, is the greatness and the power, the glory and the victory, alleluia.

Scripture Reading   *Rom 3:23-25a*
Since all have sinned and fall short of the glory of God, they are
justified by his grace as a gift, through the redemption which is in
Christ Jesus, whom God put forward as an expiation by his blood,
to be received by faith. This was to show God's righteousness.

Short Responsory
R̸ You will give me the fulness of joy in your presence, O Lord.
Repeat R̸
℣ I will find happiness at your right hand for ever. R̸ Glory be. R̸

Magnificat ant. Do great things for us, O Lord, for you are mighty,
and Holy is your name.

Intercessions
Christ is the shepherd of his flock: he loves and cares for his people.
We turn to him in trust and say: R̸ Lord, we need your care.
Christ our Lord, you are pastor of all the ages,—protect our
Bishop, N., and all the pastors of your Church. R̸
Be with those who are persecuted for their faith, and those cut off
from the support of the Church:—Good Shepherd, in their pain
and isolation may they know your care. R̸
Bring healing to the sick;—give nourishment to the hungry. R̸
We remember those who make our laws and those who apply
them:—Lord, give them wisdom and discernment. R̸
Gather the flock for which you laid down your life:—bring home
to their Father's house all who have died in your peace. R̸
Our Father

Concluding Prayer
Yours is the day and yours, the night, Lord God:
let the Sun of Justice shine so steadily in our hearts,
that we may come at length
to that light where you dwell eternally.
(We make our prayer) through our Lord.

WEEK 2: WEDNESDAY

Invitatory ant. Cry out with joy to God, all the earth: serve the Lord with gladness.
Psalm, p 371.

MORNING PRAYER

Hymn, from the appendix, for the Season.

THROUGH THE YEAR

Now that the daylight fills the sky,
we lift our hearts to God on high,
that he, in all we do or say,
would keep us free from harm today;

Would guard our hearts and tongues from strife;
from anger's din would hide our life;
from all ill sights would turn our eyes;
would close our ears from vanities.

Would keep our inmost conscience pure;
our souls from folly would secure;
would bid us check the pride of sense
with due and holy abstinence.

So we, when this new day is gone,
and night in turn is drawing on,
with conscience by the world unstained
shall praise his Name for victory gained.

PSALMODY

Ant. 1: Your ways, O God, are holy. What God is great as our God?
Holy Week: In the day of my distress I sought the Lord with outstretched arms.
Eastertide: The waters saw you. O God; you led your people through the sea, alleluia.

REMEMBERING THE WORKS OF THE LORD   PSALM 76(77)
We are in difficulties on every side, but never consumed (2 Cor 4:8)

I crý alóud to Gód,*
cry alóud to Gód that he may héar me.

In the dáy of my distréss I sought the Lórd.†
My hánds were raised at níght without céasing;*
my sóul refúsed to be consóled.
I remémbered my Gód and I gróaned.*
I póndered and my spírit fáinted.

You withhéld sléep from my éyes.*
I was tróubled, I cóuld not spéak.
I thóught of the dáys of long agó*
and remémbered the yéars long pást.
At níght I músed within my héart.*
I póndered and my spírit quéstioned.

'Will the Lórd rejéct us for éver?*
Will he shów us his fávour no móre?
Has his lóve vánished for éver?*
Has his prómise cóme to an énd?
Does Gód forgét his mércy*
or in ánger withhóld his compássion?'

I said: 'Thís is what cáuses my gríef;*
that the wáy of the Most Hígh has chánged.'
I remémber the déeds of the Lórd,*
I remémber your wónders of óld,
I múse on áll your wórks*
and pónder your míghty déeds.

Your wáys, O Gód, are hóly.*
What gód is gréat as our Gód?
Yóu are the Gód who works wónders.*
Yóu showed your pówer among the péoples.
Your stróng arm redéemed your péople,*
the sóns of Jácob and Jóseph.

The wáters sáw you, O Gód,†

the wáters sáw you and trémbled;*
the dépths were móved with térror.
The clóuds póured down ráin,†
the skíes sent fórth their vóice;*
your árrows fláshed to and fró.

Your thúnder rólled round the ský,*
your fláshes líghted up the wórld.
The éarth was móved and trémbled*
when your wáy léd through the séa,
your páth through the míghty wáters*
and nó one sáw your fóotprints.

You guíded your péople like a flóck*
by the hánd of Móses and Áaron.

Ant. Your ways, O God, are holy. What God is great as our God?
Holy Week: In the day of my distress I sought the Lord with out-stretched arms.
Eastertide: The waters saw you. O God; you led your people through the sea, alleluia.

Ant. 2: My heart exults in the Lord; he humbles and he exalts.
Holy Week: If we have died with Christ, we believe that we shall also come to life with him.
Eastertide: The Lord gives death and he gives life, alleluia.

THE POOR REJOICE IN THE LORD   CANTICLE
                                                         I SAM 2:1-10
He put down the mighty from their seats and exalted the lowly; he
filled the hungry with good things (Lk 1:52-53)

My heart exults in the Lord,*
I find my strength in my God;
my mouth laughs at my enemies*
as I rejoice in your saving help.
There is none like the Lord,†
there is none besides you.*
There is no Rock like our God.

Bring your haughty words to an end,*
let no boasts fall from your lips,
for the Lord is a God who knows all.*
It is he who weighs men's deeds.

The bows of the mighty are broken,*
but the weak are clothed with strength.
Those with plenty must labour for bread,*
but the hungry need work no more.
The childless wife has children now*
but the fruitful wife bears no more.

It is the Lord who gives life and death,*
he brings men to the grave and back;
it is the Lord who gives poverty and riches.*
He brings men low and raises them on high.

He lifts up the lowly from the dust,*
from the ash heap he raises the poor
to set him in the company of princes,*
to give him a glorious throne.

For the pillars of the earth are the Lord's,*
on them he has set the world.
He guards the steps of his faithful,*
but the wicked perish in darkness,
for no man's power gives him victory.*
The enemies of the Lord shall be broken.

The Most High will thunder in the heavens,*
the Lord will judge the ends of the earth.
He will give power to his king*
and exalt the might of his anointed.

Ant. My heart exults in the Lord; he humbles and he exalts.
Holy week: If we have died with Christ, we believe that we shall also
come to life with him.
Eastertide: The Lord gives death and he gives life, alleluia.

Ant. 3: The Lord is king, let earth rejoice.†

499

Holy Week: God has made Jesus Christ our wisdom and our virtue, our holiness and our freedom.
Eastertide: Light shines forth for the just and joy for the upright of heart, alleluia.

THE GLORY OF THE LORD'S RULE   PSALM 96(97)
This psalm tells of the salvation of the world and of the faith all peoples would have in Christ (St Athanasius)

The Lórd is kíng, let éarth rejóice,*
†let áll the cóastlands be glád.
Clóud and dárkness are his ráiment;*
his thróne, jústice and ríght.

A fíre prepáres his páth;*
it búrns up his fóes on every síde.
His líghtnings líght up the wórld,*
the éarth trémbles at the síght.

The móuntains mélt like wáx*
before the Lórd of áll the éarth.
The skíes procláim his jústice;*
all péoples sée his glóry.

Let thóse who serve ídols be ashámed,†
those who bóast of their wórthless góds.*
All you spírits, wórship hím.

Síon héars and is glád;†
the péople of Júdah rejóice*
becáuse of your júdgments O Lórd.

For yóu indéed are the Lórd†
most hígh above áll the éarth*
exálted far abóve all spírits.

The Lórd loves thóse who hate évil:†
he guárds the sóuls of his sáints;*
he séts them frée from the wícked.

Líght shines fórth for the júst*

500

and jóy for the úpright of héart.
Rejóice, you júst, in the Lórd;*
give glóry to his hóly náme.

Ant. The Lord is king, let earth rejoice.
Holy Week: God has made Jesus Christ our wisdom and our virtue,
our holiness and our freedom.
Eastertide: Light shines forth for the just and joy for the upright of
heart, alleluia.

THROUGH THE YEAR

Scripture Reading   *Rom 8:35-37*
Who will separate us from the love of Christ? Will affliction, or
distress, or persecution, or hunger, or nakedness, or peril, or the
sword? Yet in all this we are conquerors, through him who has
granted us his love.

Short Responsory
R̸ I will praise the Lord at all times. *Repeat* R̸
℣ His praise will be always on my lips. R̸ Glory be. R̸

Benedictus ant. Let us serve the Lord in holiness all our days.

Intercessions
Nothing can separate us from the love of Christ, for he promised
to be with his Church until the end of time. With confidence in his
promise we pray: R̸ Stay with us, Lord Jesus.
In all things we are victorious through your love:—take us into
your care today. R̸
Let the love of your Holy Spirit be in our hearts:—so that we may
consecrate this day to you. R̸
Help all Christians to answer your call:—may they be salt to the
earth, and light to the world. R̸
We pray for all those in industry:—may they work in harmony for
justice and for the good of the whole community. R̸
Our Father

Concluding Prayer

Shed your clear light on our hearts, Lord,
so that walking continually in the way of your commandments,
we may never be deceived or misled.
(We make our prayer) through our Lord.

EVENING PRAYER

Hymn, from the appendix, for the Season.

THROUGH THE YEAR

O Trinity of blessed light,
O unity of princely might,
the fiery sun has gone its way;
shed now within our hearts your ray.

To you our morning song of praise,
to you our evening prayer we raise;
your glory suppliant we adore
for ever and for evermore.

PSALMODY

Ant. 1: We are waiting in hope for the blessings of the glorious
coming of our Saviour.
Holy Week: The wicked men said: let us oppress the just man, since
his ways are contrary to ours.
Eastertide: Do not let your hearts be troubled; only have faith in
me alleluia.

PEACE IN GOD   PSALM 61(62)
May the God of hope fill you with all peace as you believe in him
(Rom 15:13)

In God alóne is my sóul at rést;*
my hélp comes from hím.
He alóne is my róck, my strónghold,*
my fórtress: I stand fírm.

How lóng will you áll attack one mán*
to bréak him dówn,
as thóugh he were a tóttering wáll,*
or a túmbling fénce?

Their plán is ónly to destróy:*
they take pléasure in líes.
With their móuth they útter bléssing*
but in their héart they cúrse.

In God alóne be at rést, my sóul;*
for my hópe comes from hím.
He alóne is my róck, my strónghold,*
my fórtress: I stand fírm.

In Gód is my sáfety and glóry,*
the róck of my stréngth.
Take réfuge in Gód all you péople.*
Trúst him at áll times.
Póur out your héarts befóre him*
for Gód is our réfuge.

Cómmon folk are ónly a bréath,*
gréat men an illúsion.
Pláced in the scáles, they ríse;*
they weigh léss than a bréath.

Dó not put your trúst in oppréssion*
nor vain hópes on plúnder.
Dó not set your héart on ríches*
even whén they incréase.

For Gód has sáid only óne thing:*
only twó do I knów:
that to Gód alóne belongs pówer*
and to yóu, Lord, lóve;
and that yóu repáy each mán*
accórding to his déeds.

Ant. We are waiting in hope for the blessings of the glorious coming
of our Saviour.

Holy Week: The wicked men said: let us oppress the just man, since his ways are contrary to ours.
Eastertide: Do not let your hearts be troubled; only have faith in me, alleluia.

Ant. 2: Let God bless us; let his face shed its light upon us.
Holy Week: He bore the sins of many and interceded for sinners.
Eastertide: Let the peoples praise you, O God; let them rejoice in your saving help, alleluia.

When the following psalm has been used at the Invitatory, ps. 94, p 371, is said here in place of it.

ALL THE PEOPLES WILL GIVE PRAISE TO THE LORD PSALM 66(67)
Let it be known to you that this salvation from God has been sent to all peoples (Acts 28:28)

O Gód, be grácious and bléss us*
and let your fáce shed its líght upón us.
So will your wáys be knówn upon éarth*
and all nátions learn your sáving hélp.

Let the péoples práise you, O Gód;*
let áll the péoples práise you.

Let the nátions be glád and exúlt*
for you rúle the wórld with jústice.
With fáirness you rúle the péoples,*
you guíde the nátions on éarth.

Let the péoples práise you, O Gód;*
let áll the péoples práise you.

The éarth has yíelded its frúit*
for Gód, our Gód, has bléssed us.
May Gód still gíve us his bléssing*
till the énds of the éarth revére him.

Let the péoples práise you, O Gód;*
let áll the péoples práise you.

Ant. Let God bless us; let his face shed its light upon us.
Holy Week: He bore the sins of many and interceded for sinners.
Eastertide: Let the peoples praise you, O God; let them rejoice in your saving help, alleluia.

Ant. 3: All things were created in him and he holds all things in being.
Holy Week: In Christ we gain our freedom, the forgiveness of our sins, through the shedding of his blood.
Eastertide: His majesty covers the heavens, the earth is filled with his praise, alleluia.

CHRIST IS THE FIRSTBORN OF ALL CREATION, CANTICLE
THE FIRSTBORN FROM THE DEAD COL 1:12-20

Let us give thanks to the Father,†
who has qualified us to share*
in the inheritance of the saints in light.

He has delivered us from the dominion of darkness*
and transferred us to the kingdom of his beloved Son,
in whom we have redemption,*
the forgiveness of sins.

He is the image of the invisible God,*
the firstborn of all creation,
for in him all things were created, in heaven and on earth,*
visible and invisible.

All things were created*
through him and for him.
He is before all things,*
and in him all things hold together.

He is the head of the body, the Church;*
he is the beginning,
the firstborn from the dead,*
that in everything he might be pre-eminent.

For in him all the fulness of God was pleased to dwell,*

and through him to reconcile to himself all things,
whether on earth or in heaven,*
making peace by the blood of his cross.

Ant. All things were created in him and he holds all things in being.
Holy Week: In Christ we gain our freedom, the forgiveness of our
sins, through the shedding of his blood.
Eastertide: His majesty covers the heavens, the earth is filled with
his praise, alleluia.

Scripture Reading   *1 Pet 5:5b-7*

Wrap yourselves in humility to be servants of each other, because
God refuses the proud and will always favour the humble. Bow
down, then, before the power of God now, and he will raise you
up on the appointed day; unload all your worries on to him, since
he is looking after you.

Short Responsory

R⁊ Guard us, Lord, as the apple of your eye. *Repeat* R⁊
℣ Hide us in the shadow of your wings. R⁊ Glory be. R⁊

Magnificat ant. Show the power of your arm, Lord; put down the
proud and exalt the lowly.

Intercessions

At the end of the day we give thanks to God the Father who reconciled the whole universe to himself in Christ. R⁊ Glory to you,
Lord God!
We thank you for the beauty of creation:—may the work of man not
disfigure it, but enhance it to your greater glory. R⁊
We thank you, Father, for all the good things we enjoy:—teach us
to be grateful and to use them well. R⁊
Teach us to seek the things that please you,—then we shall find you
in all that we do. R⁊
Lord, as we journey towards the promised land, feed us with bread
from heaven,—quench our thirst with living water. R⁊
To you, a thousand years are like a single day:—take up those who
have died with hope in you, and waken them into eternity. R⁊
Our Father

Concluding Prayer
Lord God,
whose name is holy
and whose mercy is proclaimed in every generation:
receive your people's prayer,
and let them sing your greatness with never-ending praise.
(We make our prayer) through our Lord.

WEEK 2: THURSDAY

Invitatory ant. Come before the Lord, singing for joy.
Psalm, p 371.

MORNING PRAYER

Hymn, from the appendix, for the Season.

THROUGH THE YEAR
Alone with none but thee, my God,
I journey on my way;
What need I fear, when thou art near,
O King of night and day?
More safe am I within thy hand,
Than if a host did round me stand.

My destined time is fixed by thee,
And death doth know his hour.
Did warriors strong around me throng,
They could not stay his power;
No walls of stone can man defend
When thou thy messenger dost send.

My life I yield to thy decree,
And bow to thy control
In peaceful calm, for from thine arm
No power can wrest my soul.
Could earthly omens e'er appal
A man that heeds the heavenly call!

507

The child of God can fear no ill,
His chosen dread no foe;
We leave our fate with thee, and wait
Thy bidding when to go.
'Tis not from chance our comfort springs,
Thou art our trust, O King of kings.

PSALMODY

Ant. 1: Lord, rouse up your might and come to our help.
Holy Week: Look, Lord, and answer quickly, for I am in distress.
Eastertide: I am the vine, you are the branches, alleluia.

LORD, COME TO VISIT YOUR VINE   PSALM 79(80)
Come, Lord Jesus (Rev 22:20)

O shépherd of Ísrael, héar us,*
you who léad Jóseph's flóck,
shine fórth from your chérubim thróne*
upon Éphraim, Bénjamin, Manásseh.
O Lórd, róuse up your míght,*
O Lórd, cóme to our hélp.

Gód of hósts, bríng us báck;*
let your fáce shine on ús and wé shall be sáved.

Lórd God of hósts, how lóng*
will you frówn on your péople's pléa?
You have féd them with téars for their bréad,*
an abúndance of téars for their drínk.
You have máde us the táunt of our néighbours,*
our énemies láugh us to scórn.

Gód of hósts, bríng us báck;*
let your fáce shine on ús and wé shall be sáved.

You bróught a víne out of Égypt;*
to plánt it you dróve out the nátions.
Befóre it you cléared the gróund;*
it took róot and spréad through the lánd.

The móuntains were cóvered with its shádow,*
the cédars of Gód with its bóughs.
It strétched out its bránches to the séa,*
to the Great Ríver it strétched out its shóots.

Then whý have you bróken down its wálls?*
It is plúcked by áll who pass bý.
It is rávaged by the bóar of the fórest,*
devóured by the béasts of the field.

God of hósts, turn agáin, we implóre,*
look dówn from héaven and sée.
Vísit this víne and protéct it,*
the víne your ríght hand has plánted.
Men have búrnt it with fíre and destróyed it.*
May they pérish at the frówn of your fáce.

May your hánd be on the mán you have chósen,*
the mán you have gíven your stréngth.
And we shall néver forsáke you agáin:*
give us lífe that we may cáll upon your náme.

Gód of hósts, bríng us báck;*
let your fáce shine on ús and wé shall be sáved.

Ant. Lord, rouse up your might and come to our help.
Holy Week: Look, Lord, and answer quickly, for I am in distress.
Eastertide: I am the vine, you are the branches, alleluia.

Ant. 2: The Lord has done marvellous things, let them be made
known to the whole world.
Holy Week: See now that God is my salvation; I have trust and no
fear.
Eastertide: With joy you will draw water from the wells of the
Saviour, alleluia.

THE REJOICING OF A REDEEMED PEOPLE   CANTICLE: IS 12:1-6
If any man is thirsty, let him come to me and drink (Jn 7:37)

I thank you Lord, you were angry with me*

509

but your anger has passed and you give me comfort.

Truly, God is my salvation,*
I trust, I shall not fear.
For the Lord is my strength, my song,*
he is my saviour.

With joy you will draw water*
from the wells of salvation.
Give thanks to the Lord, give praise to his name!*
Make his mighty deeds known to the peoples.

Declare the greatness of his name,*
sing a psalm to the Lord!
For he has done glorious deeds;*
make them known to all the earth.

People of Sion, sing and shout for joy*
for great in your midst is the Holy One of Israel.

Ant. The Lord has done marvellous things, let them be made known to the whole world.
Holy Week: See now that God is my salvation; I have trust and no fear.
Eastertide: With joy you will draw water from the wells of the Saviour, alleluia.

Ant. 3: Ring out your joy to God our strength.†
Holy Week: The Lord fed us with finest wheat, he filled us with honey from the rock.
Eastertide: The Lord has fed us with finest wheat, alleluia.

SOLEMN RENEWAL OF THE COVENANT   PSALM 80(81)
Take care that no one among you has a wicked, unbelieving heart
(Heb 3:12)

Ring out your jóy to Gód our stréngth,*
†shout in tríumph to the Gód of Jácob.

Raise a sóng and sóund the tímbrel,*
the swéet-sounding hárp and the lúte,
blów the trúmpet at the néw moon,*
when the móon is fúll, on our féast.

For thís is Ísrael's láw,*
a commánd of the Gód of Jácob.
He impósed it as a rúle on Jóseph,*
when he went óut against the lánd of Égypt.

A vóice I did not knów said to mé:*
'I fréed your shóulder from the búrden;
your hánds were fréed from the lóad.*
You cálled in distréss and I sáved you.

I ánswered, concéaled in the stórm cloud,*
at the wáters of Meríbah I tésted you.
Lísten, my péople, to my wárning,*
O Ísrael, if ónly you would héed!

Let there bé no fóreign god amóng you,*
no wórship of an álien gód.
Í am the Lórd your Gód,†
who bróught you from the lánd of Égypt.*
Ópen wide your móuth and I will fíll it.

But my péople did not héed my vóice*
and Ísrael wóuld not óbey,
so I léft them in their stúbbornness of héart*
to fóllow their ówn desígns.

Ó that my péople would héed me,*
that Ísrael would wálk in my wáys!
At ónce I would subdúe their fóes,*
turn my hánd agáinst their énemies.

The Lord's énemies would crínge at their féet*
and their subjéction would lást for éver.
But Ísrael I would féed with finest whéat*
and fíll them with hóney from the róck.'

Ant. Ring out your joy to God our strength.
Holy Week: The Lord fed us with finest wheat, he filled us with honey from the rock.
Eastertide: The Lord has fed us with finest wheat, alleluia.

THROUGH THE YEAR

Scripture Reading   *Rom 14:17-19*
The kingdom of God does not mean food and drink but righteousness and peace and joy in the Holy Spirit; he who thus serves Christ is acceptable to God and approved by men. Let us then pursue what makes for peace and for mutual upbuilding.

Short Responsory
R̷ Early in the morning I will think of you, O Lord. *Repeat* R̷
℣ You have been my help. R̷ Glory be. R̷

Benedictus ant. Give your people knowledge of salvation, Lord, and forgive us our sins.

Intercessions
Blessed be our God and Father: he hears the prayers of his children.
R̷ Lord, hear us.
We thank you, Father, for sending us your Son:—let us keep him before our eyes throughout this day. R̷
Make wisdom our guide,—help us walk in newness of life. R̷
Lord, give us your strength in our weakness:—when we meet problems give us courage to face them. R̷
Direct our thoughts, our words, our actions today,—so that we may know, and do, your will. R̷
Our Father

Concluding Prayer
Lord God, true Light and Creator of light,
grant that faithfully pondering on all that is holy,
we may ever live in the splendour of your presence.
(We make our prayer) through our Lord.

EVENING PRAYER

Hymn, from the appendix, for the Season.

THROUGH THE YEAR

Blest are the pure in heart,
For they shall see our God;
The secret of the Lord is theirs,
Their soul is Christ's abode.

The Lord, who left the heavens,
Our life and peace to bring,
To dwell in lowliness with men,
Their pattern and their King:

Still to the lowly soul
He does himself impart,
And for his dwelling and his throne
Chooses the pure in heart.

Lord, we thy presence seek;
May ours this blessing be;
Give us a pure and lowly heart,
A temple fit for thee.

PSALMODY

Ant. I: I will make you the light of the nations to bring my salvation to the ends of the earth.
Holy Week: Christ is the First-born from the dead, the Ruler of the kings of the earth. He has made us a kingdom for his God and Father.
Eastertide: God has appointed him to judge all men, both living and dead, alleluia.

THE ROYAL POWER OF THE MESSIAH PSALM 71(72)
They opened their treasures and offered him gifts of gold, frankincense and myrrh (Mt 2:11)

I

O Gód, give your júdgment to the kíng,*

to a kíng's son your jústice,
that he may júdge your péople in jústice*
and your póor in right júdgment.

May the móuntains bring forth péace for the péople*
and the hílls, jústice.
May he defénd the póor of the péople†
and save the chíldren of the néedy*
and crúsh the oppréssor.

He shall endúre like the sún and the móon*
from áge to áge.
He shall descénd like ráin on the méadow,*
like ráindrops on the éarth.

In his dáys jústice shall flóurish*
and péace till the móon fails.
He shall rúle from séa to séa,*
from the Great Ríver to earth's bóunds.

Befóre him his énemies shall fáll,*
his fóes lick the dúst.
The kíngs of Thársis and the séa coasts*
shall páy him tríbute.

The kíngs of Shéba and Séba*
shall bríng him gífts.
Before hím all kíngs shall fall próstrate,*
all nátions shall sérve him.

Ant. I will make you the light of the nations to bring my salvation
to the ends of the earth.
Holy Week: Christ is the First-born from the dead, the Ruler of the
kings of the earth. He has made us a kingdom for his God and
Father.
Eastertide: God has appointed him to judge all men, both living
and dead, alleluia.

Ant. 2: The Lord will save the poor; from oppression he will
rescue their lives.

Holy Week: The Lord shall save the poor when they cry and the needy who are helpless.
Eastertide: Every tribe shall be blessed in him, alleluia.

II

For he shall sáve the póor when they crý*
and the néedy who are hélpless.
Hé will have píty on the wéak*
and save the líves of the póor.

From oppréssion he will réscue their líves,*
to hím their blood is déar.
Lóng may he líve,*
may the góld of Shéba be gíven him.
They shall práy for hím without céasing*
and bléss him all the dáy.

May córn be abúndant in the lánd†
to the péaks of the móuntains.*
May its frúit rústle like Lébanon;
may men flóurish in the cíties*
like gráss on the éarth.

May his náme be bléssed for éver*
and endúre like the sún.
Every tríbe shall be bléssed in hím,*
all nátions bless his náme.

Bléssed be the Lórd, God of Ísrael,†
who alóne works wónders, *
ever bléssed his glórious náme.
Let his glóry fill the éarth.*
Amén! Amén!

Ant. The Lord will save the poor; from oppression he will rescue their lives.
Holy Week: The Lord shall save the poor when they cry and the needy who are helpless.
Eastertide: Every tribe shall be blessed in him, alleluia.

Ant. 3: Victory and empire have now been won by our God.
Holy Week: The saints have triumphed by the sacrifice of the Lamb, and by the testimony which they uttered.
Eastertide: Jesus Christ is the same yesterday, today and for ever, alleluia.

THE JUDGMENT OF GOD   CANTICLE
REV 11:17-18;12:10B-12A

We give thanks to you, Lord God Almighty,*
who are and who were,
that you have taken your great power*
and begun to reign.

The nations raged,*
but your wrath came,
and the time for the dead to be judged,*
for rewarding your servants, the prophets and saints,
and those who fear your name,*
both small and great.

Now the salvation and the power†
and the kingdom of our God*
and the authority of his Christ have come,
for the accuser of our brethren has been thrown down,*
who accuses them day and night before our God.

And they have conquered him*
by the blood of the Lamb
and by the word of their testimony,*
for they loved not their lives even unto death.
Rejoice, then, O heaven,*
and you that dwell therein.

Ant. Victory and empire have now been won by our God.
Holy Week: The saints have triumphed by the sacrifice of the Lamb, and by the testimony which they uttered.
Eastertide: Jesus Christ is the same yesterday, today and for ever, alleluia.

THROUGH THE YEAR

Scripture Reading   *I Pet 1:22-23*

You have been obedient to the truth and purified your souls until you can love like brothers, in sincerity; let your love for each other be real and from a pure heart—your new birth was not from any mortal seed but from the everlasting word of the living and eternal God.

Short Responsory

R℣ The Lord is my shepherd; there is nothing I shall want. *Repeat* R℣
℣ Fresh and green are the pastures where he gives me repose. R℣
Glory be. R℣

Magnificat ant. The Lord has satisfied and filled with good things those who hungered for justice.

Intercessions

Let us lift up our hearts in thankfulness to God our Father, who has blessed us in Christ with every spiritual gift. R℣ Lord, bless your people.

Father, look on the Pope, our bishops, and all Christian leaders:—sustain their faith, their love, and their courage. R℣

Almighty God, we pray for our country:—may it promote justice and brotherhood in the world. R℣

We pray for all who live the Christian life:—Father, look on them with kindness, and see in them the face of your beloved Son. R℣

Remember those who have consecrated themselves to serve you in the religious life:—enrich them in their poverty, love them in their chastity, lighten their hearts in obedience to you. R℣

Give rest to those who have died in Christ:—for with you there is mercy, and fulness of redemption. R℣

Our Father

Concluding Prayer

We beseech your mercy, Lord,
as we offer you this evening praise:
keep our hearts always engaged in meditating on your law,
and grant us the light and reward of eternal life.
(We make our prayer) through our Lord.

WEEK 2: FRIDAY

Invitatory ant. Indeed, how good is the Lord; bless his holy name.
Psalm, p 371.

MORNING PRAYER

Hymn, from the appendix, for the Season.

THROUGH THE YEAR
I am the holy vine,
Which God my Father tends.
Each branch that yields no fruit
My Father cuts away.
Each fruitful branch
He prunes with care
To make it yield
Abundant fruit.

If you abide in me,
I will in you abide.
Each branch to yield its fruit
Must with the vine be one.
So you shall fail
To yield your fruit
If you are not
With me one vine.

I am the fruitful vine,
And you my branches are.
He who abides in me
I will in him abide.
So shall you yield
Much fruit, but none
If you remain
Apart from me.

PSALMODY

Ant. 1: O God, you will not spurn a humbled, contrite heart.

Eastertide: Have courage, my son, your sins are forgiven you, alleluia.

O GOD, HAVE MERCY ON ME   PSALM 50(51)
You must be made new in mind and spirit, and put on the new nature
(Eph 4:23-24)

Have mércy on me, Gód, in your kíndness.*
In your compássion blot óut my offénce.
O wásh me more and móre from my guílt*
and cléanse me fróm my sín.

My offénces trúly I knów them;*
my sín is álways befóre me.
Against yóu, you alóne, have I sínned;*
what is évil in your síght I have dóne.

That you may be jústified whén you give séntence*
and be withóut repróach when you júdge,
O sée, in guílt I was bórn,*
a sínner was Í concéived.

Indéed you love trúth in the héart;*
then in the sécret of my héart teach me wísdom.
O púrify me, thén I shall be cléan;*
O wásh me, I shall be whíter than snów.

Make me héar rejóicing and gládness,*
that the bónes you have crúshed may revíve.
From my síns turn awáy your fáce*
and blót out áll my guílt.

A púre heart creáte for me, O Gód,*
put a stéadfast spírit withín me.
Do not cást me awáy from your présence,*
nor depríve me of your hóly spírit.

Give me agáin the jóy of your hélp;*
with a spírit of férvour sustáin me,
that I may téach transgréssors your wáys*
and sínners may retúrn to yóu.

O réscue me, Gód, my hélper,*
and my tóngue shall ríng out your góodness.
O Lórd, ópen my líps*
and my móuth shall decláre your práise.

For in sácrifice you táke no delíght,*
burnt óffering from mé you would refúse,
my sácrifice, a cóntrite spírit.*
A húmbled, contrite héart you will not spúrn.

In your góodness, show fávour to Síon:*
rebuíld the wálls of Jerúsalem.
Thén you will be pléased with lawful sácrifice,*
hólocausts óffered on your áltar.

Ant. O God, you will not spurn a humbled, contrite heart.
Eastertide: Have courage, my son, your sins are forgiven you, alleluia.

Ant. 2: In spite of your anger, Lord, have compassion.
Eastertide: Lord, you came with strength to save your people; you came with your Anointed One, alleluia.

GOD WILL APPEAR IN JUDGMENT   CANTICLE
                                                                      HAB 3:2-4,13A,15-19
Lift up your heads, for your redemption is near at hand (Lk 21:28)

Lord, I have heard of your fame,*
I stand in awe at your deeds.
Do them again in our days,†
in our days make them known!*
In spite of your anger, have compassion.

God comes forth from Teman,*
the Holy One comes from Mount Paran.
His splendour covers the sky*
and his glory fills the earth.
His brilliance is like the light,†
rays flash from his hands;*
there his power is hidden.

You march out to save your people,*
to save the one you have anointed.
You made a path for your horses in the sea,*
in the raging of the mighty waters.

This I heard and I tremble with terror,*
my lips quiver at the sound.
Weakness invades my bones,*
my steps fail beneath me
yet I calmly wait for the doom*
that will fall upon the people who assail us.

For even though the fig does not blossom,*
nor fruit grow on the vine,
even though the olive crop fail,*
and fields produce no harvest,
even though flocks vanish from the folds*
and stalls stand empty of cattle,

Yet I will rejoice in the Lord*
and exult in God my saviour.
The Lord my God is my strength.†
He makes me leap like the deer,*
he guides me to the high places.

Ant. In spite of your anger, Lord, have compassion.
Eastertide: Lord, you came with strength to save your people;
you came with your Anointed One, alleluia.

Ant. 3: O praise the Lord, Jerusalem.†
Eastertide: Sion, praise your God, for he has established peace in
your land, alleluia.

THE RENEWAL OF JERUSALEM   PSALM 147
Come, and I will show you the bride that the Lamb has chosen (Rev
21:9)

O práise the Lórd, Jerúsalem!*
†Síon, práise your Gód!

521

He has stréngthened the bárs of your gátes,*
he has bléssed the chíldren withín you.
He estáblished péace on your bórders,*
he féeds you with fínest whéat.

He sénds out his wórd to the éarth*
and swíftly rúns his commánd.
He shówers down snów white as wóol,*
he scátters hóar-frost like áshes.

He húrls down háilstones like crúmbs.*
The wáters are frózen at his tóuch;
he sénds forth his wórd and it mélts them:*
at the bréath of his móuth the waters flów.

He mákes his wórd known to Jácob,*
to Ísrael his láws and decrées.
He has not déalt thus with óther nátions;*
he has not táught them hís decrées.

Ant. O praise the Lord, Jerusalem.
Eastertide: Sion, praise your God, for he has established peace in your land, alleluia.

THROUGH THE YEAR

Scripture Reading   *Eph 2:13-16*
Now, in union with Christ Jesus, you who used to be far away have been brought near by the death of Christ. For Christ himself has brought us peace, by making the Jews and Gentiles one people. With his own body he broke down the wall that separated them and kept them enemies. He abolished the Jewish Law, with its commandments and rules, in order to create out of the two races one new people in union with himself, in this way making peace. By his death on the cross Christ destroyed the enmity; by means of the cross he united both races into one body and brought them back to God.

Short Responsory
R̓ I call to the Lord, the Most High, for he has been my help.
Repeat R̓

℣ May he send from heaven and save me. ℟ Glory be. ℟

Benedictus ant. Through the loving mercy of our God, the Rising Sun has come to visit us.

Intercessions
Father, we praise you for your Son, our Lord Jesus Christ; through the Holy Spirit he offered himself in sacrifice to you, that we might be delivered from death and selfishness, and be free to live in your peace. ℟ Father, in your will is our peace.
We accept this new day as your gift, Lord;—grant that we may live in newness of life. ℟
You made all things, and keep all things in being;—give us the insight to see your hand at work in them all. ℟
Your Son sealed the new and everlasting covenant in his blood;—help us to live by this covenant and honour it. ℟
As Jesus died on the cross, blood and water flowed from his side;—as we share in the eucharist, pour out your Spirit upon us. ℟
Our Father

Concluding Prayer
Almighty God,
as in this morning prayer we offer you our praise,
grant that, in your kingdom,
together with your saints,
we may praise you with even greater joy.
(We make our prayer) through our Lord.

EVENING PRAYER

Hymn, from the appendix, for the Season.

THROUGH THE YEAR
Day is done, but Love unfailing
Dwells ever here;
Shadows fall, but hope, prevailing,
Calms every fear.

Loving Father, none forsaking,
Take our hearts, of Love's own making,
Watch our sleeping, guard our waking,
Be always near!

Dark descends, but Light unending
Shines through our night;
You are with us, ever lending
New strength to sight;
One in love, your truth confessing,
One in hope of heaven's blessing,
May we see, in love's possessing,
Love's endless light!

PSALMODY

Ant. 1: Lord, keep my soul from death, my feet from stumbling.
Eastertide: The Lord saved my soul from the power of death,
alleluia.

THANKSGIVING   PSALM 114(116)
*We must experience many hardships before we can enter the kingdom
of God* (Acts 14:22)

I love the Lórd for hé has héard*
the crý of my appéal;
for he túrned his éar to mé*
in the dáy when I cálled him.

They surróunded me, the snáres of déath,†
with the ánguish of the tómb;*
they cáught me, sórrow and distréss.
I cálled on the Lórd's name.*

O Lórd my Gód, delíver me!

How grácious is the Lórd, and júst;*
our Gód has compássion.
The Lórd protécts the simple héarts;*
I was hélpless so he sáved me.

524

Turn báck, my sóul, to your rést*
for the Lórd has been góod;
he has képt my sóul from déath,†
my éyes from téars*
and my féet from stúmbling.

I will wálk in the présence of the Lórd*
in the lánd of the líving.

Ant. Lord, keep my soul from death, my feet from stumbling.
Eastertide: The Lord saved my soul from the power of death, alleluia.

Ant. 2: My help shall come from the Lord who made heaven and earth.
Eastertide: The Lord protected his people as the apple of his eye, alleluia.

GOD, THE PROTECTOR OF HIS PEOPLE   PSALM 120(121)
They will never hunger or thirst again; neither the sun or scorching wind will ever plague them (Rev. 7:16)

I líft up my éyes to the móuntains:*
from whére shall come my hélp?
My hélp shall cóme from the Lórd*
who made héaven and éarth.

May he néver állow you to stúmble!*
Let him sléep not, your guárd.
Nó, he sléeps not nor slúmbers,*
Ísrael's guárd.

The Lórd is your guárd and your sháde;*
at your ríght side he stánds.
By dáy the sún shall not smíte you*
nor the móon in the níght.

The Lórd will guárd you from évil,*
he will guárd your sóul.
The Lord will guárd your góing and cóming*
both nów and for éver.

Ant. My help shall come from the Lord who made heaven and earth.
Eastertide: The Lord protected his people as the apple of his eye, alleluia.

Ant. 3: Your ways are just and true, King of all the ages.
Eastertide: The Lord is my strength and protection, he is my salvation, alleluia.

HYMN OF ADORATION   CANTICLE: REV 15:3-4

Great and wonderful are your deeds,*
O Lord God the Almighty!
Just and true are your ways,*
O King of the ages!

Who shall not fear and glorify your name, O Lord?*
For you alone are holy.
All nations shall come and worship you,*
for your judgments have been revealed.

Ant. Your ways are just and true, King of all the ages.
Eastertide: The Lord is my strength and protection, he is my salvation, alleluia.

THROUGH THE YEAR

Scripture Reading   *1 Cor 2:7-10a*
The hidden wisdom of God which we teach in our mysteries is the wisdom that God predestined to be for our glory before the ages began. It is a wisdom that none of the masters of this age have ever known, or they would not have crucified the Lord of Glory; we teach what scripture calls: the things that no eye has seen and no ear has heard, things beyond the mind of man, all that God has prepared for those who love him. These are the very things that God has revealed to us through the Spirit.

Short Responsory
Ry Christ died for our sins, that he might offer us to God. *Repeat* Ry
Ⅴ In the body he was put to death, in the spirit he was raised to life.
Ry Glory be. Ry

Magnificat ant. Remember your mercy, O Lord; according to the promise you made to our fathers.

Intercessions
Christ comforted the widow who had lost her only son: let us pray to him, who will come at the last to wipe away every tear from our eyes. ℟ Come, Lord Jesus.
Lord Jesus, you consoled especially the poor and troubled:—look with mercy on those in any kind of need. ℟
The angel brought you the Father's comfort on the eve of your passion:—we pray that your comfort may strengthen those who are dying. ℟
Let all exiles know your care for them;—may they find their homelands once more, and come one day in joy to the Father's house. ℟
Look in love on all whose sins have separated them from you:—reconcile them to yourself and to your Church. ℟
The dead suffered the pain and loss of human life:—give them the fulness of life and joy in heaven. ℟
Our Father

Concluding Prayer
Lord God,
the Cross reveals the mystery of your love:
a stumbling block indeed for unbelief,
but the sign of your power and wisdom to us who believe.
Teach us so to contemplate your Son's glorious Passion
that we may always believe and glory in his Cross.
(We make our prayer) through our Lord.

WEEK 2: SATURDAY

Invitatory ant. Let us listen for the voice of the Lord and enter into his peace.
Psalm, p 371.

MORNING PRAYER

Hymn, from the appendix, for the Season.

THROUGH THE YEAR

Sing, all creation, sing to God in gladness!
Joyously serve him, singing hymns of homage!
Chanting his praises, come before his presence!
Praise the Almighty!

Know that our God is Lord of all the ages!
He is our maker; we are all his creatures,
People he fashioned, sheep he leads to pasture!
Praise the Almighty!

Great in his goodness is the Lord we worship;
Steadfast his kindness, love that knows no ending!
Faithful his word is, changeless, everlasting!
Praise the Almighty!

PSALMODY

Ant. 1: Lord, we proclaim your love in the morning and your truth in the watches of the night.
Eastertide: You have made me glad, O Lord; for the works of your hands I shout with joy, alleluia.

PRAISE OF THE LORD CREATOR   PSALM 91(92)
The deeds of God's only Son are praised (St Athanasius)

It is góod to give thánks to the Lórd*
to make músic to your náme, O Most Hígh,
to procláim your lóve in the mórning*
and your trúth in the wátches of the níght,
on the tén-stringed lýre and the lúte,*
with the múrmuring sóund of the hárp.

Your déeds, O Lórd, have made me glád;*
for the wórk of your hánds I shout with jóy.
O Lórd, how gréat are your wórks!*
How déep are yóur desígns!
The fóolish man cánnot knów this*
and the fóol cánnot understánd.

Though the wícked spring úp like gráss*
and áll who do évil thríve:
they are dóomed to be etérnally destróyed.*
But yóu, Lord, are etérnally on hígh.
Sée how your énemies pérish;*
all dóers of évil are scáttered.

To mé you give the wíld-ox's stréngth;*
you anóint me with the púrest óil.
My éyes looked in tríumph on my fóes;*
my éars heard gládly of their fáll.
The júst will flóurish like the pálm-tree*
and grów like a Lébanon cédar.

Plánted in the hóuse of the Lórd*
they will flóurish in the cóurts of our Gód,
stíll bearing frúit when they are óld,*
stíll full of sáp, still gréen,
to procláim that the Lórd is júst.*
In hím, my róck, there is no wróng.

Ant. Lord, we proclaim your love in the morning and your truth in the watches of the night.
Eastertide: You have made me glad, O Lord; for the works of your hands I shout with joy, alleluia.

Ant. 2: Proclaim the greatness of our God.
Eastertide: It is I who give death and life; it is I who strike and also heal, alleluia.

THE DEEDS OF KINDNESS WHICH GOD CANTICLE
WROUGHT FOR HIS PEOPLE DEUT 32:1-12
How often have I longed to gather your children as a hen gathers her young under her wings (Mt 23:37)

Listen, O heavens, and I will speak,*
let the earth hear the words on my lips.
May my teaching fall like the rain,*
my speech descend like the dew,

529

like rain drops on the young green,*
like showers falling on the grass.

For I shall praise the name of the Lord.*
O give glory to this God of ours!
The Rock—his deeds are perfect,*
and all his ways are just,
a faithful God, without deceit,*
a God who is right and just.

Those whom he begot unblemished*
have become crooked, false, perverse.
Is it thus you repay the Lord,*
O senseless and foolish people?
Is he not your father who created you,*
he who made you, on whom you depend?

Remember the days of old,*
consider the years that are past;
ask your father and he will show you,*
ask your elders and they will tell you.

When the Most High gave the nations their heritage*
and disposed men according to his plan,
in fixing the boundaries of the nations*
he thought first of Israel's sons.
For Israel was the Lord's possession,*
Jacob the one he had chosen.

God found him in a wilderness,*
in fearful, desolate wastes;
he surrounded him, he lifted him up,*
he kept him as the apple of his eye.

Like an eagle that watches its nest,*
that hovers over its young,
so he spread his wings; he took him,*
placed him on his outstretched wings.
The Lord alone was his guide*
and no other god was with him.

Ant. Proclaim the greatness of our God.
Eastertide: It is I who give death and life; it is I who strike and also heal, alleluia.

Ant. 3: How great is your name, Lord, through all the earth!
Eastertide: With glory and honour you crowned your Anointed One, alleluia.

THE MAJESTY OF THE LORD, THE DIGNITY OF MAN   PSALM 8
He has put all things under his feet, and appointed him to be head of the whole Church (Eph 1:22)

How gréat is your náme, O Lórd our Gód,*
   through áll the éarth!

Your májesty is práised above the héavens;*
   on the líps of chíldren and of bábes
   you have found práise to fóil your énemy,*
   to sílence the fóe and the rébel.

When I see the héavens, the wórk of your hánds,*
   The móon and the stárs which you arránged,
what is mán that you should kéep him in mínd,*
   mortal mán that you cáre for hím?

Yet you have máde him little léss than a gód;*
   with glóry and hónour you crówned him,
gave him pówer over the wórks of your hánd,*
   put áll things únder his féet.

Áll of them, shéep and cáttle,*
   yes, éven the sávage béasts,
birds of the aír, and físh*
   that máke their wáy through the wáters.

How gréat is your náme, O Lórd our Gód,*
   through áll the éarth!

Ant. How great is your name, Lord, through all the earth!
Eastertide: With glory and honour you crowned your Anointed One, alleluia.

531

THROUGH THE YEAR

Scripture Reading *Rom 12:14-16a*

Bless those who persecute you; bless and do not curse them. Rejoice with those who rejoice, weep with those who weep. Live in harmony with one another; do not be haughty, but associate with the lowly.

Short Responsory

R℣ When I sing to you my lips shall rejoice. *Repeat* R℣

℣ My tongue shall tell the tale of your justice. R℣ Glory be. R℣

Benedictus ant. Lord, guide our feet into the way of peace.

Intercessions

God the Father has adopted us as brothers of his only Son, and through the ages has stayed with us and kept us in his love. Let us ask him for the needs of the world. R℣ Lord, help us as we work.

We pray for all who plan and build in our cities:—give them respect for every human value. R℣

Pour out your Spirit on artists, craftsmen, and musicians:—may their work bring variety, joy, and inspiration to our lives. R℣

Be with us as the cornerstone of all that we build:—for we can do nothing well without your aid. R℣

You have created us anew in the resurrection of your Son:—give us the strength to create a new life, and a new world. R℣

Our Father

Concluding Prayer

Let us praise you, Lord,
with voice and mind and deed:
and since life itself is your gift,
may all we have and are be yours.
(We make our prayer) through our Lord.

WEEK 3: SUNDAY

EVENING PRAYER I

Hymn, from the appendix, for the Season.

THROUGH THE YEAR

O Light serene of God the Father's glory,
To you, O Christ, we sing,
And with the evening star, at hour of sunset,
Our worship bring.

To Father, Son and God's most Holy Spirit,
Eternal praise is due.
O Christ, who gave your life, the world gives glory
And thanks to you.

PSALMODY

ANTIPHON I

Advent: Rejoice greatly, Jerusalem, for your Saviour will come to you, alleluia.
Lent: Repent and believe the Gospel, says the Lord.
Eastertide: The Lord God is high above the heavens, and from the dust he lifts up the lowly, alleluia.

Through the Year: From the rising of the sun to its setting, great is the name of the Lord.

PRAISED BE THE NAME OF THE LORD   **PSALM 112(113)**
He put down princes from their thrones and exalted the lowly (Lk 1:52)

Práise, O sérvants of the Lórd,*
práise the náme of the Lórd!
May the náme of the Lórd be bléssed*
both nów and for évermóre!
From the rísing of the sún to its sétting*
práised be the náme of the Lórd!

533

Hígh above all nátions is the Lórd,*
abóve the héavens his glóry.
Whó is like the Lórd, our Gód,*
who has rísen on hígh to his thróne
yet stóops from the héights to look dówn,*
to look dówn upon héaven and éarth?

From the dúst he lífts up the lówly,*
from his mísery he ráises the póor
to sét him in the cómpany of prínces,*
yés, with the prínces of his péople.
To the chíldless wífe he gives a hóme*
and gláddens her héart with chíldren.

Ant. From the rising of the sun to its setting, great is the name of
the Lord.

Ant. Advent: Rejoice greatly, Jerusalem, for your Saviour will come
to you, alleluia.
Ant. 2: I, the Lord, am coming to deliver you; I am already near
and my saving act will not be delayed.

Ant. Lent: Repent and believe the Gospel, says the Lord.
Ant. 2: A thanksgiving sacrifice I make: I will call on the Lord's
name.

Ant. Eastertide: The Lord God is high above the heavens and from
the dust he lifts up the lowly, alleluia.
Ant. 2: You have loosened my bonds, Lord: a sacrifice of praise I
will make to you, alleluia.

Ant. 2: I will take the chalice of salvation, and I will call on the
name of the Lord.

THANKSGIVING IN THE TEMPLE   PSALM 115(116)
Through him (Christ), let us offer God an unending sacrifice of praise
(Heb 13:15)

I trústed, éven when I sáid:*
'I am sórely afflícted,'

534

and whén I sáid in my alárm:*
'No mán can be trústed.'

How cán I repáy the Lórd*
for his góodness to mé?
The cúp of salvátion I will ráise;*
I will cáll on the Lórd's name.

My vóws to the Lórd I will fulfíl*
befóre all his péople.
O précious in the éyes of the Lórd*
is the déath of his fáithful.

Your sérvant, Lord, your sérvant am Í;*
you have lóosened my bónds.
A thánksgiving sácrifice I máke:*
I will cáll on the Lórd's name.

My vóws to the Lórd I will fulfíl*
befóre all his péople,
in the cóurts of the hóuse of the Lórd,*
in your mídst, O Jerúsalem.

Ant. I will take the chalice of salvation, and I will call on the name of the Lord.

Ant. Advent: I, the Lord, am coming to deliver you; I am already near and my saving act will not be delayed.
Ant. 3: Send, Lord, the Lamb, the ruler of the earth, from the Rock of the desert to the mountain of the daughter of Sion.

Ant. Lent: A thanksgiving sacrifice I make: I will call on the Lord's name.
Ant. 3: No one takes my life from me, but I lay it down of my own accord, and I have power to take it up again.

Ant. Eastertide: You have loosened my bonds, Lord: a sacrifice of praise I will make to you, alleluia.
Ant. 3: The Son of God learned to obey through suffering, and he became the source of eternal salvation for all those who obey him, alleluia.

Ant. 3: The Lord Jesus humbled himself, but God exalted him on high for ever.

CHRIST, THE SERVANT OF GOD   CANTICLE: PHIL 2:6-11

Though he was in the form of God,*
Jesus did not count equality with God a thing to be grasped.

He emptied himself,†
taking the form of a servant,*
being born in the likeness of men.

And being found in human form,†
he humbled himself and became obedient unto death,*
even death on a cross.

Therefore God has highly exalted him*
and bestowed on him the name which is above every name,

That at the name of Jesus every knee should bow,*
in heaven and on earth and under the earth,

And every tongue confess that Jesus Christ is Lord,*
to the glory of God the Father.

Ant. The Lord Jesus humbled himself, but God exalted him on high for ever.

Ant. Advent: Send, Lord, the Lamb, the ruler of the earth, from the Rock of the desert to the mountain of the daughter of Sion.
Lent: No one takes my life from me, but I lay it down of my own accord, and I have power to take it up again.
Eastertide: The Son of God learned to obey through suffering and he became the source of eternal salvation for all those who obey him, alleluia.

THROUGH THE YEAR

Scripture Reading   *Heb 13:20-21*
I pray that the God of peace, who brought our Lord Jesus back from the dead to become the great Shepherd of the sheep by the

blood that sealed an eternal covenant, may make you ready to do his will in any kind of good action; and turn us all into whatever is acceptable to himself through Jesus Christ, to whom be glory for ever and ever, Amen.

Short Responsory

R̷ How great are your works, O Lord. *Repeat* R̷
V̷ In wisdom you have made them all. R̷ Glory be. R̷

Magnificat antiphon from the Proper of Seasons.

Intercessions

Christ our Lord is mindful of all who need him, and does great things for love of them. Let us not be afraid to ask him for all our needs. R̷ Show us your loving kindness.

Lord, we know that the good things we have received today have come as a gift from you:—may we receive them with thankfulness and learn how to give. R̷

Saviour and light of all people, keep missionaries in your special care:—may the light of your Spirit burn strongly in them. R̷

Grant that the world may be filled with the knowledge of your truth;—help us to carry out all you have called us to do. R̷

You healed the sickness and pain of your brothers:—Bring healing and comfort to the spirit of man. R̷

Give rest to the faithful departed;—and bring them to praise you in eternity. R̷

Our Father

The concluding prayer from the Proper of Seasons.

Invitatory

Ant. Come, ring out our joy to the Lord; hail the God who saves us, alleluia.†
Psalm, p 371.

MORNING PRAYER

Hymn, from the appendix, for the Season.

537

THROUGH THE YEAR

Transcendent God in whom we live,
The Resurrection and the Light,
We sing for you a morning hymn
To end the silence of the night.

When early cock begins to crow
And everything from sleep awakes,
New life and hope spring up again
While out of darkness colour breaks.

Creator of all things that are,
The measure and the end of all,
Forgiving God, forget our sins,
And hear our prayer before we call.

Praise Father, Son and Holy Ghost,
Blest Trinity and source of grace,
Who call us out of nothingness
To find in you our resting-place.

Alternative hymn

Christ is the world's redeemer,
The lover of the pure,
The font of heavenly wisdom,
Our trust and hope secure,
The armour of his soldiers,
The Lord of earth and sky,
Our health while we are living,
Our life when we shall die.

Down in the realm of darkness,
He lay a captive bound,
But at the hour appointed
He rose a victor crowned.
And now, to heaven ascended,
He sits upon a throne,
Whence he had ne'er departed,
His Father's and his own.

All glory to the Father,
The unbegotten One,
All honour be to Jesus,
His sole-begotten Son;
And to the Holy Spirit,
The perfect Trinity,
Let all the worlds give answer,
Amen—so let it be.

PSALMODY

ANTIPHON I

Advent: The Lord will come without delay. He will bring to light what darkness hides and he will reveal himself to all the nations, alleluia.

Lent: Truly your decrees are to be trusted. They are more wondrous than the surgings of the sea.

Eastertide: The Lord is king, with majesty enrobed, alleluia.†

Through the Year: The Lord is wonderful on high, alleluia.

THE SPLENDOUR OF THE LORD CREATOR   PSALM 92(93)
The Lord, our God, the Almighty is king; let us be glad and rejoice and give him praise (Rev 19:6-7)

The Lord is kíng, with májesty enróbed;†
†the Lórd has róbed himself with míght,*
he has gírded himsélf with pówer.

The wórld you made fírm, not to be móved;†
your thróne has stood fírm from of óld.*
From all etérnity, O Lórd, you áre.

The wáters have lífted up, O Lórd,†
the wáters have lífted up their vóice,*
the wáters have lífted up their thúnder.

Gréater than the róar of mighty wáters,†
more glórious than the súrgings of the séa,*
the Lórd is glórious on hígh.

Trúly your decrées are to be trústed.†
Hóliness is fítting to your hóuse,*
O Lórd, until the énd of tíme.

Ant. The Lord is wonderful on high, alleluia.

Ant. Advent: The Lord will come without delay. He will bring to light what darkness hides and he will reveal himself to all the nations, alleluia.
Ant. 2: Every mountain and hill shall be laid low, the rugged places shall be made smooth and the mountain-ranges become a plain. Come, Lord, and do not delay, alleluia.

Ant. Lent: Truly your decrees are to be trusted. They are more wondrous than the surgings of the sea.
Ant. 2: Springs of water, bless the Lord: give glory and eternal praise to him.

Ant. Eastertide: The Lord is king, with majesty enrobed, alleluia.
Ant. 2: The whole creation will be freed and will enjoy the glory and freedom of the children of God, alleluia.

Ant. 2: May you be praised, Lord, and extolled for ever, alleluia.

LET EVERY CREATURE PRAISE THE LORD   CANTICLE
                                                              DAN 3:57-88,56

Praise our God, all you his servants (Rev 19:5)

O all you works of the Lord, O bless the Lord.*
To him be highest glory and praise for ever.

And you, angels of the Lord, O bless the Lord.*
To him be highest glory and praise for ever.

And you, the heavens of the Lord, O bless the Lord.*
And you, clouds of the sky, O bless the Lord.
And you, all armies of the Lord, O bless the Lord.*
To him be highest glory and praise for ever.

And you, sun and moon, O bless the Lord.*
And you, the stars of the heavens, O bless the Lord.
And you, showers and rain, O bless the Lord.*
To him be highest glory and praise for ever.

And you, all you breezes and winds, O bless the Lord.*
And you, fire and heat, O bless the Lord.
And you, cold and heat, O bless the Lord.*
To him be highest glory and praise for ever.

And you, showers and dew, O bless the Lord.*
And you, frosts and cold, O bless the Lord.
And you, frost and snow, O bless the Lord.*
To him be highest glory and praise for ever.

And you, night-time and day, O bless the Lord.*
And you, darkness and light, O bless the Lord.
And you, lightning and clouds, O bless the Lord.*
To him be highest glory and praise for ever.

O let the earth bless the Lord.*
To him be highest glory and praise for ever.

And you, mountains and hills, O bless the Lord.*
And you, all plants of the earth, O bless the Lord.
And you, fountains and springs, O bless the Lord.*
To him be highest glory and praise for ever.

And you, rivers and seas, O bless the Lord.*
And you, creatures of the sea, O bless the Lord.
And you, every bird in the sky, O bless the Lord.†
And you, wild beasts and tame, O bless the Lord.*
To him be highest glory and praise for ever.

And you, children of men, O bless the Lord.*
To him be highest glory and praise for ever.

O Israel, bless the Lord. O bless the Lord.*
And you, priests of the Lord, O bless the Lord.
And you, servants of the Lord, O bless the Lord.*
To him be highest glory and praise for ever.

And you, spirits and soul of the just, O bless the Lord.*
And you, holy and humble of heart, O bless the Lord.
Ananias, Azarias, Mizael, O bless the Lord.*
To him be highest glory and praise for ever.

Let us praise the Father, the Son and Holy Spirit:*
To you be highest glory and praise for ever.
May you be blessed, O Lord, in the heavens;*
To you be highest glory and praise for ever.

The Glory be *is omitted after this canticle.*

Ant. May you be praised, Lord, and extolled for ever, alleluia.

Ant. Advent: Every mountain and hill shall be laid low, the rugged places shall be made smooth and the mountain-ranges become a plain. Come, Lord, and do not delay, alleluia.
Ant. 3: I will give salvation to Sion, I will bring my glory to Jerusalem, alleluia.

Ant. Lent: Springs of water, bless the Lord: give glory and eternal praise to him.
Ant. 3: All kings and peoples of the earth, praise God.
Ant. Eastertide: The whole creation will be freed and will enjoy the glory and freedom of the children of God, alleluia.
Ant. 3: The name of the Lord is praised, in heaven and on earth, alleluia.

Ant. 3: Praise the Lord from the heavens, alleluia.†

HYMN OF PRAISE TO THE LORD, THE CREATOR   PSALM 148
To the One who sits on the throne and to the Lamb, be all praise, honour, glory and power, for ever and ever (Rev 5:13).

Práise the Lórd from the héavens,*
†práise him in the héights.
Práise him, all his ángels,*
práise him, áll his hósts.

Práise him, sún and móon,*
práise him, shining stárs.
Práise him, highest héavens*
and the wáters abóve the héavens.

Let them práise the náme of the Lórd.*
He commánded: they were máde.
He fíxed them for éver,*
gave a láw which shall nót pass awáy.

Práise the Lórd from the éarth,*
séa creatures and all óceans,
fire and háil, snow and míst,*
stormy wínds that obéy his wórd;

áll móuntains and hílls,*
all frúit trees and cédars,
béasts, wild and táme,*
réptiles and bírds on the wíng;

áll earth's kíngs and péoples,*
earth's prínces and rúlers;
yóung men and máidens,*
old men togéther with chíldren.

Let them práise the náme of the Lórd*
for he alóne is exálted.
The spléndour of his náme*
réaches beyond héaven and éarth.

He exálts the stréngth of his péople.*
He is the práise of all his sáints,
of the sóns of Ísrael,*
of the péople to whóm he comes clóse.

Ant. Praise the Lord from the heavens, alleluia.

Ant. Advent: I will give salvation to Sion, I will bring my glory to
Jerusalem, alleluia.
Lent: All kings and peoples of the earth, praise God.

Eastertide: The name of the Lord is praised, in heaven and on earth, alleluia.

THROUGH THE YEAR

Scripture Reading   *Ezek 37:12b-14*

The Lord God says this: I am now going to open your graves; I mean to raise you from your graves, my people, and lead you back to the soil of Israel. And you will know that I am the Lord, when I open your graves and raise you from your graves, my people. And I shall put my spirit in you, and you will live, and I shall resettle you on your own soil; and you will know that I, the Lord, have said and done this—it is the Lord God who speaks.

Short Responsory

R͟ You are the Christ, the Son of the living God. Have mercy on us. *Repeat* R͟

V͟ You are seated at the right hand of the Father. R͟ Glory be. R͟

Benedictus antiphon from the Proper of Seasons.

Intercessions

We pray to the Father, who sent his Holy Spirit to bring new light to the hearts of us all. R͟ Lord, send us the light of your Spirit.

Blessed are you, the source of all light;—all creation rightly gives you praise. R͟

Through the resurrection of your Son, the world is filled with light:—through the gift of your Spirit, may your light shine out in the Church. R͟

Through your Holy Spirit, the disciples remembered all that Jesus taught them:—pour out your Spirit on the Church that she may be faithful to that teaching. R͟

Light of all the nations, look upon those who live in darkness:—open their hearts to accept you as the one true God. R͟

Our Father

The concluding prayer from the Proper of Seasons.

EVENING PRAYER II

Hymn, from the appendix, for the Season.

THROUGH THE YEAR

In the beginning God created heaven,
The dark and empty earth;
His Spirit moved across the sombre waters
And stirred them with his breath.

Then God created light, and with its coming
The dark was swept away;
The morning came, and then the quiet evening:
The end of God's first day.

To God, the Father of the world, give glory,
With Christ his only Son,
Who with the Spirit govern all creation:
Blest Trinity in One.

Alternative hymn

Praise to the holiest in the height,
And in the depth be praise,
In all his words most wonderful,
Most sure in all his ways.

O loving wisdom of our God!
When all was sin and shame,
A second Adam to the fight
And to the rescue came.

O wisest love! that flesh and blood
Which did in Adam fail,
Should strive afresh against their foe,
Should strive and should prevail.

And that a higher gift than grace
Should flesh and blood refine,
God's presence and his very self,
And essence all divine.

O generous love! that he who smote
In man for man the foe,
The double agony in man
For man should undergo.

And in the garden secretly,
And on the cross on high,
Should teach his brethren, and inspire
To suffer and to die.

Praise to the holiest in the height,
And in the depth be praise,
In all his words most wonderful,
Most sure in all his ways.

PSALMODY

ANTIPHON I

Advent: See, the Lord will come. He will sit with princes and he will mount the glorious throne.

Lent: Lord, almighty king, deliver us for the sake of your name. Give us the grade to return to you.

Eastertide: When he had made purification for sin, he sat at the right hand of the Majesty on high, alleluia.

Through the Year: The Lord's revelation to my Master: 'Sit on my right', alleluia.†

THE MESSIAH IS KING AND PRIEST   PSALM 109(110):1-5,7
He must be king so that he will put all his enemies under his feet
(1 Cor 15:25)

The Lórd's revelátion to my Máster:†
'Sít on my ríght:*
†your fóes I will pút beneath your féet.'

The Lórd will wíeld from Síon†
your scéptre of pówer:*
rúle in the mídst of all your fóes.

A prínce from the dáy of your bírth†

on the hóly móuntains;*
from the wómb before the dáwn I begót you.

The Lórd has sworn an óath he will not chánge.†
'You are a príest for éver,*
a príest like Melchízedek of óld.'

The Máster stánding at your ríght hand*
will shatter kíngs in the dáy of his wráth.

He shall drínk from the stréam by the wáyside*
and thérefore he shall líft up his héad.

Ant. The Lord's revelation to my Master: 'Sit on my right', alleluia.

Ant. Advent: See, the Lord will come. He will sit with princes and he will mount the glorious throne.
Ant. 2: The mountains will bring forth joy and the hills justice; for the Lord, the light of the world, comes in strength.

Ant. Lent: Lord, almighty king, deliver us for the sake of your name. Give us the grace to return to you.
Ant. 2: We were ransomed with the precious blood of Christ, the Lamb who is without blemish.

Ant. Eastertide: When he had made purification for sin, he sat at the right hand of the Majesty on high, alleluia.
Ant. 2: The Lord has delivered his people, alleluia.

Ant. 2: The Lord is full of merciful love; he makes us remember his wonders, alleluia.

GREAT ARE THE WORKS OF THE LORD   PSALM 110(111)
How great and wonderful are all your works, Lord God Almighty
(Rev 15:3)

I will thánk the Lórd with all my héart*
in the méeting of the júst and their assémbly.
Gréat are the wórks of the Lórd;*
to be póndered by áll who lóve them.

Majéstic and glórious his wórk,*
his jústice stands fírm for éver.
He mákes us remémber his wónders.*
The Lórd is compássion and lóve.

He gives fóod to thóse who féar him;*
keeps his cóvenant éver in mínd.
He has shówn his míght to his péople*
by gíving them the lánds of the nátions.

His wórks are jústice and trúth:*
his précepts are áll of them súre,
standing fírm for éver and éver:*
they are máde in úprightness and trúth.

He has sént delíverance to his péople†
and estáblished his cóvenant for éver.*
Hóly his náme, to be féared.
To fear the Lórd is the fírst stage of wísdom;†
all who dó so próve themselves wíse.*
His práise shall lást for éver!

Ant. The Lord is full of merciful love; he makes us remember his wonders, alleluia.

OUTSIDE LENT

Ant. Advent: The mountains will bring forth joy and the hills justice; for the Lord, the light of the world, comes in strength.
Ant. 3: Let us live justly and honestly while we are awaiting, in hope, the coming of the Lord.

Ant. Eastertide: The Lord has delivered his people, alleluia.
Ant. 3: Alleluia, the Lord our God is king; let us rejoice and give glory to him alleluia.

Ant. 3: The Lord our God almighty is king, alleluia.

When chanted, this canticle is sung with Alleluia *as set out below. When recited, it suffices to say* Alleluia *at the beginning and end of each strophe.*

THE MARRIAGE FEAST OF THE LAMB

Alleluia.
Salvation and glory and power belong to our God,*
(R℣ Alleluia.)
His judgments are true and just.
R℣ Alleluia (alleluia).

Alleluia.
Praise our God, all you his servants,*
(R℣ Alleluia.)
You who fear him, small and great.
R℣ Alleluia (alleluia).

Alleluia.
The Lord our God, the Almighty, reigns,*
(R℣ Alleluia.)
Let us rejoice and exult and give him the glory.
R℣ Alleluia (alleluia).

Alleluia.
The marriage of the Lamb has come,*
(R℣ Alleluia.)
And his bride has made herself ready.
R℣ Alleluia (alleluia).

Ant. The Lord our God almighty is king, alleluia.

Ant. Advent: Let us live justly and honestly while we are awaiting, in hope, the coming of the Lord.
Eastertide: Alleluia, the Lord our God is king; let us rejoice and give glory to him, alleluia.

LENT

Ant. Lent: We were ransomed with the precious blood of Christ, the lamb who is without blemish.
Ant. 3: Ours were the sufferings he bore, ours the sorrows he carried.

CHRIST, THE SERVANT OF GOD,
  FREELY ACCEPTS HIS PASSION

CANTICLE
I PET 2:21-24

Christ suffered for you,†
leaving you an example*
that you should follow in his steps.

He committed no sin;*
no guile was found on his lips.
When he was reviled,*
he did not revile in return.

When he suffered,*
he did not threaten;
but he trusted to him*
who judges justly.

He himself bore our sins*
in his body on the tree,
that we might die to sin*
and live to righteousness.

By his wounds you have been healed.

Ant. Ours were the sufferings he bore, ours the sorrows he carried.

THROUGH THE YEAR

Scripture Reading   *I Pet 1:3-5*
Blessed be God the Father of our Lord Jesus Christ, who in his great mercy has given us a new birth as his sons, by raising Jesus Christ from the dead, so that we have a sure hope and the promise of an inheritance that can never be spoilt or soiled and never fade away, because it is being kept for you in the heavens. Through your faith, God's power will guard you until the salvation which has been prepared is revealed at the end of time.

Short Responsory
R̷ Blessed are you, O Lord, in the vault of heaven. *Repeat* R̷
V̷ You are exalted and glorified above all else for ever. R̷ Glory be. R̷

Magnificat antiphon from the Proper of Seasons.

Intercessions

God is ever creative. His love renews all things and is the source of our hope. Let us turn to him in confidence: ℟ Lord, accept our thanks and our prayers.

We give thanks for the order of created things:—you have blessed us with the resources of the earth and the gift of human life. ℟

We give thanks for man's share in your continuing work of creation: —we praise you for your gifts to him of inventive skill and creative vision.

We pray for all the nations of the world:—may those in authority work for peace and goodwill among men. ℟

We pray for all who are homeless today:—we pray for families searching for a place to live, and for refugees driven from their homeland. ℟

Life was your first gift to us:—may those who have died come to its fulness in you. ℟

Our Father

The concluding prayer from the Proper of Seasons.

WEEK 3: MONDAY

Invitatory ant. Let us come before the Lord, giving thanks.
Psalm, p 371.

MORNING PRAYER

Hymn, from the appendix, for the Season.

THROUGH THE YEAR
> The day is filled with splendour
> When God brings light from light,
> And all renewed creation
> Rejoices in his sight.

The Father gives his children
The wonder of the world
In which his power and glory
Like banners are unfurled.

With every living creature,
Awaking with the day,
We turn to God our Father,
Lift up our hearts and pray:

O Father, Son and Spirit,
Your grace and mercy send,
That we may live to praise you
Today and to the end.

PSALMODY

Ant. 1: They are happy, who dwell in your house, Lord.
17–23 December: Behold, the Lord, the ruler of the kings of the earth, will come. Happy are those who are ready to meet him.
Eastertide: My heart and my soul ring out their joy to the living God, alleluia.

LONGING FOR THE TEMPLE OF THE LORD   PSALM 83(84)
We have no lasting city in this life but we look for one in the life to come (Heb 13:14)

How lóvely is your dwélling pláce,*
Lórd, Gód of hósts.

My sóul is lónging and yéarning,*
is yéarning for the cóurts of the Lórd.
My héart and my sóul ring out their jóy*
to Gód, the líving Gód.

The spárrow hersélf finds a hóme*
and the swállow a nést for her bróod;
she láys her yóung by your áltars,*
Lord of hósts, my kíng and my Gód.

They are háppy, who dwéll in your hóuse,*

552

for éver sínging your práise.
They are háppy, whose stréngth is in yóu,*
in whose héarts are the róads to Síon.

As they gó through the Bítter Válley†
they máke it a pláce of spríngs,*
the áutumn rain cóvers it with bléssings.
They wálk with éver growing stréngth,*
they will sée the God of góds in Síon.

O Lórd God of hósts, hear my práyer,*
give éar, O Gód of Jácob.
Turn your éyes, O Gód, our shíeld,*
lóok on the fáce of your anóinted.

Óne day withín your cóurts*
is bétter than a thóusand elsewhére.
The thréshold of the hóuse of Gód*
I prefér to the dwéllings of the wícked.

For the Lord Gód is a rámpart, a shíeld;*
he will gíve us his fávour and glóry.
The Lórd will not refúse any góod*
to thóse who wálk without bláme.

Lórd, Gód of hósts,*
háppy the mán who trusts in yóu!

Ant. They are happy, who dwell in your house, Lord.
17–23 December: Behold, the Lord, the ruler of the kings of the earth, will come. Happy are those who are ready to meet him.
Eastertide: My heart and my soul ring out their joy to the living God, alleluia.

Ant. 2: Come, let us go up to the mountain of the Lord.
17-23 December: Sing a new song to the Lord: Praise him throughout the world.
Eastertide: Great is the Temple of the Lord; all the nations will go there to worship, alleluia.

553

THE MOUNTAIN OF THE TEMPLE OF THE LORD   CANTICLE
  TOWERS ABOVE THE MOUNTAINS   IS 2:2-5
All the peoples will come and worship you (Rev 15:4)

It shall come to pass in the latter days†
that the mountain of the house of the Lord*
shall be established as the highest of the mountains,
and shall be raised above the hills;*
and all the nations shall flow to it,

And many peoples shall come, and say:†
'Come, let us go up to the mountain of the Lord,*
to the house of the God of Jacob,
that he may teach us his ways*
and that we may walk in his paths.'
For out of Sion shall go forth the law,*
and the word of the Lord from Jerusalem.

He shall judge between the nations,*
and shall decide for many peoples;
and they shall beat their swords into ploughshares,*
and their spears into pruning hooks;
nation shall not lift up sword against nation,*
neither shall they learn war any more.

O house of Jacob, come,*
let us walk in the light of the Lord.

Ant. Come, let us go up to the mountain of the Lord.
17–23 December: Sing a new song to the Lord: Praise him throughout the world.
Eastertide: Great is the Temple of the Lord; all the nations will go there to worship, alleluia.

Ant. 3: O sing to the Lord, bless his name.
17–23 December: When the Son of Man comes, will he find any faith on earth?
Eastertide: Proclaim to the nations: 'God is king', alleluia.

THE LORD IS KING AND RULER OF ALL THE EARTH   PSALM 95(96)
*They were singing a new hymn in front of the throne, in the presence
of the Lamb* (Cf Rev 14:3)

O síng a new sóng to the Lórd,†
síng to the Lórd all the éarth.*
O síng to the Lórd, bless his náme.

Procláim his hélp day by dáy,†
téll among the nátions his glóry*
and his wónders amóng all the péoples.

The Lord is gréat and wórthy of práise,†
to be féared abóve all góds;*
the góds of the héathens are náught.

It was the Lórd who máde the héavens,†
his are májesty and státe and pówer*
and spléndour in his hóly pláce.

Give the Lórd, you fámilies of péoples,†
give the Lórd glóry and pówer,*
give the Lórd the glóry of his náme.

Bring an óffering and énter his cóurts,†
wórship the Lórd in his témple.*
O éarth, trémble befóre him.

Procláim to the nátions: 'God is kíng.'†
The wórld he made fírm in its pláce;*
he will júdge the péoples in fáirness.

Let the héavens rejóice and earth be glád,*
let the séa and all withín it thunder práise,
let the lánd and all it béars rejóice,*
all the trées of the wóod shout for jóy

at the présence of the Lórd for he cómes,*
he cómes to rúle the éarth.
With jústice he will rúle the wórld,*
he will júdge the péoples with his trúth.

Ant. O sing to the Lord, bless his name,
17-23 December: When the Son of Man comes, will he find any faith on earth?
Eastertide: Proclaim to the nations: 'God is king', alleluia.

THROUGH THE YEAR

Scripture Reading   *Jas 2:12-13*
Talk and behave like people who are going to be judged by the law of freedom, because there will be judgment without mercy for those who have not been merciful themselves; but the merciful need have no fear of judgment.

Short Responsory
℞ Blessed be the Lord from age to age. *Repeat* ℞
℣ He alone has wrought marvellous works. ℞ Glory be. ℞

Benedictus ant. Blessed be the Lord, our God.

Intercessions
In the life of his incarnate Son, God has shown us the dignity of man's labour. With this in mind we pray: ℞ Lord, bless our work.
We bless you, Lord, for bringing us to this day;—we thank you for protecting our lives and giving us what we need. ℞
Be with us, Lord, as we take up our daily tasks:—and help us to remember that it is in your world we live and work. ℞
You have called us to serve you responsibly in the world:—help us to build a just and Christian society. ℞
Stay with us and with everyone we meet this day:—let us give your joy and your peace to the world. ℞
Our Father

Concluding Prayer
King of heaven and earth, Lord God,
rule over our hearts and bodies this day.
Sanctify us,
and guide our every thought, word and deed
according to the commandments of your law,

so that now and for ever
your grace may free and save us.
(We make our prayer) through our Lord.

EVENING PRAYER

Hymn, from the appendix, for the Season.

THROUGH THE YEAR

Come, praise the Lord, the Almighty, the King of all nations!
Tell forth his fame, O ye peoples, with loud acclamations!
His love is sure;
Faithful his word shall endure,
Steadfast through all generations!

Praise to the Father most gracious, the Lord of creation!
Praise to his Son, the Redeemer who wrought our salvation!
O heav'nly Dove,
Praise to thee, fruit of their love,
Giver of all consolation.

PSALMODY

Ant. 1: Our eyes are turned to the Lord; we look for his mercy.
17–23 December: Behold, the Lord, the ruler of the kings of the
earth, will come. Happy are those who are ready to meet him.
Eastertide: The Lord will be your everlasting light, your God will
be your glory, alleluia.

THE LORD IS THE HOPE OF HIS PEOPLE   PSALM 122(123)
The two blind men cried out, 'Lord, have pity on us, Son of David'
(Mt 20:30)

To you have I lífted up my éyes,*
you who dwéll in the héavens:
my éyes, like the éyes of sláves*
on the hánd of their lórds.

Líke the éyes of a sérvant*
on the hánd of her místress,

so our éyes are on the Lórd our Gód*
till he shów us his mércy.

Have mércy on us, Lórd, have mércy.*
We are fílled with contémpt.
Indéed all too fúll is our sóul†
with the scórn of the rích,*
with the próud man's disdáin.

Ant. Our eyes are turned to the Lord; we look for his mercy.
17–23 December: Behold, the Lord, the ruler of the kings of the earth, will come. Happy are those who are ready to meet him.
Eastertide: The Lord will be your everlasting light, your God will be your glory, alleluia.

Ant. 2: Our help is in the name of the Lord, who made heaven and earth.
17–23 December: Sing a new song to the Lord: praise him throughout the world.
Eastertide: The snare has been broken and we have escaped, alleluia.

OUR HELP IS IN THE NAME OF THE LORD   PSALM 123 (124)
The Lord said to Paul, 'Do not fear; for I am with you' (Acts 18:9-10)

'If the Lórd had not béen on our síde',*
this is Ísrael's sóng.
'If the Lórd had not béen on our síde*
when mén rose agáinst us,
thén would they have swállowed us alíve*
when their ánger was kíndled.

Thén would the wáters have engúlfed us,*
the tórrent gone óver us;
óver our héad would have swépt*
the ráging wáters.'

Bléssed be the Lórd who did not gíve us*
a préy to their téeth!

Our lífe, like a bírd, has escáped*
from the snáre of the fówler.

Indéed the snáre has been bróken*
and wé have escáped.
Our hélp is in the náme of the Lórd,*
who made héaven and éarth.

Ant. Our help is in the name of the Lord, who made heaven and earth.
17–23 December: Sing a new song to the Lord: praise him throughout the world.
Eastertide: The snare has been broken and we have escaped, alleluia.

Ant. 3: God has chosen us to be his adopted children through his Son.
17–23 December: When the Son of Man comes, will he find any faith on the earth?
Eastertide: When I am lifted up from the earth, I shall draw all men to myself, alleluia.

GOD, THE SAVIOUR   CANTICLE: EPH I:3-10
Blessed be the God and Father*
of our Lord Jesus Christ,
who has blessed us in Christ*
with every spiritual blessing in the heavenly places.

He chose us in him*
before the foundation of the world,
that we should be holy*
and blameless before him.

He destined us in love*
to be his sons through Jesus Christ,
according to the purpose of his will,†
to the praise of his glorious grace*
which he freely bestowed on us in the Beloved.

In him we have redemption through his blood,*

559

the forgiveness of our trespasses,
according to the riches of his grace*
which he lavished upon us.

He has made known to us†
in all wisdom and insight*
the mystery of his will,
according to his purpose*
which he set forth in Christ.

His purpose he set forth in Christ,*
as a plan for the fulness of time,
to unite all things in him,*
things in heaven and things on earth.

Ant. God has chosen us to be his adopted children through his Son.
17–23 December: When the Son of Man comes, will he find any faith on the earth?
Eastertide: When I am lifted up from the earth, I shall draw all men to myself, alleluia.

THROUGH THE YEAR

Scripture Reading   *Jas 4:11-12*
Brothers, do not slander one another. Anyone who slanders a brother, or condemns him, is speaking against the Law and condemning the Law. But if you condemn the Law, you have stopped keeping it and become a judge over it. There is only one lawgiver and he is the only judge and has the power to acquit or to sentence. Who are you to give a verdict on your neighbour?

Short Responsory
R̷ Heal my soul for I have sinned against you. *Repeat* R̷
V̷ I said: 'Lord, have mercy on me.' R̷ Glory be. R̷

Magnificat ant. My soul magnifies the Lord, since God has had regard for my humble state.

Intercessions
The will of Christ is for all men to be saved. Let us pray that his

will may be done. ℟ Draw all men to yourself, Lord.

Lord, by your sacrifice on the cross you redeemed us from the slavery of sin:—lead us to the freedom and glory of the sons of God. ℟

Be with our bishop, N., and all the bishops of your Church:—grant them courage and compassion in their ministry. ℟

Help those who seek the truth to find it:—let them be consecrated in truth. ℟

We pray especially for peace in family life, and for those orphaned and widowed:—comfort them in your love. ℟

May our departed brothers and sisters come to the heavenly city:—there, with the Father and the Holy Spirit, you will reign for ever. ℟

Our Father

Concluding Prayer

Lord God,
it is our bounden duty to proclaim you as the Light
with whom there is no alteration or shadow of change:
enlighten our darkness as we reach the close of this day,
and in your mercy forgive us our sins.
(We make our prayer) through our Lord.

WEEK 3: TUESDAY

Invitatory ant. The Lord is a great king: come, let us adore him.
Psalm, p 371.

MORNING PRAYER

Hymn, from the appendix, for the Season.

THROUGH THE YEAR
O Christ, the Light of heaven
And of the world true Light,
You come in all your radiance
To cleave the web of night.

May what is false within us
Before your truth give way.
That we may live untroubled,
With quiet hearts this day.

May steadfast faith sustain us,
And hope made firm in you;
The love that we have wasted,
O God of love, renew.

Blest Trinity we praise you
In whom our quest will cease;
Keep us with you for ever
In happiness and peace.

PSALMODY

Ant. 1: Lord, you blessed your land; you forgave the guilt of your people.

17–23 December: The Lord will come from his holy place: he will come to save his people.

Eastertide: You will restore our life again, Lord, and your people will rejoice in you, alleluia.

OUR SALVATION IS AT HAND   PSALM 84(85)
When our Saviour came on earth God blessed his land (Origen)

O Lórd, you once fávoured your lánd*
and revíved the fórtunes of Jácob,
you forgáve the guílt of your péople*
and cóvered áll their síns.
You avérted áll your ráge,*
you cálmed the héat of your ánger.

Revíve us now, Gód, our hélper!*
Put an énd to your gríevance agáinst us.
Will you be ángry with ús for éver,*
will your ánger néver céase?

562

Will you nót restóre again our lífe*
that your péople may rejóice in yóu?
Let us sée, O Lórd, your mércy*
and gíve us your sáving hélp.

I will héar what the Lord Gód has to sáy,*
a vóice that spéaks of péace,
péace for his péople and his fríends*
and those who túrn to hím in their héarts.
His help is néar for thóse who féar him*
and his glóry will dwéll in our lánd.

Mércy and faíthfulness have mét;*
jústice and péace have embráced.
Fáithfulness shall spríng from the éarth*
and jústice look dówn from héaven.

The Lórd will máke us prósper*
and our éarth shall yíeld its frúit.
Jústice shall márch befóre him*
and péace shall fóllow his stéps.

Ant. Lord, you blessed your land; you forgave the guilt of your people.
17–23 December: The Lord will come from his holy place: he will come to save his people.
Eastertide: You will restore our life again, Lord, and your people will rejoice in you, alleluia.

Ant. 2: At night my soul longs for you; I watch for you at daybreak.
17–23 December: We have a strong city, Sion. The Saviour will set up wall and rampart to guard it. Open the gates, for God is with us, alleluia.
Eastertide: We put our trust in the Lord and he gave us peace, alleluia.

HYMN AFTER VICTORY OVER THE ENEMY CANTICLE
IS 26:1-4,7-9,12

The city walls stood on twelve foundation stones (cf. Rev 21:14)

We have a strong city;*
he sets up salvation as walls and bulwarks.
Open the gates*
that the righteous nation which keeps faith may enter in.

You keep him in perfect peace,†
whose mind is stayed on you,*
because he trusts in you.
Trust in the Lord for ever,*
for the Lord God is an everlasting rock.

The way of the righteous is level;*
you make smooth the path of the righteous.
In the path of your judgments, O Lord,*
we wait for you.

My soul yearns for you in the night,*
my spirit within me earnestly seeks you;
for when your judgments are in the earth,*
the inhabitants of the world learn righteousness.

O Lord, you will ordain peace for us;*
you have wrought for us all our works.

Ant. At night my soul longs for you; I watch for you at daybreak.
17-23 December: We have a strong city, Sion. The Saviour will set
up wall and rampart to guard it. Open the gates, for God is with
us, alleluia.
Eastertide: We put our trust in the Lord and he gave us peace,
alleluia.

Ant. 3: Lord, let your face shed its light upon us.
17-23 December: Let us know your way on earth, Lord: let all the
peoples know your saving power.
Eastertide: The earth has yielded its fruit; let the nations be glad
and exult, alleluia.

When the following psalm has been used at the Invitatory ps 94, p 371,
is said here in place of it.

ALL THE PEOPLES WILL GIVE PRAISE TO THE LORD   PSALM 66(67)
Let it be known to you that this salvation from God has been sent to
all peoples (Acts 28:28)

O Gód, be grácious and bléss us*
and let your fáce shed its líght upón us.
So will your wáys be knówn upon éarth*
and all nátions learn your sáving hélp.

Let the péoples práise you, O Gód;*
let áll the péoples práise you.

Let the nátions be glád and exúlt*
for you rúle the wórld with jústice.
With fáirness you rúle the péoples,*
you guíde the nátions on éarth.

Let the péoples práise you, O Gód;*
let áll the péoples práise you.

The éarth has yíelded its frúit*
for Gód, our Gód, has bléssed us.
May Gód still gíve us his bléssing*
till the énds of the éarth revére him.

Let the péoples práise you, O Gód;*
let áll the péoples práise you.

Ant. Lord, let your face shed its light upon us.
17–23 December: Let us know your way on earth, Lord: let all the
peoples know your saving power.
Eastertide: The earth has yielded its fruit; let the nations be glad
and exult, alleluia.

THROUGH THE YEAR

Scripture Reading   *1 Jn 4:14-15*
We ourselves saw and we testify
that the Father sent his Son

as saviour of the world.
If anyone acknowledges that Jesus is the Son of God,
God lives in him, and he in God.

Short Responsory
R℟ My helper is my God; I will place my trust in him. *Repeat* R℟
℣ He is my refuge; he sets me free. R℟ Glory be. R℟

Benedictus ant. The Lord has raised up a mighty saviour for us, as he promised through the lips of his prophets.

Intercessions
By shedding his blood for us, Christ gathered together a new people from every corner of the earth. Let us pray to him: R℟ Christ, be mindful of your people.
Christ, our king and redeemer:—help us to know your power and your love. R℟
Christ, our hope and courage:—sustain us throughout the day. R℟
Christ, our refuge and strength:—fight with us against our weakness. R℟
Christ, our joy and solace:—stay with the poor and lonely. R℟
Our Father

Concluding Prayer
Almighty God,
to whom this world with all its goodness and beauty belongs,
give us grace joyfully to begin this day in your name,
and to fill it with an active love for you and our neighbour.
(We make our prayer) through our Lord.

EVENING PRAYER

Hymn, from the appendix, for the Season.

THROUGH THE YEAR
O Strength and Stay, upholding all creation,
Who ever dost thyself unmoved abide,

Yet day by day the light in due gradation
From hour to hour in all its changes guide,

Grant to life's day a calm unclouded ending,
An eve untouched by shadows of decay,
The brightness of a holy death-bed blending
With dawning glories of the eternal day.

Hear us, O Father, gracious and forgiving,
Through Jesus Christ thy co-eternal Word,
Who, with the Holy Ghost, by all things living
Now and to endless ages art adored.

PSALMODY

Ant. 1: The Lord surrounds his people.
17–23 December: The Lord will come from his holy place: he will come to save his people.
Eastertide: Peace be with you, it is I; do not be afraid, alleluia.

THE LORD, THE PROTECTOR OF HIS PEOPLE   PSALM 124(125)
Peace to the Israel of God (Gal 6:16)

Thóse who put their trúst in the Lórd†
are like Mount Síon, that cánnot be sháken,*
that stánds for éver.

Jerúsalem! The móuntains surróund her,†
so the Lórd surróunds his péople*
both nów and for éver.

For the scéptre of the wícked shall not rést*
over the lánd of the júst
for féar that the hánds of the júst*
should túrn to évil.

Do góod, Lord, to thóse who are góod,*
to the úpright of héart;
but the cróoked and thóse who do évil,†
dríve them awáy!*

On Ísrael, péace!

567

Ant. The Lord surrounds his people.

17–23 December: The Lord will come from his holy place: he will come to save his people.

Eastertide: Peace be with you, it is I; do not be afraid, alleluia.

Ant. 2: Unless you become like little children you will not enter the kingdom of heaven.

17–23 December: We have a strong city, Sion. The Saviour will set up wall and rampart to guard it. Open the gates, for God is with us, alleluia.

Eastertide: O Israel, hope in the Lord, alleluia.

CHILDLIKE CONFIDENCE IN THE LORD   PSALM 130(131)
Learn from me, for I am gentle and humble in heart (Mt 11:29)

O Lórd, my héart is not próud*
nor háughty my éyes.
I have not góne after thíngs too gréat*
nor márvels beyónd me.

Trúly I have sét my sóul*
in sílence and péace.
As a chíld has rést in its mother's árms,*
even só my sóul.

O Ísrael, hópe in the Lórd*
both nów and for éver.

Ant. Unless you become like little children you will not enter the kingdom of heaven.

17–23 December: We have a strong city, Sion. The Saviour will set up wall and rampart to guard it. Open the gates, for God is with us, alleluia.

Eastertide: O Israel, hope in the Lord, alleluia.

Ant. 3: Lord, you made us a kingdom and priests to serve our God.

17–23 December: Let us know your way on earth, Lord: let all the peoples know your saving power.

Eastertide: May your whole creation serve you; for you spoke and they came into being, alleluia.

HYMN OF THE REDEEMED   CANTICLE: REV 4:11;5:9,10,12

Worthy are you, our Lord and God,*
to receive glory and honour and power,
for you created all things,*
and by your will they existed and were created.

Worthy are you, O Lord,*
to take the scroll and to open its seals,
for you were slain,†
and by your blood you ransomed men for God*
from every tribe and tongue and people and nation.

You have made us a kingdom and priests to our God,*
and we shall reign on earth.

Worthy is the Lamb who was slain,*
to receive power and wealth,
and wisdom and might,*
and honour and glory and blessing.

Ant. Lord, you made us a kingdom and priests to serve our God.
17–23 December: Let us know your way on earth, Lord: let all the peoples know your saving power.
Eastertide: May your whole creation serve you; for you spoke and they came into being, alleluia.

THROUGH THE YEAR

Scripture Reading   *Rom 12:9-12*
Let love be genuine; hate what is evil, hold fast to what is good; love one another with brotherly affection; outdo one another in showing honour. Never flag in zeal, be aglow with the Spirit, serve the Lord. Rejoice in your hope, be patient in tribulation, be constant in prayer.

Short Responsory
R⁷ Your word, O Lord, will endure for ever. *Repeat* R⁷
V⁷ Your truth will last from age to age. R⁷ Glory be. R⁷

Magnificat ant. My spirit exults in the Lord God, my saviour.

Intercessions

God has established his people in hope. Nothing can break the confidence of those who love him. Let us proclaim: ℞ Father, our trust is in you.

We give you thanks, Lord God,—for you have made man rich in all wisdom and insight. ℞

Lord God, you know the hearts of all rulers:—may they work for the good of the people they govern. ℞

Lord, you empower mankind to glorify this world with art:—make our work live with vision and true hope. ℞

You do not allow us to be tempted beyond our limits:—strengthen the weak, raise up the fallen. ℞

Father, you have promised men a share in your Son's resurrection on the last day:—remember those who have gone before us on the path to eternal life. ℞

Our Father

Concluding Prayer

Let our evening prayer rise up before your throne of mercy, Lord, and let your blessing come down upon us:
so that now and for ever
your grace may help and save us.
(We make our prayer) through our Lord.

WEEK 3: WEDNESDAY

Invitatory ant. Let us adore the Lord, for it is he who made us.
Psalm, p 371.

MORNING PRAYER

Hymn, from the appendix, for the Season.

THROUGH THE YEAR
Lord God, your light which dims the stars
Awakes all things,
And all that springs to life in you
Your glory sings.

570

Your peaceful presence, giving strength,
Is everywhere,
And fallen men may rise again
On wings of prayer.

You are the God whose mercy rests
On all you made;
You gave us Christ, whose love through death
Our ransom paid.

We praise you, Father, with your Son
And Spirit blest.
In whom creation lives and moves,
And finds its rest.

PSALMODY

Ant. 1: Give joy to your servant, Lord, for to you I lift up my soul.
17–23 December: The Lord who is all-powerful will come from Sion
to save his people.
Eastertide: All the nations shall come to adore you, O Lord, alleluia.

PRAYER OF A POOR MAN IN DISTRESS   PSALM 85(86)
Blessed be God who comforts us in all our sorrows (2 Cor 1:3-4)

Turn your éar, O Lórd, and give ánswer*
for Í am póor and néedy.
Preserve my lífe, for Í am fáithful:*
save the sérvant who trústs in yóu.

You are my Gód, have mércy on me, Lórd,*
for I crý to you áll the day lóng.
Give jóy to your sérvant, O Lórd,*
for to yóu I líft up my sóul.

O Lórd, you are góod and forgíving,*
full of lóve to áll who cáll.
Give héed, O Lórd, to my práyer*
and atténd to the sóund of my vóice.

In the dáy of distréss I will cáll*
and súrely yóu will replý.
Among the góds there is nóne like you, O Lórd;*
nor wórk to compáre with yoúrs.

All the nátions shall cóme to adóre you*
and glórify your náme, O Lórd:
for you are gréat and do márvellous déeds,*
yóu who alóne are Gód.

Shów me, Lórd, your wáy†
so that Í may wálk in your trúth.*
Guide my héart to féar your náme.

I will práise you, Lord my Gód, with all my héart
and glórify your náme for éver;*
for your lóve to mé has been gréat:
you have sáved me from the dépths of the gráve.

The próud have rísen agáinst me;†
rúthless men séek my lífe:*
to yóu they páy no héed.

But yóu, God of mércy and compássion,*
slów to ánger, O Lórd,
abóunding in lóve and trúth,*
túrn and take píty on mé.

O gíve your stréngth to your sérvant*
and sáve your hándmaid's són.
Shów me a sígn of your fávour†
that my fóes may sée to their sháme*
that you consóle me and gíve me your hélp.

Ant. Give joy to your servant, Lord, for to you I lift up my soul.
17–23 December: The Lord who is all-powerful will come from Sion to save his people.
Eastertide: All the nations shall come to adore you, O Lord, alleluia.

Ant. 2: Blessed is the man who walks in justice and speaks what is true.

17–23 December: About Sion I will not be silent until her Holy One shines forth like light.

Eastertide: Our eyes will see the king in his splendour, alleluia.

GOD WILL RULE WITH JUSTICE   CANTICLE: IS 33:13-16
The promise that was made is for you and your children and for all those who are far away (Acts 2:39)

> Hear, you who are far off,*
> what I have done;
> and you who are near,*
> acknowledge my might.

> The sinners in Sion are afraid;*
> trembling has seized the godless:
> 'Who among us can dwell with the devouring fire?*
> Who among us can dwell with everlasting burnings?'

> He who walks righteously and speaks uprightly,†
> who despises the gain of oppressions,*
> who shakes his hands lest they hold a bribe,
> who stops his ears from hearing of bloodshed*
> and shuts his eyes from looking upon evil,

> He will dwell on the heights;*
> his place of defence will be the fortresses of rocks;
> his bread will be given him,*
> his water will be sure.

Ant. Blessed is the man who walks in justice and speaks what is true.

17–23 December: About Sion I will not be silent until her Holy One shines forth like light.

Eastertide: Our eyes will see the king in his splendour, alleluia.

Ant. 3: Acclaim the King, the Lord.

17–23 December: The Spirit of the Lord is upon me. He sent me to bring the Good News to the poor.

Eastertide: All men will see the salvation of our God, alleluia.

THE LORD IS VICTOR AND A JUST RULER   PSALM 97(98)
This psalm tells of the first coming of the Lord and of the faith of all peoples (St Athanasius)

Síng a new sóng to the Lórd*
for hé has worked wónders.
His ríght hand and his hóly árm*
have bróught salvátion.

The Lórd has made knówn his salvátion;*
has shown his jústice to the nátions.
He has remémbered his trúth and lóve*
for the hóuse of Ísrael.

All the énds of the éarth have séen*
the salvátion of our Gód.
Shóut to the Lórd all the éarth,*
ríng out your jóy.

Sing psálms to the Lórd with the hárp*
with the sóund of músic.
With trúmpets and the sóund of the hórn*
acclaim the Kíng, the Lórd.

Let the séa and all withín it, thúnder;*
the wórld, and all its péoples.
Let the rívers cláp their hánds*
and the hílls ring out their jóy.

Rejóice at the présence of the Lórd,*
for he comes to rúle the éarth.
He will rúle the wórld with jústice*
and the péoples with fáirness.

Ant. Acclaim the King, the Lord.
17–23 December: The Spirit of the Lord is upon me. He sent me to bring the Good News to the poor.
Eastertide: All men will see the salvation of our God, alleluia.

Scripture Reading   *Job 1:21;2:10b*
Naked I came from my mother's womb,
naked I shall return.
The Lord gave, the Lord has taken back.
Blessed be the name of the Lord!
If we take happiness from God's hand, must we not take sorrow too?

Short Responsory
R℣ Bend my heart to your will, O God. *Repeat* R℣
℣ By your word, give me life. R℣ Glory be. R℣

Benedictus ant. Show us your mercy, O Lord; remember your holy covenant.

Intercessions
God is love: he who dwells in love dwells in God, and God in him.
In Jesus Christ we see how God loves us. Let us renew our faith
in his love: R℣ Lord Jesus, you loved us and gave yourself for us.
You have given us life and light this morning:—let us give thanks
for such great gifts. R℣
You are sole master of the future:—keep us from despair and the
fear of what is to come. R℣
Love has no ambition to seek anything for itself:—strengthen our
will to give up selfishness today. R℣
May your love in us overcome all things:—let there be no limit to
our faith, our hope, and our endurance. R℣
Our Father

Concluding Prayer
Lord God,
in your wisdom you created us,
by your providence you rule us:
penetrate our inmost being with your holy light,
so that our way of life
may always be one of faithful service to you.
(We make our prayer) through our Lord.

EVENING PRAYER

Hymn, from the appendix, for the Season.

THROUGH THE YEAR

Christ be near at either hand,
Christ behind, before me stand
Christ with me where e'er I go,
Christ around, above, below.

Christ be in my heart and mind,
Christ within my soul enshrined,
Christ control my wayward heart;
Christ abide and ne'er depart.

Christ my life and only way,
Christ my lantern night and day;
Christ be my unchanging friend,
Guide and shepherd to the end.

PSALMODY

Ant. 1: Those who were sowing in tears, will sing when they reap.
17–23 December: The Lord who is all-powerful will come from Sion to save his people.
Eastertide: Your sorrow will turn to joy, alleluia.

JOY AND HOPE IN GOD   PSALM 125(126)
Just as you are sharing in our sufferings, so also will you share our consolations (2 Cor 1:7)

When the Lórd delivered Síon from bóndage,*
It séemed like a dréam.
Thén was our móuth filled with láughter,*
on our líps there were sóngs.

The héathens themsélves said: 'What márvels*
the Lórd worked for thém!'
What márvels the Lórd worked for ús!*
Indéed we were glád.

Delíver us, O Lórd, from our bóndage*
as stréams in dry lánd.
Thóse who are sówing in téars*
will síng when they réap.

They go óut, they go óut, full of téars,*
carrying séed for the sówing:
they come báck, they come báck, full of sóng,*
cárrying their shéaves.

Ant. Those who were sowing in tears, will sing when they reap.
17–23 December: The Lord who is all-powerful will come from Sion to save his people.
Eastertide: Your sorrow will turn to joy, alleluia.

Ant. 2: The Lord will build a house for us; he will watch over our city.
17–23 December: About Sion I will not be silent until her Holy One shines forth like light.
Eastertide: Whether we live or whether we die, we belong to the Lord, alleluia.

SUCCESS DEPENDS ON THE LORD'S BLESSING   PSALM 126(127)
You are God's building (1 Cor 3:9)

If the Lórd does not buíld the hóuse,*
in váin do its buílders lábour;
if the Lórd does not wátch over the cíty,*
in váin does the wátchman keep vígil.

In váin is your éarlier rísing,*
your góing láter to rést,
you who tóil for the bréad you éat:*
when he pours gífts on his belóved while they slúmber.

Truly sóns are a gíft from the Lórd,*
a bléssing, the frúit of the wómb.
Indéed the sóns of yóuth*
are like árrows in the hánd of a wárrior.

Ó the háppiness of the mán*
who has fílled his quíver with these árrows!
Hé will have no cáuse for sháme*
when he dispútes with his fóes in the gáteways.

Ant. The Lord will build a house for us; he will watch over our city.
17–23 December: About Sion I will not be silent until her Holy
One shines forth like light.
Eastertide: Whether we live or whether we die, we belong to the
Lord, alleluia.

Ant. 3: He is the first-born of all creation; he is supreme over all
creatures.
17–23 December: The Spirit of the Lord is upon me   He sent me to
bring the Good News to the poor.
Eastertide: From him, through him and in him are all things that
exist: to him be glory for ever, alleluia.

CHRIST IS THE FIRST-BORN OF ALL CREATION   CANCICLE
THE FIRST-BORN FROM THE DEAD   COL 1:12-20

Let us give thanks to the Father,†
who has qualified us to share*
in the inheritance of the saints in light.

He has delivered us from the dominion of darkness*
and transferred us to the kingdom of his beloved Son,
in whom we have redemption,*
the forgiveness of sins.

He is the image of the invisible God,*
the first-born of all creation,
for in him all things were created, in heaven and on earth,*
visible and invisible.

All things were created*
through him and for him.
He is before all things,*
and in him all things hold together.

He is the head of the body, the Church;*
he is the beginning,
the first-born from the dead,*
that in everything he might be pre-eminent.

For in him all the fulness of God was pleased to dwell,*
and through him to reconcile to himself all things,
whether on earth or in heaven,*
making peace by the blood of his cross.

Ant. He is the first-born of all creation; he is supreme over all creatures.

17–23 December: The Spirit of the Lord is upon me. He sent me to bring the Good News to the poor.

Eastertide: From him, through him and in him are all things that exist: to him be glory for ever, alleluia.

THROUGH THE YEAR

Scripture Reading　　　*Eph 3:20-21*
To him who is able to do so much more than we can ever ask for, or even think of, by means of the power working in us: to God be the glory in the church and in Christ Jesus, for all time, for ever and ever! Amen.

Short Responsory
R̸ Redeem me, Lord, and show me your mercy. *Repeat* R̸
V̸ Do not cast me away with sinners. R̸ Glory be. R̸

Magnificat ant. The Almighty has done great things for me; Holy is his name.

Intercessions
I may have faith strong enough to move mountains: but if I have no love, I am nothing. With this in mind we pray: R̸ Lord, grant us your love.

Lord, sustain us as we build and grow towards you:—increase our faith as we work. R̸

We are assailed by doubts, and weighed down by uncertainties,—

release our hearts, to journey towards you with hope. ℟ Lord, grant us your love.

Love keeps no score of wrong, and does not gloat over evil:—help us to delight in the truth, and rejoice in your gifts to others. ℟

Confirm the pilgrim Church in the faith of the apostles:—help us to encourage each other, sharing our gifts. ℟

Bring those who have died in your peace to that knowledge which fulfils faith and answers hope,—grant them the fulness of your love. ℟

Our Father

Concluding Prayer

Let your people's cry come into your loving presence, Lord.
Forgive them their sins,
so that by your grace they may be devoted to your service,
and rest secure under your protecting hand.
(We make our prayer) through our Lord.

WEEK 3: THURSDAY

Invitatory ant. Come, let us adore the Lord, for he is our God. *Psalm, p 371.*

MORNING PRAYER

Hymn, from the appendix, for the Season.

THROUGH THE YEAR
　　The Father's glory, Christ our light,
　　With love and mercy comes to span
　　The vast abyss of sin between
　　The God of holiness and man.

　　Christ yesterday and Christ today,
　　For all eternity the same,
　　The image of our hidden God;
　　Eternal Wisdom is his name.

He keeps his word from age to age,
Is with us to the end of days,
A cloud by day, a flame by night,
To go before us on his ways.

We bless you, Father, fount of light,
And Christ, your well-beloved Son,
Who with the Spirit dwell in us:
Immortal Trinity in One.

PSALMODY

Ant. 1: Glorious things are told of you, O city of God.
17–23 December: I look to you, Lord, for help; come and save me,
Lord, for I seek refuge in you.
Eastertide: We will dance and sing; you are the source of our life
and our joy, city of God, alleluia.

JERUSALEM, MOTHER OF ALL NATIONS   PSALM 86(87)
The Jerusalem which is above is free and is our mother (Gal 4:26)

On the hóly móuntain is his cíty*
chérished by the Lórd.
The Lórd prefers the gátes of Síon*
to áll Jacob's dwéllings.
Of yóu are told glórious thíngs,*
O cíty of Gód!

'Bábylon and Égypt I will cóunt*
among thóse who knów me;
Philístia, Týre, Ethiópia,*
thése will be her chíldren
and Síon shall be cálled "Móther"*
for áll shall be her chíldren.'

It is hé, the Lórd Most Hígh,*
who gives éach his pláce.
In his régister of péoples he wrítes:*
'Thése are her chíldren'
and whíle they dánce they will síng:*
'In yóu all find their hóme.'

581

Ant. Glorious things are told of you, O city of God.

17–23 December: I look to you, Lord, for help; come and save me, Lord, for I seek refuge in you.

Eastertide: We will dance and sing; you are the source of our life and our joy, city of God, alleluia.

Ant. 2: The Lord is coming in power; the prize of his victory is with him.

17–23 December: Lord, give those who wait for you their reward, and let your prophets be found worthy of belief.

Eastertide: He will tend his flock like a shepherd and carry them in his arms, alleluia.

THE GOOD SHEPHERD: CANTICLE
  GOD MOST-HIGH AND ALL WISE   IS 40:10-17
Behold, I come quickly, and my reward is with me (Rev 22:12)

Behold, the Lord God comes with might,*
and his arm rules for him;
behold, his reward is with him,*
and his recompense before him.

He will feed his flock like a shepherd,*
he will gather the lambs in his arms,
he will carry them in his bosom,*
and gently lead those that are with young.

Who has measured the waters in the hollow of his hand*
and marked off the heavens with a span,
enclosed the dust of the earth in a measure†
and weighed the mountains in scales*
and the hills in a balance?

Who has directed the Spirit of the Lord,*
or as his counsellor has instructed him?
Whom did he consult for his enlightenment,*
and who taught him the path of justice,
taught him knowledge,*
and showed him the way of understanding?

Behold, the nations are like a drop from a bucket,*
and are accounted as the dust on the scales;
behold, he takes up the isles*
like fine dust.

Lebanon would not suffice for fuel,*
nor are its beasts enough for a burnt offering.
All the nations are as nothing before him,*
they are accounted by him as less than nothing and emptiness.

Ant. The Lord is coming in power; the prize of his victory is with him·
17–23 December: Lord, give those who wait for you their reward,
and let your prophets be found worthy of belief.
Eastertide: He will tend his flock like a shepherd and carry them in
his arms, alleluia.

Ant. 3: Exalt the Lord our God; bow down before his holy mountain.
17–23 December: Turn to us, Lord, and make no delay in coming to
your servants.
Eastertide: The Lord is great in Sion; he is supreme above all
peoples, alleluia.

THE LORD OUR GOD IS HOLY   PSALM 98(99)
*You are higher than Cherubim; you changed the bad state of the
earth, when you came in a nature like ours* (St Athanasius)

The Lórd is kíng; the péoples trémble.†
He is thróned on the chérubim; the eárth quákes.*
The Lórd is gréat in Síon.

Hé is supréme over áll the péoples.†
Let them práise his náme, so térrible and gréat.*
He is hóly, fúll of pówer.

Yóu are a kíng who lóves what is ríght;†
you have estáblished équity, jústice and ríght;*
yóu have estáblished them in Jácob.

583

Exált the Lórd our Gód;†
bow dówn before Síon, his fóotstool.*
Hé the Lórd is hóly.

Amóng his príests were Áaron and Móses,†
among thóse who invóked his náme was Sámuel.*
They invóked the Lórd and he ánswered.

To thém he spóke in the píllar of clóud.†
They díd his wíll; they képt the láw,*
which hé, the Lórd, had gíven.

O Lórd our Gód, you ánswered thém.†
For thém yóu were a Gód who forgíves;*
yet you púnished áll their offénces.
Exált the Lórd our Gód;†
bow dówn before his hóly móuntain*
for the Lórd our Gód is hóly.

Ant. Exalt the Lord our God; bow down before his holy mountain.
17-23 December: Turn to us, Lord and make no delay in coming to your servants.
Eastertide: The Lord is great in Sion; he is supreme above all peoples, alleluia.

THROUGH THE YEAR

Scripture Reading   *1 Pet 4:10-11*
Each one of you has received a special grace, so, like good stewards responsible for all these different graces of God, put yourselves at the service of others. If you are a speaker, speak in words which seem to come from God; if you are a helper, help as though every action was done at God's orders; so that in everything God may receive the glory through Jesus Christ.

Short Responsory
R℣ I called with all my heart; Lord, hear me. *Repeat* R℣
℣ I will keep your commandments. R℣ Glory be. R℣

Benedictus ant. Let us serve the Lord in holiness, and he will deliver us from the hands of our enemies.

Intercessions

We adore and praise our God who reigns above the heavens. He is the Lord of all things and before him all creation is as nothing.

R̷ We adore you, our Lord and God.

Eternal Father, it is by your gift that we praise you:—the wonder of our making is only surpassed by the splendour and joy of our coming to life in Christ. R̷

Lord, be with us as we start a new day:—move our hearts to seek you and our wills to serve you. R̷

Deepen our awareness of your presence:—teach us reverence and love for all that you made. R̷

To know you is to love those you created:—let our lives and our work be of service to our brothers. R̷

Our Father

Concluding Prayer

Almighty, ever-living God,
shed the light of your glory
on the peoples who are living in the shadow of death,
as you did long ago,
when our Lord Jesus Christ, the Sun of Justice,
came among us from on high.
(We make our prayer) through our Lord.

EVENING PRAYER

Hymn, from the appendix, for the Season.

THROUGH THE YEAR

When God had filled the earth with life
And blessed it, to increase,
Then cattle dwelt with creeping things,
And lion with lamb, at peace.

He gave them vast, untrodden lands,
With plants to be their food;
Then God saw all that he had made
And found it very good.

Praise God the Father for all life,
His Son and Spirit blest,
By whom creation lives and moves,
In whom it comes to rest.

PSALMODY

Ant. 1: Your faithful shall ring out their joy as they enter your dwelling place, Lord.
17–23 December: I look to you, Lord, for help; come and save me, Lord, for I seek refuge in you.
Eastertide: The Lord God gave him the throne of David, his father, alleluia.

THE PROMISE OF GOD   PSALM 131(132)
    TO THE HOUSE OF DAVID
The Lord God will give him the throne of David, his father (Lk 1:32)

I

O Lórd, remémber Dávid*
and áll the many hárdships he endúred,
the óath he swóre to the Lórd,*
his vów to the Stróng One of Jácob.

'I will not énter the hóuse where I líve*
nor gó to the béd where I rést.
I will gíve no sléep to my éyes*
to my éyelids I will gíve no slúmber
till I fínd a pláce for the Lórd,*
a dwélling for the Stróng One of Jácob.'

At Éphrata we héard of the árk;*
we fóund it in the pláins of Yearím.
'Let us gó to the pláce of his dwélling;*
let us gó to knéel at his fóotstool.'

Go up, Lórd, to the pláce of your rést,*
yóu and the árk of your stréngth.
Your príests shall be clóthed with hóliness:*
your fáithful shall ríng out their jóy.

For the sáke of Dávid your sérvant*
dó not rejéct your anóinted.

Ant. Your faithful shall ring out their joy as they enter your dwelling place, Lord.
17–23 December: I look to you, Lord, for help; come and save me, Lord, for I seek refuge in you.
Eastertide: The Lord God gave him the throne of David, his father, alleluia.

Ant. 2: The Lord has chosen Sion as his dwelling place.
17–23 December: Lord, give those who wait for you their reward, and let your prophets be found worthy of belief.
Eastertide: Jesus Christ is the only Ruler over all, the King of kings and Lord of lords, alleluia.

II

The Lórd swore an óath to Dávid;*
he wíll not go báck on his wórd:
'A són, the frúit of your bódy,*
will I sét upón your thróne.

If they kéep my cóvenant in trúth*
and my láws that Í have táught them,
their sóns álso shall rúle*
on your thróne from áge to áge.'

For the Lórd has chósen Síon;*
he has desíred it fór his dwélling:
'Thís is my résting-place for éver,*
hére have I chósen to líve.

I will gréatly bléss her próduce,*
I will fíll her póor with bréad.
I will clóthe her príests with salvátion*
and her fáithful shall ríng out their jóy.

Thére David's stóck will flówer:*
I will prepáre a lámp for my anóinted.
I will cóver his énemies with sháme*
but on hím my crówn shall shíne.'   Glory be.

587

Ant. The Lord has chosen Sion as his dwelling place.

17–23 December: Lord, give those who wait for you their reward, and let your prophets be found worthy of belief.

Eastertide: Jesus Christ is the only Ruler over all, the King of kings and Lord of lords, alleluia.

Ant. 3: The Lord has given him power and honour and empire and all peoples will serve him.

17–23 December: Turn to us, Lord, and make no delay in coming to your servants.

Eastertide: Lord, who is your like, majestic in strength and holiness, alleluia?

THE JUDGMENT OF GOD   CANTICLE
                                        REV 11:17-18;12:10B-12A

We give thanks to you, Lord God Almighty,*
who are and who were,
that you have taken your great power*
and begun to reign.

The nations raged,*
but your wrath came,
and the time for the dead to be judged,*
for rewarding your servants, the prophets and saints,
and those who fear your name,*
both small and great.

Now the salvation and the power†
and the kingdom of our God*
and the authority of his Christ have come,
for the accuser of our brethren has been thrown down,*
who accuses them day and night before our God.

And they have conquered him*
by the blood of the Lamb
and by the word of their testimony,*
for they loved not their lives even unto death.
Rejoice, then, O heaven*
and you that dwell therein.

Ant. The Lord has given him power and honour and empire and all peoples will serve him.

17–23 December: Turn to us, Lord, and make no delay in coming to your servants.

Eastertide: Lord, who is your like, majestic in strength and holiness, alleluia?

THROUGH THE YEAR

Scripture Reading   *1 Pet 3:8-9*

You should all agree among yourselves and be sympathetic; love the brothers, have compassion and be modest and humble. Never pay back one wrong with another, or an angry word with another one; instead, pay back with a blessing. That is what you are called to do, so that you inherit a blessing yourself.

Short Responsory

R℣ The Lord fed us with finest wheat. *Repeat* R℣

℣ He filled us with honey from the rock. R℣ Glory be. R℣

Magnificat ant. The Lord brought down the mighty from their seats, and raised up the lowly.

Intercessions

Christ is the high priest of his people: it is in him that we come together to make our prayer to the Father of us all. R℣ Father, put new hearts within us.

We thank you for calling us into the Church:—bless us with constant faith, and make it a source of life for others. R℣

Lord, bless N., our Pope:—we pray that his faith may not fail, and that he may strengthen his brothers. R℣

Turn sinners back to you:—grant us a humble and contrite heart. R℣

Your Son knew what it was to be excluded from his homeland.— Be mindful of those who must live far from their family and country. R℣

Give eternal rest to the dead:—bring the whole Church together in heaven. R℣

Our Father

Concluding Prayer
We offer you, Lord, our thanksgiving
at the close of this day:
in your mercy forgive the faults we have committed through
  human frailty.
(We make our prayer) through our Lord.

WEEK 3: FRIDAY

Invitatory ant. Give thanks to the Lord, for his great love is without
end.
Psalm, p 371.

MORNING PRAYER

Hymn, from the appendix, for the Season.

THROUGH THE YEAR
  We bless you, Father, Lord of Life,
  To whom all living beings tend,
  The source of holiness and grace,
  Our first beginning and our end.

  We give you thanks, Redeeming Christ,
  Who bore our weight of sin and shame;
  In dark defeat you conquered sin,
  And death, by dying, overcame.

  Come, Holy Spirit, searching fire,
  Whose flame all evil burns away.
  Come down to us with light and love,
  In silence and in peace to stay.

  We praise you, Trinity in One,
  Sublime in majesty and might,
  Who reign for ever, Lord of all,
  In splendour and unending light.

PSALMODY

Ant. 1: Against you alone have I sinned; Lord, have mercy on me.
17–23 December: The one who is to rule will come from Sion: 'The Lord, Immanuel' is his great name.
Eastertide: O Lord, wash me more and more from my guilt, alleluia.

O GOD, HAVE MERCY ON ME   PSALM 50(51)
You must be made new in mind and spirit, and put on the new nature
(Eph 4:23-24)

Have mércy on me, Gód, in your kíndness.*
In your compássion blot óut my offénce.
O wásh me more and móre from my guílt*
and cléanse me fróm my sín.

My offénces trúly I knów them;*
my sín is álways befóre me.
Against yóu, you alóne, have I sínned;*
what is évil in your síght I have dóne.

That you may be jústified whén you give séntence*
and be withóut repróach when you júdge,
O sée, in guílt I was bórn,*
a sínner was Í concéived.

Indéed you love trúth in the héart;*
then in the sécret of my héart teach me wísdom.
O púrify me, thén I shall be cléan;*
O wásh me, I shall be whíter than snów.

Make me héar rejóicing and gládness,*
that the bónes you have crúshed may revíve.
From my síns turn awáy your fáce*
and blót out áll my guílt.

A púre heart creáte for me, O Gód,*
put a stéadfast spírit withín me.
Do not cást me awáy from your présence,*
nor depríve me of your hóly spírit.

Give me agáin the jóy of your hélp;*
with a spírit of férvour sustáin me,
that I may téach transgréssors your wáys*
and sínners may retúrn to yóu.

O réscue me, Gód, my hélper,*
and my tóngue shall ríng out your góodness.
O Lórd, ópen my líps*
and my móuth shall decláre your práise.

For in sácrifice you táke no delíght,*
burnt óffering from mé you would refúse,
my sácrifice, a cóntrite spírit.*
A húmbled, contrite héart you will not spúrn.

In your góodness, show fávour to Síon:*
rebuíld the wálls of Jerúsalem.
Thén you will be pléased with lawful sácrifice,*
hólocausts óffered on your áltar.

Ant. Against you alone have I sinned; Lord, have mercy on me.
17–23 December: The one who is to rule will come from Sion: 'The Lord, Immanuel' is his great name.
Eastertide: O Lord, wash me more and more from my guilt, alleluia.

Ant. 2: We know our offences, Lord; we have sinned against you.
17–23 December: Stand steadfast. You will see the helping power of the Lord.
Eastertide: Christ bore our sins in his own body on the cross, alleluia.

LAMENT OF THE PEOPLE IN TIME   CANTICLE
OF FAMINE AND WAR   JER 14:17-21
The kingdom of God is at hand. Repent, and believe in the gospel
(Mk 1:15)

Let my eyes run down with tears night and day,*
and let them not cease,
for the virgin daughter of my people is smitten with a
    great wound,*

592

with a very grievous blow.

If I go out into the field,*
behold, those slain by the sword!
And if I enter the city,*
behold, the diseases of famine!
For both prophet and priest ply their trade through the land,*
and have no knowledge.

Have you utterly rejected Judah?
Does your soul loathe Sion?
Why have you smitten us*
so that there is no healing for us?

We looked for peace,*
but no good came;
for a time of healing,*
but behold, terror.

We acknowledge our wickedness, O Lord,†
and the iniquity of our fathers,*
for we have sinned against you.
Do not spurn us, for your name's sake,†
do not dishonour your glorious throne;*
remember and do not break your covenant with us.

Ant. We know our offences, Lord; we have sinned against you.
17–23 December: Stand steadfast. You will see the helping power
of the Lord.
Eastertide: Christ bore our sins in his own body on the cross,
alleluia.

Ant. 3: The Lord is God; we are his people, the sheep of his flock.
17–23 December: I look to the Lord; I will await the God who
saves me.
Eastertide: Come before the Lord, singing for joy, alleluia.

When the following psalm has been used at the Invitatory, ps 94, p 371,
is said here in place of it.

THE JOY OF THOSE WHO ENTER   PSALM 99(100)
THE TEMPLE OF THE LORD

The Lord calls all those he has redeemed to sing a hymn of victory
(St Athanasius)

Cry out with jóy to the Lórd, all the éarth.†
Sérve the Lórd with gládness.*
Come befóre him, sínging for jóy.

Know that hé, the Lórd, is Gód.†
He máde us, we belóng to hím,*
we are his péople, the shéep of his flóck.

Gó within his gátes, giving thánks.†
Enter his cóurts with sóngs of práise.*
Give thánks to him and bléss his náme.

Indéed, how góod is the Lórd,†
etérnal his mérciful lóve.*
He is fáithful from áge to áge.

Ant. The Lord is God; we are his people, the sheep of his flock.
17–23 December: I look to the Lord; I will await the God who saves me.
Eastertide: Come before the Lord, singing for joy, alleluia.

THROUGH THE YEAR

Scripture Reading   *2 Cor 12:9b-10*
I am most happy, then, to be proud of my weaknesses, in order to
feel the protection of Christ's power over me. I am content with
weaknesses, insults, hardships, persecutions, and difficulties for
Christ's sake. For when I am weak, then I am strong.

Short Responsory
R̥ In the morning let me know your love. *Repeat* R̥
℣ Make me know the way I should walk. R̥ Glory be. R̥

Benedictus ant. The Lord has visited his people, he has come to
redeem them.

Intercessions

We have a high priest, able to sympathize with us in our weakness, one who, because of his likeness to us, has been tempted in every way, but did not sin. Let us pray to him: ℟ Show us your mercy and compassion.

Lord, for the joy which lay in the future, you willingly went to the cross:—make us share your death, that we may also share your joy. ℟

Lord, you said 'Let any man who thirsts come to me and drink':—give your Spirit now to those who thirst for you. ℟

You sent your disciples to preach the gospel to every nation:—bless those men and women who devote their lives to preaching the gospel today. ℟

Help those in pain to know that the Father cares for them—for he loves them as he loves his own Son. ℟

Our Father

Concluding Prayer

Almighty Father,
let your light so penetrate our minds,
that walking by your commandments
we may always follow you, our leader and guide.
(We make our prayer) through our Lord.

EVENING PRAYER

Hymn, from the appendix, for the Season.

THROUGH THE YEAR

When God made man he gave him all the earth,
All growing things, with every bird and beast;
Then Adam named them at the Lord's command,
Subdued the greatest of them, and the least.

In his own image God created man,
And when from dust he fashioned Adam's face,
The likeness of his only Son was formed:
His Word incarnate, filled with truth and grace.

To God the Father and to Christ his Son
And blessèd Spirit heav'n and earth give praise.
Creation with tremendous voice cries out:
All holy is the mighty Lord of days.

PSALMODY

Ant. 1: The Lord is great; our God is high above all gods.
17–23 December: The one who is to rule will come from Sion:
'The Lord, Immanuel' is his great name.
Eastertide: I, the Lord, am your Saviour, I am your Redeemer,
alleluia.

PRAISE FOR THE LORD   PSALM 134(135)
  WHO DOES MARVELLOUS THINGS
*You are a chosen race. Sing the praises of the one who called you out
of darkness into his wonderful light* (1 Pet 2:9)

I

Práise the náme of the Lórd,*
práise him, sérvants of the Lórd,
who stánd in the hóuse of the Lórd*
in the cóurts of the hóuse of our Gód.

Praise the Lórd for the Lórd is góod.*
Sing a psálm to his náme for he is lóving.
For the Lórd has chosen Jácob for himsélf*
and Ísrael for his ówn posséssion.

For I knów the Lórd is gréat,*
that our Lórd is hígh above all góds.
The Lórd does whatéver he wílls,*
in héaven, on éarth, in the séas.

He summons clóuds from the énds of the éarth;†
makes líghtning prodúce the ráin;*
from his tréasuries he sénds forth the wínd.

The fírst-born of the Egýptians he smóte,*
of mán and béast alíke.
Sígns and wónders he wórked†

in the mídst of your lánd, O Égypt,*
against Pháraoh and áll his sérvants.

Nátions in their gréatness he strúck*
and kíngs in their spléndour he sléw.
Síhon, kíng of the Ámorites,†
Óg, the kíng of Báshan,*
and áll the kíngdoms of Cánaan.
He let Ísrael inhérit their lánd;*
on his péople their lánd he bestówed.

Ant. The Lord is great; our God is high above all gods.
17–23 December: The one who is to rule will come from Sion: 'The Lord, Immanuel' is his great name.
Eastertide: I, the Lord, am your Saviour, I am your Redeemer, alleluia.

Ant. 2: Sons of Israel, bless the Lord! Sing a psalm to his name, for he is loving.
17–23 December: Stand steadfast. You will see the helping power of the Lord.
Eastertide: Blessed is the kingdom of our father David which has come among us, alleluia.

II

Lórd, your náme stands for éver,*
unforgótten from áge to áge:
for the Lórd does jústice for his péople;*
the Lórd takes píty on his sérvants.

Pagan ídols are sílver and góld,*
the wórk of húman hánds.
They have móuths but they cánnot spéak;*
they have éyes but they cánnot sée.

They have éars but they cánnot héar;*
there is néver a bréath on their líps.
Their mákers will come to bé like thém*
and so will áll who trúst in thém!

Sons of Ísrael, bléss the Lórd!*
Sons of Áaron, bléss the Lórd!
Sons of Lévi, bléss the Lórd!*
You who féar him, bléss the Lórd!

From Síon may the Lórd be bléssed,*
hé who dwélls in Jerúsalem!

Ant. Sons of Israel, bless the Lord! Sing a psalm to his name, for he is loving.
17-23 December: Stand steadfast. You will see the helping power of the Lord.
Eastertide: Blessed is the kingdom of our father David which has come among us, alleluia.

Ant. 3: All peoples will come and adore you, Lord.
17-23 December: I look to the Lord; I will await the God who saves me.
Eastertide: Let us sing to the Lord; great is his triumph, alleluia.

HYMN OF ADORATION   CANTICLE: REV 15:3-4
Great and wonderful are your deeds,*
O Lord God the Almighty!
Just and true are your ways,*
O King of the ages†

Who shall not fear and glorify your name, O Lord?*
For you alone are holy.
All nations shall come and worship you,*
for your judgments have been revealed.

Ant. All peoples will come and adore you, Lord.
17-23 December: I look to the Lord; I will await the God who saves me.
Eastertide: Let us sing to the Lord; great is his triumph, alleluia.

THROUGH THE YEAR

Scripture Reading   *Jas 1:2-4*
My brothers! Consider yourselves fortunate when all kinds of

trials come your way, because you know that when your faith succeeds in facing such trials, the result is the ability to endure. Be sure that your endurance carries you all the way, without failing, so that you may be perfect and complete, lacking nothing.

Short Responsory

R̷ Christ loved us and has washed away our sins with his blood. *Repeat* R̷

V̷ He made us a line of kings, priests to serve God. R̷ Glory be. R̷

Magnificat ant. The Lord has come to help us, his servants; he has remembered his mercy.

Intercessions

Father, Christ prayed that we be forgiven through his passion. As you accepted him, accept his prayer for all sinners. R̷ Father, into your hands I commend my spirit.

Through his beloved disciple, Jesus gave us Mary to be our mother;
—with her we pray to you for all her children. R̷

Father, heed the anguish of those who cry out to you with your Son:—'My God, my God, why have you forsaken me?' R̷

Help us to hear the cry, 'I thirst';—help us to see your Son, even in the least of his brothers. R̷

To the man dying with him, Jesus said, 'Truly I say to you, this day you will be with me in Paradise.'—Father, let those words be heard again by those who die tonight. R̷

We pray for those who have gone before us, signed with the sign of the cross:—may they rise with Christ in power when his voice resounds again through the universe: 'It is consummated.' R̷

Our Father

Concluding Prayer

Holy Father and Lord,
you willed that Christ your Son
should be the price of our salvation.
Give us grace so to live,
that through sharing his sufferings
we may be strengthened by the power of his resurrection,

who lives and reigns with you and the Holy Spirit,
God, for ever and ever.

WEEK 3: SATURDAY

Invitatory ant. The Lord's is the earth and its fulness: come, let
us adore him.
Psalm, p 371.

MORNING PRAYER

Hymn, from the appendix, for the Season.

THROUGH THE YEAR
It were my soul's desire
To see the face of God;
It were my soul's desire
To rest in his abode.

Grant, Lord, my soul's desire,
Deep waves of cleansing sighs,
Grant, Lord, my soul's desire,
From earthly cares to rise.

It were my soul's desire
To imitate my King,
It were my soul's desire
His endless praise to sing.

It were my soul's desire,
When heaven's gate is won,
To find my soul's desire,
Clear shining like the sun.

This still my soul's desire,
Whatever life afford,
To gain my soul's desire
And see thy face, O Lord.

PSALMODY

Ant. 1: You, O Lord, are close: your ways are truth.
17–23 December: God will come from Lebanon and his splendour
is like the light.
Eastertide: The words I have spoken to you are spirit and they are
life, alleluia.

PSALM 118(119):145-152 XIX(KOPH)

I cáll with all my héart; Lord, héar me,*
I will kéep your commánds.
I cáll upón you, sáve me*
and Í will do your wíll.

I ríse before dáwn and cry for hélp,*
I hópe in your wórd.
My éyes wátch through the níght*
to pónder your prómise.

In your lóve hear my vóice, O Lórd;*
give me lífe by your decrées.
Those who hárm me unjústly draw néar:*
they are fár from your láw.

But yóu, O Lórd, are clóse:*
your commánds are trúth.
Lóng have I knówn that your wíll*
is estáblished for éver.

Ant. You, O Lord, are close: your ways are truth.
17–23 December: God will come from Lebanon and his splendour
is like the light.
Eastertide: The words I have spoken to you are spirit and they are
life, alleluia.

Ant. 2: Lord, let your wisdom be with me to help me and to work
with me.
17–23 December: Send the Holy One, like the dew, you heavens,
and let the clouds rain down. Let the earth open for the Saviour to
spring forth.

Eastertide: Lord, you have set up your temple and altar on your holy mountain, alleluia.

O LORD, GIVE ME WISDOM   CANTICLE: WIS 9:1-6,9-11
I myself will give you an eloquence and a wisdom that none of your
opponents will be able to resist (Lk 21:15)

O God of my fathers and Lord of mercy,*
who have made all things by your word,
and by your wisdom have formed man*
to have dominion over the creatures you have made,
and rule the world in holiness and righteousness,*
and pronounce judgment in uprightness of soul,
give me the wisdom that sits by your throne,*
and do not reject me from among your servants.

For I am your slave*
and the son of your maidservant,
a man who is weak and short-lived,*
with little understanding of judgment and laws;
for even if one is perfect among the sons of men,†
yet without the wisdom that comes from you*
he will be regarded as nothing.

With you is wisdom, who knows your works*
and was present when you made the world,
and who understands what is pleasing in your sight*
and what is right according to your commandments.

Send her forth from the holy heavens,*
and from the throne of your glory send her,
that she may be with me and toil,*
and that I may learn what is pleasing to you;
for she knows and understands all things,†
and she will guide me wisely in my actions*
and guard me with her glory.

Ant. Lord, let your wisdom be with me to help me and to work with me.

602

17–23 December: Send the Holy One, like the dew, you heavens, and let the clouds rain down. Let the earth open for the Saviour to spring forth.
Eastertide: Lord, you have set up your temple and altar on your holy mountain, alleluia.

Ant. 3: The truth of the Lord will stand firm for ever.
17–23 December: Israel, be ready to meet the Lord, for he is coming.
Eastertide: I am the Way, the Truth and the Life, alleluia.

PRAISE TO THE GOD OF MERCIFUL LOVE   PSALM 116(117)
I ask the nations to give praise to God for his mercy (Rom 15:8-9)

> O práise the Lórd, all you nátions,*
> accláim him all you péoples!

> Stróng is his lóve for ús;*
> he is fáithful for éver.

Ant. The truth of the Lord will stand firm for ever.
17–23 December: Israel, be ready to meet the Lord, for he is coming.
Eastertide: I am the Way, the Truth and the Life, alleluia.

THROUGH THE YEAR

Scripture Reading   *Phil 2:14-15*
Do everything without complaining or arguing, so that you may be innocent and pure, as God's perfect children who live in a world of corrupt and sinful people. You must shine among them like stars lighting up the sky.

Short Responsory
R℣ I called to you, Lord, you are my refuge. *Repeat* R℣
℣ You are all I have in the land of the living. R℣ Glory be. R℣

Benedictus ant. Give your light, Lord, to those who sit in darkness and in the shadow of death.

Intercessions

From all eternity God chose Mary to be Mother of Christ. Therefore she is above all other creatures both in heaven and on earth. With her we proclaim: ℟ My soul glorifies the Lord.

Father, your Son Jesus gave his mother to the Church, a perfect example of faith:—may we accept your word in faith, as she did. ℟

Mary listened to your voice, and brought your Word into the world: —by answering your call, may we too bring your Son to men. ℟

You strengthened Mary to stand at the foot of the cross and filled her with joy at the resurrection:—by her intercession, lighten our sorrow and reinforce our hope. ℟

Our Father

Concluding Prayer

Lord God,
source and origin of our salvation,
make our lives here on earth so proclaim your glory,
that we may praise you without ceasing in heaven.
(We make our prayer) through our Lord.

WEEK 4: SUNDAY

EVENING PRAYER I

Hymn, from the appendix, for the Season.

THROUGH THE YEAR
Bless'd be the Lord our God!
With joy let heaven ring;
Before his presence let all earth
Its songs of homage bring!
His mighty deeds be told;
His majesty be praised;

To God, enthroned in heav'nly light,
Let every voice be raised!
All that has life and breath,

Give thanks with heartfelt songs!
To him let all creation sing
To whom all praise belongs!
Acclaim the Father's love,
Who gave us God his Son;
Praise too the Spirit, giv'n by both,
With both for ever one!

PSALMODY

ANTIPHON I

Advent: See, the One Desired by all the peoples will come, and the house of the Lord will be filled with glory, alleluia.
Lent: Let us enter God's house with rejoicing.
Eastertide: May the peace of Christ reign in your hearts, alleluia.

Through the Year: Pray for the peace of Jerusalem.

THE HOLY CITY OF JERUSALEM   PSALM 121(122)
You have come to Mount Zion and the city of the living God, the heavenly Jerusalem (Heb 12:22)

I rejóiced when I héard them sáy:*
'Let us gó to God's hóuse.'
And nów our féet are stánding*
within your gátes, O Jerúsalem.

Jerúsalem is búilt as a cíty*
stróngly compáct.
It is thére that the tríbes go úp,*
the tríbes of the Lórd.

For Ísrael's láw it ís,*
there to práise the Lord's náme.
Thére were set the thrónes of júdgment*
of the hóuse of Dávid.

For the péace of Jerúsalem práy:*
'Péace be to your hómes!
May péace réign in your wálls,*
in your pálaces, péace!'

605

For lóve of my bréthren and friends*
I say: 'Péace upon yóu!'
For lóve of the hóuse of the Lórd*
I will ásk for your góod.

Ant. Pray for the peace of Jerusalem.

Ant. Advent: See, the One Desired by all the peoples will come, and the house of the Lord will be filled with glory, alleluia.
Ant. 2: Come, Lord, do not delay; release your people Israel from their bonds.

Ant. Lent: Let us enter God's house with rejoicing.
Ant. 2: Sleepers, awake; rise from the dead; and Christ will give you light.

Ant. Eastertide: May the peace of Christ reign in your hearts, alleluia.
Ant. 2: In your blood, you redeemed us for God, alleluia.

Ant. 2: From the morning watch even until night my soul is longing for the Lord.

OUT OF THE DEPTHS I CRY   PSALM 129(130)
He will save his people from their sins (Mt 1:21)

Out of the dépths I crý to you, O Lórd,*
Lórd, hear my vóice!
O lét your éars be atténtive*
to the vóice of my pléading.

If you, O Lórd, should márk our guílt,*
Lórd, who would survíve?
But with yóu is fóund forgíveness:*
for thís we revére you.

My sóul is wáiting for the Lórd,*
I cóunt on his wórd.
My sóul is lónging for the Lórd*
more than wátchman for dáybreak.

606

Let the wátchman cóunt on dáybreak*
and Ísrael on the Lórd.

Becáuse with the Lórd there is mércy*
and fúlness of redémption,
Ísrael indéed he will redéem*
from áll its iníquity.

Ant. From the morning watch even until night my soul is longing
for the Lord.

Ant. Advent: Come, Lord, do not delay; release your people Israel
from their bonds.
Ant. 3: Behold, now the appointed time has come for God to send
his Son into the world.

Ant. Lent: Sleepers, awake, rise from the dead; and Christ will
give you light.
Ant. 3: God loved us so much that he was generous with his mercy:
when we were dead through our sins, he brought us to life in Christ.

Ant. Eastertide: In your blood, you redeemed us for God, alleluia.
Ant. 3: Was it not necessary that Christ should suffer thus and so
enter into his glory, alleluia?

Ant. 3: Let every creature, in heaven and on earth, bend the knee
at the name of Jesus.

CHRIST, THE SERVANT OF GOD   CANTICLE: PHIL 2:6-11
Though he was in the form of God,*
Jesus did not count equality with God a thing to be grasped.

He emptied himself,†
taking the form of a servant,*
being born in the likeness of men.

And being found in human form†
he humbled himself and became obedient unto death,*
even death on a cross.

Therefore God has highly exalted him*
and bestowed on him the name which is above every name,

That at the name of Jesus every knee should bow,*
in heaven and on earth and under the earth,

And every tongue confess that Jesus Christ is Lord,*
to the glory of God the Father.

Ant. Let every creature, in heaven and on earth, bend the knee at
the name of Jesus.

Ant. Advent: Behold, now the appointed time has come for God to
send his Son into the world.
Lent: God loved us so much that he was generous with his mercy:
when we were dead through our sins, he brought us to life in Christ.
Eastertide: Was it not necessary that Christ should suffer thus and
so enter into his glory, alleluia?

THROUGH THE YEAR

Scripture Reading   *2 Pet 1:19-20*
So we are even more confident of the message proclaimed by the
prophets. You will do well to pay attention to it, because it is like
a lamp shining in a dark place, until the Day dawns and the light
of the morning star shines in your hearts. Above all else, however,
remember this: no one can explain, by himself, a prophecy in the
Scriptures. For no prophetic message ever came from the will of
man, but men were carried along by the Holy Spirit as they spoke
the message that came from God.

Short Responsory
R̹ From the rising of the sun to its setting, great is the name of the
Lord. *Repeat* R̹
V̹ High above the heavens is his glory. R̹ Glory be. R̹

Magnificat antiphon from the Proper of Seasons.

Intercessions

Let us pray to Christ, who, of his fulness, gives his brothers love in return for love. ℟ Lord Jesus, hear our prayer.

Firstborn from the dead, you have cleansed us of our sins by your blood.—Lead us to understand what you have done for us. ℟

You have called us to be heralds of the good news:—help us to enter the depths of its message and to make it our own. ℟

King of peace, guide the actions of those who govern:—may your Spirit move them to care for those whom society rejects. ℟

Guide the steps of those who are oppressed, those persecuted for race, colour, or religion:—let their dignity be respected, and their rights upheld. ℟

Welcome all who have died in your peace;—bring them to everlasting life with our Lady and all the saints. ℟

Our Father.

The concluding prayer from the Proper of Seasons.

Invitatory

Ant. We are the people of the Lord, the flock that is led by his hand: come, let us adore him, alleluia.

Psalm, p 371.

MORNING PRAYER

Hymn, from the appendix, for the Season.

THROUGH THE YEAR

    I bind unto myself today
    The strong name of the Trinity,
    By invocation of the same,
    The Three in One, and One in Three.

    I bind unto myself today
    The power of God to hold and lead,
    His eye to watch, his might to stay,
    His ear to hearken to my need,

The wisdom of my God to teach,
His hand to guide, his shield to ward;
The word of God to give me speech,
His heavenly host to be my guard.

I bind unto myself the name,
The strong name of the Trinity;
By invocation of the same,
The Three in One, and One in Three,
Of whom all nature hath creation;
Eternal Father, Spirit, Word:
Praise to the Lord of my salvation:
Salvation is of Christ the Lord.

Alternative hymn
All people that on earth do dwell,
Sing to the Lord with cheerful voice;
Him serve with mirth, his praise forth tell,
Come ye before him, and rejoice.

The Lord, ye know, is God indeed;
Without our aid he did us make;
We are his folk, he doth us feed;
And for his sheep he doth us take.

For why, the Lord our God is good:
His mercy is for ever sure;
His truth at all times firmly stood,
And shall from age to age endure.

To Father, Son and Holy Ghost,
The God whom heaven and earth adore,
From men and from the angel-host
Be praise and glory evermore.

PSALMODY

ANTIPHON I
Advent: Sound the trumpet in Sion for the Lord is near: see, he
will come to save us, alleluia.
Lent: You are my God, I thank you. My God, I praise you.

Eastertide: I shall not die, I shall live and recount the deeds of the Lord, alleluia.

Through the Year: Give thanks to the Lord, for his great love is without end, alleluia.

SONG OF REJOICING IN SALVATION   PSALM 117(118)
This is the stone which was rejected by you builders, but which has become the cornerstone (Acts 4:11)

Give thánks to the Lórd for he is góod,*
for his lóve endures for éver.

Let the sóns of Ísrael sáy:*
'His lóve endures for éver.'
Let the sóns of Áaron sáy:*
'His lóve endures for éver.'
Let thóse who fear the Lórd sáy:*
'His lóve endures for éver.'

I cálled to the Lórd in my distréss;*
he ánswered and fréed me.
The Lórd is at my síde; I do not féar.*
What can mán do agáinst me?
The Lórd is at my síde as my hélper:*
I shall look dówn on my fóes.

It is bétter to take réfuge in the Lórd*
than to trúst in mén:
it is bétter to take réfuge in the Lórd*
than to trúst in prínces.

The nátions áll encómpassed me;*
in the Lórd's name I crúshed them.
They cómpassed me, cómpassed me abóut;*
in the Lórd's name I crúshed them.
They cómpassed me abóut like bées;†
they blázed like a fíre among thórns.*
In the Lórd's name I crúshed them.

611

I was hárd-préssed and was fálling*
but the Lórd came to hélp me.
The Lórd is my stréngth and my sóng;*
hé is my sáviour.
There are shóuts of jóy and víctory*
in the ténts of the júst.

The Lórd's right hánd has tríumphed;*
his ríght hand ráised me.
The Lórd's right hánd has tríumphed;†
I shall not díe, I shall líve*
and recóunt his déeds.
I was púnished, I was púnished by the Lórd,*
but nót doomed to díe.

Ópen to mé the gates of hóliness:*
I will énter and give thánks.
Thís is the Lórd's own gáte*
where the júst may énter.
I will thánk you for yóu have ánswered*
and yóu are my sáviour.

The stóne which the búilders rejécted*
has becóme the córner stone.
Thís is the wórk of the Lórd,*
a márvel in our éyes.
Thís day was máde by the Lórd;*
we rejóice and are glád.

O Lórd, gránt us salvátion;*
O Lórd, grant succéss.
Bléssed in the náme of the Lórd*
is hé who cómes.
We bléss you from the hóuse of the Lórd;*
the Lord Gód is our líght.

Go fórward in procéssion with bránches*
éven to the áltar.
Yóu are my Gód, I thánk you.*
My Gód, I práise you.

Give thánks to the Lórd for he is góod;*
for his lóve endures for éver.

Ant. Give thanks to the Lord, for his great love is without end, alleluia.

Ant. Advent: Sound the trumpet in Sion for the Lord is near: see, he will come to save us, alleluia.
Ant. 2: The Lord comes! Go to meet him and say: Great is his reign, and his kingdom will have no end. He is God, the Strong One, the Ruler of the world, the Prince of peace, alleluia.

Ant. Lent: You are my God, I thank you. My God, I praise you.
Ant. 2: Lord, you can deliver us from the hand of the one who is stronger than we are; save us, Lord, our God.

Ant. Eastertide: I shall not die, I shall live and recount the deeds of the Lord, alleluia.
Ant. 2: Blessed be your glorious and holy name, alleluia.

Ant. 2: Alleluia, all works of the Lord bless the Lord, alleluia.

LET EVERY CREATURE PRAISE THE LORD   CANTICLE
                                                       DAN 3:52-57

The Creator is blessed for ever (Rom 1:25)

You are blest, Lord God of our fathers.*
To you glory and praise for evermore.

Blest your glorious holy name.*
To you glory and praise for evermore.

You are blest in the temple of your glory.*
To you glory and praise for evermore.

You are blest who gaze into the depths.*
To you glory and praise for evermore.

You are blest in the firmament of heaven.*
To you glory and praise for evermore.

You who walk on the wings of the wind:*
To you glory and praise for evermore.

May they bless you, the saints and the angels.*
To you glory and praise for evermore.

From the heavens, the earth and the sea,*
To you glory and praise for evermore.

You are blest, Lord God of our fathers.*
To you glory and praise for evermore.

Ant. Alleluia, all works of the Lord bless the Lord, alleluia.

Ant. Advent: The Lord comes! Go to meet him and say: Great is his reign, and his kingdom will have no end. He is God, the Strong One, the Ruler of the world, the Prince of peace, alleluia.
Ant. 3: Your all-powerful Word, Lord, will come from the royal throne, alleluia.

Ant. Lent: Lord, you can deliver us from the hand of the one who is stronger than we are; save us, Lord, our God.
Ant. 3: Praise God in his wonderful works.

Ant. Eastertide: Blessed be your glorious and holy name, alleluia.
Ant. 3: Tell the greatness of our God. The works of God are perfect; and all his ways are right, alleluia.

Ant. 3: Let everything that breathes give praise to the Lord, alleluia.

PRAISE THE LORD   PSALM 150
Sing praise in your spirit, sing praise with your soul, that is: give glory to God in both your soul and your body (Hesychius)

Práise Gód in his hóly pláce,*
práise him in his míghty héavens.
Práise him for his pówerful déeds,*
práise his surpássing gréatness.

O práise him with sóund of trúmpet,*
práise him with lúte and hárp.
Práise him with tímbrel and dánce,*
práise him with stríngs and pípes.

O práise him with resóunding cýmbals,*
práise him with cláshing of cýmbals.
Let éverything that líves and that bréathes*
give práise to the Lórd.

Ant. Let everything that breathes give praise to the Lord, alleluia.

Ant. Advent: Your all-powerful Word, Lord, will come from the royal throne, alleluia.
Lent: Praise God in his wonderful works.
Eastertide: Tell the greatness of our God. The works of God are perfect; and all his ways are right, alleluia.

THROUGH THE YEAR

Scripture Reading   *2 Tim 2:8,11-13*
Remember the Good News that I carry, 'Jesus Christ is risen from the dead, sprung from the race of David.'
Here is a saying that you can rely on:
If we have died with him, then we shall live with him.
If we hold firm, then we shall reign with him.
If we disown him, then he will disown us.
We may be unfaithful, but he is always faithful,
for he cannot disown his own self.

Short Responsory
R⁊ We give thanks to you, O God, and call upon your name.
Repeat R⁊
V⁊ We recount your wonderful deeds. R⁊ Glory be. R⁊

Benedictus antiphon from the Proper of Seasons.

Intercessions
To the only God, our Saviour, through Jesus Christ our Lord, be glory, majesty, dominion, and authority, before all time, now, and for ever. R⁊ We praise you, O God: we acknowledge you to be the Lord.
We bless you, Lord, creator of the universe: we were sinners, in

need of your grace:—yet now you have called us to live in knowledge and service of you. ℞ We praise you, O God: we acknowledge you to be the Lord.

Your Son has shown us the way.—As we follow in his steps, may we never wander from the path that leads to life. ℞

We celebrate today the resurrection of your Son:—in suffering and in gladness, may it bring us deep joy. ℞

O Lord, give us the spirit of prayer and praise:—let us always and everywhere give you thanks. ℞

Our Father

The concluding prayer from the Proper of Seasons.

EVENING PRAYER II

Hymn, from the appendix, for the Season.

THROUGH THE YEAR

Holy God, we praise thy name;
Lord of all, we bow before thee!
All on earth thy sceptre own,
All in heaven above adore thee.
Infinite thy vast domain,
Everlasting is thy reign.

Hark! the loud celestial hymn,
Angel choirs above are raising;
Cherubim and seraphim,
In unceasing chorus praising,
Fill the heavens with sweet accord:
Holy, holy, holy, Lord.

Holy Father, holy Son,
Holy Spirit, three we name thee.
While in essence only one
Undivided God we claim thee;
And adoring bend the knee,
While we own the mystery.

Spare thy people, Lord, we pray,
By a thousand snares surrounded;
Keep us without sin today;
Never let us be confounded,
Lo, I put my trust in thee;
Never, Lord, abandon me.

Alternative hymn

Praise, my soul, the King of heaven;
To his feet your tribute bring;
Ransomed, healed, restored, forgiven,
Who like me his praise should sing?
Praise him! Praise him!
Praise him! Praise him!
Praise the everlasting King.

Praise him for his grace and favour,
To our fathers in distress;
Praise him still the same for ever,
Slow to chide and swift to bless,
Praise him! Praise him!
Praise him! Praise him!
Glorious in his faithfulness.

Fatherlike, he tends and spares us;
Well our feeble frame he knows;
In his hands he gently bears us,
Rescues us from all our foes.
Praise him! Praise him!
Praise him! Praise him!
Widely as his mercy flows.

Angels, help us to adore him;
Ye behold him face to face;
Sun and moon bow down before him,
Dwellers all in time and space.
Praise him! Praise him!
Praise him! Praise him!
Praise with us the God of grace.

PSALMODY

ANTIPHON I

Advent: See, how splendid is he who comes to save the peoples.
Lent: God has appointed him to judge everyone, living and dead.
Eastertide: You must look for the things of heaven, where Christ is, sitting at God's right hand, alleluia.

Through the Year: In holy splendour I begot you before the dawn, alleluia.

THE MESSIAH IS KING AND PRIEST   PSALM 109(110):1-5,7
He must be king so that he will put all his enemies under his feet
(1 Cor 15:25)

The Lórd's revelátion to my Máster:†
'Sít on my ríght:*
your fóes I will pút beneath your féet.'

The Lórd will wíeld from Síon†
your scéptre of pówer:*
rúle in the mídst of all your fóes.

A prínce from the dáy of your bírth†
on the hóly móuntains;*
from the wómb before the dáwn I begót you.

The Lórd has sworn an óath he will not chánge.†
'You are a príest for éver,*
a príest like Melchízedek of óld.'

The Máster stánding at your ríght hand*
will shatter kíngs in the dáy of his wráth.

He shall drínk from the stréam by the wáyside*
and thérefore he shall líft up his héad.

Ant. In holy splendour I begot you before the dawn, alleluia.

Ant. Advent: See, how splendid is he who comes to save the peoples.
Ant. 2: The rugged places shall be made smooth and the mountain-ranges shall become plains. Come, Lord, and do not delay, alleluia.

Ant. Lent: God has appointed him to judge everyone, living and dead.

Ant. 2: Happy is the man to whom the Lord shows mercy; he will never waver.

Ant. Eastertide: You must look for the things of heaven where Christ is, sitting at God's right hand, alleluia.

Ant. 2: He has risen as a light in the darkness, for the upright of heart, alleluia.

Ant. 2: Blessed are those who hunger and thirst for justice, for they shall have their fill.

THE HAPPINESS OF A JUST MAN   PSALM 111(112)
Be like children of the light; for the fruits of the light are seen in complete goodness and right living and truth (Eph 5:8-9)

Happy the mán who féars the Lórd,*
who tákes delíght in all his commánds.
His sóns will be pówerful on eárth;*
the chíldren of the úpright are bléssed.

Ríches and wéalth are in his hóuse;*
his jústice stands fírm for éver.
He is a líght in the dárkness for the úpright:*
he is génerous, mérciful and júst.

The góod man takes píty and lénds,*
he condúcts his affáirs with hónour.
The júst man will néver wáver:*
hé will be remémbered for éver.

He has no féar of évil néws;*
with a fírm heart he trústs in the Lórd.
With a stéadfast héart he will not féar;*
he will sée the dównfall of his fóes.

Open-hánded, he gíves to the póor;†
his jústice stands fírm for éver.*
His héad will be ráised in glóry.

619

The wícked man sées and is ángry,†
grinds his téeth and fádes awáy;*
the desíre of the wícked leads to dóom.

Ant. Blessed are those who hunger and thirst for justice, for they shall have their fill.

Ant. Advent: The rugged places shall be made smooth and the mountain-ranges shall become plains. Come, Lord, and do not delay, alleluia.
Ant. 3: Great will be his reign and peace will be everlasting, alleluia.

Ant. Eastertide: He has risen as a light in the darkness for the upright of heart, alleluia.
Ant. 3: Alleluia, victory and glory and power to our God, alleluia.

Ant. 3: Praise God, all you his servants, both great and small, alleluia.

When chanted, this canticle is sung with Alleluia *as set out below. When recited, it suffices to say* Alleluia *at the beginning and end of each strophe.*

THE MARRIAGE FEAST OF THE LAMB   CANTICLE
                                                        CF REV 19:1-2,5-7

Alleluia.
Salvation and glory and power belong to our God,*
(R∕ Alleluia.)
His judgments are true and just.
R∕ Alleluia (alleluia).

Alleluia.
Praise our God, all you his servants,*
(R∕ Alleluia.)
You who fear him, small and great.
R∕ Alleluia (alleluia).

Alleluia.
The Lord our God, the Almighty, reigns,*
(R7 Alleluia.)
Let us rejoice and exult and give him the glory.
R7 Alleluia (alleluia).

Alleluia.
The marriage of the Lamb has come,*
(R7 Alleluia.)
And his bride has made herself ready.
R7 Alleluia (alleluia).

Ant. Praise God, all you his servants, both great and small, alleluia.

Ant. Advent: Great will be his reign and peace will be everlasting, alleluia.
Eastertide: Alleluia, victory and glory and power to our God, alleluia.

LENT

Ant. Happy is the man to whom the Lord shows mercy; he will never waver.
Ant. 3: God fulfilled what he had foretold in the words of all the prophets: that Christ would suffer.

CHRIST, THE SERVANT OF GOD,   CANTICLE
   FREELY ACCEPTS HIS PASSION   I PET 2:21-24

Christ suffered for you,†
leaving you an example*
that you should follow in his steps.

He committed no sin;*
no guile was found on his lips.
When he was reviled,*
he did not revile in return.

When he suffered,*
he did not threaten;

but he trusted to him*
who judges justly.

He himself bore our sins*
in his body on the tree,
that we might die to sin*
and live to righteousness.

By his wounds you have been healed.

Ant. God fulfilled what he had foretold in the words of all the prophets: that Christ would suffer.

THROUGH THE YEAR

Scripture Reading   *Heb 12:22-24*
What you have come to is Mount Zion and the city of the living God, the heavenly Jerusalem where the millions of angels have gathered for the festival, with the whole Church in which everyone is a 'first-born son' and a citizen of heaven. You have come to God himself, the supreme judge, and been placed with spirits of the saints who have been made perfect; and to Jesus, the mediator who brings a new covenant and a blood for purification which pleads more insistently than Abel's.

Short Responsory
R℣ Great is our Lord; great is his might. *Repeat* R℣
℣ His wisdom can never be measured. R℣ Glory be. R℣

Magnificat antiphon from the Proper of Seasons.

Intercessions
In the Church, God has made known to us his hidden purpose: to make all things one in Christ. Let us pray that his will may be done. R℣ Father, unite all things in Christ.
We give you thanks for the presence and power of your Spirit in the Church:—give us the will to search for unity, and inspire us to pray and work together. R℣
We give you thanks for all whose work proclaims your love:—help us to serve the communities in whose life we share. R℣

622

Father, care for all who serve in the Church as ministers of your word and sacraments:—may they bring your whole family to the unity for which Christ prayed. R̸

Your people have known the ravages of war and hatred:— grant that they may know the peace left by your Son. R̸

Fulfil the hopes of those who sleep in your peace:—bring them to that final resurrection when you will be all in all. R̸

Our Father

The concluding prayer from the Proper of Seasons.

WEEK 4: MONDAY

Invitatory ant. Let us rejoice in the Lord; with songs let us praise him. *Psalm, p 371.*

MORNING PRAYER

Hymn, from the appendix, for the Season.

THROUGH THE YEAR

Come, O Creator Spirit, come,
and make within our hearts your home;
to us your grace eternal give,
who of your breathing move and live.

Our senses with your light inflame,
our hearts to heavenly love reclaim;
our bodies' poor infirmity
with strength perpetual fortify.

Our earthly foe afar repel,
grant us henceforth in peace to dwell;
and so to us, with you for guide,
no ill shall come, no harm betide.

May we by you the Father learn,
and know the Son, and you discern,

who are of both; and thus adore
in perfect faith for evermore.

PSALMODY

Ant. 1: In the morning, Lord, you fill us with your love.

17–23 December: Behold, the Lord, the ruler of the kings of the earth, will come. Happy are those who are ready to meet him.

Eastertide: Let the splendour of the Lord, our God, be upon us, alleluia.

LET THE SPLENDOUR OF THE LORD   PSALM 89(90)
COME UPON US

With the Lord one day is like a thousand years, and a thousand years is like a day (2 Pet 3:8)

O Lórd, you have béen our réfuge*
from óne generátion to the néxt.
Befóre the móuntains were bórn†
or the éarth or the wórld brought fórth,*
you are Gód, without begínning or énd.

You túrn men báck into dúst*
and say: 'Go báck, sóns of mén.'
To yóur eyes a thóusand yéars†
are like yésterday, cóme and góne,*
no móre than a wátch in the níght.

You swéep men awáy like a dréam,*
like gráss which springs úp in the mórning.
In the mórning it springs úp and flówers:*
by évening it wíthers and fádes.

So wé are destróyed in your ánger*
strúck with térror in your fúry.
Our guílt lies ópen befóre you;*
our sécrets in the líght of your fáce.

All our dáys pass awáy in your ánger.*
Our life is óver like a sígh.
Our spán is séventy yéars*

624

or éighty for thóse who are stróng.

And most of thése are émptiness and páin.*
They pass swíftly and wé are góne.
Who understánds the pówer of your ánger*
and féars the stréngth of your fúry?

Make us knów the shórtness of our lífe*
that we may gáin wísdom of héart.
Lord, relént! Is your ánger for éver?*
Show píty tó your sérvants.

In the mórning, fíll us with your lóve;*
we shall exúlt and rejóice all our dáys.
Give us jóy to bálance our afflíction*
for the yéars when we knéw misfórtune.

Show fórth your wórk to your sérvants;*
let your glóry shíne on their chíldren.
Let the fávour of the Lórd be upón us:†
give succéss to the wórk of our hánds,*
give succéss to the wórk of our hánds.

Ant. In the morning, Lord, you fill us with your love.
17–23 December: Behold, the Lord, the ruler of the kings of the earth, will come. Happy are those who are ready to meet him.
Eastertide: Let the splendour of the Lord, our God, be upon us, alleluia.

Ant. 2: Let the praise of the Lord resound from the ends of the earth.
17–23 December: Sing to the Lord a new song, his praise to the end of the earth.†
Eastertide: I will turn darkness into light before them, alleluia.

HYMN TO GOD, THE VICTOR AND SAVIOUR CANTICLE
IS 42:10-16
They were singing a new hymn before the throne of God (Rev 14:3)

Sing to the Lord a new song,*
his praise to the end of the earth!

†Let the sea roar and all that fills it,*
the coastlands and their inhabitants;
let the desert and its cities lift up their voice,*
the villages that Kedar inhabits.

Let the inhabitants of Sela sing for joy,*
let them shout from the top of the mountains.
Let them give glory to the Lord,*
and declare his praise in the coastlands.

The Lord goes forth like a mighty man,*
like a man of war he stirs up his fury;
he cries out, he shouts aloud,*
he shows himself mighty against his foes.

For a long time I have held my peace,*
I have kept still and restrained myself;
now I will cry out like a woman in travail,*
I will gasp and pant.

I will lay waste mountains and hills,*
and dry up all their herbage;
I will turn the rivers into islands,*
and dry up the pools.

And I will lead the blind*
in a way that they know not;
in paths that they have not known*
I will guide them.
I will turn the darkness before them into light,*
the rough places into level ground.

Ant. Let the praise of the Lord resound from the ends of the earth.
17–23 December: Sing to the Lord a new song, his praise to the end of the earth.
Eastertide: I will turn darkness into light before them, alleluia.

Ant. 3: Praise the name of the Lord, you who stand in the house of the Lord.
17–23 December: When the Son of Man comes, will he find any faith on earth?
Eastertide: The Lord has power to do whatever he will, alleluia.

PRAISE FOR THE LORD, PSALM 134(135):1-12
WHO DOES MARVELLOUS THINGS

You are a chosen race. Sing the praises of the one who called you out of darkness into his wonderful light (Cf 1 Pet 2:9)

Práise the náme of the Lórd,*
práise him, sérvants of the Lórd,*
who stánd in the hóuse of the Lórd*
in the cóurts of the hóuse of our Gód.

Praise the Lórd for the Lórd is góod.*
Sing a psálm to his náme for he is lóving.
For the Lórd has chosen Jácob for himsélf*
and Ísrael for his ówn posséssion.

For I knów the Lórd is gréat,*
that our Lórd is hígh above all góds.
The Lórd does whatéver he wílls,*
in héaven, on éarth, in the séas.

He summons clóuds from the énds of the éarth;†
makes líghtning prodúce the ráin;*
from his tréasuries he sénds forth the wínd.

The fírst-born of the Egýptians he smóte,*
of mán and béast alíke.
Sígns and wónders he wórked†
in the mídst of your lánd, O Égypt,*
against Pháraoh and áll his sérvants.

Nátions in their gréatness he strúck*
and kíngs in their spléndour he sléw:
Síhon, kíng of the Ámorites,†
Óg, the kíng of Báshan,*
and áll the kíngdoms of Cánaan.
He let Ísrael inhérit their lánd;*
on his péople their lánd he bestówed.

Ant. Praise the name of the Lord, you who stand in the house of the Lord.

17–23 December: When the Son of Man comes, will he find any faith on earth?
Eastertide: The Lord has power to do whatever he will, alleluia.

THROUGH THE YEAR

Scripture Reading *Jud 8:21b-23*
Remember that our fathers were put to the test to prove their love of God. Remember how our father Abraham was tested and became the friend of God after many trials and tribulations. The same was true of Isaac, Jacob, Moses, and all those who met with God's favour. They remained steadfast in the face of tribulations of every kind.

Short Responsory
℟ Rejoice in the Lord, O you just; for praise is fitting for loyal hearts. *Repeat* ℟
℣ Sing to him a new song. ℟ Glory be. ℟

Benedictus ant. Blessed be the Lord, for he has visited us and freed us.

Intercessions
Almighty Father, the heavens cannot hold your greatness: yet through your Son we have learned to say: ℟ Father, may your kingdom come!
We praise you as your children;—may your name be kept holy in the hearts of all mankind. ℟
Help us to live in the hope of heaven today:—make us ready to do your will on earth. ℟
Give us this day the courage to forgive others:—as you forgive us our trespasses. ℟
Father, be with us in all our trials:—do not allow us to fall away from you. ℟
Our Father

Concluding Prayer
Lord God,
who entrusted the earth to men

to till it and care for it,
and made the sun to serve their needs:
give us grace this day to work faithfully for your glory
and for our neighbours' good.
(We make our prayer) through our Lord.

EVENING PRAYER

Hymn, from the appendix, for the Season.

THROUGH THE YEAR
    We praise you, Father, for your gift
    Of dusk and nightfall over earth,
    Foreshadowing the mystery
    Of death that leads to endless day.

    Within your hands we rest secure;
    In quiet sleep our strength renew;
    Yet give your people hearts that wake
    In love to you, unsleeping Lord.

    Your glory may we ever seek
    In rest, as in activity,
    Until its fulness is revealed,
    O Source of life, O Trinity.

PSALMODY

Ant. 1: Give thanks to the Lord, for his great love is without end.
17–23 December: Behold, the Lord, the ruler of the kings of the
earth, will come. Happy are those who are ready to meet him.
Eastertide: Anyone who is in Christ is a new creature, alleluia.

PASCHAL HYMN   PSALM 135(136)
To tell of the works of the Lord is to give praise (Cassiodorus)

I

O give thánks to the Lórd for he is góod,*
for his lóve endúres for éver.
Give thánks to the Gód of góds,*

for his lóve endúres for éver.
Give thánks to the Lórd of lórds,*
for his lóve endúres for éver;

who alóne has wrought márvellous wórks,*
for his lóve endúres for éver;
whose wísdom it wás made the skíes,*
for his lóve endúres for éver;
who fíxed the earth fírmly on the séas,*
for his lóve endúres for éver.

It was hé who máde the great líghts,*
for his lóve endúres for éver,
the sún to rúle in the dáy,*
for his lóve endúres for éver,
the móon and stárs in the níght,*
for his lóve endúres for éver.

Ant. Give thanks to the Lord, for his great love is without end.
17–23 December: Behold, the Lord, the ruler of the kings of the
earth, will come. Happy are those who are ready to meet him.
Eastertide: Anyone who is in Christ is a new creature, alleluia.

Ant. 2: Great and wonderful are your works, Lord God Almighty.
17–23 December: Sing a new song to the Lord; Praise him throughout the world.
Eastertide: Let us love God, then, since he loved us first, alleluia.

II

The first-bórn of the Egýptians he smóte,*
for his lóve endúres for éver.
He brought Ísrael óut from their mídst,*
for his lóve endúres for éver;
arm outstrétched, with pówer in his hánd,*
for his lóve endúres for éver.

He divíded the Réd Sea in twó,*
for his lóve endúres for éver;
he made Ísrael páss through the mídst,*

630

for his lóve endúres for éver;
he flung Pháraoh and his fórce in the séa,*
for his lóve endúres for éver.

Through the désert his péople he léd,*
for his lóve endúres for éver.
Nátions in their gréatness he strúck,*
for his lóve endúres for éver.
Kíngs in their spléndour he sléw,*
for his lóve endúres for éver.

Síhon, kíng of the Ámorites,*
for his lóve endúres for éver;
and Óg, the kíng of Báshan,*
for his lóve endúres for éver.

He let Ísrael inhérit their lánd,*
for his lóve endúres for éver.
On his sérvant their lánd he bestówed,*
for his lóve endúres for éver.
He remémbered ús in our distréss,*
for his lóve endúres for éver.

And he snátched us awáy from our fóes,*
for his lóve endúres for éver.
He gives fóod to áll living thíngs,*
for his lóve endúres for éver.
To the Gód of héaven give thánks,*
for his lóve endúres for éver.

Ant. Great and wonderful are your works, Lord God Almighty.
17–23 December: Sing a new song to the Lord: Praise him throughout the world.
Eastertide: Let us love God, then, since he loved us first, alleluia.

Ant. 3: God planned to bring all things together under Christ when the fulness of time had come.
17–23 December: When the Son of Man comes, will he find any faith on earth?
Eastertide: From his fulness we have all received, grace upon grace, alleluia.

GOD, THE SAVIOUR   CANTICLE: EPH 1:3-10

Blessed be the God and Father*
of our Lord Jesus Christ,
who has blessed us in Christ*
with every spiritual blessing in the heavenly places.

He chose us in him*
before the foundation of the world,
that we should be holy*
and blameless before him.

He destined us in love*
to be his sons through Jesus Christ,
according to the purpose of his will,†
to the praise of his glorious grace*
which he freely bestowed on us in the Beloved.

In him we have redemption through his blood,*
the forgiveness of our trespasses,
according to the riches of his grace*
which he lavished upon us.

He has made known to us†
in all wisdom and insight*
the mystery of his will,
according to his purpose*
which he set forth in Christ.

His purpose he set forth in Christ,*
as a plan for the fulness of time,
to unite all things in him,*
things in heaven and things on earth.

Ant. God planned to bring all things together under Christ when the
fulness of time had come.

17–23 December: When the Son of Man comes, will he find any
faith on earth?

Eastertide: From his fulness we have all received, grace upon grace,
alleluia.

632

THROUGH THE YEAR

Scripture Reading *I Thess 3:12-13*

May the Lord be generous in increasing your love and make you love one another and the whole human race as much as we love you. And may he so confirm your hearts in holiness that you may be blameless in the sight of our God and Father when our Lord Jesus Christ comes with all his saints.

Short Responsory

R̹ Let my prayer come before you, O Lord. *Repeat* R̹
V̹ Let it rise in your presence like incense. R̹ Glory be. R̹

Magnificat ant. Let my soul proclaim your greatness for ever, O my God.

Intercessions

Let us pray to God who never deserts those who trust in him.
R̹ Lord, in your mercy, hear our prayer.
Pour out your Spirit on the Church;—let men see in her the greatness of your loving kindness. R̹
Be with the priests and ministers of your Church:—what they preach to others, may they practise in their lives. R̹
Teach us to understand one another more deeply:—by your presence free us from prejudice and fear. R̹
Give married couples constancy and mutual understanding:—may their difficulties help to deepen the love they have for each other. R̹
Pardon the sins of all our departed brothers and sisters:—may they enjoy new life in the company of your saints. R̹
Our Father

Concluding Prayer

Stay with us, Lord Jesus, as evening falls:
be our companion on our way.
In your mercy inflame our hearts and raise our hope,
so that, in union with our brethren,
we may recognize you in the scriptures,
and in the breaking of Bread.
Who live and reign with the Father and the Holy Spirit,
God, for ever and ever.

WEEK 4: TUESDAY

Invitatory ant: A mighty God is the Lord: come, let us adore him. *Psalm, p 371.*

MORNING PRAYER

Hymn, from the appendix, for the Season.

THROUGH THE YEAR

Father, we praise you, now the night is over,
active and watchful, stand we all before you;
singing, we offer prayer and meditation: thus we adore you.

Monarch of all things, fit us for your mansions;
banish our weakness, health and wholeness sending;
bring us to heaven, where your saints united joy without ending.

All-holy Father, Son and equal Spirit,
Trinity blessed, send us your salvation;
yours is the glory, gleaming and resounding through all creation.

PSALMODY

Ant. 1: I will sing to you, O Lord, and I will walk in the way of perfection.
17–23 December: The Lord will come from his holy place: he will come to save his people.
Eastertide: The man who does the will of my Father will enter the kingdom of heaven, alleluia.

DECLARATION OF A JUST RULER   PSALM 100(101)
If you love me, keep my commandments (Jn 14:15)

My sóng is of mércy and jústice;*
I síng to you, O Lórd.
I will wálk in the wáy of perféction.*
O whén, Lord, will you cóme?

I will wálk with blámeless héart*
withín my hóuse;

634

I will not sét befóre my éyes*
whatéver is báse.

I will háte the wáys of the cróoked;*
they shâll not be my friends.
The false-héarted must kéep far awáy;*
the wícked I disówn.

The man who slánders his néighbour in sécret*
I will bríng to sílence.
The mán of proud lóoks and haughty héart*
I will néver endúre.

I lóok to the fáithful in the lánd*
that they may dwéll with mé.
He who wálks in the wáy of perféction*
shall bé my friend.

No mán who práctises decéit*
shall líve within my hóuse.
No mán who utters líes shall stánd*
befóre my éyes.

Mórning by mórning I will sílence*
all the wícked in the lánd,
upróoting from the cíty of the Lórd*
áll who do évil.

Ant. I will sing to you, O Lord, and I will walk in the way of perfection.

17–23 December: The Lord will come from his holy place: he will come to save his people.

Eastertide: The man who does the will of my Father will enter the kingdom of heaven, alleluia.

Ant. 2: O Lord, do not withdraw your favour from us.

17–23 December: We have a strong city, Sion. The Saviour will set up wall and rampart to guard it. Open the gates, for God is with us, alleluia.

Eastertide: O Lord, let all the peoples see your loving mercy towards us, alleluia.

THE PRAYER OF AZARIAH IN THE FURNACE

CANTICLE
DAN 3:3,4,6,11-18

Repent and turn to God, that your sins may be wiped out (Acts 3:19)

Blessed are you, O Lord, God of our fathers,†
and worthy of praise,*
and your name is glorified for ever.

You are just*
in all that you have done to us,
for we have sinned†
and lawlessly departed from you,*
and have sinned in all things.

For your name's sake†
do not give us up utterly,*
and do not break your covenant.

Do not withdraw your mercy from us*
for the sake of Abraham your beloved,
and for the sake of Isaac your servant*
and Israel your holy one, to whom you promised
to make their descendants as many as the stars of heaven*
and as the sand on the shore of the sea.

For we, O Lord, have become fewer than any nation,†
and are brought low this day in all the world*
because of our sins;
and at this time there is no prince, or prophet, or leader,*
no burnt offering, or sacrifice, or oblation, or incense,
no place to make an offering before you*
or to find mercy.

Yet with a contrite heart and a humble spirit*
may we be accepted,
as though it were with burnt offerings of rams and bulls*
and with tens of thousands of fat lambs.

Such may our sacrifice be in your sight this day,*
and may we wholly follow you,
for there will be no shame*

for those who trust in you.

And now with all our heart we follow you,*
we fear you and seek your face.

Ant. O Lord, do not withdraw your favour from us.
17–23 December: We have a strong city, Sion. The Saviour will set
up wall and rampart to guard it. Open the gates, for God is with
us, alleluia.
Eastertide: O Lord, let all the peoples see your loving mercy towards us, alleluia.

Ant. 3: I will sing a new song to you, O God.
17–23 December: Let us know your way on earth, Lord: let all the
peoples know your saving power.
Eastertide: The Lord is my refuge and my saviour, alleluia.

FOR VICTORY AND PEACE   PSALM 143(144):1-10
I can do all things with the help of the One who gives me strength
(Phil 4:13)

Bléssed be the Lórd, my róck†
who tráins my árms for báttle,*
who prepáres my hánds for wár.

Hé is my lóve, my fórtress;*
hé is my strónghold, my sáviour,
my shíeld, my pláce of réfuge.*
He brings péoples únder my rúle.

Lórd, what is mán that you cáre for him,*
mortal mán, that you kéep him in mínd;
mán, who is mérely a bréath*
whose life fádes like a shádow?

Lówer your héavens and come dówn;*
touch the móuntains; wréathe them in smóke.
Flash your líghtnings; róut the fóe,*
shoot your árrows and pút them to flíght.

Reach dówn from héaven and sáve me;†
draw me óut from the míghty wáters,*
from the hánds of álien fóes
whose móuths are fílled with líes,*
whose hánds are ráised in pérjury.

To you, O Gód, will I síng a new sóng;*
I will pláy on the tén-stringed hárp
to yóu who give kíngs their víctory,*
who set Dávid your sérvant frée.

Ant. I will sing a new song to you, O God.

17–23 December: Let us know your way on earth, Lord: let all the peoples know your saving power.

Eastertide: The Lord is my refuge and my saviour, alleluia.

THROUGH THE YEAR

Scripture Reading   *Is 55:1*
Oh, come to the water all you who are thirsty;
though you have no money, come!
Buy corn without money, and eat,
and, at no cost, wine and milk.

Short Responsory
R℣ Hear my cry, Lord, for I hope in your word. *Repeat* R℣
℣ I rise before dawn and call for help. R℣ Glory be. R℣

Benedictus ant. Lord, save us from the hands of all who hate us.

Intercessions
Our sufferings bring acceptance, acceptance brings hope: and our hope will not deceive us, for the Spirit has been poured into our hearts. It is through the same Spirit that we pray: R℣ Stay with us, Lord, on our journey.
Help us to realize that our troubles are slight and short-lived;—they are as nothing compared with the joy we shall have when we reach our home with you. R℣
Come to the lonely, the unloved, those without friends;—show

them your love, and help them to care for their brothers and sisters.
℟
Take away our pride, temper our anger:—may we follow you in
your gentleness: may you make us humble of heart. ℟
Give us the fulness of your Spirit, the Spirit of sonship:—make our
love for each other generous and sincere. ℟
Our Father

Concluding Prayer
Increase in us, Lord, your gift of faith,
so that the praise we offer you
may ever yield its fruit from heaven.
(We make our prayer) through our Lord.

EVENING PRAYER

Hymn, from the appendix, for the Season.

THROUGH THE YEAR
  Before we end our day, O Lord,
  We make this prayer to you:
  That you continue in your love
  To guard your people here.

  Give us this night untroubled rest
  and build our strength anew:
  Your Splendour driving far away
  All darkness of the foe.

  Our hearts' desire to love you, Lord,
  Watch over while we sleep,
  That when the new day dawns on high
  We may your praises sing.

  All glory be to you, O Christ,
  Who saved mankind from death—
  To share with you the Father's love
  And in the Spirit live.

PSALMODY

Ant. 1: If I forget you, Jerusalem, let my right hand wither!
17–23 December: The Lord will come from his holy place: he will come to save his people.
Eastertide: Sing to us one of the songs of Sion, alleluia.

BY THE RIVERS OF BABYLON   PSALM 136(137):1-6
This bodily captivity of the people must be understood as pointing to their spiritual captivity (St Hilary)

By the rívers of Bábylon†
thére we sat and wépt,*
remémbering Síon;
on the póplars that gréw there*
we húng up our hárps.

For it was thére that they ásked us,†
our cáptors, for sóngs,*
our oppréssors, for jóy.
'Síng to us,' they sáid,*
'one of Síon's sóngs.'

O hów could we síng†
the sóng of the Lórd*
on álien sóil?
If I forgét you, Jerúsalem,*
let my ríght hand wíther!

O lét my tóngue†
cléave to my móuth*
if I remémber you nót,
if I príze not Jerúsalem*
abóve all my jóys!

Ant. If I forget you, Jerusalem, let my right hand wither!
17–23 December: The Lord will come from his holy place: he will come to save his people.
Eastertide: Sing to us one of the songs of Sion, alleluia.

Ant. 2: Before the angels I will bless you, my God.

17–23 December: We have a strong city, Sion. The Saviour will set up wall and rampart to guard it. Open the gates, for God is with us, alleluia.

Eastertide: In the midst of affliction you have given me life, alleluia.

THANKSGIVING   PSALM 137(138)

The kings of the earth will bring glory and honour to the holy city (cf Rev 21:24)

> I thánk you, Lórd, with all my héart,*
> you have héard the wórds of my móuth.
> In the présence of the ángels I will bléss you.*
> I will adóre before your hóly témple.

> I thánk you for your fáithfulness and lóve*
> which excél all we éver knew of yóu.
> On the dáy I cálled, you ánswered;*
> you incréased the stréngth of my sóul.

> Áll earth's kíngs shall thánk you*
> when they héar the wórds of your móuth.
> They shall síng of the Lórd's wáys:*
> 'How gréat is the glóry of the Lórd!'

> The Lord is hígh yet he lóoks on the lówly*
> and the háughty he knóws from afár.
> Though I wálk in the mídst of afflíction*
> you give me lífe and frustráte my fóes.

> You strétch out your hánd and sáve me,*
> your hánd will do áll things for mé.
> Your lóve, O Lórd, is etérnal,*
> discárd not the wórk of your hánds.

Ant. Before the angels I will bless you, my God.

17–23 December: We have a strong city, Sion. The Saviour will set up wall and rampart to guard it. Open the gates, for God is with us, alleluia.

Eastertide: In the midst of affliction you have given me life, alleluia.

Ant. 3: Worthy is the Lamb that was slain, to receive glory and honour.

17–23 December: Let us know your way on earth, Lord: let all the peoples know your saving power.

Eastertide: Yours, Lord, is the greatness and the power, the glory and the victory, alleluia.

HYMN OF THE REDEEMED   CANTICLE: REV 4:11;5:9,10,12

Worthy are you, our Lord and God,*
to receive glory and honour and power,
for you created all things,*
and by your will they existed and were created.

Worthy are you, O Lord,*
to take the scroll and to open its seals,
for you were slain,†
and by your blood you ransomed men for God*
from every tribe and tongue and people and nation.

You have made us a kingdom and priests to our God,*
and we shall reign on earth.
Worthy is the Lamb who was slain,*
to receive power and wealth,
and wisdom and might,*
and honour and glory and blessing.

Ant. Worthy is the Lamb that was slain, to receive glory and honour.

17–23 December: Let us know your way on earth, Lord: let all the peoples know your saving power.

Eastertide: Yours, Lord, is the greatness and the power, the glory and the victory, alleluia.

THROUGH THE YEAR

Scripture Reading *Col 3:16*

Christ's message, in all its richness, must live in your hearts. Teach and instruct each other with all wisdom. Sing psalms, hymns, and sacred songs; sing to God, with thanksgiving in your hearts.

Short Responsory

R7 You will give me the fulness of joy in your presence, O Lord.
Repeat R7
℣ I will find happiness at your right hand for ever. R7 Glory be. R7

Magnificat ant. Do great things for us, O Lord, for you are mighty,
and Holy is your name.

Intercessions

Christ taught us to set our hearts on the Kingdom of God, and on
its justice. In that Kingdom all that we need will be given to us.
Until then, let us pray: R7 Your Kingdom come, O Lord.
Blessed are those who know their need of God:—lead us to seek
your face in purity of heart. R7
Blessed are those who work for no reward, those who suffer for
what is right:—comfort them with your presence, lighten their
burden. R7
Blessed are the gentle, those who show mercy, and forgive;—they
shall know your forgiveness at the end of time. R7
Blessed are the peacemakers, those who reconcile conflict and hate:
—they are indeed the sons of God. R7
Bring consolation to all who mourn the dead:—may they share the
blessed hope of all who have died in the peace of Christ. R7
Our Father

Concluding Prayer

As we pray before you, Lord,
we ask you, in your mercy, for the grace
always to ponder in our hearts
what we proclaim with our lips.
(We make our prayer) through our Lord.

WEEK 4: WEDNESDAY

Invitatory ant. Cry out with joy to God all the earth: serve the Lord
with gladness.
Psalm, p 371.

MORNING PRAYER

Hymn, from the appendix, for the Season.

THROUGH THE YEAR

Now that the daylight fills the sky,
we lift our hearts to God on high,
that he, in all we do or say,
would keep us free from harm today;

Would guard our hearts and tongues from strife;
from anger's din would hide our life;
from all ill sights would turn our eyes;
would close our ears from vanities;

Would keep our inmost conscience pure;
our souls from folly would secure;
would bid us check the pride of sense
with due and holy abstinence.

So we, when this new day is gone,
and night in turn is drawing on,
with conscience by the world unstained
shall praise his Name for victory gained.

PSALMODY

Ant. 1: My heart is ready, O God, my heart is ready.†
17–22 December: The Lord who is all powerful will come from Sion
to save his people.
Eastertide: O God, arise above the heavens, alleluia.

PRAISE FOR GOD AND PRAYER FOR HELP   PSALM 107(108)
*Since the Son of God has been exalted above the heavens, his glory
is preached over all the earth* (Arnobius)

My héart is réady, O Gód;*
†I will síng, síng your práise.
Awáke, my sóul;†
awáke, lýre and hárp.*
I will awáke the dáwn.

I will thánk you, Lórd, among the péoples,*
among the nátions I will práise you,
for your lóve réaches to the héavens*
and your trúth to the skíes.
O Gód, aríse above the héavens;*
may your glóry shine on eárth!

O cóme and delíver your fríends;*
hélp with your ríght hand and replý.
From his hóly place Gód has made this prómise:†
'I will tríumph and divíde the land of Shéchem;*
I will méasure out the válley of Súccoth.

Gílead is míne and Manásseh.†
Éphraim I táke for my hélmet,*
Júdah for my commánder's stáff.
Móab I will úse for my wáshbowl,†
on Édom I will plánt my shóe.*
Over the Phílistines I will shóut in tríumph.'

But who will léad me to cónquer the fórtress?*
Who will bríng me face to fáce with Édom?
Will you útterly rejéct us, O Gód,*
and no lónger márch with our ármies?

Give us hélp agáinst the fóe:*
for the hélp of mán is vaín.
With Gód wé shall do brávely*
and hé will trámple down our fóes.

Ant. My heart is ready, O God, my heart is ready.
17–23 December: The Lord who is all-powerful will come from Sion to save his people.
Eastertide: O God, arise above the heavens, alleluia.

Ant. 2: The Lord has clothed me in a garment of justice and salvation.
17–23 December: About Sion I will not be silent until her Holy One shines forth like light.
Eastertide: The Lord will make justice and praise spring up in the sight of the nations, alleluia.

THE PROPHET REJOICES IN THE NEW JERUSALEM   CANTICLE

IS 61:10-62:5

I saw the holy city, the new Jerusalem, as beautiful as a bride prepared to meet her husband (Rev 21:2)

I will greatly rejoice in the Lord,*
my soul shall exult in my God;
for he has clothed me with the garments of salvation,*
he has covered me with the robe of righteousness,
as a bridegroom decks himself with a garland,*
and as a bride adorns herself with her jewels.

For as the earth brings forth its shoots,*
and as a garden causes what is sown in it to spring up,
so the Lord God will cause righteousness and praise*
to spring forth before all the nations.

For Sion's sake I will not keep silent,*
and for Jerusalem's sake I will not rest
until her vindication goes forth as brightness,*
and her salvation as a burning torch.

The nations shall see your vindication,*
and all the kings your glory;
and you shall be called by a new name*
which the mouth of the Lord will give.

You shall be a crown of beauty*
in the hand of the Lord,
and a royal diadem*
in the hand of your God.

You shall no more be termed Forsaken,*
and your land shall no more be termed Desolate;
but you shall be called My delight in her,*
and your land Married;
for the Lord delights in you,*
and your land shall be married.

For as a young man marries a virgin,*
so shall your sons marry you,

and as the bridegroom rejoices over the bride,*
so shall your God rejoice over you.

Ant. The Lord has clothed me in a garment of justice and salvation.
17–23 December: About Sion I will not be silent until her Holy One
shines forth like light.
Eastertide: The Lord will make justice and praise spring up in the
sight of the nations, alleluia.

Ant. 3: I will praise my God all my days.
17–23 December: The Spirit of the Lord is upon me. He sent me
to bring the Good News to the poor.
Eastertide: The Lord will reign for ever; he is your God, O Sion,
alleluia.

THE HAPPINESS OF THOSE   PSALM 145(146)
   WHO PUT THEIR TRUST IN THE LORD
Let us praise the Lord all our days, that is, in all our conduct
(Arnobius)

My sóul, give práise to the Lórd;†
I will práise the Lórd all my dáys,*
make músic to my Gód while I líve.

Pút no trúst in prínces,*
in mortal mén in whóm there is no hélp.
Take their bréath, they retúrn to cláy*
and their pláns that dáy come to nóthing.

He is háppy who is hélped by Jacob's Gód,*
whose hópe is in the Lórd his Gód,
who alóne made héaven and éarth,*
the séas and áll they contáin.

It is hé who keeps fáith for éver,*
who is júst to thóse who are oppréssed.
It is hé who gives bréad to the húngry,*
the Lórd, who sets prísoners frée,

the Lórd who gives síght to the blínd,*

who ráises up thóse who are bowed dówn,
the Lórd, who protécts the stránger*
and uphólds the wídow and órphan.

It is the Lórd who lóves the júst*
but thwárts the páth of the wícked.
The Lórd will réign for éver,*
Sion's Gód, from áge to áge.

Ant. I will praise my God all my days.
17–23 December: The Spirit of the Lord is upon me. He sent me to bring the Good News to the poor.
Eastertide: The Lord will reign for ever; he is your God, O Sion, alleluia.

THROUGH THE YEAR

Scripture Reading   *Deut 4:39-40a*
Understand this today and take it to heart: the Lord is God indeed, in heaven above as on earth beneath, he and no other. Keep his laws and commandments as I give them to you today.

Short Responsory
Ry I will praise the Lord at all times. *Repeat* Ry
Vy His praise will be always on my lips. Ry Glory be. Ry

Benedictus ant. Let us serve the Lord in holiness all our days.

Intercessions
Praise be to the God and Father of our Lord Jesus Christ. In his great mercy, he gave us new birth into a living hope by his Son's resurrection from the dead. To him we pray: Ry Father, give us your strength.
Turn our eyes to Jesus Christ your Son.—May he lead us in our faith and bring it to perfection. Ry
We pray for cheerfulness and a generous heart;—may we bring joy to our homes, to our work, and to all whom we meet. Ry
We pray for all who are working today;—be with them at home and in the city, in the factory and in the fields. Ry

We pray for those who have no work;—we pray for the disabled
and the sick, for those who cannot find work, and for those who
are retired. R℣
Our Father

Concluding Prayer
Remember, Lord, your solemn covenant,
renewed and consecrated by the blood of the Lamb,
so that your people may obtain forgiveness for their sins,
and a continued growth in grace.
(We make our prayer) through our Lord.

EVENING PRAYER

Hymn, from the appendix, for the Season.

THROUGH THE YEAR
O Trinity of blessed light
O unity of princely might,
the fiery sun has gone its way;
shed now within our hearts your ray.

To you our morning song of praise,
to you our evening prayer we raise;
your glory suppliant we adore
for ever and for evermore.

PSALMODY

Ant. 1: How wonderful is this knowledge of yours that you have
shown me, Lord.
17–23 December: The Lord who is all-powerful will come from
Sion to save his people.
Eastertide: Night will be as clear as the day, alleluia.

THE LORD SEES ALL THINGS   PSALM 138(139):1-18,23-24
*Who could ever know the mind of the Lord? Who could ever be his
counsellor?* (Rom 11:34)

I

O Lórd, you séarch me and you knów me,†

you knów my résting and my rísing,*
you discérn my púrpose from afár.
You márk when I wálk or lie dówn,*
all my wáys lie ópen to yóu.

Before éver a wórd is on my tóngue*
you knów it, O Lórd through and thróugh.
Behínd and befóre you besíege me,*
your hánd ever láid upón me.
Too wónderful for mé, this knówledge,*
too hígh, beyónd my réach.

O whére can I gó from your spírit,*
or whére can I flée from your fáce?
If I clímb the héavens, you are thére.*
If I líe in the gráve, you are thére.

If I táke the wíngs of the dáwn*
and dwéll at the séa's furthest énd,
even thére your hánd would léad me,*
your ríght hand would hóld me fást.

If I sáy: 'Let the dárkness híde me*
and the líght aróund me be níght,'
even dárkness is not dárk for yóu*
and the níght is as cléar as the dáy.

Ant. How wonderful is this knowledge of yours that you have shown me, Lord.
17–23 December: The Lord who is all-powerful will come from Sion to save his people.
Eastertide: Night will be as clear as the day, alleluia.

Ant. 2: I am the Lord, who test the mind and heart; I give each man what his conduct deserves.
17–23 December: About Sion I will not be silent until her Holy One shines forth like light.
Eastertide: I know my sheep, and they know me, alleluia.

II

For it was yóu who creáted my béing,*
knit me togéther in my móther's wómb.
I thánk you for the wónder of my béing,*
for the wónders of áll your creátion.

Alréady you knéw my sóul,*
my bódy held no sécret from yóu
when Í was being fáshioned in sécret*
and móulded in the dépths of the éarth.

Your éyes saw áll my áctions,*
they were áll of them wrítten in your bóok;
every óne of my dáys was decréed*
before óne of them cáme into béing.

To mé, how mystérious your thóughts,*
the súm of them nót to be númbered!
If I cóunt them, they are móre than the sánd;*
to fínish, I must be etérnal, like yóu.

O séarch me, Gód, and know my héart.*
O tést me and knów my thóughts.
See that I fóllow not the wróng páth*
and léad me in the páth of life etérnal.

Ant. I am the Lord, who test the mind and heart; I give each man
what his conduct deserves.
17–23 December: About Sion I will not be silent until her Holy
One shines forth like light.
Eastertide: I know my sheep, and they know me, alleluia.

Ant. 3: All things were created in him, and he holds all things in
being.
17–23 December: The Spirit of the Lord is upon me. He sent me to
bring the Good News to the poor.
Eastertide: His majesty covers the heavens, the earth is filled with
his praise, alleluia.

CHRIST IS THE FIRST-BORN OF ALL CREATION,
THE FIRST-BORN FROM THE DEAD

CANTICLE
COL 1:12-20

Let us give thanks to the Father,†
who has qualified us to share*
in the inheritance of the saints in light.

He has delivered us from the dominion of darkness*
and transferred us to the kingdom of his beloved Son,
in whom we have redemption,*
the forgiveness of sins.

He is the image of the invisible God,*
the first-born of all creation,
for in him all things were created, in heaven and on earth,*
visible and invisible.

All things were created*
through him and for him.
He is before all things,*
and in him all things hold together.

He is the head of the body, the Church;*
he is the beginning,
the first-born from the dead,*
that in everything he might be pre-eminent.

For in him all the fulness of God was pleased to dwell,*
and through him to reconcile to himself all things,
whether on earth or in heaven,*
making peace by the blood of his cross.

Ant. All things were created in him, and he holds all things in being.
17–23 December: The Spirit of the Lord is upon me. He sent me to
bring the Good News to the poor.
Eastertide: His majesty covers the heavens, the earth is filled with
his praise, alleluia.

THROUGH THE YEAR

Scripture Reading   *1 Jn 2:3-6*
We can be sure that we know God

only by keeping his commandments.
Anyone who says, 'I know him',
and does not keep his commandments,
is a liar,
refusing to admit the truth.
But when anyone does obey what he has said,
God's love comes to perfection in him.
We can be sure that we are in God
only when the one who claims to be living in him
is living the same kind of life as Christ lived.

Short Responsory
R℣ Guard us, Lord, as the apple of your eye. *Repeat* R℣
℣ Hide us in the shadow of your wings. R℣ Glory be. R℣

Magnificat ant. Show the power of your arm, Lord; put down the
proud and exalt the lowly.

Intercessions
Let us ask the Father, from whom every family in heaven and on
earth takes its name, to send the Spirit of his Son into our hearts
as we pray: R℣ Lord, in your mercy, hear our prayer.
O Lord, the creator and redeemer of all mankind, we humbly
pray for all men of every race in every kind of need:—make your
ways known to them, and reveal your salvation to all nations. R℣
May the whole Church be guided and governed by your Holy
Spirit;—let all who call themselves Christians be led into the way of
truth and hold the faith in unity of spirit. R℣
We commend to your fatherly goodness all who are afflicted or
distressed;—comfort and relieve them according to their needs, and
grant them the love and consolation of your Spirit. R℣
Father, give a place of life and rest to those who have died in your
peace:—may we share with them in the glory of Jesus Christ, who
died to save us all. R℣
Our Father

Concluding Prayer
Remember your people, Lord, and show them mercy:

as you satisfy the hungry with food from heaven,
enrich our poverty from your abundance.
(We make our prayer) through our Lord.

WEEK 4: THURSDAY

Invitatory ant. Come before the Lord, singing for joy.
Psalm, p 371.

MORNING PRAYER

Hymn, from the appendix, for the Season.

THROUGH THE YEAR

Alone with none but thee, my God,
I journey on my way;
What need I fear, when thou art near,
O King of night and day?
More safe am I within thy hand,
Than if a host did round me stand.

My destined time is fixed by thee,
And Death doth know his hour.
Did warriors strong around me throng,
They could not stay his power;
No walls of stone can man defend
When thou thy messenger dost send.

My life I yield to thy decree,
And bow to thy control
In peaceful calm, for from thine arm
No power can wrest my soul.
Could earthly omens e'er appal
A man that heeds the heavenly call!

The child of God can fear no ill,
His chosen dread no foe;

We leave our fate with thee, and wait
Thy bidding when to go.
'Tis not from chance our comfort springs,
Thou art our trust, O King of kings.

PSALMODY

Ant. 1: In the morning let me know your love, O Lord.
17–23 December: I look to you, Lord, for help; come and save me,
Lord, for I seek refuge in you.
Eastertide: For your name's sake, Lord, give me life, alleluia.

PRAYER IN DESOLATION   PSALM 142(143):1-11
*A man is made righteous not by obedience to the Law, but by faith
in Jesus Christ* (Gal 2:16)

Lórd, lísten to my práyer:†
túrn your éar to my appéal.*
You are fáithful, you are júst; give ánswer.
Do not cáll your sérvant to júdgment*
for nó one is júst in your síght.

The enémy pursúes my sóul;*
he has crúshed my lífe to the gróund;
he has máde me dwéll in dárkness*
like the déad, lóng forgótten.
Thérefore my spírit fáils;*
my héart is númb withín me.

I remémber the dáys that are pást:*
I pónder áll your wórks.
I múse on what your hánd has wróught†
and to yóu I strétch out my hánds.*
Like a párched land my sóul thirsts for yóu.

Lórd, make háste and ánswer;*
for my spírit fáils withín me.
Dó not híde your fáce*
lest I becóme like thóse in the gráve.

655

In the mórning let me knów your lóve*
for I pút my trúst in yóu.
Make me knów the wáy I should wálk:*
to yóu I líft up my sóul.

Réscue me, Lórd, from my énemies;*
I have fléd to yóu for réfuge.
Téach me to dó your wíll*
for yóu, O Lórd, are my Gód.
Let yóur good spírit guíde me*
in wáys that are lével and smóoth.

For your náme's sake, Lórd, save my lífe;*
in your jústice save my sóul from distréss.

Ant. In the morning let me know your love, O Lord.
17–23 December: I look to you, Lord, for help; come and save me, Lord, for I seek refuge in you.
Eastertide: For your name's sake, Lord, give me life, alleluia.

Ant. 2: The Lord will send peace flowing like a river upon Jerusalem.
17–23 December: Lord, give those who wait for you their reward, and let your prophets be found worthy of belief.
Eastertide: I will see you again, and then your hearts will be filled with joy, alleluia.

CONSOLATION AND JOY   CANTICLE
   IN THE HOLY CITY   IS 66:10-14A
The Jerusalem which is above is free and is our mother (Gal 4:26)

Rejoice with Jerusalem, and be glad for her,*
all you who love her;
rejoice with her in joy,*
all you who mourn over her,

That you may suck and be satisfied*
with her consoling breasts,
that you may drink deeply with delight*
from the abundance of her glory.

For thus says the Lord:†
Behold, I will extend prosperity to her like a river,*
and the wealth of the nations like an overflowing stream;
and you shall suck, you shall be carried upon her hip,*
and dandled upon her knees.

As one whom his mother comforts,†
so I will comfort you;*
you shall be comforted in Jerusalem.
You shall see, and your heart shall rejoice;*
your bones shall flourish like the grass.

Ant. The Lord will send peace flowing like a river upon Jerusalem.
17–23 December: Lord, give those who wait for you their reward,
and let your prophets be found worthy of belief.
Eastertide: I will see you again, and then your hearts will be filled
with joy, alleluia.

Ant. 3: To our God be joyful praise.
17–23 December: Turn to us, Lord, and make no delay in coming to
your servants.
Eastertide: The Lord builds up Jerusalem, he heals the broken-
hearted, alleluia.

THE POWER AND GOODNESS OF THE LORD   PSALM 146(147)
You, O God, we worship; you, O Lord, we adore

Praise the Lórd for hé is góod;†
sing to our Gód for hé is lóving:*
to hím our práise is dúe.

The Lórd buílds up Jerúsalem*
and bríngs back Ísrael's éxiles,
he héals the bróken-héarted,*
he bínds up áll their wóunds.
He fíxes the númber of the stárs;*
he cálls each óne by its náme.

Our Lórd is gréat and almíghty;*

657

his wísdom can néver be méasured.
The Lórd ráises the lówly;*
he húmbles the wícked to the dúst.
O síng to the Lórd, giving thánks;*
sing psálms to our Gód with the hárp.

He cóvers the héavens with clóuds;*
he prepáres the ráin for the éarth,
making móuntains spróut with gráss*
and with plánts to sérve man's néeds.
He provídes the béasts with their fóod*
and young rávens that cáll upón him.

His delíght is nót in hórses*
nor his pléasure in wárriors' stréngth.
The Lórd delights in thóse who revére him,*
in thóse who wáit for his lóve.

Ant. To our God be joyful praise.
17–23 December: Turn to us, Lord, and make no delay in coming to your servants.
Eastertide: The Lord builds up Jerusalem, he heals the broken-hearted, alleluia.

THROUGH THE YEAR

Scripture Reading   *Rom 8:18-21*
I consider that the sufferings of this present time are not worth comparing with the glory that is to be revealed to us. For the creation waits with eager longing for the revealing of the sons of God; for the creation was subjected to futility, not of its own will but by the will of him who subjected it in hope; because the creation itself will be set free from its bondage to decay and obtain the glorious liberty of the children of God.

Short Responsory
R̰ Early in the morning I will think of you, O Lord. *Repeat* R̰
V̰ You have been my help. R̰ Glory be. R̰

Benedictus ant. Give your people knowledge of salvation, Lord, and forgive us our sins.

Intercessions

It is the Father's will that men should see him in the face of his beloved Son. Let us honour him as we say: ℟ Hallowed be your name.

Christ greeted us with good news:—may the world hear it through us, and find hope. ℟

We praise and thank you, Lord of heaven and earth;—you are the hope and joy of men in every age. ℟

May Christ's coming transform the Church;—and renew its youth and vigour in the service of men. ℟

We pray for Christians who suffer for their belief:—sustain them in their hope. ℟

Our Father

Concluding Prayer

Grant us, Lord, a true knowledge of salvation,
so that, freed from fear and from the power of our foes,
we may serve you faithfully,
all the days of our life.
(We make our prayer) through our Lord.

EVENING PRAYER

Hymn, from the appendix, for the Season.

THROUGH THE YEAR

Blest are the pure in heart,
For they shall see our God;
The secret of the Lord is theirs,
Their soul is Christ's abode.

The Lord, who left the heavens,
Our life and peace to bring,
To dwell in lowliness with men,
Their pattern and their King:

Still to the lowly soul
He does himself impart,
And for his dwelling and his throne
Chooses the pure in heart.

Lord, we thy presence seek;
May ours this blessing be;
Give us a pure and lowly heart,
A temple fit for thee.

PSALMODY

Ant. 1: The Lord is my love and my refuge; in him I place my trust.
17–23 December: I look to you, Lord, for help; come and save me,
Lord, for I seek refuge in you.
Eastertide: The Lord is my stronghold and my saviour, alleluia.

FOR VICTORY AND PEACE   PSALM 143(144)
His arms are well trained for battle, since he has overcome the world,
for he says, 'I have overcome the world' (St Hilary)

I

Bléssed be the Lórd, my róck†
who tráins my árms for báttle,*
who prepáres my hánds for wár.

Hé is my lóve, my fórtress;*
hé is my strónghold, my sáviour,
my shíeld, my pláce of réfuge.*
He brings péoples únder my rúle.

Lórd, what is mán that you cáre for him,*
mortal mán, that you kéep him in mínd;
mán, who is mérely a bréath*
whose lífe fádes like a shádow?

Lówer your héavens and come dówn;*
touch the móuntains; wréathe them in smóke.
Flash your líghtnings; róut the fóe,*
shoot your árrows and pút them to flight.

Reach dówn from héaven and sáve me;†
draw me óut from the míghty wáters,*
from the hánds of álien fóes
whose móuths are fílled with líes,*
whose hánds are ráised in pérjury.

Ant. The Lord is my love and my refuge; in him I place my trust.
17–23 December: I look to you, Lord, for help; come and save me,
Lord, for I seek refuge in you.
Eastertide: The Lord is my stronghold and my saviour, alleluia.

Ant. 2: Blessed the people whose God is the Lord.
17–23 December: Lord, give those who wait for you their reward,
and let your prophets be found worthy of belief.
Eastretide: Thanks be to God, who has given us the victory through
our Lord, Jesus Christ, alleluia.

II

To you, O Gód, will I síng a new sóng;*
I will pláy on the tén-stringed hárp
to yóu who give kíngs their víctory,*
who set Dávid your sérvant frée.

You set him frée from the évil swórd;*
you réscued him from álien fóes
whose móuths were fílled with líes,*
whose hánds were ráised in pérjury.

Let our sóns then flóurish like sáplings*
grown táll and stróng from their yóuth:
our dáughters gráceful as cólumns,*
adórned as thóugh for a pálace.

Let our bárns be filled to overflówing*
with cróps of évery kínd;
our shéep incréasing by thóusands,†
mýriads of shéep in our fíelds,*
our cáttle héavy with yóung,

no rúined wáll, no éxile,*
no sóund of wéeping in our stréets.
Háppy the péople with such bléssings;*
happy the péople whose Gód is the Lórd.

Ant. Blessed the people whose God is the Lord.
17–23 December: Lord, give those who wait for you their reward,

and let your prophets be found worthy of belief.
Eastertide: Thanks be to God, who has given us the victory through our Lord, Jesus Christ, alleluia.

Ant. 3: Victory and empire have now been won by our God.
17–23 December: Turn to us, Lord, and make no delay in coming to your servants.
Eastertide: Jesus Christ is the same yesterday, today and for ever, alleluia.

THE JUDGMENT OF GOD   CANTICLE
                                                    REV 11:17-18;12:10B-12A

We give thanks to you, Lord God Almighty,*
who are and who were,
that you have taken your great power*
and begun to reign.

The nations raged,*
but your wrath came,
and the time for the dead to be judged,*
for rewarding your servants, the prophets and saints,
and those who fear your name,*
both small and great.

Now the salvation and the power†
and the kingdom of our God*
and the authority of his Christ have come,
for the accuser of our brethren has been thrown down,
who accuses them day and night before our God.

And they have conquered him*
by the blood of the Lamb
and by the word of their testimony,*
for they loved not their lives even unto death.
Rejoice, then, O heaven,*
and you that dwell therein.

Ant. Victory and empire have now been won by our God.

17–23 December: Turn to us, Lord, and make no delay in coming to your servants.

Eastertide: Jesus Christ is the same yesterday, today and for ever, alleluia.

THROUGH THE YEAR

Scripture Reading   *Cf Col 1:23*

You must, of course, continue faithful on a sure and firm foundation, and not allow yourselves to be shaken from the hope you gained when you heard the gospel which has been preached to everybody in the world.

Short Responsory

R̷ The Lord is my shepherd; there is nothing I shall want. *Repeat* R̷

V̷ Fresh and green are the pastures where he gives me repose. R̷

Glory be. R̷

Magnificat ant. The Lord has satisfied and filled with good things those who hungered for justice.

Intercessions

The light shines out in the darkness and the darkness cannot overcome it. Let us thank our Lord for bringing his light to our lives.

R̷ Lord Jesus Christ, you are our light.

Word of God, you have brought the light of eternity to the darkened world:—may it open the minds and hearts of all the children of the Church. R̷

Show your care for all who dedicate their lives to the service of others:—may your grace inspire their actions and sustain them to the end. R̷

Lord, you healed the paralytic and forgave him his sins:—pardon all our guilt, and heal the wounds of our sins. R̷

Men follow the light to new knowledge and discovery:—may they use your gifts to serve the whole human family, and so give glory to you. R̷

Lead the dead from darkness into your own wonderful light;—in your mercy show them the radiance of your glory. R̷

Our Father

Concluding Prayer
Listen favourably to our evening prayer, Lord,
and grant that as we follow your Son's example,
we may, by perseverance, yield a harvest of good works.
(We make our prayer) through our Lord.

WEEK 4: FRIDAY

Invitatory ant. Indeed, how good is the Lord; bless his holy name.
Psalm, p 371.

MORNING PRAYER

Hymn, from the appendix, for the Season.

THROUGH THE YEAR
I am the holy vine,
Which God my Father tends.
Each branch that yields no fruit
My Father cuts away.
Each fruitful branch
He prunes with care
To make it yield
Abundant fruit.

If you abide in me,
I will in you abide,
Each branch to yield its fruit
Must with the vine be one.
So you shall fail
To yield your fruit
If you are not
With me one vine.

I am the fruitful vine,
And you my branches are.
He who abides in me
I will in him abide.

So shall you yield
Much fruit, but none
If you remain
Apart from me.

PSALMODY

Ant. 1: A pure heart create for me, O God, put a steadfast spirit within me.

17–23 December: The one who is to rule will come from Sion: 'The Lord, Immanuel' is his great name.

Eastertide: Christ gave himself up for us as a fragrant offering and a sacrifice to God, alleluia.

O GOD, HAVE MERCY ON ME   PSALM 50(51)
You must be made new in mind and spirit, and put on the new nature
(Eph 4:23-24)

Have mércy on me, Gód, in your kíndness.*
In your compássion blot óut my offénce.
O wásh me more and móre from my guílt*
and cléanse me fróm my sín.

My offénces trúly I knów them;*
my sín is álways befóre me.
Against yóu, you alóne, have I sínned;*
what is évil in your síght I have dóne.

That you may be jústified whén you give séntence*
and be withóut repróach when you júdge,
O sée, in guílt I was bórn,*
a sínner was Í concéived.

Indéed you love trúth in the héart;*
then in the sécret of my héart teach me wísdom.
O púrify me, thén I shall be cléan;*
O wásh me, I shall be whíter than snów.

Make me héar rejóicing and gládness,*
that the bónes you have crúshed may revíve.

665

From my síns turn awáy your fáce*
and blót out áll my guílt.

A púre heart creáte for me, O Gód,*
put a stéadfast spírit withín me.
Do not cást me awáy from your présence,*
nor depríve me of your hóly spírit.

Give me agáin the jóy of your hélp;*
with a spírit of férvour sustáin me,
that I may téach transgréssors your wáys*
and sínners may retúrn to yóu.

O réscue me, Gód, my hélper,*
and my tóngue shall ríng out your góodness.
O Lórd, ópen my líps*
and my móuth shall decláre your práise.

For in sácrifice you táke no delíght,*
burnt óffering from mé you would refúse,
my sácrifice, a cóntrite spírit.*
A húmbled, contrite héart you will not spúrn.

In your góodness, show fávour to Síon:*
rebuíld the wálls of Jerúsalem.
Thén you will be pléased with lawful sácrifice,*
hólocausts óffered on your áltar.

Ant. A pure heart create for me, O God, put a steadfast spirit within me.

17–23 December: The one who is to rule will come from Sion: 'The Lord, Immanuel' is his great name.

Eastertide: Christ gave himself up for us as a fragrant offering and a sacrifice to God, alleluia.

Ant. 2: Rejoice, O Jerusalem, since through you all men will be gathered together to the Lord.

17–23 December: Stand steadfast. You will see the helping power of the Lord.

Eastertide: Jerusalem, city of God, you will be radiant with light, alleluia.

THANKSGIVING FROM A LIBERATED PEOPLE   CANTICLE

TOB 13:8-11,13-15

He showed me the holy city of Jerusalem and it had all the radiant glory of God (Rev 21:10-11)

Let all men speak,*
and give God thanks in Jerusalem.
O Jerusalem, the holy city,†
he will afflict you for the deeds of your sons,*
but again he will show mercy to the sons of the righteous.

Give thanks worthily to the Lord,†
and praise the King of the ages,*
that his tent may be raised for you again with joy.

May he cheer those within you who are captives,†
and love those within you who are distressed,*
to all generations for ever.

Many nations will come from afar*
to the name of the Lord God,
bearing gifts in their hands,*
gifts for the King of heaven.
Generations of generations*
will give you joyful praise.

Rejoice and be glad*
for the sons of the righteous,
for they will be gathered together,*
and will praise the Lord of the righteous.

How blessed are those who love you!*
They will rejoice in your peace.
Blessed are those who grieved*
over all your afflictions,
for they will rejoice for you upon seeing all your glory,†
and they will be made glad for ever.*

Let my soul praise God the great King!

Ant. Rejoice, O Jerusalem, since through you all men will be gathered together to the Lord.

17–23 December: Stand steadfast. You will see the helping power of the Lord.

Eastertide: Jerusalem, city of God, you will be radiant with light, alleluia.

Ant. 3: Sion, praise your God, who has sent out his word to the earth.

17–23 December: I look to the Lord; I will await the God who saves me.

Eastertide: I saw the new Jerusalem, coming down from heaven, alleluia.

THE RENEWAL OF JERUSALEM   PSALM 147
Come, and I will show you the bride that the Lamb has married
(Rev 21:9)

O práise the Lórd, Jerúsalem!*
Síon, práise your Gód!

He has stréngthened the bárs of your gátes,*
he has bléssed the chíldren withín you.
He estáblished péace on your bórders,*
he féeds you with fínest whéat.

He sénds out his wórd to the éarth*
and swíftly rúns his commánd.
He shówers down snów white as wóol,*
he scátters hóar-frost like áshes.

He húrls down háilstones like crúmbs.*
The wáters are frózen at his tóuch;
he sénds forth his wórd and it mélts them:*
at the bréath of his móuth the waters flów.

He mákes his wórd known to Jácob,*
to Ísrael his láws and decrées.
He has not déalt thus with óther nátions;*
he has not táught them hís decrées.

Ant. Sion, praise your God, who has sent out his word to the earth.
17–23 December: I look to the Lord; I will await the God who saves me.
Eastertide: I saw the new Jerusalem, coming down from heaven, alleluia.

THROUGH THE YEAR

Scripture Reading   *Gal 2:19b-20*

With Christ I hang upon the cross, and yet I am alive; or rather, not I; it is Christ that lives in me. True, I am living, here and now, this mortal life; but my real life is the faith I have in the Son of God, who loved me, and gave himself for me.

Short Responsory

R̷ I call to the Lord, the Most High, for he has been my help. *Repeat* R̷

V̷ May he send from heaven and save me. R̷ Glory be. R̷

Benedictus ant. Through the loving mercy of our God, the Rising Sun has come to visit us.

Intercessions

Christ is the image of the unseen God, the first-born of all creation, and the first to be born from the dead. All things are to be reconciled through him because he made peace by his death on the cross. We pray to him: R̷ Lord Jesus, come to us today.

We have been baptized into your death:—may we be cleansed of greed and envy, and clothed in the strength and gentleness of your love. R̷

We have been sealed with the Holy Spirit who has been given to us; —confirm us in your service, and help us to bear witness to you in the society in which we live. R̷

Before you suffered, you longed to eat the passover with your disciples:—as we take part in your eucharist, may we share in your resurrection. R̷

You continue to work in your faithful people:—create through them a new world where injustice and destruction will give way to growth, freedom and hope. R̷

Our Father

Concluding Prayer
Lord God,
bestow a full measure of your grace on us
who are gathered here in prayer.
As you work within us
to keep us in the path of your commandments,
may we receive consolation in this present life
and eternal joys in the next.
(We make our prayer) through our Lord.

EVENING PRAYER

Hymn, from the appendix, for the Season.

THROUGH THE YEAR
   Day is done, but Love unfailing
   Dwells ever here;
   Shadows fall, but hope, prevailing,
   Calms every fear.
   Loving Father, none forsaking,
   Take our hearts, of Love's own making,
   Watch our sleeping, guard our waking,
   Be always near!

   Dark descends, but Light unending
   Shines through our night;
   You are with us, ever lending
   New strength to sight;
   One in love, your truth confessing,
   One in hope of heaven's blessing,
   May we see, in love's possessing,
   Love's endless light!

PSALMODY

Ant. 1: I will bless you day after day and tell of your wonderful deeds, O Lord.
17–23 December: The one who is to rule will come from Sion: 'The Lord, Immanuel' is his great name.

Eastertide: God so loved the world that he gave his only Son, alleluia.

PRAISE OF GOD'S MAJESTY   PSALM 144(145)
You, O Lord, are the One who was and who is, the Just One (Rev 16:5)

I

I will give you glóry, O Gód my Kíng,*
I will bléss your náme for éver.

I will bléss you dáy after dáy*
and práise your náme for éver.
The Lord is gréat, híghly to be práised,*
his gréatness cánnot be méasured.

Age to áge shall procláim your wórks,*
shall decláre your míghty déeds,
shall spéak of your spléndour and glóry,*
tell the tále of your wónderful wórks.

They will spéak of your térrible déeds,*
recóunt your gréatness and míght.
They will recáll your abúndant góodness;*
age to áge shall ríng out your jústice.

The Lord is kínd and fúll of compássion,*
slow to ánger, abóunding in lóve.
How góod is the Lord to áll,*
compássionate to áll his créatures.

All your créatures shall thánk you, O Lórd,*
and your fríends shall repéat their bléssing.
They shall spéak of the glóry of your réign*
and decláre your míght, O Gód,

to make knówn to mén your mighty déeds*
and the glórious spléndour of your réign.
Yóurs is an éverlasting kíngdom;*
your rúle lasts from áge to áge.   (Glory be)

Ant. I will bless you day after day and tell of your wonderful deeds, O Lord.

17–23 December: The one who is to rule will come from Sion: 'The Lord, Immanuel' is his great name.

Eastertide: God so loved the world that he gave his only Son, alleluia.

Ant. 2: The eyes of all creatures look to you, Lord; you are close to all who call upon you.

17–23 December: Stand steadfast. You will see the helping power of the Lord.

Eastertide: To the eternal King, the undying, invisible and only God, be all honour and glory, alleluia.

II

The Lord is fáithful in áll his wórds*
and lóving in áll his déeds.
The Lórd suppórts all who fáll*
and ráises áll who are bowed dówn.

The éyes of all créatures look to yóu*
and you gíve them their fóod in due tíme.
You ópen wíde your hánd,*
grant the desíres of áll who líve.

The Lord is júst in áll his wáys*
and lóving in áll his déeds.
He is clóse to áll who cáll him,*
who cáll on hím from their héarts.

He gránts the desíres of those who féar him,*
he héars their crý and he sáves them.
The Lórd protécts all who lóve him;*
but the wícked he will útterly destróy.

Let me spéak the práise of the Lórd,†
let all mankínd bléss his holy náme*
for éver, for áges unénding.

Ant. The eyes of all creatures look to you, Lord; you are close to all who call upon you.

17–23 December: Stand steadfast. You will see the helping power of the Lord.

Eastertide: To the eternal King, the undying, invisible and only God, be all honour and glory, alleluia.

Ant. 3: Your ways are just and true, King of all the ages.

17–23 December: I look to the Lord; I will await the God who saves me.

Eastertide: The Lord is my strength and protection, he is my salvation, alleluia.

HYMN OF ADORATION   CANTICLE: REV 15:3-4

> Great and wonderful are your deeds,*
> O Lord God the Almighty!
> Just and true are your ways,*
> O King of the ages!

> Who shall not fear and glorify your name, O Lord?*
> For you alone are holy.
> All nations shall come and worship you,*
> for your judgments have been revealed.

Ant. Your ways are just and true, King of all the ages.

17–23 December: I look to the Lord; I will await the God who saves me.

Eastertide: The Lord is my strength and protection, he is my salvation, alleluia.

THROUGH THE YEAR

Scripture Reading   *Rom 8:1-2*
There is now no condemnation for those who are in Christ Jesus. For the law of the Spirit of life in Christ Jesus has set me free from the law of sin and death.

Short Responsory

℞ Christ died for our sins, that he might offer us to God. *Repeat* ℞
℣ In the body he was put to death, in the spirit he was raised to life.
℞ Glory be. ℞

Magnificat ant. Remember your mercy, O Lord; according to the promise you made to our fathers.

Intercessions

God's love for us was revealed when God sent into the world his only Son so that we might have life through him. We are able to love God because he loved us first. And so we pray: ℞ Lord, help us to love you and to love one another.

Jesus forgave the penitent woman her sins because she had loved much;—may we too know his healing touch and love you with all our hearts. ℞

You look with compassion on the humble and contrite of heart:— in your goodness, turn our hearts to you and help us to do what we know to be right. ℞

We acknowledge the suffering we have caused to others:—we ask forgiveness for our neglect and indifference. ℞

We ask you to remember tonight those who are in great difficulty: give new heart to those who have lost their faith in man and in God, to those who seek the truth but cannot find it. ℞

Remember all those who put their hope in you while they lived:— through the passion and death of your Son, grant them the remission of all their sins. ℞

Our Father

Concluding Prayer

God of power and mercy,
who willed that Christ your Son should suffer for the salvation of all
    the world,
grant that your people may strive to offer themselves to you as a
    living sacrifice,
and may be filled with the fulness of your love.
(We make our prayer) through our Lord.

WEEK 4: SATURDAY

Invitatory ant. Let us listen for the voice of the Lord and enter into his peace.
Psalm, p 371.

MORNING PRAYER

Hymn, from the appendix, for the season.

THROUGH THE YEAR

Sing, all creation, sing to God in gladness!
Joyously serve him, singing hymns of homage!
Chanting his praises, come before his presence!
    Praise the Almighty!

Know that our God is Lord of all the ages!
He is our maker; we are all his creatures,
People he fashioned, sheep he leads to pasture!
    Praise the Almighty!

Great in his goodness is the Lord we worship;
Steadfast his kindness, love that knows no ending!
Faithful his word is, changeless, everlasting!
    Praise the Almighty!

PSALMODY

Ant. 1: It is good to make music to your name, O Most High, to proclaim your love in the morning.
24 December: You, Bethlehem, will not be least among the towns of Juda: for the leader who will rule my people Israel will come from you.
Eastertide: O Lord, how great are your works, alleluia.

PRAISE OF THE LORD, CREATOR   PSALM 91(92)
The deeds of God's only Son are praised (St Athanasius)

It is góod to give thánks to the Lórd*

675

to make músic to your náme, O Most Hígh,
to procláim your lóve in the mórning*
and your trúth in the wátches of the níght,
on the tén-stringed lýre and the lúte,*
with the múrmuring sóund of the hárp.

Your déeds, O Lórd, have made me glád;*
for the wórk of your hánds I shout with jóy.
O Lórd, how gréat are your wórks!*
How déep are yóur desígns!
The fóolish man cánnot knów this*
and the fóol cánnot understánd.

Though the wícked spring úp like gráss*
and áll who do évil thríve,
they are dóomed to be etérnally destróyed.*
But yóu, Lord, are etérnally on hígh.
Sée how your énemies pérish;*
all dóers of évil are scáttered.

To mé you give the wíld-ox's stréngth;*
you anóint me with the púrest óil.
My éyes looked in tríumph on my fóes;*
my éars heard gládly of their fáll.
The júst will flóurish like the pálm-tree*
and grów like a Lébanon cédar.

Plánted in the hóuse of the Lórd*
they will flóurish in the cóurts of our Gód,
stíll bearing frúit when they are óld,*
stíll full of sáp, still gréen,
to procláim that the Lórd is júst.*
In hím, my róck, there is no wróng.

Ant. It is good to make music to your name, O Most High, to proclaim your love in the morning.
24 December: You, Bethlehem, will not be least among the towns of Juda: for the leader who will rule my people Israel will come from you.
Eastertide: O Lord, how great are your works, alleluia.

Ant. 2: I will give you a new heart, and put a new spirit in you.
24 December: Lift up your heads for your redemption is at hand.
Eastertide: I will pour purifying water over you, alleluia.

THE LORD WILL GIVE HIS PEOPLE NEW LIFE   CANTICLE
                                                    EZEK 36:24-28

They shall be his people, and he will be their God; his name is God-with-them (Rev 21:3)

I will take you from the nations,†
and gather you from all the countries,*
and bring you into your own land.

I will sprinkle clean water upon you,†
and you shall be clean from all your uncleannesses,*
and from all your idols I will cleanse you.

A new heart I will give you,*
and a new spirit I will put within you;
and I will take out of your flesh the heart of stone*
and give you a heart of flesh.

And I will put my spirit within you,†
and cause you to walk in my statutes*
and be careful to observe my ordinances.

You shall dwell in the land*
which I gave to your fathers;
and you shall be my people,*
and I will be your God.

Ant. I will give you a new heart, and put a new spirit in you.
24 December: Lift up your heads for your redemption is at hand.
Eastertide: I will pour purifying water over you, alleluia.

Ant. 3: On the lips of children and of babes you have found praise,
Lord.
24 December: Tomorrow your salvation will be with you, says the
Lord, God almighty.

Eastertide: All things are yours, and you are Christ's and Christ is God's, alleluia.

THE MAJESTY OF GOD, THE DIGNITY OF MAN   PSALM 8
He has put all things under his feet, and appointed him to be head of the whole Church (Eph 1:22)

How gréat is your náme, O Lórd our Gód,*
through áll the éarth!

Your májesty is práised above the héavens;*
on the líps of chíldren and of bábes
you have found práise to fóil your énemy,*
to sílence the fóe and the rébel.

When I see the héavens, the wórk of your hánds,*
the móon and the stárs which you arránged,
what is mán that you should kéep him in mínd,*
mortal mán that you cáre for hím?

Yet you have máde him little léss than a gód;*
with glóry and hónour you crówned him,
gave him pówer over the wórks of your hánd,*
put áll things únder his féet.

Áll of them, shéep and cáttle,*
yes, éven the sávage béasts,
bírds of the aír, and físh*
that máke their wáy through the wáters.

How gréat is your náme, O Lórd our Gód,*
through áll the éarth!

Ant. On the lips of children and of babes you have found praise, Lord.
24 December: Tomorrow your salvation will be with you, says the Lord, God almighty.
Eastertide: All things are yours, and you are Christ's and Christ is God's, alleluia.

THROUGH THE YEAR

Scripture Reading   *2 Pet 3:13-14*
What we are waiting for is what he promised: the new heavens and new earth, the place where righteousness will be at home. So then, my friends, while you are waiting, do your best to live lives without spot or stain so that he will find you at peace. Think of our Lord's patience as your opportunity to be saved.

Short Responsory
R℣ When I sing to you my lips shall rejoice. *Repeat* R℣
℣ My tongue shall tell the tale of your justice. R℣ Glory be. R℣

Benedictus ant. Lord, guide our feet into the way of peace.

Intercessions
God's gift was not a spirit of timidity, but the Spirit of power, and love, and self-control. With complete confidence we pray: R℣ Father, send us your Spirit.
Praise be to God, the Father of our Lord Jesus Christ:—in Christ you have given us every spiritual blessing. R℣
By the power of the Holy Spirit, Mary brought Christ into the world:—through the Church, may Christ be born again today in the hearts of men. R℣
Father, may your Spirit lead us forward out of solitude:—may he lead us to open the eyes of the blind, to proclaim the Word of light, to reap together the harvest of life. R℣
Let our striving for your kingdom not fall short through selfishness or fear:—may the universe be alive with the Spirit, and our homes be the pledge of a world redeemed. R℣
Our Father

Concluding Prayer
All-powerful, eternal God,
splendour of true light and never-ending day:
at this return of the morning hour
chase away the night of sin,
and fill our minds with the glory of your coming.
(We make our prayer) through our Lord.

109 Christ, the true light of us, true morn,
    Dispersing far the shades of night,
    Light whereof every light is born,
    Pledge of the beatific light,

    Thou all the night our guardian be
    Whose watch no sleep or slumber knows;
    Thou be our peace, that stayed on thee
    Through darkness we may find repose.

    Sleep then our eyes, but never sleep
    The watchful heaven-directed heart,
    And may thy hand in safety keep
    The servants whose desire thou art.

    Look on us, thou, and at our side
    Our foes and thine repulse afar;
    Through every ill the faithful guide
    Who in thy blood redeemèd are.

    While soul within the body clings,
    Body and soul defend us, Lord,
    Sure in the shadow of thy wings,
    Kept in thy lasting watch and ward.

8TH CENTURY
TR W. H. SHEWRING

110 Now it is evening; time to cease from labour,
    Father, according to thy will and pleasure,
    Through the night-season, have thy faithful people
    Safe in thy keeping.

    Far from our dwellings drive the evil spirits;
    Under the shadow of thy wings protect us;
    Be thou our guardian through the hours of darkness,
    Strong to defend us.

Call we, ere sleeping, on the name of Jesus;
Rise we at day-break, strong to serve thee better;
Order our doings, well begun and ended,
All to thy glory.

Fountain of goodness, bless the sick and needy;
Visit the captive, solace the afflicted;
Shelter the stranger, feed your starving children;
Strengthen the dying.

Father, who neither slumberest nor sleepest,
Thou, to whom darkness is as clear as noonday,
Have us this night-time, for the sake of Jesus,
Safe in thy keeping.

P. HERBERT D. 1571
TR G. R. WOODWARD 1848–1934
AND COMPILERS OF *The BBC Hymn Book*

111 Lead, kindly Light, amid the encircling gloom,
Lead thou me on;
The night is dark, and I am far from home,
Lead thou me on.
Keep thou my feet; I do not ask to see
The distant scene; one step enough for me.

I was not ever thus, nor prayed that thou
Shouldst lead me on;
I loved to choose and see my path; but now
Lead thou me on.
I loved the garish day, and, spite of fears,
Pride ruled my will: remember not past years.

So long thy power hath blest me, sure it still
Will lead me on
O'er moor and fen, o'er crag and torrent, till
The night is gone,
And with the morn those Angel faces smile,
Which I have loved long since, and lost awhile.

J. H. NEWMAN 1801–90

112 Abide with me; fast falls the eventide;
    The darkness deepens; Lord, with me abide;
    When other helpers fail, and comforts flee,
    Help of the helpless, O abide with me.

Swift to its close ebbs out life's little day:
Earth's joys grow dim, its glories pass away;
Change and decay in all around I see;
O thou who changest not, abide with me.

Hold thou thy Cross before my closing eyes;
Shine through the gloom, and point me to the skies;
Heaven's morning breaks, and earth's vain shadows flee;
In life, in death, O Lord, abide with me.

H. F. LYTE 1793–1847

113 The day thou gavest, Lord, is ended.
    The darkness falls at thy behest,
    To thee our morning hymns ascended,
    Thy praise shall sanctify our rest.

We thank thee that thy Church unsleeping,
While earth rolls onward into light,
Through all the world her watch is keeping,
And rests not now by day or night.

As over continent and island
The dawn leads on another day,
The voice of prayer is never silent,
Nor dies the strain of praise away.

The sun that bids us rest is waking
Our brethren 'neath the western sky,
And hour by hour fresh lips are making
Thy wondrous doings heard on high.

So be it, Lord, thy throne shall never,
Like earth's proud empires, pass away;
Thy kingdom stands, and grows for ever,
Till all thy creatures own thy sway.

J. ELLERTON 1826–93

114 Now thank we all our God,
With heart and hands and voices,
Who wondrous things hath done,
In whom his world rejoices;
Who from our mother's arms
Hath blessed us on our way
With countless gifts of love,
And still is ours today.

O may this bounteous God
Through all our life be near us,
With ever joyful hearts
And blessèd peace to cheer us;
And keep us in his grace,
And guide us when perplexed,
And free us from all ills
In this world and the next.

All praise and thanks to God
The Father now be given,
The Son, and him who reigns
With them in highest heaven,
The one eternal God,
Whom earth and heaven adore;
For thus it was, is now,
And shall be evermore.

M. RINKART 1586–1649
TR C. WINKWORTH 1829–78

115 Lord of all hopefulness, Lord of all joy,
Whose trust, ever childlike, no care could destroy,
Be there at our waking, and give us, we pray,
Your bliss in our hearts, Lord, at the break of the day.

Lord of all eagerness, Lord of all faith,
Whose strong hands were skilled at the plane and the lathe
Be there at our labours, and give us, we pray,
Your strength in our hearts, Lord, at the noon of the day.

Lord of all kindliness, Lord of all grace,
Your hands swift to welcome, your arms to embrace,
Be there at our homing, and give us, we pray,
Your love in our hearts, Lord, at the eve of the day.

Lord of all gentleness, Lord of all calm,
Whose voice is contentment, whose presence is balm,
Be there at our sleeping, and give us, we pray,
Your peace in our hearts, Lord, at the end of the day.

JAN STRUTHER 1901–53

116 Sweet Saviour, bless us e'er we go,
Thy word into our minds instil,
And make our lukewarm hearts to glow
With lowly love and fervent will.
Through life's long day and death's dark night,
O gentle Jesus, be our light.

The day is done, its hours have run,
And thou hast taken count of all,
The scanty triumphs grace hath won,
The broken vow, the frequent fall.
Through life's long day and death's dark night,
O gentle Jesus, be our light.

For all we love, the poor, the sad,
The sinful,—unto thee we call;
O let thy mercy make us glad;
Thou art our Jesus and our All.
Through life's long day and death's dark night,
O gentle Jesus, be our light.   F. W. FABER 1814–63

FINAL ANTHEMS
TO THE BLESSED VIRGIN MARY

117 Alma Redemptóris Mater, quae pérvia caeli
Porta manes, et stella maris, succúrre cadénti,
Súrgere qui curat, pópulo: tu quae genuísti,
Natúra miránte, tuum sanctum Genitórem,
Virgo prius ac postérius, Gabriélis ab ore
Sumens illud Ave, peccatórum miserére.

118 Mother of Christ! hear thou thy people's cry,
Star of the deep, and portal of the sky!
Mother of him who thee from nothing made,
Sinking we strive, and call to thee for aid:
Oh, by that joy which Gabriel brought to thee,
Thou Virgin first and last, let us thy mercy see.

119 Ave Regína caelórum!
Ave, Dómina angelórum;
Salve radix, salve porta
Ex qua mundo lux est orta.
Gaude, Virgo gloriósa,
Super omnes speciósa.
Vale, O valde decóra!
Et pro nobis Christum exóra.

120 Hail, Queen of Heaven, beyond compare,
To whom the angels homage pay;
Hail, Root of Jesse, Gate of Light,
That opened for the world's new Day.

Rejoice, O Virgin unsurpassed,
In whom our ransom was begun,
For all your loving children pray
To Christ, our Saviour, and your Son.

STANBROOK ABBEY

121 Regina caeli, laetáre! allelúia.
     Quia quem meruísti portáre, allelúia.
     Resurréxit sicut dixit; allelúia.
     Ora pro nobis Deum; allelúia.

122 Joy fill your heart, O Queen most high, alleluia!
     Your Son who in the tomb did lie, alleluia!
     Has risen as he did prophesy, alleluia!
     Pray for us, Mother, when we die, alleluia!
     Alleluia, alleluia, alleluia!

                                        JAMES QUINN SJ

or

123 Queen of heaven, rejoice, alleluia!
     for he whom you were worthy to bear, alleluia!
     has risen as he said, alleluia!
     Pray for us to God, alleluia!

124 Salve, Regína, Mater misericórdiae;
     vita, dulcédo, et spes nostra, salve.
     Ad te clamámus, éxsules fílii Hevae,
     ad te suspirámus, geméntes et flentes
     in hac lacrimárum valle.
     Eia, ergo, advocáta nostra, illos tuos
     misericórdes ocúlos ad nos convérte;
     et Iesum, benedíctum fructum ventris tui,
     nobis post hoc exílium osténde.
     O clemens, O pia, O dulcis Virgo María.

125 Hail, our Queen and Mother blest!
     Joy when all was sadness,
     Life and hope you gave mankind,
     Mother of our gladness!
     Children of the sinful Eve,
     Sinless-Eve, befriend us,
     Exiled in this vale of tears:
     Strength and comfort send us!

Pray for us, O Patroness,
Be our consolation!
Lead us home to see your Son,
Jesus, our salvation!
Gracious are you, full of grace,
Loving as none other,
Joy of heaven and joy of earth,
Mary, God's own Mother!

126 O sanctíssima, O piíssima,
Dulcis virgo María!
Mater amáta, intemeráta,
Ora, ora pro nobis.

Tu solácium et refúgium,
Virgo, mater María!
Quidquid optamus, per te sperámus;
Ora, ora pro nobis.

Ecce débiles, perquam flébiles,
Salva nos, O María!
Tolle languóres, sana dolóres,
Ora, ora pro nobis.

Virgo réspice, Mater, ádspice,
Audi nos, O María.
Tu medicínam portas divínam,
Ora, ora pro nobis.

Tua gáudia et suspíria
Iuvent nos, O María!
In te sperámus, ad te clamámus,
Ora, ora pro nobis.

127 O most holy one, O most pitiful, O sweet Virgin Mary!
Mother best beloved, Mother undefiled, pray for us!

Thou art our comfort, and our refuge, Virgin Mother Mary!
All that we long for, through thee we hope for; Pray for us!

See how weak we are, lost in tears; save us, O Mary!
Lighten our anguish; soothe our sorrows; pray for us!

Virgin, turn and look; Mother behold us; hear us, O Mary!
Thou art the bearer of health divine; pray for us!

May thy joys and thy sorrows be our help, O Mary!
In thee we hope; to thee we cry; pray for us!

NIGHT PRAYER

AFTER EVENING PRAYER I OF SUNDAYS AND SOLEMNITIES

℣ O God, come to our aid . . .

Here an examination of conscience is commended. In a common celebration this may be inserted in a penitential act using the formulas given in the Missal.

Hymn
A hymn suitable to the Hour is here said.
A selection of such hymns, nos. 109–116 is given above, pp 680 ff.

PSALMODY

Ant. 1: Lord, have mercy and hear me.
Eastertide: Alleluia, alleluia, alleluia.

THANKSGIVING   PSALM 4
The Lord raised him from the dead and made him worthy of all admiration (St Augustine)

When I cáll, ánswer me, O Gód of jústice;*
from ánguish you reléased me, have mércy and héar me!

O mén, how lóng will your héarts be clósed,*
will you lóve what is fútile and séek what is fálse?

It is the Lórd who grants fávours to thóse whom he lóves;*
the Lórd héars me whenéver I cáll him.

Fear him; do not sín: pónder on your béd and be stíll.*
Make jústice your sácrifice and trúst in the Lórd.

'What can bríng us háppiness?' mány sáy.*
Let the líght of your fáce shíne on us, O Lórd.

You have pút into my héart a gréater jóy*
than théy have from abúndance of córn and new wíne.

689

I will líe down in péace and sléep comes at ónce*
for yóu alone, Lórd, make me dwéll in sáfety.

Ant. Lord, have mercy and hear me.
Ant. 2: Bless the Lord through the night.

EVENING PRAYER IN THE TEMPLE   PSALM 133(134)
*Praise our God, all you his servants, and all who revere him, both great
and small* (Rev 19:5)

O cóme, bléss the Lórd,*
all yóu who sérve the Lórd,
who stánd in the hóuse of the Lórd,*
in the cóurts of the hóuse of our Gód.

Lift up your hánds to the hóly pláce*
and bléss the Lórd through the níght.

May the Lórd bléss you from Síon,*
he who máde both héaven and éarth.

Ant. Bless the Lord through the night.
Eastertide: Alleluia, alleluia, alleluia.

Scripture Reading   *Deut 6:4-7*
Hear, O Israel: the Lord our God is one Lord; and you shall love
the Lord your God with all your heart, and with all your soul, and
with all your might. And these words which I command you this
day shall be upon your heart; and you shall teach them diligently
to your children, and shall talk of them when you sit in your house,
and when you walk by the way, and when you lie down, and when
you rise.

Short Responsory
Outside Eastertide
R℣ Into your hands, Lord, I commend my spirit. *Repeat* R℣
℣ You have redeemed us, Lord God of truth. R℣ Glory be. R℣

Easter Octave
This is the day which was made by the Lord: let us rejoice and be glad, alleluia.

Eastertide
R̸ Into your hands, Lord, I commend my spirit, alleluia, alleluia.
Repeat R̸
V̸ You have redeemed us, Lord God of truth. R̸ Glory be. R̸

Ant. Save us, Lord, while we are awake; protect us while we sleep; that we may keep watch with Christ and rest with him in peace (alleluia).

NUNC DIMITTIS   CANTICLE: LK 2:29-32
Christ is the light of the nations and the glory of Israel

At last, all-powerful Master,†
you give leave to your servant*
to go in peace, according to your promise.

For my eyes have seen your salvation*
Which you have prepared for all nations,
the light to enlighten the Gentiles*
and give glory to Israel, your people.

Ant. Save us, Lord, while we are awake; protect us while we sleep; that we may keep watch with Christ and rest with him in peace (alleluia).

¶ *The ICET text of this canticle will be found on p 1176.*

Concluding Prayer
Sundays and Easter Octave
Come to visit us, Lord, this night,
so that by your strength we may rise at daybreak
to rejoice in the resurrection of Christ, your Son,
who lives and reigns for ever and ever.

691

Solemnities which do not occur on a Sunday
Visit this house, we pray you, Lord:
drive far away from it all the snares of the enemy.
May your holy angels stay here and guard us in peace,
and let your blessing be always upon us.
Through Christ our Lord.

Blessing
The Lord grant us a quiet night and a perfect end. R7 Amen.

This concludes the Hour even in recitation on one's own.
Anthem to the Blessed Virgin, see pp 685 ff.

AFTER EVENING PRAYER II OF SUNDAYS AND SOLEMNITIES

All as above except the following.

PSALMODY

Ant. He will conceal you with his wings; you will not fear the terror of the night.
Eastertide: Alleluia, alleluia, alleluia.

IN THE SHELTER OF THE MOST HIGH   PSALM 90(91)
Behold, I have given you power to tread underfoot serpents and scorpions (Lk 10:19)

He who dwélls in the shélter of the Most Hígh*
and abídes in the sháde of the Almíghty
sáys to the Lórd: 'My réfuge,*
my strónghold, my Gód in whom I trúst!'

It is hé who will frée you from the snáre*
of the fówler who séeks to destróy you;
hé will concéal you with his pínions*
and únder his wíngs you will find réfuge.

You will not féar the térror of the níght*
nor the árrow that flíes by dáy,

nor the plágue that prówls in the dárkness*
nor the scóurge that lays wáste at nóon.

A thóusand may fáll at your síde,*
tén thousand fáll at your ríght,
yóu, it will néver appróach;*
his fáithfulness is búckler and shíeld.

Your éyes have ónly to lóok*
to sée how the wícked are repáid,
yóu who have said: 'Lórd, my réfuge!'*
and have máde the Most Hígh your dwélling.

Upon yóu no évil shall fáll,*
no plágue appróach where you dwéll.
For yóu has he commánded his ángels,*
to kéep you in áll your wáys.

They shall béar you upón their hánds*
lest you stríke your fóot against a stóne.
On the líon and the víper you will tréad*
and trámple the young líon and the drágon.

Since he clíngs to me in lóve, I will frée him;*
protéct him for he knóws my náme.
When he cálls I shall ánswer: 'I am wíth you.'*
I will sáve him in distréss and give him glóry.

With léngth of lífe I will contént him;*
I shall lét him see my sáving pówer.

Ant. He will conceal you with his wings; you will not fear the terror of the night.
Eastertide: Alleluia, alleluia, alleluia.

Scripture Reading   *Rev 22:4-5*
They will see the Lord face to face, and his name will be written on their foreheads. It will never be night again and they will not need lamplight or sunlight, because the Lord God will be shining on them. They will reign for ever and ever.

Short Responsory
Outside Eastertide
℟ Into your hands, Lord, I commend my spirit. *Repeat* ℟
℣ You have redeemed us, Lord God of truth. ℟ Glory be. ℟

Easter Triduum
Christ humbled himself for us, and, in obedience, accepted death,
(*Good Friday, add:*) even death on a cross.
(*Holy Saturday, add further:*) Therefore God raised him to the
heights and gave him the name which is above all other names.

Easter Octave
This is the day which was made by the Lord: let us rejoice and be
glad, alleluia.

Eastertide
℟ Into your hands, Lord, I commend my spirit, alleluia, alleluia.
Repeat ℟
℣ You have redeemed us, Lord God of truth. ℟ Glory be. ℟

Ant. Save us, Lord, while we are awake; protect us while we sleep;
that we may keep watch with Christ and rest with him in peace
(alleluia).

NUNC DIMITTIS   CANTICLE: LK 2:29-32
Christ is the light of the nations and the glory of Israel

At last, all-powerful Master,†
you give leave to your servant*
to go in peace, according to your promise.

For my eyes have seen your salvation*
Which you have prepared for all nations,
the light to enlighten the Gentiles*
and give glory to Israel, your people.

Ant. Save us, Lord, while we are awake; protect us while we sleep;
that we may keep watch with Christ and rest with him in peace
(alleluia).

Concluding Prayer

Sundays and Easter Octave

God our Father,
as we have celebrated today the mystery of the Lord's resurrection,
grant our humble prayer:
free us from all harm
that we may sleep in peace
and rise in joy to sing your praise.
Through Christ our Lord.

Easter Triduum and Solemnities which do not fall on Sundays

Visit this house, we pray you, Lord:
drive far away from it all the snares of the enemy.
May your holy angels stay here and guard us in peace,
and let your blessing be always upon us.
Through Christ our Lord.

Blessing

The Lord grant us a quiet night and a perfect end. R/ Amen.

¶ *On Weekdays either the following series of Night Prayers or one of the two given for Sundays may be used.*

MONDAY

All as above, pp 689 ff, except for the following

PSALMODY

Ant. You, Lord God, are slow to anger, abounding in love.
Eastertide: Alleluia, alleluia, alleluia.

PRAYER OF A POOR MAN IN DISTRESS   PSALM 85(86)
Blessed be God who comforts us in all our sorrows (2 Cor 1:3-4)

Turn your éar, O Lórd, and give ánswer*
for Í am póor and néedy.
Preserve my lífe, for Í am fáithful:*
save the sérvant who trústs in yóu.

695

You are my Gód, have mércy on me, Lórd,*
for I crý to you áll the day lóng.
Give jóy to your sérvant, O Lórd,*
for to yóu I líft up my sóul.

O Lórd, you are góod and forgíving,*
full of lóve to áll who cáll.
Give héed, O Lórd, to my práyer*
and atténd to the sóund of my vóice.

In the dáy of distréss I will cáll*
and súrely yóu will replý.
Among the góds there is nóne like you, O Lórd;*
nor wórk to compáre with yóurs.

All the nátions shall cóme to adóre you*
and glórify your náme, O Lórd:
for you are gréat and do márvellous déeds,*
yóu who alóne are Gód.

Shów me, Lórd, your wáy†
so that Í may wálk in your trúth.*
Guide my héart to féar your náme.

I will práise you, Lord my Gód, with all my héart*
and glórify your náme for éver;
for your lóve to mé has been gréat:*
you have sáved me from the dépths of the gráve.

The próud have rísen agáinst me;†
rúthless men séek my lífe:*
to yóu they páy no héed.

But yóu, God of mércy and compássion,*
slów to ánger, O Lórd,
abóunding in lóve and trúth,*
túrn and take píty on mé.

O gíve your stréngth to your sérvant*
and sáve your hándmaid's són.
Shów me a sígn of your fávour†
that my fóes may sée to their sháme*
that you consóle me and gíve me your hélp.

Ant. You, Lord God, are slow to anger, abounding in love.
Eastertide: Alleluia, alleluia, alleluia.

Scripture Reading   *I Thess 5:9-10*
God chose us to possess salvation through our Lord Jesus Christ,
who died for us in order that we might live together with him,
whether we are alive or dead when he comes.

Short Responsory
Outside Eastertide
R̸ Into your hands, Lord, I commend my spirit. *Repeat* R̸
V̸ You have redeemed us, Lord God of truth. R̸ Glory be. R̸

Eastertide
R̸ Into your hands, Lord, I commend my spirit, alleluia, alleluia.
Repeat R̸
V̸ You have redeemed us, Lord God of truth. R̸ Glory be. R̸

Ant. Save us, Lord, while we are awake; protect us while we sleep;
that we may keep watch with Christ and rest with him in peace
(alleluia).

NUNC DIMITTIS   CANTICLE: LK 2:29-32
Christ is the light of the nations and the glory of Israel.

At last, all-powerful Master,†
you give leave to your servant*
to go in peace, according to your promise.

For my eyes have seen your salvation*
which you have prepared for all nations,
the light to enlighten the Gentiles*
and give glory to Israel, your people.

Ant. Save us, Lord, while we are awake; protect us while we sleep;
that we may keep watch with Christ and rest with him in peace
(alleluia).

Concluding Prayer
Lord, give our bodies restful sleep;
and let the work we have done today
be sown for an eternal harvest.
Through Christ our Lord.

Blessing
The Lord grant us a quiet night and a perfect end. ℟ Amen.

TUESDAY

All as above, pp 689 ff, except for the following.

PSALMODY

Ant. Do not hide your face from me, for in you have I put my trust.
Eastertide: Alleluia, alleluia, alleluia.

PRAYER IN DESOLATION   PSALM 142(143):1-11
*A man is made righteous not by obedience to the Law, but by faith in
Jesus Christ* (Gal 2:16)

Lórd, lísten to my práyer:†
túrn your éar to my appéal.*
You are fáithful, you are júst; give ánswer.
Do not cáll your sérvant to júdgment*
for nó one is júst in your síght.

The énemy pursúes my sóul;*
he has crúshed my lífe to the gróund;
he has máde me dwéll in dárkness*
like the déad, lóng forgótten.
Thérefore my spírit fáils;*
my héart is númb withín me.

I remémber the dáys that are pást:*
I pónder áll your wórks.
I múse on what your hánd has wróught†
and to yóu I strétch out my hánds.*
Like a párched land my sóul thirsts for yóu.

Lórd, make háste and ánswer;*
for my spírit fáils withín me.
Dó not híde your fáce*
lest I becóme like thóse in the gráve.

In the mórning let me knów your lóve*
for I pút my trúst in yóu.
Make me knów the wáy I should wálk:*
to yóu I líft up my sóul.

Réscue me, Lórd, from my énemies;*
I have fléd to yóu for réfuge.
Téach me to dó your wíll*
for yóu, O Lórd, are my Gód.
Let yóur good spírit guíde me*
in wáys that are lével and smóoth.

For your náme's sake, Lórd, save my lífe;*
in your jústice save my sóul from distréss.

Ant. Do not hide your face from me, for in you have I put my trust.
Eastertide: Alleluia, alleluia, alleluia.

Scripture Reading   *1 Pet 5:8-9*
Be calm but vigilant, because your enemy the devil is prowling
round like a roaring lion, looking for someone to eat. Stand up to
him, strong in faith.

Short Responsory
Outside Eastertide
R⁊ Into your hands, Lord, I commend my spirit. *Repeat* R⁊
℣ You have redeemed us, Lord God of truth. R⁊ Glory be. R⁊

Eastertide
R⁊ Into your hands, Lord, I commend my spirit, alleluia, alleluia.
Repeat R⁊
℣ You have redeemed us, Lord God of truth. R⁊ Glory be. R⁊

Ant. Save us, Lord, while we are awake; protect us while we sleep;
that we may keep watch with Christ and rest with him in peace
(alleluia).

699

NUNC DIMITTIS   CANTICLE: LK 2:29-32
Christ is the light of the nations and the glory of Israel

At last, all-powerful Master,†
you give leave to your servant*
to go in peace, according to your promise.

For my eyes have seen your salvation*
which you have prepared for all nations,
the light to enlighten the Gentiles*
and give glory to Israel, your people.

Ant. Save us, Lord, while we are awake; protect us while we sleep;
that we may keep watch with Christ and rest with him in peace
(alleluia).

Concluding Prayer
In your mercy, Lord,
dispel the darkness of this night.
Let your household so sleep in peace,
that at the dawn of a new day,
they may, with joy, waken in your name.
Through Christ our Lord.

Blessing
The Lord grant us a quiet night and a perfect end. ℞ Amen.

WEDNESDAY

All as above pp 689 ff, except for the following.

PSALMODY

Ant. 1: O God, be my protector and my refuge.
Eastertide: Alleluia, alleluia, alleluia.

CONFIDENT PRAYER IN DISTRESS   PSALM 30(31):1-6
Father, into your hands I commend my spirit (Lk 23:46)

In yóu, O Lórd, I take réfuge.*

Let me néver be pút to sháme.
In your jústice, sét me frée,
héar me and spéedily réscue me.

Be a róck of réfuge fór me,*
a míghty strónghold to sáve me,
for yóu are my róck, my strónghold.*
For your náme's sake, léad me and gúide me.

Reléase me from the snáres they have hídden*
for yóu are my réfuge, Lórd.
Into your hánds I comménd my spírit.*
It is yóu who will redéem me, Lórd.

Ant. O God, be my protector and my refuge.
Ant. 2: Out of the depths I cry to you, O Lord.†

OUT OF THE DEPTHS I CRY   PSALM 129(130)
He will save his people from their sins (Mt 1:21)

Out of the dépths I crý to you, O Lórd,*
†Lórd, hear my vóice!
O lét your éars be atténtive*
to the vóice of my pléading.

If you, O Lórd, should márk our guílt,*
Lórd, who would survíve?
But with yóu is fóund forgíveness:*
for thís we revére you.

My sóul is wáiting for the Lórd,*
I cóunt on his wórd.
My sóul is lónging for the Lórd*
more than wátchman for dáybreak.
Let the wátchman cóunt on dáybreak*
and Ísrael on the Lórd.

Becáuse with the Lórd there is mércy*
and fúlness of redémption,
Ísrael indéed he will redéem*
from áll its iníquity.   Glory be.

701

Ant. Out of the depths I cry to you, O Lord.
Eastertide: Alleluia, alleluia, alleluia.

Scripture Reading   *Eph 4:26-27*
Do not let resentment lead you into sin; the sunset must not find you still angry. Do not give the devil his opportunity.

Short Responsory
Outside Eastertide
R⁄ Into your hands, Lord, I commend my spirit. *Repeat* R⁄
V⁄ You have redeemed us, Lord God of truth. R⁄ Glory be. R⁄

Eastertide
R⁄ Into your hands, Lord, I commend my spirit, alleluia, alleluia.
Repeat R⁄
V⁄ You have redeemed us, Lord God of truth. R⁄ Glory be. R⁄

Ant. Save us, Lord, while we are awake; protect us while we sleep; that we may keep watch with Christ and rest with him in peace (alleluia).

NUNC DIMITTIS   CANTICLE: LK 2:29-32
Christ is the light of the nations and the glory of Israel

At last, all-powerful Master,†
you give leave to your servant*
to go in peace, according to your promise.

For my eyes have seen your salvation*
which you have prepared for all nations,
the light to enlighten the Gentiles*
and give glory to Israel, your people.

Ant. Save us, Lord, while we are awake; protect us while we sleep; that we may keep watch with Christ and rest with him in peace (alleluia).

Concluding Prayer
Lord Jesus Christ,
meek and humble of heart,
you offer to those who follow you
a yoke that is good to bear,
a burden that is light.
Accept, we beg you, our prayer and work of this day,
and grant us the rest we need
that we may be ever more willing to serve you,
who live and reign for ever and ever.

Blessing
The Lord grant us a quiet night and a perfect end. ℟ Amen.

THURSDAY

All as above, pp 689 ff, except for the following.

PSALMODY

Ant. My body shall rest in safety.
Eastertide: Alleluia, alleluia, alleluia.

THE LORD IS MY PORTION   PSALM 15(16)
God raised up Jesus, freeing him from the pains of death (Acts 2:24)

Presérve me, Gód, I take réfuge in yóu.†
I sáy to the Lórd: 'Yóu are my Gód.*
My háppiness líes in yóu alóne.'

He has pút into my héart a márvellous lóve*
for the fáithful ónes who dwéll in his lánd.
Those who chóose other góds incréase their sórrows.†
Néver will I óffer their ófferings of blóod.*
Néver will I táke their náme upon my líps.

O Lórd, it is yóu who are my pórtion and cúp;*
it is yóu yoursélf who áre my príze.
The lót marked óut for me is mý delíght:*
welcome indéed the héritage that fálls to mé!

I will bléss the Lórd who gíves me cóunsel,*
who éven at níght dirécts my héart.
I kéep the Lórd ever ín my síght:*
since hé is at my ríght hand, Í shall stand fírm.

And so my héart rejóices, my sóul is glád;*
éven my bódy shall rést in sáfety.
For yóu will not léave my sóul among the déad,*
nor lét your belóved knów decáy.

You will shów me the páth of lífe,†
the fúlness of jóy in your présence,*
at your ríght hand háppiness for éver.

Ant. My body shall rest in safety.
Eastertide: Alleluia, alleluia, alleluia.

Scripture Reading   *I Thess 5:23*
May the God who gives us peace make you completely his, and keep your whole being, spirit, soul, and body, free from all fault, at the coming of our Lord Jesus Christ.

Short Responsory
Outside Eastertide
R℔ Into your hands, Lord, I commend my spirit. *Repeat* R℔
V℔ You have redeemed us, Lord God of truth. R℔ Glory be. R℔

Eastertide
R℔ Into your hands, Lord, I commend my spirit, alleluia, alleluia.
Repeat R℔
V℔ You have redeemed us, Lord God of truth. R℔ Glory be. R℔

Ant. Save us, Lord, while we are awake; protect us while we sleep; that we may keep watch with Christ and rest with him in peace (alleluia).

NUNC DIMITTIS   CANTICLE: LK 2:29-32
Christ is the light of the nations and the glory of Israel

At last, all-powerfu Master,†

you give leave to your servant*
to go in peace, according to your promise.

For my eyes have seen your salvation*
which you have prepared for all nations,
the light to enlighten the Gentiles*
and give glory to Israel, your people.

Ant. Save us, Lord, while we are awake; protect us while we sleep;
that we may keep watch with Christ and rest with him in peace
(alleluia).

Concluding Prayer
Lord our God,
restore us again by the repose of sleep
after the fatigue of our daily work:
so that, continually renewed by your help,
we may serve you in body and soul.
Through Christ our Lord.

Blessing
The Lord grant us a quiet night and a perfect end. ℟ Amen.

FRIDAY

All as above, pp 689 ff, except for the following.

PSALMODY

Ant. Lord my God, I call for help by day; I cry at night before you.†
Eastertide: Alleluia, alleluia, alleluia.

PRAYER OF ONE WHO IS GRAVELY ILL   PSALM 87(88)
This is your hour; this is the reign of darkness (Lk 22:53)

Lord my Gód, I call for hélp by dáy;*
I crý at níght befóre you.
†Let my práyer cóme into your présence.*
O túrn your éar to my crý.

For my sóul is fílled with évils;*
my lífe is on the brínk of the gráve.
I am réckoned as óne in the tómb:*
I have réached the énd of my stréngth,

like óne alóne among the déad;*
like the sláin lýing in their gráves;
like thóse you remémber no móre,*
cut óff, as they áre, from your hánd.

You have láid me in the dépths of the tómb,*
in pláces that are dárk, in the dépths.
Your ánger weighs dówn upón me:*
I am drówned benéath your wáves.

You have táken awáy my fríends*
and máde me háteful in their síght
Imprísoned, I cánnot escápe;*
my éyes are súnken with gríef.

I cáll to you, Lórd, all the day lóng;*
to yóu I strétch out my hánds.
Will you wórk your wónders for the déad?*
Will the shádes stánd and práise you?

Will your lóve be tóld in the gráve*
or your fáithfulness amóng the déad?
Will your wónders be knówn in the dárk*
or your jústice in the lánd of oblívion?

As for mé, Lord, I cáll to you for hélp:*
in the mórning my práyer comes befóre you.
Lórd, whý do you rejéct me?*
Whý do you híde your fáce?

Wrétched, close to déath from my yóuth,*
I have bórne your tríals; I am númb.
Your fúry has swépt down upón me;*
your térrors have útterly destróyed me.

They surróund me all the dáy like a flóod,*
they assáil me áll togéther.

Friend and néighbour you have táken awáy:*
my óne compánion is dárkness.

Ant. Lord my God, I call for help by day; I cry at night before you.
Eastertide: Alleluia, alleluia, alleluia.

Scripture Reading   *Jer 14:9*
Lord, you are in our midst, we are called by your name. Do not
desert us, O Lord our God.

Short Responsory
Outside Eastertide
R⁷ Into your hands, Lord, I commend my spirit. *Repeat* R⁷
℣ You have redeemed us, Lord God of truth. R⁷ Glory be. R⁷

Eastertide
R⁷ Into your hands, Lord, I commend my spirit, alleluia, alleluia.
Repeat R⁷
℣ You have redeemed us, Lord God of truth. R⁷ Glory be. R⁷

Ant. Save us, Lord, while we are awake; protect us while we sleep;
that we may keep watch with Christ and rest with him in peace
(alleluia).

NUNC DIMITTIS   CANTICLE: LK 2:29-32
Christ is the light of the nations and the glory of Israel

At last, all-powerful Master,†
you give leave to your servant*
to go in peace, according to your promise.

For my eyes have seen your salvation*
which you have prepared for all nations,
the light to enlighten the Gentiles*
and give glory to Israel, your people.

Ant. Save us, Lord, while we are awake; protect us while we sleep;
that we may keep watch with Christ and rest with him in peace
(alleluia).

Concluding Prayer
Give us grace, almighty God,
so to unite ourselves in faith with your only Son,
who underwent death and lay buried in the tomb
that we may rise again in newness of life with him,
who lives and reigns for ever and ever.

Blessing
The Lord grant us a quiet night and a perfect end. ℞ Amen.

THE PROPER OF SAINTS

SAINTS OF THE GENERAL CALENDAR

THE PROPER OF SAINTS

See Introduction 113-132.

A Saint's Day may be celebrated as a Solemnity, as a Feast, or as a Memoria.

A Memoria may be either obligatory *or* optional.

A Solemnity has First and Second Evening Prayers, and the texts for all the Hours of the Office are taken from either the Proper or the appropriate Common.

A Feast has no First Evening Prayer (unless it be a feast of the Lord, celebrated on a Sunday). The texts for the Hours of the Office are taken from the Proper or the Common except for the psalms and antiphons at Prayer During the Day, which are usually *of the day or the Season. Where special psalms or antiphons are to be used at Prayer During the Day, this is indicated.*

A Memoria, whether obligatory or optional, has greater flexibility with regard to texts, except where proper texts are appointed, but normally, *the psalms and antiphons at all Hours, and the whole of Prayer During the Day, including the concluding prayer, are from the psalter or the Proper of Seasons.*

From 17 to 23 December, during the Christmas octave and in Lent, a Memoria is celebrated as an optional Commemoration by adding the antiphon and the concluding prayer of the Saint, after the concluding prayer of the day, at Morning and Evening Prayer.

¶ *In this Proper the Memorias of most of the saints have only a concluding prayer. Antiphons are given for Morning and Evening Prayer only when proper to a particular celebration. Exceptions to this general practice are the antiphons given for Memorias which are celebrated as Commemorations.*

JANUARY

2 January
SAINT BASIL THE GREAT
and
SAINT GREGORY NAZIANZEN
Bishops and Doctors of the Church

Memoria

Basil was born of a Christian family at Caesarea in Cappadocia in the year 330. Outstanding in learning and virtue he began to lead a retired life but in the year 370 he was appointed Bishop of Caesarea. He combated the Arian heresy, wrote much of value, especially the monastic rules, which even today are followed by many monks of the Eastern Church; and he was outstanding in helping the poor. He died on 1 January 379.

Gregory was born near Nazianzus in the same year, 330. He journeyed much in order to acquire knowledge and he followed his friend Saint Basil in undertaking a life of solitude, but he was ordained a priest and bishop. In 381 he was chosen Bishop of Constantinople. However, because of the divisions he encountered in the diocese he returned to his native Nazianzus where he died on 25 January in either 389 or 390. He was a man of outstanding knowledge and eloquence and was called The Theologian.

From the Common of Pastors, p 1040, or of Doctors of the Church, p 1049, except for the following:

MORNING PRAYER

Benedictus ant. The learned will shine as brightly as the vault of heaven, and those who have instructed many in virtue will shine like stars for all eternity.

Concluding Prayer
God our Father,
you enriched your Church and gave examples for us to follow
in the life and teaching of Saint Basil and Saint Gregory.
Grant that, learning your truth with humility,
we may practise it in faith and love.
(We make our prayer) through our Lord.

EVENING PRAYER

Magnificat ant. The man who keeps the commandments and teaches them will be considered great in the kingdom of heaven.

7 January

SAINT RAYMUND OF PENYAFORT, Priest

Optional Memoria

Born near Barcelona about the year 1175. He became a Canon of the Cathedral, but later joined the Dominican Order. At the command of Gregory IX he edited the *Book of Decretals.* He was chosen Master General of his Order and governed it with wise laws. His most outstanding writing was his *Summary of Cases* which gave rules for the fruitful administration of the Sacrament of Penance. He died in the year 1275.

From the Common of Pastors, p 1040.

Concluding Prayer
Almighty God,
you inspired Saint Raymund
with an immense compassion for sinners and captives.
Grant us, through his prayer, freedom from sin
and the grace to do your will.
(We make our prayer) through our Lord.

13 January

SAINT HILARY
Bishop and Doctor of the Church

Optional Memoria

Born in Poitiers at the beginning of the fourth century, Hilary was elected bishop of that city in the year 350. He combated the Arians relentlessly, for which reason he was exiled by the Emperor Constantine. For the purpose of strengthening the Catholic faith and interpreting sacred scripture he published works which are outstanding in their wisdom and learning. He died in the year 367.

From the Common of Pastors, p 1040, or of Doctors of the Church, p 1049.

Concluding Prayer
Give us grace, almighty God,
to understand aright
and faithfully maintain your Son's divinity,
which Saint Hilary so steadfastly upheld.
(We make our prayer) through our Lord.

17 January
SAINT ANTONY, Abbot
Memoria

This outstanding father of all monks was born in Egypt about the year 250. After the death of his parents he gave his worldly goods to the poor and went into the desert to live a life of penance. Many became his followers. He worked for the Church, supporting the confessors of the faith in their suffering during the persecution of Diocletian, and Saint Athanasius in his struggle against the Arians. He died in the year 356.

From the Common of Men Saints: Religious, p 1064.

Concluding Prayer
Lord God,
you bestowed on Saint Antony
the grace of serving you in the wilderness
by a strange and wonderful way of life.
Grant that through his intercession
we may deny ourselves
and love you above all things.
(We make our prayer) through our Lord.

20 January
SAINT FABIAN
Pope and Martyr
Optional Memoria

In the year 236 he was chosen to be Bishop of Rome, and in the year 250, at the beginning of the persecution of Decius, he was crowned with martyrdom, as Saint Cyprian testified. He was buried in the cemetery of Callistus.

713

From the Common of Martyrs: One Martyr, p 1029, or of Pastors, p 1040.

Concluding Prayer
Lord God,
you crown your priests in glory;
grant that by the intercession of Pope Saint Fabian,
we may share his faith
and like him give you loyal service.
(We make our prayer) through our Lord.

Also 20 January
SAINT SEBASTIAN, Martyr
Optional Memoria

He suffered martyrdom in Rome at the beginning of the persecution of Diocletian. His tomb in the place named Ad Catacumbas on the Via Appia has been venerated by the faithful from earliest times.

From the Common of Martyrs: One Martyr, p 1029.

Concluding Prayer
Grant us, Lord, the spirit of fortitude.
Teach us, by the example of Saint Sebastian,
to render obedience to you rather than to men.
(We make our prayer) through our Lord.

21 January
SAINT AGNES
Virgin and Martyr
Memoria

She suffered martyrdom at Rome either in the second half of the third century or, more probably, at the beginning of the fourth century. Pope Damasus embellished her tomb with sacred verses, and many of the Fathers, following the example of Saint Ambrose, spoke of her with great praise.

From the Common of Martyrs: One Martyr, p 1029, or Virgins, p 1053.

MORNING PRAYER

Hymn, from the psalter or the Common of Martyrs: One Martyr, p 1029, or Virgins, p 1053.

Ant. 1: My Lord, Jesus Christ, has placed a ring on my finger; he has adorned me like a bride with a crown.

Psalms and canticle of Sunday, Week 1, p 390 ff.

Ant. 2: He who is the Lord of the angels is the one to whom I am betrothed. The sun and moon reflect his beauty.

Ant. 3: Rejoice with me, and be glad, since I have taken my place with all the saints.

Scripture Reading   *2 Cor 1:3-5*

Let us give thanks to the God and Father of our Lord Jesus Christ, the merciful Father, the God from whom all help comes! He helps us in all our troubles, so that we are able to help those who have all kinds of troubles, using the same help that we ourselves have received from God. Just as we have a share in Christ's many sufferings so also through Christ we share in his great help.

Short Responsory

R℣ God is her help, she will not be moved. *Repeat* R℣
℣ The Lord is with her. R℣ Glory be. R℣

Benedictus ant. What I desired, I now see; what I hoped for, I now possess. I am united in heaven with the One I loved on earth.

Concluding Prayer

Almighty, ever-living God,
you choose what is weak in the world
to shame what is strong.
Grant that, as we celebrate the martyrdom of Saint Agnes,
we may follow her example of steadfastness in faith.
(We make our prayer) through our Lord.

EVENING PRAYER

Hymn from the psalter or the Common.

Ant. 1: The virgin of Christ was neither overcome by terror, nor won over by flattery.

Psalms and canticle from the Common of Martyrs, p 1021.

Ant. 2: I trust in him alone, to him alone do I commit myself with all my love.

Ant. 3: I give you praise, Father of my Lord Jesus Christ, because you made your servant victorious through your Son.

Scripture Reading   *1 Pet 4:13-14*
My dear people, if you can have some share in the sufferings of Christ, be glad, because you will enjoy a much greater gladness when his glory is revealed. It is a blessing for you when they insult you for bearing the name of Christ, because it means that you have the spirit of glory, the spirit of God resting on you.

Short Responsory
R̠ God chose her before she was born. *Repeat* R̠
V̠ He brought her to live in his own dwelling place. R̠ Glory be. R̠

Magnificat ant. Saint Agnes opened her arms and prayed: I pray to you, holy Father; behold, I am coming to you whom I have loved, whom I have sought, whom I have always desired.

The concluding prayer as at Morning Prayer, p 715.

22 January
SAINT VINCENT
Deacon and Martyr

Optional Memoria

Vincent, a deacon of the Church of Saragossa, suffered terrible tortures and died the death of a martyr at Valencia, in Spain, during the persecution of Diocletian. Veneration for him quickly spread throughout the Church.

From the Common of Martyrs: One Martyr, p 1029.

Concluding Prayer
Almighty, ever-living God,
fill us with your Holy Spirit,
and let a love stronger than death possess our hearts,
the love that enabled Saint Vincent
to rise above the torments of his martyrdom.
(We make our prayer) through our Lord.

24 January
SAINT FRANCIS DE SALES
Bishop and Doctor of the Church

Memoria

Born near Annecy in Savoy in the year 1567. After his ordination as a priest he worked strenuously for the renewal of the faith in his country; and after his election as Bishop of Geneva he showed himself to be a true shepherd towards his clergy and the faithful, being an example in all things, and helping all by his writings and work. He died at Lyons on 28 December 1622, and was buried at Annecy on 24 January 1623.

From the Common of Pastors, p 1040, or of Doctors of the Church, p 1049.

Concluding Prayer
Grant, Lord,
that in the service of our fellow-men
we may always reflect your own gentleness and love,
and so imitate Saint Francis de Sales,
whom you made all things to all men
for the saving of souls.
(We make our prayer) through our Lord.

717

25 January
THE CONVERSION OF
SAINT PAUL THE APOSTLE

Feast

Invitatory ant. Let us give praise to God for the conversion of the Teacher of the nations.
Psalm, p 371.

MORNING PRAYER

Hymn

Apostle of the gentiles, Paul
The greatest witness of them all,
You turned to Christ, the risen Lord,
When out of light you heard him call.

You journeyed far and wide to tell
That Christ was risen from the dead,
That all who put their faith in him
Would live for ever, as he said.

To Father, Son and Spirit blest,
The light of man's uncharted ways,
With all the Church throughout the world
Give glory and unceasing praise.

Ant. 1: I know who it is that I have put my trust in, and I am certain that he, the just judge, will be able to take care of all I have had entrusted to me until that Day.

Psalms and canticle of Sunday, Week 1, pp 390 ff.

Ant. 2: My grace is enough for you, Paul; my power is made perfect in weakness.

Ant. 3: The grace of God in me has not been fruitless; rather his grace remains with me always.

Scripture Reading   *Acts 26:16b-18*

I have appeared to you to appoint you as my servant; you are to tell others what you have seen of me today, and what I will show you in the future. I will save you from the people of Israel and from the Gentiles, to whom I will send you. You are to open their eyes and turn them from the darkness to the light, and from the power of Satan to God, so that through their faith in me they will have their sins forgiven and receive their place among God's chosen people.

Short Responsory

R/ You are the chosen instrument of God, Saint Paul, the apostle of the nations. *Repeat* R/

V/ You are the preacher of truth in all the world. R/ Glory be. R/

Benedictus ant. Let us celebrate the conversion of Saint Paul, the apostle. He who was a persecutor of the Church has become God's chosen instrument.

Intercessions

Since we have received from the apostles our heavenly inheritance, let us thank our Father for all his blessings. R/ Lord, the apostles sing your praises.

Praise to you, Lord God, for the gift of Christ's body and blood, handed on by the apostles, to give us strength and life;—Lord, the apostles sing your praises.

For the table of your word, served by the apostles, to bring us light and joy;—Lord, the apostles sing your praises.

For your holy Church, built on the apostles, to make us all one body;—Lord, the apostles sing your praises.

For the washing of baptism and penance, entrusted to the apostles, to cleanse our hearts from sin;—Lord, the apostles sing your praises.

Our Father

Concluding Prayer

Today, Lord, we celebrate the conversion of Saint Paul,
your chosen vessel for carrying your name to the whole world.
Help us to make our way towards you by following in his footsteps,

and by witnessing to your truth before the men and women of our day.
(We make our prayer) through our Lord.

EVENING PRAYER

Hymn as at Morning Prayer p 718, or from the Common, p 1006.

Ant. 1: I will freely boast of my weakness, so that the power of Christ may dwell in me.

Psalms and canticle from the Common of Apostles, Evening Prayer II, p 1007.

Ant. 2: I planted, Apollo watered, but it is God who gave the increase.

Ant. 3: For me, to live is Christ, and to die is gain; I must glory in the cross of our Lord Jesus Christ.

Scripture Reading   *1 Cor 15:9-10*
I am the least of the apostles; in fact, since I persecuted the Church of God, I hardly deserve the name apostle; but by God's grace that is what I am, and the grace that he gave me has not been fruitless. On the contrary, I, or rather the grace of God that is with me, have worked harder than any of the others.

Short Responsory
R℣ I will praise you, Lord, with all my heart. *Repeat* R℣
℣ I will tell of your name among the peoples. R℣ Glory be. R℣

Magnificat ant. Saint Paul, apostle, preacher of the truth and teacher of the nations, pray for us to God, who chose you.

Intercessions
Since we are part of a building that has the apostles for its foundation, let us pray to the Father for his holy people. R℣ Lord, remember your Church.

Father, when your Son rose from the dead, you showed him first to the apostles;—let us make him known, near and far. R̸

You sent your Son into the world to proclaim the good news to the poor;—grant that we may bring his gospel into the darkness of men's lives. R̸

You sent your Son to plant in men's hearts the seed of imperishable life;—may we labour to sow his word and reap a harvest of joy. R̸

You sent your Son to reconcile the world with yourself by the shedding of his blood;—let us become his fellow workers in restoring men to your friendship. R̸

You placed your Son at your own right hand in heaven;—receive the dead into the happiness of your kingdom. R̸

Our Father

Concluding Prayer

Today, Lord, we celebrate the conversion of Saint Paul,
your chosen vessel for carrying your name to the whole world.
Help us to make our way towards you by following in his footsteps,
and by witnessing to your truth before the men and women of our
    day.
(We make our prayer) through our Lord.

26 January

SAINT TIMOTHY
and SAINT TITUS, Bishops

Memoria

Timothy and Titus were disciples and helpers of the apostle Paul, the former being placed in charge of the Church at Ephesus, the latter the Church at Crete. Saint Paul wrote his pastoral epistles to them, containing much useful advice for the instruction of the clergy and people.

From the Common of Pastors, p 1040, except for the following:

MORNING PRAYER

Benedictus ant. Proclaim the Gospel, insist on it in season and out of season, convince, rebuke, and exhort, do all with patience and in a manner that will teach men.

721

Concluding Prayer
Almighty God,
you endowed Saint Timothy and Saint Titus
with power to preach your word;
grant that, living a life of integrity and holiness in this world,
we may, through their prayers,
come to our true home in heaven.
(We make our prayer) through our Lord.

EVENING PRAYER

Magnificat ant. Let us lead holy lives, while we await in hope the
coming of the Lord.

27 January
SAINT ANGELA MERICI, Virgin
Optional Memoria

Born about the year 1470 at Desenzano near Brescia. She took the habit
of the Third Order of Saint Francis and gathered together girls whom she
formed in the works of charity. In 1535 she formed at Brescia the institute
of the Ursulines, a society of women with the task of teaching poor girls to
be good Christians. She died in 1540.

*From the Common of Virgins, p 1053, or of Women Saints: Educators,
p 1072.*

Concluding Prayer
Lord God,
let Saint Angela ever commend us
to your love and care.
May her charity and wisdom
inspire us to treasure your teaching
and express it in our lives.
(We make our prayer) through our Lord.

28 January
SAINT THOMAS AQUINAS
Priest and Doctor of the Church

Memoria

Born about the year 1225, a member of a noble family of Aquino. He studied first at Monte Cassino and then at Naples; later as a member of the Dominican Order he completed his studies at Paris and then at Cologne with Saint Albert the Great as his teacher. He was an outstanding writer and teacher of philosophy and sacred theology. He died at Fossanuova on 7 March 1274. He is venerated on 28 January for on that date in the year 1369 his body was reburied at Toulouse.

From the Common of Doctors of the Church, p 1049, except for the following:

MORNING PRAYER

Benedictus ant. Give praise to the Lord, for love of whom Saint Thomas studied and worked at all times.

Concluding Prayer
Lord, our God,
since it was by your gift
that Saint Thomas became so great a saint and theologian,
give us grace to understand his teaching
and follow his way of life.
(We make our prayer) through our Lord.

EVENING PRAYER

Magnificat ant. God gave him great wisdom which he faithfully taught to others; he passed it on to them without keeping anything for himself.

31 January
SAINT JOHN BOSCO, Priest

Memoria

Born near Castelnuovo in the diocese of Turin in the year 1815. He had a difficult childhood in poverty but eventually was ordained priest. He put every effort into the education of youth and founded Religious Congregations to teach them and to bring them up in the Christian way of life. He wrote some short works in defence of the faith. He died in the year 1888.

From the Common of Pastors, p 1040, or of Men Saints: Educators, p 1064.

Concluding Prayer
We praise you, Lord,
for calling Saint John Bosco
to be a loving father and prudent guide of the young.
Give us his fervent zeal for souls
and enable us to live for you alone.
(We make our prayer) through our Lord.

FEBRUARY

2 February
THE PRESENTATION OF THE LORD

Feast

If 2 February is a Sunday, Evening Prayer I is as follows:

EVENING PRAYER I

Hymn as at Morning Prayer, p 726.

Ant. 1: The parents of Jesus took him up to Jerusalem to present him to the Lord.

Psalms and canticle as on 25 March, pp 757 ff.

Ant. 2: Sion, prepare your marriage chamber; behold, your king, Christ is coming to you.

Ant. 3: Blessed are you, Simeon, lover of truth; you received Christ the Lord, who was to bring freedom to his people.

Scripture Reading   *Heb 10:5-7*
This is what Christ said, on coming into the world:
You who wanted no sacrifice or oblation,
prepared a body for me.
You took no pleasure in holocausts or sacrifices for sin;
then I said,
just as I was commanded in the scroll of the book,
'God, here I am! I am coming to obey your will.'

Short Responsory
R℣ The Lord has made known his saving power. *Repeat* R℣
℣ Which he prepared in the sight of all the peoples. R℣ Glory be. R℣

Magnificat ant. **The old man held the child, but the child was his king; the virgin bore the child, yet remained a virgin after the birth; she adored as her God the child she bore.**

Intercessions
We celebrate the presentation of Jesus in the temple. He has established a new covenant and is himself the temple of the living God. Let us acclaim him as our Saviour: R℣ Our eyes have seen your salvation.
You are the true light that enlightens all men:—help us to know and accept you as our Lord and God. R℣
You are the glory of your Church:—in the fidelity of your people, let men see your saving power. R℣
Your Holy Spirit rested on Simeon and he recognized your coming: —let your Spirit dwell with us, so that we may recognize you in our lives. R℣
At your presentation, Simeon prophesied that our Lady would be pierced to the heart:—grant us the constancy and love she showed at the foot of the cross. R℣
Many have seen your promise and died in your peace:—may they share now the glory you prepared for all the nations. R℣
Our Father

Concluding Prayer
Almighty, ever-living God,

on this day your Only-begotten Son
was presented in the temple,
in flesh and blood like ours:
purify us in mind and heart
that we may meet you in your glory.
(We make our prayer) through our Lord.

Invitatory
Ant. Behold he comes to his holy temple, our Lord and Master;
come, let us adore him.
Psalm, p 371.

MORNING PRAYER

Hymn
  Hail to the Lord who comes,
  Comes to his temple gate,
  Not with his angel hosts,
  Not in his kingly state;

  But borne upon the throne
  Of Mary's gentle breast;
  Thus to his Father's house
  He comes, a humble guest.

  The world's true light draws near
  All darkness to dispel,
  The flame of faith is lit
  And dies the power of hell.

  Our bodies and our souls
  Are temples now for him,
  For we are born of grace—
  God lights our souls within.

  O Light of all the earth!
  We light our lives with thee;
  The chains of darkness gone
  All sons of God are free.

Ant. 1: Simeon was an upright and devout man; he looked for the redemption of Israel and the Holy Spirit was with him.

Psalms and canticle of Sunday, Week 1, pp 390 ff.

Ant. 2: Simeon took the child into his hands and gave thanks while praising God.

Ant. 3: A light to show the way to the pagans and the glory of your people Israel.

Scripture Reading   *Mal 3:1*
I am going to send my messenger to prepare a way before me. And the Lord you are seeking will suddenly enter his Temple; and the angel of the covenant whom you are longing for, yes, he is coming.

Short Responsory
R7 Adore the Lord in his holy court. *Repeat* R7
V Give the Lord glory and power. R7 Glory be. R7

Benedictus ant. When his parents brought in the child Jesus, Simeon took him in his arms and gave thanks to God.

Intercessions
We adore our Lord and Saviour who was presented to his Father in the temple, and who came to bring comfort to his brothers.
R7 Lord Jesus, you are the light of the world.
On the cross you consummated your sacrifice to the Father:—unite our offerings to yours in the sacrifice of your Church. R7
You brought consolation to Israel:—bring us now your wisdom, fresh understanding and new vision. R7
The Church continues to proclaim your coming;—through her bring light to those who search for truth. R7
You are the sign of contradiction, the corner-stone rejected by the builders:—build us as living stones into a temple where you will dwell. R7
Our Father

Concluding Prayer
Almighty, ever-living God,
on this day your Only-begotten Son
was presented in the temple,
in flesh and blood like ours:
purify us in mind and heart
that we may meet you in your glory.
(We make our prayer) through our Lord.

EVENING PRAYER II

*Hymn, as at Morning Prayer p726, or from the appendix, for the
Blessed Virgin Mary.*

PSALMODY

Ant. 1: The Holy Spirit had revealed to Simeon that he would not
see death until he had set eyes on the Lord.

PSALM 109(110):1-5,7

The Lórd's revelátion to my Máster:†
'Sít on my ríght:*
your fóes I will pút beneath your féet.'

The Lórd will wíeld from Síon†
your scéptre of pówer:*
rúle in the mídst of all your fóes.

A prínce from the dáy of your bírth†
on the hóly móuntains;*
from the wómb before the dáwn I begót you.

The Lórd has sworn an óath he will not chánge.†
'You are a príest for éver,*
a príest like Melchízedek of óld.'

The Máster stánding at your ríght hand*
will shatter kíngs in the dáy of his wráth.

He shall drínk from the stréam by the wáyside*
and thérefore he shall líft up his héad.

Ant. The Holy Spirit had revealed to Simeon that he would not see death until he had set eyes on the Lord.

Ant. 2: They went to offer to the Lord what the Law ordered: a pair of turtledoves or a pair of pigeons.

PSALM 129(130)

Out of the dépths I crý to you, O Lórd,*
Lórd, hear my vóice!
O lét your éars be atténtive*
to the vóice of my pléading.

If you, O Lórd, should márk our guílt,*
Lórd, who would survíve?
But with yóu is fóund forgíveness:*
for thís we revére you.

My sóul is wáiting for the Lórd,*
I cóunt on his wórd.
My sóul is lónging for the Lórd*
more than wátchman for dáybreak.
Let the wátchman cóunt on dáybreak*
and Ísrael on the Lórd.

Becáuse with the Lórd there is mércy*
and fúlness of redémption,
Ísrael indéed he will redéem*
from áll its iníquity.

Ant. They went to offer to the Lord what the Law ordered: a pair of turtledoves or a pair of pigeons.

Ant. 3: My eyes have seen your salvation which you have prepared for all the nations to see.

CANTICLE: COL 1:12-20

Let us give thanks to the Father,†
who has qualified us to share*
in the inheritance of the saints in light.

He has delivered us from the dominion of darkness*
and transferred us to the kingdom of his beloved Son,
in whom we have redemption,*
the forgiveness of sins.

He is the image of the invisible God,*
the first-born of all creation,
for in him all things were created, in heaven and on earth,*
visible and invisible.

All things were created*
through him and for him.
He is before all things,*
and in him all things hold together.

He is the head of the body, the Church;*
he is the beginning,
the first-born from the dead,*
that in everything he might be pre-eminent,

For in him all the fulness of God was pleased to dwell,*
and through him to reconcile to himself all things,
whether on earth or in heaven,*
making peace by the blood of his cross.

Ant. My eyes have seen your salvation which you have prepared for
all the nations to see.

Scripture Reading   *Heb 4:15-16*

It is not as if we had a high priest who was incapable of feeling our
weaknesses with us; but we have one who has been tempted in every
way that we are, though he is without sin. Let us be confident, then,
in approaching the throne of grace, that we shall have mercy from
him and find grace when we are in need of help.

Short Responsory

R̷ The Lord has made known his saving power. *Repeat* R̷
V̷ He has prepared this wonder in the sight of all the peoples.
R̷ Glory be. R̷

Magnificat ant. Today the Blessed Virgin Mary presented the child Jesus in the temple; there Simeon took him in his arms and gave thanks to God.

Intercessions
We celebrate the presentation of Jesus in the temple. He has established a new covenant and is himself the temple of the living God. Let us acclaim him as our Saviour: R℣ Our eyes have seen your salvation.
You are the true light that enlightens all men:—help us to know and accept you as our Lord and God. R℣
You are the glory of your Church:—in the fidelity of your people, let men see your saving power. R℣
Your Holy Spirit rested on Simeon and he recognized your coming: —let your Spirit dwell with us, so that we may recognize you in our lives. R℣
At your presentation, Simeon prophesied that our Lady would be pierced to the heart:—grant us the constancy and love she showed at the foot of the cross. R℣
Many have seen your promise and died in your peace:—may they share now the glory you prepared for all the nations. R℣
Our Father

The concluding prayer as at Morning Prayer, p 728.

3 February
SAINT BLAISE, Bishop and Martyr
Optional Memoria

He was Bishop of Sivas in Armenia in the fourth century. In the Middle Ages veneration of him spread throughout the Church.

From the Common of Martyrs: for One Martyr, p 1029, or of Pastors, p 1040.

Concluding Prayer
Peace in our present life
and help towards the life to come:
this is the prayer, Lord,
which your people offer on Saint Blaise's Day,

731

with the support of his intercession.
(We make our prayer) through our Lord.

Also 3 February
SAINT ANSGAR, Bishop

Optional Memoria

Born in France at the beginning of the ninth century. He was educated
in the monastery at Corbie and then in the year 826 he set out to preach
the gospel in Denmark. Meeting with little success he then went to Sweden.
He was chosen to be Bishop of Hamburg and was confirmed in this position
by Gregory IV who made him his legate for Denmark and Sweden. He
endured many difficulties in his work of evangelization but his spirit never
failed. He died the year 865.

From the Common of Pastors, p 1040.

Concluding Prayer
Lord God,
you sent Saint Ansgar, monk and bishop,
to bring the light of the gospel
to the peoples of northern Europe.
Through his prayer give us grace
to live always in the light of your truth.
(We make our prayer) through our Lord.

5 February
SAINT AGATHA, Virgin and Martyr

Memoria   *Lent: as a Commemoration*

She suffered martyrdom at Catania in Sicily, probably in the persecution
of Decius. She was venerated throughout the Church from earliest times
and her name was inserted into the Roman Canon.

*From the Common of Martyrs: One Martyr, p 1029, or of Virgins,
p 1053, except for the following:*

MORNING PRAYER

Benedictus ant. With joy and rejoicing as though to a feast Agatha
went to prison, and she offered her sufferings to God with many
prayers.

732

Concluding Prayer

Lord God,
let Saint Agatha who became precious in your sight
through her pure life and valiant martyrdom,
plead for our forgiveness.
(We make our prayer) through our Lord.

EVENING PRAYER

Magnificat ant. Lord Jesus Christ, my loving Master, I give you thanks for giving me the strength to overcome the torments which were brought against me; bid me come joyfully to your undying glory.

6 February
SAINT PAUL MIKI
and
HIS COMPANIONS, Martyrs

Memoria   *Lent: as a Commemoration*

Born in Japan between the years 1564 and 1566. He entered the Society of Jesus and preached the gospel with success, but when a persecution of Catholics arose he and twenty-five others were seized and subjected to terrible tortures, and finally were crucified at Nagasaki in the year 1597 on 5 February.
From the Common of Martyrs: Several Martyrs, p 1017.

MORNING PRAYER

Benedictus ant. Blessed are those who are persecuted in the cause of right: theirs is the kingdom of heaven.

Concluding Prayer

Lord God,
source of strength to all the saints,
you called your martyrs Paul and his companions
to undergo the cross that they might enter into life.

Let their prayer help us to keep the faith
to the end of our days.
(We make our prayer) through our Lord.

EVENING PRAYER

Magnificat ant. The saints, who followed in the footsteps of Christ,
rejoice in heaven. They gave their life for love of Christ; therefore
they will reign for ever.

8 February
SAINT JEROME EMILIAN
Optional Memoria   *Lent: as a Commemoration*

Born at Venice in the year 1486. At first he was a soldier but later left this
life so as to consecrate himself to helping the poor; and he gave them all
his worldly goods. He founded the Order of Clerks Regular called the
Somaschi for the purpose of helping orphan children and the poor. He died
at Somascha near Bergamo in 1537.

From the Common of Men Saints: Educators, p 1064.

MORNING PRAYER

Benedictus ant. He who has compassion teaches and guides, as a
shepherd his flock.

Concluding Prayer
Father of mercy,
you chose Saint Jerome Emilian
to be a father to orphans in their need.
Grant that through his prayer
we may keep faithfully the spirit of sonship,
by which we are not only called,
but really are your children.
(We make our prayer) through our Lord.

EVENING PRAYER

Magnificat ant. Let the children come to me; for the kingdom of heaven belongs to such as these.

SAINT SCHOLASTICA, Virgin

Memoria   *Lent: as a Commemoration*

The sister of Saint Benedict, born at Norcia in Umbria about the year 480. Together with her brother she consecrated herself to God, and she followed Benedict to Monte Cassino, where she died about the year 547.

From the Common of Virgins, p 1053.

MORNING PRAYER

Ant. See, the wise virgin has gone to Christ; she shines among the choirs of virgins like the sun in the heavens.

Concluding Prayer
Lord God,
may we, like Saint Scholastica,
serve you with an unsullied love:
and then our joy will be full
as we receive from your loving hand
all that we desire and ask.
(We make our prayer) through our Lord.

EVENING PRAYER

Ant. Come, bride of Christ, and receive the crown which the Lord has prepared for you.

OUR LADY OF LOURDES

Optional Memoria   *Lent: as a Commemoration*

In the year 1858 the Immaculate Virgin Mary appeared to Bernadette Soubirous near Lourdes in France, in the grotto of Massabielle. Through the poor child, Mary called sinners to penance, and thereby there arose in the Church a marvellous spirit of prayer and charity, especially in helping the poor and the sick.

From the Common of the Blessed Virgin Mary, p 987, except for the following:

MORNING PRAYER

Benedictus ant. Bright dawn of salvation, Virgin Mary; from you rose the Sun of justice, the Rising Sun who came to visit us from on high.

Concluding Prayer
Lord of mercy,
as we keep the memory of Mary,
the immaculate Mother of God,
who appeared to Bernadette at Lourdes:
grant us through her prayer
strength in our weakness
and grace to rise up from our sins.
(We make our prayer) through our Lord.

EVENING PRAYER

Magnificat ant. Hail Mary, full of grace: the Lord is with you. You are the most blessed of all women and blessed is the fruit of your womb.

14 February
SAINT CYRIL, Monk, and
SAINT METHODIUS, Bishop
Memoria *Lent: as a Commemoration*

Cyril was born in Salonika and was educated at Constantinople. With his brother Methodius he went to Moravia to preach the faith. They both translated the liturgical books into the Slavonic language using the Cyrillic alphabet which they invented. They were called to Rome and here Cyril died on 14 February in the year 869. Methodius was made a bishop and went to Pannonia (Hungary) where he laboured ceaselessly in preaching the gospel, while enduring many hardships as a result of jealousy, though he had the support of the Holy See. He died on 6 April in the year 885 at Velehrad in Czechoslovakia.

From the Common of Pastors, p 1040, except for the following:

MORNING PRAYER

Benedictus ant. They served the Lord in holiness and virtue all their days.

Concluding Prayer

Saint Cyril and Saint Methodius were your instruments, Lord,
in bringing the light of the gospel to the Slavonic peoples.
May we take your word into our hearts
and be at one in professing the true faith.
(We make our prayer) through our Lord.

EVENING PRAYER

Magnificat ant. These saints were made friends of God, glorious for preaching the truth of God.

17 February
THE SEVEN HOLY FOUNDERS
OF THE SERVITE ORDER

Optional Memoria   *Lent: as a Commemoration*

These seven men were born at Florence and led lives as hermits on Monte Senario, especially venerating the Blessed Virgin Mary. They then preached through the length and breadth of Tuscany, and founded the Order of Servites which in 1304 received the approval of the Holy See. They are venerated on this day which is said to be the day on which Saint Alexis Falconieri, one of the seven, died, in the year 1310.

From the Common of Men Saints: Religious, p 1064, except for the following:

MORNING PRAYER

Benedictus ant. How good and how pleasant it is, brothers dwelling in unity.

Concluding Prayer
Inspire us, Lord, with the great love
the Seven Founders had for Mary, the Mother of God,
and as they drew your people to you by their devotion,
so may we proclaim your love to all.
(We make our prayer) through our Lord.

EVENING PRAYER

Magnificat ant. Where brothers are united in praising God, there the
Lord will bestow his blessing.

21 February
SAINT PETER DAMIAN
Bishop and Doctor of the Church
Optional Memoria   *Lent: as a Commemoration*

Born at Ravenna in the year 1007. After completing his studies he taught
for a short while but then gave it up and became a hermit at Fonte Avellana.
He was elected Prior of the community and strenuously promoted religious
observance both there and in other parts of Italy. In the difficult times in
which he lived he helped the Roman Pontiffs by his writings and acted as
legate to reform the Church. He was created a Cardinal and Bishop of
Ostia by Stephen IX. On his death in the year 1072 he was immediately
venerated as a saint.

*From the Common of Pastors, p 1040, or of Doctors of the Church,
p 1049.*

MORNING PRAYER

Benedictus ant. The learned will shine as brightly as the vault of
heaven, and those who have instructed many in virtue will shine like
stars for all eternity.

Concluding Prayer
Almighty God,
teach us by the example and doctrine of Saint Peter Damian
to prefer nothing whatever to Christ,

and to make the service of your Church our chief concern,
and so come to the joy of your eternal kingdom.
(We make our prayer) through our Lord.

EVENING PRAYER

Magnificat ant. O holy doctor, Saint Peter, you light of the Church,
you love the law of heaven; pray for us to the Son of God.

22 February
THE SEE OF SAINT PETER
THE APOSTLE

Feast

The feast of the See of Saint Peter has been kept at Rome on this day from
the fourth century as a symbol of the unity of the Church founded on the
Apostle Saint Peter.

Invitatory ant. The Lord is the King of Apostles; come, let us adore
him.
Psalm, p 371.

MORNING PRAYER

Hymn

O Peter, who were named by Christ
The guardian-shepherd of his flock,
Protect the Church he built on you
To stand unyielding, firm on rock.

Your weakness Christ exchanged for strength,
You faltered, but he made you true;
He knew the greatness of your love
And gave the keys of heaven to you.

Unseen, eternal Trinity,
We give you glory, praise your name;
Your love keeps faith with faithless men,
Through change and stress you are the same.

739

Alternative hymn

Jesus, true God and Rock of our salvation!
Yours is the title that you gave to Simon,
Naming him Peter as the Church's bedrock,
First of apostles!

Jesus, sole Ruler in the Church, your kingdom,
Yours are the keys that open David's city!
Yet till your coming Peter is your viceroy,
Keys in his keeping!

Jesus, we thank you for the Church, your Body!
Keep us all one with you and with each other,
One with our bishop, one with your chief shepherd,
Peter's successor!

Ant. 1: The Lord said to Simon, 'Do not fear, from now on you will be a fisher of men.'

Psalms and canticle of Sunday, Week 1, pp 390 ff.

Ant. 2: 'You are the Christ, the Son of the living God'; 'Blessed are you, Simon Peter.'

Ant. 3: The Lord said to Peter, 'To you I will give the keys of the kingdom of heaven.'

Scripture Reading   *Acts 15:7b-9*
God chose me from among you to preach the message of Good News to the Gentiles, so that they could hear and believe. And God, who knows the hearts of men, showed his approval of the Gentiles by giving the Holy Spirit to them, just as he had to us. He made no difference between us and them; he forgave them their sins because they believed.

Short Responsory
R̶7 You will make them rulers over all the land. *Repeat* R̶7
V̶ Your name, Lord, will be remembered. R̶7 Glory be. R̶7

Benedictus ant. The Lord said to Simon Peter. 'I have prayed for you that your faith may not fail, and when you have repented, you must strengthen your brothers.'

Intercessions
Since we have received from the apostles our heavenly inheritance, let us thank our Father for all his blessings. R℣ Lord, the apostles sing your praises.
Praise to you, Lord God, for the gift of Christ's body and blood, handed on by the apostles, to give us strength and life;—Lord, the apostles sing your praises.
For the table of your word, served by the apostles, to bring us light and joy;—Lord, the apostles sing your praises.
For your holy Church, built on the apostles, to make us all one body;—Lord, the apostles sing your praises.
For the washing of baptism and penance, entrusted to the apostles, to cleanse our hearts from sin;—Lord, the apostles sing your praises.
Our Father

Concluding Prayer
Almighty God,
as you built your Church
on the rock of Peter's faith,
grant that with such a firm foundation
we may hold fast in every storm.
(We make our prayer) through our Lord.
(Through Christ our Lord.)

EVENING PRAYER

Hymn as at Morning Prayer, p 739.

Ant. 1: Peter, do you love me? You know that I love you, Lord. Feed my sheep.

Psalms and canticle from the Common of Apostles, Evening Prayer II, pp 1007 ff.

Ant. 2: While Peter was held in prison the Church prayed unceasingly to God for him.

Ant. 3: You are Peter, and on this rock I will build my Church.

Scripture Reading   *I Pet 1:3-5*

Blessed be God the Father of our Lord Jesus Christ, who in his great mercy has given us a new birth as his sons, by raising Jesus Christ from the dead, so that we have a sure hope and the promise of an inheritance that can never be spoilt or soiled and never fade away, because it is being kept for you in the heavens. Through your faith, God's power will guard you until the salvation which has been prepared is revealed at the end of time.

Short Responsory

R⁷ Tell of the glory of the Lord; announce it among the nations.
Repeat R⁷
V⁷ Speak of his wonderful deeds to all the peoples. R⁷ Glory be. R⁷

Magnificat ant. You are the shepherd of the flock, the prince of the apostles: to you were given the keys of the kingdom of heaven.

Intercessions

Since we are part of a building that has the apostles for its foundation, let us pray to the Father for his holy people. R⁷ Lord, remember your Church.
Father, when your Son rose from the dead, you showed him first to the apostles;—let us make him known, near and far. R⁷
You sent your Son into the world to proclaim the good news to the poor;—grant that we may bring his gospel into the darkness of men's lives. R⁷
You sent your Son to plant in men's hearts the seed of imperishable life;—may we labour to sow his word and reap a harvest of joy. R⁷
You sent your Son to reconcile the world with yourself by the shedding of his blood;—let us become his fellow workers in restoring men to your friendship. R⁷
You placed your Son at your own right hand in heaven;—receive the dead into the happiness of your kingdom. R⁷
Our Father

Concluding Prayer
Almighty God,
as you built your Church
on the rock of Peter's faith,
grant that with such a firm foundation
we may hold fast in every storm.
(We make our prayer) through our Lord.

23 February
SAINT POLYCARP
Bishop and Martyr

Memoria   *Lent: as a Commemoration*

Polycarp was a disciple of the apostles and bishop of Smyrna, as well as a friend of Saint Ignatius of Antioch. He went to Rome to confer with Pope Saint Anicetus about the celebration of Easter. He suffered martyrdom about the year 155 by being burnt to death in the city stadium.

From the Common of Martyrs: for One Martyr, p 1029, or of Pastors, p 1040, except for the following:

MORNING PRAYER

Benedictus ant. I have been a servant of Christ for eighty-six years and no evil has come near me; how can I now speak against my king who has saved me?

Concluding Prayer
Lord of all creation,
you gave Saint Polycarp a place in the company of the martyrs.
Grant that, through his intercession,
we may, like him, drink from that cup which Christ drank,
and so rise to eternal life.
(We make our prayer) through our Lord.

EVENING PRAYER

Magnificat ant. Lord, God almighty, I give you praise because you have numbered me among the martyrs who partake of the chalice of your Christ.

MARCH

4 March
SAINT CASIMIR

Optional Memoria   *Lent: as a Commemoration*

Born in the year 1458, the son of the King of Poland. He practised the Christian virtues especially chastity and love of the poor. He was conspicuous for a firm faith and for his veneration for the Holy Eucharist and the Blessed Virgin Mary. He died of phthisis in the year 1484.

From the Common of Men Saints, p 1064.

MORNING PRAYER

Ant. The man who lives by the truth comes out into the light, so that it may be plainly seen that what he does is done in God.

Concluding Prayer
Almighty God,
to serve you is to reign with you.
At the intercession of Saint Casimir
grant that we may always serve you
by just and holy living.
(We make our prayer) through our Lord.

EVENING PRAYER

Ant. Well done, good and faithful servant, come and join in your Master's joy.

7 March
SAINT PERPETUA and
SAINT FELICITY, Martyrs

Memoria   *Lent: as a Commemoration*

Died in the persecution of Septimius Severus in the year 203, at Carthage. There is an impressive narrative of their martyrdom in existence, partly written by the saints themselves and partly by a contemporary writer.

From the Common of Martyrs: Several Martyrs, p 1017.

MORNING PRAYER

Ant. Blessed are those who are persecuted in the cause of right; theirs is the kingdom of heaven.

Concluding Prayer
With overwhelming love for you, Lord God,
your martyrs Perpetua and Felicity defied the persecutor
and overcame the pain of death.
Listen to their prayers
and grant that we may love you daily more and more.
(We make our prayer) through our Lord.

EVENING PRAYER

Ant. The saints, who followed in the footsteps of Christ, rejoice in heaven. They gave their life for love of Christ: therefore, they will reign for ever.

8 March
SAINT JOHN OF GOD, Religious
Optional Memoria   *Lent: as a Commemoration*

Born in Portugal in 1495. After leading a dangerous life as a soldier, and wishing to devote the rest of his life to good works, he gave himself up completely to looking after the sick. He founded a hospital at Granada in Spain and with his followers set up the Order of Hospitallers of Saint John of God. He was outstanding in his love for the sick and needy. He died at Granada in the year 1550.
From the Common of Men Saints: Religious, or Saints Noted for Works of Mercy, p 1064.

MORNING PRAYER

Ant. If there is love among you, then all will know that you are my disciples.

Concluding Prayer
Lord,
you filled the heart of Saint John of God
with compassion for his fellow-men.
Grant that, loving our neighbour as he did,
we may be called to share with your saints
in the joys of your kingdom.
(We make our prayer) through our Lord.

EVENING PRAYER

Ant. Truly I tell you, anything you did for the least of those who are mine, you did for me. Come, you blessed of my Father, inherit the kingdom prepared for you from the foundation of the world.

9 March
SAINT FRANCES OF ROME
Religious

Optional Memoria   *Lent: as a Commemoration*

Born in Rome in the year 1384. She was married when very young and gave birth to three children. She lived in troubled times and gave her goods to the poor and tended the sick. She was outstanding in virtue especially in humility, patience and devotion to the needy. In the year 1425 she founded a Congregation of Oblates following the rule of Saint Benedict, and died in 1440.

From the Common of Women Saints: Religious, p 1072.

MORNING PRAYER

Ant. Whoever does the will of my Father, says the Lord, is my brother, and sister, and mother.

Concluding Prayer
In the life of Saint Frances of Rome, Lord God,
you gave us an outstanding example
of the married state and of the religious life.
Grant that we may discern your presence

in all the circumstances of our lives,
and follow you to the end of our days.
(We make our prayer) through our Lord.

EVENING PRAYER

Ant. You have left all things and have followed me; you will be repaid a hundred times over, and gain eternal life.

17 March
SAINT PATRICK, Bishop
As a Commemoration

Born in Great Britain about the year 385. As a youth he was taken captive to Ireland as a slave and worked as a herdsman. After making his escape he wished to become a priest and after being made Bishop for Ireland he was untiring in preaching the Gospel and he converted many to the faith. In addition he organized the Church throughout Ireland. It is believed that he died in 461 and was buried at Downpatrick.

MORNING PRAYER

Ant. Go, and teach all peoples; baptize them in the name of the Father, and of the Son, and of the Holy Spirit.

Concluding Prayer
We give you thanks, almighty God,
for sending Saint Patrick to preach your glory to the people of
 Ireland.
Grant that we who are proud to call ourselves Christians
may never cease to proclaim to the world
the good news of salvation.
(We make our prayer) through our Lord.

EVENING PRAYER

Ant. Many will come from the east and the west to take their places with Abraham and Isaac and Jacob in the kingdom of heaven.

18 March
SAINT CYRIL OF JERUSALEM
Bishop and Doctor of the Church
As a Commemoration

Born of Christian parents in the year 315. He succeeded Maximus as Bishop of Jerusalem in 348. He was involved in the Arian controversy and more than once was sentenced to exile. His *Catecheses* in which he explained the true doctrine of the faith and Sacred Scripture as well as the tradition of the Church for the sake of the people show his pastoral zeal. He died in the year 386.

MORNING PRAYER

Ant. The learned will shine as brightly as the vault of heaven, and those who have instructed many in virtue will shine like the stars for all eternity.

Concluding Prayer
By your grace, Lord God,
Saint Cyril led your Church to a deeper understanding
of the mysteries of baptism and the eucharist.
May his prayer help us to grow in knowledge of your Son,
that we may have life, and have it more abundantly.
(We make our prayer) through our Lord.

19 March
SAINT JOSEPH
Husband of the Blessed Virgin Mary
Solemnity

EVENING PRAYER I

Hymn
Joseph, the scriptures love to trace
The glories of thy kingly line;
Yet no succession of thy race,
No long posterity was thine—
Of her the everlasting spouse

Who must a Virgin ever be,
The faithful ruler of his house
Who owns no fatherhood in thee.

There were no songs of old renown,
No crowds to greet you when you came,
Two wanderers, to your native town,
That lost inheritance to claim;
But hard the hearts, and cold the air,
And mean the lodging where you lay,
And long the exile you must bear
Till upstart Herod's dying day.

Joseph, the Church of God protect;
Her priests with holy care endow;
Shield of the virgin-souls elect,
Hope of the fatherless, be thou:
And, when our parting spirits cling
To earthly joys that cannot bide,
Make Nazareth in our homes, and bring
Jesus and Mary to our side.

The alleluia *given in parentheses is added to the antiphons in Eastertide.*

Ant. 1: Jacob was the father of Joseph, the husband of Mary; of her was born Jesus who is called Christ (alleluia).

Psalms and canticle from the Common of Pastors, pp 1036 ff.

Ant. 2: The angel Gabriel was sent by God to a town in Galilee called Nazareth, to the virgin who was betrothed to a man named Joseph (alleluia).

Ant. 3: Mary, the mother of Jesus, was betrothed to Joseph; but before they came to live together she was found to be with child through the Holy Spirit (alleluia).

Scripture Reading   *Col 3:23-24*
Whatever you do, work at it with all your heart, as though you were

working for the Lord, and not for men. Remember that the Lord will reward you; you will receive what he has kept for his people. For Christ is the real Master you serve.

Short Responsory

R̷ The virtuous man will bloom like the lily. *Repeat* R̷
V̷ He will grow for ever before the Lord. R̷ Glory be. R̷

Eastertide

R̷ The virtuous man will bloom like the lily, alleluia, alleluia.
Repeat R̷
V̷ He will grow for ever before the Lord. R̷ Glory be. R̷

Magnificat ant. Behold the faithful and wise servant, whom the Master placed over his household (alleluia).

Intercessions

Let us pray to God our Father, for from him, all fatherhood in heaven and on earth takes its name. R̷ Father, hallowed be your name.

Father, in your Son you revealed to Joseph the mystery kept secret for endless ages:—help us to acknowledge your Son as God and man. R̷

Father, you enabled Joseph to spend his life in your service:—set our minds on your kingdom and your justice before all other things. R̷

Father, your will is that every man should accept and answer your call:—by the prayer of Joseph, give us the grace to live in accord with your will. R̷

Creator of all things, you have entrusted your work to our hands:—grant that our labours may prove worthy of you. R̷

Father, in whom all men live, grant to those who have died new life, through your Son:—with Mary, and Joseph, and all your saints for ever. R̷

Our Father

Concluding Prayer

Almighty God,

at the beginnings of our salvation,
when Mary conceived your Son and brought him forth into the
 world,
you placed them under Joseph's watchful care.
May his prayer still help your Church
to be an equally faithful guardian of your mysteries,
and a sign of Christ to mankind.
(We make our prayer) through our Lord.

Invitatory
Ant. Today we are celebrating the feast of Saint Joseph; come, let
us worship Christ the Lord (alleluia).
Psalm, p 371.

MORNING PRAYER

Hymn
> Joseph, wise ruler of God's earthly household,
> Nearest of all men to the heart of Jesus,
> Be still a father, lovingly providing
> For us, his brethren.
>
> Saint strong and manly, chosen by the Father,
> As trusted guardian of the Son eternal,
> Guide us as once you guided Wisdom's footsteps
> With sure direction.
>
> Husband of Mary, loving and beloved,
> Teach us the joy of love so pure and holy,
> Warming our hearts with love for God's own Mother
> By your example.
>
> Saint of the dying, blest with Mary's presence,
> In death you rested in the arms of Jesus;
> So at our ending, Jesus, Mary, Joseph,
> Come to assist us!

Ant. 1: The shepherds came quickly and they found Mary and
Joseph and the child lying in the manger (alleluia).

Psalms and canticle of Sunday, Week 1, pp 390 ff.

Ant. 2: Joseph and Mary, the mother of Jesus, marvelled at what was being said of him, and Simeon gave them his blessing (alleluia).

Ant. 3: Joseph arose from sleep and, taking the child and his mother with him, left that night for Egypt, where he stayed until the death of Herod (alleluia).

Scripture Reading   *2 Sam 7:28-29*

Lord, you are God indeed, your words are true and you have made this fair promise to your servant. Be pleased, then, to bless the house of your servant, that it may continue for ever in your presence; for you, Lord God, have spoken; and with your blessing the house of your servant will be for ever blessed.

Short Responsory

R̸ The Lord made him master of his house. *Repeat* R̸
Ỿ He constituted him ruler of all he possessed. R̸ Glory be. R̸

Eastertide

R̸ The Lord made him master of his house, alleluia, alleluia.
Repeat R̸
Ỿ He constituted him ruler of all he possessed. R̸ Glory be. R̸

Benedictus ant. Joseph settled in a town called Nazareth. This was to fulfil the words spoken about Christ by the prophets: He will be called a Nazarene (alleluia).

Intercessions

Whatever we do or say, let us do it in the name of the Lord Jesus, giving thanks to God the Father through him. R̸ Lord, hear us.
As Joseph believed what you had told him, and became the guardian of your only Son:—so may we put our faith in you, and receive the fulfilment of your promise. R̸
Father, give us that faith which gives substance to our hopes,—and make us certain of realities we do not see. R̸
Joseph took the child Jesus into his care, loving and accepting him

as his own Son:—may we accept all that God gives us, and care for those entrusted to us. ℟

You have given man authority over the work of your hands and invited him to share in your creation:—help us to accept our responsibility by working for your glory and the good of all mankind. ℟

Our Father

Concluding Prayer

Almighty God,
at the beginnings of our salvation,
when Mary conceived your Son and brought him forth into the
  world,
you placed them under Joseph's watchful care.
May his prayer still help your Church
to be an equally faithful guardian of your mysteries,
and a sign of Christ to mankind.
(We make our prayer) through our Lord.

EVENING PRAYER II

Hymn as at Morning Prayer, p 751.

Ant. 1: The parents of Jesus found him in the Temple, sitting among the doctors, listening to them and asking them questions (alleluia).

Psalms and canticle from the Common of Pastors, pp 1044 ff.

Ant. 2: The mother of Jesus said to him, 'Son, why have you treated us like this? Your father and I have been looking for you anxiously.'

Ant. 3: Jesus went down with them to Nazareth and lived under their authority (alleluia).

Scripture Reading   *Col 3:23-24*
Whatever you do, work at it with all your heart, as though you were working for the Lord, and not for men. Remember that the Lord

will reward you; you will receive what he has kept for his people. For Christ is the real Master you serve.

Short Responsory
R℣ The virtuous man will bloom like the lily. *Repeat* R℣
℣ He will grow for ever before the Lord. R℣ Glory be. R℣

Eastertide
R℣ The virtuous man will bloom like the lily, alleluia, alleluia. *Repeat* R℣
℣ He will grow for ever before the Lord. R℣ Glory be. R℣

Magnificat ant. When Jesus started to teach, he was about thirty years old, being the son, as it was thought, of Joseph (alleluia).

Intercessions
Let us pray to God our Father, for from him, all fatherhood in heaven and on earth takes its name. R℣ Father, hallowed be your name.
Father, in your Son you revealed to Joseph the mystery kept secret for endless ages:—help us to acknowledge your Son as God and man. R℣
Father, you enabled Joseph to spend his life in your service:—set our minds on your kingdom and your justice before all other things. R℣
Father, your will is that every man should accept and answer your call:—by the prayer of Joseph, give us the grace to live in accord with your will. R℣
Creator of all things, you have entrusted your work to our hands:—grant that our labours may prove worthy of you. R℣
Father, in whom all men live, grant to those who have died new life, through your Son:—with Mary, and Joseph, and all your saints for ever. R℣
Our Father

The concluding prayer as at Morning Prayer, p 753.

23 March
SAINT TURIBIUS OF MONGROVEJO, Bishop

As a Commemoration

Born in Spain about the year 1538. He studied law in Salamanca and in 1580 was chosen to be Bishop of Lima and went to America. He was on fire with apostolic zeal and called together synods and councils for the purpose of reforming religion in the whole country. He strenuously defended the rights of the Church and looked after the flock committed to his care by going among them on visitation, as well as spending much time and labour for the good of the native Indian population. He died in 1606.

MORNING PRAYER

Ant. It is not you who speak: the Spirit of your Father speaks in you.

Concluding Prayer
Lord, through the pastoral care and zeal for truth of Saint Turibius,
you built up your church in Peru.
Grant that the people of God
may continually grow in faith and holiness.
(We make our prayer) through our Lord.

EVENING PRAYER

Ant. This is the faithful and wise steward whom the Master placed over his household to give them their measure of food at the proper time.

25 March
THE ANNUNCIATION OF THE LORD

Solemnity

EVENING PRAYER I

Hymn

All creation was renewed
By the power of God most high,
When his promise was fulfilled
Adam's sons to justify.

By the Holy Spirit's love,
God pronounced his saving Word,
Then, with free consent and trust,
Mary bore creation's Lord.

Moment of unequalled faith,
Here in any time or place—
Thus did God put on our flesh
In his Virgin, full of grace.

Christ, the holy One of God,
Son of David, Light from light,
Dwells with men, his glory dimmed
Till he comes again with might.

Father, Son and Spirit praise
For this marvel they have done;
In this act of perfect love,
Undivided, always One.

The alleluia *given in parentheses is added to the antiphons in Eastertide.*

PSALMODY

Ant. 1: A shoot shall spring from the stock of Jesse; a flower shall grow out from his roots. The spirit of the Lord shall rest upon him (alleluia).

Práise, O sérvants of the Lórd,*
práise the náme of the Lórd!
May the náme of the Lórd be bléssed*
both nów and for évermóre!
From the rísing of the sún to its sétting*
práised be the náme of the Lórd!

Hígh above all nátions is the Lórd,*
abóve the héavens his glóry.
Whó is like the Lórd, our Gód,*
who has rísen on hígh to his thróne
yet stóops from the héights to look dówn,*
to look dówn upon héaven and éarth?

From the dúst he lífts up the lówly,*
from his mísery he ráises the póor
to sét him in the cómpany of prínces,*
yés, with the prínces of his péople.
To the chíldless wífe he gives a hóme*
and gláddens her héart with chíldren.

Ant. A shoot shall spring from the stock of Jesse; a flower shall grow
out from his roots. The Spirit of the Lord shall rest upon him
(alleluia).
Ant. 2: The Lord will give him the throne of David, his father, and
he will rule for ever (alleluia).

O práise the Lórd, Jerúsalem!*
Síon, práise your Gód!

He has stréngthened the bárs of your gátes,*
he has bléssed the chíldren withín you.

He estáblished péace on your bórders,*
he féeds you with fínest whéat.

He sénds out his wórd to the éarth*
and swiftly rúns his commánd.

He shówers down snów white as wóol,*
he scátters hóar-frost like áshes.

He húrls down háilstones like crúmbs.*
The wáters are frózen at his tóuch;
he sénds forth his wórd and it mélts them:*
at the bréath of his móuth the waters flów.

He mákes his wórd known to Jácob,*
to Ísrael his láws and decrées.
He has not déalt thus with óther nátions;*
he has not táught them hís decrées.

Ant. The Lord will give him the throne of David, his father, and he will rule for ever (alleluia).
Ant. 3: The Word of God, born of the Father before time began, humbled himself today for us and became man (alleluia).

CANTICLE: PHIL 2:6-11

Though he was in the form of God,*
Jesus did not count equality with God a thing to be grasped.

He emptied himself,†
taking the form of a servant,*
being born in the likeness of men.

And being found in human form,†
he humbled himself and became obedient unto death,*
even death on a cross.

Therefore God has highly exalted him*
and bestowed on him the name which is above every name,

That at the name of Jesus every knee should bow,*
in heaven and on earth and under the earth,

And every tongue confess that Jesus Christ is Lord,*
to the glory of God the Father.

Ant. The Word of God, born of the Father before time began, humbled himself today for us and became man (alleluia).

Scripture Reading   *1 Jn 1:1-2*
Something which has existed since the beginning,
that we have heard,
and we have seen with our own eyes;
that we have watched
and touched with our hands:
the Word who is life—
this is our subject.
That life was made visible:
we saw it and we are giving our testimony,
telling you of the eternal life
which was with the Father and has been made visible to us.

Short Responsory
R℣ A shoot has sprung from the stock of Jesse; a star has risen from Jacob. *Repeat* R℣
℣ The Virgin has given birth to the Saviour. R℣ Glory be. R℣

Eastertide
R℣ A shoot has sprung from the stock of Jesse; a star has risen from Jacob, alleluia, alleluia. *Repeat* R℣
℣ The Virgin has given birth to the Saviour. R℣ Glory be. R℣

Magnificat ant. The Holy Spirit will come upon you, Mary, and the power of the Most High will overshadow you (alleluia).

Intercessions
Eternal Father, on this day through your angel you made known our salvation to Mary. Full of confidence we earnestly pray: R℣ Lord, fill us with your grace.
You chose the Virgin Mary to be the mother of your Son.—Have mercy on all who wait for your redemption. R℣
Through your angel Gabriel you brought a message of peace and joy to Mary.—Give to the world the joy and peace of salvation. R℣
By the consent of your handmaid and the power of the Holy Spirit, your Word came to dwell among us.—Open our hearts to receive Christ, as Mary the Virgin received him. R℣
You look with compassion on the lowly and fill the starving with

good things.—Encourage the downhearted, help all those in need
and comfort those near to death. ℞ Lord, fill us with your grace.
To you, O God, nothing is impossible, and you alone do marvellous
things;—save us, and on the last day along with all the faithful
departed, bring us to yourself. ℞
Our Father

Concluding Prayer
Shape us in the likeness of the divine nature of our Redeemer,
whom we believe to be true God and true man,
since it was your will, Lord God,
that he, your Word,
should take to himself our human nature
in the womb of the Blessed Virgin Mary.
(We make our prayer) through our Lord.

Invitatory
Ant. The Word was made flesh; come, let us adore him (alleluia).
Psalm, p 371.

MORNING PRAYER

Hymn
> All creation was renewed
> By the power of God most high,
> When his promise was fulfilled
> Adam's sons to justify.
>
> By the Holy Spirit's love,
> God pronounced his saving Word
> Then, with free consent and trust,
> Mary bore creation's Lord.
>
> Moment of unequalled faith,
> Here in any time or place—
> Thus did God put on our flesh
> In his Virgin, full of grace.
>
> Christ, the holy One of God,

Son of David, Light from Light,
Dwells with men, his glory dimmed
Till he comes again with might.

Father, Son and Spirit praise
For this marvel they have done;
In this act of perfect love,
Undivided, always One.

Ant. 1: The angel Gabriel was sent to the virgin Mary who was betrothed to Joseph (alleluia).

Psalms and canticle of Sunday, Week 1, pp 390 ff.

Ant. 2: You are the most blessed of all women, and blessed is the fruit of your womb (alleluia).

Ant. 3: Through her word the Virgin conceived; she remained a virgin; as a virgin she gave birth to the Saviour (alleluia).

Scripture Reading   *Phil 2:6-7*
In your minds you must be the same as Christ Jesus: his state was divine, yet he did not cling to his equality with God but emptied himself to assume the condition of a slave and became as men are.

Short Responsory
R⁷ Hail, Mary, full of grace: the Lord is with you. *Repeat* R⁷
V̷ You are the most blessed of all women and blessed is the fruit of your womb. R⁷ Glory be. R⁷

Eastertide
R⁷ Hail, Mary, full of grace: the Lord is with you, alleluia, alleluia. *Repeat* R⁷
V̷ You are the most blessed of all women and blessed is the fruit of your womb. R⁷ Glory be. R⁷

Benedictus ant. God loved us so much that he sent his own Son in a mortal nature like ours (alleluia).

Intercessions

Today we celebrate the beginning of our salvation in the Annunciation of the Lord, and full of joy we pray: R℣ Holy Mother of God, intercede for us.

The Blessed Virgin received the joyful message from the angel.—O God, let us receive the Saviour in the same generous spirit. R℣

You looked with compassion on the lowliness of your handmaid. —Merciful Father, remember us and all men, and have mercy on us. R℣

The new Eve was obedient to your divine Word.—Give us the grace to submit to your holy will. R℣

Holy Mary, comfort the miserable, help the faint-hearted, cheer those that weep.—Pray for the people, be the advocate of the clergy, intercede for all women consecrated to God. R℣

Our Father

Concluding Prayer

Shape us in the likeness of the divine nature of our Redeemer,
whom we believe to be true God and true man,
since it was your will, Lord God,
that he, your Word,
should take to himself our human nature
in the womb of the Blessed Virgin Mary.
(We make our prayer) through our Lord.

EVENING PRAYER II

Hymn, from the appendix, for the Blessed Virgin Mary.

PSALMODY

Ant. 1: The angel of the Lord brought the good news to Mary and she conceived by the power of the Holy Spirit (alleluia).

PSALM 109(110):1-5,7

The Lórd's revelátion to my Máster:†
'Sít on my ríght:*
your fóes I will pút beneath your féet.'

The Lórd will wíeld from Síon†
your scéptre of pówer:*
rule in the mídst of all your fóes.

A prínce from the dáy of your bírth†
on the hóly móuntains;*
from the wómb before the dáwn I begót you.

The Lórd has sworn an óath he will not chánge.†
'You are a príest for éver,*
a príest like Melchízedek of óld.'

The Máster stánding at your ríght hand*
will shatter kíngs in the dáy of his wráth.

He shall drínk from the stréam by the wáyside*
and thérefore he shall líft up his héad.

Ant. The angel of the Lord brought the good news to Mary and she conceived by the power of the Holy Spirit (alleluia).
Ant. 2: Do not be afraid, Mary, for you have found favour with God. Behold, you will conceive and bear a son, and he will be called the Son of the Most High (alleluia).

PSALM 129(130)

Out of the dépths I crý to you, O Lórd,*
Lórd, hear my vóice!
O lét your éars be atténtive*
to the vóice of my pléading.

If you, O Lórd, should márk our guílt,*
Lórd, who would survíve?
But with yóu is fóund forgíveness:*
for thís we revére you.

My sóul is wáiting for the Lórd,*
I cóunt on his wórd.
My sóul is lónging for the Lórd*
more than wátchman for dáybreak*
Let the wátchman cóunt on dáybreak*
and Ísrael on the Lórd.

Becáuse with the Lórd there is mércy*
and fúlness of redémption,
Ísrael indéed he will redéem*
from áll its iníquity.

Ant. Do not be afraid, Mary, for you have found favour with God.
Behold, you will conceive and bear a son, and he will be called the
Son of the Most High (alleluia).
Ant. 3: I am the servant of the Lord; let it be done to me as you have
said (alleluia).

CANTICLE: COL I:12-20

Let us give thanks to the Father,†
who has qualified us to share*
in the inheritance of the saints in light.

He has delivered us from the dominion of darkness*
and transferred us to the kingdom of his beloved Son,
in whom we have redemption,*
the forgiveness of sins.

He is the image of the invisible God,*
the first-born of all creation,
for in him all things were created, in heaven and on earth,*
visible and invisible.

All things were created*
through him and for him.
He is before all things,*
and in him all things hold together.

He is the head of the body, the Church;*
he is the beginning,*
the first-born from the dead,*
that in everything he might be pre-eminent,

For in him all the fulness of God was pleased to dwell,*
and through him to reconcile to himself all things,
whether on earth or in heaven,*
making peace by the blood of his cross.

Ant. I am the servant of the Lord; let it be done to me as you have said (alleluia).

Scripture Reading   *I Jn 1:1-2*
Something which has existed since the beginning,
that we have heard,
and we have seen with our own eyes;
that we have watched
and touched with our hands:
the Word who is life—
this is our subject.
That life was made visible:
we saw it and we are giving our testimony,
telling you of the eternal life
which was with the Father and has been made visible to us.

Short Responsory
R/ The Word was made flesh and dwelt amongst us. *Repeat* R/
V/ He was with God in the beginning. R/ Glory be. R/

Eastertide
R/ The Word was made flesh and dwelt amongst us, alleluia, alleluia.
Repeat R/
V/ He was with God in the beginning. R/ Glory be. R/

Magnificat ant. The angel Gabriel said to Mary: Hail, full of grace: the Lord is with you. You are the most blessed of all women (alleluia).

Intercessions
Eternal Father, on this day through your angel you made known our salvation to Mary. Full of confidence we earnestly pray: R/ Lord, fill us with your grace.
You chose the Virgin Mary to be the mother of your Son.—Have mercy on all who wait for your redemption. R/
Through your angel Gabriel you brought a message of peace and joy to Mary.—Give to the world the joy and peace of salvation. R/
By the consent of your handmaid and the power of the Holy Spirit,

your Word came to dwell among us.—Open our hearts to receive Christ, as Mary the Virgin received him. R̹ Lord, fill us with your grace.

You look with compassion on the lowly and fill the starving with good things.—Encourage the downhearted, help all those in need and comfort those near to death. R̹

To you, O God, nothing is impossible, and you alone do marvellous things;—save us, and on the last day along with all the faithful departed, bring us to yourself. R̹

Our Father

The concluding prayer as at Morning Prayer, p 762.

APRIL

2 April
SAINT FRANCIS OF PAOLA, Hermit

Optional Memoria   *Lent: as a Commemoration*

Born at Paola in Calabria in the year 1416. He founded a congregation of hermits which was later changed to the Order of Minims and received approval of the Holy See in 1506. He died at Tours in France in 1507.

From the Common of Men Saints: Religious, p 1064.

MORNING PRAYER

Benedictus ant. Behold, I am standing at the door. If anyone hears me calling and opens the door, I will come in to eat with him, and he with me (alleluia).

Concluding Prayer
Lord God,
by whom the holy are exalted,
and Saint Francis was raised to share in the glory of the saints,
let his prayer and example bring us the reward
you have promised to the humble.
(We make our prayer) through our Lord.

EVENING PRAYER

Magnificat ant. If a man were to give away all his possessions for love, he would consider that he had lost nothing (alleluia).

4 April

SAINT ISIDORE,
Bishop and Doctor of the Church

Optional Memoria   *Lent: as a Commemoration*

Born about the year 560 at Seville in Spain. After the death of his father he was brought up by his brother Leander. He was appointed Bishop of Seville and was a prolific writer as well as calling together and presiding over councils in which wise regulations were made for the Church in Spain. He died in the year 636.

From the Common of Pastors, p 1040, or of Doctors of the Church, p 1049.

MORNING PRAYER

Ant. The learned will shine as brightly as the vault of heaven, and those who have instructed many in virtue will shine like the stars for all eternity.

Concluding Prayer
As we keep the memory of Saint Isidore, Lord God,
hear our prayer that he may support your Church
by his intercession
as he enriched it with his teaching while here on earth.
(We make our prayer) through our Lord.

EVENING PRAYER

Ant. O holy doctor, Saint Isidore, light of the Church; lover of the law of God, pray for us to the Son of God.

5 April
SAINT VINCENT FERRER, Priest

Optional Memoria   *Lent: as a Commemoration*

Born in Valencia in Spain in the year 1350. He joined the Dominican Order
and taught theology. He journeyed much as a preacher and reaped much
fruit in protecting the true faith and reforming morals. He died at Vannes
in France in the year 1419.

From the Common of Pastors, p 1040.

MORNING PRAYER

Ant. It is not you who speak: the Spirit of your Father speaks in you.

Concluding Prayer
Lord God,
who sent Saint Vincent Ferrer
to preach the gospel of Christ,
grant that we may see the Son of Man reigning in heaven
whom he proclaimed as judge of mankind.
(We make our prayer) through our Lord.

EVENING PRAYER

Ant. I made myself all things to all men in order to save them all.

7 April
SAINT JOHN BAPTIST DE LA SALLE, Priest

Memoria   *Lent: as a Commemoration*

Born at Rheims in France in the year 1651. He was ordained priest and
devoted himself mainly to educating children and founding schools for the
poor. He formed his companions into a Religious Congregation, and this
caused him many hardships. He died at Rouen in 1719.

*From the Common of Pastors, p 1040, or of Men Saints: Educators,
p 1064.*

MORNING PRAYER

Ant. He who has compassion teaches men, as a shepherd his flock.

Concluding Prayer
In your providence, Lord God,
you chose Saint John Baptist de la Salle
to educate the young in Christian faith.
Raise up, Lord, in the church of today
teachers who will devote themselves wholeheartedly
to the human and Christian education of youth.
(We make our prayer) through our Lord.

EVENING PRAYER

Ant. Let the children come to me; for the kingdom of heaven belongs
to such as these.

11 April

SAINT STANISLAUS
Bishop and Martyr

Optional Memoria   *Lent: as a Commemoration*

Born in the town of Szczepanow in Poland about the year 1030. He studied
at Paris. He became a priest and in 1071 succeeded Lambert as the Bishop
of Cracow. He ruled his diocese as a good shepherd, helping the poor and
making a visitation of his clergy every year. He fearlessly rebuked the king
Boleslav and was murdered by him in the year 1097.

*From the Common of Martyrs: One Martyr, p 1029, or of Pastors,
p 1040.*

MORNING PRAYER

Ant. Anyone who hates his soul in this world will save it for the
eternal life.

Concluding Prayer
Lord God,
we praise you for Saint Stanislaus,

slain by the sword of the persecutor.
Grant that, strong in faith,
we may persevere until death.
(We make our prayer) through our Lord.

EVENING PRAYER

Ant. The saints will dwell in the kingdom of heaven; their peace will
last for ever.

13 April
SAINT MARTIN
Pope and Martyr

Optional Memoria   *Lent: as a Commemoration*

Born at Todi in Umbria. He joined the diocese of Rome and in the year
649 was elected Pope. That same year he presided over the Council that
condemned the heresy of the Monothelites. In 653 he was seized by the
Emperor Constans and taken to Constantinople where he was treated
harshly; then he was moved to Kherson in the Crimea where he died in
the year 656.

*From the Common of Martyrs: One Martyr, p 1029, or of Pastors,
p 1040.*

MORNING PRAYER

Ant. Anyone who hates his soul in this world will save it for the
eternal life.

Concluding Prayer
Almighty, ever living God,
give us grace to bear the hardships of this life
with a steadfast mind,
even as you strengthened Pope Saint Martin,
whom no threats could daunt, no pains or penalties break.
(We make our prayer) through our Lord.

EVENING PRAYER

Ant. The saints will dwell in the kingdom of heaven; their peace will last for ever.

21 April
ST ANSELM
Bishop and Doctor of the Church
Optional Memoria

Born in the year 1033 in Aosta in Piedmont. He entered the Benedictine Order in the monastery of Le Bec in France where he taught theology to the students while he himself quickly progressed in the spiritual life. He went to England where he was chosen to be Archbishop of Canterbury. There he fought strenuously for the freedom of the Church and was twice condemned to exile. He is renowned for his writings, particularly in mystical theology. He died in the year 1109.

From the Common of Pastors, p 1040, or of Doctors of the Church, p 1049.

Concluding Prayer
Lord God,
you led Saint Anselm
to search out the depth of your wisdom,
and teach it to his brethren.
Let your gift of faith so help our minds
that what you command us to believe
we may love in our hearts.
(We make our prayer) through our Lord.

23 April
SAINT GEORGE, Martyr
Optional Memoria

In the fourth century there is evidence of the veneration of Saint George in Lydda in Palestine where a church was built in his honour. From the earliest times this veneration has spread throughout both the East and the West.

From the Common of Martyrs: One Martyr, Eastertide, p 1029.

Concluding Prayer
Proclaiming your glory, Lord,
we humbly ask
that as Saint George imitated Christ in his passion,
so he may be a ready helper in our weakness.
(We make our prayer) through our Lord.

24 April
SAINT FIDELIS OF SIGMARINGEN
Priest and Martyr

Optional Memoria

Born in the town of Sigmaringen in Germany in the year 1578. He entered
the Order of Friars Minor Capuchin where he led a hard life of penance,
vigils and prayer. He had a reputation as an indefatigable preacher and he
was ordered by the Sacred Congregation for the Propagation of the Faith
to preach in the canton of the Grisons in Switzerland. There he was
pursued by the heretics and suffered martyrdom in 1622 at Seewis.

*From the Common of Martyrs: One Martyr, Eastertide, p 1029, or of
Pastors, p 1040.*

Concluding Prayer
Lord God,
you crowned Saint Fidelis with a martyr's death,
when, filled with your love, he was preaching the faith.
Let our lives be rooted in love,
so that with him, and by his prayer,
we may know the power of Christ's resurrection.
(We make our prayer) through our Lord.

25 April
SAINT MARK, Evangelist

Feast

He was a cousin of Saint Barnabas. He accompanied Saint Paul the Apostle
on his first missionary journey and later followed him to Rome. He was a
disciple of Saint Peter and reproduced his teaching in his Gospel. He is said
to have founded the Church of Alexandria.

Invitatory ant. The Lord is speaking to us in the gospel: come, let us adore him, alleluia.
Psalm, p 371.

MORNING PRAYER

Hymn, from the Common of Apostles, p 1004.

Ant. 1: The holy evangelists sought out the wisdom of the ancients; in their gospels they confirmed the prophecies of old, alleluia.

Psalms and canticle from Sunday, Week 1, pp 390 ff.

Ant. 2: Through the gospel, God called us to faith in the truth so that we might share the glory of our Lord Jesus Christ, alleluia.

Ant. 3: Many will praise their wisdom, and it will never be forgotten, alleluia.

Scripture Reading   *1 Cor 15:1-2a, 3-4*
Brothers, I want to remind you of the gospel I preached to you, the gospel that you received and in which you are firmly established, because the gospel will save you. I taught you what I had been taught myself, namely that Christ died for our sins, in accordance with the scriptures; that he was buried, and that he was raised to life on the third day, in accordance with the scriptures.

Short Responsory
R7 They told of the glories of the Lord and of his might, alleluia, alleluia. *Repeat* R7
V They spoke of the marvellous deeds he had done. R7 Glory be. R7

Benedictus ant. Let us give thanks to Jesus Christ, who has sent teachers and evangelists to be ministers of faith to all peoples who believe in him, alleluia.

Intercessions
Our Saviour destroyed death and through the gospel revealed

eternal life to us. With joyful praises let us make him known, and let us say: ℟ Strengthen your Church in faith and love.

Lord Jesus, in times past you have lighted the way for your people through wise and holy leaders;—may Christians always enjoy this sign of your loving kindness. ℟

You forgave the sins of your people when holy pastors prayed;—continually cleanse your Church through their powerful intercession. ℟

In the presence of their brothers, you anointed your holy ones and poured on them your Spirit;—fill with your Holy Spirit all the leaders of your people. ℟

Nothing could ever separate the holy pastors from your love;—do not lose even one of those whom you redeemed by your passion. ℟

Our Father

Concluding Prayer
Almighty God,
you chose out the evangelist Saint Mark
and ennobled him with grace to preach the gospel.
Let his teaching so improve our lives
that we may walk faithfully in the footsteps of Christ.
(We make our prayer) through our Lord.

EVENING PRAYER

Hymn, from the Common of Apostles, p 1006.

Ant. 1: I have become a minister of the gospel according to the bountiful gift of God, alleluia.

Psalms and canticle from the Common of Apostles, p 1007.

Ant. 2: I do all things for the sake of the gospel, to have a share in its blessings, alleluia.

Ant. 3: To me this grace was given, to preach to the peoples the unsearchable riches of Christ, alleluia.

Scripture Reading   *Col 1:3a-6*

We always give thanks to God, the Father of our Lord Jesus Christ, when we pray for you. For we have heard of your faith in Christ Jesus and of your love for all God's people. When the true message, the Good News, first came to you, you heard of the hope it offers. So your faith and love are based on what you hope for, which is kept safe for you in heaven. The gospel is bringing blessings and spreading through the whole world, just as it has among you ever since the day you first heard of the grace of God and came to know it as it really is.

Short Responsory

R℣ Tell of the glory of the Lord, announce it among the nations, alleluia, alleluia. *Repeat* R℣
℣ Speak of his wonderful deeds to all the peoples. R℣ Glory be. R℣

Magnificat ant. The word of the Lord endures for ever; and that word is the gospel which has been preached to you, alleluia.

Intercessions

O God and Father of light, you called us to the true faith through the gospel of your Son. We pray to him now for all his holy people, saying: R℣ Remember your Church, O Lord.
Father, you raised your Son from the dead to be the Shepherd of a huge flock;—make us his witnesses to the ends of the earth. R℣
You sent your Son into the world to proclaim the good news to the poor;—grant that we may bring his gospel into the darkness of men's lives. R℣
You sent your Son to plant in men's hearts the seed of imperishable life;—may we labour to sow his word and reap a harvest of joy. R℣
You sent your Son to reconcile the world with yourself by the shedding of his blood;—let us become his fellow workers in restoring men to your friendship. R℣
You placed your Son at your own right hand in heaven;—receive the dead into the happiness of your kingdom. R℣
Our Father

The concluding prayer as at Morning Prayer, p 774.

28 April
SAINT PETER CHANEL
Priest and Martyr

Optional Memoria

Born in the town of Cuet in France in the year 1803. He entered the ranks of the clergy and for a few years did pastoral work. He then entered the Marist Society and went to Oceania to preach the Gospel. In spite of many difficulties he did manage to convert a number to the true faith. In hatred of the faith he was clubbed to death on the island of Futuna in the year 1841.

From the Common of Martyrs: One Martyr, Eastertide, p 1029.

Concluding Prayer
Lord God,
you made the martyrdom of Saint Peter Chanel
serve the growth of your Church.
Give us grace, in these days of Easter joy,
so to celebrate the mysteries of Christ's death and resurrection
that we may give witness of newness of life.
(We make our prayer) through our Lord.

29 April
SAINT CATHERINE OF SIENA
Virgin and Doctor of the Church

Memoria

Born at Siena in the year 1347. Wishing to follow the way of perfection she entered the Third Order of Saint Dominic while still an adolescent. She was on fire with love of God and her neighbour; she brought peace and harmony between her fellow citizens, strenuously fought for the rights and liberty of the papacy, and did much for the renewal of religious life. She dictated a number of writings which are renowned for their spirituality and sound doctrine. She died in the year 1380.

From the Common of Virgins, p 1057, except for the following:

MORNING PRAYER

Benedictus ant. The holy virgin, Saint Catherine, never ceased praying to God to let peace return to his holy Church, alleluia.

Concluding Prayer
Almighty God,
you made Saint Catherine of Siena
a contemplative lover of the Lord's sufferings
and an ardent servant of your Church.
Grant through her prayer
that your people may be united to Christ in his mystery,
and rejoice for ever in the revelation of his glory.
(We make our prayer) through our Lord.

EVENING PRAYER

Magnificat ant. At all times and in all places, Catherine sought God. She found him and was united to him in love, alleluia.

30 April
SAINT PIUS V, Pope
Optional Memoria

Born near Alessandria in Italy in the year 1504. He entered the Dominican Order and taught theology. After being made a bishop and a cardinal, he became pope in 1566. He vigorously carried out the reform of the Church which was begun by the Council of Trent, actively promoted the spreading of the faith and restored the sacred liturgy. He died on 1 May, 1572.

From the Common of Pastors, p 1040.

Concluding Prayer
Lord God, in your providence
you called Pope Saint Pius to defend the faith
and to enhance the dignity of divine worship.
Give us grace, through his prayer,
to worship you in your sacred mysteries
with an ardent faith and an active charity.
(We make our prayer) through our Lord.

MAY

1 May
SAINT JOSEPH THE WORKER
Optional Memoria

Where this Memoria is celebrated with proper texts, those not given here are taken from 19 March, pp 748 ff.

Invitatory ant. Christ the Lord allowed himself to be considered the son of a carpenter: come, let us adore him, alleluia.

MORNING PRAYER

Hymn

Joseph, the scriptures love to trace
The glories of thy kingly line;
Yet no succession of thy race,
No long posterity was thine—
Of her the everlasting spouse
Who must a Virgin ever be,
The faithful ruler of his house
Who owns no fatherhood in thee.

And though thy Son were God indeed,
Over that home no angels sang,
But still, through years of toil and need,
Hammer and mallet bravely rang;
And surely 'twas a gracious thing
When, standing at his father's knee,
The world's great Craftsman and its King
Not king but craftsman learned to be.

But king or craftsman, die we must:
Who would not change his lot with thine,
In such sweet peace and holy trust
His earthly being to resign?
With Mary's comfort at thy side

Thy spirit, freed from mortal clay,
Out of God's presence satisfied
Into God's presence passed away.

Scripture Reading   *2 Sam 7:28-29*

Lord, you are God indeed, your words are true and you have made this fair promise to your servant. Be pleased, then, to bless the house of your servant, that it may continue for ever in your presence; for you, Lord God, have spoken; and with your blessing the house of your servant will be for ever blessed.

Short Responsory

R̥ The Lord made him master of his house, alleluia, alleluia. *Repeat* R̥

V̥ He made him ruler of all he possessed. R̥ Glory be. R̥

Benedictus ant. Saint Joseph worked faithfully as a carpenter; he shines as an example to all workmen, alleluia.

Intercessions

Whatever we do or say, let us do it in the name of the Lord Jesus, giving thanks to God the Father through him. R̥ Lord, hear us.

As Joseph believed what you had told him, and became the guardian of your only Son:—so may we put our faith in you, and receive the fulfilment of your promise. R̥

Father, give us that faith which gives substance to our hopes,—and make us certain of realities we do not see. R̥

Joseph took the child Jesus into his care, loving and accepting him as his own Son:—may we accept all that God gives us, and care for those entrusted to us. R̥

You have given man authority over the work of your hands and invited him to share in your creation:—help us to accept our responsibility by working for your glory and the good of all mankind. R̥

Our Father

Concluding Prayer

Lord God and Creator of the universe,

you imposed on mankind the law of work.
Give us grace, by Saint Joseph's example and at his intercession,
to finish the works you give us to do,
and to come to the rewards you promise.
(We make our prayer) through our Lord.

EVENING PRAYER

Hymn as at Morning Prayer, p 778.

Scripture Reading   *Col 3:23-24*
Whatever you do, work at it with all your heart, as though you were
working for the Lord, and not for men. Remember that the Lord
will reward you; you will receive what he has kept for his people.
For Christ is the real Master you serve.

Short Responsory
R̷ The virtuous man will bloom like the lily, alleluia, alleluia.
Repeat R̷
V̷ He will grow for ever before the Lord. R̷ Glory be. R̷

Magnificat ant. Christ the Lord allowed himself to be considered the
son of a carpenter, alleluia.

Intercessions
Let us pray to God our Father, for from him, all fatherhood in
heaven and on earth takes its name. R̷ Father, hallowed be your
name.
Father, in your Son you revealed to Joseph the mystery kept secret
for endless ages:—help us to acknowledge your Son as God and
man. R̷
Father, you enabled Joseph to spend his life in your service:—set
our minds on your kingdom and your justice before all other things.
R̷
Father, your will is that every man should accept and answer your
call:—by the prayer of Joseph, give us the grace to live in accord
with your will. R̷
Creator of all things, you have entrusted your work to our hands:

—grant that our labours may prove worthy of you. ℞
Father, in whom all men live, grant to those who have died new life,
through your Son:—with Mary, and Joseph, and all your saints for
ever. ℞
Our Father

The concluding prayer as at Morning Prayer, p 779.

2 May
SAINT ATHANASIUS
Bishop and Doctor of the Church

Memoria

Born at Alexandria in the year 295. He accompanied his bishop, Alexander,
to the Council of Nicaea and later he himself succeeded as bishop. He
fought ceaselessly against the Arian heresy and as a result he had to endure
much tribulation and he was several times sent into exile. He wrote out-
standingly to illustrate and defend true doctrine. He died in the year 373.

*From the Common of Pastors, p 1040, or of Doctors of the Church,
p 1049.*

Concluding Prayer
Almighty, ever-living God and Father,
you raised up Saint Athanasius
as the great champion of your Son's divinity.
Through the doctrine and patronage of your saint,
in which we rejoice,
let our knowledge and love of you
grow ever deeper and stronger.
(We make our prayer) through our Lord.

3 May
SAINTS PHILIP AND JAMES
Apostles

Feast

Philip was born at Bethsaida. Formerly a disciple of John the Baptist, he
became a follower of Christ.

James, the son of Alphaeus and a cousin of the Lord, ruled the Church at Jerusalem, wrote an Epistle, and led a life of penance. He converted many of the Jews to the true faith and was martyred in the year 62.

Invitatory ant. Alleluia, the Lord is king of apostles: come, let us adore him, alleluia.
Psalm, p 371.

MORNING PRAYER

Hymn, from the Common of Apostles, p 1004.

Ant. 1: Lord, let us see the Father and then we shall be satisfied, alleluia.

Psalms and canticle of Sunday, Week 1, pp 390 ff.

Ant. 2: Have I been with you all this time and you still do not know me? Philip, to see me is to see the Father, alleluia.

Ant. 3: Do not let your hearts be troubled. Trust in God still, and trust in me. There are many rooms in my Father's house, alleluia.

Scripture Reading   *Eph 2:19-20*
You are no longer aliens in a foreign land, but fellow-citizens with God's people, members of God's household. You are built upon the foundation laid by the apostles and prophets, and Christ Jesus himself is the foundation-stone. In him the whole building is bound together and grows into a holy temple in the Lord. In him you too are being built with all the rest into a spiritual dwelling for God.

Short Responsory
R̸ You will make them rulers over all the earth, alleluia, alleluia.
Repeat R̸
V̸ Your name, Lord, will be remembered. R̸ Glory be. R̸

Benedictus ant. Philip found Nathanael and said to him, 'We have found the one about whom Moses wrote in the Law and whom the prophets foretold: he is Jesus, son of Joseph, from Nazareth, alleluia.'

Intercessions

Since we have received from the apostles our heavenly inheritance, let us thank our Father for all his blessings. R℣ Lord, the apostles sing your praises.

Praise to you, Lord God, for the gift of Christ's body and blood, handed on by the apostles to give us strength and life;—Lord, the apostles sing your praises.

For the table of your word, served by the apostles, to bring us light and joy;—Lord, the apostles sing your praises.

For your holy Church, built on the apostles, to make us all one body;—Lord, the apostles sing your praises.

For the washing of baptism and penance, entrusted to the apostles, to cleanse our hearts from sin;—Lord, the apostles sing your praises.

Our Father

Concluding Prayer

Lord God, you give us the joy every year
of celebrating the feastday of the apostles Philip and James.
Make us partners, by their prayers,
in the passion and resurrection of your only-begotten Son,
so that we may come to the eternal vision of your glory.
(We make our prayer) through our Lord.

EVENING PRAYER

Hymn, from the Common of Apostles, p 1006.

Ant. 1: Philip, to see me is to see the Father, alleluia.

Psalms and canticle from the Common of Apostles, p 1007.

Ant. 2: If you know me, you know my Father too. From this moment you know him and you have seen him, alleluia.

Ant. 3: If you love me you will keep my commandments, alleluia.

Scripture Reading   *Eph 4:11-13*

Christ has appointed some to be apostles, others to be prophets, others to be evangelists, or pastors, or teachers. They are to order the lives of the faithful, minister to their needs, build up the frame of Christ's body, until we all realize our common unity through faith in the Son of God, and fuller knowledge of him. So we shall reach perfect manhood, that maturity which is proportioned to the completed growth of Christ.

Short Responsory

R⁊ Tell of the glory of the Lord; announce it among the nations, alleluia, alleluia. *Repeat* R⁊

℣ Speak of his wonderful deeds to all the peoples. R⁊ Glory be. R⁊

Magnificat ant. If you remain in me and my word remains in you, you may ask what you will and you will receive it, alleluia.

Intercessions

Since we are part of a building that has the apostles for its foundation, let us pray to the Father for his holy people. R⁊ Lord, remember your Church.

Father, when your Son rose from the dead, you showed him first to the apostles;—let us make him known, near and far. R⁊

You sent your Son into the world to proclaim the good news to the poor;—grant that we may bring his gospel into the darkness of men's lives. R⁊

You sent your Son to plant in men's hearts the seed of imperishable life;—may we labour to sow his word and reap a harvest of joy. R⁊

You sent your Son to reconcile the world with yourself by the shedding of his blood;—let us become his fellow workers in restoring men to your friendship. R⁊

You placed your Son at your own right hand in heaven;—receive the dead into the happiness of your kingdom. R⁊

Our Father

The concluding prayer as at Morning Prayer, p 783.

12 May
SAINTS NEREUS AND ACHILLEUS
Martyrs

Optional Memoria

These martyrs were Roman soldiers who were converted to the true faith and refused to serve any longer. Because of this they were put to death, probably in the time of Diocletian. Their tomb is in the cemetery on the Via Ardeatina, where a basilica was erected in their honour.

From the Common of Martyrs: Several Martyrs (Eastertide), p 1017.

Concluding Prayer
Almighty God,
we have seen that the holy martyrs Nereus and Achilleus
proved themselves strong in their hour of trial.
Let us feel their loving intercession with you on our behalf.
(We make our prayer) through our Lord.

Also 12 May
SAINT PANCRAS, Martyr

Optional Memoria

He suffered martyrdom at Rome probably in the persecution of Diocletian and was buried on the Via Aurelia. Pope Symmachus built a church over his tomb.

From the Common of Martyrs: One Martyr (Eastertide), p 1029.

Concluding Prayer
Almighty God, let your Church rejoice,
relying as she does on the prayers
of the blessed martyr Pancras.
Helped by his intercession from heaven,
may she stand firmly secure
and persevere in your service.
(We make our prayer) through our Lord.

14 May
SAINT MATTHIAS, Apostle

Feast

He was chosen by the apostles to take the place of Judas so that he might be a witness of the resurrection of the Lord. The story of how he was numbered with the other apostles is found in the Acts of the Apostles (1:15-26).

From the Common of Apostles (Eastertide), p 1004, except for the following:

MORNING PRAYER

Benedictus ant. One of those who were with us all the time that the Lord Jesus was travelling round with us must be chosen to act with us as a witness to his resurrection (alleluia).

Concluding Prayer
Lord God, you chose Saint Matthias
to complete the number of the twelve apostles.
By his prayer, include us among your chosen ones,
since we rejoice to see
that the lot marked out for us is your love.
(We make our prayer) through our Lord.

EVENING PRAYER

Magnificat ant. You did not choose me: I chose you. I appointed you to go on and bear fruit, fruit that shall last (alleluia).

18 May
SAINT JOHN I, Pope and Martyr

Optional Memoria

Born in Tuscany. In the year 523 he was elected pope. He was sent by the king Theodoric to the Emperor Justin at Constantinople, but on his return the king, angry at the outcome of the mission, had him imprisoned at Ravenna where he died in the year 526.

From the Common of Martyrs: One Martyr (Eastertide), p 1029, or of Pastors, p 1040.

786

Concluding Prayer

Lord God, who give faithful souls their reward,
you have consecrated this day
by the martyrdom of Pope Saint John the First.
Listen to your people's prayer:
grant that, as we honour his sanctity,
we may follow his constancy in faith.
(We make our prayer) through our Lord.

20 May
SAINT BERNARDINE OF SIENA
Priest

Optional Memoria

Born near Siena in the year 1380. He joined the Friars Minor and was ordained priest and then went throughout Italy preaching, with great spiritual success. He propagated devotion to the holy name of Jesus. In addition he wrote some theological works and did much to further discipline and study in his order. He died in the year 1444.

From the Common of Pastors, p 1040.

Concluding Prayer

God our Father,
you gave Saint Bernardine of Siena
a most tender love of the holy Name of Jesus.
Grant, by his merits and prayers,
that your Spirit of love may always inflame us.
(We make our prayer) through our Lord.

25 May
SAINT BEDE THE VENERABLE
Priest and Doctor of the Church

Optional Memoria

Born near the monastery of Wearmouth in the year 673. He received his education from Saint Benedict Biscop. Joining the monastery he became a priest and spent his time teaching and writing. He wrote theological and historical works, and especially upheld the tradition of the Fathers and explained the Scriptures. He died in the year 735.

*From the Common of Doctors of the Church, p 1049, or of Men Saints:
Religious, p 1067.*

Concluding Prayer
Lord God, you enrich your Church
with the grace of Saint Bede's learning.
In your love grant to us who serve you
that his wisdom may always enlighten us,
and his prayer help us.
(We make our prayer) through our Lord.

Also 25 May

SAINT GREGORY VII, Pope

Optional Memoria

Hildebrand was born in Tuscany about the year 1028, and after being
educated at Rome he became a monk. He was of great assistance at the
time to the popes who were working to reform the Church, and when he
himself was elected pope in 1073, taking the name of Gregory VII, he
strenuously carried on this work. He was opposed especially by the
emperor Henry IV, and he had to flee to Salerno where he died in the year
1085.

From the Common of Pastors, p 1040.

Concluding Prayer
Lord God, give your Church
that spirit of fortitude and zeal for justice
with which you so richly endowed Pope Saint Gregory.
Let your Church rebuke everything sinful,
and carry out, in the freedom of charity,
all that is right and true.
(We make our prayer) through our Lord.

Also 25 May

SAINT MARY MAGDALENE
OF PAZZI, Virgin

Optional Memoria

Born in Florence in the year 1566. After a pious upbringing she entered the

Carmelites where she led a hidden life of prayer and self-denial. She prayed especially for the reform of the Church. She was endowed by God with many spiritual gifts and directed her fellow sisters along the road of perfection. She died in the year 1607.

From the Common of Virgins, p 1057, or of Women Saints: Religious, p 1074.

Concluding Prayer

God our Father, you love Christian virginity.
You enriched the virgin Saint Mary Magdalene of Pazzi with your grace.
Grant that, as we celebrate her feastday,
we may imitate her purity and love.
(We make our prayer) through our Lord.

26 May
SAINT PHILIP NERI, Priest

Memoria

Born in Florence in the year 1515. He came to Rome and began to devote himself to work among the young men, while at the same time he led a Christian life and formed a brotherhood to look after the sick poor. In 1551 he became a priest and formed the Oratory in which he held services consisting of spiritual readings and hymns, as well as performing charitable works. He was outstanding for love of his neighbour, an evangelical simplicity and joyfulness in the service of God. He died in the year 1595.

From the Common of Pastors, p 1040, or of Men Saints: Religious, p 1067.

Concluding Prayer

God our Father,
you are continually raising to the glory of holiness
those who serve you faithfully.
In your love, hear our prayer:
let the Holy Spirit inflame us with that fire,
with which, in so admirable a way,
he took possession of Saint Philip's heart.
(We make our prayer) through our Lord.

27 May
SAINT AUGUSTINE OF CANTERBURY, Bishop

Optional Memoria

He was sent by Saint Gregory the Great in the year 597 from the monastery of Saint Andrew at Rome to preach the gospel in England. He was helped there by the king Ethelbert and he became Archbishop of Canterbury. He converted many to the faith and set up some dioceses especially in the kingdom of Kent. He died on 26 May about the year 605.

From the Common of Pastors, p 1040.

Concluding Prayer
Almighty God,
you led the English people to the gospel
by the preaching of Saint Augustine of Canterbury.
Grant that his work may last on in the Church,
and bear fruit in every generation.
(We make our prayer) through our Lord.

31 May
THE VISITATION OF THE BLESSED VIRGIN MARY

Feast

Invitatory ant. Today we are celebrating the Visitation of the Blessed Virgin Mary; come, let us sing to the Lord (alleluia).
Psalm, p 371.

MORNING PRAYER

Hymn, from the Common or the appendix, for the Blessed Virgin Mary, nos. 42-47.

Ant. 1: Mary arose and went with haste into the hill country, to a city of Judah (alleluia).

Psalms and canticle of Sunday, Week 1, pp 390 ff.

Ant. 2: When Elizabeth heard the greeting of Mary, the child in her womb leapt for joy and she was filled with the Holy Spirit (alleluia).

Ant. 3: Blessed are you, Mary, because you have believed: all those things which were said to you by the Lord will be fulfilled (alleluia).

Scripture Reading   *Joel 2:27-3:1a*
You will know that I am in the midst of Israel, that I am the Lord your God, with none to equal me. My people will not be disappointed any more. After this, I will pour out my spirit on all mankind, and your sons and daughters will prophesy.

Short Responsory
Eastertide
R⁷ The Lord chose her. He chose her before she was born, alleluia, alleluia. *Repeat* R⁷
V⁷ He made her live in his own dwelling place. R⁷ Glory be. R⁷

Outside Eastertide
R⁷ The Lord chose her. He chose her before she was born. *Repeat* R⁷
V⁷ He made her live in his own dwelling place. R⁷ Glory be. R⁷

Benedictus ant. When Elizabeth heard the greeting of Mary she cried out with joy and said, 'Why should I be honoured with a visit from the mother of my Lord?' (allelluia).

Intercessions
Let us proclaim the greatness of our Saviour who chose to be born of the Virgin Mary. Confident that he will hear us, we ask: R⁷ Lord, may your mother pray for us.
Sun of justice, you showed your day was dawning in the immaculate Virgin Mary;—help us to walk in the daylight of your presence. R⁷
Eternal Word, you taught your mother Mary to choose the part that was best;—let us follow her example and hunger for the food of everlasting life. R⁷
Saviour of the world, by your redemptive power you preserved your mother Mary from every stain of sin;—deliver us from the evil that lies hidden in our hearts. R⁷

Christ, our Redeemer, you made the Virgin Mary the sanctuary of
your presence and the temple of the Spirit;—make us bearers of your
Spirit, in mind, heart and body. ℟ Lord, may your mother pray for
us.
Our Father

Concluding Prayer
Almighty, ever-living God,
you inspired the Blessed Virgin Mary,
when she was carrying your Son,
to visit Elizabeth
Grant that, always docile to the voice of the Spirit,
we may, together with our Lady, glorify your Name.
(We make our prayer) through our Lord.

EVENING PRAYER

*Hymn, from the Common or the appendix, for the Blessed Virgin
Mary, nos. 42-47.*

Ant. 1: Mary entered the house of Zachary, and greeted Elizabeth
(alleluia).

*Psalms and canticle from the Common of the Blessed Virgin Mary, p
992.*

Ant. 2: When I heard your greeting, the child in my womb leapt for
joy (alleluia).

Ant. 3: You are the most blessed of all women, and blessed is the
fruit of your womb (alleluia).

Scripture Reading   *1 Pet 5:5b-7*
Wrap yourselves in humility to be servants of each other, because
God refuses the proud and will always favour the humble. Bow
down then before the power of God now, and he will raise you up
on the appointed day; unload all your worries on to him, since he is
looking after you.

Short Responsory

Eastertide

R̷ Hail, Mary, full of grace: the Lord is with you, alleluia, alleluia.
Repeat R̷
V̷ You are the most blessed of all women, and blessed is the fruit of your womb. R̷ Glory be. R̷

Outside Eastertide

R̷ Hail, Mary, full of grace: the Lord is with you. *Repeat* R̷
V̷ You are the most blessed of women, and blessed is the fruit of your womb. R̷ Glory be. R̷

Magnificat ant. All generations will call me blessed, because God has had regard for his servant in her lowliness (alleluia).

Intercessions

Let us praise God the Father who chose Mary as the mother of his Son and wanted all generations to call her blessed. With confidence we pray: R̷ May the Virgin Mary intercede for us.
Through the prayers of Mary, our mother, heal the sick, comfort the sorrowful, pardon sinners;—grant peace and salvation to all. R̷
May the Church be united heart and soul, held fast by love;—and may your faithful be joined in continuous prayer, with Mary the mother of Jesus. R̷
Father, you have looked on the Virgin Mary and made her the mother of mercy;—may those who are in danger experience the depth of her love. R̷
You called Mary to be the mother in the house of Jesus and Joseph; —through her prayers help all mothers to make their homes places of love and holiness. R̷
Father, you have exalted the Virgin Mary and crowned her queen of heaven;—may the dead enter your kingdom and rejoice with your saints for ever. R̷
Our Father

The concluding prayer as at Morning Prayer, p 792.

Saturday after the Second Sunday after Pentecost
THE IMMACULATE HEART
OF MARY

Optional Memoria

From the Common of the Blessed Virgin Mary, p 987, except for the following:

MORNING PRAYER

Benedictus ant. My heart and my soul ring out their joy to God, the living God.

Concluding Prayer
God our Father,
you created a worthy dwelling place for the Holy Spirit
in the heart of the Blessed Virgin Mary.
Grant that through her prayers
we may become
a temple fit for your glory.
(We make our prayer) through our Lord.

EVENING PRAYER

Magnificat ant. My heart rejoices in the Lord, the Almighty, who works marvels for me.

JUNE

1 June
SAINT JUSTIN, Martyr

Memoria

Born of a pagan family in Nablus in Samaria at the beginning of the second century. He was a philosopher and on his conversion to the faith he wrote in defence of religion, though the only works now extant are his two *Apologies* and his *Dialogue* addressed to Trypho. He opened a school in Rome and he took part in public disputations. He suffered a martyr's death with his companions during the time of Marcus Aurelius, about the year 165.

From the Common of Martyrs: One Martyr (Eastertide), p 1029, except for the following:

MORNING PRAYER

Benedictus ant. In everything we offer up let us worship the creator of all things, through his Son Jesus Christ, and through the Holy Spirit (alleluia).

Concluding Prayer
Lord God, in a wonderful way,
through the folly of the cross,
you taught your martyr, Saint Justin,
the surpassing knowledge of Jesus Christ.
Heed his prayer for us:
dispel every deceiving error,
and ground us firmly in the faith.
(We make our prayer) through our Lord.

EVENING PRAYER

Magnificat ant. A fire was enkindled in my soul; I was filled with love for the prophets and for those holy men who are the friends of Christ (alleluia).

2 June
SAINTS MARCELLINUS and PETER, Martyrs

Optional Memoria

The account of the death of these two martyrs, who died in the persecution of Diocletian, comes from Pope Damasus who in turn obtained it from the executioner. They were beheaded in a wood and then buried in the cemetery called *The Two Laurels* on the Via Labicana. When peace came to the Church a basilica was erected over their tomb.

From the Common of Martyrs: Several Martyrs (Eastertide), p 1017.

Concluding Prayer
Lord God,
you give us an abiding, protecting grace
in the martyrdom of Saints Marcellinus and Peter.
Grant that their example may improve our lives,
and their prayer support our weakness.
(We make our prayer) through our Lord.

3 June

SAINT CHARLES LWANGA and HIS COMPANIONS, Martyrs

Memoria

During the years 1885 to 1887 many Christians were killed in Uganda by the king Mwanga in hatred of religion. Some of those put to death served in the king's palace and some even were the king's personal attendants, and among these were Charles Lwanga and twenty-one of his companions, who were fervent Catholics. Because they would not acquiesce in the impure desires of the king some of them were killed by the sword while others were burned to death.

From the Common of Martyrs: Several Martyrs (Eastertide), p 1017.

Concluding Prayer
Lord God,
you have made the blood of martyrs
become the seed of Christians.
In your love grant that your Church,
the field that was moistened by the blood
of Saint Charles and his companions,
may always yield a fertile harvest for you.
(We make our prayer) through our Lord.

5 June

SAINT BONIFACE
Bishop and Martyr

Memoria

Born in England about the year 673. He became a monk in the monastery of Exeter, and in 719 he went to Germany to preach the faith. He had great success and was consecrated Bishop of Mainz and with the help of his companions he founded or restored dioceses in Bavaria, Thuringia and Franconia. He presided over a number of councils and promulgated laws. While he was engaged in the evangelization of Friesland he was killed by the pagans in the year 754, and his body was buried in the monastery of Fulda.

From the Common of Martyrs: One Martyr (Eastertide), p 1029, or of Pastors, p 1040.

Concluding Prayer
Almighty God,
the martyr Saint Boniface sealed with his blood
the faith he preached.
Let him pray that we may hold fast to the faith,
and profess it courageously in our lives.
(We make our prayer) through our Lord.

6 June
SAINT NORBERT, Bishop
Optional Memoria

Born about the year 1080 in the Rhineland. He became a canon of the cathedral of Xanten, but later underwent a conversion from his worldly life and adopted a regular rule of life and became a priest in 1115. He went through France and Germany and other places preaching the word of God, and with the help of companions who had joined him, laid the foundations of the Premonstratensian Order and set up a number of monasteries. In 1126 he was elected Archbishop of Magdeburg, in which position he carried out reforms in the religious life of the people and spread the faith among the pagans living nearby. He died in the year 1134.

From the Common of Pastors, p 1040.

Concluding Prayer
Almighty God, you made Saint Norbert
to be an outstanding minister of your Church,
through his practice of prayer and pastoral zeal.
Grant, at his intercession,
that your faithful flock may find shepherds

797

to lead them, according to your will,
to pastures of holiness.
(We make our prayer) through our Lord.

9 June
SAINT EPHRAEM
Deacon and Doctor of the Church

Optional Memoria

Born of a Christian family in Nisibis about the year 306. He was ordained a deacon and worked both in his own country and at Edessa where he laid the foundations of the School of Theology. He lived a life of asceticism though at the same time he did not neglect the ministry of preaching; and he wrote a number of works to refute the errors in doctrine current at the time. He died in the year 373.

From the Common of Doctors of the Church, p 1049.

Concluding Prayer
Lord God,
in your kindness open our hearts to the Holy Spirit,
under whose inspiration
Saint Ephraem loved to sing of your mysteries,
and by whose power he served you alone.
(We make our prayer) through our Lord.

11 June
SAINT BARNABAS, Apostle

Memoria

Born in the island of Cyprus. He was one of the first converts in Jerusalem and preached at Antioch. He became a companion of Saint Paul and went with him on his first missionary journey, and he took part in the Council of Jerusalem. He returned to his native land to preach the gospel and there he died.

Invitatory ant. The Holy Spirit has spoken to us through the prophets and teachers of the Church: come, let us adore him (alleluia).
Psalm, p 371.

MORNING PRAYER

Hymn, from the Common of Apostles, p 1004.

Scripture Reading   *1 Cor 15:1-2a,3-4*

Brothers, I want to remind you of the gospel I preached to you, the gospel that you received and in which you are firmly established, because the gospel will save you. I taught you what I had been taught myself, namely that Christ died for our sins, in accordance with the scriptures; that he was buried, and that he was raised to life on the third day, in accordance with the scriptures.

Short Responsory

℟ They told of the glories of the Lord and of his might. *Repeat* ℟
℣ They spoke of the marvellous deeds he had done. ℟ Glory be. ℟

In Eastertide, Short Responsory as on 25 April, p 773.

Benedictus ant. Barnabas set out for Tarsus to look for Saul, and when he found him he brought him to Antioch, where they worked together in the Church and instructed a large number of people (alleluia).

Intercessions

Our Saviour destroyed death and through the gospel revealed eternal life to us. With joyful praises let us make him known, and let us say: ℟ Strengthen your Church in faith and love.

Lord Jesus, in times past you have lighted the way for your people through wise and holy leaders;—may Christians always enjoy this sign of your loving kindness. ℟

You forgave the sins of your people when holy pastors prayed; —continually cleanse your Church through their powerful intercession. ℟

In the presence of their brothers, you anointed your holy ones and poured on them your Spirit;—fill with your Holy Spirit all the leaders of your people. ℟

Nothing could ever separate the holy pastors from your love;—do not lose even one of those whom you redeemed by your passion. ℟

Our Father

Concluding Prayer
Lord God,
you filled Saint Barnabas with faith and the Holy Spirit,
and set him apart for the conversion of the nations.
Grant that the gospel of Christ
which he preached so strenuously,
may, in our day, be faithfully proclaimed
by word and deed.
(We make our prayer) through our Lord.

EVENING PRAYER

Hymn, from the Common of Apostles, p 1006.

Scripture Reading   *Col 1:3a-6*
We always give thanks to God, the Father of our Lord Jesus Christ,
when we pray for you. For we have heard of your faith in Christ
Jesus and of your love for all God's people. When the true message,
the Good News, first came to you, you heard of the hope it offers.
So your faith and love are based on what you hope for, which is kept
safe for you in heaven. The gospel is bringing blessings and spreading
through the whole world, just as it has among you ever since the day
you first heard of the grace of God and came to know it as it really is.

Short Responsory
R⁷ Tell of the glory of the Lord; announce it among the nations.
Repeat R⁷
V̷ Speak of his wonderful deeds to all the peoples. R⁷ Glory be. R⁷

In Eastertide, Short Responsory as on 25 April, p 775.

Magnificat ant. The entire assembly kept silence, and they listened
to Barnabas and Paul describing all the signs and wonders God had
worked through them among the Gentiles (alleluia).

Intercessions
O God and Father of light, you called us to the true faith through
the gospel of your Son. We pray to him now for all his holy people,

saying: ℞ Remember your Church, O Lord.

Father, you raised your Son from the dead to be the Shepherd of a huge flock;—make us his witnesses to the ends of the earth. ℞

You sent your Son into the world to proclaim the good news to the poor;—grant that we may bring his gospel into the darkness of men's lives. ℞

You sent your Son to plant in men's hearts the seed of imperishable life;—may we labour to sow his word and reap a harvest of joy. ℞

You sent your Son to reconcile the world with yourself by the shedding of his blood;—let us become his fellow workers in restoring men to your friendship. ℞

You placed your Son at your own right hand in heaven;—receive the dead into the happiness of your kingdom. ℞

Our Father

The concluding prayer as at Morning Prayer, p 800.

13 June
SAINT ANTONY OF PADUA
Priest and Doctor of the Church
Memoria

Born at Lisbon in Portugal about the end of the twelfth century. He became a canon regular of Saint Augustine but after being ordained priest he joined the Friars Minor so that he might preach the gospel among the people of Africa. But it was in France and Italy that he exercised the ministry of preaching with great profit and brought many heretics back to the faith. He became the first theologian of his Order and wrote a number of sermons which are renowned for their doctrine and their gentleness. He died at Padua in the year 1231.

From the Common of Pastors, p 1040, or of Doctors of the Church, p 1049, or of Men Saints: Religious, p 1067.

Concluding Prayer
Almighty, ever-living God,
you gave Saint Antony of Padua to your people
as a preacher of great power
and a patron in their needs.

Grant that, with his help,
we may follow the Christian way of life,
and feel your aid in all our trials.
(We make our prayer) through our Lord.

19 June
SAINT ROMUALD, Abbot

Optional Memoria

Born at Ravenna about the middle of the tenth century. He embraced the life of a hermit. For many years he went from place to place seeking true solitude, and built a number of small monasteries. He fought against the depraved morals of many of the monks at the time and by the exercise of virtue advanced along the path of perfection. He died about the year 1027.

From the Common of Men Saints: Religious, p 1064.

Concluding Prayer
Lord God,
you chose Saint Romuald
to restore the religious life of hermits in your Church.
Grant that, by denying ourselves and following Christ,
we may come safely to the kingdom of heaven.
(We make our prayer) through our Lord.

21 June
SAINT ALOYSIUS GONZAGA
Religious

Memoria

Born in the year 1568 near Mantua in Lombardy, of the noble family of Castiglione. He was brought up piously by his mother and had a vocation to the religious life. He resigned his birthright to his brother and at Rome entered the Society of Jesus. While working among the sick in a hospital he was stricken by the plague and died in the year 1591.

From the Common of Men Saints: Religious, p 1064.

Concluding Prayer
Lord God, source of every grace,
you joined an innocent heart to a penitent's sorrow

in the life of Saint Aloysius Gonzaga.
Grant, through his intercession,
that we, who have failed to imitate his innocence,
may follow his example of penance.
(We make our prayer) through our Lord.

22 June
SAINT PAULINUS OF NOLA
Bishop
Optional Memoria

Born at Bordeaux in France in the year 355. He rose high in public service,
married and had a son, but wishing to embrace a more austere life he
received baptism, gave up all his worldly goods and in 393 he began to live
the monastic life at Nola in Campagna. He became Bishop of Nola where
he did much to promote the veneration of Saint Felix of Nola, helping the
pilgrims and doing what he could to relieve the misery of that time. He
composed a number of poems which are outstanding for their literary
quality. He died in the year 431.

From the Common of Pastors, p 1040.

Concluding Prayer
God our Father,
you willed that Saint Paulinus
should be renowned as a bishop
for his love of poverty and his pastoral zeal.
Give us grace to imitate his charity
while we venerate him as a saint.
(We make our prayer) through our Lord.

Also 22 June
SAINT JOHN FISHER, Bishop
and SAINT THOMAS MORE
Martyrs
Optional Memoria

John Fisher was born in the year 1469. He studied theology at the Univer-

803

sity of Cambridge in England and was ordained priest. He was appointed Bishop of Rochester. His life was austere and he became an outstanding pastor of his flock, often visiting them. In addition he wrote against the doctrinal errors of the time.

Thomas More was born in the year 1477. He studied at the University of Oxford, married and had a son and three daughters. He was appointed Chancellor of the kingdom. He wrote a number of works about civil affairs and in defence of religion.

They resisted the king, Henry VIII, on the question of dissolving his marriage and on the king's orders they were executed in the year 1535, Fisher on 22 June and More on 6 July. While Fisher had been held in prison he had been created a cardinal of the Church of Rome by Paul III.

From the Common of Martyrs: Several Martyrs, p 1017.

Concluding Prayer
Almighty, ever-living God,
you set the perfection of true faith in martyrdom.
Strengthen us by the prayers of the martyrs
Saint John Fisher and Saint Thomas More,
so that our lives may bear witness
to the faith we profess.
(We make our prayer) through our Lord.

24 June
THE BIRTHDAY OF
SAINT JOHN THE BAPTIST
Solemnity

EVENING PRAYER I

Hymn as at Morning Prayer, p 806.

Ant. 1: Elizabeth, the wife of Zachary, gave birth to a great man, John the Baptist, the man who went before the Lord.

Psalms and canticle from the Common of Pastors, p 1036.

Ant. 2: John, who went before the Lord, was born when his mother was old and considerable incapable of bearing a child.

Ant. 3: Among those born of women there was no man greater than John the Baptist.

Scripture Reading   *Acts 13:23-25*

It was Jesus, one of the descendants of David, that God made the Saviour of the people of Israel, as he had promised. Before the coming of Jesus, John preached to all the people of Israel that they should turn from their sins and be baptized. And as John was about to finish his mission, he said to the people: 'Who do you think I am? I am not the one you are waiting for. But look! He is coming after me, and I am not good enough to take his sandals off his feet.'

Short Responsory

R⁷ Prepare a way for the Lord, make his paths straight. *Repeat* R⁷.
V̷ There is one coming after me who existed before me. R⁷ Glory be.
R⁷

Magnificat ant. When Zachary had entered the temple of the Lord, the angel Gabriel appeared to him, standing on the right of the altar of incense.

Intercessions

God our Father, you chose John the Baptist to announce the kingdom of Christ to all men. Joyfully we pray, therefore: R⁷ Lord, guide us in the way of peace.

Even in his mother's womb you chose John to prepare the way for your Son:—give us the faith to know Christ, and to make him known. R⁷

You inspired the Baptist to recognize the Lamb of God;—through us, let the world recognize your Son, our Lord Jesus Christ. R⁷

You disposed your prophet to give way before Christ;—give us the humility to let his light shine in the world. R⁷

You called John even to die for you:—grant that we may share his burning zeal for the truth. R⁷

Remember the dead who have walked in the path of life:—bring them to new life, cleansed from all stain of sin. R⁷

Our Father

Concluding Prayer
Almighty God,
give your people grace to enter on the way of salvation.
As they hearken to the voice of John, the Lord's herald,
bring them safely to Jesus, whom John foretold.
(We make our prayer) through our Lord.

Invitatory
Ant. John rejoiced and pointed out the Lamb of God: come, let us
adore him.
Psalm, p 371.

MORNING PRAYER

Hymn
> God called great prophets to foretell
> The coming of his Son;
> The greatest, called before his birth,
> Was John, the chosen one.
>
> John searched in solitude for Christ
> And knew him when he came.
> He showed the world the Lamb of God
> And hailed him in our name.
>
> That lonely voice cried out the truth,
> Derided and denied.
> As witness to the law of God
> His mighty martyr died.
>
> We praise you, Trinity in One,
> The light of unknown ways,
> The hope of all who search for you,
> Whose love fills all our days.

Ant. 1: His name will be called John; many will rejoice at his birth.

Psalms and canticle of Sunday, Week 1, pp 390 ff.

Ant. 2: With the spirit and power of Elijah he will go before the Lord God to prepare a people fit for him.

Ant. 3: You, little child, you shall be called the Prophet of the Most High, you will go before the Lord to prepare the way for him.

Scripture Reading   *Mal 4:5-6*
Behold, I will send you Elijah the prophet before the great and terrible day of the Lord comes. And he will turn the hearts of fathers to their children and the hearts of children to their fathers, lest I come and smite the land with a curse.

Short Responsory
R̰ He will be great in the sight of God; he will be filled with the Holy Spirit. *Repeat* R̰.
V̰ He will go before the Lord to prepare a people fit for him. R̰
Glory be. R̰

Benedictus ant. Zachary opened his mouth and spoke this prophecy: Blessed be the Lord, the God of Israel.

Intercessions
Let us make our prayer to Christ who sent John before him to prepare his way: R̰ Lord, prepare us for your coming.
John leaped in the womb of Elizabeth as she met your mother:—Lord, make us always glad to welcome your coming. R̰
John showed in his life what he preached by his words:—give us the courage to practise what we preach. R̰
John baptized you in the Jordan and the Spirit of justice rested upon you:—help us, Lord, to work for a world of justice. R̰
Lord, you called men to preach your word:—send heralds to carry the gospel to the world. R̰
Our Father

Concluding Prayer
Almighty God and Father,
you sent Saint John the Baptist to the people of Israel
to make them ready for Christ the Lord.

Give us the grace of joy in the Spirit,
and guide the hearts of all the faithful
in the way of salvation and peace.
(We make our prayer) through our Lord.

EVENING PRAYER II

Hymn as at Morning Prayer, p 806.

Ant. 1: There was a man sent by God, whose name was John.

Psalms and canticle from the Common of Pastors, p 1044.

Ant. 2: He came as a witness to the truth.

Ant. 3: John was like a brightly shining light.

Scripture Reading   *Acts 13:23-25*
It was Jesus, one of the descendants of David, that God made the
Saviour of the people of Israel, as he had promised. Before the
coming of Jesus, John preached to all the people of Israel that they
should turn from their sins and be baptized. And as John was about
to finish his mission, he said to the people: 'Who do you think I am?
I am not the one you are waiting for. But look! He is coming after
me, and I am not good enough to take his sandals off his feet.'

Short Responsory
R⁷ Prepare a way for the Lord, make his paths straight. *Repeat* R⁷
V⁷ There is one coming after me who existed before me. R⁷ Glory be.
R⁷

Magnificat ant. The child that is born to us today is greater than any
prophet: this is he of whom the Saviour said, 'Among those born of
women there was no man greater than John the Baptist.'

Intercessions
God our Father, you chose John the Baptist to announce the kingdom of Christ to all men. Joyfully we pray, therefore: R⁷ Lord,

guide us in the way of peace.

Even in his mother's womb you chose John to prepare the way for your Son;—give us the faith to know Christ, and to make him known. ℟

You inspired the Baptist to recognize the Lamb of God:—through us, let the world recognize your Son, our Lord Jesus Christ. ℟

You disposed your prophet to give way before Christ;—give us the humility to let his light shine in the world. ℟

You called John even to die for you;—grant that we may share his burning zeal for the truth. ℟

Remember the dead who have walked in the path of life:—bring them to new life, cleansed from all stain of sin. ℟

Our Father

The concluding prayer as at Morning Prayer, p 807.

27 June

SAINT CYRIL OF ALEXANDRIA
Bishop and Doctor of the Church

Optional Memoria

Born in the year 370. He entered a monastery, became a priest and then succeeded his uncle as Bishop of Alexandria in 412. He fought strenuously against the teachings of Nestorius and took the lead at the Council of Ephesus. He wrote many works to explain and defend the Catholic faith. He died in the year 444.

From the Common of Pastors, p 1040, or of Doctors of the Church, p 1049.

Concluding Prayer

Almighty God and Father,
you gave Saint Cyril of Alexandria
the grace to defend victoriously
the divine motherhood of the Virgin Mary.
We believe that she is truly the Mother of God;
grant that we may be saved by Christ your Son, made man,
who lives and reigns with you and the Holy Spirit,
God, for ever and ever.

28 June
SAINT IRENAEUS, Bishop and Martyr
Memoria

Born about the year 130. He was brought up at Smyrna, a disciple of Saint Polycarp, the bishop of that city. By the year 177 he was a priest at Lyons in France and shortly afterwards he was made bishop of that city. In his writings he sought to defend the Catholic faith against the errors of the Gnostics. Tradition has it that he was martyred about the year 200.

From the Common of Martyrs: One Martyr, p 1029, or of Pastors, p 1040, except for the following:

MORNING PRAYER

Benedictus ant. Irenaeus, in keeping with his name, was a man of peace; he fought strenuously for the peace of the Church.

Concluding Prayer
Lord God,
you strengthened the true faith
and established the peace of the Church
by the ministry and writings of Saint Irenaeus.
Through his prayer renew our faith and charity,
so that we may always work for unity and peace.
(We make our prayer) through our Lord.

29 June
SAINTS PETER AND PAUL
Apostles

Solemnity

EVENING PRAYER I

Hymn as at Morning Prayer, p 812.

Ant. 1: 'You are the Christ, the Son of the living God'; 'Blessed are you, Simon Bar Jona.'

Psalms and canticle from the Common of Apostles, p 1001.

Ant. 2: You are Peter, and on this Rock I will build my Church.

Ant. 3: You are the chosen instrument of God, Saint Paul, apostle; the preacher of truth in all the world.

Scripture Reading   *Rom 1:1-2,7*
Paul, servant of Christ Jesus, apostle by God's call, set apart for the service of the gospel. This gospel God announced beforehand in sacred scriptures through his prophets. It is about his Son. I send greetings to all of you in Rome whom God loves and has called to be his dedicated people. Grace and peace to you from God our Father and the Lord Jesus Christ.

Short Responsory
R7 The apostles proclaimed the word of God and feared no one.
Repeat R7
V They gave testimony to the resurrection of Jesus Christ. R7 Glory be. R7

Magnificat ant. Glorious are the apostles of Christ; they loved each other in this life; they are not separated in death.

Intercessions
We pray to Christ who built his Church on the foundation of the apostles and prophets. R7 Lord, be with your people.
Simon the fisherman was called by you to be a fisher of men:—call others today to share in his task. R7
When the disciples feared that the ship was sinking, you commanded the sea and there was calm:—protect your Church in the midst of trouble, and give her the peace that the world cannot give. R7
After your resurrection you gathered your Church around Peter: —gather all your people now into the unity for which you prayed. R7
You sent Paul as an apostle to all men:—let your good news be preached today through all creation. R7
You entrusted the keys of your kingdom to your Church:—open

the gates of life to the dead who put their trust in you. ℟
Our Father

Concluding Prayer
Lord our God,
may the blessed apostles Peter and Paul
support us by their prayers.
Through them you first taught your Church
the Christian faith.
Provide us now, by their intercession,
with help for our eternal salvation.
(We make our prayer) through our Lord.

Invitatory
Ant. The Lord is the king of apostles: come, let us adore him.
Psalm, p 371.

MORNING PRAYER

Hymn
What fairer light is this than time itself doth own,
The golden day with beams more radiant brightening?
The princes of God's church this feast-day doth enthrone,
To sinners heavenward bound their burden lightening.

One taught mankind its creed, one guards the heavenly gate.
Founders of Rome, they bind the world in loyalty;
One by the sword achieved, one by the cross his fate;
With laurelled brows they hold eternal royalty.

Rejoice, O Rome, this day, thy walls they once did sign
With princely blood, who now their glory share with thee.
What city's vesture glows with crimson deep as thine?
What beauty else has earth that may compare with thee?

Ant. 1: I know who it is that I have put my trust in, and I am certain
that he, the just judge, will be able to take care of all I have had
entrusted to me until that Day.

Psalms and canticle of Sunday, Week 1, pp 390 ff.

Ant. 2: The grace of God in me has not been fruitless; rather his grace remains with me always.

Ant. 3: I have fought the good fight, I have finished the race; I have kept the faith.

Scripture Reading   *1 Pet 4:13-14*
My dear people, if you can have some share in the sufferings of Christ, be glad, because you will enjoy a much greater gladness when his glory is revealed. It is a blessing for you when they insult you for bearing the name of Christ, because it means that you have the spirit of glory, the spirit of God resting on you.

Short Responsory
Ry They laid down their lives for the sake of our Lord Jesus Christ.
Repeat Ry
Vy They went away rejoicing that they had had the honour of suffering humiliation. Ry Glory be. Ry

Benedictus ant. Simon Peter said, 'Lord, to whom shall we go? You have the words of eternal life; we believe and we know that you are the Christ, the Son of God,' alleluia.

Intercessions
We pray to Christ who built his Church on the rock, and sent his apostles as witnesses to his victory over death: Ry Lord, be with your Church.
You prayed that the faith of Peter might not fail:—strengthen and sustain the faith of your Church. Ry
When you had risen from the dead you appeared to Peter and revealed yourself to Paul:—help us to live in the power of your resurrection. Ry
You chose Paul to proclaim your good news to the nations:—like him, may we be committed to spreading the truths of your gospel. Ry
Peter denied you, but your love drew him back to you:—whatever we have done in the past, keep us close to your merciful love. Ry
Our Father

Concluding Prayer
Almighty, ever-living God,
you give us the great joy of devoting this day
to the honour of the apostles Peter and Paul.
Grant that your Church
may follow their teaching to the full,
because these are the men
who first taught us to worship you in Christ, your Son,
who lives and reigns with you and the Holy Spirit,
God, for ever and ever.
(Who lives and reigns for ever and ever.)

EVENING PRAYER II

Hymn as at Morning Prayer, p 812.

Ant. 1: I have prayed for you, Peter, that your faith may not fail, and when you have repented, you must strengthen your brothers.

Psalms and canticle from the Common of Apostles, p 1007.

Ant. 2: I will boast freely of my weakness, so that the power of Christ may dwell in me.

Ant. 3: You are the shepherd of God's people, the prince of the apostles: to you were given the keys of the kingdom of heaven.

Scripture Reading   *1 Cor 15:3-5,8*
In the first place, I taught you what I had been taught myself, namely that Christ died for our sins, in accordance with the scriptures; that he was buried, and that he was raised to life on the third day, in accordance with the scriptures; that he appeared first to Cephas and secondly to the Twelve and last of all he appeared to me too.

Short Responsory
R̷ The apostles proclaimed the word of God and feared no one.
Repeat R̷
V̷ They gave testimony to the resurrection of Jesus Christ. R̷ Glory be. R̷

Magnificat ant. Peter the apostle and Paul the teacher of the nations taught us your law, Lord.

Intercessions
We pray to Christ who built his Church on the foundation of the apostles and prophets. R̸ Lord, be with your people.
Simon the fisherman was called by you to be a fisher of men:—call others today to share in his task. R̸
When the disciples feared that the ship was sinking, you commanded the sea and there was calm:—protect your Church in the midst of trouble, and give her the peace that the world cannot give. R̸
After your resurrection you gathered your Church around Peter: —gather all your people now into the unity for which you prayed. R̸
You sent Paul as an apostle to all men:—let your good news be preached today through all creation. R̸
You entrusted the keys of your kingdom to your Church:—open the gates of life to the dead who put their trust in you. R̸
Our Father

The concluding prayer as at Morning Prayer, p 814.

30 June

THE FIRST MARTYRS OF
THE SEE OF ROME

Optional Memoria

In the first persecution against the Church, that of the Emperor Nero, after the City of Rome had been burnt in the year 64, many of the faithful suffered death after terrible tortures. Testimony to their deaths is found in the writings of the pagan Tacitus (*Annales*, 15, 44) as well as in the letter to the Corinthians of Pope Saint Clement (cap. 5-6).

From the Common of Martyrs: Several Martyrs, p 1017, except for the following:

MORNING PRAYER

Benedictus ant. The great number of martyrs remained constant in

815

their love for the brotherhood, because they shared the one spirit and the one faith.

Concluding Prayer
Lord God,
you consecrated with the blood of martyrs
the fertile beginnings of the Roman Church.
Give us grace to rejoice at the martyrs' victory,
and strengthen us with firm courage
as we remember their endurance of such a trial.
(We make our prayer) through our Lord.

EVENING PRAYER

Magnificat ant. They loved Christ in their lives and imitated him in their death; therefore, they will reign with him for ever.

JULY

3 July
SAINT THOMAS, Apostle

Feast

Thomas is renowned among the apostles chiefly because of his lack of faith which was dispelled when the risen Christ appeared to him. He proclaimed what is in fact the Easter faith of the Church when he said: *My Lord and my God.* Nothing certain is known of his life apart from what is given in the gospels, but tradition has it that he preached to the people of India. From the sixth century a feast of the translation of his relics has been kept at Edessa on 3 July.

Invitatory ant. The Lord is king of apostles; come, let us adore him. *Psalm, p 371.*

MORNING PRAYER

Hymn from the Common of Apostles, p 1004.

Ant. 1: Thomas said, 'Lord, we do not know where you are going, so how can we know the way?' Jesus said to him, 'I am the way, the truth and the life.'

Psalms and canticle of Sunday, Week 1, pp 390 ff.

Ant. 2: Thomas, called Didymus, was not with them when Jesus came. The other disciples said to him, 'We have seen the Lord, alleluia.'

Ant. 3: Put your hands here and see the holes that the nails made. Doubt no longer but believe, alleluia.

Scripture Reading   *Eph 2:19-22*
You are no longer aliens in a foreign land, but fellow-citizens with God's people, members of God's household. You are built upon the foundations laid by the apostles and prophets, and Christ Jesus himself is the foundation-stone. In him the whole building is bonded together and grows into a holy temple in the Lord. In him you too are being built with all the rest into a spiritual dwelling for God.

Short Responsory
R̸ You will make them rulers over all the earth. *Repeat* R̸
V̸ Your name, Lord, will be remembered. R̸ Glory be. R̸

Benedictus ant. Thomas, you believe because you have seen me. Blessed are those who have not seen and yet believe.

Intercessions
Since we have received from the apostles our heavenly inheritance, let us thank our Father for all his blessings. R̸ Lord, the apostles sing your praises.
Praise to you, Lord God, for the gift of Christ's body and blood, handed on by the apostles, to give us strength and life;—Lord, the apostles sing your praises.
For the table of your word, served by the apostles, to bring us light and joy;—Lord, the apostles sing your praises.
For your holy Church, built on the apostles, to make us all one body;—Lord, the apostles sing your praises.

For the washing of baptism and penance, entrusted to the apostles,
to cleanse our hearts from sin;—Lord, the apostles sing your praises.
Our Father

Concluding Prayer
Father,
let our celebration of the feast of Saint Thomas the apostle
be the source of his unfailing help and protection.
Fill us with your life-giving grace
through faith in your Son, Jesus,
whom Thomas acknowledged to be his Lord and God.
(We make our prayer) through our Lord.

EVENING PRAYER

Hymn from the Common of Apostles, p 1006.
Antiphons as at Morning Prayer, p 817.
Psalms and canticle from the Common of Apostles, p 1007.

Scripture Reading   *Eph 4:11-13*
Some Christ has appointed to be apostles, others to be prophets,
others to be evangelists, or pastors, or teachers. They are to order the
lives of the faithful, minister to their needs, build up the frame of
Christ's body, until we all realize our common unity through faith
in the Son of God, and fuller knowledge of him. So we shall reach
perfect manhood, that maturity which is proportioned to the completed growth of Christ.

Short Responsory
R⁊ Tell of the glory of the Lord; announce it among the nations.
Repeat R⁊
℣ Speak of his wonderful deeds to all the peoples. R⁊ Glory be. R⁊

Magnificat ant. I put my fingers into the holes that the nails made in
his hands; I put my hand into his side; I said, 'My Lord and my
God, alleluia.'

Intercessions

Since we are part of a building that has the apostles for its foundation, let us pray to the Father for his holy people. R̸ Lord, remember your Church.

Father, when your Son rose from the dead, you showed him first to the apostles;—let us make him known, near and far. R̸

You sent your Son into the world to proclaim the good news to the poor;—grant that we may bring his gospel into the darkness of men's lifes. R̸

You sent your Son to plant in men's hearts the seed of imperishable life;—may we labour to sow his word and reap a harvest of joy. R̸

You sent your Son to reconcile the world with yourself by the shedding of his blood;—let us become his fellow workers in restoring men to your friendship. R̸

You placed your Son at your own right hand in heaven;—receive the dead into the happiness of your kingdom. R̸

Our Father

The concluding prayer as at Morning Prayer, p 818.

4 July
SAINT ELIZABETH OF PORTUGAL
Optional Memoria

Born of the royal family of Aragon in the year 1271. As a girl she was given in marriage to the king of Portugal, by whom she had two sons. She overcame many trials and difficulties by prayer and works of charity. When her husband died she gave her worldly goods to the poor and took the habit of the Third Order of Saint Francis. While effecting a reconciliation between her son and son-in-law, she died in the year 1336.

From the Common of Women Saints: Saints Noted for Works of Mercy, p 1074.

Concluding Prayer

Father of peace and love,
you endowed Saint Elizabeth of Portugal
with the gift of reconciling enemies.
Through her intercession

give us grace to work for peace
and so deserve to be called children of God.
(We make our prayer) through our Lord.

5 July
SAINT ANTONY MARY ZACCARIA, Priest

Optional Memoria

Born at Cremona in Lombardy in the year 1502. He first studied medicine at Padua and then became a priest. He founded the Congregation of Clerics of Saint Paul, known as Barnabites, which worked for the reform of morals among the faithful. He died in the year 1539.

From the Common of Pastors, p 1040, or of Men Saints: Educators or Religious, p 1067.

Concluding Prayer
God our Father,
in the spirit of Paul the apostle
Saint Antony Mary Zaccaria came to know the mystery of Christ
and preached the gospel unceasingly in the Church.
Give us a deeper knowledge of our Saviour
and a greater zeal in bearing witness to his gospel.
(We make our prayer) through our Lord.

6 July
SAINT MARIA GORETTI
Virgin and Martyr

Optional Memoria

Born at Ancona in Italy of a poor family in the year 1890. She spent her childhood near Nettuno in poverty, helping her mother in the domestic chores. She was a religious girl and much given to prayer. In the year 1902, while defending her chastity against a man attempting to violate her, she preferred to die rather than give way, and was repeatedly stabbed with a knife.

From the Common of Martyrs: One Martyr, p 1029, or of Virgins, p 1057.

Concluding Prayer
Lord God,
you alone can give the grace of innocence
and you love those who are chaste.
By your grace Saint Maria Goretti,
though as yet but a young girl,
was able to offer herself in death for your sake.
As you crowned her virginity with martyrdom,
grant us, at her intercession,
constancy in your love.
(We make our prayer) through our Lord.

11 July
SAINT BENEDICT, Abbot

Memoria

Born at Norcia in Umbria about the year 480. After studying at Rome, he led a life of solitude in Subiaco and gathered disciples around him, and then went on to Monte Cassino. Here he founded a well-known monastery and wrote his Rule, as a result of which he has been called the Father of monasticism in the West. He died on 21 March 547, but from the end of the eighth century he has been venerated on 11 July in many places.

From the Common of Men Saints: Religious, p 1067, except for the following:

MORNING PRAYER

Benedictus ant. He was a man of venerable life; Saint Benedict, blessed in name and with the grace of God.

Concluding Prayer
Lord God,
you appointed Saint Benedict
to be a wise master in the school of your service.
Give us grace to put your love before all else,
and so to run with joy
in the way of your commandments.
(We make our prayer) through our Lord.

EVENING PRAYER

Magnificat ant. He has received blessings from the Lord, and reward from the God who saves him. Such are the men who seek the Lord.

13 July
SAINT HENRY

Optional Memoria

Born in Bavaria in the year 973. He succeeded his father as Duke of Bavaria and later was elected Holy Roman Emperor. He was outstanding for his reforms in the Church and for his encouragement of missionary activity; he set up many dioceses and founded monasteries. He died in the year 1024 and was canonized by Eugene III in 1146.

From the Common of Men Saints, p 1067.

Concluding Prayer
Lord God,
you endowed Saint Henry with abundant grace
and led him from an earthly to a heavenly kingdom.
Grant, at his intercession,
that, amid this world's changes,
we may, with pure minds, hasten on our way to you.
(We make our prayer) through our Lord.

14 July
SAINT CAMILLUS OF LELLIS
Priest

Optional Memoria

Born near Chieti in Abruzzi in the year 1550. At first he was a soldier and then, after his conversion to a more religious life, he dedicated himself to the care of the sick. He completed his studies and was ordained priest, then founded a religious congregation which set up hospitals to look after the sick. He died at Rome in the year 1614.

From the Common of Men Saints: Saints Noted for Works of Mercy, p 1067.

Concluding Prayer
Almighty, ever-living God,
you gave your priest Saint Camillus
an extraordinary love for the sick.
Help us, through his intercession,
to love and serve you in our brethren,
so that, at the hour of our death,
we may come before you with confidence.
(We make our prayer) through our Lord.

15 July
SAINT BONAVENTURE
Bishop and Doctor of the Church

Memoria

Born about the year 1218 at Bagnoregio in Tuscany. He studied philosophy and theology at Paris, where he gained his Master's degree, and then taught the students of the order. He became Minister General of the Franciscan Order and ruled the order with great wisdom and prudence, and later became Cardinal Bishop of Albano. He wrote many influential works in philosophy and theology, and died at Lyons in the year 1274.

From the Common of Pastors, p 1040, or of Doctors of the Church, p 1049.

Concluding Prayer
Almighty God and Father,
on this feast of Saint Bonaventure,
enlighten our minds with the splendour of his teaching,
and help us to imitate his ardent love of you.
(We make our prayer) through our Lord.

16 July
OUR LADY OF MOUNT CARMEL
Optional Memoria

The sacred sciptures speak of the beauty of Mount Carmel where the prophet Elijah defended the faith of the people of Israel in the living God. In the twelfth century a group of hermits settled there and afterwards set up the Carmelite Order to lead a contemplative life under the patronage of the holy Mother of God.

From the Common of the Blessed Virgin Mary, p 987, except for the following:

MORNING PRAYER

Benedictus ant. I sought wisdom openly in my prayer; it has come to flower like early grapes.

Concluding Prayer
Almighty Lord and God,
let the gracious intercession of our Lady of Mount Carmel help us.
Under her protection,
may we come to the mountain of God, Christ the Lord,
who lives and reigns with you and the Holy Spirit,
God, for ever and ever.

EVENING PRAYER

Magnificat ant. Mary treasured the word of God and pondered it in her heart.

21 July
SAINT LAURENCE OF BRINDISI
Priest and Doctor of the Church
Optional Memoria

Born in the year 1559. He entered the Capuchin Order where he taught theology to the students and engaged in many of the works of the Order. As a renowned preacher he travelled throughout Europe and he wrote many works to explain the Catholic faith. He died at Lisbon in the year 1619.

From the Common of Pastors, p 1040, or of Doctors of the Church, p 1049.

Concluding Prayer
Lord God,
you bestowed on Saint Laurence of Brindisi
the spirit of counsel and fortitude,

so that your name might be glorified
and souls be saved.
At the intercession of Saint Laurence
grant that we may see what we have to do,
and, in your mercy, give us the strength to do it.
(We make our prayer) through our Lord.

22 July
SAINT MARY MAGDALEN
Memoria

She was one of Christ's disciples and was present at his death. On the morning of Easter day she was the first to whom the risen Redeemer appeared, according to Saint Mark's Gospel (16:9). Devotion to her spread throughout the Western Church especially in the twelfth century.

Invitatory ant. How wonderful is God among his saints; come, let us adore him.
Alternative invitatory ant, p 1074.
Psalm, p 371.

MORNING PRAYER

Hymn

Christ died, but soon revived again, alleluia,
And even death by him was slain, alleluia.
Say, happy Magdalen, oh, say, alleluia.
What didst thou see there by the way? alleluia,
Alleluia, alleluia, alleluia.

'I saw the tomb of my dear Lord, alleluia;
I saw himself, and him adored, alleluia.
I saw the napkin and the sheet, alleluia,
That bound his head and wrapt his feet, alleluia.
Alleluia, alleluia, alleluia.

'I heard the angels witness bear, alleluia,
"Jesus is risen; he is not here: alleluia,
Go, tell his followers they shall see, alleluia,
Thine and their hope in Galilee, alleluia."'
Alleluia, alleluia, alleluia.

Ant. 1: Very early on the Sunday morning, just as the sun was rising, Mary Magdalen came to the tomb.

Psalms and canticle of Sunday, Week 1, pp 390 ff.

Ant. 2: My heart is on fire; I desire to see my Lord; I look for him, but I cannot find where they have put him, alleluia.

Ant. 3: Mary was weeping and she looked into the tomb; there she saw two angels in brilliant clothes, alleluia.

Scripture Reading   *Rom 12:1-2*
My brothers, I implore you by God's mercy to offer your very selves to him: a living sacrifice, dedicated and fit for his acceptance, the worship offered by mind and heart. Adapt yourselves no longer to the pattern of this present world, but let your minds be remade and your whole nature thus transformed. Then you will be able to discern the will of God, and to know what is good, acceptable, and perfect.

Short Responsory
Ry Mary, do not weep; the Lord is risen from the dead. *Repeat* Ry
Y Go to my brethren and tell them. Ry Glory be. Ry

Benedictus ant. When Jesus had risen from the dead early on the Sunday morning, he appeared first to Mary Magdalen, from whom he had cast out seven devils.

Intercessions
The following or those of the occurring weekday may be said.
With all the holy women let us praise our Saviour and call on him in prayer. Ry Come, Lord Jesus.
Lord Jesus, you said of the woman who was a sinner, 'Her many sins are forgiven, because she has loved much';—grant us your forgiveness for our many sins. Ry
Lord Jesus, women ministered to your needs on your saving journeys;—open our eyes to see you in those who need our help. Ry
Lord and master, Mary listened to your teaching and Martha did the serving;—may our faith grow ever deeper and our love go out to others. Ry

Lord Jesus, you called those who do God's will your brother and sister and mother;—teach us to live as members of your family. ℟
Our Father

Concluding Prayer
Almighty, ever-living God,
your Only-begotten Son Jesus Christ
made Mary Magdalen
the first herald of Easter joy.
Grant that, following her example and helped by her prayers,
we may, in this life, proclaim the living Christ,
and come to see him reigning with you in glory.
(We make our prayer) through our Lord.

EVENING PRAYER

Hymn as at Morning Prayer, p 825.

Ant. 1: Jesus said to Mary, 'Woman, why are you weeping? Whom do you seek?'

Psalm and canticle from the Commons of Virgins, p 1057.

Ant. 2: They have taken my Lord away and I do not know where they have put him.

Ant. 3: Jesus said, 'Mary.' She turned to him and said, 'Rabboni', which means Master.

Scripture Reading   *Rom 8:28-30*
We are well assured that everything helps to secure the good of those who love God, those whom he has called in fulfilment of his design. All those who from the first were known to him, he has destined from the first to be moulded into the image of his Son, who is thus to become the eldest-born among many brethren. So pre-destined, he called them; so called, he justified them; so justified, he glorified them.

Short Responsory

R̸ Mary, do not weep; the Lord has risen from the dead. *Repeat* R̸
V̸ Go to my brethren and tell them. R̸ Glory be. R̸

Magnificat ant. Mary came and told the disciples that she had seen
the Lord, alleluia.

Intercessions as at Morning Prayer or of the occurring weekday.
The concluding prayer as at Morning Prayer, p 827.

23 July
SAINT BRIDGET, Religious
Optional Memoria

Born in Sweden in the year 1303. She married while still a girl and gave
birth to eight children whom she brought up in a religious spirit. She was
a member of the Third Order of Saint Francis, but after the death of her
husband she decided to lead a more ascetical life even though still in the
world. Later she founded the Bridgettine Order and went to Rome where
she became outstanding in her practice of virtue. She wrote many works
describing the mystical experiences she had and went on a penitential
pilgrimage to the Holy Land. She died at Rome in the year 1373.

From the Common of Women Saints: Religious, p 1074.

Concluding Prayer
Lord our God,
as Saint Bridget contemplated your Son our Lord Jesus Christ,
you revealed to her the mysteries of his passion.
Grant that we may rejoice, in time to come,
in the revelation of your glory.
(We make our prayer) through our Lord.

25 July
SAINT JAMES, Apostle
Feast

Born at Bethsaida, the son of Zebedee and the brother of the apostle John.
He was present when Christ performed his more important miracles. He
was killed by King Herod about the year 42, and is venerated especially at

Compostella in Spain where there is a magnificent church dedicated in his honour.

Invitatory ant. The Lord is king of apostles; come, let us adore him. *Psalm, p 371.*

MORNING PRAYER

Hymn from the Common of Apostles, p 1004.

Ant. 1: As he was passing by, Jesus saw James, the son of Zebedee, and John his brother, and he called them both.

Psalms and canticle of Sunday, Week 1, pp 390 ff.

Ant. 2: At once, leaving their nets and their father, they followed him.

Ant. 3: You will drink from the chalice that I shall drink and you will be baptized as I shall be baptized.

Scripture Reading   *Eph 2:19-22*
You are no longer aliens in a foreign land, but fellow-citizens with God's people, members of God's household. You are built upon the foundations laid by the apostles and prophets, and Christ Jesus himself is the foundation-stone. In him the whole building is bonded together and grows into a holy temple in the Lord. In him you too are being built with all the rest into a spiritual dwelling for God.

Short Responsory
R7 You will make them rulers over all the land. *Repeat* R7
V7 Your name, Lord, will be remembered. R7 Glory be. R7

Benedictus ant. Jesus took Peter, James, and John the brother of James, and led them up a high mountain where they were alone; and in their presence he was transfigured.

Intercessions
Since we have received from the apostles our heavenly inheritance,

let us thank our Father for all his blessings. ℟ Lord, the apostles sing your praises.

Praise to you, Lord God, for the gift of Christ's body and blood, handed on by the apostles, to give us strength and life;—Lord, the apostles sing your praises.

For the table of your word, served by the apostles, to bring us light and joy;—Lord, the apostles sing your praises.

For your holy Church, built on the apostles, to make us all one body;—Lord, the apostles sing your praises.

For the washing of baptism and penance, entrusted to the apostles, to cleanse our hearts from sin;—Lord, the apostles sing your praises.

Our Father

Concluding Prayer
Lord God,
you accepted the sacrifice of Saint James,
the first of your apostles to give his life for your sake.
May your Church find strength in his martyrdom
and support in his constant prayer.
(We make our prayer) through our Lord.

EVENING PRAYER

Hymn from the Common of Apostles, p 1006.

Ant. 1: Jesus took Peter and James and John with him, and a sudden fear came over him and he began to tremble.

Psalms and canticle from the Common of Apostles, p 1007.

Ant. 2: Then he said to them, 'Keep awake, and pray that you be not tempted.'

Ant. 3: Herod began persecuting some members of the Church. He had James, the brother of John, put to death by the sword.

Scripture Reading   *Eph 4:11-13*
Some Christ has appointed to be apostles, others to be prophets,

others to be evangelists, or pastors, or teachers. They are to order the lives of the faithful, minister to their needs, build up the frame of Christ's body, until we all realize our common unity through faith in the Son of God, and fuller knowledge of him. So we shall reach perfect manhood, that maturity which is proportioned to the completed growth of Christ.

Short Responsory

℟ Tell of the glory of the Lord; announce it among the nations.
Repeat ℟
℣ Speak of his wonderful deeds to all the peoples. ℟ Glory be. ℟

Magnificat ant. Anyone who wishes to become great among you must be your servant; anyone who wishes to be the first among you must be the slave to all.

Intercessions

Since we are part of a building that has the apostles for its foundation, let us pray to the Father for his holy people. ℟ Lord, remember your Church.
Father, when your Son rose from the dead, you showed him first to the apostles;—let us make him known, near and far. ℟
You sent your Son into the world to proclaim the good news to the poor;—grant that we may bring his gospel into the darkness of men's lives. ℟
You sent your Son to plant in men's hearts the seed of imperishable life;—may we labour to sow his word and reap a harvest of joy. ℟
You sent your Son to reconcile the world with yourself by the shedding of his blood;—let us become his fellow workers in restoring men to your friendship. ℟
You placed your Son at your own right hand in heaven;—receive the dead into the happiness of your kingdom. ℟
Our Father

The concluding prayer as at Morning Prayer, p 830.

831

26 July
SAINT JOACHIM AND SAINT ANNE
Parents of the Blessed Virgin Mary

Memoria

An old tradition going back to the second century gives these names to the parents of the Blessed Virgin Mary. The veneration of Saint Anne dates from the sixth century in the East and spread throughout the West in the tenth century; that of Saint Joachim is more recent.

Invitatory ant. How wonderful is God among his saints; come, let us adore him.
Psalm, p 371.

MORNING PRAYER

Hymn

Lord God, we give you thanks for all your saints
Who sought the trackless footprints of your feet,
Who took into their own a hand unseen,
And heard a voice whose silence was complete.

Blest Trinity, may yours be endless praise
For all who lived so humbly in your sight;
Your holy ones who walked dark ways in faith
Now share the joy of your unfailing light.

Scripture Reading   *Is 55:3*

Come to me and listen to my words, hear me, and you shall have life: I will make a covenant with you, this time for ever, to love you faithfully as I have loved David.

Short Responsory

R̸ Because of his tender mercy the Lord has come to visit us.
Repeat R̸
V̸ He raised up the saviour Jesus from the house of David. R̸ Glory be. R̸

Benedictus ant. Blessed be the Lord, the God of Israel. He has raised up for us a great saviour in the house of his servant David.

832

Intercessions from the Common of Men Saints, p 1068, or the occurring weekday.

Concluding Prayer
Lord, God of our fathers,
you bestowed on Saint Joachim and Saint Anne
this singular grace
that their daughter, Mary,
should become the Mother of your Son, Jesus Christ.
Grant, at their intercession,
the salvation you promised to your people.
(We make our prayer) through our Lord.

EVENING PRAYER

Hymn as at Morning Prayer, p 832.

Scripture Reading   *Rom 9:4-5*
They are Israelites: they were made God's sons; theirs is the splendour of the divine presence, theirs the covenants, the law, the temple worship, and the promises. Theirs are the patriarchs, and from them, in natural descent, sprang the Messiah. May God, supreme above all, be blessed for ever. Amen.

Short Responsory
R℧ He has come to help Israel his servant, mindful of his mercy.
Repeat R℧
℣ According to the promise he made to our fathers. R℧ Glory be. R℧

Magnificat ant. The noble stem of Jesse put forth a branch from which there blossomed a flower full of beauty and rich in scent.

Intercessions from the Common of Men Saints, p 1070, or the occurring weekday.

The concluding prayer as at Morning Prayer, above.

29 July
SAINT MARTHA

Memoria

Saint Martha was the sister of Mary and Lazarus. She received the Lord into her house and provided for his needs with great care. At her request the Lord raised her brother from the dead.

From the Common of Women Saints, p 1074, except for the following:

MORNING PRAYER

Benedictus ant. Martha said to Jesus, 'You are the Christ, the Son of the living God, the One who has come into the world.'

Concluding Prayer
Almighty, ever-living God,
your Son graciously came as a guest
to the home of Saint Martha.
By her prayers give us grace
to serve Christ faithfully in our brethren,
and bring us to your home in heaven.
(We make our prayer) through our Lord.

EVENING PRAYER

Magnificat ant. Jesus loved Martha and Mary her sister and Lazarus her brother.

30 July
SAINT PETER CHRYSOLOGUS
Priest and Doctor of the Church

Optional Memoria

Born about the year 380 at Imola in Emilia. He entered the clerical state and in the year 424 was chosen to be Bishop of Ravenna. He looked after his flock with meticulous care and taught the people with his sermons and writings. He died about the year 450.

From the Common of Pastors, p 1040, or of Doctors of the Church, p 1049.

Concluding Prayer

God our Father,
you made Saint Peter Chrysologus
a most eloquent preacher of Christ, your Word made man.
By the intercession of your saint
help us to meditate constantly in our hearts
on the mysteries by which you saved us,
and to manifest them faithfully in our lives.
(We make our prayer) through our Lord.

31 July
SAINT IGNATIUS LOYOLA, Priest
Memoria

Born in the year 1491 at Loyola in northern Spain. His early life was led at court and in the army, and later he was converted to a life of holiness. He studied theology at Paris and gathered companions around him, and afterwards at Rome he formed the Society of Jesus. He exercised a very fruitful apostolate by his written work and by the formation of his disciples who were outstanding in the reform of the Church. He died at Rome in the year 1556.

From the Common of Pastors, p 1040, or of Men Saints: Religious, p 1067, except for the following.

MORNING PRAYER

Benedictus ant. How I want to know Christ and the power of his resurrection! I wish to have part in his passion.

Concluding Prayer

Lord God,
you raised up Saint Ignatius Loyola in your Church
to give greater glory to your name.
Grant that, aided by his prayers,
we may fight against all that is evil on earth,
and with him receive the crown of victory in heaven.
(We make our prayer) through our Lord.

EVENING PRAYER

Magnificat ant. What will a man gain if he wins the whole world and suffers the loss of his own soul?

AUGUST

1 August
SAINT ALPHONSUS MARY DE LIGUORI
Bishop and Doctor of the Church

Memoria

Born at Naples in the year 1696. He studied law and took his doctor's degree in both civil and canon law, became a priest and later founded the Congregation of the Most Holy Redeemer (Redemptorists). In order to promote among the faithful a truly Christian life he spent his time in preaching and in writing, especially about moral theology of which discipline he is looked upon as the master. He was chosen to be Bishop of Sant' Agata dei Goti, but soon gave up the post and returned to his own Congregation where he died at Nocera dei Pagani in Campagna in the year 1787.

From the Common of Pastors, p 1040, or of Doctors of the Church, p 1067.

Concluding Prayer
Lord God,
you never cease to give new saints to your Church
as a pattern for holy living.
Help us to imitate Saint Alphonsus
in his zeal for souls,
that we may share his reward in heaven.
(We make our prayer) through our Lord.

2 August
SAINT EUSEBIUS OF VERCELLI
Bishop

Optional Memoria

Born in Sardinia at the beginning of the fourth century. He became a cleric at Rome and in the year 345 he was chosen to be the first Bishop of Vercelli. He spread the true faith by his preaching and he set up the monastic life in his diocese. He was sent into exile by the emperor Constantius and suffered much for the sake of the faith. When he returned to his own country he worked unceasingly for the restoration of religion against the Arian heresy. He died at Vercelli in the year 371.

From the Common of Pastors, p 1040.

Concluding Prayer
Lord God,
help us to imitate the constancy of Saint Eusebius
in proclaiming the godhead of your Only-begotten Son.
By maintaining the faith as Saint Eusebius taught it
may we come to share the life of our Lord Jesus Christ your Son,
who lives and reigns with you and the Holy Spirit,
God, for ever and ever.

4 August
SAINT JOHN MARY VIANNEY
Priest

Memoria

Born at Lyons in the year 1786. After overcoming tremendous difficulties he was finally ordained priest. He was given charge of the parish of Ars in the diocese of Belley, and by his forthright preaching, personal mortification, prayer and charity renewed it and increased it in a wonderful way. His help to those who came to the sacrament of confession was renowned and people flocked to him from all sides to obtain his advice. He died in the year 1859.

From the Common of Pastors, p 1040.

Concluding Prayer
Almighty and merciful God,

by your grace Saint John Mary Vianney
was remarkable for his zeal as priest and pastor.
Help us by his example and prayers
to win our brethren for Christ by love,
and to share with them in eternal glory.
(We make our prayer) through our Lord.

5 August

DEDICATION OF THE BASILICA
OF SAINT MARY MAJOR

Optional Memoria

The doctrine of Mary, Mother of God, was solemnly proclaimed at the
Council of Ephesus (431), and afterwards Pope Sixtus III (432–440)
erected a basilica at Rome on the Esquiline Hill in honour of the Holy
Mother of God, later to be known as Saint Mary Major. This is the oldest
church in the west dedicated to the Blessed Virgin Mary.

*From the Common of the Blessed Virgin Mary, p 987, except for the
following:*

MORNING PRAYER

Benedictus ant. Holy Mary, Mother of God, ever virgin: you are the
most blessed of all women, and blessed is the fruit of your womb.

Concluding Prayer
Forgive the sins of your people, Lord,
and since of ourselves we are unable to do what pleases you,
lead us on the way of salvation
by the prayers of Mary, the Mother of your Son,
our Lord Jesus Christ,
who lives and reigns with you and the Holy Spirit,
God, for ever and ever.

EVENING PRAYER

Magnificat ant. Holy Mary, Mother of God, pray for us sinners,
now, and at the hour of our death.

6 August
THE TRANSFIGURATION
OF THE LORD

Feast

EVENING PRAYER I
(Said when this feast occurs on a Sunday)

Hymn as at Morning Prayer.

PSALMODY

Ant. 1: Jesus took his disciples and led them up the mountain where he was transfigured in their presence.

PSALM 112(113)

Práise, O sérvants of the Lórd,*
práise the náme of the Lórd!
May the náme of the Lórd be bléssed*
both nów and for évermóre!
From the rísing of the sún to its sétting*
práised be the náme of the Lórd!

Hígh above all nátions is the Lórd,*
abóve the héavens his glóry.
Whó is like the Lórd, our Gód,*
who has rísen on hígh to his thróne
yet stóops from the héights to look dówn,*
to look dówn upon héaven and éarth?

From the dúst he lífts up the lówly,*
from his mísery he ráises the póor
to sét him in the cómpany of prínces,*
yés, with the prínces of his péople.
To the chíldless wífe he gives a hóme*
and gláddens her héart with chíldren.

Ant. Jesus took his disciples and led them up the mountain where he was transfigured in their presence.

Ant. 2: Moses and Elijah appeared to them and spoke with Jesus.

PSALM 116(117)

O práise the Lórd, all you nátions,*
accláim him all you péoples!
Stróng is his lóve for ús;*
he is fáithful for éver.

Ant. Moses and Elijah appeared to them and spoke with Jesus.

Ant. 3: Lord, it is good for us to be here; if you wish we will make three holy dwelling places here, one for you, one for Moses and one for Elijah.

When chanted this canticle is sung with Alleluia *as set out below; when recited it suffices to repeat* Alleluia *at the beginning and end of each strophe.*

CANTICLE: CF REV 19:1-2,5-7

Alleluia.
Salvation and glory and power belong to our God,*
(R̷ Alleluia.)
His judgments are true and just.
R̷ Alleluia (alleluia).

Alleluia.
Praise our God, all you his servants,*
(R̷ Alleluia.)
You who fear him, small and great.
R̷ Alleluia (alleluia).

Alleluia.
The Lord our God, the Almighty, reigns,*
(R̷ Alleluia.)
Let us rejoice and exult and give him the glory.
R̷ Alleluia (alleluia).

Alleluia.
The marriage of the Lamb has come,*
(R̷ Alleluia.)
And his bride has made herself ready.
R̷ Alleluia (alleluia).

Ant. Lord, it is good for us to be here; if you wish we will make three holy dwelling places here, one for you, one for Moses and one for Elijah.

Scripture Reading   *Phil 3:20-21*

We are citizens of heaven, and we eagerly wait for our Saviour to come from heaven, the Lord Jesus Christ. He will change our weak mortal bodies and make them like his own glorious body, using that power by which he is able to bring all things under his rule.

Short Responsory

R̸ In glory you appeared before the Lord, alleluia, alleluia.
Repeat R̸
℣ Therefore the Lord has clothed you in splendour. R̸ Glory be. R̸

Magnificat ant. Jesus Christ is the radiant light of the Father's glory and flawless expression of his nature, sustaining the universe by his powerful word; now he has destroyed the defilement of sin and appeared in glory today on the high mountain.

Intercessions

On this day we pray to the Son of God, who revealed himself to his friends in the fulness of his glory, and we say: R̸ Lord, that we may see.

Bless the Church ever more with your risen life:—so that the world may see in her the integrity of your mission. R̸

You appeared with Elijah and Moses, accepting their homage:—may the world accept your word, and live by your law of love. R̸

Even before your passion your disciples saw your risen glory:—give us the vision to accept both suffering and joy. R̸

Emptied of glory, you preached the kingdom of God, and your own people did not accept you:—help us to find you in the poor and deprived, and to love them in your name. R̸

You showed to your friends the splendour of the living God:—take to yourself those who have died and make them glorious. R̸

Our Father

Concluding Prayer

Father,
at the Transfiguration in glory of your Only-begotten Son,
you confirmed the mysteries of faith
by the witness to Jesus
of the prophets Moses and Elijah.
You foreshadowed there what we shall be
when you bring our sonship to its perfection.
Grant that by listening to the voice of Jesus
we may become heirs with him,
who lives and reigns with you and the Holy Spirit,
God, for ever and ever.

Invitatory

Ant. The Lord is the Great King of glory; come, let us adore him.

Psalm, p 371.

MORNING PRAYER

Hymn

More ancient than the primal world
And older than the morning star,
Before the first things took their shape,
Creator of them all, you are.

Your image is the Lord of life,
Your Son from all eternity;
All that must perish, he restores;
In him all reconciled will be.

Transfigured Christ, believed and loved,
In you our only hope has been;
Grant us, in your unfathomed love,
Those things no eye has ever seen.

O Father, Son and Spirit blest,
With hearts transfigured by your grace,
May we your matchless splendour praise
And see the glory of your face.

PSALMODY

Ant. 1: Today Jesus Christ was transfigured: his face shone like the sun and his clothes became as white as snow.

Psalms and canticle of Sunday, Week 1, pp 390 ff.

Ant. 2: Today the Lord was transfigured and the voice of the Father bore witness to him; Moses and Elijah appeared with him in glory, and spoke with him about the death he was to accomplish.

Ant. 3: The Law was given by Moses, prophecy by Elijah: they were seen in majesty, shining with the Lord on the mountain.

Scripture Reading *Rev 21:10-23*

In the spirit, the angel took me to the top of an enormous high mountain and showed me Jerusalem, the holy city, coming down from God out of heaven. And the city did not need the sun or the moon for light, since it was lit by the radiant glory of God and the Lamb was a lighted torch for it.

Short Responsory

℟ Lord, you have crowned him with glory and honour, alleluia, alleluia. *Repeat* ℟

℣ You set him over the works of your hands. ℟ Glory be. ℟

Benedictus ant. A voice came from the cloud, saying, 'This is my beloved Son, with whom I am well pleased; listen to him', alleluia.

Intercessions

Let us pray to Christ, for he is with God the Father, and all power is given to him, in heaven and on earth. ℟ Lord, that we may see.

Help us to work well today:—transfigure our hearts with your presence. ℟

We do not always feel the joy and power of your presence:—when we are weak and tired, help us to look forward to the glory that is to come. ℟

Remember all who live in depression and distress:—bring to them new vision, and the hope of the gospel. ℟

We praise you, Lord, and thank you for the greatness of your glory:

—be with us as we set out to build up your new creation. ℟ Lord, that we may see.

Our Father

Concluding Prayer
Father,
at the Transfiguration in glory of your Only-begotten Son,
you confirmed the mysteries of faith
by the witness to Jesus
of the prophets Moses and Elijah.
You foreshadowed there what we shall be
when you bring our sonship to its perfection.
Grant that by listening to the voice of Jesus
we may become heirs with him,
who lives and reigns with you and the Holy Spirit,
God, for ever and ever.

EVENING PRAYER II

Hymn as at Morning Prayer, p 842.

PSALMODY

Ant. 1: Jesus took Peter, James, and John the brother of James and led them up a high mountain where they were alone; and in their presence he was transfigured.

PSALM 109(110):1-5,7

The Lórd's revelátion to my Máster:†
'Sít on my ríght:*
your fóes I will pút beneath your féet.'

The Lórd will wíeld from Síon†
your scéptre of pówer:*
rúle in the mídst of all your fóes.

A prínce from the dáy of your bírth†
on the hóly móuntains;*
from the wómb before the dáwn I begót you.

The Lórd has sworn an óath he will not chánge.†

'You are a príest for éver,*
a príest like Melchízedek of óld.'

The Máster stánding at your ríght hand*
will shatter kíngs in the dáy of his wráth.

He shall drínk from the stréam by the wáyside*
and thérefore he shall líft up his héad.

Ant. Jesus took Peter, James, and John the brother of James and led them up a high mountain where they were alone; and in their presence he was transfigured.

Ant. 2: A bright cloud overshadowed them and they heard the voice of the Father, saying, 'This is my beloved Son, with whom I am well pleased.'

PSALM 120(121)

I líft up my éyes to the móuntains:*
from whére shall come my hélp?
My hélp shall cóme from the Lórd*
who made héaven and éarth.

May he néver állow you to stúmble!*
Let him sléep not, your guárd.
Nó, he sléeps not nor slúmbers,*
Ísrael's guárd.

The Lórd is your guárd and your sháde;*
at your ríght side he stánds.
By dáy the sún shall not smíte you*
nor the móon in the níght.

The Lórd will guárd you from évil,*
he will guárd your sóul.
The Lord will guárd your góing and cóming*
both nów and for éver.

Ant. A bright cloud overshadowed them and they heard the voice of the Father, saying, 'This is my beloved Son, with whom I am well pleased.'

Ant. 3: As they were coming down from the mountain Jesus said to them, 'Tell no man about the vision until the Son of Man has risen from the dead,' alleluia.

THE MYSTERY AND GLORY OF CHRIST   CANTICLE
                                                  CF 1 TIM 3:16

R̷ O praise the Lord, all you nations!

He was manifested in the flesh,*
vindicated in the Spirit.
R̷ O praise the Lord, all you nations!

He was seen by angels,*
preached among the nations.
R̷ O praise the Lord, all you nations!

He was believed on in the world,*
taken up in glory.
R̷ O praise the Lord, all you nations!

Ant. As they were coming down from the mountain Jesus said to them, 'Tell no man about the vision until the Son of Man has risen from the dead,' alleluia.

Scripture Reading   *Rom 8:16-17*
The Spirit himself thus assures our spirit, that we are children of God; and if we are his children, then we are his heirs too; heirs of God, sharing the inheritance of Christ; only we must share his sufferings if we are to share his glory.

Short Responsory
R̷ Majesty and power are his, alleluia, alleluia. *Repeat* R̷
℣ State and splendour are in his holy place. R̷ Glory be. R̷

Magnificat ant. When the disciples heard they fell on their faces, overcome with fear. But Jesus came up and touched them, saying, 'Stand up and do not be afraid,' alleluia.

Intercessions
On this day we pray to the Son of God, who revealed himself to his

friends in the fulness of his glory, and we say: ℞ Lord, that we may see.

Bless the Church ever more with your risen life:—so that the world may see in her the integrity of your mission. ℞

You appeared with Elijah and Moses, accepting their homage:—may the world accept your word, and live by your law of love. ℞

Even before your passion your disciples saw your risen glory:—give us the vision to accept both suffering and joy. ℞

Emptied of glory, you preached the kingdom of God, and your own people did not accept you:—help us to find you in the poor and deprived, and to love them in your name. ℞

You showed to your friends the splendour of the living God:—take to yourself those who have died and make them glorious. ℞

Our Father

The concluding prayer as at Morning Prayer, p 844.

7 August

SAINT SIXTUS II, Pope
and
HIS COMPANIONS, Martyrs

Optional Memoria

Saint Sixtus was ordained Bishop of Rome in the year 257. In the following year, while saying Mass in the cemetery of Saint Callistus, he was seized by the soldiers under the orders of the Emperor Valerian, and together with four deacons of the Church of Rome was put to death on 6 August. He was buried in the same cemetery.

From the Common of Martyrs: Several Martyrs, p 1017.

Concluding Prayer
Almighty God,
by the power of the Holy Spirit
you enabled Saint Sixtus and his companions
to lay down their lives for your word,
and to bear witness to Jesus.
Give us a ready faith
and the courage to profess it.
(We make our prayer) through our Lord.

Also 7 August
SAINT CAJETAN, Priest
Optional Memoria

Born at Vicenza in the year 1480. He studied law at Padua and after being ordained priest, founded at Rome a Congregation of Clerks Regular (Theatines) in order to help the work of the apostolate. He worked to make this congregation spread throughout the regions of Venice and Naples. He was outstanding for his personal prayer and for his love of his neighbour. He died at Naples in the year 1547.

From the Common of Pastors, p 1040, or of Men Saints: Religious, p 1067.

Concluding Prayer
Lord God,
you inspired Saint Cajetan
to live and work like the apostles.
Help us, by his example and prayers,
to trust in you at all times,
and continually to seek your kingdom.
(We make our prayer) through our Lord.

8 August
SAINT DOMINIC, Priest
Memoria

Born at Calaruega in Spain about the year 1170. He studied theology at Palencia and became a canon of the Cathedral of Osma. He preached against the Albigensian heresy and because of the example of his own life this bore great fruit. In order to carry on and increase this work he gathered around him a group of companions and formed the Order of Preachers (Dominicans). He died on 6 August in the year 1221 at Bologna.

From the Common of Pastors, p 1040, or of Men Saints: Religious, p 1067.

Concluding Prayer
Lord God,
you gave Saint Dominic to the Church of his day
as a great preacher of your truth.

We pray that he will help us in our time
by his merits, his teaching and his unfailing prayer.
(We make our prayer) through our Lord.

10 August
SAINT LAURENCE
Deacon and Martyr

Feast

Laurence was a deacon of the Church of Rome and died in the persecution
of Valerian four days after Pope Saint Sixtus II and his four fellow-
deacons. He was buried on the Via Tiburtina at the Campo Verano near to
where Constantine the Great built a basilica. He has been venerated
throughout the Church from the fourth century.

MORNING PRAYER

Hymn from the Common of Martyrs: One Martyr, p 1029.

Ant. 1: My soul thirsts for you, my God, since my body was burnt
in the fire for you.

Psalms and canticle of Sunday, Week 1, pp 390 ff.

Ant. 2: The Lord sent his angel to free me from the fire and I was
not burnt.

Ant. 3: Blessed Laurence prayed, saying, 'I give thanks to you, O
Lord, because you have found me worthy to enter your gates.'

Scripture Reading   *2 Cor 1:3-5*
Let us give thanks to the God and Father of our Lord Jesus Christ,
the merciful Father, the God from whom all help comes. He helps
us in all our troubles, so that we are able to help those who have all
kinds of troubles, using the same help that we ourselves have
received from God. Just as we have a share in Christ's many
sufferings, so also through Christ we share in his great help.

Short Responsory

R̷ The Lord is my strength; it is him I praise. *Repeat* R̷
V̷ He has become my Saviour. R̷ Glory be. R̷

Benedictus ant. Do not fear, my son, for I am with you; though you should walk through fire the flames will not harm you, neither will the smell of burning be about you.

Intercessions

Through the martyrs who were slain for God's word, let us give glory to our Saviour, the faithful and true witness. R̷ You redeemed us by your precious blood.

Through the martyrs, who bore witness to your love,—set us free to live for you. R̷

Through the martyrs, who proclaimed your saving death,—give us a deep and constant faith. R̷

Through the martyrs, who took up your cross,—grant us courage for every trial. R̷

Through the martyrs, washed in the blood of the Lamb,—give us grace to conquer our weakness. R̷

Our Father

Concluding Prayer

Lord God,
you inspired Saint Laurence
with so ardent a love,
that his life was renowned for the service of your people
and his death for the splendour of his martyrdom.
Help us to love what he loved
and to live as he showed us.
(We make our prayer) through our Lord.

EVENING PRAYER

Hymn from the Common of Martyrs, p 1021.

Ant. 1: Laurence entered heaven as a martyr; he bore witness to the name of the Lord Jesus Christ.

Psalms and canticle from the Common, p 1021.

Ant. 2: Blessed Laurence cried out, saying, 'I will rejoice openly, since I have been found worthy to be a consumed sacrifice for Christ.'

Ant. 3: I give thanks to you, O Lord Jesus Christ, because you have found me worthy to enter your gates.

Scripture Reading   *1 Pet 4:13-14*
My dear people, if you can have some share in the sufferings of Christ, be glad, because you will enjoy a much greater gladness when his glory is revealed. It is a blessing for you when they insult you for bearing the name of Christ, because it means that you have the Spirit of glory, the Spirit of God resting on you.

Short Responsory
R̷ You have tested us, God, and you have brought us out into freedom again. *Repeat* R̷
V̷ You have refined us like silver. R̷ Glory be. R̷

Magnificat ant. Blessed Laurence said, 'This night of mine is not dark; rather everything shines with light.'

Intercessions
Let us give thanks to the King of martyrs, for this is the hour when he offered himself in the last supper and laid down his life on the cross. R̷ We praise you, Christ the Lord.
We praise you, Christ our Saviour, example and strength of the martyrs, because you have loved us to the end;—we praise you, Christ the Lord.
Because you have promised repentant sinners the reward of eternal life,—we praise you, Christ the Lord.
Because you have called the Church to offer the blood of the new and eternal covenant, the blood shed for the remission of sins,—we praise you, Christ the Lord.
Because you have brought us to this day with the gift of faith intact, —we praise you, Christ the Lord.
Because of the many brothers who today have come to share in your saving death,—we praise you, Christ the Lord.
Our Father

The concluding prayer as at Morning Prayer, p 850.

11 August
SAINT CLARE, Virgin

Memoria

Born at Assisi in the year 1193. She followed her fellow countryman Saint Francis in his life of poverty and was the founder and ruler of an order of nuns (Poor Clares). She led a very austere life, abounding in works of piety and charity. She died in the year 1253.

From the Common of Virgins, p 1057, or of Women Saints: Religious, p 1074.

Concluding Prayer
Lord God,
in your mercy
you led Saint Clare to the love of poverty.
Help us, by her intercession,
to follow Christ in poverty of spirit,
so that, in the kingdom of heaven,
we may see you in your glory.
(We make our prayer) through our Lord.

13 August
SAINTS PONTIANUS, Pope
and HIPPOLYTUS, Priest, Martyrs
Optional Memoria

Pontianus was ordained Bishop of Rome in the year 231, and in the year 235 was exiled by the Emperor Maximinus to Sardinia, together with the priest Hippolytus. Here he abdicated the papacy. After his death in Sardinia his body was buried in the cemetery of Callistus, while the body of Hippolytus was taken to the cemetery on the Via Tiburtina. Both of these martyrs have been venerated by the Church of Rome from the beginning of the fourth century.

From the Common of Martyrs: Several Martyrs, p 1017, or of Pastors, p 1040.

Concluding Prayer

Lord God,
may the martyrs' patient endurance,
which is precious in your sight,
increase our love for you,
and keep the faith firm in our hearts.
(We make our prayer) through our Lord.

15 August

THE ASSUMPTION OF
THE BLESSED VIRGIN MARY

Solemnity

EVENING PRAYER I

Hymn

Who is she ascends so high,
Next the heavenly King,
Round about whom angels fly
And her praises sing?

Who is she, adorned with light,
Makes the sun her robe,
At whose feet the queen of night
Lays her changing globe?

This is she in whose pure womb
Heaven's Prince remained;
Therefore in no earthly tomb
Can she be contained.

Heaven she was, which held that fire,
Whence the world took light,
And to heaven doth now aspire
Flames with flames t' unite.

She that did so clearly shine
When our day begun,
See how bright her beams decline:
Now she sits with the Sun.

Ant. 1: When Christ ascended into heaven, he prepared there an immortal place for his most chaste Mother, alleluia.

Psalms and canticle from the Common of the Blessed Virgin Mary, p 982.

Ant. 2: The gates of paradise were closed to all men because of Eve, but they have been opened again through the Virgin Mary, alleluia.

Ant. 3: The Virgin Mary has been exalted high above the heavens; come, let us all glorify Christ the king, whose kingdom has no end.

Scripture Reading   *Rom 8:30*
Those whom God predestined, he also called; and those whom he called, he also justified; and those whom he justified, he also glorified.

Short Responsory
R̸ Mary has been assumed into heaven; the angels rejoice. *Repeat* R̸
V̸ They sing for joy and praise the Lord. R̸ Glory be. R̸

Magnificat ant. Behold, all generations will call me blessed, for he who is mighty has done great things for me, alleluia.

Intercessions
Let us praise God the Father who chose Mary as the mother of his Son and wanted all generations to call her blessed. With confidence we pray: R̸ May the Virgin Mary intercede for us.
Father, you did great things for the Virgin Mary and brought her, body and soul, to the glory of heaven;—fill the hearts of your children with the hope of Christ's glory. R̸
Through the prayers of Mary, our mother, heal the sick, comfort the sorrowful, pardon sinners;—grant peace and salvation to all. R̸
You favoured Mary with the fulness of grace;—bestow on all men your overflowing blessings. R̸
May your Church be united heart and soul, held fast by love;— and may your faithful be joined in continuous prayer, with Mary the mother of Jesus. R̸

Father, you exalted the Virgin Mary and crowned her queen of heaven;—may the dead enter your kingdom and rejoice with your saints for ever. R̦
Our Father

Concluding Prayer
God our Father,
you crowned the Blessed Virgin Mary
on the day of her Assumption
with a glory beyond compare.
You had looked on her lowliness
and had made her the mother of our Lord Jesus Christ,
your Only-begotten Son.
Grant that, by her prayers,
we may be saved by the mystery of your redemption,
and share with her in the glory of eternal life.
(We make our prayer) through our Lord.

Invitatory
Ant. Come, let us adore the King of kings: today his Virgin Mother
was taken up to heaven.
Psalm, p 371.

MORNING PRAYER

Hymn
The ark which God has sanctified,
Which he has filled with grace,
Within the temple of the Lord
Has found a resting-place.

More glorious than the seraphim,
This ark of love divine,
Corruption could not blemish her
Whom death could not confine.

God-bearing Mother, Virgin chaste,
Who shines in heaven's sight;
She wears a royal crown of stars
Who is the door of Light.

855

To Father, Son and Spirit blest
May we give endless praise
With Mary, who is Queen of heaven,
Through everlasting days.

Ant. 1: Blessed are you, O Mary, for through you salvation came into the world; now you are in glory and rejoice before the Lord.

Psalms and canticle of Sunday, Week 1, pp 390 ff.

Ant. 2: The Virgin Mary is exalted high above the choirs of angels; let all the faithful rejoice and bless the Lord.

Ant. 3: Your name has been so exalted by the Lord that your praises will never cease on the lips of men.

Scripture Reading　　　*Is 61:10*
I exult for joy in the Lord, my soul rejoices in my God, for he has clothed me in the garments of salvation, he has wrapped me in the cloak of integrity, like a bride adorned in her jewels.

Short Responsory
R̷ Today the Virgin Mary was assumed into heaven. *Repeat* R̷
V̷ For ever she will share in the victory of Christ. R̷ Glory be. R̷

Benedictus ant. See the beauty of the daughter of Jerusalem, who ascended to heaven like the rising sun at dawn.

Intercessions
Let us proclaim the greatness of our Saviour who chose to be born of the Virgin Mary. Confident that he will hear us, we ask: R̷ Lord, may your mother pray for us.
Eternal Word, in the living flesh of Mary you found a dwelling place on earth;—remain with us for ever in hearts free from sin. R̷
Christ, our Redeemer, you made the Virgin Mary the sanctuary of your presence and the temple of the Spirit;—make us bearers of your Spirit, in mind, heart and body. R̷
Eternal Word, you taught your mother Mary to choose the part that

was best;—let us follow her example and hunger for the food of everlasting life. ℟

King of kings, you assumed Mary into heaven to be with you completely in body and soul;—may we seek the things that are above and keep our lives fixed on you. ℟

King of heaven and earth, you placed Mary at your side to reign as queen for ever;—grant us the joy of sharing in your glory. ℟

Our Father

Concluding Prayer
Almighty, ever-living God,
you have taken the mother of your Son,
the immaculate Virgin Mary,
body and soul into the glory where you dwell.
Keep our hearts set on heaven
so that, with her, we may share in your glory.
(We make our prayer) through our Lord.

EVENING PRAYER II

Hymn as at Evening Prayer I, p 853.

Ant. 1: Mary has been assumed into heaven, the angels rejoice. They sing for joy and praise the Lord.

Psalms and canticle from the Common of the Blessed Virgin Mary, p 992.

Ant. 2: The Virgin Mary has been assumed to the heavenly dwelling-place where the King of kings sits on a throne of stars.

Ant. 3: You, O daughter, are blessed by the Lord; through you we have partaken of the fruit of life.

Scripture Reading   *1 Cor 15:22-23*
Just as all men die in Adam, so all men will be brought to life in Christ; but all of them in their proper order: Christ as the first-fruits and then, after the coming of Christ, those who belong to him.

Short Responsory

℟ The Virgin Mary has been exalted high above the choirs of angels.
Repeat ℟
℣ Blessed is the Lord who raised her up. ℟ Glory be. ℟

Magnificat ant. Today the Virgin Mary was assumed into heaven;
rejoice and be glad, for she will reign for ever with Christ.

Intercessions

Let us praise God the Father who chose Mary as the mother of his
Son and wanted all generations to call her blessed. With confidence
we pray: ℟ May the Virgin Mary intercede for us.
Father, you did great things for the Virgin Mary and brought her,
body and soul, to the glory of heaven;—fill the hearts of your
children with the hope of Christ's glory. ℟
Through the prayers of Mary, our mother, heal the sick, comfort the
sorrowful, pardon sinners;—grant peace and salvation to all. ℟
You favoured Mary with the fulness of grace;—bestow on all men
your overflowing blessings. ℟
May your Church be united heart and soul, held fast by love;—and
may your faithful be joined in continuous prayer, with Mary the
mother of Jesus. ℟
Father, you exalted the Virgin Mary and crowned her queen of
heaven;—may the dead enter your kingdom and rejoice with your
saints for ever. ℟
Our Father

The concluding prayer as at Morning Prayer, p 857.

*After Night Prayer the anthems nos 119 and 120 are particularly
suitable.*

16 August
SAINT STEPHEN OF HUNGARY
Optional Memoria

Born in Hungary about the year 969. He received baptism and in the year
1000 was crowned King of Hungary. He was a just, peaceful and religious
king, keeping strictly to the laws of the Church and always seeking the good

of his subjects. He established many dioceses and did much to strengthen the life of the Church. He died at Szekesfehérvar in the year 1038.

From the Common of Men Saints p 1067.

Concluding Prayer
Almighty God,
under the reign of Saint Stephen as king,
the Church in his country
increased in numbers and strength.
Grant that he may continue to defend your Church
from his place in heaven.
(We make our prayer) through our Lord.

19 August
SAINT JOHN EUDES, Priest
Optional Memoria

Born in the diocese of Séez in France in the year 1601. After being ordained priest he spent many years preaching as a missioner. He founded congregations with the object of educating priests in seminaries and of rescuing women who were in moral danger. He strenuously promoted devotion to the Sacred Hearts of Jesus and Mary. He died in 1680.

From the Common of Pastors, p 1040, or of Men Saints: Religious, p 1067.

Concluding Prayer
Almighty God and Father,
you gave Saint John Eudes the wonderful grace
of making known the inexhaustible riches of Christ.
Help us, by his example and teaching,
to grow in knowledge of you,
and faithfully to live by the light of the gospel.
(We make our prayer) through our Lord.

20 August
SAINT BERNARD
Abbot and Doctor of the Church

Memoria

Born near Dijon in France in the year 1090. He was brought up religiously and joined the Cistercians in 1111. Soon afterwards he was elected Abbot of the monastery of Clairvaux. He was outstanding in directing the monks in virtue both by his work and by his example. On account of divisions which had arisen in the Church he travelled through Europe trying to restore peace and unity. He wrote many works dealing with theology and the spiritual life. He died in 1153.

From the Common of Doctors of the Church, p 1049, or of Men Saints: Religious, p 1067, except for the following:

MORNING PRAYER

Benedictus ant. O blessed Bernard, whose soul was enlightened with the wonders of the eternal Word. He spread the light of faith and true teaching throughout the Church.

Concluding Prayer
Lord God,
you made Saint Bernard burn with zeal for your house,
and gave him grace
to enkindle and enlighten others in your Church.
Grant that by his prayer
we may be filled with the same spirit,
and always live as children of the light.
(We make our prayer) through our Lord.

EVENING PRAYER

Magnificat ant. Bernard, doctor of the Church from whom teaching flowed like sweet honey, friend of the divine Bridegroom and herald telling of the wonders of the Virgin Mother, became famous at Clairvaux as a pastor of souls.

SAINT PIUS X, Pope

Memoria

Born at Riese in the province of Venice in the year 1835. He became a priest and excelled in the duties given to him. After being first Bishop of Mantua and then Patriarch of Venice, he was elected pope in the year 1903. He made it his object in his pontificate to restore all things in Christ, and he did this by his simplicity, his poverty and his fortitude. He renewed the true Christian life among the faithful and he fought strenuously against the errors which were sweeping through the Church at the time. He died on 20 August in the year 1914.

From the Common of Pastors, p 1040.

Concluding Prayer
Lord God,
you filled Pope Saint Pius with wisdom
and gave him the strength of an apostle
to defend the Catholic faith
and to renew all things in Christ.
Grant that we may follow his example and teaching,
and so come to our reward in heaven.
(We make our prayer) through our Lord.

22 August
OUR LADY, QUEEN AND MOTHER

Memoria

From the Common of the Blessed Virgin Mary, p 987, except for the following:

Invitatory ant. Christ the king crowned his Mother as Queen of Heaven: come, let us adore him.
Psalm, p 371.

MORNING PRAYER

Benedictus ant. Hail, O Queen of all the world, ever virgin Mary. You bore Christ the Lord, the Saviour of all creation.

Concluding Prayer
Almighty God, our Father,
you have given us Mary, the Mother of your Son,
to be our Mother and Queen.
Grant that, supported by her prayers,
we may come to the kingdom of heaven
and to the glory destined for your children.
(We make our prayer) through our Lord.

EVENING PRAYER

Magnificat ant. Blessed are you, O Virgin Mary, because you
believed in all the things which were told you by the Lord: you will
reign for ever with Christ.

*After Night Prayer the anthems nos 119 and 120 are particularly
suitable.*

23 August
SAINT ROSE OF LIMA, Virgin
Optional Memoria

Born at Lima in Peru in the year 1586. She advanced in virtue in her daily
life at home, and after taking the habit of the Third Order of Saint
Dominic she made great progress in a life of penance and mystical contemplation. She died on 24 August in the year 1617.

*From the Common of Virgins, p 1053, or of Women Saints: Religious,
p 1074.*

Concluding Prayer
God our Father,
for love of you Saint Rose left the world
and gave herself to a life of penitence and austerity.
Help us, by her prayers,
so to follow the path of life on earth,
that we may obtain the fulness of joy
in your presence in heaven.
(We make our prayer) through our Lord.

24 August
SAINT BARTHOLOMEW
Apostle

Feast

Born at Cana. He was led to Jesus by the apostle Philip, and after the Lord's Ascension tradition has it that he preached the gospel in India and there suffered martyrdom.

From the Common of Apostles, p 1004.

Concluding Prayer
Almighty Lord and Father,
strengthen in us that faith
with which Saint Bartholomew
gave himself wholeheartedly to Christ your Son.
Grant, at his intercession,
that your Church may become
the sacrament of salvation
for all the nations of the earth.
(We make our prayer) through our Lord.

25 August
SAINT LOUIS

Optional Memoria

Born in the year 1214. He became King of France in his twenty-second year. He married and had eleven children whom he brought up religiously. He was outstanding in penance and prayer and in his love for the poor. In ruling his kingdom he was concerned not only with peace and the temporal good of his subjects but also with their spiritual good. He undertook Crusades to the Holy Land and died in the year 1270 near Carthage.

From the Common of Men Saints, p 1067.

Concluding Prayer
Almighty, ever-living God,
you took Saint Louis from his cares
as a ruler in this world,
and brought him to the glory of heaven.

Help us, by his intercession,
to seek your eternal kingdom
through the tasks we perform on earth.
(We make our prayer) through our Lord.

Also 25 August
SAINT JOSEPH OF CALASANZ
Priest

Optional Memoria

Born in Aragon in the year 1557. After receiving a good education he was ordained priest and worked in his own country, then went to Rome where he gave himself to the education of poor children. He founded a religious congregation for this purpose. As a result of jealousy he had to suffer many trials. He died at Rome in the year 1648.

From the Common of Men Saints: Educators, p 1067, or of Pastors, p 1040.

Concluding Prayer
God our Father,
for the education and religious upbringing of the young
you gave Saint Joseph of Calasanz
remarkable gifts of priestly charity and patience.
Grant that while we honour him as a master of wisdom,
we may imitate him
by teaching the true way of life.
(We make our prayer) through our Lord:

27 August
SAINT MONICA

Memoria

Born at Thagaste in Africa of a Christian family about the year 331. While still young she was married to Patricius and had children, one of whom was Augustine. She was unceasing in her prayers to God for his conversion and shed many tears for him. She strengthened her faith by her prayer and was outstanding in virtue, a wonderful example of a Christian mother. She died at Ostia in the year 387.

From the Common of Women Saints, p 1074, except for the following:

864

MORNING PRAYER

Benedictus ant. You listened to her, O Lord, and did not despise those tears of hers which moistened the earth wherever she prayed.

Concluding Prayer
God our Father,
comforter of the sorrowful,
you accepted Saint Monica's offering of tears
for the conversion of her son, Augustine.
Help us, by their intercession,
to be truly contrite for our sins
so that we may receive the grace of your forgiveness.
(We make our prayer) through our Lord.

EVENING PRAYER

Magnificat ant. Monica lived in Christ while still living in this world; she so lived that the name of God was praised in both her faith and her works.

28 August
SAINT AUGUSTINE
Bishop and Doctor of the Church

Memoria

Born at Thagaste in Africa in the year 354. As a young man he led an unsettled life both in the philosophy he professed and in his moral behaviour, but later, in the year 387, he was converted and received baptism at Milan from the bishop Saint Ambrose. He came back to his own country and led the life of an ascetic. Elected Bishop of Hippo, for thirty-four years he was an exemplary bishop to his flock, teaching his people by his sermons and writings, striving to combat the errors of the time and to make the faith understood. He died in the year 430.

From the Common of Pastors, p 1040, or of Doctors of the Church, p 1049, except for the following:

MORNING PRAYER

Benedictus ant. You stir us up, O Lord, and make us find joy in praising you, since you have made us for yourself; and our hearts find no rest until they rest in you.

Concluding Prayer
Lord God,
renew your Church
with the Spirit of wisdom and love
which you gave so fully to Saint Augustine.
Lead us by that same Spirit
to seek you, the only fountain of true wisdom
and the source of everlasting love.
(We make our prayer) through our Lord.

EVENING PRAYER

Magnificat ant. Late have I loved you, O beauty both ancient and new, late have I loved you. You called, you cried out and you rid me of my deafness.

29 August

THE BEHEADING OF
SAINT JOHN THE BAPTIST

Memoria

Invitatory ant. Come, let us adore the Lamb of God; Saint John went before him in his passion.
Psalm, p 371.

MORNING PRAYER

Hymn
God called great prophets to foretell
The coming of his Son;
The greatest, called before his birth,
Was John, the chosen one.

John searched in solitude for Christ
And knew him when he came.
He showed the world the Lamb of God
And hailed him in our name.

That lonely voice cried out the truth,
Derided and denied.
As witness to the law of God
His mighty martyr died.

We praise you, Trinity in One,
The light of unknown ways,
The hope of all who search for you
Whose love fills all our days.

Ant. 1: The Lord stretched out his hand and touched my mouth, and set me up as a prophet for the peoples.

Psalms and canticle of Sunday, Week 1, pp 390 ff.

Ant. 2: Herod feared John who was a virtuous and holy man, and he had him put in prison.

Ant. 3: Herod listened to John, and when he had heard him he did many things.

Scripture Reading　　　*Is 49:1b-2*
The Lord called me before I was born, from my mother's womb he pronounced my name. He made my mouth a sharp sword, and hid me in the shadow of his hand. He made me into a sharpened arrow, and concealed me in his quiver.

Short Responsory
R7 You sent to John and he gave testimony to the truth. *Repeat* R7
V He was like a bright shining light. R7 Glory be. R7

Benedictus ant. The friend of the bridegroom, who stands and listens for him, rejoices greatly when he hears the voice of the bridegroom: therefore my joy is now complete.

Intercessions

Let us make our prayer to Christ who sent John before him to prepare his way: R℣ Lord, prepare us for your coming.

John leaped in the womb of Elizabeth as she met your mother:— Lord, make us always glad to welcome your coming. R℣

John showed in his life what he preached by his words:—give us the courage to practise what we preach. R℣

John baptized you in the Jordan and the spirit of Justice rested upon you:—help us, Lord, to work for a world of justice. R℣

Lord, you called men to preach your word:—send heralds to carry the gospel to the world. R℣

Our Father

Concluding Prayer

God our Father,
you appointed Saint John the Baptist
to be the herald
of the birth and death of Christ your Son.
Grant that as he died a martyr for justice and truth,
so we also may courageously bear witness to your word.
(We make our prayer) through our Lord.

EVENING PRAYER

Hymn as at Morning Prayer, p 866.

Ant. 1: Do not fear them, for I am with you, says the Lord.

Psalms and canticle from the Common of Martyrs, p 1021.

Ant. 2: Herod sent one of his bodyguard to behead John, who was in prison.

Ant. 3: The disciples of John came and took his body and placed it in a tomb.

Scripture Reading   *Acts 13:23-25*

It was Jesus, one of the descendants of David, that God made the

Saviour of the people of Israel, as he had promised. Before the coming of Jesus, John preached to all the people of Israel that they should turn from their sins and be baptized. And as John was about to finish his mission, he said to the people: 'Who do you think I am? I am not the one you are waiting for. But look! He is coming after me, and I am not good enough to take his sandals off his feet.'

Short Responsory
R̸ The friend of the bridegroom rejoices when he hears the bridegroom's voice. *Repeat* R̸
V̸ Now my joy is complete. R̸ Glory be. R̸

Magnificat ant. I am not the Christ, but I have been sent before him. He must increase in importance, I must decrease.

Intercessions
God our Father, you chose John the Baptist to announce the kingdom of Christ to all men. Joyfully we pray, therefore: R̸ Lord, guide us in the way of peace.
Even in his mother's womb you chose John to prepare the way for your Son;—give us the faith to know Christ, and to make him known. R̸
You inspired the Baptist to recognize the Lamb of God;—through us, let the world recognize your Son, our Lord Jesus Christ. R̸
You disposed your prophet to give way before Christ;—give us the humility to let his light shine in the world. R̸
You called John even to die for you;—grant that we may share his burning zeal for the truth. R̸
Remember the dead who have walked in the path of life;—bring them to new life, cleansed from all stain of sin. R̸
Our Father

The concluding prayer as at Morning Prayer, p 868.

SEPTEMBER

3 September
SAINT GREGORY THE GREAT
Pope and Doctor of the Church

Memoria

Born at Rome about the year 540. He entered the public service and was appointed a Prefect of the City. Then he entered a monastery, was ordained deacon and performed the office of a papal legate to Constantinople. On 3 September 590 he became pope and showed himself a true pastor in his administration, his care of the poor, and in spreading and consolidating the faith. In addition he wrote many works on faith and morals. He died on 12 March 604.

From the Common of Pastors, p 1040, or of Doctors of the Church, p 1049, except for the following:

MORNING PRAYER

Benedictus ant. The chosen pastor Gregory passed on an example by the life he led as a pastor and he also left us a rule.

Concluding Prayer
God our Father,
your rule is a rule of love,
your providence is full of mercy for your people.
Through the intercession of Saint Gregory
grant the spirit of wisdom
to those you have placed in authority,
so that the spiritual growth of the people
may bring eternal joy to the pastors.
(We make our prayer) through our Lord.

EVENING PRAYER

Magnificat ant. Gregory fulfilled in deeds what he preached by word, so that he might be an example while speaking about mystical things.

8 September
THE BIRTHDAY OF
THE BLESSED VIRGIN MARY
Feast

Invitatory ant. Let us celebrate the birth of the Virgin Mary: let us adore her Son, Christ the Lord.
Psalm, p 371.

MORNING PRAYER

Hymn from the Common, p 987, or the appendix.

Ant. 1: Today is the birthday of the glorious Virgin Mary, of the seed of Abraham, who rose from the tribe of Judah and the stock of David.

Psalms and canticle of Sunday, Week 1, pp 390 ff.

Ant. 2: When the sacred Virgin was born, then the world was filled with light; blessed and holy is the stock which bore such blessed fruit.

Ant. 3: With joy let us celebrate the nativity of blessed Mary, that she may intercede for us with the Lord Jesus Christ.

Scripture Reading   *Is 11:1-3*
A shoot shall grow from the stock of Jesse, and a branch shall spring from his roots. The spirit of the Lord shall rest upon him, a spirit of wisdom and understanding, a spirit of counsel and power, a spirit of knowledge and the fear of the Lord.

Short Responsory
Ry The Lord chose her, he chose her before she was born. *Repeat* Ry
Vy He made her live in his own dwelling place. Ry Glory be. Ry

Benedictus ant. Your birth, O Virgin Mother of God, announced joy to the whole world, for from you has risen the Sun of justice, Christ our God. He released us from the ancient curse and made us blessed; he destroyed death and gave us eternal life.

Intercessions
The alternative intercessions, p 988, may be used.
Let us proclaim the greatness of our Saviour who chose to be born of the Virgin Mary. Confident that he will hear us, we ask: ℟ Lord, may your mother pray for us.
Sun of justice, you showed your day was dawning in the immaculate Virgin Mary;—help us to walk in the daylight of your presence. ℟
Eternal Word, in the living flesh of Mary you found a dwelling place on earth;—remain with us for ever in hearts free from sin. ℟
Christ, our Saviour, you willed that your mother should be there when you died;—through her intercession may we rejoice to share your suffering. ℟
Loving Saviour, while hanging on the cross, you gave your mother Mary to be the mother of John;—let us be known as her children by our way of living. ℟
Our Father

Concluding Prayer
Lord God,
the day of our salvation dawned
when the Blessed Virgin gave birth to your Son.
As we celebrate her nativity
grant us your grace and your peace.
(We make our prayer) through our Lord.
(Through Christ our Lord.)

EVENING PRAYER

Hymn from the appendix.

Ant. 1: The Virgin Mary was born from the stock of Jesse and the Spirit of the Most High came to dwell with her.

Psalms and canticle from the Common of the Blessed Virgin Mary, p 992.

Ant. 2: Today is the birthday of the holy Virgin Mary. God looked on her beauty and came to visit her in her lowliness.

Ant. 3: Blessed and worthy of our veneration is holy Mary, the Virgin Mother of God: her birthday we celebrate that she may intercede for us with the Lord.

Scripture Reading   *Rom 9:4-5*
They are Israelites: they were made God's sons; theirs is the splendour of the divine presence, theirs the covenants, the law, the temple worship, and the promises. Theirs are the patriarchs, and from them, in natural descent, sprang the Messiah. May God, supreme above all, be blessed for ever. Amen.

Short Responsory
R⁷ Hail, full of grace, the Lord is with you. *Repeat* R⁷
V⁷ You are the most blessed of all women, and blessed is the fruit of your womb. R⁷ Glory be. R⁷

Magnificat ant. Let us remember the worthy birth of the glorious Virgin Mary. The Lord looked on her in her lowliness and sent his angel to announce to her that she would conceive and bear the Redeemer of the world.

Intercessions
The alternative intercessions, p 996, may be used.
Let us praise God the Father who chose Mary as the mother of his Son and wanted all generations to call her blessed. With confidence we pray: R⁷ May the Virgin Mary intercede for us.
Father, you did great things for the Virgin Mary and brought her, body and soul, to the glory of heaven;—fill the hearts of your children with the hope of Christ's glory. R⁷
Through the prayers of Mary, our mother, heal the sick, comfort the sorrowful, pardon sinners;—grant peace and salvation to all. R⁷
You favoured Mary with the fulness of grace;—bestow on all men your overflowing blessing. R⁷
May your Church be united heart and soul, held fast by love,—and may your faithful be joined in continuous prayer, with Mary the mother of Jesus. R⁷
Father, you exalted the Virgin Mary and crowned her queen of heaven;—may the dead enter your kingdom and rejoice with your

saints for ever. ℟ May the Virgin Mary intercede for us.
Our Father

The concluding prayer as at Morning Prayer, p 872.

13 September
SAINT JOHN CHRYSOSTOM
Bishop and Doctor of the Church

Memoria

Born at Antioch about the year 349. After a brilliant course of studies he began to lead a life of austerity. He was ordained priest and laboured in preaching, with great fruit. In 397 he became Bishop of Constantinople and showed himself a true pastor, striving to reform the morals of both clergy and people. He incurred the hatred of the imperial court and his work was undermined because of jealousy, and twice he was sent into exile. Overcome by exhaustion he died at Comana in Pontus on 14 September 407. Because of his sermons and writings to explain the faith and to encourage the practice of the Christian life he was called John of the Golden Mouth.

From the Common of Pastors, p 1040, or of Doctors of the Church, p 1049.

Concluding Prayer
Lord God, strength of those who hope in you,
by your will
Saint John Chrysostom became renowned in the Church
for his astounding eloquence
and his forbearance in persecution.
Grant that we may be enriched by his teaching,
and encouraged by the example of his unconquerable fortitude.
(We make our prayer) through our Lord.

14 September
THE EXALTATION OF
THE HOLY CROSS

Feast

EVENING PRAYER I
(When the feast occurs on a Sunday)

Hymn as at Morning Prayer, p 878.

PSALMODY

Ant. 1: After he had been crucified he rose from the dead and brought us redemption, alleluia.

PSALM 146(147)

Praise the Lórd for hé is góod;†
sing to our Gód for hé is lóving:*
to hím our práise is dúe.

The Lórd buílds up Jerúsalem*
and bríngs back Ísrael's éxiles,
he héals the bróken-héarted,*
he bínds up áll their wóunds.
He fíxes the númber of the stárs;*
he cálls each óne by its náme.

Our Lórd is gréat and almíghty;*
his wísdom can néver be méasured.
The Lórd ráises the lówly;*
he húmbles the wícked to the dúst.
O sing to the Lórd, giving thánks;*
sing psálms to our Gód with the hárp.

He cóvers the héavens with clóuds;*
he prepáres the ráin for the éarth,
making móuntains spróut with gráss*
and with plánts to sérve man's néeds.
He provídes the béasts with their fóod*
and young rávens that cáll upón him.

875

His delíght is nót in hórses*
nor his pléasure in wárriors' stréngth.
The Lórd delights in thóse who revére him,*
in thóse who wáit for his lóve.

Ant. After he had been crucified he rose from the dead and brought
us redemption, alleluia.
Ant. 2: In the centre of the holy city of Jerusalem stands the tree of
life, and the leaves of that tree will bring salvation to all peoples,
alleluia.

PSALM 147

O práise the Lórd, Jerúsalem!*
Síon, práise your Gód!

He has stréngthened the bárs of your gátes,*
he has bléssed the chíldren withín you.
He estáblished péace on your bórders,*
he féeds you with fínest whéat.

He sénds out his wórd to the éarth*
and swíftly rúns his commánd.
He shówers down snów white as wóol,*
he scátters hóar-frost like áshes.

He húrls down háilstones like crúmbs.*
The wáters are frózen at his tóuch;
he sénds forth his wórd and it mélts them:*
at the bréath of his móuth the waters flów.

He mákes his wórd known to Jácob,*
to Ísrael his láws and decrées.
He has not déalt thus with óther nátions;*
he has not táught them hís decrées.

Ant. In the centre of the holy city of Jerusalem stands the tree of life,
and the leaves of that tree will bring salvation to all peoples, alleluia.
Ant. 3: It is right for us to glory in the cross of our Lord Jesus Christ.

Though he was in the form of God,*
Jesus did not count equality with God a thing to be grasped.

He emptied himself,†
taking the form of a servant,*
being born in the likeness of men.

And being found in human form,†
he humbled himself and became obedient unto death,*
even death on a cross.

Therefore God has highly exalted him*
and bestowed on him the name which is above every name,

That at the name of Jesus every knee should bow,*
in heaven and on earth and under the earth,

And every tongue confess that Jesus Christ is Lord,*
to the glory of God the Father.

Ant. It is right for us to glory in the cross of our Lord Jesus Christ.

Scripture Reading *1 Cor 1:23-24*
We proclaim Christ—yes, Christ nailed to the cross: and though it is a stumbling-block to Jews and folly to Greeks, yet to those who have heard his call, Jews and Greeks alike, he is the power of God and the wisdom of God.

Short Responsory
R̷ This sign will appear in heaven when the Lord comes. *Repeat* R̷
V̷ Lift up your heads: your salvation is at hand. R̷ Glory be. R̷

Magnificat ant. It was fitting that Christ should suffer and rise from the dead, and so enter into his glory.

Intercessions
Let us pray to our Redeemer, who went to the cross for our sakes.
R̷ Lead us into your kingdom through the cross.
Lord Jesus, you took the form of a slave and became like us:—grant us a share in your humility. R̷

877

Lord Jesus, you humbled yourself, becoming obedient even unto the death of the cross:—let us share your obedience in suffering.

℞ Lead us into your kingdom through the cross.

Lord Jesus, you were raised on high by God, and given a name above every other name:—grant us perseverance, and a share in your glory. ℞

Let every knee bow at the name of Jesus:—fire the hearts of all men with your love. ℞

Son of God, grant salvation to those who have called you their Lord:—take our deceased brothers and sisters into your kingdom. ℞

Our Father

Concluding Prayer

God our Father,

in obedience to your will

your Only-begotten Son endured the cross for our salvation.

Grant that as we have come to know the mystery of the cross here
    on earth,

we may receive its rewards in heaven.

(We make our prayer) through our Lord.

Invitatory

Ant. Christ the king was raised up on the cross for our sake: come, let us adore him.

Psalm, p 371.

MORNING PRAYER

Hymn

O Cross of Christ, immortal tree
On which our Saviour died,
The world is sheltered by your arms
That bore the Crucified.

From bitter death and barren wood
The tree of life is made;
Its branches bear unfailing fruit
And leaves that never fade.

O faithful Cross, you stand unmoved
While ages run their course;
Foundation of the universe,
Creation's binding force.

Give glory to the risen Christ
And to his Cross give praise,
The sign of God's unfathomed love,
The hope of all our days.

Ant. 1: He who suffered on the cross, crushed the power of hell. On the third day he rose again to clothe himself with power.

Psalms and canticle of Sunday, Week 1, pp 390 ff.

Ant. 2: The holy cross shines in splendour. The Lord hung upon it to wash our wounds clean with his blood.

Ant. 3: The holy cross shines upon us. In the cross is victory, in the cross is power. By the cross every sin is overcome, alleluia.

Scripture Reading   *Heb 2:9-10*
We see in Jeus one who was for a short while made lower than the angels and is now crowned with glory and splendour because he submitted to death; by God's grace he had to experience death for all mankind. As it was his purpose to bring a great many of his sons into glory, it was appropriate that God, for whom everything exists and through whom everything exists, should make perfect, through suffering, the leader who would take them to their salvation.

Short Responsory
R̰ We worship you, Christ, and we bless you. *Repeat* R̰
V̰ By your cross you have redeemed the world. R̰ Glory be. R̰

Benedictus ant. We venerate your cross, Lord: we praise and glorify your holy resurrection: because of the wood of the cross, joy has come into the world.

Intercessions

Let us pray to Christ, who saved us by his cross. ℟ Lord, we find glory in your cross.

Son of God, you were raised up to draw all men to yourself:—may we never run away from our cross, but suffer it gladly in union with you. ℟

Son of Man, your death brought life to the world:—may we accept your call to die to sin and live as children of light. ℟

Only Son of the Father, you save your brothers from eternal death: —may all who seek you find eternal life. ℟

Beloved Son of the Father, you did not come to condemn the world but to die for its salvation:—we pray for the salvation of all whom we know and love. ℟

Eternal Son of the Father, you came to cast fire on the earth, and longed for it to be kindled:—bring us into all truth that we may live in your presence. ℟

Our Father

Concluding Prayer

God our Father,
in obedience to your will
your Only-begotten Son endured the cross for our salvation.
Grant that as we have come to know the mystery of the cross here
    on earth,
we may receive its rewards in heaven.
(We make our prayer) through our Lord.

EVENING PRAYER II

Hymn as at Morning Prayer, p 878.

PSALMODY

Ant. 1: This was Love's great deed that death should die, when Life itself was slain upon the tree.

PSALM 109(110):1-5,7

The Lórd's revelátion to my Máster:†

'Sít on my ríght:*
your fóes I will pút beneath your féet'.

The Lórd will wíeld from Síon†
your scéptre of pówer:*
rúle in the mídst of all your fóes.

A prínce from the dáy of your bírth†
on the hóly móuntains;*
from the wómb before the dáwn I begót you.

The Lórd has sworn an óath he will not chánge.†
'You are a príest for éver,*
a príest like Melchízedek of óld.'

The Máster stánding at your ríght hand*
will shatter kíngs in the dáy of his wráth.

He shall drínk from the stréam by the wáyside*
and thérefore he shall líft up his héad.

Ant. This was Love's great deed that death should die, when Life
itself was slain upon the tree.
Ant. 2: Lord, we venerate your cross as we recall your blessed passion. You suffered for our sake, have mercy on us.

PSALM 115(116)

I trústed, éven when I sáid:*
'I am sórely afflícted,'
and whén I sáid in my alárm:*
'No mán can be trústed.'

How cán I repáy the Lórd*
for his góodness to mé?
The cúp of salvátion I will ráise;*
I will cáll on the Lórd's name.

My vóws to the Lórd I will fulfíl*
befóre all his péople.
O précious in the éyes of the Lórd*
is the déath of his fáithful.

881

Your sérvant, Lord, your sérvant am Í;*
you have lóosened my bónds.
A thánksgiving sácrifice I máke:*
I will cáll on the Lórd's name.

My vóws to the Lórd I will fulfíl*
befóre all his péople,
in the cóurts of the hóuse of the Lórd,*
in your mídst, O Jerúsalem.

Ant. Lord, we venerate your cross as we recall your blessed passion.
You suffered for our sake, have mercy on us.
Ant. 3: We worship you, Christ, and we bless you. By your cross,
you have redeemed the world.

CANTICLE: REV 4:11;5:9,10,12

Worthy are you, our Lord and God,*
to receive glory and honour and power,
for you created all things,*
and by your will they existed and were created.

Worthy are you, O Lord,*
to take the scroll and to open its seals,
for you were slain,†
and by your blood you ransomed men for God*
from every tribe and tongue and people and nation.

You have made us a kingdom and priests to our God,*
and we shall reign on earth.

Worthy is the Lamb who was slain,*
to receive power and wealth,
and wisdom and might,*
and honour and glory and blessing.

Ant. We worship you, Christ, and we bless you. By your cross, you
have redeemed the world.

Scripture Reading   *1 Cor 1:23-24*
We proclaim Christ—yes, Christ nailed to the cross; and though it is

a stumbling-block to Jews and folly to Greeks, yet to those who have heard his call, Jews and Greeks alike, he is the power of God and the wisdom of God.

Short Responsory

R̷ The King of angels held his triumph on the cross of glory. *Repeat* R̷
V̷ He washed our wounds clean with his blood. R̷ Glory be. R̷

Magnificat ant. Hail holy cross, standard of victory. Lead us to the triumph of Christ Jesus in the kingdom of heaven.

Intercessions

Let us pray to our Redeemer, who went to the cross for our sakes.
R̷ Lead us into your kingdom through the cross.
Lord Jesus, you took the form of a slave and became like us:—grant us a share in your humility. R̷
Lord Jesus, you humbled yourself becoming obedient even unto the death of the cross:—let us share your obedience in suffering. R̷
Lord Jesus, you were raised on high by God, and given a name above every other name:—grant us perseverance, and a share in your glory. R̷
Let every knee bow at the name of Jesus:—fire the hearts of all men with your love. R̷
Son of God, grant salvation to those who have called you their Lord:—take our deceased brothers and sisters into your kingdom. R̷
Our Father

The concluding prayer as at Morning Prayer, p 880.

15 September
OUR LADY OF SORROWS

Memoria

From the Common of the Blessed Virgin Mary, p 987, except for the following:

Invitatory ant. Let us adore the Saviour, who gave his Mother a share in his passion.
Psalm, p 371.

MORNING PRAYER

Hymn, from the Common, p 987, or the appendix, for the Blessed Virgin Mary.

Ant. 1: Lord Jesus, my soul clings to you.

Psalms and canticle of Sunday, Week 1, pp 390 ff.

Ant. 2: As sharers in Christ's sufferings, let us rejoice.

Ant. 3: God has been pleased to reconcile all creation to himself by the blood of Christ.

Scripture Reading   *Col 1:24-25*
It is now my happiness to suffer for you. This is my way of helping to complete, in my poor human flesh, the full tale of Christ's afflictions still to be endured, for the sake of his body which is the church. I became its servant by virtue of the task assigned to me by God for your benefit: to deliver his message in full.

Short Responsory
R̰ May we obtain salvation through you, Mary, ever-virgin. *Repeat* R̰
V̰ May we find life in the passion of Christ. R̰ Glory be. R̰

Benedictus ant. Rejoice, grief-stricken Mother, for now you share the triumph of your Son. Enthroned in heavenly splendour, you reign as queen of all creation.

Intercessions
The alternative intercessions, p 988, may be used.
Let us proclaim the greatness of our Saviour who chose to be born of the Virgin Mary. Confident that he will hear us, we ask: R̰ Lord,

may your mother pray for us.

Sun of justice, you showed your day was dawning in the immaculate
Virgin Mary;—help us to walk in the daylight of your presence. R̷
Eternal Word, in the living flesh of Mary you found a dwelling place
on earth;—remain with us for ever in hearts free from sin. R̷
Christ, our Saviour, you willed that your mother should be there
when you died;—through her intercession may we rejoice to share
your suffering. R̷
Loving Saviour, while hanging on the cross, you gave your mother
Mary to be the mother of John;—let us be known as her children
by our way of living. R̷
Our Father

Concluding Prayer
God our Father,
when Jesus, your Son, was raised up on the cross,
it was your will that Mary, his mother, should stand there
and suffer with him in her heart.
Grant that, in union with her,
the Church may share in the passion of Christ,
and so be brought to the glory of his resurrection.
(We make our prayer) through our Lord.

EVENING PRAYER

*Hymn, from the Common, p 991, or the appendix, for the Blessed
Virgin Mary.*

Ant. 1: Christ by his cross gained for us peace and forgiveness from
God.

*Psalms and canticle from the Common of the Blessed Virgin Mary,
p 992.*

Ant. 2: Let us draw near to Jesus, high priest of the new covenant,
city of the living God.

Ant. 3: We have obtained salvation through the blood of Christ.

Scripture Reading   *2 Tim 2:10-12a*

I endure everything for the sake of God's chosen people, in order that they too may obtain the salvation that is in Christ Jesus, together with eternal glory. This is a true saying: 'If we have died with him, we shall also live with him; if we continue to endure, we shall also rule with him.'

Short Responsory

R̷ By the cross of her Lord stood Mary all-holy, queen of heaven and of earth. *Repeat* R̷

V̷ She won the crown of martyrdom without suffering the pain of death. R̷ Glory be. R̷

Magnificat ant. Jesus, seeing his Mother and beloved disciple standing by the cross, said, 'Woman, behold, your son!' And to the disciple, 'Son, behold, your mother.'

Intercessions

The alternative intercessions, p 996, may be used.

Let us praise God the Father who chose Mary as the mother of his Son, and wanted all generations to call her blessed. With confidence we pray: R̷ May the Virgin Mary intercede for us.

Father, you did great things for the Virgin Mary and brought her, body and soul, to the glory of heaven;—fill the hearts of your children with the hope of Christ's glory. R̷

Through the prayers of Mary, our mother, heal the sick, comfort the sorrowful, pardon sinners;—grant peace and salvation to all. R̷

You favoured Mary with the fulness of grace;—bestow on all men your overflowing blessings. R̷

May your Church be united heart and soul, held fast by love,—and may your faithful be joined in continuous prayer, with Mary the mother of Jesus. R̷

Father, you exalted the Virgin Mary and crowned her queen of heaven;—may the dead enter your kingdom and rejoice with your saints for ever. R̷

Our Father

The concluding prayer as at Morning Prayer, p 885.

16 September
SAINT CORNELIUS, Pope and
SAINT CYPRIAN, Bishop, Martyrs
Memoria

Cornelius was ordained Bishop of Rome in the year 251. He laboured to combat the Novatian schism and with the help of Cyprian he was able to enforce his authority. He was sent into exile by the Emperor Gallus, and he died at Civitavecchia in the year 253. His body was brought to Rome and interred in the cemetery of Callistus.

Cyprian was born in Carthage about the year 210. He was converted to the faith in mature life and ordained priest. He was ordained bishop of Carthage in 249. He guided his church excellently during much troubled times both by his deeds and his writings. During the persecution of Valerian he was first exiled, then, on 14 September 258, martyred for the faith.

From the Common of Martyrs: Several Martyrs, p 1017, or of Pastors, p 1040, except for the following:

MORNING PRAYER

Benedictus ant. Death is of value when eternal life is purchased at the cost of one's blood.

Concluding Prayer
Lord God,
you gave Saint Cornelius and Saint Cyprian to your Church
as faithful pastors and steadfast martyrs.
Strengthen our faith and our courage by their prayers,
so that we may strive with all our power
for the unity of the Church.
(We make our prayer) through our Lord.

EVENING PRAYER

Magnificat ant. The blood of Christ's martyrs bathes our holy Church with radiance.

17 September
SAINT ROBERT BELLARMINE
Bishop and Doctor of the Church
Optional Memoria

Born in the year 1542 in Montepulciano in Tuscany. He entered the Society of Jesus at Rome and was ordained priest. He engaged in arguments in defence of the Catholic faith and he taught in the Collegio Romano. After being created a Cardinal and later Bishop of Capua, he was of considerable help to the Roman Congregations in solving the many difficult questions which arose. He died at Rome in the year 1621.

From the Common of Pastors, p 1040, or of Doctors of the Church, p 1049.

Concluding Prayer
Lord God,
to defend the faith of the Church
you bestowed on Saint Robert Bellarmine
great gifts of learning and holiness.
Grant, through his intercession,
that your people may always rejoice to possess
the fulness of that same faith.
(We make our prayer) through our Lord.

19 September
SAINT JANUARIUS
Bishop and Martyr

Optional Memoria

He was Bishop of Benevento and together with his companions he suffered martyrdom, in the persecution of Diocletian, at Naples. He is especially venerated in that city.

From the Common of Martyrs: One Martyr, p 1029, or of Pastors, p 1040.

Concluding Prayer
Lord God,
as, by your grace,

we keep the memory of Saint Januarius,
grant that we may share with him
the eternal joy you have promised us.
(We make our prayer) through our Lord.

21 September
SAINT MATTHEW
Apostle and Evangelist

Feast

Born at Capernaum. He was a tax gatherer when called by Jesus. He wrote his Gospel in the Hebrew language, and tradition has it that he preached the faith in the East.

From the Common of Apostles, p 1004, except for the following:

MORNING PRAYER

Benedictus ant. Jesus saw a man called Matthew seated at the tax office and said to him, 'Follow me.' And he rose and followed him.

Concluding Prayer
Lord,
you showed your great mercy to Matthew the tax-gatherer
by calling him to become your apostle.
Supported by his prayer and example
may we always answer your call,
and live in close union with you.
(We make our prayer) through our Lord.

EVENING PRAYER

Magnificat ant. The Lord says, 'I desire mercy, not sacrifice. For I came not to call the righteous, but sinners '

26 September
SAINTS COSMAS AND DAMIAN
Martyrs

Optional Memoria

From early writings there is evidence that the tomb of Cosmas and Damian was at Cyrrhus in Syria where a basilica was built in their honour. Their veneration spread from there to Rome and then throughout the Church.

From the Common of Martyrs: Several Martyrs, p 1017.

Concluding Prayer
Lord God,
we proclaim your great power
as we keep the memory of Saint Cosmas and Saint Damian.
In your providence
you have exalted them to glory,
and you have given us the patronage of their prayers.
(We make our prayer) through our Lord.

27 September
SAINT VINCENT DE PAUL,
Priest

Memoria

Born in Gascony in France in the year 1581. He completed his studies and was ordained priest, and became a parish priest in Paris. He founded the Congregation of the Mission (Vincentians) for the purpose of the spiritual formation of the clergy and the relief of the poor, and with the help of Saint Louise de Marillac he founded also the Congregation of the Sisters of Charity. He died at Paris in the year 1660.

From the Common of Pastors, p 1040, or of Men Saints: Saints Noted for Works of Mercy, p 1067, except for the following:

MORNING PRAYER

Benedictus ant. Vincent comforted those in grief. He was the protector of orphans, and benefactor of widows.

Concluding Prayer

Father,
you endowed Saint Vincent de Paul with the spirit of an apostle
to give himself to the service of the poor
and to the training of priests.
Give us a share of the same spirit
that we may love what he loved
and do as he taught us.
(We make our prayer) through our Lord.

EVENING PRAYER

Magnificat ant. The Lord says, 'What you did to one of the least of
these my brethren, you did to me.'

28 September
SAINT WENCESLAUS, Martyr
Optional Memoria

Born in Bohemia about the year 907. He was brought up in the Christian
religion by his grandmother and took over power in the kingdom about
the year 925. He encountered many difficulties both in ruling his kingdom
and in promoting the Christian faith. He was betrayed by his brother
Boleslaus and was murdered in the year 935. He was immediately proclaimed a martyr and is venerated as the principal patron of Bohemia.

From the Common of Martyrs: One Martyr, p 1029.

Concluding Prayer

Almighty, ever-living God,
under your guidance Saint Wenceslaus learnt
to lay aside an earthly kingdom
for the sake of the kingdom of heaven.
Help us, by his prayers, to deny ourselves
and to follow you with all our heart.
(We make our prayer) through our Lord.

29 September
SAINTS MICHAEL, GABRIEL and RAPHAEL, Archangels

Feast

Invitatory ant. In the presence of the angels, come let us adore the Lord.

Psalm, p 371.

MORNING PRAYER

Hymn

Angels of God, you see the Father's face,
Sharing his splendour, clothed in fire and flame,
Worshipping him, the terrible and great,
Singing for ever: Holy is his name!

Angels, you sang when Christ came down to earth,
Gave him your comfort in the hour of dread,
Solaced his spirit, anguished and alone,
Shouted his triumph, risen from the dead.

Angels, archangels, when he comes again,
Compassed in glory, fearful in his might,
Open for him the King's eternal gates:
Then will he lead his faithful into light.

When to the Father, Son and Spirit blest,
Angels and men united worship bring,
From all creation, from the world unseen,
Up to the Godhead perfect praise will spring.

Ant. 1: Let us praise the Lord, united with the angels; holy, holy, holy, is the song of the cherubim and seraphim.

Psalms and canticle of Sunday, Week 1, pp 390 ff.

Ant. 2: Angels of the Lord, give thanks to him for ever.

Ant. 3: Holy Lord, all the angels in heaven glorify you; with one accord they say, 'Our praise is your due, O God.'

Scripture Reading   *Gen 28:12-13a*

Jacob had a dream: a ladder was there standing on the ground with its top reaching to heaven; and there were angels of God going up it and coming down. And the Lord was there, standing over him saying: 'I am the Lord, the God of Abraham your father and the God of Isaac.'

Short Responsory

R̷ There the angel stood, by the altar in the temple. *Repeat* R̷
V̷ In his hand he held a golden censer. R̷ Glory be. R̷

Benedictus ant. Truly, I say to you, you will see heaven opened, and God's angels ascending and descending upon the Son of Man.

Intercessions

Father, as you laid the foundation of creation, the stars of the morning sang for joy, and the sons of God in chorus chanted your praise: R̷ All you spirits, worship the Lord.

Lord, your heavenly servants were sent to men to guard and lead them.—Keep us faithful to your call today. R̷

Lord, the angels stand before your throne to praise you:—help us to seek your face today. R̷

Lord, your sons are called to be like angels of light:—keep us pure in heart and body. R̷

Lord, we thank you for your glorious power; we praise your victory over the powers of darkness:—for yours is the kingdom, the power, and the glory, for all ages to come. R̷

Our Father

Concluding Prayer

Lord God of hosts,
in your all-wise plan
you assign to angels and to men
the services they have to render you.
Grant that the angels who adore you in heaven,
may protect us here on earth.
(We make our prayer) through our Lord.

EVENING PRAYER

Hymn as at Morning Prayer, p 892.

Hymn as at Morning Prayer, p 892.

PSALMODY

Ant. 1: King of the angels, your splendour surpasses that of the heavens.

PSALM 8

How gréat is your náme, O Lórd our Gód,*
through áll the éarth!

Your májesty is práised above the héavens;*
on the líps of chíldren and of bábes
you have found práise to fóil your énemy,*
to sílence the fóe and the rébel.

When I see the héavens, the wórk of your hánds,*
the móon and the stárs which you arránged,
what is mán that you should kéep him in mínd,*
mortal mán that you cáre for hím?

Yet you have máde him little léss than a gód;*
with glóry and hónour you crówned him,
gave him pówer over the wórks of your hánd,*
put áll things únder his féet.

Áll of them, shéep and cáttle,*
yes, éven the sávage béasts,
bírds of the aír, and físh*
that máke their wáy through the wáters.

How gréat is your náme, O Lórd our Gód,*
through áll the éarth!

Ant. King of the angels, your splendour surpasses that of the heavens.
Ant. 2: Before the angels, I will bless you, my God.

PSALM 137(138)

I thánk you, Lórd, with all my héart,*
you have héard the wórds of my móuth.

In the présence of the ángels I will bléss you.*
I will adóre before your hóly témple.

I thánk you for your fáithfulness and lóve*
which excél all we éver knew of yóu.
On the dáy I cálled, you ánswered;*
you incréased the stréngth of my sóul.

Áll earth's kíngs shall thánk you*
when they héar the wórds of your móuth.
They shall síng of the Lórd's wáys:*
'How gréat is the glóry of the Lórd!'

The Lord is hígh yet he lóoks on the lówly*
and the háughty he knóws from afár.
Though I wálk in the mídst of afflíction*
you give me lífe and frustráte my fóes.

You strétch out your hánd and sáve me,*
your hánd will do áll things for mé.
Your lóve, O Lórd, is etérnal,*
discárd not the wórk of your hánds.

Ant. Before the angels I will bless you, my God.
Ant. 3: I saw the Lamb standing, as it were, slain, and occupying the throne; all around arose the sound of angel choirs.

CANTICLE: COL 1:12-20

Let us give thanks to the Father,†
who has qualified us to share*
in the inheritance of the saints in light.

He has delivered us from the dominion of darkness*
and transferred us to the kingdom of his beloved Son,
in whom we have redemption,*
the forgiveness of sins.

He is the image of the invisible God,*
the firstborn of all creation,
for in him all things were created, in heaven and on earth,*
visible and invisible.

All things were created*
through him and for him.
He is before all things,*
and in him all things hold together.

He is the head of the body, the Church;*
he is the beginning,
the firstborn from the dead,*
that in everything he might be pre-eminent,

For in him all the fulness of God was pleased to dwell,*
and through him to reconcile to himself all things,
whether on earth or in heaven,*
making peace by the blood of his cross.

Ant. I saw the Lamb standing, as it were, slain, and occupying the throne; all around arose the sound of angel choirs.

Scripture Reading   *Rev 1:4b-5*
Grace and peace be yours from God, who is, who was, and who is to come, and from the seven spirits in front of his throne, and from Jesus Christ, the faithful witness, the first-born Son who was raised from death, who is also the ruler of the kings of the earth. He loves us, and by his death he has freed us from our sins.

Short Responsory
R℣ Sweet-scented smoke went up in the Lord's presence. *Repeat* R℣
℣ From an angel's hand. R℣ Glory be. R℣

Magnificat ant. The angel Gabriel said to Mary, 'You will conceive in your womb and bear a son and you shall call his name Jesus.'

Intercessions
The powers of heaven stand at God's throne to serve him. Let us ask our Father to make us ready to do his will on earth. R℣ Let us praise the Father with the hosts of heaven.
Lord, you made the angels to be ministers of your word:—by their help may we bring your word to our brothers. R℣
Lord, your holiness is sung by the eternal angels:—may the Church

on earth never fail in your praise. ℟
You sent your angels to watch over your servants,—protect all those who travel, and guide them safely home. ℟
At Christmas your angels sang of peace toward men:—may their message of peace inspire the hearts of rulers and peoples. ℟
When the angels summon the dead from the four corners of the world,—may your people be gathered as one into your joy. ℟
Our Father

The concluding prayer as at Morning Prayer, p 893.

30 September
SAINT JEROME
Priest and Doctor of the Church

Memoria

Born at Strido in Dalmatia about the year 340. He studied at Rome and was later baptized. Then he began to lead a life of asceticism, went to the East and was there ordained priest. Returning to Rome he was secretary to Pope Saint Damasus and began the task of translating the Bible into Latin as well as promoting the monastic life. He then settled in Bethlehem where he gave great help in the needs of the Church. He wrote many works, especially commentaries on the scriptures. He died at Bethlehem in the year 420.

From the Common of Doctors of the Church, p 1049.

Concluding Prayer
Almighty, ever-living God,
you endowed Saint Jerome
with a deep reverence for Holy Scripture,
which he loved with all his heart.
Sustain us ever more with your word
and help us to find in it the source of life.
(We make our prayer) through our Lord.

OCTOBER

1 October
SAINT TERESA
OF THE CHILD JESUS
Virgin

Memoria

Born at Alençon in France in the year 1873. While still young she entered the Carmelite monastery at Lisieux and practised the virtues of humility, evangelical simplicity and a firm confidence in God. By her words and example she taught the novices. Offering her life for the salvation of souls and for the spreading of the faith in the missions, she died on 30 September in the year 1897.

From the Common of Virgins, p 1057, except for the following:

MORNING PRAYER

Benedictus ant. Indeed I tell you that, unless you undergo a change of heart and become more like children, you shall not enter my heavenly kingdom.

Concluding Prayer
God our Father,
you promised your kingdom
to the little ones and the humble of heart.
Give us grace to walk confidently
in the way of Saint Teresa of the Child Jesus,
so that, helped by her prayers,
we may see your eternal glory.
(We make our prayer) through our Lord.

EVENING PRAYER

Magnificat ant. Rejoice and be glad because your names have been recorded in heaven.

898

2 October
THE GUARDIAN ANGELS
Memoria

Invitatory ant. Come, let us adore the Lord, whom the angels serve.
Psalm, p 371.

MORNING PRAYER

Hymn

They come, God's messengers of love,
They come from realms of peace above,
From homes of never-fading light,
From blissful mansions ever bright.

They come to watch around us here,
To soothe our sorrow, calm our fear:
Ye heavenly guides, speed not away,
God willeth you with us to stay.

But chiefly at its journey's end
'Tis yours the spirit to befriend,
And whisper to the willing heart,
'O Christian soul, in peace depart.'

To us the zeal of angels give,
With love to serve thee while we live;
To us an Angel-guard supply,
When on the bed of death we lie.

Ant. 1: The Lord will send his angels with you, to guide your footsteps.

Psalms and canticle of Sunday, Week 1, pp 390 ff.

Ant. 2: Thanks be to God, who sent his angel to rescue his faithful followers.

Ant. 3: All hosts of angels, praise the Lord.

Scripture Reading   *Ex 23:20-21*
Behold, I send an angel before you, to guard you on the way and to

bring you to the place which I have prepared. Give heed to him and hearken to his voice.

Short Responsory

℟ In the presence of the angels I shall sing to you, my God. *Repeat* ℟

℣ I shall bear witness to you. ℟ Glory be. ℟

Benedictus ant. These are all ministering spirits sent out to serve, for the sake of those who are to obtain salvation.

Intercessions

Father, as you laid the foundations of creation, the stars of the morning sang for joy, and the sons of God in chorus chanted your praise: ℟ All you spirits, worship the Lord.

Lord, your heavenly servants were sent to men to guard and lead them.—Keep us faithful to your call today. ℟

Lord, the angels stand before your throne to praise you:—help us to seek your face today. ℟

Lord, your sons are called to be like angels of light:—keep us pure in heart and body. ℟

Lord, we thank you for your glorious power; we praise your victory over the powers of darkness:—for yours is the kingdom, the power, and the glory, for all ages to come. ℟

Our Father

Concluding Prayer

Lord God of hosts,
in your all-wise providence
you send angels to guard and protect us.
Surround us with their watchful care on earth,
and give us the joy of their company for ever in heaven.
(We make our prayer) through our Lord.

EVENING PRAYER

Hymn as at Morning Prayer, p 899.

PSALMODY

Ant. 1: The angel of the Lord is encamped around those who revere him, to rescue them.

PSALM 33(34)

I

I will bléss the Lórd at all tímes,*
his práise álways on my líps;
in the Lórd my sóul shall make its bóast.*
The húmble shall héar and be glád.

Glórify the Lórd with mé.*
Togéther let us práise his náme.
I sóught the Lórd and he ánswered me;*
from all my térrors he sét me frée.

Lóok towards hím and be rádiant;*
let your fáces nót be abáshed.
This póor man cálled; the Lord héard him*
and réscued him from áll his distréss.

The ángel of the Lórd is encámped*
around thóse who revére him, to réscue them.
Taste and sée that the Lórd is góod.*
He is háppy who seeks réfuge in hím.

Revére the Lórd, you his sáints.*
They lack nóthing, thóse who revére him.
Strong líons suffer wánt and go húngry*
but thóse who seek the Lórd lack no bléssing.

Ant. The angel of the Lord is encamped around those who revere him, to rescue them.
Ant. 2: As God lives, so has his angel protected me.

II

Cóme, chíldren, and héar me*
that I may téach you the féar of the Lórd.
Who is hé who lóngs for lífe*
and many dáys, to enjóy his prospérity?

Then kéep your tóngue from évil*
and your líps from spéaking decéit.
Turn asíde from évil and do góod;*
séek and stríve after péace.

The Lórd turns his fáce against the wícked*
to destróy their remémbrance from the éarth.
The Lórd turns his éyes to the júst*
and his éars to théir appéal.

They cáll and the Lórd héars*
and réscues them in áll their distréss.
The Lord is clóse to the bróken-héarted;*
those whose spírit is crúshed he will sáve.

Mány are the tríals of the júst man*
but from them áll the Lórd will réscue him.
He will keep guárd over áll his bónes,*
not óne of his bónes shall be bróken.

Évil brings déath to the wícked;*
those who háte the góod are dóomed.
The Lord ránsoms the sóuls of his sérvants.*
Those who híde in him shall nót be condémned.

Ant. As God lives, so has his angel protected me.
Ant. 3: Give thanks to the God of heaven, glorify him with all living
things, for he has shown to you his loving kindness.

CANTICLE: REV 11:17-18;12:10B-12A

We give thanks to you, Lord God Almighty,*
who are and who were,
that you have taken your great power*
and begun to reign.

The nations raged,*
but your wrath came,
and the time for the dead to be judged,*
for rewarding your servants, the prophets and saints,
and those who fear your name,*
both small and great.

Now the salvation and the power†
and the kingdom of our God*
and the authority of his Christ have come,
for the accuser of our brethren has been thrown down,*
who accuses them day and night before our God.

And they have conquered him*
by the blood of the Lamb
and by the word of their testimony,*
for they loved not their lives even unto death.
Rejoice, then, O heaven,*
and you that dwell therein.

Ant. Give thanks to the God of heaven, glorify him with all living things, for he has shown to you his loving kindness.

Scripture Reading   *Rev 8:3-4*
Another angel who had a gold incense container came and stood at the altar. He was given much incense to add to the prayers of all God's people and offer on the altar that stands before the throne. The smoke of the burning incense went up with the prayers of God's people from the hands of the angel standing before God.

Short Responsory
R̸ God has entrusted you to the care of his angels. *Repeat* R̸
V̸ May they protect you wherever you go. R̸ Glory be. R̸

Magnificat ant. The angels always look on the face of my Father in heaven.

Intercessions
The powers of heaven stand at God's throne to serve him. Let us ask our Father to make us ready to do his will on earth. R̸ Let us praise the Father with the hosts of heaven.
Lord, you made the angels to be ministers of your word:—by their help may we bring your word to our brothers. R̸
Lord, your holiness is sung by the eternal angels:—may the Church on earth never fail in your praise. R̸

You sent your angels to watch over your servants,—protect all those who travel, and guide them safely home. ℟ Let us praise the Father with the hosts of heaven.

At Christmas your angels sang of peace towards men:—may their message of peace inspire the hearts of rulers and peoples. ℟

When the angels summon the dead from the four corners of the world,—may your people be gathered as one into your joy. ℟

Our Father

Concluding Prayer
Lord God of hosts,
in your all-wise providence
you send angels to guard and protect us.
Surround us with their watchful care on earth,
and give us the joy of their company for ever in heaven.
(We make our prayer) through our Lord.

4 October
SAINT FRANCIS OF ASSISI
Memoria

Born at Assisi in the year 1182. From being a light-hearted youth he changed, gave up his inheritance and bound himself to God, embracing poverty and living the life of the gospels. He preached to all the love of God. He gave to his followers wise rules which were approved by the Holy See. He laid the foundations of an order of nuns, of groups of penitents living in the world, and of preaching the gospel to infidels. He died in the year 1226.

From the Common of Men Saints: Religious, p 1067, except for the following:

MORNING PRAYER

Benedictus ant. Francis, the destitute and lowly, enters heaven a rich man, acclaimed by the songs of angels.

Concluding Prayer
Lord God,

you made Saint Francis of Assisi
Christ-like in his poverty and humility.
Help us so to walk in his ways
that, with joy and love,
we may follow Christ your Son,
and be united to you.
(We make our prayer) through our Lord.

EVENING PRAYER

Magnificat ant. I make no boast, save in the cross of our Lord Jesus
Christ, the marks of whose wounds I bear in my body.

6 October
SAINT BRUNO, Priest
Optional Memoria

Born at Cologne about the year 1035. After being educated at Paris and
ordained priest, he taught theology; but wanting to lead the life of a soli-
tary he founded the monastery of La Grande Chartreuse. He was called to
Rome by Pope Urban II to be his adviser and helper in the needs of the
Church. He died at Squillace in Calabria in the year 1101.

*From the Common of Pastors, p 1040, or of Men Saints: Religious,
p 1067.*

Concluding Prayer
Lord God,
you called Saint Bruno to serve you
in a life of solitude.
Amidst this world's changes
help us, by his prayers,
to set our hearts always on you.
(We make our prayer) through our Lord.

7 October
OUR LADY OF THE ROSARY
Memoria

This feast was instituted by Pope Saint Pius V on the anniversary of the naval battle at Lepanto (1571). It was said that the Christians were victorious because of the help of the holy Mother of God, invoked by the saying of the Rosary. Today's celebration urges all to meditate on the mysteries of Christ, following the example of the Blessed Virgin Mary who was in a special manner associated with the incarnation, passion and glorious resurrection of the Son of God.

Invitatory antiphon from the Common of the Blessed Virgin Mary, p 986.

MORNING PRAYER

Hymn, from the Common, p 987, or the appendix, for the Blessed Virgin Mary.

Ant. 1: Jesus, who is called Christ, was born of Mary.

Psalms and canticle of Sunday, Week 1, pp 390 ff.

Ant. 2: We give thanks to the Lord, with you, our Mother; as he was dying he gave us into your care.

Ant. 3: The Virgin Mary is exalted high above the choirs of angels; on her head is a crown of twelve stars.

Scripture Reading   *Cf Is 61:10*
I will greatly rejoice in the Lord, my soul shall exult in my God; for he has clothed me with the garments of salvation, he has covered me with the robe of righteousness, as a bride adorns herself with her jewels.

Short Responsory
R̸ Hail Mary, full of grace: the Lord is with you. *Repeat* R̸
V̸ You are the most blessed of all women and blessed is the fruit of your womb. R̸ Glory be. R̸

Benedictus ant. Blessed Mother, and pure Virgin, renowned queen of creation, may all who keep your festival experience the power of your intercession.

Intercessions

The first alternative intercessions, p 988, may be used.

Let us proclaim the greatness of our Saviour who chose to be born of the Virgin Mary. Confident that he will hear us, we ask: ℟ Lord, may your mother pray for us.

Saviour of the world, by your redemptive power you preserved your mother Mary from every stain of sin;— deliver us from the evil that lies hidden in our hearts. ℟

Christ, our Redeemer, you made the Virgin Mary the sanctuary of your presence and the temple of the Spirit;—make us bearers of your Spirit, in mind, heart and body. ℟

Eternal Word, you taught your mother Mary to choose the part that was best;—let us follow her example and hunger for the food of everlasting life. ℟

King of kings, you assumed Mary into heaven to be with you completely in body and soul;—may we seek the things that are above and keep our lives fixed on you. ℟

King of heaven and earth, you placed Mary at your side to reign as queen for ever;—grant us the joy of sharing in your glory. ℟

Our Father

Concluding Prayer

Lord, open our hearts to your grace.
May we who learned to believe,
through the angel's message,
in the incarnation of Christ your Son,
be brought by his passion and cross,
at the intercession of the Blessed Virgin Mary,
to the glory of his resurrection.
(We make our prayer) through our Lord.

EVENING PRAYER

Hymn from the Common or from the appendix, for the Blessed Virgin Mary.

Ant. 1: The angel Gabriel brought the good news to Mary and she conceived by the power of the Holy Spirit.

Psalms and canticle from the Common of the Blessed Virgin Mary, p 992.

Ant. 2: The mother of Jesus stood by the cross.

Ant. 3: Rejoice, O Virgin Mother; Christ has risen from the tomb, alleluia.

Scripture Reading   *Gal 4:4-5*
When the appointed time came, God sent his Son, born of a woman, born a subject of the Law, to redeem the subjects of the Law and to enable us to be adopted as sons.

Short Responsory
R̷ Hail Mary, full of grace: the Lord is with you. *Repeat* R̷
V̷ You are the most blessed of all women and blessed is the fruit of your womb. R̷ Glory be. R̷

Magnificat ant. Mary treasured all these things and pondered them in her heart.

Intercessions
The first alternative intercessions, p 996, may be used.
Let us praise God the Father who chose Mary as the mother of his Son and wanted all generations to call her blessed. With confidence we pray: R̷ May the Virgin Mary intercede for us.
Father, you have looked on the Virgin Mary and made her the mother of mercy;—may those who are in danger experience the depth of her love. R̷
You called Mary to be the mother in the house of Jesus and Joseph; —through her prayers help all mothers to make their homes places of love and holiness. R̷
You gave Mary the strength to stand beneath the cross and made her radiant with joy in the resurrection;—raise up the sorrowful and transform their lives with hope. R̷
Mary was your faithful handmaid who treasured your words in her heart;—through her intercession let us become true disciples of your Son, devoted to his service. R̷

Father, you exalted the Virgin Mary and crowned her queen of heaven;—may the dead enter your kingdom and rejoice with your saints for ever. R̷
Our Father

The concluding prayer as at Morning Prayer, p 907.

9 October
SAINT DENIS, Bishop
and HIS COMPANIONS, Martyrs
Optional Memoria

It is recounted by St Gregory of Tours that Denis came from Rome to France in the middle of the third century, that he became the first Bishop of Paris, and that he died a martyr with two members of his clergy in the neighbourhood of the city.

From the Common of Martyrs: Several Martyrs, p 1017.

Concluding Prayer
Lord God,
you sent Saint Denis and his companions
to proclaim your glory to the nations,
and gave them the fortitude to die for your sake.
Help us, by their example,
to meet with a like indifference
the triumphs and afflictions
this world has to offer.
(We make our prayer) through our Lord.

Also 9 October
SAINT JOHN LEONARDI, Priest
Optional Memoria

Born at Lucca in Tuscany in the year 1541. At first he was a pharmacist but abandoned that to become a priest. He undertook the work of preaching and teaching Christian doctrine to children. He founded the Order of Clerks Regular of the Mother of God in the year 1574, a task which involved him in many difficulties. He formed a body of priests for the purpose of spreading the faith and because of this he is rightly looked upon

909

as the founder of the Institute which, extended by the Popes, is called the Work of the Propagation of the Faith. By his wisdom and charity he restored discipline in various Congregations. He died at Rome in the year 1609.

From the Common of Pastors, p 1040, or of Men Saints; Saints Noted for Works of Mercy, p 1067.

Concluding Prayer
Father, source of all that is good,
you sent Saint John Leonardi
to preach the gospel to the nations.
Grant, at his intercession,
that the true faith
may everywhere go forward unhindered.
(We make our prayer) through our Lord.

14 October
SAINT CALLISTUS
Pope and Martyr

Optional Memoria

Tradition has it that he was a slave who, when he obtained his freedom, was made a deacon by Pope Zephyrinus and later succeeded him. He fought strenuously against the heresies of Modalism and Adoptionism. He was martyred in the year 222 and buried on the Via Aurelia.

From the Common of Martyrs: One Martyr, p 1029, or of Pastors, p 1040.

Concluding Prayer
Lord God,
listen in your kindness to your people's prayer
as we joyfully celebrate the martyrdom of Saint Callistus:
may his merits come to our aid.
(We make our prayer) through our Lord.

SAINT TERESA OF AVILA
Virgin and Doctor of the Church

Memoria

Born at Avila in Spain in the year 1515. She joined the Carmelite Order and she made great progress in the way of perfection and enjoyed mystic revelations. She undertook the reform of the Order and in this she had to endure great trials, but overcame them all by her indomitable spirit. She wrote works which are renowned for the depth of their doctrine and which showed her own spiritual experiences. She died at Alba in the year 1582.

From the Common of Virgins, p 1053, or of Doctors of the Church, p 1049.

Concluding Prayer
Almighty God, our Father,
you sent Saint Teresa of Avila
to be a witness in the Church
to the way of perfection.
Sustain us by her spiritual doctrine,
and kindle in us the longing for true holiness.
(We make our prayer) through our Lord.

16 October
SAINT HEDWIG, Religious
Optional Memoria

Born in Bavaria about the year 1174. She married the Duke of Silesia by whom she had seven children. Her life was renowned for her devotion and for her kindness to the sick and poor for whom she built hostels. On the death of her husband she retired to a monastery at Trebnitz where she died in the year 1243.

From the Common of Women Saints: Saints Noted for Works of Mercy, or Religious, p 1074.

Concluding Prayer
Almighty God,
grant us your help
as we pray to Saint Hedwig,

whose holy life was a pattern of humility to all.
(We make our prayer) through our Lord.

Also 16 October
SAINT MARGARET MARY ALACOQUE, Virgin

Optional Memoria

Born in the year 1647 in the diocese of Autun in France. She joined the Visitation Sisters at Paray-le-Monial where she led a life of rapid progress along the way of perfection and was granted mystical revelations especially concerning the Sacred Heart of Jesus. She spared no effort in bringing about veneration of the Sacred Heart in the Church. She died on 17 October in the year 1690.

From the Common of Virgins, p 1053, or of Women Saints: Religious, p 1074.

Concluding Prayer
God our Father,
fill our hearts with the spirit of charity
which you gave so abundantly to Saint Margaret Mary.
May we experience the love of Christ
which surpasses all knowledge,
and attain to the fulness of life you destine for us.
(We make our prayer) through our Lord.

17 October
SAINT IGNATIUS OF ANTIOCH
Bishop and Martyr

Memoria

He became the second bishop of Antioch after Saint Peter. He was sentenced to death by being thrown to wild beasts and for this purpose he was sent to Rome and in the year 107 under the Emperor Trajan suffered a glorious martyrdom. On the journey to Rome he wrote seven letters to the various churches in which he dealt wisely and deeply with the theology of Christ, the constitution of the Church and the Christian life. He has been venerated at Antioch on this date since the time of the fourth century.

From the Common of Martyrs: One Martyr, p 1029, or of Pastors, p 1040, except for the following:

MORNING PRAYER

Benedictus ant. I seek him who died for us; I yearn for him who rose from the dead for us.

Concluding Prayer
Almighty, ever-living God,
the sufferings of the martyrs
adorn the Church, which is the Body of Christ.
As we celebrate the martyrdom of Saint Ignatius of Antioch,
grant that it may be for us a constant source of strength,
as it was for him the entry into glory.
(We make our prayer) through our Lord.

EVENING PRAYER

Magnificat ant. I seek the bread of heaven, the body of Jesus Christ, born of David's line; for drink, I seek the blood of Christ, pledge of his undying love.

18 October
SAINT LUKE, Evangelist
Feast

Born of a pagan family and converted to the true faith, he was the companion of the apostle Paul and wrote his Gospel in accordance with the apostle's preaching. He also wrote the account of the early days of the Church, up to the time of Paul's first sojourn in Rome, in the book called *The Acts of the Apostles.*

Invitatory ant. The Lord is speaking to us in the gospel: come, let us adore him.
Psalm, p 371.

MORNING PRAYER

Hymn from the Common of Apostles, p 1004.

Ant. 1: The holy evangelists sought out the wisdom of the ancients; in their gospels they confirmed the prophecies of old.

Psalms and canticle of Sunday, Week 1, pp 390 ff.

Ant. 2: Through the gospel, God called us to faith in the truth so that we might share the glory of our Lord Jesus Christ.
Ant. 3: Many will praise their wisdom, and it will never be forgotten.

Scripture Reading   *1 Cor 15:1-2a,3-4*
Brothers, I want to remind you of the gospel I preached to you, the gospel that you received and in which you are firmly established, because the gospel will save you. I taught you what I had been taught myself, namely that Christ died for our sins, in accordance with the scriptures; that he was buried, and that he was raised to life on the third day, in accordance with the scriptures.

Short Responsory
R/ They told of the glories of the Lord and of his might. *Repeat* R/
V/ They spoke of the marvellous deeds he had done. R/ Glory be. R/

Benedictus ant. By giving us the gospel of Christ, Saint Luke proclaimed the rising of the Sun from on high.

Intercessions
Our Saviour destroyed death and through the gospel revealed eternal life to us. With joyful praises let us make him known, and let us say: R/ Strengthen your Church in faith and love.
Lord Jesus, in times past you have lighted the way for your people through wise and holy leaders;—may Christians always enjoy this sign of your loving kindness. R/
You forgave the sins of your people when holy pastors prayed;—continually cleanse your Church through their powerful intercession. R/
In the presence of their brothers, you anointed your holy ones and poured on them your Spirit;—fill with your Holy Spirit all the leaders of your people. R/
Nothing could ever separate the holy pastors from your love;—do

not lose even one of those whom you redeemed by your passion. ℟
Our Father

Concluding Prayer
Lord God,
you chose Saint Luke
to reveal the mystery of your love for the poor
in his preaching and his writings.
Grant that those who already acknowledge your name
may continue to be one in mind and heart,
and that all the nations may see your salvation.
(We make our prayer) through our Lord.

EVENING PRAYER

Hymn from the Common of Apostles, p 1006.

Ant. 1: I have become a minister of the gospel according to the
bountiful gift of God.

Psalms and canticle from the Common of Apostles, p 1007.

Ant. 2: I do all things for the sake of the gospel, to have a share in its
blessings.

Ant. 3: To me this grace was given, to preach to the peoples the
unsearchable riches of Christ.

Scripture Reading   *Col 1:3a-6*
We always give thanks to God, the Father of our Lord Jesus Christ,
when we pray for you. For we have heard of your faith in Christ
Jesus and of your love for all God's people. When the true message,
the Good News, first came to you, you heard of the hope it offers.
So your faith and love are based on what you hope for, which is
kept safe for you in heaven. The gospel is bringing blessings and
spreading through the whole world, just as it has among you ever
since the day you first heard of the grace of God and came to know it
as it really is.

Short Responsory

R⁷ Tell of the glory of the Lord; announce it among the nations.
Repeat R⁷
V⁷ Speak of his wonderful deeds to all the peoples. R⁷ Glory be. R⁷

Magnificat ant. Luke, the saintly evangelist, achieved well-merited glory in the Church, by telling of the gentle nature of Christ.

Intercessions

God, the Father of light, called us to the true faith through the gospel of his Son. We pray to him now for all his holy people, saying:
R⁷ Remember your Church, O Lord.
Father, you raised your Son from the dead to be the great shepherd of the sheep;—make us his witnesses to the ends of the earth. R⁷
You sent your Son into the world to proclaim the good news to the poor;—grant that we may bring his gospel into the darkness of men's lives. R⁷
You sent your Son to plant in men's hearts the seed of imperishable life;—may we labour to sow his word and reap a harvest of joy. R⁷
You sent your Son to reconcile the world with yourself by the shedding of his blood;—let us become his fellow workers in restoring men to your friendship. R⁷
You placed your Son at your own right hand in heaven;—receive the dead into the happiness of your kingdom. R⁷
Our Father

The concluding prayer as at Morning Prayer, p 915.

19 October
SAINTS JOHN de BRÉBEUF
and ISAAC JOGUES, Priests
and THEIR COMPANIONS, Martyrs
Optional Memoria

Between the years 1642 and 1649 these eight members of the Society of Jesus, who had gone to North America to preach the true faith to the pagans of that land, were killed by the Huron Indians and the Iroquois tribes after they had suffered terrible tortures. Isaac Jogues died on 18 October 1647 and John de Brébeuf on 16 March 1648.

From the Common of Martyrs: Several Martyrs, p 1017, or of Pastors, p 1040.

Concluding Prayer
Lord God,
you consecrated the first-fruits of the faith in North America
by the preaching and martyrdom of Saint John de Brébeuf, Saint
Isaac Jogues and their companions.
Through their intercession
may the Church of Christ flourish abundantly
in every nation.
(We make our prayer) through our Lord.

Also 19 October
SAINT PAUL OF THE CROSS
Priest

Optional Memoria

Born at Ovada in Liguria in the year 1694. As a young man he helped his father who was a merchant but afterwards, feeling himself called to a life of perfection, he gave up his worldly goods and looked after the poor and the sick, and in this work assembled a body of companions to help him. After becoming a priest he spent more and more time for the salvation of souls and set up houses for his congregation. He spent himself in apostolic works and practised austere mortification. He died at Rome on 18 October in the year 1775.

From the Common of Pastors, p 1040, or of Men Saints: Religious, p 1067.

Concluding Prayer
Almighty God,
your priest Saint Paul
loved only the cross.
May he obtain your grace for us
so that, inspired with a new courage by his example,
we may take up our cross without flinching.
(We make our prayer) through our Lord.

23 October
SAINT JOHN of CAPESTRANO
Priest

Optional Memoria

Born at Capestrano in the Abruzzi in the year 1386. He studied law at Perugia and for a time held the office of judge. Then he entered the Order of Friars Minor, was ordained priest, and went throughout Europe leading an apostolic life, seeking to strengthen Christian morals and to argue against the errors of the heretics. He died at Villach in Austria in the year 1456.

From the Common of Pastors, p 1040.

Concluding Prayer
Almighty God,
you sent Saint John of Capestrano
to comfort Christian people in a time of distress.
Keep us, we pray, in the safety of your protection,
and give your Church lasting peace.
(We make our prayer) through our Lord.

24 October
SAINT ANTONY MARY CLARET
Bishop

Optional Memoria

Born at Sallent in Spain in the year 1807. After becoming a priest he spent several years preaching to the people throughout Catalonia. He founded a society of missionaries (Claretian Fathers) and was made a bishop in the island of Cuba where he worked for the good of souls with great profit. Coming back to Spain he had to endure many trials for the sake of the Church. He died at Fontfroide in France in the year 1870.

From the Common of Pastors, p 1040.

Concluding Prayer
Lord God,
you strengthened Saint Antony Mary
with great charity and patience

in his work as a missionary bishop.
Help us, at his intercession,
to seek your will in all things,
and to devote ourselves, in Christ,
to winning our brethren.
(We make our prayer) through our Lord.

28 October
SAINTS SIMON AND JUDE
Apostles

Feast

The name of Simon is placed eleventh in the list of apostles and nothing is known of him except that he was born at Cana and was known as the Zealot.

Jude, also known as Thaddaeus, was the apostle who, at the Last Supper, asked the Lord why he showed himself only to his disciples and not to the world (John 14:22).

From the Common of Apostles, p 1004, except for the following:

Concluding Prayer
Lord God,
you taught us to call upon your name
through the preaching of the apostles.
At the intercession of Saint Simon and Saint Jude
may your Church continue to grow
by an increase in the number of believing nations.
(We make our prayer) through our Lord.

NOVEMBER

1 November
ALL SAINTS

EVENING PRAYER I

Solemnity

Hymn

The hymn from the Common of Men Saints, p 1067, may be used as an alternative.

O fair is our Lord's own city,
With clearest light abloom,
And full of joy and music,
Where woe can never come.

No guilt or condemnation
Its citizens may know,
None weary is, none anxious,
No head by grief bent low.

The saints and martyrs countless,
Who in this world found woe,
Find there a peace and pleasure
The world cannot bestow.

From earth our faces turning
Towards the King of grace,
In prayer let us beseech him
To bring us to that place.

PSALMODY

Ant. 1: Undying light will shine about your saints, Lord; they will live for ever, alleluia.

PSALM 112(113)

Práise, O sérvants of the Lórd,*
práise the náme of the Lórd!
May the náme of the Lórd be bléssed*

both nów and for évermóre!
From the rísing of the sún to its sétting*
práised be the náme of the Lórd!

Hígh above all nátions is the Lórd,*
abóve the héavens his glóry.
Whó is like the Lórd, our Gód,*
who has rísen on hígh to his thróne
yet stóops from the héights to look dówn,*
to look dówn upon héaven and éarth?

From the dúst he lífts up the lówly,*
from his mísery he ráises the póor
to sét him in the cómpany of prínces,*
yés, with the prínces of his péople.
To the chíldless wífe he gives a hóme*
and gláddens her héart with chíldren.

Ant. Undying light will shine about your saints, Lord; they will live
for ever, alleluia.
Ant. 2: Jerusalem, city of God, you shall rejoice in your children.
They shall all be blessed, and shall be gathered together to the Lord,
alleluia.

PSALM 147

O práise the Lórd, Jerúsalem!*
Síon, práise your Gód!

He stréngthened the bárs of your gátes,*
he has bléssed the chíldren withín you.
He estáblished péace on your bórders.*
he féeds you with fínest whéat.

He sénds out his wórd to the éarth*
and swíftly rúns his commánd.
He shówers down snów white as wóol.*
he scátters hóar-frost like áshes.

He húrls down háilstones like crúmbs.*
The wáters are frózen at his tóuch;

he sénds forth his wórd and it mélts them:*
at the bréath of his móuth the waters flów.

He mákes his wórd known to Jácob,*
to Ísrael his láws and decrées.
He has not déalt thus with óther nátions;*
he has not táught them hís decrées.

Ant. Jerusalem, city of God, you shall rejoice in your children. They shall all be blessed, and shall be gathered together to the Lord, alleluia.

Ant. 3: The saints were singing a new song at the throne of God and of the Lamb, and the earth rang to the sound of their voices, alleluia.

When chanted, this canticle is sung with Alleluia *as set out below. When recited, it suffices to say* Alleluia *at the beginning and end of each strophe.*

CANTICLE: CF REV 19:1-2,5-7

Alleluia.
Salvation and glory and power belong to our God,*
(R⁊ Alleluia.)
His judgments are true and just.
R⁊ Alleluia (alleluia).

Alleluia.
Praise our God, all you his servants,*
(R⁊ Alleluia.)
You who fear him, small and great.
R⁊ Alleluia (alleluia).

Alleluia.
The Lord our God, the Almighty, reigns,*
(R⁊ Alleluia.)
Let us rejoice and exult and give him the glory.
R⁊ Alleluia (alleluia).

Alleluia.
The marriage of the Lamb has come,*

922

(℟ Alleluia.)
And his bride has made herself ready.
℟ Alleluia (alleluia).

Ant. The saints were singing a new song at the throne of God and of the Lamb, and the earth rang to the sound of their voices, alleluia.

Scripture Reading   *Heb 12:22-24a*
What you have come to is Mount Zion and the city of the living God, the heavenly Jerusalem where the millions of angels have gathered for the festival with the whole Church in which everyone is a 'first-born son' and a citizen of heaven. You have come to God himself, the supreme Judge, and been placed with spirits of the saints who have been made perfect; and to Jesus, the mediator who brings a new covenant and a blood for purification which pleads more insistently than Abel's.

Short Responsory
℟ The just shall rejoice at the presence of God. *Repeat* ℟
℣ They shall exult and dance for joy. ℟ Glory be. ℟

Magnificat ant. The glorious band of apostles, the noble company of prophets, the white-robed army who shed their blood for Christ and all the saints in heaven together proclaim: We praise you, Holy Trinity, one God.

Intercessions
With so many witnesses in a great cloud on every side of us, we are encouraged to run steadily in the race we have started. We pray to Christ, for he is the author of our faith, and he will bring it to fulfilment: ℟ With all the saints we praise and thank you, Lord.
Lord, you chose the apostles to be the foundation of your Church:
—keep us faithful to all that you left in their care. ℟
Your martyrs testified to you, even to the shedding of their blood:
—make all Christians faithful witnesses to your word. ℟
Lord, be with those who have consecrated their lives to you in virginity:—may their hope and generosity be a sign to the world of

the glorious life they await at the end of time. R̷ With all the saints
we praise and thank you, Lord.

In the saints you reveal your presence and your care:—as we
venerate them, may we be drawn closer to you. R̷

Welcome our departed brothers and sisters into the company of
Mary, Joseph, and all the saints:—through their intercession, grant
us a place in your kingdom. R̷

Our Father

Concluding Prayer
Almighty, ever-living God,
we are celebrating with joy
the triumph of your grace in all the saints.
With so vast a multitude praying for us,
may we receive from you
the fulness of mercy we have always desired.
(We make our prayer) through our Lord.

Invitatory
Ant. How wonderful is God among his saints; come, let us adore
him.
Psalm, p 371.

MORNING PRAYER

Hymn
The Father's holy ones, the blest,
Who drank the chalice of the Lord,
Have learned that bitterness is sweet
And courage keener than the sword.

In darkness they were unafraid,
And kept alight their living fire.
They now keep timeless days of joy
Where God gives all their heart's desire.

May all that splendid company,
Whom Christ in glory came to meet,
Help us on our uneven road
Made smoother by their passing feet.

O Father, Son and Holy Ghost,
May we keep faith till time shall cease.
Grant us a place among your saints:
The poor in spirit, men of peace.

Ant. 1: The saints will dwell in the kingdom of heaven; their peace will last for ever.

Psalms and canticle of Sunday, Week 1, pp 390 ff.

Ant. 2: You, saints of the Lord, O bless the Lord for ever.

Ant. 3: He is the praise of all his saints, of the sons of Israel, of the people to whom he comes close.

Scripture Reading *Eph 1:17-18*
May the God of our Lord Jesus Christ, the Father of glory, give you a spirit of wisdom and perception of what is revealed, to bring you to full knowledge of him. May he enlighten the eyes of your mind so that you can see what hope his call holds for you, what rich glories he has promised the saints will inherit.

Short Responsory
R̷ Rejoice in the Lord. Let the just shout for joy. *Repeat* R̷
V̷ Let the upright sing praise. R̷ Glory be. R̷

Benedictus ant. The just will shine out, clear as the sun, in their Father's kingdom, alleluia.

Intercessions
We are planted in love and built on love. With all the saints we are given the power to grasp the breadth and the length, the height and the depth of Christ's love, which is beyond all telling. Let us pray, therefore: R̷ Father, be with your people.
O God, source of all holiness, the glory of your gift shines out in all your saints:—we glorify you for the riches of your grace, revealed in them. R̷
Father, you have moved the saints to offer their lives to you, and

have showed us in them the face of your Son:—move us to follow in their steps, to journey in hope towards the Lord of life. R̸ Father, be with your people.

We venerate today with great devotion the saints in heaven:—we pray for the unity and peace of your holy people on earth. R̸

Father, through the sacrifice of your incarnate Son, you have bound yourself forever to mankind:—as we celebrate this feast, we pray that we may be numbered among the saints who see your face. R̸

Our Father

Concluding Prayer

Almighty, ever-living God
we are celebrating with joy
the triumph of your grace in all the saints.
With so vast a multitude praying for us,
may we receive from you
the fulness of mercy we have always desired.
(We make our prayer) through our Lord.

EVENING PRAYER II

Hymn as at Evening Prayer I, p 920.
The hymn from the Common of Men Saints, p 1067, may be used as an alternative.

PSALMODY

Ant. 1: I saw a vast throng, which no man could number, from every nation, standing before the throne.

PSALM 109(110):1-5,7

The Lórd's revelátion to my Máster:†
'Sít on my ríght:*
your fóes I will pút beneath your féet.'

The Lórd will wíeld from Síon†
your scéptre of pówer:*
rúle in the mídst of all your fóes.

A prínce from the dáy of your bírth†
on the hóly móuntains;*
from the wómb before the dáwn I begót you.

The Lórd has sworn an óath he will not chánge.†
'You are a príest for éver,*
a príest like Melchízedek of óld.'

The Máster stánding at your ríght hand*
will shatter kíngs in the dáy of his wráth.

He shall drínk from the stréam by the wáyside*
and thérefore he shall líft up his héad.

Ant. I saw a vast throng, which no man could number, from every
nation, standing before the throne.
Ant. 2: God has tried them and found them worthy of himself.
Royal splendour shall be theirs from the Lord.

PSALM 115(116)

I trústed, éven when I sáid:*
'I am sórely afflícted,'
and whén I sáid in my alárm:*
'No mán can be trústed.'

How cán I repáy the Lórd*
for his góodness to mé?
The cúp of salvátion I will ráise;*
I will cáll on the Lórd's name.

My vóws to the Lórd I will fulfíl*
befóre all his péople.
O précious in the éyes of the Lórd*
is the déath of his fáithful.

Your sérvant, Lord, your sérvant am Í;*
you have lóosened my bónds.
A thánksgiving sácrifice I máke:*
I will cáll on the Lórd's name.

My vóws to the Lórd I will fulfíl*
befóre all his péople,
in the cóurts of the hóuse of the Lórd,*
in your mídst, O Jerúsalem.

Ant. God has tried them and found them worthy of himself. Royal splendour shall be theirs from the Lord.

Ant. 3: You have redeemed us, Lord God, in your blood, from every tribe and tongue and people and nation. You have made us a kingdom to our God.

CANTICLE: REV 4:11;5:9,10,12

Worthy are you, our Lord and God,*
to receive glory and honour and power,
for you created all things,*
and by your will they existed and were created.

Worthy are you, O Lord,*
to take the scroll and to open its seals,*
for you were slain,†
and by your blood you ransomed men for God*
from every tribe and tongue and people and nation.

You have made us a kingdom and priests to our God,*
and we shall reign on earth.

Worthy is the Lamb who was slain,*
to receive power and wealth,
and wisdom and might,*
and honour and glory and blessing.

Ant. You have redeemed us, Lord God, in your blood, from every tribe and tongue and people and nation. You have made us a kingdom to our God.

Scripture Reading   *2 Cor 6:16b;7:1*

The temple of the living God is what we are. God's own words are: 'I will live and move and have my being among them; I will be their God, and they shall be my people.' Such are the promises that have been made to us, dear friends. Let us therefore cleanse ourselves from all that can defile our spirit, and in the fear of God complete our consecration.

Short Responsory

℟ Let the saints rejoice in the Lord. Alleluia, alleluia. *Repeat* ℟
℣ God has chosen you for his own. ℟ Glory be. ℟

Magnificat ant. How full of splendour is the kingdom where all the saints exult with Christ! The white-robed throng follows the Lamb of God in all his ways.

Intercessions

With so many witnesses in a great cloud on every side of us, we are encouraged to run steadily in the race we have started. We pray to Christ, for he is the author of our faith, and he will bring it to fulfilment: ℟ With all the saints we praise and thank you, Lord.

Lord, you chose the apostles to be the foundation of your Church: —keep us faithful to all that you left in their care. ℟

Your martyrs testified to you, even to the shedding of their blood: —make all Christians faithful witnesses to your word. ℟

Lord, be with those who have consecrated their lives to you in virginity:—may their hope and generosity be a sign to the world of the glorious life they await at the end of time. ℟

In the saints you reveal your presence and your care:—as we venerate them, may we be drawn closer to you. ℟

Welcome our departed brothers and sisters into the company of Mary, Joseph, and all the saints:—through their intercession, grant us a place in your kingdom. ℟

Our Father

The concluding prayer as at Morning Prayer, p 926.

2 November
ALL SOULS DAY

When 2 November is a Sunday, even though Mass may be of the Commemoration of All Souls, the Office celebrated is that of the Sunday, and the Office for the Dead is omitted. However, Morning Prayer and Evening Prayer for the Dead, in which the people participate, may be celebrated.

From the Office for the Dead, p 1087.

Concluding Prayer
Grant, Lord, we pray,
that as our faith is built on the Risen Christ,
so too our hope may be steadfast
as we await the resurrection of all the faithful departed.
(We make our prayer) through our Lord.

3 November
SAINT MARTIN DE PORRES
Religious

Optional Memoria

He was born at Lima in Peru in the year 1579, the son of a Spanish father
and a coloured mother. As a young man he learnt the art of a dispenser of
medicines, and afterwards when he joined the Dominican Order he
practised this for the sake of the poor. He led a humble and austere life
and had a great devotion towards the Holy Eucharist. He died in the year
1639.

*From the Common of Men Saints: Religious, p 1067, except for the
following:*

MORNING PRAYER

Benedictus ant. Blessed be the Lord. He has set all the nations free,
calling them all out of darkness into his amazing light.

Concluding Prayer
Lord God,
you led Saint Martin de Porres by the path of humility
to the glory of heaven.
Help us so to follow his splendid example
that we may obtain from you, as he did,
a place in your kingdom.
(We make our prayer) through our Lord.

EVENING PRAYER

Magnificat ant. Let us glorify the Lord. With grace from heaven he
raised up his lowly servant Martin.

930

4 November
SAINT CHARLES BORROMEO
Bishop

Memoria

Born at Arona in Lombardy in the year 1538. After obtaining his doctorate in both civil and canon law he was created a cardinal by his uncle Pius IV and was chosen to be bishop of Milan. He became a true shepherd of his flock and frequently went around his diocese, called synods, made wise regulations for the good of souls, and worked for the good of Christian morality. He died on 3 November in the year 1584.

From the Common of Pastors, p 1040.

Concluding Prayer
Lord,
keep alive in your people
the spirit you gave to your bishop Saint Charles Borromeo.
Shape and renew your Church
until it bears the image of Christ,
and shows his true likeness to the world.
(We make our prayer) through our Lord.

9 November
DEDICATION OF
THE LATERAN BASILICA

Feast

This feast commemorates the dedication of the basilica built by the Emperor Constantine on the Lateran Hill which, by a tradition dating from the twelfth century, is said to have taken place on this day. At first the feast was kept only in the City of Rome but then, in honour of the basilica which is called the Mother and Head of all Churches of the City and the World, it was extended to the whole of the Roman Rite as a sign of unity and respect towards the Holy See, which, as St Ignatius of Antioch wrote, presides over the whole assembly of charity.

From the Common of the Dedication of a Church, p 967.

10 November
SAINT LEO THE GREAT
Pope and Doctor of the Church

Memoria

Born in Tuscany, he became Pope in the year 440. He was a true father and shepherd of his people. He constantly strove to preserve the integrity of the faith, defended the unity of the Church, repelled or alleviated the incursions of the barbarians, and in very truth he is called the Great. He died in the year 461.

From the Common of Pastors, p 1040, or of Doctors of the Church, p 1049, except for the following:

MORNING PRAYER

Benedictus ant. Peter, firm as the rock in the strength given him by Christ, has not ceased to guide the Church.

Concluding Prayer
Lord God,
you built your Church
on the firm foundation of the apostle Peter,
and you promised
that the gates of hell would never overcome it.
Supported by the prayers of Pope Saint Leo,
we ask that you will keep the Church faithful to your truth,
and maintain it in enduring peace.
(We make our prayer) through our Lord.

EVENING PRAYER

Magnificat ant. Throughout the Church, Peter proclaims every day:
You are the Christ, the Son of the living God.

11 November
SAINT MARTIN OF TOURS
Bishop

Memoria

Born in Pannonia of pagan parents about the year 316. He received baptism, gave up his career as a soldier and founded a monastery in Ligugé in France where he lived the religious life under the guidance of Saint Hilary. Then he was ordained priest and was chosen bishop of Tours. He always gave the example of a good shepherd, founding new monasteries, instructing the clergy and preaching the gospel to the poor. He died in the year 397.

Invitatory ant. Today we are honouring Saint Martin: come, let us adore the Lord our God.
Psalm, p 371.

MORNING PRAYER

Hymn from the Common of Pastors, p 1040.

Ant. 1: Martin, priest of God, my Father's kingdom is ready to receive you.

Psalms and canticle for Sunday, Week 1, pp 390 ff.

Ant. 2: With eyes and hands raised up to heaven, he kept his undaunted spirit fixed in prayer, allelua.

Ant. 3: Martin is received with joy by Abraham. Martin, once poor and lowly, enters heaven with riches, alleluia.

Scripture Reading   *Heb 13:7-8*
Remember your leaders who preached the word of God to you, and as you reflect on the outcome of their lives, imitate their faith. Jesus Christ is the same today as he was yesterday, and as he will be for ever.

Short Responsory
R⁷ I placed watchmen on your towers, Jerusalem. *Repeat* R⁷
℣ They will never cease to tell of the name of the Lord, by day and by night. R⁷ Glory be. R⁷

Benedictus ant. How blessed this man, whose soul inherits paradise! For this, the angels exult, the archangels rejoice, the choirs of saints are calling, throngs of virgins sing welcome: abide with us for ever.

Intercessions

Christ, the good shepherd, laid down his life for his sheep. Let us praise him with grateful hearts, as we pray: R̷ Lord, nourish the lives of your people.

Christ our Lord, in the holy pastors you reveal your love for us;—may we never be deprived of the care you show through them. R̷

Through your sacred ministers you are present in our midst as the shepherd of our souls;—never cease to guide us through their teaching and encouragement. R̷

In the saints who lead your people, you manifest your power of healing souls and bodies;—remain always with us to renew our lives in holiness. R̷

By the example of the saints you instruct your faithful in the ways of wisdom and love;—through our pastors help us to grow to the full stature of perfection. R̷

Our Father

Concluding Prayer

Lord God,
you were glorified
by the life and death of Saint Martin.
Renew the wonders of your grace in our hearts
so that neither death nor life
may separate us from your love.
(We make our prayer) through our Lord.

EVENING PRAYER

Hymn from the Common of Pastors, p 1043.

Ant. 1: Neither overcome by toil, nor to be overcome by death, this great man did not fear to die, nor was he unwilling to live.

Psalms and canticle from the Common of Pastors, p 1044.

Ant. 2: Lord, if your people still need me, I do not refuse to do your work: may your will be done.

Ant. 3: Bishop Martin bade farewell to the world; this most noble of priests now lives in Christ.

Scripture Reading   *1 Pet 5:1-4*

Now I have something to tell your elders: I am an elder myself, and a witness to the sufferings of Christ, and with you I have a share in the glory that is to be revealed. Be the shepherds of the flock of God that is entrusted to you; watch over it, not simply as a duty but gladly, because God wants it; not for sordid money, but because you are eager to do it. Never be a dictator over any group that is put in your charge, but be an example that the whole flock can follow. When the chief shepherd appears, you will be given the crown of unfading glory.

Short Responsory

R̥ This is a man who loves his brothers and intercedes for the people.
Repeat R̥
V̥ He laid down his life for his brothers. R̥ Glory be. R̥

Magnificat ant. The blessed bishop Martin loved Christ the King with his whole heart, and did not fear the imperial power. His holy soul, though spared the sword of persecution, was not deprived of the martyr's palm.

Intercessions

Let us pray to Christ, the high priest, who was appointed to represent men in their relations with God. R̥ Lord, save your people.
Lord Jesus, in times past you have lighted the way for your people through wise and holy leaders;—may Christians always enjoy this sign of your loving kindness. R̥
You forgave the sins of your people when holy pastors prayed;—continually cleanse your Church through their powerful intercession. R̥
In the presence of their brothers, you anointed your holy ones and poured on them your Spirit;—fill with your Holy Spirit all the leaders of your people. R̥
Nothing could ever separate the holy pastors from your love;—do

not lose even one of those whom you redeemed by your passion.
R℣ Lord, save your people.
Through the pastors of your Church you give your sheep eternal
life, and no one can steal them from you;—save the faithful departed,
for whom you laid down your life. R℣
Our Father

Concluding Prayer
Lord God,
you were glorified
by the life and death of Saint Martin.
Renew the wonders of your grace in our hearts
so that neither death nor life
may separate us from your love.
(We make our prayer) through our Lord.

12 November
SAINT JOSAPHAT
Bishop and Martyr

Memoria

Born in the Ukraine of Orthodox parents about the year 1580. He became
a Catholic and joined the monks of Saint Basil. He became a priest and
was elected Bishop of Polock, and worked strenuously for the unity of the
Church. He suffered martyrdom at the hands of his enemies in the year
1623.

*From the Common of Martyrs: One Martyr, p 1029, or of Pastors,
p 1040.*

Concluding Prayer
Lord,
filled with your Holy Spirit
Saint Josaphat laid down his life for his flock.
Renew that Spirit in your Church,
strengthen our hearts with your grace,
so that, with the help of his prayers,
we may be ready to lay down our lives for our brethren.
(We make our prayer) through our Lord.

15 November
SAINT ALBERT THE GREAT
Bishop and Doctor of the Church

Optional Memoria

Born at Lauingen on the Danube in Germany about the year 1206. He studied at Padua and Paris and then entered the Dominican Order and was engaged in teaching in a number of places with great merit. He was ordained Bishop of Regensburg and made great efforts to secure peace between peoples and between cities. He wrote many eminent works of doctrine and natural science. He died at Cologne in the year 1280.

From the Common of Pastors, p 1040, or of Doctors of the Church, p 1049.

Concluding Prayer
Lord God,
you made Saint Albert great by his gift
for reconciling human wisdom with divine faith.
Help us so to follow his teaching
that every advance in science
may lead us to a deeper knowledge and love of you.
(We make our prayer) through our Lord.

16 November
SAINT MARGARET OF SCOTLAND

Optional Memoria

Born in Hungary, where her father lived in exile, about the year 1046. She was given in marriage to Malcom III, king of the Scots, and she bore him eight children. She was an outstanding example of a true mother and queen. She died at Edinburgh in the year 1093.

From the Common of Women Saints: Saints Noted for Works of Mercy, p 1074.

Concluding Prayer
Almighty God,
you made Saint Margaret of Scotland outstanding

937

for her great love of the poor.
Following her example and helped by her prayers
may we, by our lives,
bear witness among men to your goodness and love.
(We make our prayer) through our Lord.

Also 16 November
SAINT GERTRUDE, Virgin
Optional Memoria

Born at Eisleben in Thuringia in the year 1256. As a girl she was brought up by the Cistercian nuns at Helfta, where she did well at her studies especially philosophy and the humanities. She gave herself to God and progressed in a wonderful manner along the paths of perfection, spending her time in prayer and contemplation. She died on 17 November in the year 1301.

From the Common of Virgins, p 1057, or of Women Saints: Religious, p 1074.

Concluding Prayer
Lord God,
you made the heart of Saint Gertrude
the dwelling-place of your love.
Lighten our darkness
so that, through her intercession,
we may experience the joy of your presence in our hearts.
(We make our prayer) through our Lord.

17 November
SAINT ELIZABETH OF HUNGARY, Religious
Memoria

She was born in the year 1207, the daughter of King Andrew of Hungary. While still young she was given in marriage to Ludwig the landgrave of Thuringia, by whom she had three children. She was assiduous in mental prayer; after the death of her husband she embraced poverty and spent her days in caring for the sick in a hospice which she had built. She died at Marburg in the year 1231.

938

From the Common of Women Saints: Saints Noted for Works of Mercy, p 1074.

Concluding Prayer
Lord God,
you taught Saint Elizabeth of Hungary
to see and reverence Christ in the poor.
May her prayers help us
to give constant love and service
to the afflicted and the needy.
(We make our prayer) through our Lord.

18 November

DEDICATION OF THE BASILICAS
OF SAINT PETER AND SAINT PAUL

Apostles

Optional Memoria

From the twelfth century the dedications of the Vatican Basilica of Saint Peter and the Basilica of Saint Paul on the Via Ostiense have been celebrated on this day as the anniversary of their dedication by Pope Saint Silvester and Pope Saint Siricius in the fourth century. In more recent times this feast has been extended to the whole Roman Rite. As the anniversary of the dedication of the Basilica of Saint Mary Major (5 August) honours the motherhood of Our Lady, so this feast honours the memory of the two Princes of the Apostles.

From the Common of Apostles, p 1004, except for the following:

MORNING PRAYER

Benedictus ant. Peter the apostle and Paul the teacher of the nations taught us your law, Lord.

Concluding Prayer
Lord God,
give your Church the help of the apostles Peter and Paul,
who first brought it the knowledge of the faith;
may they always obtain for it an increase of grace.
(We make our prayer) through our Lord.

EVENING PRAYER

Magnificat ant. The bodies of the saints have been buried in peace, and their name lives on for all generations.

21 November
THE PRESENTATION OF
THE BLESSED VIRGIN MARY
Memoria

On this day, which was the dedication in the year 543 of the Church of Our Lady near to the Temple in Jerusalem, together with the Christians of the Eastern rites we celebrate that dedication of herself which Mary made to God from her very childhood under the inspiration of the Holy Spirit who filled her with grace at her Immaculate Conception.

From the Common of the Blessed Virgin Mary, p 987, except for the following:

MORNING PRAYER

Benedictus ant. Blessed are you, Mary, because you believed that all those things which were said to you by the Lord would be fulfilled.

Concluding Prayer
Lord,
as we honour the memory of the Blessed Virgin Mary
and seek her help,
grant that we, like her, may share in the fulness of your grace.
(We make our prayer) through our Lord.

EVENING PRAYER

Magnificat ant. Holy Mother of God, Mary ever-virgin, temple of the Lord, sacred dwelling-place of the Holy Spirit, you alone without an equal found favour with our Lord Jesus Christ.

22 November
SAINT CECILIA, Virgin and Martyr
Memoria

The veneration of Saint Cecilia, in whose honour a basilica was erected at

Rome in the fifth century, has extended far and wide because of the *Passion of Saint Cecilia*, which presented her as a perfect example of Christian womanhood who preserved her virginity and suffered martyrdom for the love of Christ.

From the Common of Martyrs: One Martyr, p 1029, or of Virgins, p 1057, except for the following:

MORNING PRAYER

Benedictus ant. Day had almost dawned as Cecilia cried out: Soldiers of Christ, throw off the deeds of darkness and put on your armour as soldiers of the light.

Concluding Prayer
Lord God,
in your mercy listen to our prayers,
which we offer you
under the patronage of Saint Cecilia.
(We make our prayer) through our Lord.

EVENING PRAYER

Magnificat ant. Cecilia the virgin always bore the gospel of Christ in her heart: day or night she never ceased from prayer and converse with God.

23 November
SAINT CLEMENT, Pope and Martyr
Optional Memoria

Clement was the third pope after Saint Peter to rule the Church, at about the end of the first century. He wrote a renowned letter to the Corinthians with the object of preserving peace and concord among them.

From the Common of Martyrs: One Martyr, p 1029, or of Pastors, p 1040.

Concluding Prayer
Almighty, ever-living God,

the holiness of the saints is your glory.
Let us rejoice in the memory of Saint Clement,
priest and martyr of Christ your Son.
His life confirmed his teaching
and his death bore witness to the mystery of faith.
(We make our prayer) through our Lord.

Also 23 November
SAINT COLUMBANUS, Abbot

Optional Memoria

Born in Ireland before the middle of the sixth century. After studying the humanities and the sacred sciences he embraced the monastic life and went to France where he founded a number of monasteries which he ruled with very strict discipline. He was sentenced to exile but went to Italy where he founded the monastery of Bobbio. Renowned for his example of the Christian and the religious life, he died in the year 615.

From the Common of Pastors, p 1040, or of Men Saints: Religious, p 1067.

Concluding Prayer
Lord God,
in the life of Saint Columbanus
you combined a zeal for mission
and a love of the monastic life.
May his prayer and example
prompt us to love you above all things
and to increase the household of the faith.
(We make our prayer) through our Lord.

30 November
SAINT ANDREW, Apostle

Feast

Born at Bethsaida. He was formerly a disciple of John the Baptist and then followed Christ, to whom he brought his brother Peter. With Philip he introduced the Gentiles to Christ and he was the apostle who pointed out the boy with the loaves and fishes. Tradition has it that after Pentecost he preached the gospel in many different places and finally suffered death on a cross in Achaia.

MORNING PRAYER

Hymn from the Common of Apostles, p 1004.

Ant. 1: Andrew, the brother of Simon Peter, was one of the two who followed the Lord.

Psalms and canticle of Sunday, Week 1, pp 390 ff.

Ant. 2: The Lord loved Andrew; he accepted him like a fragrant offering.

Ant. 3: Andrew said to Simon, his brother, 'We have found the Messiah', and he brought him to Jesus.

Scripture Reading   *Eph 2:19-22*
You are no longer aliens in a foreign land, but fellow-citizens with God's people, members of God's household. You are built upon the foundation laid by the apostles and prophets, and Christ Jesus himself is the foundation-stone. In him the whole building is bound together and grows into a holy temple in the Lord. In him you too are being built with all the rest into a special dwelling for God.

Short Responsory
R̸ You will make them rulers over all the land. *Repeat* R̸
Ỹ Your name, Lord, will be remembered. R̸ Glory be. R̸

Benedictus ant. Hail, precious cross; receive the disciple of my Master, Jesus Christ, who hung upon you.

Intercessions
Since we have received from the apostles our heavenly inheritance, let us thank our Father for all his blessings. R̸ Lord, the apostles sing your praises.
Praise to you, Lord God, for the gift of Christ's body and blood, handed on by the apostles, to give us strength and life;—Lord, the apostles sing your praises.
For the table of your word, served by the apostles, to bring us light and joy;—Lord, the apostles sing your praises.

For your holy Church, built on the apostles, to make us all one body;—Lord, the apostles sing your praises.

For the washing of baptism and penance, entrusted to the apostles, to cleanse our hearts from sin;—Lord, the apostles sing your praises.

Our Father

Concluding Prayer
Lord God,
you called Saint Andrew your apostle
to preach the gospel and to guide your Church.
We humbly pray
that he may always plead for us in your presence.
(We make our prayer) through our Lord.

EVENING PRAYER

Hymn from the Common of Apostles, p 1006.

Ant. 1: The Lord saw Peter and Andrew, and he called them.

Psalms and canticle from the Common of Apostles, p 1007.

Ant. 2: Come, follow me, said the Lord; I will make you fishers of men.

Ant. 3: They left their nets and followed the Lord, the redeemer.

Scripture Reading   *Eph 4:11-13*
Some Christ has appointed to be apostles, others to be prophets, others to be evangelists, or pastors, or teachers. They are to order the lives of the faithful, minister to their needs, build up the frame of Christ's body, until we all realize our common unity through faith in the Son of God, and fuller knowledge of him. So we shall reach perfect manhood, that maturity which is proportioned to the completed growth of Christ.

Short Responsory

R̸ Tell of the glory of the Lord; announce it among the nations.
Repeat R̸
V̸ Speak of his wonderful deeds to all the peoples. R̸ Glory be. R̸

Magnificat ant. Let us remember Saint Andrew, the servant of
Christ and apostle of God. He was the brother of Peter and suffered
with him for his Master.

Intercessions

Since we are part of a building that has the apostles for its foundation, let us pray to the Father for his holy people. R̸ Lord, remember
your Church.
Father, when your Son rose from the dead, you showed him first to
the apostles;—let us make him known, near and far. R̸
You sent your Son into the world to proclaim the good news to the
poor;—grant that we may bring his gospel into the darkness of
men's lives. R̸
You sent your Son to plant in men's hearts the seed of imperishable
life;—may we labour to sow his word and reap a harvest of joy. R̸
You sent your Son to reconcile the world with yourself by the
shedding of his blood;—let us become his fellow workers in restoring
men to your friendship. R̸
You placed your Son at your own right hand in heaven;—receive
the dead into the happiness of your kingdom. R̸
Our Father

Concluding Prayer

Lord God,
you called Saint Andrew your apostle
to preach the gospel and to guide your Church.
We humbly pray
that he may always plead for us in your presence.
(We make our prayer) through our Lord.

945

DECEMBER

3 December
SAINT FRANCIS XAVIER, Priest

Memoria

Born in Spain in the year 1506. When studying at Paris he joined Saint Ignatius and was ordained priest at Rome in 1537. He spent himself in works of charity and in 1541 he went to the East where for ten years he preached the gospel in India and Japan and brought many to the true faith. He died in the year 1552 on the Chinese island of Shangchwan.

From the Common of Pastors, p 1040.

Concluding Prayer
Lord God,
you won many peoples to yourself
by the preaching of Saint Francis Xavier.
Give us the same zeal that he had for the faith,
and let your Church rejoice
to see the virtue and the number of her children
increase throughout the world.
(We make our prayer) through our Lord.

4 December
SAINT JOHN DAMASCENE
Priest and Doctor of the Church

Optional Memoria

Born in Damascus of a Christian family in the latter part of the seventh century. He became a monk in the monastery of Saint Sabbas near Jerusalem and there was ordained priest. Proficient in philosophy, he wrote extensively about doctrine, especially against those who urged the destruction of sacred images. He died in the middle of the eighth century.

From the Common of Doctors of the Church, p 1049.

Concluding Prayer
Lord God,
let Saint John Damascene help us by his prayers,

so that the true faith
of which he was so outstanding a teacher,
may always bring us light and strength.
(We make our prayer) through our Lord.

6 December
SAINT NICHOLAS, Bishop
Optional Memoria

He was Bishop of Myra in Lycia (now in Turkey), where he died about the middle of the fourth century. He is honoured throughout the Church, especially from the tenth century.

From the Common of Pastors, p 1040.

Concluding Prayer
We implore your love and mercy, Lord,
to protect us from all danger.
Through the prayer of Saint Nicholas
lead us to salvation
by paths that are swift and sure.
(We make our prayer) through our Lord.

7 December
SAINT AMBROSE
Bishop and Doctor of the Church
Memoria

Born at Trier of a Roman family about the year 340. He studied law at Rome, entered the public service and then, while living in Milan, he was unexpectedly chosen to be bishop and ordained on 7 December in the year 374. He carried out the work of his office assiduously, being a true shepherd and teacher of the faithful, and especially did he show charity towards all. He strenuously guarded the rights of the Church, and in his writings and his work defended the true faith against the Arians. He died on 4 April, Holy Saturday, in the year 397.

From the Common of Doctors of the Church, p 1049.

Concluding Prayer
Lord God,

you made Saint Ambrose
a teacher of the Catholic faith
and a pattern of apostolic fortitude.
Raise up in the Church today
men after your own heart
to lead your people with wisdom and strength.
(We make our prayer) through our Lord.

8 December

THE IMMACULATE CONCEPTION OF THE BLESSED VIRGIN MARY

Solemnity

EVENING PRAYER I

Hymn, as at Morning Prayer, p 950, or from the Common of the Blessed Virgin Mary, p 981.

Ant. 1: I will put enmity between you and the woman, between your seed and her seed.

Psalms and canticle from the Common of the Blessed Virgin Mary, p 982.

Ant. 2: The Lord has clothed me in the garments of salvation; he has wrapped me in the cloak of integrity.

Ant. 3: Hail, Mary, full of grace; the Lord is with you.

Scripture Reading   *Rom 8:29,30*
All those who from the first were known to God, he has destined from the first to be moulded to the image of his Son. So predestined, he called them; so called, he justified them.

Short Responsory
R̠ I will praise you, Lord, you have rescued me. *Repeat* R̠
V̠ You have not let my enemies rejoice over me. R̠ Glory be. R̠

Magnificat ant. All generations will call me blessed, for the Almighty has done great things for me, alleluia.

Intercessions

Let us praise God the Father who chose Mary as the mother of his Son and wanted all generations to call her blessed. With confidence we pray: R̸ May the Virgin Mary intercede for us.

Father, you did great things for the Virgin Mary and brought her, body and soul, to the glory of heaven;—fill the hearts of your children with the hope of Christ's glory. R̸

Through the prayers of Mary, our mother, heal the sick, comfort the sorrowful, pardon sinners;—grant peace and salvation to all. R̸

You looked on the Virgin Mary and made her the mother of mercy;
—may those who are in danger experience the depth of her love. R̸

You called Mary to be the mother in the house of Jesus and Joseph;
—through her prayers help all mothers to make their homes places of love and holiness. R̸

You exalted the Virgin Mary and crowned her queen of heaven;
—may the dead enter your kingdom and rejoice with your saints for ever. R̸

Our Father

Concluding Prayer

Father,
we rejoice in the privilege of our Lady's Immaculate Conception,
which preserved her from the stain of sin
by the power of Christ's redeeming death,
and prepared her to be the Mother of God.
Grant that through her prayers
we ourselves may come to you,
cleansed from all sin.
(We make our prayer) through our Lord.

Invitatory

Ant. Let us celebrate the Immaculate Conception of the Virgin Mary. Let us adore her Son, who is Christ the Lord.
Psalm, p 371.

MORNING PRAYER

Hymn

Holy light on earth's horizon,
Star of hope to fallen man,
Light amid a world of shadows,
Dawn of God's redemptive plan.
Chosen from eternal ages,
Thou alone of all our race,
By thy Son's atoning merits
Wast conceived in perfect grace.

Mother of the world's Redeemer,
Promised from the dawn of time:
How could one so highly favoured
Share the guilt of Adam's crime?
Sun and moon and stars adorn thee,
Sinless Eve, triumphant sign;
Thou art she who crushed the serpent,
Mary, pledge of life divine.

Earth below and highest heaven
Praise the splendour of thy state,
Thou who now art crowned in glory
Wast conceived immaculate.
Hail, beloved of the Father,
Mother of his only Son,
Mystic bride of Love eternal,
Hail, thou fair and spotless one!

Ant. 1: Behold, the chaste Mother who knew no stain; she was chosen to be the Mother of God.

Psalms and canticle of Sunday, Week 1, pp 390 ff.

Ant. 2: Blessed are you, O Virgin Mary, above all women on earth. The Lord God himself has chosen you.

Ant. 3: Fragrant is the scent of your perfume, immaculate Virgin. Let us follow in your footsteps.

Scripture Reading   *Is 43:1*

Now, thus says the Lord, who created you, Jacob, who formed you, Israel: Do not be afraid for I have redeemed you; I have called you by your name, you are mine.

Short Responsory

R⁷ The Lord God Almighty girds me with strength. *Repeat* R⁷
℣ He preserves me from stain of sin. R⁷ Glory be. R⁷

Benedictus ant. The Lord God said to the serpent: I will put enmity between you and the woman, between your seed and her seed. She will crush your head, alleluia.

Intercessions

Let us proclaim the greatness of our Saviour who chose to be born of the Virgin Mary. Confident that he will hear us, we ask: R⁷ Lord, may your mother pray for us.

Sun of justice, you showed your day was dawning in the immaculate Virgin Mary;—help us to walk in the daylight of your presence. R⁷

Saviour of the world, by your redemptive power you preserved your mother Mary from every stain of sin;—deliver us from the evil that lies hidden in our hearts. R⁷

Christ, our Redeemer, you made the Virgin Mary the sanctuary of your presence and the temple of the Spirit;—make us bearers of your Spirit, in mind, heart and body. R⁷

King of kings, you assumed Mary into heaven to be with you completely in body and soul;—may we seek the things that are above and keep our lives fixed on you. R⁷

Our Father

Concluding Prayer

Father,
we rejoice in the privilege of our Lady's Immaculate Conception,
which preserved her from the stain of sin
by the power of Christ's redeeming death,

and prepared her to be the Mother of God.
Grant that through her prayers
we ourselves may come to you,
cleansed from all sin.
(We make our prayer) through our Lord.

EVENING PRAYER II

Hymn, as at Morning Prayer, p 950, or from the Common of the Blessed Virgin Mary, p 991.

Ant. 1: You are all fair, O Mary; without orginal sin.

Psalms and canticle from the Common of the Blessed Virgin Mary, p 992.

Ant. 2: You are the glory of Jerusalem, you are the joy of Israel! You are the highest honour of our race.

Ant. 3: Your garments are white as snow, your face shines like the sun.

Scripture Reading   *Rom 5:20-21*
As our fault was amplified, grace has been more amply bestowed than ever; that so, where guilt held its reign of death, justifying grace should reign instead, to bring us eternal life through Jesus Christ our Lord.

Short Responsory
℟ By this I shall know that you have chosen me. *Repeat* ℟
℣ If my enemy does not shout in triumph over me. ℟ Glory be. ℟

Magnificat ant. Hail, Mary, full of grace: the Lord is with you. You are the most blessed of all women, and blessed is the fruit of your womb, alleluia.

Intercessions
Let us praise God the Father who chose Mary as the mother of his

Son and wanted all generations to call her blessed. With confidence we pray: ℟ May the Virgin Mary intercede for us.

Father, you did great things for the Virgin Mary and brought her, body and soul, to the glory of heaven;—fill the hearts of your children with the hope of Christ's glory. ℟

Through the prayers of Mary, our mother, heal the sick, comfort the sorrowful, pardon sinners;—grant peace and salvation to all. ℟

You looked on the Virgin Mary and made her the mother of mercy;—may those who are in danger experience the depth of her love. ℟

You called Mary to be the mother in the house of Jesus and Joseph;—through her prayers help all mothers to make their homes places of love and holiness. ℟

You exalted the Virgin Mary and crowned her queen of heaven;—may the dead enter your kingdom and rejoice with your saints for ever. ℟

Our Father

The concluding prayer as at Morning Prayer, p 951.

11 December
SAINT DAMASUS I, Pope
Optional Memoria

Born about the year 305, of Spanish descent. He became a cleric in Rome and in the year 366, during very troublesome times, he was ordained Bishop of Rome. He called together a number of synods against the heretics and schismatics, and he did much to promote the veneration of martyrs, whose tombs he embellished with sacred verse. He died in the year 384.

From the Common of Pastors, p 1040.

Concluding Prayer
Give us grace. Lord,
always to celebrate the holiness of your martyrs,
for whom Pope Saint Damasus
showed such great love and veneration.
(We make our prayer) through our Lord.

12 December
SAINT JANE FRANCES
DE CHANTAL, Religious

Optional Memoria

Born in Dijon in France in the year 1572. She was married to a nobleman named de Chantal, by whom she had six children whom she brought up religiously. After the death of her husband she placed herself under the direction of St Francis de Sales and made great progress along the way of perfection, performing many works of charity especially among the poor and sick. She founded and wisely directed the Visitation Order, and died in the year 1641.

From the Common of Women Saints: Religious, p 1074.

Concluding Prayer
Lord God,
you enriched Saint Jane Frances de Chantal
with the graces both of marriage
and of the religious life:
grant that through her prayer
we may continue faithful to our vocation,
and always bear witness to the light.
(We make our prayer) through our Lord.

13 December
SAINT LUCY, Virgin
and Martyr

Memoria

She suffered martyrdom at Syracuse probably during the persecution of Diocletian. Devotion to her spread almost throughout the whole Church and dates back to the earliest times. Her name was inserted into the Roman Canon.

From the Common of Martyrs, p 1029, or of Virgins, p 1057, except for the following:

MORNING PRAYER

Benedictus ant. I am the lowly servant of the Lord, who wished only to offer everything to the living God. Now since there is nothing left to be offered, I give myself to him.

Concluding Prayer
Let the prayer of the virgin martyr Lucy
support us, Lord,
so that with each passing year
we may celebrate her entry into life,
and finally see you face to face in heaven.
(We make our prayer) through our Lord.

EVENING PRAYER

Magnificat ant. By your endurance you gained eternal life, Saint Lucy, bride of Christ. You despised the things of this world; now you are in glory with the angels. With your own blood you overcame the enemy.

14 December
SAINT JOHN OF THE CROSS
Priest and Doctor of the Church
Memoria

Born at Fontiveros in Old Castile in Spain about the year 1542. He was a Carmelite friar and about the year 1568 he was persuaded by Saint Teresa of Avila to be the first to undertake the reform of his Order, which cost him much hard work and many trials. He died at Ubeda in Andalusia in 1591. He was outstanding in holiness and knowledge as his many spiritual writings testify.

From the Common of Doctors of the Church, p 1049.

Concluding Prayer
Lord God,
you gave Saint John of the Cross
the grace of complete self-denial
and an ardent love for the cross of Christ.
Grant that by following always in his footsteps
we may come to the eternal vision of your glory.
(We make our prayer) through our Lord.

21 December
SAINT PETER CANISIUS
Priest and Doctor of the Church
As a commemoration

Born at Nijmegen in Holland in 1521. He studied at Cologne and joined the Society of Jesus, being ordained priest in 1546. He was sent to Germany where for many years he worked to defend and to strengthen the Catholic faith by his writings and preaching. Of his many works *The Catechism* is outstanding. He died at Fribourg in Switzerland in 1597.

MORNING PRAYER

Ant. The learned will shine as brightly as the vault of heaven, and those who have instructed many in virtue will shine like stars for all eternity.

Concluding Prayer
Almighty God,
you strengthened Saint Peter Canisius
in sanctity and doctrine
for the defence of the Catholic faith.
Grant that every seeker after truth
may have the joy of finding you,
and that all believers may persevere in the one true faith.
(We make our prayer) through our Lord.

EVENING PRAYER

Ant. O holy doctor, Saint Peter, light of the Church, lover of the law of God; pray for us to the Son of God.

23 December
SAINT JOHN OF KENTY, Priest
As a Commemoration

Born in Kenty in the diocese of Cracow in 1390. He became a priest and for many years taught in the University of Cracow and then was parish priest of Olkusz. Besides being an outstanding professor of the Catholic faith, he excelled in personal holiness and in charity to his neighbour, so that he was a true example to his colleagues and to his students. He died in the year 1473.

MORNING PRAYER

Ant. If there is love among you, then all will know that you are my disciples.

Concluding Prayer
Grant, almighty God and Father,
that like Saint John of Kenty
we may grow in the wisdom of the saints.
By showing compassion to all
may we experience your love and mercy.
(We make our prayer) through our Lord.

EVENING PRAYER

Ant. Truly I tell you, anything you did for the least of these who are mine, you did for me. Come, you blessed of my Father, inherit the kingdom prepared for you from the foundation of the world.

26 December
SAINT STEPHEN
The First Martyr

Feast

Invitatory ant. Let us adore the new-born Christ; today he has crowned Saint Stephen.
Psalm, p 371.

MORNING PRAYER

Hymn from the Common of Martyrs, p 1017.

Ant. 1: My soul clings to you, my God; for your sake my body was stoned.

Psalms and canticle of Sunday, Week 1, pp 390 ff.

Ant. 2: Stephen saw the heavens opened and he entered in there; blessed is the man for whom the heavens stood open.

Ant. 3: Behold, I see the heavens thrown open, and Jesus standing at the right hand of God.

Scripture Reading   *Acts 6:2b-5a*
It is not right for us to neglect the preaching of God's word in order to handle finances. So then, brothers, choose seven men among you who are known to be full of the Holy Spirit and wisdom, and we will put them in charge of this matter. We ourselves, then, will give our full time to prayers and the work of preaching. The whole group was pleased with the apostles' proposal.

Short Responsory
R̸ The Lord is my strength. I will sing praise to him. *Repeat* R̸
V̸ He is my salvation. R̸ Glory be. R̸

Benedictus ant. The gates of heaven were thrown open for Saint Stephen, who was the first follower of Christ to receive the martyr's crown.

Intercessions
Let us give thanks for Saint Stephen, whose life on earth was lived in the service of Christ, and who came at his death to witness to Christ with his blood. R̸ We give you thanks, O Lord.
For all who have found the freedom to lay down their lives for your sake—We give you thanks, O Lord.
For all whose desire for you has brought them through death with a joyful heart—We give you thanks, O Lord.
For all who have followed, through suffering, the way of the cross—We give you thanks, O Lord.
For all who have undergone martyrdom for the gospel—We give you thanks, O Lord.
Our Father

Concluding Prayer
Give us grace, Lord, to practise what we worship.
Teach us to love our enemies
as we keep the feast of Saint Stephen,
who prayed even for the men who stoned him to death.
(We make our prayer) through our Lord.

EVENING PRAYER

*Evening Prayer is of the Octave of Christmas for 26 December, p 64.
When the feast of St Stephen is celebrated as a solemnity, antiphons,
scripture reading, responsory and concluding prayer are from Morning
Prayer, p 957; the psalms, canticle and intercessions are from the
Common of Martyrs, p 1021.*

27 December
SAINT JOHN
Apostle and Evangelist

Feast

Invitatory ant. The Lord is the king of apostles: come, let us adore
him.
Psalm, p 371.

MORNING PRAYER

Hymn from the Common of Apostles, p 1004.

Ant. 1: John, the apostle and evangelist, was chosen by the Lord
because of his virginal purity. He was the disciple whom the Lord
especially loved.

Psalms and canticle of Sunday, Week 1, pp 390 ff.

Ant. 2: This is John the virgin to whose trust Christ, when he was
dying on the cross, commended his Mother, the Virgin Mary.

Ant. 3: The disciple that Jesus loved said, 'It is the Lord', alleluia.

Scripture Reading   *Acts 4:19-20*

Peter and John answered: 'You yourselves judge which is right in God's sight, to obey you or to obey God. For we cannot stop speaking of what we ourselves have seen and heard.'

Short Responsory

R̷ You will make them rulers over all the land. *Repeat* R̷
V̷ Your name, Lord, will be remembered. R̷ Glory be. R̷

Benedictus ant. The Word was made flesh and dwelt among us, and we saw his glory, alleluia.

Intercessions

Since we are part of that building which has the apostles for its foundation, let us pray to our Father for his holy people. R̷ Lord, remember your Church.

Father, you made the apostles the first witnesses of the risen Lord:
—may we reveal Christ to the world. R̷

Father, you gave your Son to those in need:—help us to bring the gospel to all men. R̷

Father, you sent to us your Word of life:—may we labour to sow his word and reap a harvest of joy. R̷

Father, your Son became our reconciliation:—may we help to give peace to troubled hearts. R̷

Our Father

Concluding Prayer

Almighty God,
who through your apostle John
unlocked for us the hidden treasures of your Word,
grant that we may grasp with fuller understanding
the message he so admirably proclaimed.
(We make our prayer) through our Lord.

EVENING PRAYER

Evening Prayer is of the Octave of Christmas for 27 December, p 65. Where the feast of St John is celebrated as a solemnity, the antiphons, scripture reading, responsory and concluding prayer are from Morning Prayer, p 959; the psalms, canticle and intercessions are from the Common of Apostles, p 1007.

28 December
THE HOLY INNOCENTS
Martyrs
Feast

Invitatory ant. Let us adore the new-born Christ; today he gave the Holy Innocents the martyrs' crown.
Psalm, p 371.

MORNING PRAYER

Hymn from the Common of Martyr , p 1029.

Ant. 1: They will walk with me dressed in white garments, says the Lord, because they are worthy.

Psalms and canticle of Sunday, Week 1, pp 390 ff.

Ant. 2: The children sing praise to God; in death they preach what their young mouths could not utter.

Ant. 3: On the lips of children and of babes you have found praise to foil your enemy.

Scripture Reading   *Jer 31:15*
A voice is heard in Rama, of lamentation and bitter mourning; it is Rachel weeping for her children, and she will not be comforted, because none is left.

Short Responsory

℟ These were saints of God. They will live for ever. *Repeat* ℟
℣ The Lord himself is their reward. ℟ Glory be. ℟

Benedictus ant. The innocent children were put to death in place of
Christ; the infants were murdered by the evil king: they follow the
sinless Lamb and sing his praises, saying: Glory to you, O Lord.

Intercessions

Lord Jesus, even at your birth, you met with the hatred of men, and
children were the first to suffer for your sake. We proclaim our trust
in you: ℟ The Lord is at my side: I shall not fear.

As you were persecuted, so will be your brothers.—Lord Jesus, we
look to you for help. ℟

You committed no sin: yet you, like us, were called to suffer.—Help
us to take up our cross and follow you. ℟

The Holy Innocents were your silent witnesses—may we proclaim
you to others by word and deed. ℟

As a child you were persecuted and driven into exile:—save all the
children of men, in exile or under persecution. ℟

Our Father

Concluding Prayer

Lord God,
the Holy Innocents bore witness to you
not by speaking but by dying:
grant that the faith we proclaim in words,
may be borne out by deeds.
(We make our prayer) through our Lord.

EVENING PRAYER

*Evening Prayer is of the Octave of Christmas for 28 December, p 67.
Where the feast of the Holy Innocents is celebrated as a solemnity, the
antiphons, scripture reading, responsory and concluding prayer are
from Morning Prayer, p 961; the psalms, canticle and intercessions
from the Common of Martyrs, p 1021.*

29 December

SAINT THOMAS BECKET
Bishop and Martyr

As a Commemoration

Born in London in 1118. He was a cleric of the Church of Canterbury and became Chancellor of the kingdom, and then in 1162 was chosen to be Archbishop. He strenuously defended the rights of the Church against King Henry II and he was exiled to France for six years. On his return to his country he again had to bear many trials and finally in 1170 he was murdered by the king's followers.

MORNING PRAYER

Ant. Anyone who hates his soul in this world will save it for the eternal life.

Concluding Prayer
Almighty God,
you enabled Saint Thomas Becket
to lay down his life with undaunted spirit
for the rights of your Church.
Let his prayer help us to deny ourselves for Christ in this life,
and so find our true life in heaven.
(We make our prayer) through our Lord.

EVENING PRAYER

Ant. The saints will dwell in the kingdom of heaven; their peace will last for ever.

31 December

SAINT SILVESTER I, Pope
As a Commemoration

He was ordained Bishop of the Church of Rome in the year 314 and ruled the Church during the reign of Constantine the Great, at the time when the Donatist schism and the Arian heresy brought troubles on the Church. He died in 335 and was buried in the cemetery of Priscilla on the Via Salaria.

963

MORNING PRAYER

Ant. It is not you who speak: the Spirit of your Father speaks in you.

Concluding Prayer
Help your people, Lord,
who are supported by the prayer of Saint Silvester.
Under your guidance let our voyage through this life
come safely into harbour at the end.
(We make our prayer) through our Lord.

THE COMMON OFFICES

THE COMMON OFFICES

¶ *The Magnificat antiphon given for Evening Prayer I may be used at Evening Prayer on the memorias of Saints.*
¶ *The* alleluia *printed in parentheses is added to the antiphons in Eastertide.*

THE COMMON OF
THE DEDICATION OF A CHURCH

EVENING PRAYER I

Hymn

The Church's one foundation
Is Jesus Christ, her Lord;
She is his new creation
By water and the word:
From heaven he came and sought her
To be his holy bride,
With his own blood he bought her,
And for her life he died.

Elect from every nation,
Yet one o'er all the earth,
Her charter of salvation
One Lord, one faith, one birth;
One holy name she blesses,
Partakes one holy food,
And to one hope she presses
With every grace endued.

Though with a scornful wonder
Men see her sore oppressed,
By schisms rent asunder,
By heresies distrest,
Yet saints their watch are keeping,
Their cry goes up, 'How long?'

967

And soon the night of weeping
Shall be the morn of song.

Mid toil and tribulation,
And tumult of her war,
She waits the consummation
Of peace for everymore;
Till with the vision glorious
Her longing eyes are blest,
And the great Church victorious
Shall be the Church at rest.

Yet she on earth hath union
With God the three in one,
And mystic sweet communion
With those whose rest is won:
O happy ones and holy!
Lord, give us grace that we
Like them, the meek and lowly,
On high may dwell with thee.

PSALMODY

Ant. 1: The very streets of Jerusalem will rejoice; every one of its paths will be filled with a song of joy, alleluia.
Lent: In the temple of the Lord they all cry: 'Glory!'

PSALM 146(147)

Praise the Lórd for hé is góod;†
sing to our Gód for hé is lóving:*
to hím our práise is dúe.

The Lórd buílds up Jerúsalem*
and bríngs back Ísrael's éxiles,
he héals the bróken-héarted,*
he bínds up áll their wóunds.
He fíxes the númber of the stárs;*
he cálls each óne by its náme.

Our Lórd is gréat and almíghty;*
his wísdom can néver be méasured.

The Lórd ráises the lówly;*
he húmbles the wícked to the dúst.
O síng to the Lórd, giving thánks;*
sing psálms to our Gód with the hárp.

He cóvers the héavens with clóuds;*
he prepáres the ráin for the éarth,
making móuntains spróut with gráss*
and with plánts to sérve man's néeds.
He provídes the béasts with their fóod*
and young rávens that cáll upón him.

His delíght is nót in hórses*
nor his pléasure in wárriors' stréngth.
The Lórd delights in thóse who revére him,*
in thóse who wáit for his lóve.

Ant. The very streets of Jerusalem will rejoice; every one of its paths
will be filled with a song of joy, alleluia.
Lent: In the temple of the Lord they all cry: 'Glory!'

Ant. 2: The Lord has strengthened the bars of your gates, he has
blessed the children within you (alleluia).

PSALM 147

O práise the Lórd, Jerúsalem!*
Síon, práise your Gód!

He has stréngthened the bárs of your gátes,*
he has bléssed the chíldren withín you.
He estáblished péace on your bórders,*
he féeds you with fínest whéat.

He sénds out his wórd to the éarth*
and swíftly rúns his commánd.
He shówers down snów white as wóol,*
he scátters hóar-frost like áshes.

He húrls down háilstones like crúmbs.*
The wáters are frózen at his tóuch;

he sénds forth his wórd and it mélts them:*
at the bréath of his móuth the waters flów.

He mákes his wórd known to Jácob,*
to Ísrael his láws and decrées.
He has not déalt thus with óther nátions;*
he has not táught them hís decrées.

Ant. The Lord has strengthened the bars of your gates, he has blessed the children within you (alleluia).

OUTSIDE LENT

Ant. 3: The holy ones, who are assembled in the city of God, rejoice; the angels chant before the throne of God, alleluia.

When chanted, this canticle is sung with Alleluia *as set out below. When recited it suffices to say* Alleluia *at the beginning and end of each strophe.*

CANTICLE: CF REV 19:1-2,5-7

Alleluia.
Salvation and glory and power belong to our God,*
(R⁷ Alleluia.)
His judgments are true and just.
R⁷ Alleluia (alleluia).

Alleluia.
Praise our God, all you his servants,*
(R⁷ Alleluia.)
You who fear him, small and great.
R⁷ Alleluia (alleluia).

Alleluia.
The Lord our God, the Almighty, reigns,*
(R⁷ Alleluia.)
Let us rejoice and exult and give him the glory.
R⁷ Alleluia (alleluia).

Alleluia.
The marriage of the Lamb has come,*

(R͗ Alleluia.)
And his bride has made herself ready.
R͗ Alleluia (alleluia).

Ant. The holy ones, who are assembled in the city of God, rejoice;
the angels chant before the throne of God, alleluia.

LENT

Ant. 3: Glory to you, O Lord, through Christ in the Church!

CANTICLE: COL 1:12-20

Let us give thanks to the Father,†
who has qualified us to share*
in the inheritance of the saints in light.

He has delivered us from the dominion of darkness*
and transferred us to the kingdom of his beloved Son,
in whom we have redemption,*
the forgiveness of sins.

He is the image of the invisible God,*
the first-born of all creation,
for in him all things were created, in heaven and on earth,*
visible and invisible.

All things were created*
through him and for him.
He is before all things,*
and in him all things hold together.

He is the head of the body, the Church;*
he is the beginning,
the first-born from the dead,*
that in everything he might be pre-eminent.

For in him all the fulness of God was pleased to dwell,*
and through him to reconcile to himself all things,
whether on earth or in heaven,*
making peace by the blood of his cross.

Ant. Glory to you, O Lord, through Christ in the Church!

Scripture Reading   *Eph 2:19-22*

You are no longer aliens in a foreign land, but fellow-citizens with God's people, members of God's household. You are built upon the foundation laid by the apostles and prophets, and Christ Jesus himself is the foundation-stone. In him the whole building is bonded together and grows into a holy temple in the Lord. In him you too are being built with all the rest into a spiritual dwelling for God.

Short Responsory

Outside Eastertide

R͡ Your house, Lord, is set apart. It is distinguished by holiness. *Repeat* R͡

V͡ As long as time shall last. R͡ Glory be. R͡

Eastertide

R͡ Your house, Lord, is set apart, alleluia, alleluia. *Repeat* R͡

V͡ As long as time shall last. R͡ Glory be. R͡

Magnificat ant. Rejoice with Jerusalem and exult in her for ever all you who love her (alleluia).

Intercessions

Let us pray to our Saviour who gave up his life to gather into unity the scattered children of God. R͡ Lord, remember your Church.

Lord Jesus, you commanded your disciples to hear your words and put them into action;—constantly strengthen your Church in faith, courage and trust. R͡

Lord Jesus, from your opened side there poured out blood and water;—make your Church vigorously alive through the sacraments of the new and everlasting covenant. R͡

Lord Jesus, you are present among those who are gathered in your name;—hear your Church, united in prayer. R͡

Lord Jesus, you come with the Father to dwell in those who love you;—perfect your Church all over the world in your divine love. R͡

Lord Jesus, anyone who comes to you is never turned away;—admit all those who have died into your Father's house. R͡

Our Father

Concluding Prayer
In the dedicated church only
Almighty God,
as we recall with joy
the dedication of this house of yours
on each recurring anniversary:
listen to your people's prayer,
and grant that our worship here
may be a sincere and holy service,
honouring your name
and bringing us the fulness of redemption.
(We make our prayer) through our Lord.

INVITATORY
Ant. Christ is the spouse of the Church: come, let us adore him (alleluia).

Alternative
Christ has shown his love for the Church: come, let us adore him (alleluia).

MORNING PRAYER

Hymn
When time began, God walked with man,
With Adam in the evening light;
And when his people bore the ark
Through trackless desert, day and night,
God led them with a cloud by day;
At night, with fire lit up their way.

The Lord dwelt in Jerusalem,
Enthroned above the Cherubim,
And there the tribes of Israel
Went up to praise and worship him
Whose hand had made them strong to build
The temple that his glory filled.

The Body of the risen Christ
Is God's new dwelling-place sublime
And man's eternal temple here,
Secure against eroding time.
Built up of stones that live, it stands:
God's holy house, not made with hands.

The loving Father bless and praise
And Christ, his uncreated Son,
Who with the Holy Spirit reigns
In peace and love, for ever One:
Blest Trinity, since time began
Abiding in the heart of man.

Ant. 1: My house will be called a house of prayer (alleluia).

Psalms and canticle from Sunday, Week 1, pp 390 ff.

Ant. 2: May you be blessed, Lord, in your sacred temple (alleluia).

Ant. 3: Praise the Lord in his holy Church (alleluia).

Scripture Reading   *Is 56:7*
I will bring them to my holy mountain. I will make them joyful in my house of prayer. Their holocausts and their sacrifices will be accepted on my altar, for my house will be called a house of prayer for all the peoples.

Short Responsory
Outside Eastertide
R℟ Great is the Lord. He is worthy of our greatest praise. *Repeat* R℟
V℣ In the city of our God, upon his holy mountain. R℟ Glory be. R℟

Eastertide
R℟ The Lord is great and worthy to be praised, alleluia, alleluia. *Repeat* R℟
V℣ In the city of our God, upon his holy mountain. R℟ Glory be. R℟

Benedictus ant. 'Zacchaeus, make haste and come down; for I must stay with you today.' He came down with great haste and received the Lord joyfully in his house. Today salvation has come from God to this house, alleluia. (*Lent, omit* alleluia.)

Intercessions

Since we are living stones in the temple of Christ's body, let us pray to the Father for his beloved Church and profess our faith in her.

℟ This is the house of God and the gate of heaven.

Father, cleanse the vineyard of your Church,—watch over it with care and cultivate it with love, until it fills the world and is wonderful to see. ℟

Eternal shepherd, protect and extend the sheepfold of your Church; —let there be one flock, with your Son its only shepherd. ℟

Almighty Father, sow your word in the field of the Church;—produce its crop a hundredfold for your eternal harvest. ℟

God of all wisdom, sanctify your house and all the members of your family;—let men see the heavenly city, the new Jerusalem, the bride adorned with glory. ℟

Our Father

Concluding Prayer

In the dedicated church only

Almighty God,
as we recall with joy
the dedication of this house of yours
on each recurring anniversary:
listen to your people's prayer,
and grant that our worship here
may be a sincere and holy service,
honouring your name
and bringing us the fulness of redemption.
(We make our prayer) through our Lord.

Outside the dedicated church itself

Lord God,
you choose men as living stones to become an eternal dwelling,
built to the glory of your name.

Increase your gifts of grace to the Church,
and let your faithful people throng in ever greater numbers
to form the heavenly Jerusalem.
(We make our prayer) through our Lord.

Alternative
Lord God,
you have called your people to become your Church,
grant that all who are gathered in your name
may fear you and love you,
may follow you and, under your guidance,
attain to your promises in heaven.
(We make our prayer) through our Lord.

EVENING PRAYER II

Hymn

The Church's one foundation
Is Jesus Christ, her Lord;
She is his new creation
By water and the word:
From heaven he came and sought her
To be his holy bride,
With his own blood he bought her,
And for her life he died.

Elect from every nation,
Yet one o'er all the earth,
Her charter of salvation
One Lord, one faith, one birth;
One holy name she blesses,
Partakes one holy food,
And to one hope she presses
With every grace endued.

Though with a scornful wonder
Men see her sore oppressed,
By schisms rent asunder,
By heresies distrest,

Yet saints their watch are keeping,
Their cry goes up, 'How long?'
And soon the night of weeping
Shall be the morn of song.

Mid toil and tribulation,
And tumult of her war,
She waits the consummation
Of peace for evermore;
Till with the vision glorious
Her longing eyes are blest,
And the great Church victorious
Shall be the Church at rest.

Yet she on earth hath union
With God the three in one,
And mystic sweet communion
With those whose rest is won:
O happy ones and holy!
Lord, give us grace that we
Like them, the meek and lowly,
On high may dwell with thee.

PSALMODY

Ant. 1: The Lord has made holy the place where he dwells: God is within, it cannot be shaken (alleluia).

PSALM 45(46)

Gód is for ús a réfuge and stréngth,*
a hélper close at hánd, in tíme of distréss:
so wé shall not féar though the éarth should róck,*
though the móuntains fáll into the dépths of the séa,
even thóugh its wáters ráge and fóam,*
even thóugh the móuntains be sháken by its wáves.

The Lórd of hósts is wíth us:*
the Gód of Jácob is our strónghold.

The wáters of a ríver give jóy to God's cíty,*
the hóly pláce where the Móst High dwélls.

Gód is withín, it cánnot be sháken;*
Gód will hélp it at the dáwning of the dáy.
Nátions are in túmult, kíngdoms are sháken:*
he lífts his vóice, the éarth shrinks awáy.

The Lórd of hósts is wíth us:*
the Gód of Jácob is our strónghold.

Cóme, consíder the wórks of the Lórd*
the redóubtable déeds he has dóne on the éarth.
He puts an énd to wárs over áll the éarth;†
the bów he bréaks, the spéar he snáps.*
He búrns the shíelds with fíre.
'Be stíll and knów that Í am Gód,*
supréme among the nátions, supréme on the éarth!'

The Lórd of hósts is wíth us:*
the Gód of Jácob is our strónghold.

Ant. The Lord has made holy the place where he dwells: God is
within, it cannot be shaken (alleluia).
Ant. 2: Let us enter the house of the Lord with rejoicing (alleluia).

PSALM 121(122)

I rejóiced when I héard them sáy:*
'Let us gó to God's hóuse.'
And nów our féet are stánding*
within your gátes, O Jerúsalem.

Jerúsalem is búilt as a cíty*
stróngly compáct.
It is thére that the tríbes go úp,*
the tríbes of the Lórd.

For Ísrael's láw it ís,*
there to práise the Lord's náme.
Thére were set the thrónes of júdgment*
of the hóuse of Dávid.

For the péace of Jerúsalem práy:*
'Péace be to your hómes!

May péace réign in your wálls,*
in your pálaces, péace!'

For lóve of my bréthren and fríends*
I say: 'Péace upon yóu!'
For lóve of the hóuse of the Lórd*
I will ásk for your góod.

Ant. Let us enter the house of the Lord with rejoicing (alleluia).

OUTSIDE LENT

Ant. 3: Praise our God, all you his saints (alleluia).

When chanted, this canticle is sung with Alleluia *as set out below. When recited it suffices to say* Alleluia *at the beginning and end of each strophe.*

CANTICLE: CF REV 19:1-2,5-7

Alleluia.
Salvation and glory and power belong to our God,*
(R/ Alleluia.)
His judgments are true and just.
R/ Alleluia (alleluia).

Alleluia.
Praise our God, all you his servants,*
(R/ Alleluia.)
You who fear him, small and great.
R/ Alleluia (alleluia).

Alleluia.
The Lord our God, the Almighty, reigns,*
(R/ Alleluia.)
Let us rejoice and exult and give him the glory.
R/ Alleluia (alleluia).

Alleluia.
The marriage of the Lamb has come,*
(R/ Alleluia.)
And his bride has made herself ready.
R/ Alleluia (alleluia).

979

Ant. Praise our God, all you his saints (alleluia).

LENT

Ant. 3: All the nations shall come and adore you, Lord.

CANTICLE: REV 15:3-4

Great and wonderful are your deeds,*
O Lord God the Almighty!
Just and true are your ways,*
O King of the ages!

Who shall not fear and glorify your name, O Lord?*
For you alone are holy.
All nations shall come and worship you,*
for your judgments have been revealed.

Ant. All the nations shall come and adore you, Lord.

Scripture Reading   *Rev 21:2-3,22,27*
I saw the Holy City, the new Jerusalem, coming down out of heaven from God, prepared and ready, like a bride dressed to meet her husband. I heard a loud voice speaking from the throne: 'Now God's home is with men! He will live with them, and they shall be his people. God himself will be with them, and he will be their God.' I did not see a temple in the city, because its temple is the Lord God, the Almighty, and the Lamb. Nothing that is defiled will enter the city, nor anyone who does shameful things or tells lies. Only those whose names are written in the Lamb's book of the living will enter the city.

Short Responsory
Outside Eastertide
R⁊ Happy are they that dwell in your house, O Lord. *Repeat* R⁊
℣ They will sing your praise for ever. R⁊ Glory be. R⁊

Eastertide
R⁊ Happy are they that dwell in your house, O Lord, alleluia,

alleluia. *Repeat* ℟

℣ They will sing your praise for ever. ℟ Glory be. ℟

Magnificat ant. The Lord has made holy the place where he dwells: this is the house of God in which his name will be invoked; as it is written: My name shall be there, says the Lord (alleluia).

Intercessions

Let us pray to our Saviour who gave up his life to gather into unity the scattered children of God. ℟ Lord, remember your Church.

Lord Jesus, you commanded your disciples to hear your words and put them into action;—constantly strengthen your Church in faith, courage and trust. ℟

Lord Jesus, from your opened side there poured out blood and water;—make your Church vigorously alive through the sacraments of the new and everlasting covenant. ℟

Lord Jesus, you are present among those who are gathered in your name;—hear your Church, united in prayer. ℟

Lord Jesus, you come with the Father to dwell in those who love you;—perfect your Church all over the world in your divine love. ℟

Lord Jesus, anyone who comes to you is never turned away;— admit all those who have died into your Father's house. ℟

Our Father

The concluding prayer as at Morning Prayer, p 975.

THE COMMON OF
THE BLESSED VIRGIN MARY

EVENING PRAYER I

Hymn
Other suitable hymns are in the appendix, nos. 42–47.

Star of sea and ocean,
gateway to man's heaven,

mother of our Maker,
hear our pray'r, O Maiden.

Welcoming the *Ave*
of God's simple greeting
you have borne a Saviour
far beyond all dreaming.

Loose the bonds that hold us
bound in sin's own blindness
that with eyes now open'd
God's own light may guide us.

Show yourself our mother
he will hear your pleading
whom your womb has sheltered
and whose hand brings healing.

Gentlest of all virgins,
that our love be faithful
keep us from all evil
gentle, strong and grateful.

Guard us through life's dangers
never turn and leave us,
may our hope find harbour
in the calm of Jesus.

Sing to God our Father
through the Son who saves us
joyful in the Spirit
everlasting praises.

PSALMODY

Ant. 1: Blessed are you, Virgin Mary: you carried the Creator of all
things (alleluia).

PSALM 112(113)

Práise, O sérvants of the Lórd,*
práise the náme of the Lórd!

May the náme of the Lórd be bléssed*
both nów and for évermóre!
From the rísing of the sún to its sétting*
práised be the náme of the Lórd!

Hígh above all nátions is the Lórd,*
abóve the héavens his glóry.
Whó is like the Lórd, our Gód,*
who has rísen on hígh to his thróne
yet stóops from the héights to look dówn,*
to look dówn upon héaven and éarth?

From the dúst he lífts up the lówly,*
from his mísery he ráises the póor
to sét him in the cómpany of prínces,*
yés, with the prínces of his péople.
To the chíldless wífe he gives a hóme*
and gláddens her héart with chíldren.

Ant. Blessed are you, Virgin Mary: you carried the Creator of all things (alleluia).
Ant. 2: You bore him who created you; yet forever you remain a virgin (alleluia).

PSALM 147

O práise the Lórd, Jerúsalem!*
Síon, práise your Gód!

He has stréngthened the bárs of your gátes,*
he has bléssed the chíldren withín you.
He estáblished péace on your bórders,*
he féeds you with fínest whéat.

He sénds out his wórd to the éarth*
and swiftly rúns his commánd.
He shówers down snów white as wóol,*
he scátters hóar-frost like áshes.

He húrls down háilstones like crúmbs.*
The wáters are frózen at his tóuch;
he sénds forth his wórd and it mélts them:*
at the bréath of his móuth the waters flów.

He mákes his wórd known to Jácob,*
to Ísrael his láws and decrées.
He has not déalt thus with óther nátions;*
he has not táught them hís decrées.

Ant. You bore him who created you; yet forever you remain a virgin (alleluia).

Ant. 3: You are blessed, daughter, by the Lord your God; through you we partake of the fulness of life (alleluia).

CANTICLE: EPH 1:3-10

Blessed be the God and Father*
of our Lord Jesus Christ,
who has blessed us in Christ*
with every spiritual blessing in the heavenly places.

He chose us in him*
before the foundation of the world,
that we should be holy*
and blameless before him.

He destined us in love*
to be his sons through Jesus Christ,
according to the purpose of his will,†
to the praise of his glorious grace*
which he freely bestowed on us in the Beloved.

In him we have redemption through his blood,*
the forgiveness of our trespasses,
according to the riches of his grace*
which he lavished upon us.

He has made known to us†
in all wisdom and insight*
the mystery of his will,
according to his purpose*
which he set forth in Christ.

His purpose he set forth in Christ,*
as a plan for the fulness of time,

to unite all things in him,*
things in heaven and things on earth.

Ant. You are blessed, daughter, by the Lord your God; through you we partake of the fulness of life (alleluia).

Scripture Reading   *Gal 4:4-5*
When the appointed time came, God sent his Son, born of a woman, born a subject of the Law, to redeem the subjects of the Law and to enable us to be adopted as sons.

Short Responsory
Outside Eastertide
Ry After the birth of your child you remained a virgin. *Repeat* Ry
Ꝟ Mother of God, intercede for us. Ry Glory be. Ry

Eastertide
Ry After the birth of your child you remained a virgin, alleluia, alleluia. *Repeat* Ry
Ꝟ Mother of God, intercede for us. Ry Glory be. Ry

Magnificat ant. The Lord has looked upon my lowliness; the Almighty has done great things for me (alleluia).

Alternative
All generations will call me blessed, because God has had regard for his servant in her lowliness (alleluia).

Intercessions
Let us praise God the Father who chose Mary as the mother of his Son and wanted all generations to call her blessed. With confidence we pray: Ry May the Virgin Mary intercede for us.
Father, you did great things for the Virgin Mary and brought her, body and soul, to the glory of heaven;—fill the hearts of your children with the hope of Christ's glory. Ry
Through the prayers of Mary, our mother, heal the sick, comfort the sorrowful, pardon sinners;—grant peace and salvation to all. Ry
You favoured Mary with the fulness of grace;—bestow on all men

your overflowing blessings. ℟ May the Virgin Mary intercede for us.
May your Church be united heart and soul, held fast by love;—and
may your faithful be joined in continuous prayer, with Mary the
mother of Jesus. ℟

Father, you exalted the Virgin Mary and crowned her queen of
heaven;—may the dead enter your kingdom and rejoice with your
saints for ever. ℟

Our Father

Alternative

Let us praise God the Father who chose Mary as the mother of his
Son and wanted all generations to call her blessed. With confidence
we pray: ℟ May the Virgin Mary intercede for us.

Father, you have looked on the Virgin Mary and made her the
mother of mercy;—may those who are in danger experience the
depth of her love. ℟

You called Mary to be the mother in the house of Jesus and Joseph;
—through her prayers help all mothers to make their homes places
of love and holiness. ℟

You gave Mary the strength to stand beneath the cross and made
her radiant with joy in the resurrection;—raise up the sorrowful and
transform their lives with hope. ℟

Mary was your faithful handmaid who treasured your words in her
heart;—through her intercession let us become true disciples of your
Son, devoted to his service. ℟

Father, you exalted the Virgin Mary and crowned her queen of
heaven;—may the dead enter your kingdom and rejoice with your
saints for ever. ℟

Our Father

The concluding prayer as at Morning Prayer, pp 988 ff.

INVITATORY

Ant. Christ is the Son of Mary: come, let us adore him (alleluia).

Alternative

Come, ring out our joy to the Lord, as we venerate the Blessed
Virgin Mary (alleluia).

MORNING PRAYER

Hymn
Other suitable hymns are in the appendix, nos. 42–47.

Mary, crowned with living light,
Temple of the Lord,
Place of peace and holiness,
Shelter of the Word.

Mystery of sinless life
In our fallen race,
Free from shadow you reflect
Plenitude of grace.

Virgin-mother of our God,
Lift us when we fall,
Who were named upon the Cross
Mother of us all.

Father, Son and Holy Ghost,
Heaven sings your praise,
Mary magnifies your name
Through eternal days.

Ant. 1: Blessed are you, Mary; the salvation of the world came from you; now you rejoice in glory in the presence of the Lord; intercede for us with your Son (alleluia).

Psalms and canticle from Sunday, Week 1, pp 390 ff.

Ant. 2: You are the glory of Jerusalem! You are the joy of Israel! You are the highest honour of our race! (alleluia).

Ant. 3: Rejoice always, Virgin Mary; you were found worthy to bear Christ the Saviour (alleluia).

Scripture Reading   *Cf Is 61:10*
I will greatly rejoice in the Lord, my soul shall exult in my God; for he has clothed me with the garments of salvation, he has covered

me with the robe of righteousness, as a bride adorns herself with her jewels.

Short Responsory
Outside Eastertide

℟ The Lord chose her. He chose her before she was born. *Repeat* ℟
℣ He made her live in his own dwelling place. ℟ Glory be. ℟

Eastertide

℟ The Lord chose her before she was born, alleluia, alleluia. *Repeat* ℟
℣ He made her live in his own dwelling place. ℟ Glory be. ℟

Benedictus ant. The door of Paradise was closed to all men because of the sin of Eve; it has been opened again by the Virgin Mary (alleluia).

Intercessions

Let us proclaim the greatness of our Saviour who chose to be born of the Virgin Mary. Confident that he will hear us, we ask: ℟ Lord, may your mother pray for us.

Sun of justice, you showed your day was dawning in the immaculate Virgin Mary;—help us to walk in the daylight of your presence. ℟

Eternal Word, in the living flesh of Mary you found a dwelling place on earth;—remain with us for ever in hearts free from sin. ℟

Christ, our Saviour, you willed that your mother should be there when you died;—through her intercession may we rejoice to share your suffering. ℟

Loving Saviour, while hanging on the cross, you gave your mother Mary to be the mother of John;—let us be known as her children by our way of living. ℟

Our Father

Alternative

Let us proclaim the greatness of our Saviour who chose to be born of the Virgin Mary. Confident that he will hear us, we ask: ℟ Lord, may your mother pray for us.

Saviour of the world, by your redemptive power you preserved your

mother Mary from every stain of sin;—deliver us from the evil that
lies hidden in our hearts. R̹

Christ, our Redeemer, you made the Virgin Mary the sanctuary of
your presence and the temple of the Spirit;—make us bearers of your
Spirit, in mind, heart and body. R̹

Eternal Word, you taught your mother Mary to choose the part that
was best;—let us follow her example and hunger for the food of
everlasting life. R̹

King of kings, you assumed Mary into heaven to be with you
completely in body and soul;—may we seek the things that are above
and keep our lives fixed on you. R̹

King of heaven and earth, you placed Mary at your side to reign as
queen for ever;—grant us the joy of sharing in your glory. R̹

Our Father

Concluding Prayer
If no proper prayer is given one of the following is said:

Advent
As it was your will, heavenly Father.
that, at the angel's message,
your Word should be conceived by the Blessed Virgin Mary,
grant, that as we believe her to be truly the Mother of God,
so may we be helped by her intercession.
(We make our prayer) through our Lord.

Christmastide
God, our Father,
since you gave mankind a saviour through Blessed Mary, virgin and
    mother,
grant that we may feel the power of her intercession,
when she pleads for us with Jesus Christ, your Son,
the author of life,
who lives and reigns with you and the Holy Spirit,
God, for ever and ever.

Lent
Lord, open our hearts to your grace.

Through the angel's message to Mary
we have learned to believe
in the incarnation of Christ your Son.
Lead us by his passion and cross
to the glory of his resurrection.
(We make our prayer) through our Lord.

Alternative for Lent, and also Through the Year
Forgive the sins of your people, Lord,
and as nothing we can do is worthy in your sight,
save us through the intercession of the Mother of our Lord Jesus
    Christ
who lives and reigns with you and the Holy Spirit,
God, for ever and ever.

Eastertide
Lord God,
as you brought joy to the world through the resurrection of our
    Lord Jesus Christ, your Son,
grant that through his Virgin Mother
we may come to the joys of eternal life.
(We make our prayer) through our Lord.

Alternative
Lord God
you bestowed the Holy Spirit on your apostles
while they were at prayer with Mary the Mother of Jesus:
grant that by her prayer
we may give you faithful service
and spread abroad the glory of your name by word and example.
(We make our prayer) through our Lord.

Through the Year
Grant us, Lord, we pray,
the joy of continued health of mind and body:
and through the intercession of Blessed Mary ever-virgin,
free us of this present sadness,
fill us with eternal joy.
(We make our prayer) through our Lord.

Alternative
Come to help us in our weakness, God of mercy,
and as we celebrate the memory of the Mother of God,
may we rise from our sins by the help of her prayer.
(We make our prayer) through our Lord.

Alternative
Let the gracious intercession of Blessed Mary ever-virgin help us,
    Lord:
may she protect us in all dangers
and make us rejoice in your peace.
(We make our prayer) through our Lord.

Alternative
Lord God,
as we venerate the memory of the Virgin Mary, now in glory,
grant that by her intercession
we ourselves may share in the fulness of your grace.
(We make our prayer) through our Lord.

Alternative
Almighty God,
grant that your faithful who rejoice in the protection of the Blessed
    Virgin Mary,
may be delivered from every evil here on earth through her prayer,
and come to the enduring joys of heaven.
(We make our prayer) through our Lord.

EVENING PRAYER II

Hymn
Other suitable hymns are in the appendix, nos. 42–47.

Maiden, yet a Mother,
Daughter of thy Son,
High beyond all other—
Lowlier is none;

Thou the consummation
Planned by God's decree,
When our lost creation
Nobler rose in thee!

Thus his place preparèd,
He who all things made
'Mid his creatures tarried,
In thy bosom laid;
There his love he nourished,—
Warmth that gave increase
To the Root whence flourished
Our eternal peace.

Nor alone thou hearest
When thy name we hail;
Often thou art nearest
When our voices fail;
Mirrored in thy fashion
All creation's good,
Mercy, might, compassion
Grace thy womanhood.

Lady, lest our vision
Striving heavenward, fail,
Still let thy petition
With thy Son prevail,
Unto whom all merit,
Power and majesty,
With the Holy Spirit
And the Father be.

PSALMODY

Ant. 1: Hail Mary, full of grace: the Lord is with you (alleluia).

PSALM 121(122)

I rejóiced when I héard them sáy:*
'Let us gó to God's hóuse.'

992

And nów our féet are stánding*
within your gátes, O Jerúsalem.

Jerúsalem is buílt as a cíty*
stróngly compáct.
It is thére that the tríbes go úp,*
the tríbes of the Lórd.

For Ísrael's láw it ís,*
there to práise the Lord's náme.
Thére were set the thrónes of júdgment*
of the hóuse of Dávid.

For the péace of Jerúsalem práy:*
'Péace be to your hómes!
May péace réign in your wálls,*
in your pálaces, péace!'

For lóve of my bréthren and fríends*
I say: 'Péace upon yóu!'
For lóve of the hóuse of the Lórd*
I will ásk for your góod.

Ant. Hail Mary, full of grace: the Lord is with you (alleluia).
Ant. 2: I am the servant of the Lord; let it be as you have said (alleluia).

PSALM 126(127)

If the Lórd does not buíld the hóuse,*
in váin do its buílders lábour;
if the Lórd does not wátch over the cíty,*
in váin does the wátchman keep vígil.

In váin is your éarlier rísing,*
your góing láter to rést,
you who tóil for the bréad you éat:*
when he pours gífts on his belóved while they slúmber.

Truly sóns are a gíft from the Lórd,*
a bléssing, the frúit of the wómb.
Indéed the sóns of yóuth*
are like árrows in the hánd of a wárrior.

993

Ó the háppiness of the mán*
who has fílled his quíver with these árrows!
Hé will have no cáuse for sháme*
when he dispútes with his fóes in the gáteways.

Ant. I am the servant of the Lord; let it be as you have said (alleluia).
Ant. 3: You are the most blessed of all women, and blessed is the fruit of your womb (alleluia).

CANTICLE: EPH 1:3-10

Blessed be the God and Father*
of our Lord Jesus Christ,
who has blessed us in Christ*
with every spiritual blessing in the heavenly places.

He chose us in him*
before the foundation of the world,
that we should be holy*
and blameless before him.

He destined us in love*
to be his sons through Jesus Christ,
according to the purpose of his will,†
to the praise of his glorious grace*
which he freely bestowed on us in the Beloved.

In him we have redemption through his blood,*
the forgivenesss of our trespasses,
according to the riches of his grace*
which he lavished upon us.

He has made known to us†
in all wisdom and insight*
the mystery of his will,
according to his purpose*
which he set forth in Christ.

His purpose he set forth in Christ,*
as a plan for the fulness of time,
to unite all things in him,*
things in heaven and things on earth.

Ant. You are the most blessed of all women, and blessed is the fruit of your womb (alleluia).

Scripture Reading   *Gal 4:4-5*
When the appointed time came, God sent his Son, born of a woman, born a subject of the Law, to redeem the subjects of the Law and to enable us to be adopted as sons.

Short Responsory
Outside Eastertide
R̸ Hail Mary, full of grace: the Lord is with you. *Repeat* R̸
V̸ You are the most blessed of all women and blessed is the fruit of your womb. R̸ Glory be. R̸

Eastertide
R̸ Hail Mary, full of grace: the Lord is with you, alleluia, alleluia. *Repeat* R̸
V̸ You are the most blessed of all women and blessed is the fruit of your womb. R̸ Glory be. R̸

Magnificat ant. Blessed are you, Mary, because you believed that all those things which were said to you by the Lord will be fulfilled (alleluia).

Intercessions
Let us praise God the Father who chose Mary as the mother of his Son and wanted all generations to call her blessed. With confidence we pray: R̸ May the Virgin Mary intercede for us.
Father, you did great things for the Virgin Mary and brought her, body and soul, to the glory of heaven;—fill the hearts of your children with the hope of Christ's glory. R̸
Through the prayers of Mary, our mother, heal the sick, comfort the sorrowful, pardon sinners;—grant peace and salvation to all. R̸
You favoured Mary with the fulness of grace;—bestow on all men your overflowing blessings. R̸
May your Church be united heart and soul, held fast by love,—and may your faithful be joined in continuous prayer, with Mary the mother of Jesus. R̸

Father, you exalted the Virgin Mary and crowned her queen of heaven;—may the dead enter your kingdom and rejoice with your saints for ever. R⁷ May the Virgin Mary intercede for us.
Our Father

Alternative
Let us praise God the Father who chose Mary as the mother of his Son and wanted all generations to call her blessed. With confidence we pray: R⁷ May the Virgin Mary intercede for us.
Father, you have looked on the Virgin Mary and made her the mother of mercy;—may those who are in danger experience the depth of her love. R⁷
You called Mary to be the mother in the house of Jesus and Joseph; —through her prayers help all mothers to make their homes places of love and holiness. R⁷
You gave Mary the strength to stand beneath the cross and made her radiant with joy in the resurrection;—raise up the sorrowful and transform their lives with hope. R⁷
Mary was your faithful handmaid who treasured your words in her heart;—through her intercession let us become true disciples of your Son, devoted to his service. R⁷
Father, you exalted the Virgin Mary and crowned her queen of heaven;—may the dead enter your kingdom and rejoice with your saints for ever. R⁷
Our Father

The concluding prayer as at Morning Prayer, pp 989 ff.

MEMORIA OF THE BLESSED VIRGIN MARY ON SATURDAY

On ordinary Saturdays Through the Year on which optional Memorias are allowed, an optional Memoria of the Blessed Virgin Mary may be celebrated.

INVITATORY

Ant. Christ is the Son of Mary; come, let us adore him.

Alternative
Come, ring out our joy to the Lord, as we venerate the Blessed
Virgin Mary.

MORNING PRAYER

*Hymn from the Common of the Blessed Virgin Mary, p 987, or the
appendix.*

Antiphons, psalms and canticle from the current Saturday.

*The Scripture Reading with its short responsory may be chosen from
among the following:*

Scripture Reading *Gal 4:4-5*
When the appointed time came, God sent his Son, born of a woman,
born a subject of the Law, to redeem the subjects of the Law and to
enable us to be adopted as sons.

Short Responsory
R/ After the birth of your child you remained a virgin. *Repeat* R/
V/ Mother of God, intercede for us. R/ Glory be. R/

Alternative
Scripture Reading *Cf Is 61:10*
I will greatly rejoice in the Lord, my soul shall exult in my God; for
he has clothed me with the garments of salvation, he has covered me
with the robe of righteousness, as a bride adorns herself with her
jewels.

Short Responsory
R/ The Lord chose her. He chose her before she was born. *Repeat* R/
V/ He made her live in his own dwelling place. R/ Glory be. R/

Alternative
Scripture Reading *Rev 12:1*
A great sign appeared in heaven: a woman, adorned with the sun,
standing on the moon, and with the twelve stars on her head for a
crown.

Short Responsory

R⁷ Hail Mary, full of grace: the Lord is with you. *Repeat* R⁷
V⁷ You are the most blessed of all women and blessed is the fruit of your womb. R⁷ Glory be. R⁷

Benedictus Antiphon

One of the following may be chosen:

1 Let us celebrate the commemoration of the Blessed Virgin Mary, that she may intercede for us with the Lord Jesus Christ.

2 Blessed are you, O Virgin Mary, above all women on earth. The Lord God himself has chosen you.

3 Through you, immaculate Virgin, the life we had lost was returned to us. You received a child from heaven, and brought forth to the world a Saviour.

4 Hail Mary, full of grace; the Lord is with you. You are the most blessed of all women, alleluia.

5 How shall I fittingly praise you, holy and immaculate virginity of Mary? Through you we received our Redeemer, our Lord Jesus Christ.

6 You are the glory of Jerusalem! You are the joy of Israel! You are the highest honour of our race.

Intercessions

Let us proclaim the greatness of our Saviour who chose to be born of the Virgin Mary. Confident that he will hear us, we ask: R⁷ Lord, may your mother pray for us.

Sun of justice, you showed your day was dawning in the immaculate Virgin Mary;—help us to walk in the daylight of your presence. R⁷

Eternal Word, in the living flesh of Mary you found a dwelling place on earth;—remain with us for ever in hearts free from sin. R⁷

Christ, our Saviour, you willed that your mother should be there when you died;—through her intercession may we rejoice to share your suffering. R⁷

Loving Saviour, while hanging on the cross, you gave your mother Mary to be the mother of John;—let us be known as her children by our way of living. R⁷

Our Father

Alternative

Let us proclaim the greatness of our Saviour who chose to be born
of the Virgin Mary. Confident that he will hear us, we ask: ℟ Lord,
may your mother pray for us.

Saviour of the world, by your redemptive power you preserved your
mother Mary from every stain of sin;—deliver us from the evil that
lies hidden in our hearts. ℟

Christ, our Redeemer, you made the Virgin Mary the sanctuary of
your presence and the temple of the Spirit;—make us bearers of your
Spirit, in mind, heart and body. ℟

Eternal Word, you taught your mother Mary to choose the part that
was best;—let us follow her example and hunger for the food of
everlasting life. ℟

King of kings, you assumed Mary into heaven to be with you
completely in body and soul;—may we seek the things that are above
and keep our lives fixed on you. ℟

King of heaven and earth, you placed Mary at your side to reign as
queen for ever;—grant us the joy of sharing in your glory. ℟

Our Father

Concluding Prayer
One of the following may be chosen:

Grant us, Lord, we pray
the joy of continued health of mind and body:
and through the intercession of Blessed Mary ever-virgin,
free us of this present sadness,
fill us with eternal joy.
(We make our prayer) through our Lord.

Alternative

Forgive the sins of your people, Lord,
and as nothing we can do is worthy in your sight,
save us through the intercession of the Mother of our Lord
    Jesus Christ
who lives and reigns with you and the Holy Spirit,
God, for ever and ever.

Alternative

Come to help us in our weakness, God of mercy,
and as we celebrate the memory of the Mother of God,
may we rise from our sins by the help of her prayer.
(We make our prayer) through our Lord.

Alternative

Let the gracious intercession of Blessed Mary ever-virgin help us,
  Lord:
may she protect us in all dangers
and make us rejoice in your peace.
(We make our prayer) through our Lord.

Alternative

Lord God,
as we venerate the memory of the Virgin Mary, now in glory,
grant that by her intercession
we ourselves may share in the fulness of your grace.
(We make our prayer) through our Lord.

Alternative

Almighty God,
grant that your faithful who rejoice in the protection of the
  Blessed Virgin Mary,
may be delivered from every evil here on earth through her prayer,
and come to the enduring joys of heaven.
(We make our prayer) through our Lord.

THE COMMON OF APOSTLES

EVENING PRAYER I

Hymn

Let all on earth their voices raise,
Re-echoing heav'ns triumphant praise,
To him who gave th' apostles grace
To run on earth their glorious race.

Thou at whose word they bore the light
Of gospel truth o'er heathen night,
To us that heavenly light impart,
To glad our eyes and cheer our heart.

Thou at whose will to them was given
To bind and loose in earth and heaven,
Our chains unbind, our sins undo,
And in our hearts thy grace renew.

Thou in whose might they spoke the word
Which cured disease and health restored,
To us its healing power prolong,
Support the weak, confirm the strong.

PSALMODY

Ant. 1: Jesus called his disciples to him, and from among them he
chose twelve and called them apostles (alleluia).

PSALM 116(117)

O práise the Lórd, all you nátions,*
accláim him all you péoples!

Stróng is his lóve for ús;*
he is fáithful for éver.

Ant. Jesus called his disciples to him, and from among them he
chose twelve and called them apostles (alleluia).
Ant. 2: They left their nets and followed their Lord and Redeemer
(alleluia).

PSALM 147

O práise the Lórd, Jerúsalem!*
Síon, práise your Gód!

He has stréngthened the bárs of your gátes,*
he has bléssed the chíldren withín you.
He estáblished péace on your bórders,*
he féeds you with fínest whéat.

He sénds out his wórd to the éarth*
and swíftly rúns his commánd.
He shówers down snów white as wóol,*
he scátters hóar-frost like áshes.

He húrls down háilstones like crúmbs.*
The wáters are frózen at his tóuch;
he sénds forth his wórd and it mélts them:*
at the bréath of his móuth the waters flów.

He mákes his wórd known to Jácob,*
to Ísrael his láws and decrées.
He has not déalt thus with óther nátions;*
he has not táught them hís decrées.

Ant. They left their nets and followed their Lord and Redeemer
(alleluia).
Ant. 3: You are my friends since you have remained in my love
(alleluia).

CANTICLE: EPH 1:3-10

Blessed be the God and Father*
of our Lord Jesus Christ,
who has blessed us in Christ*
with every spiritual blessing in the heavenly places.

He chose us in him*
before the foundation of the world,
that we should be holy*
and blameless before him.

He destined us in love*
to be his sons through Jesus Christ,

according to the purpose of his will,†
to the praise of his glorious grace*
which he freely bestowed on us in the Beloved.

In him we have redemption through his blood,*
the forgiveness of our trespasses,
according to the riches of his grace*
which he lavished upon us.

He has made known to us†
in all wisdom and insight*
the mystery of his will,
according to his purpose*
which he set forth in Christ.

His purpose he set forth in Christ,*
as a plan for the fulness of time,
to unite all things in him,*
things in heaven and things on earth.

Ant. You are my friends since you have remained in my love
(alleluia).

Scripture Reading   *Acts 2:42-45*
They met constantly to hear the apostles teach, and to share the
common life, to break bread, and to pray. A sense of awe was everywhere, and many marvels and signs were brought about through the
apostles. All whose faith had drawn them together held everything
in common: they would sell their property and make a general dis-
tribution as the need of each required.

Short Responsory
Outside Eastertide
R̸ All will know that you are my disciples. *Repeat* R̸
V̸ If there is love among you. R̸ Glory be. R̸

Eastertide
R̸ All will know that you are my disciples, alleluia, alleluia.
Repeat R̸
V̸ If there is love among you. R̸ Glory be. R̸

Magnificat ant. You did not choose me: I chose you. I appointed you to go on and bear fruit, fruit that shall last (alleluia).

Intercessions
Since we are part of a building that has the apostles for its foundation, let us pray to the Father for his holy people. ℟ Lord, remember your Church.
Father, when your Son rose from the dead, you showed him first to the apostles;—let us make him known, near and far. ℟
You sent your Son into the world to proclaim the good news to the poor;—grant that we may bring his gospel into the darkness of men's lives. ℟
You sent your Son to plant in men's hearts the seed of imperishable life;—may we labour to sow his word and reap a harvest of joy. ℟
You sent your Son to reconcile the world with yourself by the shedding of his blood;—let us become his fellow workers in restoring men to your friendship. ℟
You placed your Son at your own right hand in heaven;—receive the dead into the happiness of your kingdom. ℟
Our Father

The concluding prayer is from the Proper of Saints.

INVITATORY

Outside Eastertide
Ant. The Lord is the king of apostles: come, let us adore him.

Eastertide
Ant. Alleluia, the Lord is king of apostles: come, let us adore him, alleluia.

MORNING PRAYER

Hymn
O fathers of our ancient faith,
With all the heav'ns we sing your fame
Whose sound went forth in all the earth
To tell of Christ, and bless his name.

You took the gospel to the poor,
The word of God alight in you,
Which in our day is told again:
That timeless word, for ever new.

You told of God who died for us
And out of death triumphant rose,
Who gave the truth that made us free,
And changeless through the ages goes.

Praise Father, Son and Holy Ghost
Whose gift is faith that never dies:
A light in darkness now, until
The day-star in our hearts arise.

Ant. 1: This is my commandment: love one another, as I have loved you (alleluia).

Psalms and canticle of Sunday, Week 1, pp 390 ff.

Ant. 2: A man can have no greater love than to lay down his life for his friends (alleluia).

Ant. 3: You are my friends if you do what I command you, says the Lord (alleluia).

Scripture Reading   *Eph 2:19-22*
You are no longer aliens in a foreign land, but fellow-citizens with God's people, members of God's household. You are built upon the foundation laid by the apostles and prophets, and Christ Jesus himself is the foundation-stone. In him the whole building is bonded together and grows into a holy temple in the Lord. In him you too are being built with all the rest into a spiritual dwelling for God.

Short Responsory
Outside Eastertide
R̄ You will make them rulers over all the land. *Repeat* R̄
V̄ Your name, Lord, will be remembered. R̄ Glory be. R̄

Eastertide

℞ You will make them rulers over all the land, alleluia, alleluia.
Repeat ℞
℣ Your name, Lord, will be remembered. ℞ Glory be. ℞

Benedictus ant. The holy city of Jerusalem had twelve foundation-stones, and on them were the names of the twelve apostles of the Lamb. The Lamb himself was the light of that city (alleluia).

Intercessions

Since we have received from the apostles our heavenly inheritance, let us thank our Father for all his blessings. ℞ Lord, the apostles sing your praises.

Praise to you, Lord God, for the gift of Christ's body and blood, handed on by the apostles, to give us strength and life;—Lord, the apostles sing your praises.

For the table of your word, served by the apostles, to bring us light and joy;—Lord, the apostles sing your praises.

For your holy Church, built on the apostles, to make us all one body;—Lord, the apostles sing your praises.

For the washing of baptism and penance, entrusted to the apostles, to cleanse our hearts from sin;—Lord, the apostles sing your praises.

Our Father

The concluding prayer is from the Proper of Saints.

EVENING PRAYER II

Hymn

Let all on earth their voices raise,
Re-echoing heav'ns triumphant praise,
To him who gave th' apostles grace
To run on earth their glorious race.

Thou at whose word they bore the light
Of gospel truth o'er heathen night,
To us that heavenly light impart,
To glad our eyes and cheer our heart.

Thou at whose will to them was given
To bind and loose in earth and heaven,
Our chains unbind, our sins undo,
And in our hearts thy grace renew.

Thou in whose might they spoke the word
Which cured disease and health restored,
To us its healing power prolong,
Support the weak, confirm the strong.

PSALMODY

Ant. 1: You are the men who have stood faithfully by me in my trials (alleluia).

PSALM 115(116)

I trústed, éven when I sáid:*
'I am sórely afflícted,'
and whén I sáid in my alárm:*
'No mán can be trústed.'

How cán I repáy the Lórd*
for his góodness to mé?
The cúp of salvátion I will ráise;*
I will cáll on the Lórd's name.

My vóws to the Lórd I will fulfíl*
befóre all his péople.
O précious in the éyes of the Lórd*
is the déath of his fáithful.

Your sérvant, Lord, your sérvant am Í;*
you have lóosened my bónds.
A thánksgiving sácrifice I máke:*
I will cáll on the Lórd's name.

My vóws to the Lórd I will fulfíl*
befóre all his péople,
in the cóurts of the hóuse of the Lórd,*
in your mídst, O Jerúsalem.

Ant. You are the men who have stood faithfully by me in my trials (alleluia).

Ant. 2: I am here among you as one who serves (alleluia).

PSALM 125(126)

When the Lórd delivered Síon from bóndage,*
It séemed like a dréam.
Thén was our móuth filled with láughter,*
on our líps there were sóngs.

The héathens themsélves said: 'What márvels*
the Lórd worked for thém!'
What márvels the Lórd worked for ús!*
Indéed we were glád.

Delíver us, O Lórd, from our bóndage*
as stréams in dry lánd.
Thóse who are sówing in téars*
will síng when they réap.

They go óut, they go óut, full of téars,*
carrying séed for the sówing:
they come báck, they come báck, full of sóng,*
cárrying their shéaves.

Ant. I am here among you as one who serves (alleluia).

Ant. 3: I shall not call you servants any more, I call you friends, because I have made known to you everything I learnt from my Father (alleluia).

CANTICLE: EPH 1:3-10

Blessed be the God and Father*
of our Lord Jesus Christ,
who has blessed us in Christ*
with every spiritual blessing in the heavenly places.

He chose us in him*
before the foundation of the world,
that we should be holy*
and blameless before him.

He destined us in love*
to be his sons through Jesus Christ,
according to the purpose of his will,†
to the praise of his glorious grace*
which he freely bestowed on us in the Beloved.

In him we have redemption through his blood,*
the forgiveness of our trespasses,
according to the riches of his grace*
which he lavished upon us.

He has made known to us†
in all wisdom and insight*
the mystery of his will,
according to his purpose*
which he set forth in Christ.

His purpose he set forth in Christ,*
as a plan for the fulness of time,
to unite all things in him,*
things in heaven and things on earth.

Ant. I shall not call you servants any more, I call you friends, because I have made known to you everything I learnt from my Father (alleluia).

Scripture Reading   *Eph 4:11-13*
Some Christ has appointed to be apostles, others to be prophets, others to be evangelists, or pastors, or teachers. They are to order the lives of the faithful, minister to their needs, build up the frame of Christ's body, until we all realize our common unity through faith in the Son of God, and fuller knowledge of him. So we shall reach perfect manhood, that maturity which is proportioned to the completed growth of Christ.

Short Responsory
Outside Eastertide
R̷ Tell of the glory of the Lord; announce it among the nations.
Repeat R̷
V̷ Speak of his wonderful deeds to all the peoples. R̷ Glory be. R̷

Eastertide
℞ Tell of the glory of the Lord among the nations, alleluia, alleluia.
Repeat ℞
℣ Speak of his wonderful deeds to all the peoples. ℞ Glory be. ℞

Magnificat ant. When all is made new and the Son of Man sits on his throne of glory, you will sit on twelve thrones to judge the twelve tribes of Israel (alleluia).

Intercessions
Since we are part of a building that has the apostles for its foundation, let us pray to the Father for his holy people. ℞ Lord, remember your Church.
Father, when your Son rose from the dead, you showed him first to the apostles;—let us make him known, near and far. ℞
You sent your Son into the world to proclaim the good news to the poor;—grant that we may bring his gospel into the darkness of men's lives. ℞
You sent your Son to plant in men's hearts the seed of imperishable life;—may we labour to sow his word and reap a harvest of joy. ℞
You sent your Son to reconcile the world with yourself by the shedding of his blood;—let us become his fellow workers in restoring men to your friendship. ℞
You placed your Son at your own right hand in heaven;—receive the dead into the happiness of your kingdom. ℞
Our Father

The concluding prayer is from the Proper of Saints.

THE COMMON OF MARTYRS
SEVERAL MARTYRS

EVENING PRAYER I

Hymn
In Lent, the hymn as at Morning Prayer is used, p 1017.

Our Lord the path of suffering trod,
And, since his blood for man has flowed,
'Tis meet that man should yield to God
The life he owes. Alleluia!

No shame to own the crucified!
Nay, 'tis our immortality
That we confess our God who died,
And for him die. Alleluia!

Beholding his predestined crown,
Into death's arms the martyr goes;
Dying, he conquers death; o'erthrown,
O'erthrows his foes. Alleluia!

Lord, make us your own soldiers true;
Grant us brave faith, a spirit pure;
That for your name, your cross in view,
We may endure. Alleluia!

PSALMODY

ANTIPHON I
Several Martyrs: These saints suffered many torments to win the
honour of the martyr's palm (alleluia).
One Martyr: If anyone openly declares himself for me in the presence
of men, I will declare myself for him in the presence of my Father
(alleluia).

I

Give thánks to the Lórd for he is góod,*
for his lóve endures for éver.

Let the sóns of Ísrael sáy:*
'His lóve endures for éver.'
Let the sóns of Áaron sáy:*
'His lóve endures for éver.'
Let thóse who fear the Lórd sáy:*
'His lóve endures for éver.'

I cálled to the Lórd in my distréss;*
he ánswered and fréed me.
The Iórd is at my síde; I do not féar.*
What can mán do agáinst me?
The Lórd is at my síde as my hélper:*
I shall look dówn on my fóes.

It is bétter to take réfuge in the Lórd*
than to trúst in mén:
it is bétter to take réfuge in the Lórd*
than to trúst in prínces.

The nátions áll encómpassed me;*
in the Lórd's name I crúshed them.
They cómpassed me, cómpassed me abóut;*
in the Lórd's name I crúshed them.
They cómpassed me abóut like bées;†
they blázed like a fíre among thórns.*
In the Lórd's name I crúshed them.

I was hárd-préssed and was fálling*
but the Lórd came to hélp me.
The Lórd is my stréngth and my sóng;*
hé is my sáviour.
There are shóuts of jóy and víctory*
in the ténts of the júst.

The Lórd's right hánd has tríumphed;*
his ríght hand ráised me.

The Lórd's right hánd has tríumphed;†
I shall not díe, I shall líve*
and recóunt his déeds.
I was púnished, I was púnished by the Lórd,*
but nót doomed to díe.

Ant. Several Martyrs: These saints suffered many torments to win
the honour of the martyr's palm (alleluia).
One Martyr: If anyone openly declares himself for me in the
presence of men, I will declare myself for him in the presence of my
Father (alleluia).

ANTIPHON 2
Several Martyrs: These saints came to the kingdom of heaven
carrying palm branches: they were found worthy to receive crowns
from the hand of God (alleluia).
One Martyr: Anyone who follows me will not be walking in the
dark; he will have the light of life (alleluia).

II

Ópen to mé the gates of hóliness:*
I will énter and give thánks.
Thís is the Lórd's own gáte*
where the júst may énter.
I will thánk you for yóu have ánswered*
and yóu are my sáviour.

The stóne which the buílders rejécted*
has becóme the córner stone.
Thís is the wórk of the Lórd,*
a márvel in our éyes.
Thís day was máde by the Lórd;*
we rejóice and are glád.

O Lórd, gránt us salvátion;*
O Lórd, grant succéss.
Bléssed in the náme of the Lórd*
is hé who cómes.
We bléss you from the hóuse of the Lórd;*
the Lord Gód is our líght.

Go fórward in procéssion with bránches*
éven to the áltar.
Yóu are my Gód, I thánk you.*
My Gód, I práise you,
Give thánks to the Lórd for he is góoᴅ;*
for his lóve endures for éver.

Ant. Several Martyrs: These saints came to the kingdom of heaven
carrying palm branches: they were found worthy to receive crowns
from the hand of God (alleluia).
One Martyr: Anyone who follows me will not be walking in the
dark; he will have the light of life (alleluia).

ANTIPHON 3
Several Martyrs: The martyrs died as witnesses to Christ; they will
live for ever (alleluia).
One Martyr: As the sufferings of Christ overflow to us, so, through
Christ, does our consolation overflow (alleluia).

CANTICLE: I PET 2:21-24

Christ suffered for you†
leaving you an example*
that you should follow in his steps.

He committed no sin;*
no guile was found on his lips.
When he was reviled,*
he did not revile in return.

When he suffered,*
he did not threaten;
but he trusted to him*
who judges justly.

He himself bore our sins*
in his body on the tree,
that we might die to sin*
and live to righteousness.

By his wounds you have been healed.

Ant. Several Martyrs: The martyrs died as witnesses to Christ; they will live for ever (alleluia).

One Martyr: As the sufferings of Christ overflow to us, so, through Christ, does our consolation overflow (alleluia).

OUTSIDE EASTERTIDE

Scripture Reading   *Rom 8:35,37-39*

Who will separate us from the love of Christ? Will affliction, or distress, or persecution, or hunger, or nakedness, or peril, or the sword? Yet in all this we are conquerors, through him who has granted us his love. Of this I am fully persuaded; neither death nor life, nor angels or principalities or powers, neither what is present nor what is to come, no force whatever, neither the height above us nor the depth beneath us, nor any other created thing, will be able to separate us from the love of God, which comes to us in Christ Jesus our Lord.

Short Responsory

R̷ The souls of the virtuous are in the hands of God. *Repeat* R̷
Ỵ No torment shall ever touch them. R̷ Glory be. R̷

Magnificat ant. The kingdom of heaven belongs to those who hated their life in the present world and have now come to the rewards of the kingdom. They have washed their robes in the blood of the Lamb.

Intercessions

Let us give thanks to the king of martyrs, for this is the hour when he offered himself in the last supper and laid down his life on the cross. R̷ We praise you, Christ the Lord.

We praise you, Christ our Saviour, example and strength of the martyrs, because you have loved us to the end;—we praise you, Christ the Lord.

Because you have promised repentant sinners the reward of eternal life,—we praise you, Christ the Lord.

Because you have called the Church to offer the blood of the new and eternal covenant, the blood shed for the remission of sins,—we praise you, Christ the Lord.

Because you have brought us to this day with the gift of faith intact,

—we praise you, Christ the Lord.

Because of the many brothers who today have come to share in your saving death,—we praise you, Christ the Lord.

Our Father

Concluding Prayer

If no proper prayer is given one of those at Morning Prayer is said, p 1019.

EASTERTIDE

Scripture Reading   *Rev 3:10-12*

Because you have kept my order to be patient, I will also keep you safe from the time of trouble which is coming upon the whole world, to test all the people on earth. I am coming soon. Keep safe what you have, so that no one will rob you of your victory prize. I will make him who is victorious a pillar in the temple of my God, and he will never again leave it. I will write on him the name of my God, and the name of the city of my God, the new Jerusalem, which will come down out of heaven from my God. I will also write on him my new name.

Short Responsory

R⁊ Let the saints rejoice in the Lord. Alleluia, alleluia. *Repeat* R⁊
V⁊ God has chosen you for his own. R⁊ Glory be. R⁊

Magnificat ant. Undying light will shine about your saints, Lord; they will live for ever, alleluia.

Intercessions

Let us give thanks to the king of martyrs, for this is the hour when he offered himself in the last supper and laid down his life on the cross. R⁊ We praise you, Christ the Lord.

We praise you, Christ our Saviour, example and strength of the martyrs, because you have loved us to the end;—we praise you, Christ the Lord.

Because you have promised repentant sinners the reward of eternal life,—we praise you, Christ the Lord.

Because you have called the Church to offer the blood of the new and eternal covenant, the blood shed for the remission of sins,—we

1016

praise you, Christ the Lord.
Because you have brought us to this day with the gift of faith intact,
—we praise you, Christ the Lord.
Because of the many brothers who today have come to share in your
saving death,—we praise you, Christ the Lord.
Our Father

Concluding Prayer

*If no proper prayer is given, one of those at Morning Prayer is said,
p 1020.*

INVITATORY

Ant. The Lord is the king of martyrs; come, let us adore him
(alleluia).

MORNING PRAYER

Hymn

The martyrs living now with Christ
In suffering were tried,
Their anguish overcome by love,
When on his cross they died.

Across the centuries they come,
In constancy unmoved.
Their loving hearts make no complaint;
In silence they are proved.

No man has ever measured love,
Or weighed it in his hand,
But God who knows the inmost heart,
Gives them the promised land.

Praise Father, Son and Spirit blest
Who guide us through the night
In ways that reach beyond the stars
To everlasting light.

Ant. 1: When the martyrs of Christ were in torment they fixed their minds on heavenly things, and said: Lord, come to our help (alleluia).

Psalms and canticle of Sunday, Week 1, pp 390 ff.

Ant. 2: Let the souls of the saints sing praise to God, alleluia.
Lent. Ant. 2: Martyrs of the Lord, bless the Lord for ever.

Ant. 3: Choirs of martyrs, praise the Lord in the highest (alleluia).

OUTSIDE EASTERTIDE

Scripture Reading　　　*2 Cor 1:3-5*

Let us give thanks to the God and Father of our Lord Jesus Christ, the merciful Father, the God from whom all help comes: he helps us in all our troubles, so that we are able to help those who have all kinds of troubles, using the same help that we ourselves have received from God. Just as we have a share in Christ's many sufferings, so also through Christ we share in his great help.

Short Responsory

R̠ These were holy men: they will live for ever! *Repeat* R̠
V̠ The Lord himself is their reward. R̠ Glory be. R̠

Benedictus ant. Blessed are those who are persecuted in the cause of right: theirs is the kingdom of heaven.

Intercessions

Through the martyrs who were slain for God's word, let us give glory to our Saviour, the faithful and true witness. R̠ You redeemed us by your precious blood.

Through the martyrs, who bore witness to your love,—set us free to live for you. R̠

Through the martyrs, who proclaimed your saving death,—give us a deep and constant faith. R̠

Through the martyrs, who took up your cross,—grant us courage for every trial. R̠

Through the martyrs, washed in the blood of the Lamb,—give us grace to conquer our weakness. R̠

Our Father

1018

Concluding Prayer
If no proper prayer is given one of the following is said:

Almighty, ever-living God
you gave your martyrs N. and N.
grace to lay down their lives for Christ.
Help our weakness too:
give us the strength to live for you
even as they did not shrink from dying for your sake.
(We make our prayer) through our Lord.

Alternative
May the prayers of your martyrs N. and N.
prevail with you, Lord, on our behalf:
let them strengthen us in our witness to your truth.
(We make our prayer) through our Lord.

For Virgin Martyrs
May Saints N. and N. pray for us, Lord,
as we celebrate with joy their yearly feast:
their purity and strength of soul are precious gifts
which light us on our way.
(We make our prayer) through our Lord.

For Women Martyrs
Your power comes to its full strength, Lord, in our weakness:
grant to us who are celebrating the martyrdom of Saints N. and N.,
that as they obtained from you the power to conquer,
so they may obtain for us the grace of final victory.
(We make our prayer) through our Lord.

EASTERTIDE

Scripture Reading   *I Jn* 5:3-5
This is what loving God is—keeping his commandments; and his
commandments are not difficult, because anyone who has been
begotten by God has already overcome the world; this is the victory

over the world—our faith. Who can overcome the world? Only the man who believes that Jesus is the Son of God.

Short Responsory

℟ Everlasting joy shall be on their faces, alleluia, alleluia. *Repeat* ℟
℣ Joy and gladness will go with them. ℟ Glory be. ℟

Benedictus ant. Rejoice, all you saints, and be glad, for your reward is great in heaven, alleluia.

Intercessions

Through the martyrs who were slain for God's word, let us give glory to our Saviour, the faithful and true witness. ℟ You redeemed us by your precious blood.

Through the martyrs, who bore witness to your love,—set us free to live for you. ℟

Through the martyrs, who proclaimed your saving death,—give us a deep and constant faith. ℟

Through the martyrs, who took up your cross,—grant us courage for every trial. ℟

Through the martyrs, washed in the blood of the Lamb,—give us grace to conquer our weakness. ℟

Our Father

Concluding Prayer

If no proper prayer is given, one of the following is said:

Human weakness finds its anchor in you, Lord,
and our faith is built on you as on a rock:
give us a share in the passion and resurrection of Christ
through the prayers of your martyrs N. and N.,
so that we may come to joys that never fail.
(We make our prayer) through our Lord.

Alternative
Lord,
may our joy today be full
as we recall the martyrdom of N. and N.:

they sealed their faith with their life's blood,
fearlessly proclaiming the passion and resurrection of your
   Only-begotten Son,
who lives and reigns with you and the Holy Spirit,
God, for ever and ever.

For Virgin Martyrs: see p 1019.
For Women Martyrs: see p 1019.

EVENING PRAYER II

Hymn
In Lent, the hymn as at Morning Prayer is used, p 1017.

Our Lord the path of suffering trod,
And, since his blood for man has flowed,
'Tis meet that man should yield to God
The life he owes. Alleluia!

No shame to own the crucified!
Nay, 'tis our immortality
That we confess our God who died,
And for him die. Alleluia!

Beholding his predestined crown,
Into death's arms the martyr goes;
Dying, he conquers death; o'erthrown,
O'erthrows his foes. Alleluia!

Lord, make us your own soldiers true;
Grant us brave faith, a spirit pure;
That for your name, your cross in view,
We may endure. Alleluia!

PSALMODY

ANTIPHON I
Several Martyrs: The bodies of the saints have been buried in peace,
and their name lives on for all generations (alleluia).
One Martyr: If anyone wishes to be a follower of mine, he must deny
himself; he must take up his cross and come with me (alleluia).

PSALM 114(116)

I love the Lórd for hé has héard*
the crý of my appéal;
for he túrned his éar to mé*
in the dáy when I cálled him.

They surróunded me, the snáres of déath,†
with the ánguish of the tómb;*
they cáught me, sórrow and distréss.
⎧I cálled on the Lórd's name.*
⎩O Lórd my Gód, delíver me!

How grácious is the Lórd, and júst;*
our Gód has compássion.
The Lórd protécts the simple héarts;*
I was hélpless so he sáved me.

Turn báck, my sóul, to your rést*
for the Lórd has been góod;
he has képt my sóul from déath,†
my éyes from téars*
and my féet from stúmbling.

I will wálk in the présence of the Lórd*
in the lánd of the living.

Ant. Several Martyrs: The bodies of the saints have been buried in
peace, and their name lives on for all generations (alleluia).
One Martyr: If anyone wishes to be a follower of mine, he must deny
himself; he must take up his cross and come with me (alleluia).

ANTIPHON 2
Several Martyrs: I saw the souls of all who had been killed for
having witnessed to Jesus and for having preached God's word
(alleluia).
One Martyr: If anyone serves me, my Father will honour him
(alleluia).

I trústed, éven when I sáid:*
'I am sórely afflícted,'
and whén I sáid in my alárm:*
'No mán can be trústed.'

How cán I repáy the Lórd*
for his góodness to mé?
The cúp of salvátion I will ráise;*
I will cáll on the Lórd's name.

My vóws to the Lórd I will fulfíl*
befóre all his péople.
O précious in the éyes of the Lórd*
is the déath of his fáithful.

Your sérvant, Lord, your sérvant am Í;*
you have lóosened my bónds.
A thánksgiving sácrifice I máke:*
I will cáll on the Lórd's name.

My vóws to the Lórd I will fulfíl*
befóre all his péople,
in the cóurts of the hóuse of the Lórd,*
in your mídst, O Jerúsalem.

Ant. Several Martyrs: I saw the souls of all who had been killed for having witnessed to Jesus and for having preached God's word (alleluia).
One Martyr: If anyone serves me, my Father will honour him (alleluia).

ANTIPHON 3
Several Martyrs: These are the saints who bore witness to God by laying aside earthly life. They have washed their robes clean in the blood of the Lamb (alleluia).
One Martyr: If anyone denies himself for my sake, he will receive eternal life (alleluia).

CANTICLE: REV 4:11;5:9,10,12

Worthy are you, our Lord and God,*
to receive glory and honour and power,
for you created all things,*
and by your will they existed and were created.

Worthy are you, O Lord,*
to take the scroll and to open its seals,
for you were slain,†
and by your blood you ransomed men for God*
from every tribe and tongue and people and nation.

You have made us a kingdom and priests to our God,*
and we shall reign on earth.

Worthy is the Lamb who was slain,*
to receive power and wealth,
and wisdom and might,*
and honour and glory and blessing.

Ant. Several Martyrs: These are the saints who bore witness to God
by laying aside earthly life. They have washed their robes clean in the
blood of the Lamb (alleluia).

One Martyr: If anyone denies himself for my sake, he will receive
eternal life (alleluia).

OUTSIDE EASTERTIDE

Scripture Reading   *1 Pet 4:13-14*
My dear people, if you can have some share in the sufferings of
Christ, be glad, because you will enjoy a much greater gladness
when his glory is revealed. It is a blessing for you when they insult
you for bearing the name of Christ, because it means that you have
the Spirit of glory, the Spirit of God resting on you.

Short Responsory
Ry Rejoice in the Lord. Let the just shout for joy. *Repeat* Ry
Vy Let the upright sing praise. Ry Glory be. Ry

Magnificat ant. The saints, who followed in the footsteps of Christ, rejoice in heaven. They gave their life for love of Christ: therefore, they will reign with him for ever.

Intercessions

Let us give thanks to the king of martyrs, for this is the hour when he offered himself in the last supper and laid down his life on the cross. ℟ We praise you, Christ the Lord

We praise you, Christ our Saviour, example and strength of the martyrs, because you have loved us to the end;—we praise you, Christ the Lord.

Because you have promised repentant sinners the reward of eternal life,—we praise you, Christ the Lord.

Because you have called the Church to offer the blood of the new and eternal covenant, the blood shed for the remission of sins,— we praise you, Christ the Lord.

Because you have brought us to this day with the gift of faith intact, —we praise you, Christ the Lord.

Because of the many brothers who today have come to share in your saving death,—we praise you, Christ the Lord.

Our Father

The concluding prayer as at Morning Prayer, p 1019.

EASTERTIDE

Scripture Reading   *Rev 7:14-17*

These are the people who have come safely through the great persecution. They washed their robes and made them white with the blood of the Lamb. That is why they stand before God's throne and serve him day and night in his temple. He who sits on the throne will protect them with his presence. Never again will they hunger or thirst; neither sun nor any scorching heat will burn them; for the Lamb, who is in the centre of the throne, will be their shepherd, and guide them to springs of living water; and God will wipe away every tear from their eyes.

Short Responsory

℟ The virtuous will shine before God, alleluia, alleluia. *Repeat* ℟

℣ The pure of heart will rejoice. ℟ Glory be. ℟

Magnificat ant. Rejoice, you saints, before the Lamb; the kingdom was prepared for you from the beginning of the world, alleluia.

Intercessions
Let us give thanks to the king of martyrs, for this is the hour when he offered himself in the last supper and laid down his life on the cross. ℟ We praise you, Christ the Lord.
We praise you, Christ our saviour, example and strength of the martyrs, because you have loved us to the end;—we praise you, Christ the Lord.
Because you have promised repentant sinners the reward of eternal life,—we praise you, Christ the Lord.
Because you have called the Church to offer the blood of the new and eternal covenant, the blood shed for the remission of sins,—we praise you, Christ the Lord.
Because you have brought us to this day with the gift of faith intact, —we praise you, Christ the Lord.
Because of the many brothers who today have come to share in your saving death,—we praise you, Christ the Lord.
Our Father

The concluding prayer as at Morning Prayer, pp 1020 ff.

THE COMMON OF MARTYRS
ONE MARTYR

EVENING PRAYER I

Hymn as on p 1011
Psalms and canticle with antiphons for One Martyr, pp 1011 ff

OUTSIDE EASTERTIDE
Scripture Reading   *Rom 8:35,37-39*
Who will separate us from the love of Christ? Will affliction, or

distress, or persecution, or hunger, or nakedness, or peril, or the sword? Yet in all this we are conquerors, through him who has granted us his love. Of this I am fully persuaded; neither death nor life, no angels or principalities or powers, neither what is present nor what is to come, no force whatever, neither the height above us nor the depth beneath us, nor any other created thing, will be able to separate us from the love of God, which comes to us in Christ Jesus our Lord.

Short Responsory
For a man

℟ Lord, you have shown him honour. You have crowned him with glory. *Repeat* ℟
℣ You set him over the works of your hands. ℟ Glory be. ℟

For a woman

℟ The Lord chose her. He chose her before she was born. *Repeat* ℟
℣ He made her live in his own dwelling place. ℟ Glory be. ℟

Magnificat Antiphon
For a man

This saint fought unto death for the law of his God. He was not afraid of the words of evil men; for he was like a house that is founded on a rock.

For a woman

She set about her duty with courage and braced herself for the work; her lamp will never go out.

Intercessions

Let us give thanks to the king of martyrs, for this is the hour when he offered himself in the last supper and laid down his life on the cross. ℟ We praise you, Christ the Lord

We praise you, Christ our Saviour, example and strength of the martyrs, because you have loved us to the end;—we praise you, Christ the Lord.

Because you have promised repentant sinners the reward of eternal life,—we praise you, Christ the Lord.

Because you have called the Church to offer the blood of the new and eternal covenant, the blood shed for the remission of sins,—we praise you, Christ the Lord.

Because you have brought us to this day with the gift of faith intact, —we praise you, Christ the Lord.

Because of the many brothers who today have come to share in your saving death,—we praise you, Christ the Lord

Our Father

The concluding prayer as at Morning Prayer, p 1031.

EASTERTIDE

Scripture Reading   *Rev 3:10-12*

Because you have kept my order to be patient, I will also keep you safe from the time of trouble which is coming upon the whole world, to test all the people on earth. I am coming soon. Keep safe what you have, so that no one will rob you of your victory prize. I will make him who is victorious a pillar in the temple of my God, and he will never again leave it. I will write on him the name of my God, and the name of the city of my God, the new Jerusalem, which will come down out of heaven from my God. I will also write on him my new name.

Short Responsory

R̷ Let the saints rejoice in the Lord. Alleluia, alleluia. *Repeat* R̷
V̷ God has chosen you for his own. R̷ Glory be. R̷

Magnificat ant. Undying light will shine about your saints, Lord, they will live for ever, alleluia.

Intercessions

Let us give thanks to the king of martyrs, for this is the hour when he offered himself in the last supper and laid down his life on the cross. R̷ We praise you, Christ the Lord.

We praise you, Christ our Saviour, example and strength of the martyrs, because you have loved us to the end;—we praise you, Christ the Lord.

Because you have promised repentant sinners the reward of eternal life,—we praise you, Christ the Lord.

Because you have called the Church to offer the blood of the new and eternal covenant, the blood shed for the remission of sins,—we praise you, Christ the Lord.

Because you have brought us to this day with the gift of faith intact, —we praise you, Christ the Lord.

Because of the many brothers who today have come to share in your saving death,—we praise you, Christ the Lord.

Our Father

Concluding Prayer

If no proper prayer is given, one of those at Morning Prayer is said, p 1032.

INVITATORY

Ant. The Lord is the king of martyrs: come, let us adore him (alleluia).

MORNING PRAYER

Hymn

The martyrs living now with Christ
In suffering were tried,
Their anguish overcome by love,
When on his cross they died.

Across the centuries they come,
In constancy unmoved.
Their loving hearts make no complaint;
In silence they are proved.

No man has ever measured love,
Or weighed it in his hand,
But God who knows the inmost heart,
Gives them the promised land.

Praise Father, Son and Spirit blest
Who guide us through the night

In ways that reach beyond the stars
To everlasting light.

Ant. 1: Your love is better than life itself, my lips will recite your praise (alleluia).

Psalms and canticle of Sunday, Week 1, pp 390 ff.

Ant. 2: Martyrs of the Lord, bless the Lord for ever (alleluia).

Ant. 3: The one who proves victorious I will make into a pillar in my temple, says the Lord (alleluia).

OUTSIDE EASTERTIDE

Scripture Reading *2 Cor 1:3-5*
Let us give thanks to the God and Father of our Lord Jesus Christ, the merciful Father, the God from whom all help comes! He helps us in all our troubles, so that we are able to help those who have all kinds of troubles, using the same help that we ourselves have received from God. Just as we have a share in Christ's many sufferings, so also through Christ we share in his great help.

Short Responsory
R̷ The Lord is my strength. I will sing praise to him. *Repeat* R̷
Ẏ He is my salvation. R̷ Glory be. R̷

Benedictus ant. Anyone who hates his soul in this world will save it for the eternal life.

Intercessions
Through the martyrs who were slain for God's word, let us give glory to our Saviour, the faithful and true witness. R̷ You redeemed us by your precious blood.
Through the martyrs, who bore witness to your love,—set us free to live for you. R̷
Through the martyrs, who proclaimed your saving death,—give us a deep and constant faith. R̷
Through the martyrs, who took up your cross,—grant us courage for

every trial. ℟
Through the martyrs, washed in the blood of the Lamb,—give us
grace to conquer our weakness. ℟
Our Father

Concluding Prayer
If no proper prayer is given one of the following is said:

God of power and mercy,
you gave Saint N. grace to overcome the sufferings of martyrdom:
grant to us who celebrate his victory
that the power of your protecting hand
may keep us unshaken in the face of our ancient enemy
and all his hidden snares.
(We make our prayer) through our Lord.

Alternative
Almighty and everlasting God,
you gave Saint N.
grace to fight to the death for the true faith.
Let his prayer
enable us to endure every trial for love of you,
and to make all haste on our way to you,
in whom alone is life.
(We make our prayer) through our Lord.

For a Virgin Martyr
May Saint N. pray for us, Lord,
as we celebrate with joy her yearly feast:
her purity and strength of soul are precious gifts
which light us on our way.
(We make our prayer) through our Lord.

For a Woman Martyr
Your power comes to its full strength, Lord, in our weakness:
grant to us who are celebrating the martyrdom of Saint N.,
that as she obtained from you the power to conquer,
so she may obtain for us the grace of final victory.
(We make our prayer) through our Lord.

Scripture Reading *1 Jn 5:3-5*

This is what loving God is—keeping his commandments; and his commandments are not difficult, because anyone who has been begotten by God has already overcome the world; this is the victory over the world—our faith. Who can overcome the world? Only the man who believes that Jesus is the Son of God.

Short Responsory

R̸ Everlasting joy shall be on their faces, alleluia, alleluia. *Repeat* R̸
V̸ Joy and gladness will go with them. R̸ Glory be. R̸

Benedictus ant. Rejoice, all you saints, and be glad, for your reward is great in heaven, alleluia.

Intercessions

Through the martyrs who were slain for God's word, let us give glory to our Saviour, the faithful and true witness. R̸ You redeemed us by your precious blood.

Through the martyrs, who bore witness to your love,—set us free to live for you. R̸

Through the martyrs, who proclaimed your saving death,—give us a deep and constant faith. R̸

Through the martyrs, who took up your cross,—grant us courage for every trial. R̸

Through the martyrs, washed in the blood of the Lamb,—give us grace to conquer our weakness. R̸

Our Father

Concluding Prayer

If no proper prayer is given one of the following is said:

Lord God,
Saint N. imitated Christ in his suffering and death:
grant that as his martyrdom brings glory to your Church,
so we may follow in his footsteps and come to the joys that endure.
(We make our prayer) through our Lord.

Alternative
Proclaiming your glory, Lord.
we humbly ask
that as Saint N. imitated Christ in his passion,
so he may be a ready helper in our weakness.
(We make our prayer) through our Lord.

For a Virgin Martyr: As above, p 1031.
For a Woman Martyr: As above, p 1031.

EVENING PRAYER II

Hymn from p 1021.
Psalms and canticle with antiphons for One Martyr, pp 1021 ff.

OUTSIDE EASTERTIDE

Scripture Reading   *1 Pet 4:13-14*
My dear people, if you can have some share in the sufferings of
Christ, be glad, because you will enjoy a much greater gladness when
his glory is revealed. It is a blessing for you when they insult you for
bearing the name of Christ, because it means that you have the
Spirit of glory, the Spirit of God resting on you.

Short Responsory
R℣ You have tested us, God, and you have brought us out into
freedom again. *Repeat* R℣
℣ You have refined us like silver. R℣ Glory be. R℣

Magnificat ant. The saints will dwell in the kingdom of heaven; their
peace will last for ever.

Intercessions
Let us give thanks to the king of martyrs, for this is the hour when
he offered himself in the last supper and laid down his life on the
cross. R℣ We praise you, Christ the Lord.
We praise you, Christ our Saviour, example and strength of the

martyrs, because you have loved us to the end;—we praise you, Christ the Lord.

Because you have promised repentant sinners the reward of eternal life,—we praise you, Christ the Lord.

Because you have called the Church to offer the blood of the new and eternal covenant, the blood shed for the remission of sins,—we praise you, Christ the Lord.

Because you have brought us to this day with the gift of faith intact, —we praise you, Christ the Lord.

Because of the many brothers who today have come to share in your saving death,—we praise you, Christ the Lord.

The concluding prayer as at Morning Prayer, p 1031.

EASTERTIDE

Scripture Reading   *Rev 7:14-17*

These are the people who have come safely through the great persecution. They washed their robes and made them white with the blood of the Lamb. That is why they stand before God's throne and serve him day and night in his temple. He who sits on the throne will protect them with his presence. Never again will they hunger or thirst; neither sun nor any scorching heat will burn them; for the Lamb, who is in the centre of the throne, will be their shepherd, and guide them to springs of living water; and God will wipe away every tear from their eyes.

Short Responsory

R̷ The virtuous will shine before God, alleluia, alleluia. *Repeat* R̷
V̷ The pure of heart will rejoice. R̷ Glory be. R̷

Magnificat ant. Unless the wheat grain falls on the earth and dies, it remains itself alone; but if it dies it yields much fruit, alleluia.

Intercessions

Let us give thanks to the king of martyrs, for this is the hour when he offered himself in the last supper and laid down his life on the cross. R̷ We praise you, Christ the Lord.

We praise you, Christ our Saviour, example and strength of the martyrs, because you have loved us to the end;—we praise you, Christ the Lord.

Because you have promised repentant sinners the reward of eternal life,—we praise you, Christ the Lord.

Because you have called the Church to offer the blood of the new and eternal covenant, the blood shed for the remission of sins,—we praise you, Christ the Lord.

Because you have brought us to this day with the gift of faith intact, —we praise you, Christ the Lord.

Because of the many brothers who today have come to share in your saving death,—we praise you, Christ the Lord.

Our Father

The concluding prayer as at Morning Prayer, p 1032.

THE COMMON OF PASTORS

EVENING PRAYER I

Hymn
During Lent, the hymn as at Morning Prayer is used, p 1040.

Who are these, like stars appearing,
These before God's throne who stand?
Each a golden crown is wearing;
Who are all this glorious band?
Alleluia, hark! they sing,
Praising loud their heav'nly King.

These are they who have contended
For their Saviour's honour long,
Wrestling on till life was ended,
Following not the sinful throng;
These, who well the fight sustained,
Triumph through the Lamb have gained.

These your priests have watched and waited,
Offering up to Christ their will,
Soul and body consecrated,

1035

Day and night to serve him still:
Now, in God's most holy place
Blest they stand before his face.

PSALMODY

ANTIPHON I
Pastors: I will give you shepherds after my own heart, and these
shall feed you on knowledge and true doctrine (alleluia).
Men Saints: Sing praise to our God, all his saints (alleluia).

PSALM 112(113)

Práise, O sérvants of the Lórd,*
práise the náme of the Lórd!
May the náme of the Lórd be bléssed*
both nów and for evermóre!
From the rísing of the sún to its sétting*
práised be the náme of the Lórd!

Hígh above all nátions is the Lórd,*
abóve the héavens his glóry.
Whó is like the Lórd, our Gód,*
who has rísen on hígh to his thróne
yet stóops from the héights to look dówn,*
to look dówn upon héaven and éarth?

From the dúst he lífts up the lówly,*
from his mísery he ráises the póor
to sét him in the cómpany of prínces,*
yés, with the prínces of his péople.
To the chíldless wífe he gives a hóme*
and gláddens her héart with chíldren.

Ant. Pastors: I will give you shepherds after my own heart, and these
shall feed you on knowledge and true doctrine (alleluia).
Men Saints: Sing praise to our God, all his saints (alleluia).

ANTIPHON 2
Pastors: I will feed my sheep; I will look for the lost one, bring back the stray (alleluia).
Men Saints: Blessed are those who hunger and thirst for what is right: they shall be satisfied (alleluia).

PSALM 145(146)

My sóul, give práise to the Lórd;†
I will práise the Lórd all my dáys,*
make músic to my Gód while I líve.

Pút no trúst in prínces,*
in mortal mén in whóm there is no hélp.
Take their bréath, they retúrn to cláy*
and their pláns that dáy come to nóthing.

He is háppy who is hélped by Jacob's Gód,*
whose hópe is in the Lórd his Gód,
who alóne made héaven and éarth,*
the séas and áll they contáin.

It is hé who keeps fáith for éver,*
who is júst to thóse who are oppréssed.
It is hé who gives bréad to the húngry,*
the Lórd, who sets prísoners frée,

the Lórd who gives síght to the blínd,*
who ráises up thóse who are bowed dówn,
the Lórd, who protécts the stránger*
and uphólds the wídow and órphan.

It is the Lórd who lóves the júst*
but thwárts the páth of the wícked.
The Lórd will réign for éver,*
Sion's Gód, from áge to áge.

Ant. Pastors: I will feed my sheep; I will look for the lost one, bring back the stray (alleluia).
Men Saints: Blessed are those who hunger and thirst for what is right; they shall be satisfied (alleluia).

ANTIPHON 3

Pastors: The good shepherd is one who lays down his life for his sheep (alleluia).

Men Saints: Blessed be God who chose us to be holy and spotless and live in love (alleluia).

CANTICLE: EPH I :3-10

Blessed be the God and Father*
of our Lord Jesus Christ,
who has blessed us in Christ*
with every spiritual blessing in the heavenly places.

He chose us in him*
before the foundation of the world,
that we should be holy*
and blameless before him.

He destined us in love*
to be his sons through Jesus Christ,
according to the purpose of his will,†
to the praise of his glorious grace*
which he freely bestowed on us in the Beloved.

In him we have redemption through his blood,*
the forgiveness of our trespasses,
according to the riches of his grace*
which he lavished upon us.

He has made known to us†
in all wisdom and insight*
the mystery of his will,
according to his purpose*
which he set forth in Christ.

His purpose he set forth in Christ,*
as a plan for the fulness of time,
to unite all things in him,*
things in heaven and things on earth.

Ant. Pastors: The good shepherd is one who lays down his life for

his sheep (alleluia).
Men Saints: Blessed be God who chose us to be holy and spotless and live in love (alleluia).

Scripture Reading   *1 Pet 5:1-4*

Now I have something to tell your elders: I am an elder myself, and a witness to the sufferings of Christ, and with you I have a share in the glory that is to be revealed. Be the shepherds of the flock of God that is entrusted to you; watch over it, not simply as a duty but gladly, because God wants it; not for sordid money, but because you are eager to do it. Never be a dictator over any group that is put in your charge, but be an example that the whole flock can follow. When the chief shepherd appears, you will be given the crown of unfading glory.

Short Responsory
Outside Eastertide
R̷ Priests of the Lord, bless the Lord. *Repeat* R̷
V̷ You holy and humble of heart, praise God. R̷ Glory be. R̷

Eastertide
R̷ Priests of the Lord, bless the Lord, alleluia, alleluia. *Repeat* R̷
V̷ You holy and humble of heart, praise God. R̷ Glory be. R̷

Magnificat Antiphon
For a Pope or a Bishop: Priest of the Most High and mirror of all that is good in man; you were a good shepherd of the people who pleased the Lord (alleluia).
For a Priest: I made myself all things to all men in order to save them all (alleluia).

Intercessions
Let us pray to Christ, the high priest, who was appointed to represent men in their relations with God. R̷ Lord, save your people.
Lord Jesus, in times past you have lighted the way for your people through wise and holy leaders;—may Christians always enjoy this sign of your loving kindness. R̷
You forgave the sins of your people when holy pastors prayed;—

continually cleanse your Church through their powerful intercession.
R7 Lord, save your people.

In the presence of their brothers, you anointed your holy ones and
poured on them your Spirit;—fill with your Holy Spirit all the leaders
of your people. R7

Nothing could ever separate the holy pastors from your love;—do
not lose even one of those whom you redeemed by your passion. R7

Through the pastors of your Church you give your sheep eternal life,
and no one can steal them from you;—save the faithful departed,
for whom you laid down your life. R7

Our Father

Concluding Prayer

*If no proper prayer is given one of those at Morning Prayer is said,
p 1042.*

INVITATORY

Ant. Christ is the chief shepherd, the leader of his flock; come, let us
adore him (alleluia).

MORNING PRAYER

Hymn

 The saints who toiled from place to place,
 Spreading the Gospel of God's grace,
 Now in their heavenly homeland dwell
 With Christ, whom here they served so well.

 Alert at thy command to go,
 And everywhere thy word to sow,
 They went, O Master, far and wide,
 Eager, but yet unsatisfied.

 Thine was the task they took in hand,
 Thine their good news for every land,
 Thine was their power, and thine again
 Their passion for the souls of men.

Ant. 1: You are the light of the world. A city built on a hill-top
cannot be hidden (alleluia).

Psalms and canticle of Sunday, Week 1, pp 390 ff.

Ant. 2: Your light must shine in the sight of men, so that, seeing your good works, they may give the praise to your Father in heaven (alleluia).

Ant. 3: The word of God is alive and active; it cuts more finely than any double-edged sword (alleluia).

Scripture Reading   *Heb 13:7-9a*
Remember your leaders, who preached the word of God to you, and as you reflect on the outcome of their lives, imitate their faith. Jesus Christ is the same today as he was yesterday and as he will be for ever. Do not let yourselves be led astray by all sorts of strange doctrines.

Short Responsory
Outside Eastertide
R̥ I placed watchmen on your towers, Jerusalem. *Repeat* R̥
V̥ They will never cease to tell of the name of the Lord, by day and by night. R̥ Glory be. R̥

Eastertide
R̥ I placed watchmen on your towers, Jerusalem, alleluia, alleluia. *Repeat* R̥
V̥ They will never cease to tell of the name of the Lord, by day and by night. R̥ Glory be. R̥

Benedictus ant. It is not you who speak: the Spirit of your Father speaks in you (alleluia).

Intercessions
Christ, the good shepherd, laid down his life for his sheep. Let us praise him with grateful hearts, as we pray: R̥ Lord, nourish the lives of your people.
Christ our Lord, in the holy pastors you reveal your love for us;—
may we never be deprived of the care you show through them. R̥
Through your sacred ministers you are present in our midst as the shepherd of our souls;—never cease to guide us through their

teaching and encouragement. R︎℣ Lord, nourish the lives of your people.

In the saints who lead your people, you manifest your power of healing souls and bodies;—remain always with us to renew our lives in holiness. R︎℣

By the example of the saints you instruct your faithful in the ways of wisdom and love;—through our pastors help us to grow to the full stature of perfection. R︎℣

Our Father

Concluding Prayer
If no proper prayer is given one of the following is said:

For a Pope
Almighty, ever-living God,
by whose choice blessed N. was placed over your whole people
and served them by word and example,
at his intercession protect the pastors of your Church
together with the flocks committed to their care
and lead them on the way to salvation.
(We make our prayer) through our Lord.

For a Bishop
Lord God,
who made blessed N. a bishop in your Church,
eminent for his ardent love and that faith which overcomes the world,
at his intercession grant that we ourselves,
persevering in faith and love,
may join him in your glory.
(We make our prayer) through our Lord.

For the Founder of a Church
Lord God,
who called our forefathers to the admirable light of the gospel
    through the preaching of blessed N.,
grant that by his intercession
we may grow in grace and in the knowledge of our Lord Jesus Christ
    your Son,
who lives and reigns with you and the Holy Spirit,
God, for ever and ever.

For a Pastor
Lord God,
light of the faithful and shepherd of souls,
who gave blessed N. to your Church to feed your flock by his
    teaching and form them by his example,
grant that by his intercession
we may keep the faith which he taught
and follow in the way he walked.
(We make our prayer) through our Lord.

Alternative
Lord God,
who bestowed your spirit of truth and of love in full measure
on blessed N. as pastor of your people,
grant that we who are celebrating his feast
may be supported by his prayer
and grow in perfection as we follow his example.
(We make our prayer) through our Lord.

For a Missionary
Lord God,
by whose surpassing mercy blessed N. made known the
    unfathomable riches of Christ,
grant, at his intercession,
that we may grow in knowledge of you,
yield fruit in every good work,
and by the truth of the gospel
live faithfully in your presence.
(We make our prayer) through our Lord.

EVENING PRAYER II

Hymn
During Lent, the hymn as at Morning Prayer is used, p 1040.

Who are these, like stars appearing,
These before God's throne who stand?
Each a golden crown is wearing;

Who are all this glorious band?
Alleluia, hark! they sing,
Praising loud their heav'nly King.

These are they who have contended
For their Saviour's honour long,
Wrestling on till life was ended,
Following not the sinful throng;
These, who well the fight sustained,
Triumph through the Lamb have gained.

These your priests have watched and waited,
Offering up to Christ their will,
Soul and body consecrated,
Day and night to serve him still:
Now, in God's most holy place
Blest they stand before his face.

PSALMODY

ANTIPHON I
Pastors: I have become a minister of the gospel according to the
bountiful gift of God (alleluia).
Men Saints: This man was found to be blameless and faithful;
eternal glory will be his (alleluia).

PSALM 14(15)

Lord, whó shall be admítted to your tént*
and dwéll on your hóly móuntain?

Hé who wálks without fáult;*
hé who ácts with jústice
and spéaks the trúth from his héart;*
hé who does not slánder with his tóngue;

hé who does no wróng to his bróther,*
who cásts no slúr on his néighbour,
who hólds the gódless in disdáin,*
but hónours those who féar the Lórd;

hé who keeps his plédge, come what máy;†
who tákes no ínterest on a lóan*

and accépts no bríbes against the ínnocent.
Such a mán will stand fírm for éver.

Ant. Pastors: I have become a minister of the gospel according to the bountiful gift of God (alleluia).
Men Saints: This man was found to be blameless and faithful; eternal glory will be his (alleluia).

ANTIPHON 2

Pastors: This is the wise and faithful servant whom the Master placed in charge of his household (alleluia).
Men Saints: Grace and mercy await the chosen ones of God; he comes to the help of his holy people (alleluia).

PSALM 111(112)

Happy the mán who féars the Lórd,*
who tákes delíght in all his commánds.
His sóns will be pówerful on éarth;*
the chíldren of the úpright are bléssed.

Ríches and wéalth are in his hóuse;*
his jústice stands fírm for éver.
He is a líght in the dárkness for the úpright:*
he is génerous, mérciful and júst.

The góod man takes píty and lénds,*
he condúcts his affáirs with hónour.
The júst man will néver wáver:*
hé will be remémbered for éver.

He has no féar of évil néws;*
with a fírm heart he trústs in the Lórd.
With a stéadfast héart he will not féar;*
he will sée the dównfall of his fóes.

Open-hánded, he gíves to the póor;†
his jústice stands fírm for éver.*
His héad will be ráised in glóry.

The wícked man sées and is ángry,†
grinds his téeth and fádes awáy;*
the desíre of the wícked leads to dóom.   (Glory be)

Ant. Pastors: This is the wise and faithful servant whom the Master placed in charge of his household (alleluia).
Men Saints: Grace and mercy await the chosen ones of God; he comes to the help of his holy people (alleluia).

ANTIPHON 3
Pastors: The sheep that belong to me listen to my voice; there will be only one flock and one shepherd (alleluia).
Men Saints: The saints will sing a new song before the throne of God and of the Lamb; their voices will fill the whole world (alleluia).

CANTICLE: REV 15:3-4

Great and wonderful are your deeds,*
O Lord God the Almighty!
Just and true are your ways,*
O King of the ages!

Who shall not fear and glorify your name, O Lord?*
For you alone are holy.
All nations shall come and worship you,*
for your judgments have been revealed.

Ant. Pastors: The sheep that belong to me listen to my voice; there will be only one flock and one shepherd (alleluia).
Men Saints: The saints will sing a new song before the throne of God and of the Lamb; their voices will fill the whole world (alleluia).

Scripture Reading   *1 Pet 5:1-4*
Now I have something to tell your elders: I am an elder myself, and a witness to the sufferings of Christ, and with you I have a share in the glory that is to be revealed. Be the shepherds of the flock of God that is entrusted to you; watch over it, not simply as a duty but gladly, because God wants it; not for sordid money, but because you are eager to do it. Never be a dictator over any group that is put in your charge, but be an example that the whole flock can follow. When the chief shepherd appears, you will be given the crown of unfading glory.

Short Responsory
Outside Eastertide
R̷ This is a man who loves his brothers and intercedes for the people.

Repeat R̰
V̰ He laid down his life for his brothers. R̰ Glory be. R̰

Eastertide
R̰ This is a man who loves his brothers and intercedes for the people, alleluia, alleluia. *Repeat* R̰
V̰ He laid down his life for his brothers. R̰ Glory be. R̰

Magnificat ant. This is the faithful and wise steward whom the Master placed over his household to give them their measure of food at the proper time (alleluia).

Alternative
I thank you, Christ, for honouring me by leading me to this glory. You are the good shepherd; I pray that the sheep which you have placed in my charge will share with me in your glory for ever (alleluia).

Intercessions
Let us pray to Christ, the high priest, who was appointed to represent men in their relations with God. R̰ Lord, save your people.
Lord Jesus, in times past you have lighted the way for your people through wise and holy leaders;—may Christians always enjoy this sign of your loving kindness. R̰
You forgave the sins of your people when holy pastors prayed;—continually cleanse your Church through their powerful intercession. R̰
In the presence of their brothers, you anointed your holy ones and poured on them your Spirit;—fill with your Holy Spirit all the leaders of your people. R̰
Nothing could ever separate the holy pastors from your love;—do not lose even one of those whom you redeemed by your passion. R̰
Through the pastors of your Church you give your sheep eternal life, and no one can steal them from you;—save the faithful departed, for whom you laid down your life. R̰
Our Father

The concluding prayer as at Morning Prayer, p 1042.

THE COMMON OF DOCTORS
OF THE CHURCH

EVENING PRAYER I

Hymn from the Common of Pastors, Evening Prayer I, p 1035.
Psalms and canticle, with antiphons, from the Common of Pastors,
p 1036.

Scripture Reading   *Jas 3:17-18*
The wisdom which comes from above is marked chiefly indeed by its
purity, but also by its peacefulness; it is courteous and ready to be
convinced, always taking the better part; it carries mercy with it,
and a harvest of all that is good; it is uncensorious and without
affectation. Peace is the seed-ground of holiness, and those who make
peace will win its harvest.

Short Responsory
Outside Eastertide
R⁄ The mouth of the good man utters wisdom. *Repeat* R⁄
V⁄ His lips speak what is right. R⁄ Glory be. R⁄

Eastertide
R⁄ The mouth of the good man utters wisdom, alleluia, alleluia.
Repeat R⁄
V⁄ His lips speak what is right. R⁄ Glory be. R⁄

Magnificat ant. The man who keeps the commandments and teaches
them will be considered great in the kingdom of heaven (alleluia).

Intercessions
Let us pray to Christ, the high priest, who was appointed to represent men in their relations with God. R⁄ Lord, save your people.
Lord Jesus, in times past you have lighted the way for your people
through wise and holy leaders;—may Christians always enjoy this
sign of your loving kindness. R⁄
You forgave the sins of your people when holy pastors prayed;—

continually cleanse your Church through their powerful intercession.
R7
In the presence of their brothers, you anointed your holy ones and
poured on them your Spirit;—fill with your Holy Spirit all the
leaders of your people. R7
Nothing could ever separate the holy pastors from your love;—do
not lose even one of those whom you redeemed by your passion. R7
Through the pastors of your Church you give your sheep eternal
life, and no one can steal them from you;—save the faithful departed, for whom you laid down your life. R7
Our Father

The concluding prayer as at Morning Prayer, p 1051.

INVITATORY

Ant. The Lord is the source of all wisdom: come, let us adore him
(alleluia).

MORNING PRAYER

Hymn

The saints who toiled from place to place,
Spreading the Gospel of God's grace,
Now in their heavenly homeland dwell
With Christ, whom here they served so well.

Alert at thy command to go,
And everywhere thy word to sow,
They went, O Master, far and wide,
Eager, but yet unsatisfied.

Thine was the task they took in hand,
Thine their good news for every land,
Thine was their power, and thine again
Their passion for the souls of men.

Ant. 1: You are the light of the world. A city built on a hill-top
cannot be hidden (alleluia).

Psalms and canticle of Sunday, Week 1, pp 390 ff.

Ant. 2: Your light must shine in the sight of men, so that, seeing your good works, they may give the praise to your Father in heaven (alleluia).

Ant. 3: The word of God is alive and active; it cuts more finely than any double-edged sword (alleluia).

Scripture Reading *Wis 7:13-14*
What I learned without self-interest, I pass on without reserve; I do not intend to hide wisdom's riches. For she is an inexhaustible treasure to men, and those who acquire it win God's friendship, commended as they are to him by the benefits of her teaching.

Short Responsory
Outside Eastertide
R⁷ The people tell about the wisdom of the saints. *Repeat* R⁷
℣ The Church sings their praises. R⁷ Glory be. R⁷

Eastertide
R⁷ The people tell about the wisdom of the saints, alleluia, alleluia. *Repeat* R⁷
℣ The Church sings their praises. R⁷ Glory be. R⁷

Benedictus ant. The learned will shine as brightly as the vault of heaven, and those who have instructed many in virtue will shine like stars for all eternity (alleluia).

Intercessions
Christ, the good shepherd, laid down his life for his sheep. Let us praise him with grateful hearts, as we pray: R⁷ Lord, nourish the lives of your people.
Christ our Lord, in the holy pastors you reveal your love for us;
—may we never be deprived of the care you show through them. R⁷
Through your sacred ministers you are present in our midst as the shepherd of our souls;—never cease to guide us through their

teaching and encouragement. ℟
In the saints who lead your people, you manifest your power of
healing souls and bodies;—remain always with us to renew our lives
in holiness. ℟
By the example of the saints you instruct your faithful in the ways
of wisdom and love;—through our pastors help us to grow to the
full stature of perfection. ℟
Our Father

Concluding Prayer
If no proper prayer is given the following is said:

Lord God,
who enlightened blessed N. with your heavenly truth,
give us grace, at his intercession,
to maintain that same doctrine faithfully,
and to show it forth in the conduct of our lives.
(We make our prayer) through our Lord.

EVENING PRAYER II

Hymn from the Common of Pastors, p 1043.
Psalms and canticle, with antiphons, from the Common of Pastors,
p 1044.

Scripture Reading   *Jas 3:17-18*
The wisdom which comes from above is marked chiefly indeed by its
purity, but also by its peacefulness; it is courteous and ready to be
convinced, always taking the better part; it carries mercy with it,
and a harvest of all that is good; it is uncensorious and without
affectation. Peace is the seed-ground of holiness, and those who make
peace will win its harvest.

Short Responsory
Outside Eastertide
℟ This man became a teacher in the Church of God. *Repeat* ℟
℣ The Lord filled him with the spirit of wisdom and understanding.
℟ Glory be. ℟

Eastertide

R℣ This man became a teacher in the Church of God, alleluia, alleluia. *Repeat* R℣

℣ The Lord filled him with the spirit of wisdom and understanding. R℣ Glory be. R℣

Magnificat ant. O holy doctor, Saint N., light of the Church, lover of the law of God, pray for us to the Son of God (alleluia).

Intercessions

Let us pray to Christ, the high priest, who was appointed to represent men in their relations with God. R℣ Lord, save your people.

Lord Jesus, in times past you have lighted the way for your people through wise and holy leaders;—may Christians always enjoy this sign of your loving kindness. R℣

You forgave the sins of your people when holy pastors prayed; —continually cleanse your Church through their powerful intercession. R℣

In the presence of their brothers, you anointed your holy ones and poured on them your Spirit;—fill with your Holy Spirit all the leaders of your people. R℣

Nothing could ever separate the holy pastors from your love;—do not lose even one of those whom you redeemed by your passion. R℣

Through the pastors of your Church you give your sheep eternal life, and no one can steal them from you;—save the faithful departed, for whom you laid down your life. R℣

Our Father

The concluding prayer as at Morning Prayer, p 1051.

THE COMMON OF VIRGINS

EVENING PRAYER I

Hymn
Alternative hymn, appendix, no. 55.

For all thy saints, O Lord,
Who strove in thee to live,
Who followed thee, obeyed, adored,
Our grateful hymn receive.

They all in life and death,
With thee their Lord in view,
Learned from thy Holy Spirit's breath
To suffer and to do.

For this thy name we bless,
And humbly beg that we
May follow them in holiness,
And live and die in thee.

PSALMODY

ANTIPHON I
Virgins: Come, daughters, look to the Lord and you will shine with glory (alleluia).
Women Saints: Blessed be the name of the Lord; he has shown his love to his servant (alleluia).

PSALM 112(113)

Práise, O sérvants of the Lórd,*
práise the náme of the Lórd!
May the náme of the Lórd be bléssed*
both nów and for évermóre!
From the rísing of the sún to its sétting*
práised be the náme of the Lórd!

Hígh above all nátions is the Lórd,*
abóve the héavens his glóry.

1053

Whó is like the Lórd, our Gód,*
who has rísen on hígh to his thróne.
yet stóops from the héights to look dówn,*
to look dówn upon héaven and éarth?

From the dúst he lífts up the lówly,*
from his mísery he ráises the póor
to sét him in the cómpany of prínces,*
yés, with the prínces of his péople.
To the chíldless wífe he gives a hóme*
and gláddens her héart with chíldren.

Ant. Virgins: Come, daughters, look to the Lord and you will shine
with glory (alleluia).
Women Saints: Blessed be the name of the Lord; he has shown his
love to his servant (alleluia).

ANTIPHON 2
Virgins: We follow you with all our heart, Lord, we seek your
presence; do not disappoint us (alleluia).
Women Saints: Praise the Lord, Jerusalem; he has blessed your
children within your walls (alleluia).

PSALM 147

O práise the Lórd, Jerúsalem!*
Síon, práise your Gód!

He has stréngthened the bárs of your gátes,*
he has bléssed the chíldren withín you.
He estáblished péace on your bórders,*
he féeds you with fínest whéat.

He sénds out his wórd to the éarth*
and swíftly rúns his commánd.
He shówers down snów white as wóol,*
he scátters hóar-frost like áshes.

He húrls down háilstones like crúmbs.*
The wáters are frózen at his tóuch;
he sénds forth his wórd and it mélts them:*
at the bréath of his móuth the waters flów.

He mákes his wórd known to Jácob,*
to Ísrael his laws and decrées.
He has not déalt thus with óther nátions;*
he has not táught them hís decrées.

Ant. Virgins: We follow you with all our heart, Lord, we seek your presence; do not disappoint us (alleluia).
Women Saints: Praise the Lord, Jerusalem; he has blessed your children within your walls (alleluia).

ANTIPHON 3
Virgins: Rejoice, virgins of Christ; the Lord himself will be your spouse for ever (alleluia).
Women Saints: The Lord has taken delight in you; your God rejoices over you (alleluia).

CANTICLE: EPH 1:3-10

Blessed be the God and Father*
of our Lord Jesus Christ,
who has blessed us in Christ*
with every spiritual blessing in the heavenly places.

He chose us in him*
before the foundation of the world,
that we should be holy*
and blameless before him.

He destined us in love*
to be his sons through Jesus Christ,
according to the purpose of his will,†
to the praise of his glorious grace*
which he freely bestowed on us in the Beloved.

In him we have redemption through his blood,*
the forgiveness of our trespasses,
according to the riches of his grace*
which he lavished upon us.

He has made known to us†
in all wisdom and insight*

1055

the mystery of his will,
according to his purpose*
which he set forth in Christ.

His purpose he set forth in Christ,*
as a plan for the fulness of time,
to unite all things in him,*
things in heaven and things on earth.

Ant. Virgins: Rejoice, virgins of Christ; the Lord himself will be
your spouse for ever (alleluia).
Women Saints: The Lord has taken delight in you; your God
rejoices over you (alleluia).

Scripture Reading   *1 Cor 7:32,34*
He who is unmarried is concerned with God's claim, asking how he
is to please God; a woman who is free of wedlock, or a virgin, is
concerned with the Lord's claim, intent on holiness, bodily and
spiritual.

Short Responsory
Outside Eastertide
R︣ My portion is the Lord, says my soul. *Repeat* R︣
V︣ The Lord is good to those who trust him. R︣ Glory be. R︣

Eastertide
R︣ My portion is the Lord, says my soul, alleluia, alleluia. *Repeat* R︣
V︣ The Lord is good to those who trust him. R︣ Glory be. R︣

Magnificat Antiphon
For a Virgin Martyr: See, how the virgin follows unhesitatingly in the
path of the Lamb who was crucified for us; she is a pure oblation, a
chaste victim (alleluia).

For one Virgin: The bridegroom came and the wise virgin who was
ready went in with him to the marriage feast (alleluia).

For several Virgins: Prepare your lamps, you wise virgins: the
bridegroom is here! Go out and meet him (alleluia).

Intercessions

Christ the Lord praised those who follow the way of virginity for the sake of the kingdom of heaven. Let us proclaim his love and pray:

R⁷ Jesus, king of virgins, hear us.

Christ our Lord, you presented the Church to yourself, as a chaste virgin to her only husband;—make her pure, holy and faultless. R⁷

Christ Jesus, the holy virgins went to meet you with lamps burning bright;—keep alive the flame of fidelity in the hearts of religious. women. R⁷

Lord, you have always preserved your Church in purity and soundness of faith;—grant to all Christians a faith that is true and complete. R⁷

You bring joy to the lives of your faithful as they celebrate the feast of your holy virgin N.;—may they also rejoice in her constant intercession. R⁷

You have welcomed your holy virgins to the wedding feast of heaven;—invite all the dead to the feast of eternal life. R⁷

Our Father

Concluding Prayer

*If no proper prayer is given one of those at Morning Prayer is said,
p 1059.*

INVITATORY

Ant. The Lord is the king of virgins: come, let us adore him (alleluia)

Alternative

Virgins follow the Lamb wherever he goes; come, let us adore him (alleluia).

MORNING PRAYER

Hymn
Alternative hymn, appendix, no. 55.

God's blessèd Spirit moved his virgin saint
To wield strong weapons in a life-long fight,
To make a lonely journey from the flesh,
That she might live unfettered in his sight.

She turned her face towards the cross of Christ,
And he himself prepared her as his bride;
She bore the Holy Spirit's timeless fruits
By which God's pledge of love is ratified.

Her life showed forth the kingdom of the Lord,
When humbly, for his sake, she dwelt apart,
To wait on him in silence with the poor,
The chaste of body and the clean of heart.

O blessèd Trinity, the virgins' crown,
They sing your praises with unending song,
Rejoicing in the hope you have fulfilled,
Lord God, unfailing strength of all the strong.

Ant. 1: I will bear witness to Christ; it is Christ that I seek; with Christ I desire to be united (alleluia).

Psalms and canticle of Sunday, Week 1, pp 390 ff.

Ant. 2: Virgins, bless the Lord; he who planted his wisdom in you now crowns the fruit that you have borne (alleluia).

Ant. 3: The saints will rejoice in glory; their victory shines forth in their bodies (alleluia).

Scripture Reading   *Song 8:7*
Love is a fire no waters avail to quench, no floods to drown; for love, a man will give up all that he has in the world, and think nothing of his loss.

Short Responsory
Outside Eastertide
R̸ My heart has said of you: I have sought your presence, Lord.
Repeat R̸
V̸ It is your face that I will continue to seek. R̸ Glory be. R̸

Eastertide
℟ My heart has said of you, I have sought your presence, Lord, alleluia, alleluia. *Repeat* ℟
℣ It is your face that I will continue to seek. ℟ Glory be. ℟

Benedictus Antiphon
For a Virgin Martyr: Blessed is the virgin who denied herself and took up her cross; she has imitated the Lord; he is the spouse of virgins, the prince of martyrs (alleluia).

For one Virgin: See, the wise virgin has gone to Christ: she shines among the choirs of virgins like the sun in the heavens (alleluia).

For several Virgins: Virgins of the Lord, bless the Lord for ever (alleluia).

Intercessions
With great joy let us praise Christ, the bridegroom of all virgins.
℟ Jesus, crown of virgins, hear us.
Lord Jesus, the holy virgins loved you as their only spouse;—may we never be separated from you. ℟
You crowned your mother Mary as queen of all virgins;—by her prayers grant that we may serve you in purity of life. ℟
The holy virgins followed you with undivided hearts;—do not allow us to be fascinated by this passing world and drawn away from you. ℟
Lord Jesus, you are the bridegroom that the wise virgins were ready to meet;—let us watch for your coming with longing and hope. ℟
May Saint N., who reigns in your kingdom, intercede for us;—through her prayers grant us wisdom and innocence of life. ℟
Our Father

Concluding Prayer
If no proper prayer is given one of the following is said:

To those who love you, Lord,
you promise to come with your Son
and make your home within them.
Come then with your purifying grace,

and, at the intercession of Saint N. your virgin,
make our hearts a place where you can dwell.
(We make our prayer) through our Lord.

Alternative
Accept our prayer, Lord,
as we recall the life and virtues of blessed N.:
grant that we may abide in your love
and continually grow in it
to the end of our days.
(We make our prayer) through our Lord.

For several Virgins
Enfold us yet more in your love and mercy, Lord:
and even as we rejoice on this feast of the virgins N. and N.
so may we, through the gift of your grace, live in their company
    forever.
(We make our prayer) through our Lord.

EVENING PRAYER II

Hymn as at Evening Prayer I, p 1053.
Alternative hymn, appendix, no. 55.

PSALMODY

ANTIPHON I
Virgins: I will keep myself chaste for you. I will meet you, the
bridegroom, carrying a brightly shining lamp (alleluia).
Women Saints: Lord, your servant rejoices, because you have saved
her (alleluia).

PSALM 121(122)

I rejóiced when I héard them sáy:*
'Let us gó to God's hóuse.'
And nów our féet are stánding*
within your gátes, O Jerúsalem.

Jerúsalem is buílt as a cíty*
stróngly compáct.
It is thére that the tríbes go úp,*
the tríbes of the Lórd.

For Ísrael's láw it ís,*
there to práise the Lord's náme.
Thére were set the thrónes of júdgment*
of the hóuse of Dávid.

For the péace of Jerúsalem práy:*
'Péace be to your hómes!
May péace réign in your wálls,*
in your pálaces, péace!'

For lóve of my bréthren and fríends*
I say: 'Péace upon yóu!'
For lóve of the hóuse of the Lórd*
I will ásk for your góod.

Ant. Virgins: I will keep myself chaste for you. I will meet you, the
bridegroom, carrying a brightly shining lamp (alleluia).
Women Saints: Lord, your servant rejoices, because you have saved
her (alleluia).

ANTIPHON 2
Virgins: Blessed are the pure in heart: they shall see God (alleluia).
Women Saints: Like everlasting foundations on a rock are the
commandments of God in the heart of a good woman (alleluia).

PSALM 126(127)

If the Lórd does not buíld the hóuse,*
in váin do its buílders lábour;
if the Lórd does not wátch over the cíty,*
in váin does the wátchman keep vígil.

In váin is your éarlier rísing,*
your góing láter to rést,
you who tóil for the bréad you éat:*
when he pours gífts on his belóved while they slúmber.

Truly sóns are a gíft from the Lórd,*
a bléssing, the frúit of the wómb.
Indéed the sóns of yóuth*
are like árrows in the hánd of a wárrior.

Ó the háppiness of the mán*
who has fílled his quíver with these árrows!
Hé will have no cáuse for sháme*
when he dispútes with his fóes in the gáteways.

Ant. Virgins: Blessed are the pure in heart: they shall see God
(alleluia).
Women Saints: Like everlasting foundations on a rock are the
commandments of God in the heart of a good woman (alleluia).

ANTIPHON 3
Virgins: My firm hope will not be moved; it is based on Christ like
a house on a rock (alleluia).
Women Saints: God's own hand has given her strength; she will be
blessed for ever (alleluia).

CANTICLE: EPH 1:3-10

Blessed be the God and Father*
of our Lord Jesus Christ,
who has blessed us in Christ*
with every spiritual blessing in the heavenly places.

He chose us in him*
before the foundation of the world,
that we should be holy*
and blameless before him.

He destined us in love*
to be his sons through Jesus Christ,
according to the purpose of his will,†
to the praise of his glorious grace*
which he freely bestowed on us in the Beloved.

In him we have redemption through his blood,*
the forgiveness of our trespasses,

according to the riches of his grace*
which he lavished upon us.

He has made known to us†
in all wisdom and insight*
the mystery of his will,
according to his purpose*
which he set forth in Christ.

His purpose he set forth in Christ,*
as a plan for the fulness of time,
to unite all things in him,*
things in heaven and things on earth.

Ant. Virgins: My firm hope will not be moved; it is based on Christ
like a house on a rock (alleluia).
Women Saints: God's own hand has given her strength; she will be
blessed for ever (alleluia).

Scripture Reading   *1 Cor 7:32,34*
He who is unmarried is concerned with God's claim, asking how he
is to please God; a woman who is free of wedlock, or a virgin, is
concerned with the Lord's claim, intent on holiness, bodily and
spiritual.

Short Responsory
Outside Eastertide
R︎ The virgins come before the king. They sing for joy. *Repeat* R︎
V︎ They enter the temple of the king. R︎ Glory be. R︎

Eastertide
R︎ The virgins come before the king, singing for joy, alleluia,
alleluia. *Repeat* R︎
V︎ They enter the temple of the king. R︎ Glory be. R︎

Magnificat Antiphon
For a Virgin Martyr: We celebrate, in one victim, the reward of both
purity and religious devotion. This saint remained a virgin and also
attained the martyr's crown (alleluia).

For one Virgin: Come, bride of Christ, and receive the crown which the Lord has prepared for you (alleluia).

For several Virgins: Such are the saints who seek the Lord, who seek the presence of our God (alleluia).

Intercessions
Christ the Lord praised those who follow the way of virginity for the sake of the kingdom of heaven. Let us proclaim his love and pray:
R/ Jesus, king of virgins, hear us.
Christ our Lord, you presented the Church to yourself, as a chaste virgin to her only husband;—make her pure, holy and faultless. R/
Christ Jesus, the holy virgins went to meet you with lamps burning bright;—keep alive the flame of fidelity in the hearts of religious women. R/
Lord, you have always preserved your Church in purity and soundness of faith;—grant to all Christians a faith that is true and complete. R/
You bring joy to the lives of your faithful as they celebrate the feast of your holy virgin N.;—may they also rejoice in her constant intercession. R/
You have welcomed your holy virgins to the wedding feast of heaven;—invite all the dead to the feast of eternal life. R/
Our Father

The concluding prayer as at Morning Prayer, pp 1059-60.

THE COMMON OF MEN SAINTS

EVENING PRAYER I

Hymn
In Lent the hymn as at Morning Prayer is used, p 1067.

For all the saints who from their labours rest,
Who thee by faith before the world confest,
Thy name, O Jesu, be for ever blest.
Alleluia! Alleluia!

Thou wast their rock, their fortress and their might;
Thou, Lord, their captain in the well-fought fight;
Thou in the darkness drear their one true Light.
Alleluia! Alleluia!

O may thy soldiers, faithful, true and bold,
Fight as the saints who nobly fought of old,
And win, with them, the victor's crown of gold.
Alleluia! Alleluia!

O blest communion! fellowship divine!
We fight as they did, 'neath the holy sign;
And all are one in thee, for all are thine.
Alleluia! Alleluia!

Psalms and canticle with antiphons for Men Saints, pp 1035 ff.

Scripture Reading   *Phil 3:7-8a*
Because of Christ I have come to consider all these advantages that I had as disadvantages. Not only that, but I believe nothing can happen that will outweigh the supreme advantage of knowing Christ Jesus my Lord. For him, I have accepted the loss of everything, and I look on everything as so much rubbish, if only I can have Christ.

Short Responsory
Outside Eastertide
R℣ The Lord has shown him his love and covered him in glory.
Repeat R℣
℣ He has clothed him in a splendid garment. R℣ Glory be. R℣

Eastertide
R℣ The Lord has shown him his love and covered him in glory, alleluia, alleluia. *Repeat* R℣
℣ He has clothed him in a splendid garment. R℣ Glory be. R℣

Magnificat Antiphon
For one Saint: He is like a wise man who built his house upon the rock (alleluia).

For several Saints: The Lord looks on those who fear him, on those who rely on his merciful love (alleluia).

For a Religious: No one can be my disciple, says the Lord, unless he gives up all his possessions (alleluia).

Alternative for a Religious: He shall receive blessings from the Lord, and reward from the God who saves him. Such are the men who seek the Lord (alleluia).

For a Saint Noted for Works of Mercy: He who takes pity on the poor will receive a blessing; he who puts his trust in the Lord loves compassion (alleluia).

For an Educator: My child, keep your father's commands and do not reject the teaching of your mother; wear them always next your heart (alleluia).

Intercessions

Let us ask the Father to lead us to holiness through the intercession and example of the saints. R℣ Make us holy as you are holy.

Father, it was your will that we be called your children, and that is what we are;—may your Church all over the world bear witness to your goodness. R℣

Father, you have called us to walk in your light and do always the things that please you;—may our lives be rich in every kind of good work. R℣

Father, through Christ you have reconciled us to yourself;—keep us in your name that we may all be one. R℣

Father, you have invited us to the festival of eternal life;—make us perfect in your love through the bread that comes from heaven. R℣

Father, grant all sinners peace and forgiveness;—let the dead live in the light of your presence. R℣

Our Father

Concluding Prayer

If no proper prayer is given one of those at Morning Prayer is said, p 1069.

INVITATORY

Ant. How wonderful is God among his saints; come, let us adore him (alleluia).

Alternative

Today we are celebrating a feast in honour of Saint N.; come, let us adore the Lord our God (alleluia).

MORNING PRAYER

Hymn

This is the day whereon the Lord's true witness,
Whom all the nations lovingly do honour,
Worthy at last was found to wear for ever
 Glory transcendent.

Oft hath it been thro' his sublime deserving
Poor human bodies, howsoever stricken,
Broke and cast off the bondage of their sickness
 Healèd divinely.

Healing and power, grace and beauteous honour
Always be his, who shining in the highest,
Ruleth and keepeth all the world's vast order,
 One God, three Persons.

Ant. 1: The Lord gave them everlasting honour; an immortal name
will be their heritage (alleluia).

Psalms and canticle of Sunday, Week 1, pp 390 ff.

Ant. 2: Servants of the Lord, bless the Lord for ever (alleluia).

Ant. 3: The saints will rejoice in glory; they will sing for joy day and
night (alleluia).

Scripture Reading   *Rom 12:1-2*

My brothers, I implore you by God's mercy to offer your very selves
to him: a living sacrifice, dedicated and fit for his acceptance, the
worship offered by mind and heart. Adapt yourselves no longer to the
pattern of this present world, but let your minds be remade and your
whole nature thus transformed. Then you will be able to discern the
will of God, and to know what is good, acceptable, and perfect.

Short Responsory
Outside Eastertide
For one Saint
R̷ The law of God guides him; his mind is fixed on God. *Repeat* R̷
V̷ His steps will never falter. R̷ Glory be. R̷

For Several Saints
℞ The just shall rejoice in the sight of God. *Repeat* ℞
℣ They shall be filled with gladness. ℞ Glory be. ℞

Eastertide
℞ The law of God guides him; his mind is fixed on God, alleluia, alleluia. *Repeat* ℞
℣ His steps will never falter. ℞ Glory be. ℞

Benedictus Antiphon
For one Saint: The man who lives by the truth comes out into the light, so that it may be plainly seen that what he does is done in God (alleluia).

For several Saints: Blessed are the peacemakers, blessed are the pure in heart: they shall see God (alleluia).

For a Religious: Whoever does the will of my Father, says the Lord, is my brother, and sister, and mother (alleluia).

Alternative for a Religious: The Lord is all that I have; the Lord is good to the soul that seeks him (alleluia).

For a Saint Noted for Works of Mercy: If there is love among you, then all will know that you are my disciples (alleluia).

For an Educator: He who has compassion teaches and guides as a shepherd his flock (alleluia).

Intercessions
Let us praise Christ, the holy God, and ask that we may serve him in justice and holiness all the days of our life. ℞ Lord, you alone are holy.
You were tempted in every way that we are, but you did not sin;—Lord Jesus, have mercy on us. ℞
You have called us to grow in love until there is no longer any fear;—Lord Jesus, make us holy. ℞
You have told us to be the salt of the earth and the light of the world;—Lord Jesus, enlighten our minds and hearts. ℞
In a world of human need it was your will to serve and not to be served;—let us become like you, Lord Jesus, in the humble service of our brothers. ℞

You are the radiant brightness of God's glory, the perfect likeness of his nature;—Lord Jesus, let us see the splendour of your face. ℟
Our Father

Concluding Prayer
If no proper prayer is given one of the following is said:

Lord God,
you alone are holy,
the only source of goodness:
at the intercession of blessed N.
make us such
that we may not be shut out from your kingdom.
(We make our prayer) through our Lord.

Alternative
Almighty God,
grant that the example of your saints may spur us on to perfection,
so that we who are celebrating the feast of Saint N.
may follow him step by step in his way of life.
(We make our prayer) through our Lord.

For several Saints
Almighty, ever-living God,
who in the lives of the saints
continually give us new proofs of your love:
lead us to the faithful imitation of Christ,
by the help of their prayer and the spur of their example.
(We make our prayer) through our Lord.

For a Religious
Almighty God,
by whose grace Saint N. persevered
in imitation of Christ's humility and poverty:
grant through his prayer
that we also may remain faithful to our vocation,
and so come to that perfection
which you have set forth for us in your Son.
(We make our prayer) through our Lord.

For an Abbot
Give us grace, Lord,
amid the changing scenes of this life,
to set our hearts firmly on the things of heaven,
even as you gave us an example of the perfect life of the gospel
through your saint, Abbot N.
(We make our prayer) through our Lord.

For a Saint Noted for Works of Mercy
Lord God,
as you have taught your Church
that all the commandments are summed up in the love of you and
   of our neighbour,
grant that as we follow Saint N. in doing works of charity,
we may be numbered among the blessed in your kingdom.
(We make our prayer) through our Lord.

For an Educator
Lord God,
who gave blessed N. to the Church
to show the way of salvation to his fellow-men,
grant that inspired by his example
we may so follow Christ our Master,
that, together with our brethren, we may come at length into your
   presence.
(We make our prayer) through our Lord.

EVENING PRAYER II

Hymn
In Lent the hymn at Morning Prayer is used, p 1067.
Through the Year as at Evening Prayer I, p 1064.
Psalms and canticle with antiphons for Men Saints, p 1044.

Scripture Reading   *Rom 8:28-30*
We are well assured that everything helps to secure the good of those
who love God, those whom he has called in fulfilment of his design.
All those who from the first were known to him, he has destined

from the first to be moulded into the image of his Son, who is thus to become the eldest-born among many brethren. So predestined, he called them; so called, he justified them; so justified, he glorified them.

Short Responsory
Outside Eastertide
℟ The Lord is good; he loves good deeds. *Repeat* ℟
℣ His face is turned towards the upright man. ℟ Glory be. ℟

Eastertide
℟ The Lord is good; he loves good deeds, alleluia, alleluia.
Repeat ℟
℣ His face is turned towards the upright man. ℟ Glory be. ℟

Magnificat Antiphon
For one Saint: Well done, good and faithful servant; come and join in your Master's joy (alleluia).

For several Saints: They were faithful till death, and the Lord has given them the crown of life (alleluia).

For a Religious: You have left all things and have followed me; you will be repaid a hundred times over, and gain eternal life (alleluia).

Alternative for a Religious: Where brothers are united in praising God, there the Lord will bestow his blessing (alleluia).

For a Saint Noted for Works of Mercy: Truly I tell you, anything you did for the least of these who are mine, you did for me. Come, you blessed of my Father, inherit the kingdom prepared for you from the foundation of the world (alleluia).

For an Educator: Let the children come to me; for the kingdom of heaven belongs to such as these (alleluia).

Intercessions
Let us ask the Father to lead us to holiness through the intercession and example of the saints. ℟ Make us holy as you are holy.
Father, it was your will that we be called your children, and that is

what we are;—may your Church all over the world bear witness to your goodness. R̸ Make us holy as you are holy.

Father, you have called us to walk in your light and do always the things that please you;—may our lives be rich in every kind of good work. R̸

Father, through Christ you have reconciled us to yourself;—keep us in your name that we may all be one. R̸

Father, you have invited us to the festival of eternal life;—make us perfect in your love through the bread that comes from heaven. R̸

Father, grant all sinners peace and forgiveness;—let the dead live in the light of your presence. R̸

Our Father

The concluding prayer as at Morning Prayer, p 1069.

THE COMMON OF WOMEN SAINTS

EVENING PRAYER I

Hymn

Praise we the woman who, endued
With high heroic fortitude,
Has won renown that shall not die,
A place among the saints on high.

Such holy love inflamed her breast,
She would not seek on earth her rest,
But, strong in faith and patience, trod
The narrow path that leads to God.

Restraining every forward sense
By gentle bonds of abstinence,
With prayer her hungry soul she fed,
And thus to heavenly joys hath sped.

O Christ, the strength of all the strong,
To whom alone high deeds belong,

Through her prevailing prayer on high
In mercy hear thy people's cry.

All praise to God the Father be,
All praise, eternal Son, to thee,
Whom with the Spirit we adore
For ever and for evermore. Amen.

Psalms and canticle with antiphons for Women Saints, pp 1053 ff.

Scripture Reading   *Phil 3:7-8a*
Because of Christ I have come to consider all these advantages that
I had as disadvantages. Not only that, but I believe nothing can
happen that will outweigh the supreme advantage of knowing
Christ Jesus my Lord. For him, I have accepted the loss of everything, and I look on everything as so much rubbish, if only I can
have Christ.

Short Responsory
Outside Eastertide
R/ I will exult and rejoice in your merciful love. *Repeat* R/
V/ You have looked upon my wretchedness. R/ Glory be. R/

Eastertide
R/ I will exult and rejoice in your merciful love, alleluia, alleluia.
Repeat R/
V/ You have looked upon my lowliness. R/ Glory be. R/

Magnificat Antiphon
For one Saint: Give her a share in what her hands have worked for,
and let her works tell her praises at the city gates (alleluia).

For several Saints: Glory in his holy name; let the hearts that seek
the Lord rejoice (alleluia).

For a Woman Religious: The Lord has betrothed her to himself for
ever; he has betrothed her with faithfulness and with merciful love
(alleluia).

For a Saint Noted for Works of Mercy: She who takes pity on the
poor will receive a blessing; she who puts her trust in the Lord loves
compassion (alleluia).

For an Educator: My child, keep your father's commands and do not reject the teaching of your mother; wear them always next to your heart (alleluia).

Intercessions
Through the holy women let us pray to the Lord for all the needs of his Church. ℟ Lord, remember your Church.
Through the women martyrs who overcame death with undying courage—strengthen your Church in time of trial. ℟
Through the married women who graced the lives of the human family—renew the Church in her apostolic mission. ℟
Through all the widows who sanctified loneliness with prayer and hospitality—make your Church a telling sign of your love for all the world. ℟
Through all the mothers who introduced their children to the kingdom of God and true human life in society—may your Church bring mankind to eternal life and salvation. ℟
Through all the holy women who live in the light of your glory—grant to the faithful departed the everlasting vision of happiness. ℟
Our Father

Concluding Prayer
If no proper prayer is given one of those at Morning Prayer is said,
pp 1076-7

INVITATORY

Ant. How wonderful is God among his saints; come, let us adore him (alleluia).

Alternative
Today we are celebrating a feast in honour of Saint N.; come, let us adore the Lord our God (alleluia).

MORNING PRAYER

Hymn
    Lord God, we give you thanks for all your saints
    Who sought the trackless footprints of your feet,

Who took into their own a hand unseen
And heard a voice whose silence was complete.

In every word and deed they spoke of Christ,
And in their life gave glory to his name;
Their love was unconsumed, a burning bush
Of which the Holy Spirit was the flame.

Blest Trinity, may yours be endless praise
For all who lived so humbly in your sight;
Your holy ones who walked dark ways in faith
Now share the joy of your unfailing light.

Ant. 1: My soul clings to you; your right hand holds me fast
(alleluia).

Psalms and canticle of Sunday, Week 1, pp 390 ff.

Ant. 2: God's own right hand has given you strength; may you be
blessed for ever (alleluia).

Ant. 3: I will exult, Lord, and rejoice in your love (alleluia).

Scripture Reading   *Rom 12:1-2*
My brothers, I implore you by God's mercy to offer your very selves
to him: a living sacrifice, dedicated and fit for his acceptance, the
worship offered by mind and heart. Adapt yourselves no longer to
the pattern of this present world, but let your minds be remade and
your whole nature thus transformed. Then you will be able to discern
the will of God, and to know what is good, acceptable, and perfect.

Short Responsory
Outside Eastertide
For one Saint
R God is her help; she will not be moved. *Repeat* R
V The Lord is with her. R Glory be. R

For several Saints
R The just shall rejoice in the sight of God. *Repeat* R
V They shall be filled with gladness. R Glory be. R

Eastertide
℟ God is her help, she will not be moved, alleluia, alleluia. *Repeat* ℟
℣ The Lord is with her. ℟ Glory be. ℟

Benedictus ant. The kingdom of heaven is like a merchant looking for fine pearls; when he found one of great value he went and sold everything he had and bought it (alleluia).

For a Religious: Whoever does the will of my Father, says the Lord, is my brother, and sister, and mother (alleluia).

Alternative for a Religious: The Lord is all that I have; the Lord is good to the soul that seeks him (alleluia).

For a Saint Noted for Works of Mercy: If there is love among you, then all will know that you are my disciples (alleluia).

For an Educator: She who has compassion teaches and guides, as a shepherd his flock (alleluia).

Intercessions
With all the holy women let us praise our Saviour and call on him in prayer. ℟ Come, Lord Jesus.
Lord Jesus, you said of the woman who was a sinner, 'Her many sins are forgiven, because she has loved much';—grant us your forgiveness for our many sins. ℟
Lord Jesus, women ministered to your needs on your saving journeys;—open our eyes to see you in those who need our help. ℟
Lord and master, Mary listened to your teaching and Martha did the serving;—may our faith grow ever deeper and our love go out to others. ℟
Lord Jesus, you called those who do God's will your brother and sister and mother;—teach us to live as members of your family. ℟
Our Father

Concluding Prayer
If no proper prayer is given one of the following is said:

Lord God,
as you offer us each year the joy of blessed N.'s feast,
grant that as we celebrate her in worship,
    we may imitate her in holiness of life.
(We make our prayer) through our Lord.

Alternative
Grant us in full measure, Lord,
that spirit of knowledge and love of you,
which you gave so abundantly to your handmaid, Saint N.,
so that by closely following her example
and offering you loyal service
we may please you by our faith and actions.
(We make our prayer) through our Lord.

For several Saints
Almighty God,
grant that the prayer of Saints N. and N. may bring us support from
   heaven,
even as their admirable lives offer to us all an example of Christian
   living.
(We make our prayer) through our Lord.

For a Religious
Almighty God,
by whose grace Saint N. persevered
in imitation of Christ's humility and poverty:
grant through her prayer
that we also may remain faithful to our vocation,
and so come to that perfection
which you have set forth for us in your Son.
(We make our prayer) through our Lord.

For a Saint Noted for Works of Mercy
Lord God,
as you have taught your Church
that all the commandments are summed up in the love of you and
   of our neighbour,
grant that as we follow Saint N. in doing works of charity,
we may be numbered among the blessed in your kingdom.
(We make our prayer) through our Lord.

For an Educator
Lord God,
who gave blessed N. to the Church

to show to others the way of salvation,
grant that inspired by her example
we may so follow Christ our Master,
that, together with our brethren, we may come at length into your
    presence.
(We make our prayer) through our Lord.

EVENING PRAYER II

Hymn as at Evening Prayer I, p 1072.
Psalms and canticle with antiphons for Women Saints, p 1060.

Scripture Reading   *Rom 8:28-30*
We are well assured that everything helps to secure the good of those
who love God, those whom he has called in fulfilment of his design.
All those who from the first were known to him, he has destined
from the first to be moulded into the image of his Son, who is thus
to become the eldest-born among many brethren. So predestined, he
called them; so called, he justified them; so justified, he glorified
them.

Short Responsory
Outside Eastertide
R̷ God has chosen her. He chose her before she was born. *Repeat* R̷
V̷ He brought her to live in his own dwelling place. R̷ Glory be. R̷

Eastertide
R̷ God has chosen her. He chose her before she was born, alleluia,
alleluia. *Repeat* R̷
V̷ He brought her to live in his own dwelling place. R̷ Glory be. R̷

Magnificat Ant. My heart exults in the Lord, and I am filled with
gladness; I rejoice because you have saved me (alleluia).

For a Religious: You have left all things and have followed me; you
will be repaid a hundred times over, and gain eternal life (alleluia).

Alternative for a Religious: Where sisters are united in praising God,
there the Lord will bestow his blessing (alleluia).

For a Saint Noted for Works of Mercy: Truly I tell you, anything you did for the least of these who are mine, you did for me. Come, you blessed of my Father, inherit the kingdom prepared for you from the foundation of the world (alleluia).

For an Educator: Let the children come to me; for the kingdom of heaven belongs to such as these (alleluia).

Intercessions

Through the holy women let us pray to the Lord for all the needs of his Church. ℟ Lord, remember your Church.

Through the women martyrs who overcame death with undying courage—strengthen your Church in time of trial. ℟

Through the married women who graced the lives of the human family—renew the Church in her apostolic mission. ℟

Through all the widows who sanctified loneliness with prayer and hospitality—make your Church a telling sign of your love for all the world. ℟

Through all the mothers who introduced their children to the kingdom of God and true human life in society—may your Church bring all men to eternal life and salvation. ℟

Through all the holy women who live in the light of your glory—grant to the faithful departed the everlasting vision of happiness. ℟

Our Father

The concluding prayer as at Morning Prayer, pp 1076-7.

BENEDICTUS AND MAGNIFICAT ANTIPHONS
from the Common Offices

¶ *The Magnificat antiphon given for Evening Prayer I may be said at Evening Prayer on the Memorias of Saints.*

THE COMMON OF THE DEDICATION OF
A CHURCH

Evening Prayer I: Rejoice with Jerusalem and exult in her for ever all you who love her (alleluia).

Morning Prayer: 'Zacchaeus, make haste and come down; for I must stay with you today.' He came down with great haste and received the Lord joyfully in his house. Today salvation has come from God to this house (alleluia).

Evening Prayer II: The Lord has made holy the place where he dwells; this is the house of God in which his name will be invoked; as it is written: My name shall be there, says the Lord (alleluia).

THE COMMON OF THE BLESSED
VIRGIN MARY

Evening Prayer I: The Lord has looked upon my lowliness; the Almighty has done great things for me (alleluia).

Alternative: All generations will call me blessed, because God has had regard for his servant in her lowliness (alleluia).

Morning Prayer: The door of Paradise was closed to all men because of the sin of Eve; it has been opened again by the Virgin Mary (alleluia).

Evening Prayer II: Blessed are you, Mary, because you have believed: all those things which were said to you by the Lord will be fulfilled (alleluia).

THE COMMON OF APOSTLES

Evening Prayer I: You did not choose me: I chose you. I appointed you to go on and bear fruit, fruit that shall last (alleluia).

Morning Prayer: The holy city of Jerusalem had twelve foundation-stones, and on them were the names of the twelve apostles of the Lamb. The Lamb himself was the light of that city (alleluia).

Evening Prayer II: When all is made new and the Son of Man sits on his throne of glory, you will sit on twelve thrones to judge the twelve tribes of Israel (alleluia).

THE COMMON OF SEVERAL MARTYRS

OUTSIDE EASTERTIDE

Evening Prayer I: The kingdom of heaven belongs to those who hated their life in the present world and have now come to the rewards of the kingdom. They have washed their robes clean in the blood of the Lamb.

Morning Prayer: Blessed are those who are persecuted in the cause of right: theirs is the kingdom of heaven.

Evening Prayer II: The saints, who followed in the footsteps of Christ, rejoice in heaven. They gave their life for love of Christ: therefore, they will reign with him for ever.

EASTERTIDE

Evening Prayer I: Undying light will shine about your saints, Lord; they will live for ever, alleluia.

Morning Prayer: Rejoice, all you saints, and be glad, for your reward is great in heaven, alleluia.

Evening Prayer II: Rejoice, you saints, before the Lamb; the kingdom was prepared for you from the beginning of the world, alleluia.

THE COMMON OF ONE MARTYR

OUTSIDE EASTERTIDE

Evening Prayer I
For a Man: This saint fought unto death for the law of his God. He was not afraid of the words of evil men; for he was like a house that is founded on a rock.

For a Woman: She set about her duty with courage and braced herself for the work; her lamp will never go out.

Morning Prayer: Anyone who hates his soul in this world will save it for the eternal life.

Evening Prayer II: The saints will dwell in the kingdom of heaven; their peace will last for ever.

EASTERTIDE

Evening Prayer I: Undying light will shine about your saints, Lord; they will live for ever, alleluia.

Morning Prayer: Rejoice, all you saints, and be glad, for your reward is great in heaven, alleluia.

Evening Prayer II: Unless the wheat grain falls on the earth and dies it remains itself alone; but if it dies it yields much fruit, alleluia.

THE COMMON OF PASTORS

Evening Prayer I
For a Pope or a Bishop: Priest of the Most High and mirror of all that is good in man; you were a good shepherd of the people who pleased the Lord (alleluia).

For a Priest: I made myself all things to all men in order to save them all (alleluia).

Morning Prayer: It is not you who speak: the Spirit of your Father speaks in you (alleluia).

Evening Prayer II: This is the faithful and wise steward whom the master placed over his household to give them their measure of food at the proper time (alleluia).

Alternative: I thank you, Christ, for honouring me by leading me to this glory. You are the good shepherd; I pray that the sheep which you have placed in my charge will share with me in your glory for ever (alleluia).

THE COMMON OF DOCTORS OF THE CHURCH

Evening Prayer I: The man who keeps the commandments and teaches them will be considered great in the kingdom of heaven (alleluia).

Morning Prayer: The learned will shine as brightly as the vault of heaven, and those who have instructed many in virtue will shine like the stars for all eternity (alleluia).

Evening Prayer II: O holy doctor, Saint N., light of the Church; lover of the law of God; pray for us to the Son of God (alleluia).

THE COMMON OF VIRGINS

Evening Prayer 1
For a Virgin Martyr: See, how the virgin follows unhesitatingly in the path of the Lamb who was crucified for us; she is a pure oblation, a chaste victim (alleluia).

For one Virgin: The bridegroom came and the wise virgin who was ready went in with him to the marriage feast (alleluia).

For several Virgins: Prepare your lamps, you wise virgins: the bridegroom is here! Go out and meet him (alleluia).

Morning Prayer
For a Virgin Martyr: Blessed is the virgin who denied herself and took up her cross; she has imitated the Lord; he is the spouse of virgins, the prince of martyrs (alleluia).

For one Virgin: See, the wise virgin has gone to Christ: she shines among the choirs of virgins like the sun in the heavens (alleluia).

For several Virgins: Virgins of the Lord, bless the Lord for ever (alleluia).

Evening Prayer II
For a Virgin Martyr: We celebrate, in one victim, the reward of both purity and religious devotion. This saint remained a virgin and also attained the martyr's crown (alleluia).

For one Virgin: Come, bride of Christ, and receive the crown which the Lord has prepared for you (alleluia).

For several Virgins: Such are the saints who seek the Lord, who seek the presence of our God (alleluia).

THE COMMON OF MEN SAINTS

Evening Prayer I
For one Saint: He is like a wise man who built his house upon the rock (alleluia).

For several Saints: The Lord looks on those who fear him, on those who rely on his merciful love (alleluia).

Morning Prayer
For one Saint: The man who lives by the truth comes out into the light, so that it may be plainly seen that what he does is done in God (alleluia).

For several Saints: Blessed are the peacemakers, blessed are the pure in heart: they shall see God (alleluia).

Evening Prayer II
For one Saint: Well done, good and faithful servant; come and join in your Master's joy (alleluia).

For several Saints: They were faithful till death, and the Lord has given them the crown of life (alleluia).

THE COMMON OF WOMEN SAINTS

Evening Prayer I
For one Saint: Give her a share in what her hands have worked for, and let her works tell her praises at the city gates (alleluia).

For several Saints: Glory in his holy name; let the hearts that seek the Lord rejoice (alleluia).

Morning Prayer: The kingdom of heaven is like a merchant looking for fine pearls; when he found one of great value he went and sold everything he had and bought it (alleluia).

Evening Prayer II: My heart exults in the Lord, and I am filled with gladness; I rejoice because you have saved me (alleluia).

FOR RELIGIOUS

Evening Prayer I: No one can be my disciple, says the Lord, unless he gives up all his possessions (alleluia).

Alternative for a Male Religious: He shall receive blessings from the Lord, and reward from the God who saves him. Such are the men who seek the Lord (alleluia).

For a Woman Religious: The Lord has betrothed her to himself for ever; he has betrothed her with faithfulness and with merciful love (alleluia).

Morning Prayer: Whoever does the will of my Father, says the Lord, is my brother, and sister, and mother (alleluia).

Alternative: The Lord is all that I have; the Lord is good to the soul that seeks him (alleluia).

Evening Prayer II: You have left all things and have followed me; you will be repaid a hundred times over, and gain eternal life (alleluia).

Alternative: Where brothers (sisters) are united in praising God, there the Lord will bestow his blessing (alleluia).

FOR SAINTS NOTED FOR
WORKS OF MERCY

Evening Prayer I: He (she) who takes pity on the poor will receive a blessing; he (she) who puts his (her) trust in the Lord loves compassion (alleluia).

Morning Prayer: If there is love among you, then all will know that you are my disciples (alleluia).

Evening Prayer II: Truly I tell you, anything you did for the least of these who are mine, you did for me. Come, you blessed of my Father, inherit the kingdom prepared for you from the foundation of the world (alleluia).

FOR EDUCATORS

Evening Prayer I: My child, keep your father's commands and do not reject the teaching of your mother; wear them always next your heart (alleluia).

Morning Prayer: He (she) who has compassion teaches and guides, as a shepherd his flock (alleluia).

Evening Prayer II: Let the children come to me; for the kingdom of heaven belongs to such as these (alleluia).

THE OFFICE FOR THE DEAD

The concluding prayers are to be changed in gender and number according to circumstances.
In Eastertide, Alleluia *may be added, if judged fitting, to the end of antiphons, versicles and responsories.*

INVITATORY

Ant. Come, let us adore the King for whom all men are alive.

MORNING PRAYER

Hymn
Remember those, O Lord,
Who in your peace have died,
Yet may not gain love's high reward
Till love is purified.

With you they faced death's night,
Sealed with your victory sign,
Soon may the splendour of your light
On them for ever shine.

Sweet is their pain, yet deep,
Till perfect love is born;
Their lone night-watch they gladly keep
Before your radiant morn.

Your love is their great joy;
Your will their one desire;
As finest gold without alloy
Refine them in love's fire.

For them we humbly pray:
Perfect them in your love.
O may we share eternal day
With them in heaven above.

PSALMODY

Ant. 1: The bones you have crushed will rejoice in you, Lord.

PSALM 50(51)

Have mércy on me, Gód, in your kíndness.*
In your compássion blot óut my offénce.
O wásh me more and móre from my guílt*
and cléanse me fróm my sín.

My offénces trúly I knów them;*
my sín is álways befóre me.
Against yóu, you alóne, have I sínned;*
what is évil in your síght I have dóne.

That you may be jústified whén you give séntence*
and be withóut repróach when you júdge
O sée, in guílt I was bórn,*
a sínner was Í concéived.

Indéed you love trúth in the héart;*
then in the sécret of my héart teach me wísdom.
O púrify me, thén I shall be cléan;*
O wásh me, I shall be whíter than snów.

Make me héar rejóicing and gládness,*
that the bónes you have crúshed may revíve.
From my síns turn awáy your fáce*
and blót out áll my guílt.

A púre heart creáte for me, O Gód,*
put a stéadfast spírit withín me.
Do not cást me awáy from your présence,*
nor depríve me of your hóly spírit.

Give me agáin the jóy of your hélp;*
with a spírit of férvour sustáin me,
that I may téach transgréssors your wáys*
and sínners may retúrn to yóu.

O réscue me, Gód, my hélper,*
and my tóngue shall ríng out your góodness.

O Lórd, ópen my líps*
and my móuth shall decláre your práise.

For in sácrifice you táke no delíght,*
burnt óffering from mé you would refúse,
my sácrifice, a cóntrite spírit.*
A húmbled, contrite héart you will not spúrn.

In your góodness, show fávour to Síon:*
rebuíld the wálls of Jerúsalem.
Thén you will be pléased with lawful sácrifice,*
hólocausts óffered on your áltar.

Ant. The bones you have crushed will rejoice in you, Lord.
Ant. 2: Rescue my soul, Lord, from the gate of death.

CANTICLE: IS 38:10-14,17-20

I said, In the noontide of my days I must depart;†
I am consigned to the gates of Sheol*
for the rest of my years.

I said, I shall not see the Lord*
in the land of the living;
I shall look upon man no more*
among the inhabitants of the world.

My dwelling is plucked up and removed from me*
like a shepherd's tent;
like a weaver I have rolled up my life;*
he cuts me off from the loom;

From day to night you bring me to an end;*
I cry for help until morning;
like a lion he breaks all my bones;*
from day to night you bring me to an end.

Like a swallow or a crane I clamour,*
I moan like a dove.
My eyes are weary with looking upward.*
O Lord, I am oppressed; be my security.

Lo, it was for my welfare*
that I had great bitterness;
but you have held back my life*
from the pit of destruction,
for you have cast all my sins*
behind your back.

For Sheol cannot thank you,*
death cannot praise you;
those who go down to the pit*
cannot hope for your faithfulness.

The living, the living, he thanks you†
as I do this day;*
the father makes known to the children your faithfulness.

The Lord will save me,*
and we will sing to stringed instruments
all the days of our life,*
at the house of the Lord.

Ant. Rescue my soul, Lord, from the gate of death.
Ant. 3: I will praise God all my days.

PSALM 145(146)

My sóul, give práise to the Lórd;†
I will práise the Lórd all my dáys,*
make músic to my Gód while I líve.

Pút no trúst in prínces,*
in mortal mén in whóm there is no hélp.
Take their bréath, they retúrn to cláy*
and their pláns that dáy come to nóthing.

He is háppy who is hélped by Jacob's Gód,*
whose hópe is in the Lórd his Gód,
who alóne made héaven and éarth,*
the séas and áll they contáin.

It is hé who keeps fáith for éver,*
who is júst to thóse who are oppréssed.

It is hé who gives bréad to the húngry,*
the Lórd, who sets prísoners frée,

the Lórd who gives síght to the blínd,*
who ráises up thóse who are bowed dówn,
the Lórd, who protécts the stránger*
and uphólds the wídow and órphan.

It is the Lórd who lóves the júst
but thwárts the páth of the wícked.
The Lórd will réign for éver,
Sion's Gód, from áge to áge.

Ant. I will praise God all my days.

Alternative psalm
Ant. 3: Let everything that lives praise the Lord.

PSALM 150

Práise Gód in his hóly pláce,*
práise him in his míghty héavens.
Práise him for his pówerful déeds,*
práise his surpássing gréatness.

O práise him with sóund of trúmpet,*
práise him with lúte and hárp.
Práise him with tímbrel and dánce,*
práise him with stríngs and pípes.

O práise him with resóunding cýmbals,*
práise him with cláshing of cýmbals.
Let éverything that líves and that bréathes*
give práise to the Lórd.

Ant. Let everything that lives praise the Lord.

Scripture Reading   *1 Thess 4:14*
We believe that Jesus died and rose again; so we believe that God
will bring with Jesus those who have died believing in him.

Short Responsory

R7 I will praise you, Lord. You have rescued me. *Repeat* R7
V7 You have changed my mourning into gladness. R7 Glory be. R7

Benedictus ant. I am the resurrection and the life; he who believes in me, though he die, yet shall he live, and whoever lives and believes in me shall never die.

Alternative for Eastertide
Christ has risen; he is the light of his people, whom he has redeemed with his blood, alleluia.

Intercessions

God, the Father almighty, raised Jesus from the dead and he will give life to our own mortal bodies. We pray to him in faith: R7 Lord, bring us to life in Christ.

Holy Father, we have been buried with your Son in baptism to rise with him in glory;—may we always live in Christ and not see death for ever. R7

Father, you have given us the living bread from heaven to be eaten with faith and love;—grant that we may have eternal life and be raised up on the last day. R7

Lord, when your Son was in agony you sent an angel to console him; —at the hour of our death take away all fear and fill our hearts with hope. R7

You delivered the three young men from the blazing furnace;—free the souls of the dead from the punishments their sins have deserved. R7

God of the living and the dead, you brought Jesus back to life;— raise up the faithful departed, and let us come with them into your heavenly glory. R7

Our Father

Concluding Prayer

Grant, Lord, we pray,
that as our faith is built on the Risen Christ,
so too may our hope be steadfast,
as we await the resurrection of your servant N. from the dead.
(We make our prayer) through our Lord.

Alternative: For a Man
God, our Father,
by whose Son's death and resurrection we have been redeemed,
you are the glory of your faithful, the life of your saints:
have mercy on your servant N.,
and as he professed his faith in the mystery of our resurrection,
so may he gain possession of eternal joy.
(We make our prayer) through our Lord.

For a Woman
God, our Father,
by whose Son's death and resurrection we have been redeemed,
you are the glory of your faithful, the life of your saints:
have mercy on your servant N.,
and as she professed her faith in the mystery of our resurrection,
so may she gain possession of eternal joy.
(We make our prayer) through our Lord.

Alternative: Through the Year
For a Man
Let our prayer come into your presence, Lord,
as we humbly ask for mercy:
and as in your love
you counted your servant N. among your people in this world,
so bring him now to the abode of peace and light,
and number him among your saints.
(We make our prayer) through our Lord.

For a Woman
Let our prayer come into your presence, Lord,
as we humbly ask for mercy:
and as in your love
you counted your handmaid N. among your people in this world,
so bring her now to the abode of peace and light,
and number her among your saints.
(We make our prayer) through our Lord.

Eastertide
God of mercy and power,
whose Son of his own free will
underwent a human death on our behalf:
let your servant N.
share in the admirable victory of Christ's resurrection.
(We make our prayer) through our Lord.

For several deceased
Lord God,
who gave your only-begotten Son
his place on high as conqueror of death:
grant to your servants N. and N. who have died,
that they in their turn may triumph over death,
and may live forever before you, their creator and redeemer.
(We make our prayer) through our Lord.

For Brethren, Relatives and Benefactors
Lord God,
as you are the fount of mercy and wish all men to be saved:
have mercy then on our deceased brethren, relatives and
    benefactors.
Through the intercession of Blessed Mary ever-virgin,
and of all your saints,
bring them to the fellowship of eternal joy.
(We make our prayer) through our Lord.

EVENING PRAYER

Hymn
    Merciful Saviour, hear our humble prayer,
    For all your servants passed beyond life's care;
    Though sin has touched them, yet their weakness spare.

    Refrain:
    O grant them pardon, Jesus Saviour blest,
    And give their spirits light and endless rest.

O gentle Saviour, Lamb for sinners slain,
Look on your brothers, cleanse their hearts of stain:
Your cross has won them everlasting gain. (*Refrain:*)

Lord, at your passion love did conquer fear;
Now share that triumph with these souls so dear:
Banish their sorrows, let your light appear. (*Refrain:*)

PSALMODY

Ant. 1: The Lord will guard you from every evil, he will guard your soul.

PSALM 120(121)

I lift up my éyes to the móuntains:*
from whére shall come my hélp?
My hélp shall cóme from the Lórd*
who made héaven and éarth.

May he néver állow you to stúmble!*
Let him sléep not, your guárd.
Nó, he sléeps not nor slúmbers,*
Ísrael's guárd.

The Lórd is your guárd and your sháde;*
at your ríght side he stánds.
By dáy the sún shall not smíte you*
nor the móon in the níght.

The Lórd will guárd you from évil,*
he will guárd your sóul.
The Lord will guárd your góing and cóming*
both nów and for éver.

Ant. The Lord will guard you from every evil, he will guard your soul.
Ant. 2: If you, O Lord, should mark our guilt, Lord, who would survive?

PSALM 129(130)

Out of the dépths I crý to you, O Lórd,*

Lórd, hear my vóice!
O lét your éars be atténtive*
to the vóice of my pléading.

If you, O Lórd, should márk our guílt,*
Lórd, who would survíve?
But with yóu is fóund forgíveness:*
for thís we revére you.

My sóul is wáiting for the Lórd,*
I cóunt on his wórd.

My sóul is lónging for the Lórd*
more than wátchman for dáybreak.
Let the wátchman cóunt on dáybreak*
and Ísrael on the Lórd.

Becáuse with the Lórd there is mércy*
and fúlness of redémption,
Ísrael indéed he will redéem*
from áll its iníquity.

Ant. If you, O Lord, should mark our guilt, Lord, who would
survive?
Ant. 3: As the Father raises the dead and gives them life, so the Son
gives life to anyone he chooses.

CANTICLE: PHIL 2:6-11

Though he was in the form of God,*
Jesus did not count equality with God a thing to be grasped.

He emptied himself,†
taking the form of a servant,*
being born in the likeness of men.

And being found in human form,*
he humbled himself and became obedient unto death,*
even death on a cross.

Therefore God has highly exalted him*
and bestowed on him the name which is above every name,

That at the name of Jesus every knee should bow,*
in heaven and on earth and under the earth,

And every tongue confess that Jesus Christ is Lord,*
to the glory of God the Father.

Ant. As the Father raises the dead and gives them life, so the Son gives life to anyone he chooses.

Scripture Reading   *1 Cor 15:55-57*
Death, where is your victory? Death, where is your sting? Now the sting of death is sin, and sin gets its power from the Law. So let us thank God for giving us the victory through our Lord Jesus Christ.

Short Responsory
R̂ In you, O Lord, I take refuge. Let me not be lost for ever.
Repeat R̂
V̂ I will rejoice and be glad because of your merciful love. R̂ Glory be. R̂

Alternative
R̂ Show them your merciful love, Lord, give them eternal rest.
Repeat R̂
V̂ You are coming to rule over both the living and the dead. R̂ Glory be. R̂

Magnificat ant. All that the Father gives me will come to me; and I will never turn away the one who comes to me.

Alternative in Eastertide
Christ was crucified and rose from the dead; he has redeemed us, alleluia.

Intercessions
Let us pray to Christ who gives us the hope that our mortal bodies will become like his in glory. R̂ Lord, you are our life and our resurrection.
Christ, Son of the living God, you raised your friend Lazarus from the dead;—grant life and glory to the faithful departed, redeemed by

your precious blood. ℟ Lord, you are our life and our resurrection.
Compassionate Saviour, you wiped away all tears when you gave
back to the widow of Naim her only son;—comfort those who
mourn because the one they love has died. ℟

Christ, our Redeemer, destroy the reign of sin in our mortal bodies;
—let us not receive the wages of death but the reward of eternal
life. ℟

Christ, our Saviour, look on those who live without hope and do not
know you;—let them believe in the resurrection and the life of the
world to come. ℟

You restored sight to the man born blind and opened the eyes of his
faith;—reveal your face to the dead who have not seen your glory.
℟

Lord, be merciful to us when we leave this earthly dwelling;—make
for us a home in heaven that will last for ever. ℟

Our Father

The concluding prayer as at Morning Prayer, pp 1092–4.

NIGHT PRAYER

All as on a Sunday, After Evening Prayer II, pp 692 ff.

Appendix I
SHORT INTERCESSIONS FOR
USE AT EVENING PRAYER

The following short Intercessions may always be used at Evening Prayer in place of those given elsewhere.

Sunday
In real humility of heart let us pray to God who cares for everyone.

℟ Lord, have mercy on your people.

Defend the Church against all danger.

Protect N. our pope.

Be the strength of N. our bishop.

Save your people.

Preserve the world in peace.

Bring light to those who do not believe.

Guide the rulers of all nations.

Come to the aid of the poor.

Comfort the afflicted.

Show to orphans your loving kindness.

Have mercy on the dead.

Monday
In real humility let us pray to God who cares for everyone.

℟ Lord, visit your people.

Unite your Church all over the world.

Keep N. our pope safe from harm.

Protect N. our bishop.

Guide missionaries in their saving work.

Clothe your priests with perfect love.

Reveal your holiness in religious men and women.

Change hatred into friendship.

Make children live with your grace.

Lead young people along the path of wisdom.

Comfort the aged and renew their courage.

Bestow your blessings on our friends.

Welcome the dead into the company of the saints.

Tuesday
In humility of heart let us pray to God who cares for everyone.

℟ Lord, hear us.

Remember your Church with love.

Defend N. our pope in time of trial.

Come to the aid of N. our bishop.

Grant prosperity to our country.

Bless those who have been good to us.

Deepen the love between husband and wife.

Help engaged couples to plan their future.

Give work to the unemployed.

Show the needy that you care for them.

Uphold the persecuted with your strength.

Come to those who have lost their way.

Grant to the dead eternal glory.

Wednesday

In humility of heart let us pray to God who cares for everyone.

℟ Lord, save your people.

Keep alive in your Church all the joy of believing.

Grant to N. our pope every good gift.

Strengthen N. our bishop in grace and knowledge.

Preserve the nations in your peace.

Make every home your dwelling place.

Rid the world of all injustice.

Give farmers joy as they reap the harvest.

Be the companion of those who travel.

Direct the skill of every craftsman.

Help widows in their loneliness.

Grant to the dead eternal life.

Thursday

In humility of heart let us pray to God who cares for everyone.

℟ Lord, you are our hope.

Strengthen the unity of your Church.

Give N. our pope long life in your service.

Lead N. our bishop by the light of your wisdom.

Call men and women for the work of your gospel.

Bless our relatives and friends.

Restore health to the sick.

Comfort the dying.

Bring back exiles to their homeland.
Deliver us from all disaster.
Grant sunshine and fine weather.
Refresh the earth with rain.
Grant eternal rest to the faithful departed.

Friday
In real humility let us pray to God who cares for everyone.
   ℟ In you, Lord, we place our trust.
Make your Church perfect in love.
Watch over N. our pope with your fatherly care.
Sustain N. our bishop in the service of your people.
Be close to the college of bishops.
Give food to the hungry.
Restore sight to the blind.
Comfort the aged with contentment of heart.
Take care of the homeless.
Strengthen those who have chosen a life of virginity.
Call the Jewish people to share in your new covenant.
Give wisdom to those who make our laws.
Do not abandon those who are tempted.
Let eternal light shine on the dead.

Saturday
In real humility let us pray to God who cares for everyone.
   ℟ Lord, come to the aid of your people.
Gather the nations into your Church.
Protect N. our pope.
Bless N. our bishop.
Rule the hearts of your priests.
Display your holiness in the lives of the laity.
Guide the daily work of every man and woman.
Make the rich generous in serving others.
Give strength to the weak.
Restore freedom to prisoners.
Shelter us from the violence of nature.
Save us from sudden death.
Grant to the dead the vision of glory.

HYMNS AND RELIGIOUS POEMS

The hymns given in this book and this appendix are recommended for use in Morning and Evening Prayer from The Divine Office. *Any other hymn approved by the local Episcopal Conference may be substituted provided it is suitable for the Hour, season or feast (cf General Instruction no. 178. Introduction no. 80).*

Except where the sense of the hymn demands it, hymns are not assigned particularly to Morning or Evening Prayer.

Attention is drawn to the religious poetry which may be used in place of the hymns.

HYMNS

ADVENT I
To 16 December

Morning Prayer

1   Hear the herald voice resounding:
     'Christ is near', it seems to say,
     'Cast away the dreams of darkness,
     Welcome Christ, the light of day!'

     Wakened by this solemn warning,
     Let the earth-bound soul arise;
     Christ her sun, all sloth dispelling,
     Shines upon the morning skies.

     So when next he comes with glory,
     Shrouding all the earth in fear,
     May he then as our defender
     On the clouds of heav'n appear.

                                        6TH CENTURY
                                        TR E. CASWALL 1814-78

Evening Prayer

2   Creator of the stars of night,
     The people's everlasting light,

Redeemer, Saviour of us all,
O hear your servants when they call.

As once through Mary's flesh you came,
To save us from our sin and shame,
So now, Redeemer, by your grace,
Come heal again our fallen race.

And when on that last judgment day,
We rise to glory from decay,
Then come again, O Saviour blest,
And bring us to eternal rest.

IRVIN UDULUTSCH OFM CAP

ADVENT II
From 17 December

3   The co-eternal Son,
       A maiden's offspring see;
       A servant's form Christ putteth on,
       To set his people free.

Daughter of Sion, rise
To greet thine infant King;
Nor let thy stubborn heart despise
The pardon he doth bring.

Let deeds of darkness fly
Before the approaching morn,
For unto sin 'tis ours to die
And serve the Virgin-born.

Our joyful praises sing
To Christ, that set us free;
Like tribute to the Father bring,
And, Holy Ghost, to thee.

CHARLES COFFIN 1676-1749
TR ROBERT CAMPBELL 1814-68 AND
COMPILERS *Parish Hymn Book*

4   O come, O come, Emmanuel,
And ransom captive Israel,
That mourns in lonely exile here
Until the Son of God appear.
   Rejoice! Rejoice! Emmanuel
   Shall come to you, O Israel!

O come, now Wisdom from on high,
Who orders all things mightily;
To us the path of knowledge show,
And teach us in her ways to go.
Rejoice! etc. . . .

O come, O come, now Lord of might,
Who to your tribes on Sinai's height
In ancient times you gave the law,
In cloud, and majesty, and awe.
Rejoice! etc. . . .

5   O come, now Rod of Jesse's stem,
From every foe deliver them
That trust your mighty power to save,
And give them vict'ry o'er the grave.
   Rejoice! Rejoice! Emmanuel
   Shall come to you, O Israel!

O come, now Key of David, come,
And open wide our heav'nly home;
Make safe the way that leads on high,
And close the path to misery.
Rejoice! etc. . . .

O come, now Day-spring from on high,
And cheer us by your drawing nigh;
Disperse the gloomy clouds of night,
And death's dark shadow put to flight.
Rejoice! etc. . . .

O come, Desire of nations, bind
In one the hearts of all mankind;

Bid now our sad divisions cease,
And be yourself our King of Peace.
Rejoice! etc. . . . .

TR THOMAS HELMORE 1811-90

¶ *Hymns nos 4 and 5 may be joined to form one.*

CHRISTMASTIDE I
Before Epiphany

6   A noble flow'r of Juda from tender roots has sprung,
A rose from stem of Jesse, as prophets long had sung,
A blossom fair and bright,
That in the midst of winter will change to dawn our night.

The rose of grace and beauty of which Isaiah sings
Is Mary, virgin mother, and Christ the flow'r she brings.
By God's divine decree
She bore our loving Saviour, who died to set us free.

To Mary, dearest Mother, with fervent hearts we pray:
Grant that your tender infant will cast our sins away,
And guide us with his love
That we shall ever serve him, and live with him above.

15TH CENTURY

7   Afar from where the sun doth rise
To lands beneath the western skies,
Homage to Christ our King we pay,
Born of the virgin's womb this day.

Blessèd Creator, thou didst take
A servant's likeness for our sake,
And didst in flesh our flesh restore
To bid thy creature live once more.

Chaste was the womb where thou didst dwell,
Of heavenly grace the hidden cell:

Nor might the blessed Maid proclaim
Whence her dread Guest in secret came.

Down from on high God came to rest
His glory in a sinless breast;
Obedience at his word believed,
And virgin innocence conceived.

Ere long, that holy Child she bore
By Gabriel's message named before,
Whom, yet unborn, with eager pride,
The swift fore-runner prophesied.

Fast doth he sleep, where straw doth spread
A humble manger for his bed;
A Mother's milk that strength renewed
Which gives the birds of heaven their food.

Glory to God, the angels cry;
Earth hears the echo from on high;
Mankind's true Shepherd and its Lord
By shepherd hearts is first adored.   5TH CENTURY
                                        TR R. A. KNOX 1888-1957

8   Christ, whose blood for all men streamed,
     Light that shone ere morning beamed,
     God and God's eternal Son,
     Ever with the Father one;

     Splendour of the Father's light,
     Star of hope for ever bright,
     Hearken to the prayers that flow
     From thy servants here below.

     Lord, remember that in love
     Thou didst leave thy throne above,
     Man's frail nature to assume
     In the holy Virgin's womb.

     Let not earth alone rejoice,
     Seas and skies unite their voice

In a new song, to the morn
When the Lord of life was born.

Virgin-born, to thee be praise,
Now and through eternal days;
Father, equal praise to thee,
With the Spirit, ever be.

9 O come, all ye faithful,
   Joyful and triumphant,
   O come ye, O come ye to Bethlehem;
   Come and behold him
   Born the King of Angels.
       O come, let us adore him,
       O come, let us adore him,
       O come, let us adore him, Christ the Lord.

God of God,
Light of Light,
Lo! he abhors not the virgin's womb;
Very God,
Begotten, not created.
O come let us adore him, etc. . . .

Sing, choirs of angels,
Sing in exultation,
Sing, all ye citizens of heaven above;
'Glory to God
In the highest.'
O come let us adore him, etc. . . .

Yea, Lord we greet thee,
Born this happy morning,
Jesu, to thee be glory given;
Word of the Father
Now in flesh appearing.
O come, let us adore him, etc. . . .

18TH CENTURY
TR F. OAKLEY 1802-80

10 Unto us a Child is given,
     Christ our Saviour brings release;
     Counsellor, Eternal Father,
     God made man and Prince of Peace.

     Born of Mary, gentle Virgin,
     By the Spirit of the Lord;
     From eternal ages spoken:
     This, the mighty Father's Word.

     Love and truth in him shall flower,
     From his strength their vigour take.
     Branches that are bare shall blossom;
     Joy that slept begins to wake.

     Praise the everlasting Father
     And the Word, his only Son;
     Praise them with the Holy Spirit,
     Perfect Trinity in One.

STANBROOK ABBEY HYMNAL

11 Of the Father's love begotten,
     Ere the worlds began to be,
     He is Alpha and Omega,
     He the source, the ending he,
     Of all things that are and have been
     And that future years shall see:
     Evermore and evermore.

     Blessèd was the day for ever
     When the Virgin, full of grace,
     By the Holy Ghost conceiving,
     Bore the Saviour of our race,
     And the child, the world's Redeemer,
     First revealed his sacred face:
     Evermore and evermore.

     Glory be to God the Father,
     Glory be to God the Son,
     Glory to the Holy Spirit,

Persons three, yet Godhead one.
Glory be from all creation
While eternal ages run:
Evermore and evermore.

AURELIUS C. PRUDENTIUS 348-*c.* 413
TR J. M. NEALE 1818-66

12 Christ is here, Emmanuel!
Majesty so mild:
Wisdom dwells with grace and truth,
Hidden in this Child.

Born of God's creative will,
Christ is light from light,
Come to rescue Adam's sons
Waiting in the night.

Father, Son and Spirit blest,
Heav'n their glory sings,
While the earth with mighty voice
Praise and worship brings.

STANBROOK ABBEY HYMNAL

CHRISTMASTIDE II
After Epiphany

Hymns 10, 11, 12 are also suitable.

13 Bethlehem, of noblest cities
None can once with thee compare:
Thou alone the Lord from heaven
Didst for us incarnate bear.

Fairer than the sun at morning
Was the star that told his birth;
To the lands their God announcing,
Seen in human form on earth.

By its peerless beauty guided
See the eastern kings appear;
Bowing low, their gifts they offer,
Gifts of incense, gold and myrrh.

Sacred gifts of mystic meaning:
Incense doth the God disclose,
Gold the King of Kings proclaimeth,
Myrrh a future tomb foreshows.

In thy glory, O Lord Jesus,
To the Gentile world displayed,
With the Father and the Spirit
Endless praise to thee be paid.

AURELIUS C. PRUDENTIUS 348-*c* 413
TR E. CASWALL 1814-78 AND OTHERS

14   Songs of thankfulness and praise,
Jesu, Lord, to thee we raise,
Manifested by the star
To the sages from afar;
Branch of royal David's stem
In thy birth at Bethlehem;
Anthems be to thee addressed,
God in man made manifest.

Manifest at Jordan's stream,
Prophet, priest and king supreme;
And at Cana wedding-guest
In thy Godhead manifest;
Manifest in power divine,
Changing water into wine;
Anthems be to thee addressed,
God in man made manifest.

Grant us grace to see thee, Lord,
Mirrored in thy holy word;
May we imitate thee now,
And be pure, as pure art thou;

That we like to thee may be
At thy great Epiphany,
And may praise thee, ever blest,
God in man made manifest.

C. WORDSWORTH 1807-85

LENT

15 God, of thy pity, unto us thy children
Bend down thy ear in thine own loving kindness,
And all thy people's prayers and vows ascending,
Hear, we beseech thee.

Look down in mercy from thy seat of glory,
Pour on our souls the radiance of thy presence,
Drive from our weary hearts the shades of darkness,
Lightening our footsteps.

Free us from sin by might of thy great loving,
Cleanse thou the sordid, loose the fettered spirit,
Spare every sinner, raise with thine own right hand,
All who are fallen.

Glory to God the Father everlasting,
Glory for ever to the Sole-begotten,
With whom thy Holy Spirit through the ages
Reigneth co-equal.

ANTE-TRIDENTINE BREVIARY
TR ALAN G. MCDOUGALL 1895-1964

16 O God, creator of us all,
From whom we come, to whom we go,
You look with pity on our hearts,
The weakness of our wills you know.

Forgive us all the wrong we do,
And purify each sinful soul.
What we have darkened, heal with light,
And what we have destroyed, make whole.

The fast by law and prophets taught,
By you, O Christ, was sanctified.
Bless all our penance, give us strength
To share the cross on which you died.

O God of mercy, hear our prayer,
With Christ your Son, and Spirit blest,
Transcendent Trinity in whom
Created things all come to rest.

STANBROOK ABBEY HYMNAL

17   Lord Jesus, think on me
     And purge away my sins;
     From earth-born passions set me free,
     And make me pure within.

     Lord Jesus, think on me,
     With care and woe oppressed;
     Let me thy loving servant be,
     And taste thy promised rest.

     Lord Jesus, think on me
     Amid the battle's strife;
     In all my pain and misery
     Be thou my health and life.

     Lord Jesus, think on me,
     Nor let me go astray;
     Through darkness and perplexity
     Point thou the heavenly way.

BISHOP SYNESIUS 375-430

The following hymn is more suitable for Morning Prayer.

18   Jesus, the sun of ransomed earth,
     Shed in our inmost souls thy light,
     As in spring days a fairer birth
     Heralds, each morn, the doom of night.

     This hour of grace thou dost impart;
     Teach us with flowing tears the stain

1112

To cleanse from every victim-heart
That longs to feel love's welcome pain.

The day is come, the accepted day,
When grace, like nature, flowers anew;
Trained by thy hand the surer way
Rejoice we in our spring-time too.

Let the whole earth in worship bow,
Great God, before thy mercy-seat,
As we, renewed by grace, do now
With praises new thy presence greet.

6TH CENTURY
TR R. A. KNOX 1888-1957

19 Now let us all with one accord,
In fellowship with ages past,
Keep vigil with our heav'nly Lord,
In his temptation and his fast.

The covenant so long revealed
To faithful men in former time,
Christ by his own example sealed;
The Lord of love, in love sublime.

Remember, Lord, though frail we be,
By your own kind hand were we made;
And help us, lest our frailty
Cause your great name to be betrayed.

Hear us, O Trinity sublime,
And undivided un'ty;
So let this consecrated time
Bring forth its fruit abundantly.

ST GREGORY THE GREAT 540-604

HOLY WEEK

20   Man of sorrows, wrapt in grief,
Bow your ear to our relief;
You for us the path have trod
Of the dreadful wrath of God;
You the cup of fire have drained
Till its light alone remained.
Lamb of love, our comfort be:
Hear our mournful litany.

By the garden filled with woe,
Where to rest you oft would go;
By your agony of prayer
In the desolation there;
By the dire and deep distress
More than human mind can guess,
Lord, our grief in mercy see:
Hear our fervent litany.

By that bitter cup of pain,
When your strength began to wane;
By those lips which once did pray
That it might but pass away;
By the heart that drank it dry
Lest the human race should die,
In your pity grant our plea,
Hear our solemn litany.

Man of sorrows, let your grief
Purchase for us our relief;
Lord of mercy, bow your ear,
Slow to anger, swift to hear:
By the cross's royal road,
Lead us to the throne of God,
There to sing triumphantly
Heaven's glorious litany.

MATTHEW BRIDGES 1800-94
ADAPTED BY AGP AND GL

21   O Cross of Christ, immortal tree
On which our Saviour died,
The world is sheltered by your arms
That bore the Crucified.

From bitter death and barren wood
The tree of life is made;
Its branches bear unfailing fruit
And leaves that never fade.

O faithful Cross, you stand unmoved
While ages run their course:
Foundation of the universe,
Creation's binding force.

Give glory to the risen Christ
And to his Cross give praise,
The sign of God's unfathomed love,
The hope of all our days.

STANBROOK ABBEY HYMNAL

22   Abroad the regal banners fly,
Now shines the Cross's mystery;
Upon it Life did death endure,
And yet by death did life procure.

That which the prophet-king of old
Hath in mysterious verse foretold,
Is now accomplished, whilst we see
God ruling nations from a tree.

Blest Tree, whose happy branches bore
The wealth that did the world restore;
The beam that did that body weigh
Which raised up hell's expected prey.

Hail Cross, our hope; on thee we call,
Who keep this mournful festival;
Grant to the just increase of grace,
And every sinner's crimes efface.

Blest Trinity, we praises sing
To thee, from whom all graces spring;
Celestial crowns on those bestow
Who conquer by the Cross below.

VENANTIUS FORTUNATUS 530-609

23   O sacred head ill-usèd,
By reed and bramble scarred,
That idle blows have bruisèd,
And mocking lips have marred,
How dimmed that eye so tender,
How wan those cheeks appear,
How overcast the splendour
That angel hosts revere!

Thy face is drawn with anguish
That once did love display.
In death's grip thou dost languish,
Thy strength is drained away.
O thou who bore this burden,
Who felt this bitter pain,
It was for sinners' pardon
Which thou alone couldst gain.

In this thy sacred passion
O that some share had I!
O may thy cross's fashion
O'erlook me when I die!
For these dear pains that rack thee
A sinner's thanks receive;
O, lest in death I lack thee,
A sinner's care relieve.

Since death must be my ending,
In that dread hour of need,
My friendless cause befriending,
Lord, to my rescue speed:
Thyself, dear Jesus, trace me
That passage to the grave,

And from thy cross embrace me
With arms outstretched to save.

13TH CENTURY
TR R. A. KNOX 1888-1957

24 My song is love unknown,
My Saviour's love to me,
Love to the loveless shown,
That they might lovely be.
O who am I,
That for my sake
My Lord should take
Frail flesh and die?

Sometimes they strew his way
And his sweet praises sing;
Resounding all the day
Hosannas to their King;
Then 'Crucify!'
Is all their breath,
And for his death
They thirst and cry.

They rise, and needs will have
My dear Lord made away;
A murderer they save,
The Prince of life they slay;
Yet cheerful he
To suffering goes,
That he his foes
From thence might free.

S. CROSSMAN 1624-83

EASTERTIDE I
Before Ascension Day

25   Christ the Lord is risen again!
Christ hath broken every chain,
Hark, the angels shout for joy,
Singing evermore on high,
              Alleluya!

He who gave for us his life,
Who for us endured the strife,
Is our Paschal Lamb today!
We too sing for joy, and say
              Alleluya!

He who bore all pain and loss
Comfortless upon the Cross,
Lives in glory now on high,
Pleads for us, and hears our cry.
              Alleluya!

Now he bids us tell abroad
How the lost may be restored,
How the penitent forgiven,
How we too may enter heaven.
              Alleluya!

MICHAEL WEISSE *c.* 1480-1534
TR C. WINKWORTH 1829-78

26   Easter glory fills the sky! Alleluia!
Christ now lives, no more to die! Alleluia!
Darkness has been put to flight, Alleluia!
By the living Lord of light! Alleluia!

Mary, Mother, greet your Son,
Radiant from his triumph won!
By his cross you shared his pain,
So for ever share his reign!

Shepherd, seek the sheep that strayed!
Come to contrite Peter's aid!

Strengthen him to be the rock;
Make him shepherd of your flock!

Seek not life within the tomb;
Christ stands in the upper room!
Risen glory he conceals,
Risen body he reveals!

Though we see his face no more,
He is with us as before!
Glory veiled, he is our priest,
His true flesh and blood our feast!

JAMES QUINN SJ

27 Alleluia, sing to Jesus, his the sceptre, his the throne.
Alleluia, his the triumph, his the victory alone.
Hark, the songs of holy Sion, thunder like a mighty flood:
Jesus out of every nation hath redeemed us by his blood.

Alleluia, not as orphans are we left in sorrow now;
Alleluia, he is near us faith believes nor questions how.
Though the clouds from sight received him when the forty
    days were o'er,
Shall our hearts forget his promise: 'I am with you evermore'?
S. S. WESLEY 1810-76

28 At the Lamb's high feast we sing
Praise to our victorious king,
Who hath washed us in the tide
Flowing from his piercèd side.
Praise we him whose love divine
Gives the guests his blood for wine,
Gives his body for the feast,
Love the victim, love the priest.

Where the Paschal blood is poured,
Death's dark angel sheathes his sword;
Israel's hosts triumphant go
Through the wave that drowns the foe.

1119

Christ, the Lamb, whose blood was shed,
Paschal victim, Paschal bread;
With sincerity and love
Eat we manna from above.

Mighty victim from the sky,
Powers of hell beneath thee lie;
Death is conquered in the fight;
Thou has brought us life and light.
Now thy banner thou dost wave;
Vanquished Satan and the grave;
Angels join his praise to tell—
See o'erthrown the prince of hell.

Paschal triumph, Paschal joy,
Only sin can this destroy;
From the death of sin set free,
Souls re-born, dear Lord, in thee.
Hymns of glory, songs of praise,
Father, unto thee we raise;
Risen Lord, all praise to thee,
Ever with the Spirit be.

7TH CENTURY
TR R. CAMPBELL 1814-68

29 Proclaim his triumph, heav'n and earth,
For Christ is risen as he said:
The Crucified, the living God,
Who dwelt three days among the dead.

Christ died for us in bitter shame,
But now he lives in power and might;
His fire unquenched, his vital flame
Fills all the world with joy and light.

The Uncreated Father praise,
His living and unconquered Son,
Who with the Spirit reigns supreme,
Triumphant Trinity in One.

STANBROOK ABBEY HYMNAL

30 Come, ye faithful, raise the strain
    Of triumphant gladness;
    God hath brought his Israel
    Into joy from sadness;
    Loosed from Pharaoh's bitter yoke
    Jacob's sons and daughters;
    Led them with unmoistened foot
    Through the Red Sea waters.

    'Tis the spring of souls today;
    Christ hath burst his prison,
    And from three days' sleep in death
    As a sun hath risen;
    All the winter of our sins,
    Long and dark, is flying
    From his light, to whom we give
    Laud and praise undying.

    Neither might the gates of death,
    Nor the tomb's dark portal,
    Nor the watchers, nor the seal,
    Hold thee as a mortal;
    But today amidst the twelve
    Thou didst stand, bestowing
    That thy peace which evermore
    Passeth human knowing.

    ST JOHN DAMASCENE *c.* 750
    TR J. M. NEALE 1818-66

31 Battle is o'er, hell's armies flee;
    Raise we the cry of victory
    With abounding joy resounding, alleluia.

    Christ, who endured the shameful tree,
    O'er death triumphant welcome we,
    Our adoring praise outpouring, alleluia.

    On the third morn from death rose he,
    Clothed with what light in heaven shall be,
    Our unswerving faith deserving, alleluia.

Hell's gloomy gates yield up their key,
Paradise door thrown wide we see;
Never-tiring be our choiring, alleluia.

Lord, by the stripes men laid on thee,
Grant us to live from death set free,
This our greeting still repeating, alleluia.

Simphonia Sirenum 1695
TR R. A. KNOX 1888-1957

EASTERTIDE II
After Ascension Day

32   Come, Holy Ghost, Creator, come
From thy bright heavenly throne,
Come, take possession of our souls,
And make them all thy own.

Thou who art called the Paraclete,
Best gift of God above,
The living spring, the living fire,
Sweet unction and true love.

Thou who art sev'nfold in thy grace,
Finger of God's right hand;
His promise, teaching little ones
To speak and understand.

O guide our minds with thy blest light,
With love our hearts inflame;
And with thy strength, which ne'er decays,
Confirm our mortal frame.

Far from us drive our deadly foe,
True peace unto us bring;
And through all perils lead us safe
Beneath thy sacred wing.

Through thee may we the Father know,
Through thee th'eternal Son,

And thee the Spirit of them both,
Thrice-blessed Three in One.

All glory to the Father be,
With his co-equal Son:
The same to thee, great Paraclete,
While endless ages run.

ATTR TO RABANUS MAURUS 766-856
TR ANON

33   Come, O Creator, Spirit blest,
And in our souls take up thy rest;
Come with thy grace and heavenly aid,
To fill the hearts which thou hast made.

Great Paraclete, to thee we cry,
O highest gift of God most high,
O Fount of Life, O Fire of Love,
And sweet anointing from above!

Thou in thy sevenfold gifts art known;
The finger of God's hand we own;
The promise of the Father thou,
Who dost the tongue with pow'r endow.

Our senses kindle from above,
And make our hearts o'erflow with love;
With patience firm and virtue high
The weakness of our flesh supply.

Drive far from us the foe we dread
And grant us thy true peace instead;
So shall we not, with thee for Guide,
Turn from the path of life aside.

Oh, may thy grace on us bestow
The Father and the Son to know,
And thee, through endless times confess'd,
Of both th' eternal Spirit blest.

All glory while the ages run
Be to the Father and the Son,
Who rose from death; the same to thee,
O Holy Ghost, eternally!

34 Spirit of God, on the waste and the darkness
hov'ring in power as creation began,
drawing forth beauty from clay and from chaos,
breathing God's life in the nostrils of man,

Come and sow life in the waste of our being,
pray in us, form us as sons in the Son.
Open our hearts to yourself, mighty Spirit,
bear us to life in the Three who are One.

STANBROOK ABBEY HYMNAL

35 Come down, O love divine,
Seek thou this soul of mine,
And visit it with thine own ardour glowing;
O Comforter draw near,
Within my heart appear,
And kindle it, thy holy flame bestowing.

O let it freely burn,
Till earthly passions turn
To dust and ashes in its heat consuming;
And let thy glorious light
Shine ever on my sight,
And clothe me round, the while my path illuming.

Let holy charity
Mine outward vesture be,
And lowliness become mine inner clothing.
True lowliness of heart,
Which takes the humbler part,
And o'er its own shortcomings weeps with loathing.

And so the yearning strong,
With which the soul will long,

Shall far outpass the power of human telling;
For none can guess its grace,
Till he become the place
Wherein the Holy Spirit makes his dwelling.

BIANCO DA SIENA D 1434
TR R. F. LITTLEDALE 1833-90

36 Love of the Father, Love of God the Son,
From whom all came, in whom was all begun;
Who formest heavenly beauty out of strife,
Creation's whole desire and breath of life:

Thou the All-holy, thou supreme in might,
Thou dost give peace, thy presence maketh right;
Thou with thy favour all things dost enfold,
With thine all-kindness free from harm wilt hold.

Purest and highest, wisest and most just,
There is no truth save only in thy trust;
Thou dost the mind from earthly dreams recall,
And bring, through Christ, to him for whom are all.

Eternal Glory, all men thee adore,
Who art and shalt be worshipped evermore:
Us whom thou madest, comfort with thy might,
And lead us to enjoy thy heavenly light.

ROBERT BRIDGES 1844-1930
BASED ON *Amor Patris et Filii* 12TH CENTURY

THROUGH THE YEAR

37 Firmly I believe and truly
God is Three, and God is One;
And I next acknowledge duly
Manhood taken by the Son;

And I trust and hope most fully
In that manhood crucified;
And each thought and deed unruly
Do to death, as he has died.

Simply to his grace and wholly
Light and life and strength belong;
And I love supremely, solely,
Him the holy, him the strong.

Adoration aye be given,
With and through the angelic host,
To the God of earth and heaven,
Father, Son and Holy Ghost.

J. H. NEWMAN 1801-90

Alternative Hymns to The Sacred Heart
38   To Christ, the prince of peace,
And Son of God most high,
The father of the world to come,
Sing we with holy joy.

Deep in his heart for us
The wound of love he bore;
That love wherewith he still inflames
The hearts that him adore.

O Jesu, victim blest,
What else but love divine
Could thee constrain to open thus
That sacred heart of thine?

O fount of endless life,
O spring of water clear,
O flame celestial, cleansing all
Who unto thee draw near!

Praise to the Father be,
And sole-begotten Son;
Praise, holy Paraclete, to thee
While endless ages run.

Catholicum Hymnologium Germanicum 1587
TR E. CASWALL 1814-78

39   O sacred Heart,
Our home lies deep in thee;
On earth thou art an exile's rest,
In heaven the glory of the blest.
    O sacred Heart.

O sacred Heart,
Thou fount of contrite tears;
Where'er those living waters flow,
New life to sinners they bestow,
    O sacred Heart.

O sacred Heart,
Our trust is all in thee;
For though earth's night be dark and drear,
Thou breathest rest where thou art near,
    O sacred Heart.

O sacred Heart,
When shades of death shall fall,
Receive us 'neath thy gentle care,
And save us from the tempter's snare,
    O sacred Heart.

O sacred Heart,
Lead exiled children home,
Where we may ever rest near thee,
In peace and ioy eternally,
    O sacred Heart.

F. STANFIELD 1835-1914

¶ *Hymns nos. 40-62 for the Common Offices and the Office for the Dead are given in the appendix in Vols I-III of* The Divine Office. *In this volume some of these hymns are given at Morning and Evening Prayer of the Commons to which they are assigned. The others are given here.*

THE COMMON OF THE BLESSED
VIRGIN MARY

42 Star of sea and ocean,
gateway to man's heaven,
mother of our Maker,
hear our pray'r, O Maiden.

Welcoming the *Ave*
of God's simple greeting
you have borne a Saviour
far beyond all dreaming.

Loose the bonds that hold us
bound in sin's own blindness
that with eyes now open'd
God's own light may guide us.

Show yourself our mother
he will hear your pleading
whom your womb has sheltered
and whose hand brings healing.

Gentlest of all virgins,
that our love be faithful
keep us from all evil
gentle, strong and grateful.

Guard us through life's dangers
never turn and leave us,
may our hope find harbour
in the calm of Jesus.

Sing to God our Father
through the Son who saves us
joyful in the Spirit
everlasting praises.   RALPH WRIGHT

43 Maiden, yet a Mother,
Daughter of thy Son,
High beyond all other—
Lowlier is none;

Thou the consummation
Planned by God's decree,
When our lost creation
Nobler rose in thee!

Thus his place preparéd,
He who all things made
'Mid his creatures tarried,
In thy bosom laid;
There his love he nourished,—
Warmth that gave increase
To the Root whence flourished
Our eternal peace.

Nor alone thou hearest
When thy name we hail;
Often thou art nearest
When our voices fail;
Mirrored in thy fashion
All creation's good,
Mercy, might, compassion
Grace thy womanhood.

Lady, lest our vision
Striving heavenward, fail,
Still let thy petition
With thy Son prevail,
Unto whom all merit,
Power and majesty,
With the Holy Spirit
And the Father be.

DANTE ALIGHIERI 1265-1321
TR R. A. KNOX 1888-1957

44   Mary, crowned with living light,
Temple of the Lord,
Place of peace and holiness,
Shelter of the Word.

Mystery of sinless life
In our fallen race,

1129

Free from shadow you reflect
Plenitude of grace.

Virgin-mother of our God,
Lift us when we fall,
Who were named upon the Cross
Mother of us all.

Father, Son and Holy Ghost,
Heaven sings your praise,
Mary magnifies your name
   Through eternal days.   STANBROOK ABBEY HYMNAL

45 Hail, Queen of heav'n, the ocean star,
     Guide of the wand'rer here below;
     Thrown on life's surge, we claim thy care:
     Save us from peril and from woe.
     Mother of Christ, star of the sea,
     Pray for the wand'rer, pray for me.

O gentle, chaste and spotless maid,
We sinners make our prayers through thee;
Remind thy son that he has paid
The price of our iniquity.
Virgin most pure, star of the sea,
Pray for the sinner, pray for me.

Sojourners in this vale of tears,
To thee, blest advocate, we cry;
Pity our sorrow, calm our fears,
And sooth with hope our misery.
Refuge in grief, star of the sea,
Pray for the mourner, pray for me.

And while to him who reigns above,
In godhead one, in persons three,
The source of life, of grace, of love,
Homage we pay on bended knee;
Do thou, bright Queen, star of the sea,
Pray for thy children, pray for me.

                 JOHN LINGARD 1771-1851

46 God, who made the earth and sky
    And the changing sea,
    Clothed his glory in our flesh:
    Man, with men to be.

    Mary, Virgin filled with light,
    Chosen from our race,
    Bore the Father's only Son
    By the Spirit's grace.

    He whom nothing can contain,
    No one can compel,
    Bound his timeless Godhead here,
    In our time to dwell.

    God, our Father, Lord of days,
    And his only Son,
    With the Holy Spirit praise:
    Trinity in One.   STANBROOK ABBEY HYMNAL

47 Queen, on whose starry brow doth rest
    The crown of perfect maidenhood,
    The God who made thee, from thy breast
    Drew, for our sakes, his earthly food.

    The grace that sinful Eve denied,
    With thy Child-bearing, reappears;
    Heaven's lingering door, set open wide,
    Welcomes the children of her tears.

    Gate, for such royal progress meet,
    Beacon, whose rays such light can give,
    Look, how the ransomed nations greet
    The virgin-womb that bade them live!

    O Jesus, whom the Virgin bore,
    Be praise and glory unto thee;
    Praise to the Father evermore
    And his life-giving Spirit be.

                        VENANTIUS FORTUNATUS 530-609
                        TR R. A. KNOX 1888-1957

THE COMMON OF VIRGINS

55 O Jesu, thou the virgins' crown,
    Thy gracious ear to us bow down,
    Born of that Virgin whom alone
    The Mother and the Maid we own.

    In thee, their Bridegroom and their Lord,
    The virgins find their bright reward,
    And wheresoe'r thy footsteps wend
    With hymns and praises thee attend.

    O gracious Lord, we thee implore
    Thy grace into our minds to pour;
    From all defilement keep us free,
    And make us pure in heart for thee.

    All praise to God the Father be,
    All praise, eternal Son, to thee,
    Whom with the Spirit we adore,
    For ever and for evermore.

ST AMBROSE
Tr Compilers *Hymns Ancient and Modern Revised*

POEMS

ADVENT AND CHRISTMAS

63   *O Felix Culpa*

Adam lay y-bounden
    Bounden in a bond;
Four thousand winter
    Thought he not too long;
And all was for an apple,
    An apple that he took,
As clerkès finden written
    In theirè book.

Ne had the apple taken been,
   The apple taken been,
Ne haddè never our Lady
   A been heaven's queen.
Blessed be the time
   That apple taken was!
Therefore we may singen
   '*Deo Gracias*!'

                                      ANON

64   *I sing of a maiden*

I sing of a maiden
That is matchless;
King of all kings
For her son she chose.

He came all so still
Where his mother was,
As dew in April
That falleth on the grass.

He came all so still
To his mother's bowr,
As dew in April
That falleth on the flower.

He came all so still
where his mother lay,
As dew in April
That falleth on the spray.

Mother and maiden
Was never none but she;
Well may such a lady
Godes mother be.

                                      ANON

65   *Sussex Carol*

On Christmas night all Christians sing,
To hear the news the angels bring—
News of great joy, news of great mirth,
News of our merciful King's birth.

Then why should men on earth be so sad,
Since our Redeemer made us glad,
When from our sin he set us free,
All for to gain our liberty?

When sin departs before his grace,
Then life and health come in its place;
Angels and men with joy may sing,
All for to see the new-born King.

All out of darkness we have light,
Which made the angels sing this night:
'Glory to God and peace to men,
Now and for evermore. Amen.'

                                        TRADITIONAL

66   From *La Corona*

Deign at my hands this crown of prayer and praise,
Weav'd in my low devout melancholy,
Thou which of good, hast, yea art treasury,
All changing unchang'd Ancient of days,
But do not, with a vile crown of frail bays,
Reward my muses white sincerity,
But what thy thorny crown gain'd, that give me,
A crown of glory, which doth flower always;
The end crown our works, but thou crown'st our ends,
For, at our end begins our endless rest,
The first last end, now zealously possess'd,
With a strong sober thirst, my soul attends.
'Tis time that heart and voice be lifted high,
Salvation to all that will is nigh.

                                        JOHN DONNE

1134

67   *The Nativity of Christ*

Behold the father is his daughter's son,
The bird that built the nest is hatched therein,
The old of years an hour hath not outrun,
Eternal life to live doth now begin,
The Word is dumb, the mirth of heaven doth weep,
Might feeble is, and force doth faintly creep.

O dying souls, behold your living spring;
O dazzled eyes, behold your sun of grace;
Dull ears, attend what word this Word doth bring;
Up, heavy hearts, with joy your joy embrace.
From death, from dark, from deafness, from despairs,
This life, this light, this Word, this joy repairs.

Gift better than himself God doth not know;
Gift better than his God no man can see.
This gift doth here the giver given bestow;
Gift to this gift let each receiver be.
God is my gift, himself he freely gave me;
God's gift am I, and none but God shall have me.

Man altered was by sin from man to beast;
Beast's food is hay, hay is all mortal flesh.
Now God is flesh and lies in manger pressed
As hay, the brutest sinner to refresh.
O happy field wherein this fodder grew,
Whose taste doth us from beasts to men renew.

ROBERT SOUTHWELL

68   Who would have thought my shrivell'd heart
Could have recovered greenness? It was gone
Quite underground, as flowers depart
To feed their mother-root when they have blown;
Where they together
All the hard weather,
Dead to the world, keep house unknown.

These are thy wonders, Lord of Power,
Killing and quickning, bringing down to hell
And up to heaven in an hour;
Making a chiming of a passing-bell.
We say amiss,
This or that is:
Thy word is all, if we could spell.

GEORGE HERBERT

LENT AND EASTER

*The following poems, nos. 69-86, although specifically allotted to Lent
and Eastertide, may be used at other times.*

69   *Corpus Christi Carol*

*Lully, lullay, lully, lullay,
The falcon hath borne my make away.*

He bore him up, he bore him down;
He bore him into an orchard brown.

In that orchard there was an hall,
That was hanged with purple and pall.

And in that hall there was a bed
It was hanged with gold so red.

And in that bed there lieth a knight,
His woundès bleeding day and night.

By that bed's side there kneeleth a may,
And she weepeth both night and day.

And by that bed's side there standeth a stone,
Corpus Christi written thereon.   ANON

70   O King of the Friday
          Whose limbs were stretched on the cross,
          O Lord who did suffer
          The bruises, the wounds, the loss.

1136

We stretch ourselves
Beneath the shield of thy might,
Some fruit from the tree of thy passion
Fall on us this night!

FROM THE IRISH

71   *Easter*

Most glorious Lord of life, that on this day
    Didst make thy triumph over death and sin;
    And having harrowed hell didst bring away
    Captivity thence captive, us to win:
This joyous day, dear Lord, with joy begin,
    And grant that we for whom thou didest die
    Being with thy dear blood clean washed from sin,
    May live forever in felicity.
And that thy love we weighing worthily,
    May likewise love thee for the same again;
    And for thy sake that all like dear didst buy,
    With love may one another entertain.
So let us love, dear love, like as we ought.
Love is the lesson which the Lord us taught.

EDWARD SPENSER

72   *Holy Sonnets iii*

At the round earth's imagined corners blow
Your trumpets, angels, and arise, arise
From death, you numberless infinities
Of souls, and to your scattered bodies go:
All whom the flood did, and fire shall o'erthrow,
All whom war, dearth, age, agues, tyrannies,
Despair, law, chance hath slain, and you whose eyes
Shall behold God and never taste death's woe.
But let them sleep, Lord, and me mourn a space,
For if above all these my sins abound,
'Tis late to ask abundance of thy grace
When we are there. Here on this lowly ground

Teach me how to repent; for that's as good
As if thou hadst sealed my pardon with thy blood.

JOHN DONNE

73   *Holy Sonnets v*

Batter my heart, three-personed God, for you
As yet but knock, breathe, shine, and seek to mend;
That I may rise and stand, o'erthrow me and bend
Your force to break, blow, burn, and make me new.
I, like an usurped town to another due,
Labour to admit you, but O, to no end.
Reason, your viceroy in me, me should defend,
But is captived and proves weak or untrue.
Yet dearly I love you and would be loved fain,
But am betrothed unto your enemy.
Divorce me, untie, or break that knot again,
Take me to you, imprison me, for I,
Except you enthrall me, never shall be free,
Nor ever chaste except you ravish me.

JOHN DONNE

74   *Holy Sonnets vi*

O, to vex me contraries meet in one;
Inconstancy unnaturally hath begot
A constant habit, that when I would not
I change in vows and in devotion.
As humorous is my contrition
As my profane love, and as soon forgot,
As riddlingly distempered, cold and hot;
I durst not view heaven yesterday, and today
In prayers and flattering speeches I court God;
Tomorrow I quake with true fear of his rod.
So my devout fits come and go away
Like a fantastic ague, save that here
Those are my best days when I shake with fear.

JOHN DONNE

75 *A Hymn to God the Father*

Hear me, O God!
   A broken heart
   Is my best part:
Use still thy rod
   That I may prove
   Therein thy love.

If thou hadst not
   Been stern to me,
   But let me free,
I had forgot
   Myself and thee.

For sin's so sweet,
   As minds ill bent
   Rarely repent,
Until they meet
   Their punishment.

Who more can crave
   Than thou hast done,
   That gav'st a son
To free a slave,
   First made of nought,
   With all since bought?

Sin, Death, and Hell
   His glorious Name
   Quite overcame,
Yet I rebel,
   And slight the same.

But I'll come in,
   Before my loss
   Me farther toss,
As sure to win
   Under his cross.

BEN JONSON

76 *De Profundis*

Out of my soul's depth to thee my cries have sounded:
Let thine ears my plaints receive, on just fear grounded.
Lord, should'st thou weigh our faults, who's not confounded?

But with grace thou censur'st thine when they have errèd,
Therefore shall thy blessed name be loved and fearèd.
E'en to thy throne my thoughts and eyes are rearèd.

Thee alone my hopes attend, on thee relying;
In thy sacred word I'll trust, to thee fast flying,
Long ere the watch shall break, the morn descrying.

In the mercies of our God who live securèd,
May of full redemption rest in him assurèd,
Their sin-sick souls by him shall be recurèd.

THOMAS CAMPION

77 *To Keep a True Lent*

Is this a Fast, to keep
The larder lean?
And clean
From fat of veals and sheep?

Is it to quit the dish
Of flesh, yet still
To fill
The platter high with fish?

Is it to fast an hour,
Or ragg'd to go,
Or show
A down-cast look and sour?

No: 'tis a Fast to dole
Thy sheaf of wheat
And meat
Unto the hungry soul.

It is to fast from strife
And old debate,
        And hate;
To circumcise thy life.

To show a heart grief-rent;
To starve thy sin,
        Not bin;
And that's to keep thy Lent.

ROBERT HERRICK

78   *The Call*

Come, my Way, my Truth, my Life:
Such a Way, as gives us breath:
Such a Truth, as ends all strife:
Such a Life, as killeth death.

Come, my Light, my Feast, my Strength:
Such a Light, as shows a feast:
Such a Feast, as mends in length:
Such a Strength, as makes his guest.

Come, my Joy, my Love, my Heart:
Such a Joy, as none can move:
Such a Love, as none can part:
Such a Heart, as joys in Love.

GEORGE HERBERT

79   *Love*

Love bade me welcome; yet my soul drew back,
        Guilty of dust and sin.
But quick-eyed Love, observing me grow slack
        From my first entrance in,
Drew nearer to me, sweetly questioning,
        If I lacked anything.

'A guest', I answered, 'worthy to be here.'
        Love said, 'You shall be he.'

'I, the unkind, ungrateful? Ah, my dear,
            I cannot look on thee.'
Love took my hand, and smiling did reply,
            'Who made the eyes but I?'

'Truth, Lord, but I have marred them; let my shame
            Go where it doth deserve.'
'And know you not', says Love, 'who bore the blame?'
            'My dear, then I will serve.'
'You must sit down', says Love, 'and taste my meat.'
            So I did sit and eat.

GEORGE HERBERT

80   *Easter*

Rise heart; thy Lord is risen. Sing his praise
            Without delays,
Who takes thee by the hand, that thou likewise
            With him mayst rise:
That, as his death calcined thee to dust,
His life may make thee gold, and much more just.

Awake, my lute, and struggle for thy part
            With all thy art.
The cross taught all wood to resound his name,
            Who bore the same.
His stretched sinews taught all strings, what key
Is best to celebrate this most high day.

Consort both heart and lute, and twist a song
            Pleasant and long:
Or since all music is but three parts vied
            And multiplied;
O let thy blessed Spirit bear a part,
And make up our defects with his sweet art.

I got me flowers to straw thy way;
I got me boughs off many a tree:
But thou wast up by break of day,
And brought'st thy sweets along with thee.

The Sun arising in the East,
Though he give light, & th' East perfume;
If they should offer to contest
With thy arising, they presume.
Can there by any day but this,
Though many suns to shine endeavour?
We count three hundred, but we miss:
There is but one, and that one ever.   GEORGE HERBERT

81   *The Windhover*
                     To Christ our Lord

I caught this morning morning's minion, king-
    dom of daylight's dauphin, dapple-dawn-drawn Falcon,
        in his riding
    Of the rolling level underneath him steady air, and
        striding
High there, how he rung upon the rein of a wimpling wing
In his ecstasy! then off, off forth on swing,
    As a skate's heel sweeps smooth on a bow-bend: the
        hurl and gliding
    Rebuffed the big wind. My heart in hiding
Stirred for a bird, the achieve of, the mastery of the thing!
Brute beauty and valour and act, oh, air, pride, plume here
    Buckle! AND the fire that breaks from thee then, a
        billion
Times told lovelier, more dangerous, O my chevalier!
    No wonder of it: shéer plód makes plough down sillion
Shine, and blue-bleak embers, ah my dear,
    Fall, gall themselves, and gash gold-vermilion.

                                        GERARD MANLEY HOPKINS

82   *Marina*
            Quis hic locus, quae regio, quae mundi plaga?

What seas what shores—what grey rocks and what islands
What water lapping the bow

And scent of pine and the woodthrush singing through the fog
What images return
O my daughter.
   Those who sharpen the tooth of the dog, meaning
Death
Those who glitter with the glory of the humming bird, meaning
Death
Those who sit in the sty of contentment, meaning
Death
Those who suffer the ecstasy of the animals, meaning
Death

   Are become unsubstantial, reduced by a wind,
A breath of pine, and the woodsong fog
By this grace dissolved in place

   What is this face, less clear and clearer
The pulse in the arm, less strong and stronger—
Given or lent? more distant than stars and nearer than the eye

   Whispers and small laughter between leaves and hurrying feet
Under sleep, where all the waters meet.

   Bowsprit cracked with ice and paint cracked with heat.
I made this, I have forgotten
And remember.
The rigging weak and the canvas rotten
Between one June and another September.
Made this unknowing, half conscious,—unknown, my own.
The garboard strake leaks, the seams need caulking.
This form, this face, this life
Living to live in a world of time beyond me; let me
Resign my life for this life, my speech for that unspoken,
The awakened, lips parted, the hope, the new ships.
   What seas what shores what granite islands towards my timbers
And woodthrush calling through the fog
My daughter.
                                        T. S. ELIOT

83 ### From *The Rock*

O perpetual revolution of configured stars,
O perpetual recurrence of determined seasons,
O world of spring and autumn, birth and dying!
The endless cycle of idea and action,
Endless invention, endless experiment,
Brings knowledge of motion, but not of stillness;
Knowledge of speech, but not of silence;
Knowledge of words, and ignorance of the Word.
All our knowledge brings us nearer to our ignorance,
All our ignorance brings us nearer to death,
But nearness to death no nearer to God.   T. S. ELIOT

84 ### *One Foot in Eden*

One foot in Eden still, I stand
And look across the other land.
The world's great day is growing late,
Yet strange these fields that we have planted
So long with crops of love and hate.
Time's handiworks by time are haunted,
And nothing now can separate
The corn and tares compactly grown.
The armorial weed in stillness bound
About the stalk; these are our own.
Evil and good stand thick around
In the fields of charity and sin
Where we shall lead our harvest in.

Yet still from Eden springs the root
As clean as on the starting day.
Time takes the foliage and the fruit
And burns the archetypal leaf
To shapes of terror and of grief
Scattered along the winter way.
But famished field and blackened tree
Bear flowers in Eden never known.

Blossoms of grief and charity
Bloom in these darkened fields alone.
What had Eden ever to say
Of hope and faith and pity and love
Until was buried all its day
And memory found its treasure trove?
Strange blessings never in Paradise
Fall from these beclouded skies.

EDWIN MUIR

85   *The Killing*

That was the day they killed the Son of God
On a squat hill-top by Jerusalem.
Zion was bare, her children from their maze
Sucked by the demon curiosity
Clean through the gates. The very halt and blind
Had somehow got themselves up to the hill.

After the ceremonial preparation,
The scourging, nailing, nailing against the wood,
Erection of the main-trees with their burden,
While from the hill rose an orchestral wailing,
They were there at last, high up in the soft spring day.
We watched the writhings, heard the moanings, saw
The three heads turning on their separate axles
Like broken wheels left spinning. Round his head
Was loosely bound a crown of plaited thorn
That hurt at random, stinging temple and brow
As the pain swung into its envious circle.
In front the wreath was gathered in a knot
That as he gazed looked like the last stump left
Of a death-wounded deer's great antlers. Some
Who came to stare grew silent as they looked,
Indignant or sorry. But the hardened old
And the hard-hearted young, although at odds
From the first morning, cursed him with one curse,
Having prayed for a Rabbi or an armed Messiah

And found the Son of God. What use to them
Was a God or a Son of God? Of what avail
For purposes such as theirs? Beside the cross-foot
Alone, four women stood and did not move
All day. The sun revolved, the shadow wheeled,
The evening fell. His head lay on his breast,
But in his breast they watched his heart move on
By itself alone, accomplishing its journey.
Their taunts grew louder, sharpened by the knowledge
That he was walking in the park of death,
Far from their rage. Yet all grew stale at last,
Spite, curiosity, envy, hate itself.
They waited only for death and death was slow
And came so quietly they scarce could mark it.
They were angry then with death and death's deceit.

I was a stranger, could not read these people
Or this outlandish deity. Did a God
Indeed in dying cross my life that day
By chance, he on his road and I on mine?

EDWIN MUIR

86   *Discipline*

Throw away thy rod,
Throw away thy wrath:
        O my God,
Take the gentle path.

For my heart's desire
Unto thine is bent:
        I aspire
To a full consent.

Though I fail, I weep:
Though I halt in pace,
        Yet I creep
To the throne of grace.

Then let wrath remove;
Love will do the deed:
     For with love
Stony hearts will bleed.

Love is swift of foot;
Love's a man of war,
     And can shoot,
And can hit from far.

Who can scape his bow?
That which wrought on thee,
     Brought thee low,
Needs must work on me.

Throw away thy rod;
Though man frailties hath,
     Thou art God:
Throw away thy wrath.   GEORGE HERBERT

FOR ALL SEASONS OF THE YEAR

87   *Saint Patrick's Breastplate*

I bind unto myself today
The strong name of the Trinity:
By invocation of the same,
The Three in One and One in Three.

I bind this day to me for ever,
By power of faith, Christ's incarnation,
His baptism in the Jordan River,
His death on the Cross for my salvation.
His bursting from the spicèd tomb,
His riding up the heavenly way,
His coming at the day of doom
I bind unto myself today!

I bind unto myself today
The power of God to hold and lead:

His eye to watch, his might to stay,
His ear to hearken to my need;
The wisdom of my God to teach,
His hand to guide, his shield to ward;
The Word of God to give me speech,
His heavenly host to be my guard!

Christ be with me, Christ within me,
Christ behind me, Christ before me,
Christ beside me, Christ to win me,
Christ to comfort and restore me.
Christ beneath me, Christ above me,
Christ in quiet, Christ in danger,
Christ in hearts of all that love me,
Christ in mouth of friend and stranger.

I bind unto myself the name,
The strong name of the Trinity:
By invocation of the same,
The Three in One and One in Three;
Of whom all nature hath creation,
Eternal Father, Spirit, Word;
Praise to the Lord of my salvation—
Salvation is of Christ the Lord!   Amen.

ASCR. ST PATRICK. TR. MRS. C. F. ALEXANDER

88   *True Love*

My true love hath my heart and I have his,
    By just exchange one for another given;
I hold his dear, and mine he cannot miss,
    There never was a better bargain driven.
        My true love hath my heart and I have his.

His heart in me keeps him and me in one,
    My heart in him his thoughts and senses guides;
He loves my heart, for once it was his own,
    I cherish his, because in me it bides.
        My true love hath my heart and I have his.

SIR PHILIP SIDNEY

89   *'O come quickly!'*

Never weather-beaten sail more willing bent to shore,
Never tirèd pilgrim's limbs affected slumber more,
Than my wearied spright now longs to fly, out of my
         troubled breast:
    O come quickly, sweetest Lord, and take my soul
       to rest.
Ever-blooming are the joys of Heaven's high Paradise,
Cold age deafs not there our ears, nor vapour dims our
    eyes:
Glory there the sun outshines, whose beams the blessed
         only see:
    O come quickly, glorious Lord, and raise my spright
       to thee.

                                        THOMAS CAMPION

90   *Good Lord, deliver us!*

     From being anxious, or secure,
Dead clods of sadness, or light squibs of mirth,
     From thinking that great courts immure
All, or no happiness, or that this earth
          Is only for our prison framed,
          Or that thou art covetous
To them whom thou lov'st, or that they are maimed
From reaching this world's sweet who seek thee thus
With all their might, good Lord, deliver us.

     From needing danger to be good,
From owing thee yesterday's tears today,
     From trusting so much to thy blood
That in that hope we would our souls away,
          From bribing thee with alms to excuse
          Some sin more burdenous,
From light affecting, in religion, news,
From thinking us all soul, neglecting thus
Our mutual duties, Lord, deliver us.

From tempting Satan to tempt us
By our connivance or slack company,
From measuring ill by vicious,
Neglecting to choke sin's spawn, vanity,
From indiscreet humility,
Which might be scandalous
And cast reproach on Christianity,
From being spies, or to spies pervious,
From thirst, or scorn of fame, deliver us.

When senses, which thy soldiers are,
We arm against thee, and they fight for sin,
When want, sent but to tame, doth war
And work despair a breach to enter in,
When plenty, God's image and seal,
Makes us idolatrous,
And love it, not him, whom it should reveal,
When we are moved to seem religious
Only to vent wit, Lord deliver us.

JOHN DONNE

91 *A Hymn to God the Father*

Wilt thou forgive that sin where I begun,
Which is my sin, though it were done before?
Wilt thou forgive those sins through which I run,
And do run still, though still I do deplore?
When thou hast done, thou hast not done,
For I have more.

Wilt thou forgive that sin by which I won
Others to sin, and made my sin their door?
Wilt thou forgive that sin which I did shun
A year or two, but wallowed in a score?
When thou hast done, thou hast not done,
For I have more.

I have a sin of fear, that when I've spun
My last thread, I shall perish on the shore;
Swear by thyself that at my death thy Sun
Shall shine as it shines now, and heretofore;

> And having done that, thou hast done,
>   I have no more.   JOHN DONNE

92   *Hymn to God my God, in my Sickness*

Since I am coming to that Holy room,
    Where, with thy Quire of Saints for evermore,
I shall be made thy Music; As I come
    I tune the Instrument here at the door,
    And what I must do then, think here before.

Whilst my Physicians by their love are grown
    Cosmographers, and I their Map, who lie
Flat on this bed, that by them may be shown
    That this is my South-west discovery
    Per fretum febris, by these straits to die,

I joy, that in these straits, I see my West;
    For, though their currents yield return to none,
What shall my West hurt me? As West and East
    In all flat Maps (and I am one) are one,
    So death doth touch the Resurrection.

Is the Pacific Sea my home? Or are
    The Eastern riches? Is Jerusalem?
Anyan, and Magellan, and Gibraltar,
    All straits, and none but straits, are ways to them,
    Whether where Japhet dwelt, or Cham, or Sem.

We think that Paradise and Calvary,
    Christ's Cross, and Adam's tree, stood in one place;
Look, Lord, and find both Adams met in me;
    As the first Adam's sweat surrounds my face,
    May the Last Adam's blood my soul embrace.

So, in his purple wrapp'd receive me Lord,
    By these his thorns give me his other Crown;
And as to other's soul I preach'd thy word,
    Be this my Text, my Sermon to mine own,
    Therefore that he may raise the Lord throws down.

                                                           JOHN DONNE

Thou who has put the times and seasons in thine own power
Grant that we make our prayer unto thee in a time
Convenient and when Thou may'st be found

> and save us.

Thou who for us men and for our salvation wast born
 at dead of night:
Give us daily to be born again by renewing of the Holy
 Ghost,
Till Christ be formed in us unto a perfect man,

> and save us.

Thou who very early in the morning while the sun was
 yet arising didst rise from the dead:
Raise us up daily unto newness of life
Suggesting to us ways of repentance which thyself knowest

> and save us.

Thou who at the third hour didst send down thy Holy
 Ghost on the apostles:
Take not away the same Spirit from us,
but renew him daily within us,

> and save us.

Thou who hast willed the ninth hour to be an hour of
 prayer:
Hear us while we pray in the hour of prayer and
Make us to obtain our prayer and our desires

> and save us.

Thou who didst vouchsafe even at the eleventh hour of
 the day to send men into thy vineyard and to fix a wage,
notwithstanding they had stood all the day idle:
do unto us like favour and, though it be late, as it were
 about the eleventh hour, accept us graciously when we
 return to thee,

> and save us.

BISHOP LANCELOT ANDREWES

94 *Trinity Sunday*

Lord, who hast form'd me out of mud,
    And hast redeem'd me through thy blood,
    And sanctifi'd me to do good;

Purge all my sins done heretofore:
    For I confess my heavy score,
    And I will strive to sin no more.

Enrich my heart, mouth, hands in me,
    With faith, with hope, with charity;
    That I may run, rise, rest with thee.

GEORGE HERBERT

95 *Antiphon*

Cho. Let all the world in ev'ry corner sing,
             My God and King.

    Vers. The heav'ns are not too high,
          His praise may thither fly:
          The earth is not too low,
          His praises there may grow.

Cho. Let all the world in ev'ry corner sing,
             My God and King.

    Vers. The church with psalms must shout,
          No door can keep them out:
          But above all, the heart
          Must bear the longest part.

Cho. Let all the world in ev'ry corner sing,
             My God and King.

GEORGE HERBERT

96 *His Litany to the Holy Spirit*

In the hour of my distress,
When temptations me oppress,

And when I my sins confess,
    Sweet Spirit comfort me!

When I lie within my bed,
Sick in heart and sick in head,
And with doubts discomforted,
    Sweet Spirit comfort me!

When the house doth sigh and weep,
And the world is drowned in sleep,
Yet mine eyes the watch do keep,
    Sweet Spirit comfort me!

When the artless Doctor sees
No one hope but of his fees,
And his skill runs on the lees,
    Sweet Spirit comfort me!

When his potion and his pill,
Has, or none, or little skill,
Meet for nothing but to kill,
    Sweet Spirit comfort me!

When the passing-bell doth toll,
And the Furies in a shoal,
Come to fright a parting soul,
    Sweet Spirit comfort me!

When the tapers now burn blue,
And the comforters are few,
And that number more than true,
    Sweet Spirit comfort me!

When the priest his last hath prayed,
And I nod to what is said,
'Cause my speech is now decayed,
    Sweet Spirit comfort me!

When (God knows) I'm tossed about,
Either with despair or doubt,
Yet before the glass be out,
    Sweet Spirit comfort me!

When the Tempter me pursu'th
With the sins of all my youth,
And half damns me with untruth,
    Sweet Spirit comfort me!

When the flames and hellish cries
Fright mine ears and fright mine eyes,
And all terrors me surprise,
    Sweet Spirit comfort me!

When the judgment is revealed,
And that opened which was sealed,
When to thee I have appealed,
    Sweet Spirit comfort me!

ROBERT HERRICK

97   *At a Solemn Music*

Blest pair of Sirens, pledges of Heav'n's joy,
Sphere-born harmonious sisters, Voice and Verse,
Wed your divine sounds, and mixed power employ
Dead things with inbreath'd sense able to pierce,
And to our high-rais'd phantasy present,
That undisturbèd song of pure concent,
Aye sung before the sapphire-colour'd throne
To him that sits thereon
With saintly shout, and solemn jubilee,
Where the bright seraphim in burning row
Their loud up-lifted angel-trumpets blow,
And the cherubic host in thousand choirs
Touch their immortal harps of golden wires,
With those just spirits that wear victorious palms,
Hymns devout and holy psalms
Singing everlastingly;
That we on earth with undiscording voice
May rightly answer that melodious noise;
As once we did, till disproportion'd sin
Jarr'd against Nature's chime, and with harsh din
Broke the fair music that all creatures made

To their great Lord, whose love their motion sway'd
In perfect diapason, whilst they stood
In first obedience, and their state of good.
O may we soon again renew that song,
And keep in tune with heaven, will God ere long
To his celestial consort us unite,
To live with him, and sing in endless morn of light.

JOHN MILTON

98   *The Morning-Watch*

O Joys! Infinite sweetness! with what flowers,
And shoots of glory, my soul breaks, and buds!
                    All the long hours
                    Of night, and rest,
                    Through the still shrouds
                    Of sleep, and clouds,
                    This dew fell on my breast;
                    O, how it bloods,
And spirits all my earth! Hark! in what rings,
And hymning circulations the quick world
                    Awakes, and sings;
                    The rising winds
                    And falling springs,
                    Birds, beasts, all things
                    Adore him in their kinds.
                    Thus all is hurled
In sacred hymns and order, the great chime
And symphony of nature. Prayer is
                    The world in tune,
                    A spirit-voice,
                    And vocal joys
                    Whose echo's heaven's bliss.
                    O, let me climb,
When I lie down. The pious soul by night
Is like a clouded star, whose beams, though said
                    To shed their light
                    Under some cloud,

Yet are above,
And shine and move
Beyond that misty shroud.
So in my bed,
That curtained grave, though sleep, like ashes, hide
My lamp, and life, both shall in thee abide.

HENRY VAUGHAN

99   *Peace*

My soul, there is a country
　　Far beyond the stars,
Where stands a wingèd sentry
　　All skilful in the wars:
There above noise and danger
　　Sweet Peace sits crowned with smiles,
And One born in a manger
　　Commands the beauteous files.
He is thy gracious friend
　　And—O my soul, awake!—
Did in pure love descend
　　To die here for thy sake.
If thou canst get but thither,
　　There grows the flower of Peace,
The Rose that cannot whither,
　　Thy fortress, and thy ease.
Leave then thy foolish ranges,
　　For none can thee secure,
But one who never changes,
　　Thy God, thy life, thy cure.

HENRY VAUGHAN

100   *The World*

I saw Eternity the other night
Like a great Ring of pure and endless light,
　　All calm, as it was bright;

And round beneath it, Time, in hours, days, years,
    Driven by the spheres
Like a vast shadow moved, in which the world
    And all her train were hurled.
The doting Lover in his quaintest strain
    Did there complain;
Near him, his lute, his fancy, and his flights,
    Wit's sour delights;

With gloves and knots, the silly snares of pleasure;
    Yet his dear treasure
All scattered lay, while he his eyes did pour
    Upon a flower.

The darksome Statesman hung with weights and woe,
Like a thick midnight fog, moved there so slow
    He did not stay nor go;
Condemning thoughts, like sad eclipses, scowl
    Upon his soul,
And clouds of crying witnesses without
    Pursued him with one shout.
Yet digged the mole, and, lest his ways be found,
    Worked underground,
Where he did clutch his prey; but One did see
    That policy.
Churches and altars fed him, perjuries
    Were gnats and flies;
It rained about him blood and tears, but he
    Drank them as free.

The fearful Miser on a heap of rust
Sat pining all his life there, did scarce trust
    His own hands with the dust;
Yet would not place one piece above, but lives
    In fear of thieves.
Thousands there were as frantic as himself,
    And hugged each one his pelf.
The downright Epicure placed heaven in sense
    And scorned pretence;

While others, slipped into a wide excess,
    Said little less;
The weaker sort, slight, trivial wares enslave,
    Who think them brave;
And poor despisèd Truth sat counting by
    Their victory.

Yet some, who all this while did weep and sing,
And sing and weep, soared up into the Ring;
    But most would use no wing.
O fools (said I), thus to prefer dark night
    Before true light,
To live in grots, and caves, and hate the day
    Because it shows the way,
The way which from this dead and dark abode
    Leads up to God,
A way where you might tread the sun, and be
    More bright than he.
But as I did their madness so discuss,
    One whispered thus,
This Ring the Bridegroom did for none provide
    But for his Bride.

HENRY VAUGHAN

101   *In No Strange Land*

O world invisible, we view thee,
O world intangible, we touch thee,
O world unknowable, we know thee,
Inapprehensible, we clutch thee!

Does the fish soar to find the ocean,
The eagle plunge to find the air—
That we ask of the stars in motion
If they have rumour of thee there?

Not where the wheeling systems darken,
And our benumb'd conceiving soars!—
The drift of pinions, would we hearken,
Beats at our own clay-shuttered doors.

The angels keep their ancient places;—
Turn but a stone, and start a wing!
'Tis ye, 'tis your estrangèd faces,
That miss the many-splendour'd thing.

But (when so sad thou canst not sadder)
Cry—and upon thy so sore loss
Shall shine the traffic of Jacob's ladder
Pitched between Heaven and Charing Cross.

Yea, in the night, my Soul, my daughter,
Cry—clinging heaven by the hems;
And lo, Christ walking on the water,
Not of Gennesareth, but Thames!

FRANCIS THOMPSON

102   *That Nature is a Heraclitean Fire*
                         and
            of the Comfort of the Resurrection

¹Cloud-puffball, torn tufts, tossed pillows ¹ flaunt forth,
    then chevy on an air-
built thoroughfare: heaven-roysterers, in gay-gangs ¹ they
    throng; they glitter in marches.
Down roughcast, down dazzling whitewash, ¹ wherever
    an elm arches,
Shivelights and shadowtackle in long ¹ lashes, lace,
    lance, and pair.
Delightfully the bright wind boisterous ¹ ropes, wrestles,
    beats earth bare
Of yestertempest's creases; ¹ in pool and rut peel parches
Squandering ooze to squeezed ¹ dough, crust, dust;
    stanches, starches
Squadroned masks and manmarks ¹ treadmire toil there
Footfretted in it. Million-fuelèd, ¹ nature's bonfire
    burns on.
But quench her bonniest, dearest ¹ to her, her clearest-
    selvèd spark

1161

Man, how fast his firedint, [|] his mark on mind, is gone!
Both are in an unfathomable, all is in an enormous dark
Drowned. O pity and indig [|] nation! Manshape, that
    shone
Sheer off, disseveral, a star, [|] death blots black out; nor
    mark
              Is any of him at all so stark
But vastness blurs and time [|] beats level. Enough! the
    Resurrection,
A heart's-clarion! Away grief's gasping, [|] joyless days,
    dejection.
             Across my foundering deck shone
A beacon, an eternal beam. [|] Flesh fade, and mortal trash
Fall to the residuary worm; [|] world's wildfire, leave but
    ash:
In a flash, at a trumpet crash,
I am all at once what Christ is, [|] since he was what I am
    and
This Jack, joke, poor potsherd, [|] patch, matchwood,
    immortal diamond,
             Is immortal diamond.

                             GERARD MANLEY HOPKINS

103   *Pied Beauty*

    Glory be to God for dappled things—
        For skies of couple-colour as a brinded cow;
            For rose-moles all in stipple upon trout that swim;
    Fresh firecoal chestnut-falls; finches' wings;
    Landscape plotted and pieced—fold, fallow, and plough;
        And áll trádes, their gear and tackle and trim.

    All things counter, original, spare, strange;
        Whatever is fickle, freckled (who knows how?)
           With swift, slow; sweet, sour; adazzle, dim;
    He fathers-forth whose beauty is past change:
                     Praise him.

                             GERARD MANLEY HOPKINS

104 *God's Grandeur*

The world is charged with the grandeur of God.
   It will flame out, like shining from shook foil;
   It gathers to a greatness, like the ooze of oil
Crushed. Why do men then now not reck his rod?
Generations have trod, have trod, have trod;
   And all is seared with trade; bleared, smeared with toil;
   And wears man's smudge and shares man's smell: the soil
Is bare now, nor can foot feel, being shod.

And for all this, nature is never spent;
   There lives the dearest freshness deep down things;
And though the last lights off the black West went
   Oh, morning, at the brown brink eastward, springs—
Because the Holy Ghost over the bent
   World broods with warm breast and with ah! bright wings.

GERARD MANLEY HOPKINS

105 From Choruses from *The Rock*, X

O Light Invisible, we praise Thee!
Too bright for mortal vision.
O Greater Light, we praise Thee for the less;
The eastern light our spires touch at morning,
The light that slants upon our western doors at evening,
The twilight over stagnant pools at batflight,
Moon light and star light, owl and moth light,
Glow-worm glowlight on a grassblade.
O Light Invisible, we worship Thee!

We thank Thee for the lights that we have kindled,
The light of altar and of sanctuary;
Small lights of those who meditate at midnight
And lights directed through the coloured panes of windows
And light reflected from the polished stone,
The gilded carven wood, the coloured fresco.
Our gaze is submarine, our eyes look upward

And see the light that fractures through unquiet water.
We see the light but see not whence it comes.
O Light Invisible, we glorify Thee!

T. S. ELIOT

106 *The Incarnation*

Then He summoned an archangel,
Saint Gabriel: and when he came,
Sent him forth to find a maiden,
    Mary was her name.

Only through her consenting love
Could the mystery be preferred
That the Trinity in human
    Flesh might clothe the Word.

Though the three Persons worked the wonder
It only happened in the One.
So was the Word made incarnation
    In Mary's womb, a son.

So He who only had a Father
Now had a Mother undefiled,
Though not as ordinary maids
    Had she conceived the Child.

By Mary, and with her own flesh
He was clothed in His own frame:
Both Son of God and Son of Man
    Together had one name.

ST JOHN OF THE CROSS. TR ROY CAMPBELL

107 *Concerning the Divine Word*

With the divinest Word, the Virgin
Made pregnant, down the road
Comes walking, if you'll grant her
A room in your abode.

ST JOHN OF THE CROSS. TR ROY CAMPBELL

Of the Birth of Christ

When the ancient dispensation
Its predestin'd course had run,
Straight from out His bridal chamber
Came the Bridegroom, God the Son.

Once on earth, with arms extended
He embrac'd His heavenly Bride,
And His blessèd Mother laid Him
In the manger, at her side.

All around that helpless baby
Animals were standing by;
Men sang songs of glad rejoicing;
Angels join'd their songs on high,

Celebrating the betrothal
'Twixt the Bridegroom and the Bride,
While the Almighty, in the manger,
As an infant, wept and cried.

Gems these tears which human nature
Brought to the betrothal-rite,
And the Maid was lost in wonder
As she witness'd such a sight.

Man was full of joy and gladness;
God was weeping, weak and lone.
Ne'er before throughout the ages
Had so strange a thing been known.

ST JOHN OF THE CROSS
TR E. ALLISON PEERS

*Nos. 109-127 for Night Prayer are given after Week 4 in the psalter,
pp 680 ff.*

INDEXES

INDEX OF HYMN METRES AND SUGGESTED TUNES

The tunes listed here are suggested only as an aid to the user, and are given because they are readily available in standard hymn collections. Any suitable hymn tunes may be used.

First words	Tune	Metre
Abide with me	Eventide	10.10.10.10.
Abroad the regal banners	Andernach	LM
Afar from where the sun	St Venantius	LM
All creation was renewed	Gott sei dank (Lübeck)	77.77.
Alleluia, sing to Jesus	Hyfrydol	87.87.D.
All people that on earth	Old hundredth	LM
All ye who seek a comfort	St Bernard	CM
Alone with none but thee	Auch jetzt macht	86.86.88
A mighty wind invades	Herongate	LM
Angels of God, you see	Trisagion	10.10.10.10.
A noble flow'r of Juda	Es ist ein Ros entsprungen	76.76.676.
Apostle of the Gentiles	Wareham	LM
At the Lamb's high feast	Salzburg	77.77.D.
Battle is o'er	Surrexit	888.Alleluias
Before we end our day	St Bernard	CM
Bethlehem, of noblest cities	Stuttgart	87.87.
Bless'd be the Lord our God	Corona	DSM
Blest are the pure in heart	Franconia	SM
Bring, all ye dear-bought nations, bring, Alleluia	Lasst uns erfreuen	LM. Alleluias
Christ be near at either hand	Greystones	77.77.
Christ died, but soon revived, alleluia	Lasst uns erfreuen	LM. Alleluias
Christ is here, Emmanuel	Ravenshaw (66.66.)	75.75.
Christ is the world's Redeemer	O king of might Moville	76.76.D.
Christ the Lord is risen	Easter hymn	77.77.
Christ, the true light of us, true morn	O amor quam exstaticus	LM

First words	Tune	Metre
Christ, whose blood	Greystones	77.77.
Come down, O Love divine	Down Ampney	66.11.D.
Come, Holy Ghost, Creator	Tallis ordinal	CM
Come, O Creator, Spirit blest	Veni Creator	LM
Come, O Creator Spirit, come	Veni Creator	LM
Come, praise the Lord	Lobe den Herren	14.14.4.7.8.
Come, ye faithful, raise	Ach wie kurz	76.76.D.
Creator of the stars of night	Creator alme siderum	LM
Day is done	Ar hyd y nos	84.84.8884.
Easter glory fills the sky	Francois	77.77.Alleluias
Father most holy	Theophila	11.11.11.5.
Father, we praise you	Christe sanctorum	11.11.11.5.
Firmly I believe and truly	Stuttgart	87.87.
For all the saints	Sine nomine	10.10.10.Alleluias
Forth from on high	Melcombe	LM
Gall he drinks: his strength	St Thomas	87.87.87.
God called great prophets	Richmond	CM
God, of thy pity, unto us thy children	Herzliebster Jesu	11.11.11.5.
God's blessèd Spirit	Eventide	10.10.10.10.
God, who made the earth	Paderborn (76.76.)	75.75.
Hail, our Queen and Mother blest	Ave Virgo virginum	76.76.D.
Hail our Saviour's glorious body	St Thomas	87.87.87.
Hail, Queen of heaven, beyond compare	Rottenburg	DLM
Hail, Queen of heav'n, the ocean star	Stella	88.88.88.
Hail to the Lord who comes	Psalm 32	66.66.
Hail, Redeemer, King divine	King divine	77.77.D.
Hear the herald voice	Merton	87.87.
Holy God, we praise thy name	Grosser Gott	78.78.77.
Holy light on earth's horizon	Blaenwern	87.87.D.
I am the holy vine	Love unknown	66.66.44.44.
I bind unto myself today	St Patrick's Breastplate	Irregular
In the beginning, God created		11.6.11.6.
It were my soul's desire	Maria jung und zart	66.66.
	Fingal	

First words	Tune	Metre
Jesus, the sun of ransomed earth	O invidenda martyrum	LM
Jesus, true God and Rock	Iste confessor	11.11.11.5.
Joseph, the scriptures	Aimable enfant	DLM
Joseph, wise ruler	Diva servatrix	11.11.11.5.
Joy fill your heart, O queen most high	Lasst uns erfreuen	LM. Alleluias
Leader now on earth no longer	Swavesey	87.87.D.
Lead, kindly Light	Lux benigna	10.4.10.4.10.10.
Let all on earth their voices	Hurley	LM
Lord God, we give you thanks	Woodlands	10.10.10.10.
Lord God, your light which dims the stars	Providence	84.84.
Lord Jesus, think on me	Southwell	SM
Love of the Father, love of God the Son	Song 22	10.10.10.10.
Lord of all hopefulness	Slane	10.11.11.12.
Maiden, yet a Mother	Grace soit rendue	65.65.D.
Man of sorrows	Afron	77.77.D.
Mary, crowned with living light	Parvulus (76.76.)	75.75.
Merciful Saviour, hear	Old 124th	10.10.10.10.10.
More ancient than the primal world	Creator alme siderum	LM
Mother of Christ, hear thou	Song 1	10.10.10.10.10.10.
My God, I love thee though	Everlasting love	CM
My song is love unknown	Love unknown	66.66.44.44.
Now it is evening	Christus sanctorum	11.11.11.5.
Now let us all with one accord	Rerum Deus tenax vigor	LM
Now thank we all our God	Nun Danket	67.67.66.66.
Now that the daylight fills	Saxony	LM
O blessed Lord, creator God	O Mensch sieh	8.8.8.
O Christ, the light of heaven	Narenza	SM
O come, all ye faithful	Adeste fideles	Irregular
O come, now Rod of Jesse's stem	Veni Emmanuel	88.88.88.
O come, O come, Emmanuel	Veni Emmanuel	88.88.88.
O cross of Christ, immortal	St Flavian	CM
O fair is our Lord's own city	Attracta	76.76.
O fathers of our ancient faith	Creator alme siderum	LM

First words	Tune	Metre
Of the Father's love begotten	Divinum mysterium	87.87.877.
O God, creator of us all	Severn view	LM
O great St David	Saint David	11 10.11 10.11 10.11.9.
O Jesu, thou the virgin's crown	Rex gloriose martyrum	LM
O light serene of God		11.6.11.4.
O loving wisdom of our God	Billing	CM
O most holy one	O Sanctissima (10.7.10.7.)	Irregular.
O Peter, who were named by Christ	Gonfalon Royal	LM
O sacred Head ill-usèd	Passion chorale	76.76.D.
O sacred Heart, our home lies		4.6.8.8.4.
O strength and stay	Strength and stay	11.10.11.10.
O Trinity of blessed light	Tallis' canon	LM
Our Lord the path of suffering trod	Mein Seel, O Gott, muss loben dich	LM
Praise, my soul, the king	Praise my soul	87.87.87.
Praise to the holiest	Billing	CM
Proclaim his triumph	Eisenach	LM
Praise we the woman	Morning hymn	LM
Queen of heaven, rejoice		
Queen, on whose starry brow	Eisenach	LM
Remember those, O Lord	Franconia	SM
Sing all creation, sing	Diva servatrix	11.11.11.5.
Songs of thankfulness and praise	Werde munter mein Gemüte	77.77.D.
Sower and seed of man's reprieving	Les commandements de Dieu	98.98.
Spirit of God, on the waste	Liebster Immanuel	11.10.11.10.
Star of sea and ocean	Ave Maris stella	66.66.
Sweet Saviour, bless us	Sunset	88.88.88.
The ark which God has sanctified	St Peter	CM
The co-eternal Son	Optatus	SM
The Church's one foundation	Aurelia	76.76.D.
The day is filled with splendour	Paderborn	76.76.
The day thou gavest, Lord	St Clement	98.98.

First words	Tune	Metre
The Father's glory, Christ	Creator alme siderum	LM
The Father's holy ones	Auctoritate saeculi	LM
The Lord goes up with shouts of joy	Duke Street	LM
The love of God was shown	Abends	LM
The martyrs living now	Horsley	CM
The saints who toiled	Old hundredth	LM
They come, God's messengers	Angels' song	LM
This is the day	Iste confessor	11.11.11.5.
To Christ the Lord of worlds	Deus tuorum militum	LM
Transcendent God	Morning hymn	LM
To Christ, the prince of peace	Ave Maria klare	SM
Unto us a Child is given	Drakes Boughton	87.87.
We bless you, Father	Saxony	LM
What fairer light is this	Decora lux	12.12.12.12.
When Christ our Lord to Andrew cried	St Andrew	DCM
When God had filled the earth	St Bernard	CM
When God made man he gave him	Woodlands	10.10.10.10.
When Jesus comes to be baptized	Winchester New	LM
When time began, God walked	Melita	88.88.88.
Who are these like stars	All saints	87.87.77.
Who is she ascends so high	Assumpta est	75.75.

SCRIPTURE VERSIONS USED
FOR CANTICLES

Grail Version

Exodus 15:1-4a,8-13,17-18	Daniel 3:52-57
Deuteronomy 32:1-12	3:57-88 56
1 Samuel 2:1-10	Hab 3:2-4,13a,15-19
Sirach 36:1-7,13-16	Luke 1:46-55
Isaiah 12:1-6	1:68-79
45:15-26	2:29-32
Jeremiah 31:10-14	

Revised Standard Version

1 Chron 29:10-13	Isaiah 66:10-14a
Tobit 13:1-5b,7-8	Jeremiah 14:17-21
13:8-11,13-15	Ezekiel 36:24-28
Judith 16:2-3a,15-19	Daniel 3:3,4,6,11-18
Wisdom 9:1-6,9-11	Ephesians 1:3-10
Proverbs 9:1-6,10-12	Philippians 2:6-11
Isaiah 2:2-5	Colossians 1:12-20
26:1-4,7-9,12	1 Timothy 3:16
33:13-16	1 Peter 2:21-24
38:10-14,17-20	Revelation 4:11; 5:9,10,12
40:10-17	11:17-18; 12:10b-12a
42:10-16	15:3-4
61:10-62:5	19:1-2,5-7

1171

INDEX OF PSALMS

The division of the psalms into strophes has been maintained as well as the accents, so the psalms may be sung to the Gelineau melodies; yet, in order to facilitate recitation or singing according to the verses the latter have been marked in the traditional manner with † and * depending on whether there are three or only two lines to the verse.

Instead of *Glory be to the Father*, any approved doxology, suitable for singing, may be used.

NUMBERING OF THE PSALMS
The following is a note from the Grail Psalter on the numbering of the psalms. In *Morning and Evening Prayer* the Hebrew numbering is given in parentheses at the head of each psalm.

The numbering of the psalms to be found in most Christian liturgies is taken from the Greek Septuagint. The numeration differs from that found in the Hebrew text and the Authorised Version. Since books with a liturgical emphasis (such as the present one) generally follow the Septuagint numbering, and other Biblical and exegetical works the Hebrew, it seems useful to give the comparative numbering of the two systems:

Greek Septuagint	*Hebrew*
1-8	1-8
9	9-10
10-112	11-113
113	114-115
114-115	116
116-145	117-146
146-147	147
148-150	148-150

Therefore for most of the psalms the Greek numeration is one behind that of the Hebrew.

The numbering of the verses is also slightly different from that of the later English versions. These generally begin numbering the verses from the body of the psalm, and leave its preceding title out of account. The liturgical texts on the other hand have included the title in their reckoning, and when this is more than a few words long, they have counted the beginning of the psalm as its second or third verse. It is this latter system which has been followed here, though the wording of the titles themselves has not been included. Very occasionally the sequence of verses within a psalm has been disturbed (as for instance in Psalm 21:16-18) in an attempt to restore what appears to have been the order of the original.

INDEX OF PSALMS

INDEX OF CANTICLES

ACKNOWLEDGEMENTS

ACKNOWLEDGMENTS

The Publishers are grateful to the following for permission to reproduce copyright material:

SCRIPTURE TEXTS
The following versions have been used:
Knox Bible, © 1945, 1949, the Hierarchy of England and Wales.
New English Bible, 2nd edition copyright 1970, Oxford and Cambridge University Presses.
Revised Standard Version, Common Bible, copyrighted © 1973, by the Division of Christian Education, National Council of the Churches of Christ in the USA. Special permission has been obtained to use in this publication the 'you-your-yours' forms of the personal pronoun in the address to God.
Today's English Version (Good News for Modern Man), United Bible Societies of America and Collins Publishers, London.
See *Index of Canticles* for details of versions used in the Canticles.
Psalm texts are translated from the Hebrew by The Grail, © The Grail (England) 1963, and published by Collins in Fontana Books, London, 1963. They are reprinted from the Singing Version first published in Fontana Books in 1966.
The practical needs of choral recitation prompted a number of revisions in the psalms and canticles of this Breviary. These revisions are made with the agreement of The Grail.
Alternative texts of the Gospel Canticles given on the last pages, are © 1970, 1971, International Consultation on English Texts.

HYMNS AND RELIGIOUS POETRY
Ampleforth Abbey Trustees, for Ralph Wright OSB, 'Star of sea and ocean'.
Benedictine Nuns of St Mary's Abbey, West Malling, Kent, for 'We praise you, Father, for your gift'.
Geoffrey Chapman Publishers, for James Quinn SJ, 'Blessed be the Lord our God', 'Come praise the Almighty', 'Day is done but love unfailing', 'Easter glory fills the sky', 'Forth from on high the Father sends', 'Hail our Saviour's glorious body', 'I am the holy vine', 'Jesus, true God and rock', 'Jesus, your church was built', 'Joseph, wise ruler', 'Joy fill your heart, O Queen most high', 'Remember those, O Lord', 'Sing all creation'; and, from *Praise the Lord* (revised), 'Now let us all with one accord', 'Of the Father's love begotten' (adaptations), 'Osacred head ill-used' (verse 2).
Chatto & Windus and the literary estate of Eleanor Henrietta Hull, for 'It were my soul's desire'.

1175

ACKNOWLEDGEMENTS

Faber Music Ltd, London, from *New Catholic Hymnal*, 'A noble flow'r of Juda' (paraphrased by Anthony Petti), 'Man of sorrows wrapt in grief' (adapted by Anthony Petti and Geoffrey Laycock), 'Hear the herald voice resounding' (adapted by Anthony Petti).

Faber & Faber Ltd, Publishers, and Harcourt Brace Jovanovich Inc, for T. S. Eliot, two extracts from 'Choruses from "The Rock"' (in USA copyright 1936 Harcourt Brace Jovanovich Inc, and copyright © 1963, 1964, T. S. Eliot); and for 'Marina' (in USA copyright 1935 by Harcourt Brace Jovanovich Inc, and copyright © 1963, 1964, by T. S. Eliot); all from *Collected Poems 1909–1962*.

Faber & Faber Ltd, Publishers, and Oxford University Press Inc, for Edwin Muir, 'One Foot in Eden', and 'The Killing', from *Collected Poems 1921–1958* (in USA, copyright © 1960 Willa Muir).

The literary executors of Canon J. Fennelly, for 'Christ be near at either hand'.

Harvill Press, and Roy Campbell (translator), for St John of the Cross, 'The Incarnation' and 'Concerning the Divine Word'.

Hymn Society of America, for G. W. Briggs, 'God hath spoken by his prophets', from *Ten New Hymns on the Bible*, copyright 1953 Hymn Society of America.

Proprietors of *Hymns Ancient and Modern*, for Bishop W. H. Frere, 'The saints who toiled from place to place'.

Oxford University Press, for 'Lord of all hopefulness', © Jan Struther 1901–1955, from *Enlarged Songs of Praise*; 'Love of the Father, love of God the Son', © R. S. Bridges 1844–1930, from *The Yattendon Hymnal* (edited by Robert Bridges and H. Ellis Wooldridge); 'Father, we praise thee, now the night is over', © translation Percy Dearmer 1867–1936, from *The English Hymnal*.

Canon Coslett Quin, for 'O fair is our Lord's own city', translation from the Irish of Rev. Owen Donnelly b. 1647.

Search Press, for E. Allison Peers, trans, John of the Cross, 'Of the Birth of Christ'; for hymn texts from *Westminster Hymnal*: R. A. Knox, 'Afar from where the sun doth rise', 'Battle is o'er', 'Father most holy', 'Jesus the sun', 'Joseph, the scriptures', 'Maiden yet a mother', 'My God I love thee', 'O sacred head', 'Queen on whose starry brow', 'Sing my tongue of warfare ended', 'Sower and seed', 'What fairer light'; Walter Shewring, 'Christ the true light', 'To Christ the Lord'; A. G. McDougall, 'God of thy pity'; P. Brennan, 'Hail Redeemer'; F. E. Mostyn, 'O great St David'; J. O'Connor, 'This is the day'; from *Day Hours of the Roman Breviary*, 'Praise we the woman who endued'.

Benedictine Nuns of Stanbrook Abbey, from *Stanbrook Abbey Hymnal*, 'All creation was renewed', 'A mighty wind invades the world', 'Angels of God, you see the Father's face', 'Apostle of the Gentiles, Paul', 'Christ is here, Emmanuel', 'Eternal Father, through your word', 'God's blessed

1176

Spirit moved his virgin saint', 'God called great prophets to foretell', 'God who made the earth and sky', 'Hail Queen of heaven beyond compare', 'In the beginning God created heaven', 'Lord God, we give you thanks', 'Lord God, your light which dims the stars', 'Mary, crowned with living light', 'More ancient than the primal world', 'O blessed Lord, creator God', 'O Christ the light of heaven', 'O cross of Christ, immortal tree', 'O fathers of our ancient faith', 'O God, creator of us all', 'O light serene of God the Father's glory', 'O Peter, who were named', 'Proclaim his triumph', 'Spirit of God on the waste and the darkness', 'The ark which God has sanctified', 'The day is filled with splendour', 'The Father's glory, Christ our light', 'The Father's holy ones, the blest', 'The Lord goes up with shouts of joy', 'The love of God was shown to man', 'The martyrs living now with Christ', 'They come, God's messengers of love', 'Transcendent God in whom we live', 'Unto us a child is given', 'We bless you, Father, Lord of life', 'When God had filled the earth with life', 'When God made man, he gave him all the earth', 'When time began, God walked with man', 'When Jesus comes to be baptized'.

Schott & Co Ltd, for P. Hebert, trans G. R. Woodward, 'Now it is evening'.

Irvin Udulutsch OFM Cap, for 'Creator of the stars of night'.

World Library Publications Inc, Cincinnati OH45214, for M. Farrel, 'Merciful Saviour, hear our humble prayer', © copyright 1955, 1966, World Library Publications Inc. Cincinnati, OH45214.

ICET TEXTS FOR THE GOSPEL CANTICLES

THE SONG OF ZECHARIAH

Blessed be the Lord, the God of Israel;*
he has come to his people and set them free.
He has raised up for us a mighty saviour,*
born of the house of his servant David.

Through his holy prophets he promised of old†
    that he would save us from our enemies,*
from the hands of all who hate us.
He promised to show mercy to our fathers*
and to remember his holy covenant.

This was the oath he swore to our father Abraham:*
to set us free from the hand of our enemies,
free to worship him without fear,*
holy and righteous in his sight
    all the days of our life.

You, my child, shall be called the prophet of the Most High*
for you will go before the Lord to prepare his way,
to give his people knowledge of salvation*
by forgiving them their sins.

In the tender compassion of our God*
the dawn from on high shall break upon us,
to shine on those who dwell in darkness and the shadow of death,*
and to guide our feet on the road of peace.

THE SONG OF THE VIRGIN MARY

My soul proclaims the greatness of the Lord,*
my spirit rejoices in God my Saviour;
for he has looked with favour on his lowly servant,*
and from this day all generations will call me blessed.

The Almighty has done great things for me:*
holy is his Name.
He has mercy on those who fear him*
in every generation.

He has shown the strength of his arm,*
he has scattered the proud in their conceit.
He has cast down the mighty from their thrones,*
and has lifted up the lowly.
He has filled the hungry with good things,*
and has sent the rich away empty.

He has come to the help of his servant Israel*
for he has remembered his promise of mercy,
the promise he made to our fathers,*
to Abraham and his children for ever.

THE SONG OF SIMEON

Now, Lord, you have kept your word:*
let your servant go in peace.

With my own eyes I have seen the salvation*
which you have prepared in the sight of every people:

a light to reveal you to the nations*
and the glory of your people Israel.

Appendix III
SAINTS OF THE NATIONAL CALENDARS

Australia
England and Wales
Ireland
Scotland

The asterisk denotes a celebration which occurs in the Calendar of the Universal Church.

AUSTRALIA

17 March
SAINT PATRICK, Bishop*

Solemnity

From the Proper of Saints, p 747, and the Common of Pastors, p 1035. Hymn as on p 1193.

28 April
SAINT PETER CHANEL
Priest and Martyr*

Memoria

As in the Proper of Saints, p 776.

24 May
OUR LADY HELP OF CHRISTIANS
Patroness of Australia

Solemnity

In 1844 at the First Provincial Synod of Sydney, Our Lady Help of Christians was chosen as the patroness of Australia. In her maternal love Mary cares for the brethren of her Son who still journey on earth amidst trials and dangers, until they reach their home in heaven.

From the Common of the Blessed Virgin Mary, p 982, except for the following:

EVENING PRAYER I

Intercessions

Let us praise God the Father who chose Mary as the mother of his Son and wanted all generations to call her blessed. ℞ Our Lady Help of Christians, pray for us.

Father, you did great things for the Virgin Mary and brought her, body and soul, to the glory of heaven;—fill the hearts of your children with the hope of Christ's glory. ℞

Through the prayers of Mary, our help, protect our country, comfort the sorrowful, pardon sinners;—grant peace and salvation to all. ℞

You favoured Mary with the fulness of grace;—bestow on all men your overflowing blessings. ℞

May your Church be united heart and soul, held fast together by love,—and your faithful joined in continuous prayer, with Mary the mother of Jesus. ℞

Father, you have exalted the Virgin Mary and crowned her queen of heaven;—may the dead enter your kingdom and rejoice with your saints for ever. ℞

Our Father

The concluding prayer as at Morning Prayer, p 1182.

Invitatory

Ant. Let us rejoice in the Lord as we celebrate the feast of our Lady Help of Christians (alleluia).

MORNING PRAYER

Intercessions

Let us proclaim the greatness of our Saviour who chose to be born of the Virgin Mary. ℞ Lord, may your mother be our help.

Sun of justice, you showed your day was dawning in the immaculate Virgin Mary;—help us to walk in the daylight of your presence. ℞

Eternal Word, in the living flesh of Mary you found a dwelling place on earth;—remain with us for ever in hearts free from sin. ℞

Christ, our Saviour, you willed that your mother should be there when you died;—through her intercession may we rejoice to share your suffering. R꜖ and, may your mother be our help.

Loving Saviour, while hanging on the cross, you gave your mother Mary to be the mother of John;—let us be known as her children by our way of living. R꜖

Our Father

Concluding Prayer

Lord, place deep in our hearts
the love of Mary, our help.
May we fight vigorously for the faith
   on earth
and praise your victories in heaven.
(We make our prayer) through our Lord.

EVENING PRAYER II

Intercessions

Let us praise God the Father who chose Mary as the mother of his Son and wanted all generations to call her blessed. R꜖ Our Lady Help of Christians, pray for us.

Father, you did great things for the Virgin Mary and brought her, body and soul, to the glory of heaven;—fill the hearts of your children with the hope of Christ's glory. R꜖

Through the prayers of Mary, our help, protect our country, comfort the sorrowful, pardon sinners;—grant peace and salvation to all. R꜖

You favoured Mary with the fulness of grace—bestow on all men your overflowing blessings. R꜖

May your Church be united heart and soul, held fast together by love,—and your faithful joined in continuous prayer, with Mary the mother of Jesus. R꜖

Father, you have exalted the Virgin Mary and crowned her queen of heaven;—may the dead enter your kingdom and rejoice with your saints for ever. R꜖

Our Father

The concluding prayer as at Morning Prayer, above.

I October
SAINT TERESA
OF THE CHILD JESUS
Virgin*

Feast

From the Proper of Saints, p 898, and the Common of Virgins, p 1053.

3 December
SAINT FRANCIS XAVIER
Priest*

Feast

From the Proper of Saints, p 946, and the Common of Pastors, p 1040.

ENGLAND AND WALES

I March
SAINT DAVID, Bishop
Patron of Wales

Feast in England
Solemnity in Wales

Born probably in Cardigan about the year 520, he received his early training from St Illtyd. He attracted many postulants to the monasteries he founded, all of which were remarkable for the austerity of their rule of life. Consecrated bishop, according to his biographer, in Jerusalem, he was recognized as primate of Wales and established his see at Mynyw (Menevia), the monastery of which he was abbot and where he died about the year 588. He is the principal patron of Wales.

From the Common of Pastors, p 1035, except for the following:

MORNING PRAYER

Hymn
O great Saint David, still we hear thee call us,
Unto a life that knows no fear of death;
Yea, down the ages will thy words enthral us,

Strong, happy words: 'Be joyful, keep the faith.'
On Cambria's sons stretch out thy hands in blessing;
For our dear land thy help we now implore.
Lead us to God, with humble hearts confessing
Jesus, Lord and king for evermore.

Christ was the centre rock of all thy teaching,
God's holy will—the splendour of its theme.
His grace informed, his love inflamed thy preaching;
Christ's sway on earth, the substance of thy dream.
On Cambria's sons stretch out thy hands in blessing;
For our dear land thy help we now implore.
Lead us to God, with humble hearts confessing
Jesus, Lord and king for evermore.

Concluding Prayer
Grant, we beseech you, almighty God,
that the loving intercession of blessed David,
your confessor and bishop,
may protect us,
and that while we celebrate his festival
we may also imitate his firmness in defending the
    Catholic faith.
(We make our prayer) through our Lord.

17 March
SAINT PATRICK, Bishop*
Feast in England and Wales

From the Proper of Saints, p 747, and the Common of Pastors, p 1040.
Hymn as on p 1193.

23 April
SAINT GEORGE, Martyr*
Principal Patron of England
Feast in England and Wales

From the Proper of Saints, p 771, and the Common of Martyrs: One
Martyr, Eastertide, p 1029, except:

1184

MORNING PRAYER

Hymn
> Leader now on earth no longer,
> Soldier of th'eternal King,
> Victor in the fight for heaven,
> We thy loving praises sing.
> > Great Saint George, our patron, help us,
> > In the conflict be thou nigh;
> > Help us in that daily battle,
> > Where each one must win or die.
>
> Praise him who in deadly battle
> Never shrank from foeman's sword,
> Proof against all earthly weapon,
> Gave his life for Christ the Lord.
> > Great Saint George, etc.
>
> Who, when earthly war was over,
> Fought, but not for earth's renown;
> Fought, and won a nobler glory,
> Won the martyr's purple crown.
> > Great Saint George, etc.

4 May
THE BEATIFIED MARTYRS OF ENGLAND AND WALES

Feast in England
Optional Memoria in Wales

During the sixteenth and seventeenth centuries innumerable men and women from England and Wales suffered persecution for the ancient faith of their country. Many gave their lives for the supremacy of the Pope, the unity of the Church and the Holy Sacrifice of the Mass. Of these martyrs forty-two have now been canonized. Some one hundred and sixty others have been declared Blessed, and their common celebration is kept on this day.

From the Common of Martyrs: Several Martyrs, Eastertide, p 1017.

Concluding Prayer

O God almighty and everlasting,
you fashioned the blessed Martyrs of England and Wales
 after the likeness of your Son,
who is glorified in his death for the world's salvation:
listen now to their prayers,
and grant us the strength that their love and faith imparts,
so that we may come to the fulness of life.
(We make our prayer) through our Lord.

25 May

SAINT BEDE THE VENERABLE
Priest and Doctor of the Church*

Memoria in England

From the Proper of Saints, p 787, and the Common of Doctors of the Church, p 1049, or of Men Saints: Religious, p 1064.

27 May

SAINT AUGUSTINE OF CANTERBURY*
Apostle of England

Feast in England

From the Proper of Saints, p 790, and the Common of Pastors, p 1040.

20 June

SAINT ALBAN, Martyr

Memoria in England

Saint Alban, the first martyr in Britain, suffered during a persecution late in the third century. He was beheaded at Verulamium (St Albans), probably *c* 287. His cult was already well established by 429, when St Germanus of Auxerre visited Britain. The earliest account of his martyrdom is that of St Gildas, who wrote *c* 540. By the time St Bede wrote his Ecclesiastical History (*c* 731), Saint Alban was commemorated by a church and shrine.

From the Common of Martyrs: One Martyr, p 1029.

Concluding Prayer
Father,
by your grace
Saint Alban gave himself up for his friend
and was the first in this land
to shed his blood for Christ.
May we who celebrate his feast
be helped continually by his prayers.
(We make our prayer) through our Lord.

Also 20 June

SAINTS ALBAN, JULIUS and AARON, Martyrs

Memoria in Wales

Along with Saint Alban, Gildas mentions two other British Christians who were martyred: Julius and Aaron, who were described as citizens of Caerleon (Monmouthshire). They were put to death probably late in the third century. Nothing else is recorded about them.

From the Common of Martyrs: Several Martyrs, p 1017.

22 June

SAINT JOHN FISHER, Bishop and SAINT THOMAS MORE, Martyrs*

Feast in England
Memoria in Wales

From the Proper of Saints, p 803, and the Common of Martyrs: Several Martyrs, p 1017.

26 August

BLESSED DOMINIC OF THE MOTHER OF GOD, Priest

Optional Memoria in England

Dominic Barberi was born of devout farming people near Viterbo in Italy on 22 June, 1792. In 1814 he joined the Congregation of the Passion and became known as Dominic of the Mother of God. He felt a divine call to work especially in England, although it was not until 1841 that he eventually arrived. In the space of eight years he had founded four Passionist houses and exercised an extensive apostolate by preaching missions and retreats throughout the country. His writings and personal zeal brought many to the faith; most prominent among those he received into the Church was John Henry Newman. Broken finally by his labours, he died at Reading on 27 August, 1849, at the age of 57. He was enrolled among the Blessed by Pope Paul VI during the Second Vatican Council, on 23 October, 1963.

From the Common of Pastors, p 1040.

Concluding Prayer
Father,
you chose Dominic as a minister of your love
so that his teaching and example helped many
to find pardon and peace in the unity of your Church.
Grant that we may follow the same way of love
and so gain an eternal reward.
(We make our prayer) through our Lord.

3 September
SAINT GREGORY THE GREAT
Pope and Doctor*
Apostle of the English

Feast in England

From the Proper of Saints, p 870, and the Common of Pastors, p 1040.

24 September
OUR LADY OF RANSOM

Memoria in England

The only feast of our Lady proper to England, it reminds us that we are the Dowry of Mary. Originating in Spain for ransoming Christians enslaved by the Moors, devotion to our Lady of Ransom came to express the desire of Catholics to restore her dowry to Mary. Pope Leo XIII personally encouraged the devotion by making this feast proper to all the dioceses of England and by becoming the first President of the Guild of our Lady of Ransom, founded to foster the reconversion of our country.

From the Common of the Blessed Virgin Mary, p 987.

Concluding Prayer
Lord,
we have long been the dowry of Mary
and subjects of Peter, prince of the apostles.
Let us hold to the Catholic faith
and remain devoted to the blessed Virgin
and obedient to Peter.
(We make our prayer) through our Lord.

13 October
SAINT EDWARD THE CONFESSOR
King

Memoria in England

Saint Edward, known as 'the Confessor', came to the throne of England in 1042. 'Then was seen', says an early biographer, 'how great is the influence of a king who is truly the father of his people.' He was remarkable for his generosity to the poor, and was never happier than when giving alms. He died on 5 January, 1066, just one week after the opening of the Abbey Church of Westminster, which he had refounded and endowed. There his bodily remains were enshrined behind the High Altar on 13 October, 1268.

From the Common of Men Saints, p. 1064.

Concluding Prayer
Lord,
you raised Saint Edward, king and confessor,
to excel in good government and faithful service.
May these ideals survive and flourish among us
through his prayers.
(We make our prayer) through our Lord.

25 October
SAINTS CUTHBERT MAYNE, JOHN HOUGHTON, EDMUND CAMPION, RICHARD GWYNN, and THIRTY-SIX COMPANIONS
Martyrs

Feast in England and Wales

These seven laymen and women, thirteen secular priests and twenty religious suffered during the sixteenth and seventeenth centuries, a turbulent age when the Christian family was tragically torn apart. But although they died in the hatred engendered by religious controversy, many of them surrendered their lives with the greatest willingness for the spiritual welfare of their fellow countrymen. They were canonized by Pope Paul VI on 25 October, 1970, for two reasons: 'They will assist in advancing an ecumenism worthy of the name. They will be a true safeguard of those real values in which the genuine peace and prosperity of human society are rooted.'

From the Common of Martyrs: Several Martyrs, p 1017.

Concluding Prayer
God our Father,
you raised up martyr-saints among our countrymen
from every walk of life.
They vindicated the authority of your Church
in teaching and worship.
Through their prayers
may our whole nation be gathered once again
to celebrate the same sacraments
under one Pastor.
(We make our prayer) through our Lord.

29 December
SAINT THOMAS BECKET
Bishop and Martyr*
Patron of the English Pastoral Clergy

Feast in England

From the Proper of Saints, p 963, and the Common of Pastors, p 1040.
Evening Prayer of the Octave of Christmas, p 69.

IRELAND

Limerick   3 January
SAINT MAINCHIN, Bishop
Principal Patron

Feast

Mainchin, 'the Wise', who lived in the seventh century, is commemorated in the early Irish martyrologies and is venerated as the patron of the diocese of Limerick.

From the Common of Pastors, p 1040.

Limerick   15 January
SAINT ITA, Virgin

Optional Memoria

Ita was by birth of the Munster Deisi. She established her monastery at the place now known by her name, Killeedy, in county Limerick. She died about the year 570.

From the Common of Virgins, p 1053, or of Women Saints: Religious, p 1072.

Ferns, Kilmore   30 January
SAINT AIDAN, Bishop
Principal Patron of the Diocese of Ferns   *Feast*
Optional Memoria in Kilmore

Aidan, born in Breifne, established his chief church at Ferns in Ui

1191

Cennsalaigh, and founded many churches in the area. He died in the year 626.

From the Common of Pastors, p 1040.

All dioceses

1 February
SAINT BRIGID, Virgin
Secondary Patron of Ireland *Feast*
Kildare & Leighlin Principal Patron *Feast*

Brigid, who died about the year 525, founded her monastery at Kildare, and took an active part with Bishop Conleth in preaching the gospel. She became widely venerated in Europe as well as in Ireland, where she has always been honoured as one of the three national patrons.

From the Common of Virgins, p 1053, or of Women Saints: Religious, p 1072.

Concluding Prayer
Lord,
you inspired in Saint Brigid such whole-hearted
  dedication to your work
that she is known as Mary of the Gael;
through her intercession bless our country;
may we follow the example of her life
and be united with her and the Virgin Mary in your presence.
(We make our prayer) through our Lord.

Ardagh
& Clonmacnois

7 February
SAINT MEL, Bishop
Principal Patron of Ardagh *Feast*

Mel was one of Patrick's disciples, and by him placed as bishop over the church of Ardagh, which venerates him as its founder. He died in the year 488.

From the Common of Pastors, p 1040.

Leighlin   17 February
SAINT FINTAN, Abbot
Optional Memoria

Fintan was a native of Leinster. He entered the monastery of Terryglass and later became abbot of Clonenagh, where his austere life drew many disciples. He died in the year 603.

From the Common of Men Saints: Religious, p 1064.

Ossory   5 March
SAINT KIERAN, Bishop
Principal Patron   *Feast*

Kieran's mother was a native of Clear Island, county Cork, and he was born there in the fifth century. He became a bishop in his father's native territory of Ossory, where he is venerated as patron of the diocese.

From the Common of Pastors, p 1040.

Killaloe, Limerick   8 March
SAINT SENAN, Bishop
Optional Memoria

Senan was born in Munster. After many wanderings he settled on Scattery Island in the Shannon estuary, where he was consecrated bishop. He died in the middle of the sixth century.

From the Common of Pastors, p 1040.

All dioceses   17 March
SAINT PATRICK, Bishop*
Principal Patron of Ireland   *Solemnity*

From the Proper of Saints, p 747, and the Common of Pastors, p 1040.

MORNING PRAYER

Hymn
    I bind unto myself today
    The strong name of the Trinity:

By invocation of the same
The Three in One and One in Three.

I bind this day to me for ever,
By power of faith, Christ's incarnation,
His baptism in the Jordan River,
His death on the Cross for my salvation.
His bursting from the spicèd tomb,
His riding up the heavenly way,
His coming at the day of doom
I bind unto myself today!

I bind unto myself today
The power of God to hold and lead:
His eye to watch, his might to stay,
His ear to hearken to my need;
The wisdom of my God to teach,
His hand to guide, his shield to ward;
The Word of God to give me speech,
His heavenly host to be my guard!

Christ be with me, Christ within me,
Christ behind me, Christ before me,
Christ beside me, Christ to win me,
Christ to comfort and restore me,
Christ beneath me, Christ above me,
Christ in quiet, Christ in danger,
Christ in hearts of all that love me,
Christ in mouth of friend and stranger.

I bind unto myself the name,
The strong name of the Trinity:
By invocation of the same,
The Three in One and One in Three;
Of whom all nature hath creation,
Eternal Father, Spirit, Word:
Praise to the Lord of my salvation—
Salvation is of Christ the Lord.

Clogher   24 March
SAINT MACARTAN, Bishop
Principal Patron   *Feast*

Macartan, a native of Ulster, was one of Patrick's disciples, and by him placed as bishop over the church of Clogher. He died in the year 506.

From the Common of Pastors, p 1040.

Armagh   1 April
SAINT CEALLACH (CELSUS)
Bishop
Optional Memoria

When Celsus or Ceallach became bishop in Armagh he initiated a programme of Church reform. He attended the synod of Rathbreasail, where under the presidency of a papal legate the boundaries of the Irish dioceses were defined. He died in the year 1129 and was succeeded by Malachy.

From the Common of Pastors, p 1040.

Leighlin   18 April
SAINT LASERIAN, Bishop
Principal Patron   *Feast*

Laserian, patron of the diocese of Leighlin, was a defender of the Roman Easter usage. After the return of an Irish mission sent to Rome from the synod of Magh Lena, Laserian was present at a further synod of Magh Ailbe, after which the Roman usage began to prevail in Ireland. He died about the year 639.

From the Common of Pastors, p 1040.

Derry   21 April
DEDICATION OF THE
CATHEDRAL
Solemnity in the cathedral   *Feast in the diocese*

From the Common of the Dedication of a Church, pp 967 ff.

Elphin

27 April

SAINT ASICUS, Bishop

Principal Patron   *Feast*

Asicus was a disciple of Patrick, and was by him set as bishop over the church of Elphin. Seven years before his death he retired to live the contemplative life at Rath Cunga in county Donegal, where he was buried.

From the Common of Pastors, p 1040.

Kildare

4 May

SAINT CONLETH, Bishop

Principal Patron   *Feast*

Conleth was persuaded by Brigid to abandon the eremitical life in order to become the first bishop of Kildare. He died in the year 519.

From the Common of Pastors, p 1040.

Down & Connor

10 May

SAINT COMGALL, Abbot   *Memoria*

Comgall was the founder of the great monastery of Bangor, famed for the austerity of its religious observance and for its traditions of learning. Both qualities are exemplified in the best known of its monks, Gall and Columban. Comgall died in the year 603.

From the Common of Men Saints: Religious, p 1064.

Lismore

15 May

SAINT CARTHAGE, Bishop

Principal Patron   *Feast*

Carthage was born in county Kerry and became abbot of the midland monastery of Rathan. After he had been expelled by a local ruler he founded the great monastery of Lismore among the Deisi of county Waterford. Here he died in the year 637.

From the Common of Pastors, p 1040.

Kerry, Clonfert

16 May

SAINT BRENDAN, Abbot

Principal Patron   *Feast*

Brendan, a native of county Kerry, founded many churches in that area.

He travelled widely in Britain, and became renowned for his 'sea-voyag-ings'. In later life he founded the monastery of **Clonfert**, where he died about the year 580.

From the Common of Men Saints: Religious, p 1064.

Ardagh
& Clonmacnois   19 May
# DEDICATION OF THE CATHEDRAL
Solemnity in the cathedral   *Feast in the diocese*

From the Common of the Dedication of a Church, pp 969 ff.

Dublin   4 June
SAINT KEVIN, Abbot
Principal Patron   *Feast*

Kevin was born in Leinster. In search of the contemplative life he retired to the valley of **Glendalough**, where, however, many disciples gathered around him. He died in the year 612.

From the Common of Men Saints: Religious, p 1064.

Tuam   6 June
SAINT JARLATH, Bishop
Principal Patron   *Feast*

He lived in the middle of the sixth century, and was founder and first bishop of the church of **Tuam**.

From the Common of Pastors, p 1040.

Dromore   7 June
SAINT COLMAN, Bishop
Principal Patron   *Feast*

Colman lived at the beginning of the sixth century, and was founder and first bishop of the church of **Dromore**.

From the Common of Pastors, p 1040.

All dioceses   9 June
SAINT COLUMBA (COLUM CILLE)
Abbot
Secondary Patron of Ireland   *Feast*

Derry, Raphoe

Principal Patron   *Feast*

Columba was born of royal blood in Gartan, county Donegal. He founded a number of monasteries, notably Durrow and Derry. In the year 563 he left Ireland for Iona, an island off the Scottish coast, where he spent the remainder of his life and died in 597. With Patrick and Brigid he has always been venerated as a national patron.

From the Common of Men Saints: Religious, p 1064.

Concluding Prayer
Lord,
warm our hearts
with zeal for your kingdom
and a longing for its fulfilment:
make our lives rich in good works
and so bring us to share the glory of Saint Columba,
when we see you face to face
and are one with you always.
(We make our prayer) through our Lord.

Raphoe   14 June
DEDICATION OF THE CATHEDRAL
Solemnity in the cathedral   *Feast in the diocese*

From the Common of the Dedication of a Church, p 967.

Limerick   19 June
DEDICATION OF THE CATHEDRAL
Solemnity in the cathedral   *Feast in the diocese*

From the Common of the Dedication of a Church, p 967.

Cashel & Emly,
Ferns
22 June
DEDICATION OF THE CATHEDRAL

Solemnity in the cathedral   *Feast in the diocese*

From the Common of the Dedication of a Church, p 967.

Elphin
1 July
DEDICATION OF THE CATHEDRAL

Solemnity in the cathedral   *Feast in the diocese*

From the Common of the Dedication of a Church, p 967.

Kilmore
8 July
SAINT KILIAN, Bishop and Martyr
Optional Memoria

Kilian preached the gospel in Franconia, which venerates him as its apostle. With two of his companions he was martyred about the year 689.

From the Common of Martyrs: One Martyr, p 1029, or of Pastors, p 1040.

Armagh, Meath,
Down & Connor
10 July
SAINT OLIVER PLUNKETT, Bishop and Martyr
Memoria

Educated in the Irish College in Rome, after his ordination he was unable to return to Ireland because of the Cromwellian persecution. He remained in Rome for fifteen years, until nominated archbishop of Armagh in 1669. He was arrested during the Popish Plot, condemned on the testimony of perjured witnesses, and executed at Tyburn in 1681. Canonized 1975.

From the Common of Martyrs: One Martyr, p 1029, or of Pastors, p 1040.

Concluding Prayer
O God,
you were pleased to endow your blessed Martyr Bishop Oliver
with a wonderful spirit of courage
in defence of the Catholic faith:
grant that by his prayers and his example
we may follow his firmness in faith
and enjoy his protection in danger.
(We make our prayer) through our Lord.

Armagh   20 July
DEDICATION OF THE
CATHEDRAL

Solemnity in the cathedral   *Feast in the diocese*

From the Common of the Dedication of a Church p 969.

Dromore   21 July
DEDICATION OF THE
CATHEDRAL

Solemnity in the cathedral   *Feast in the diocese*

From the Common of the Dedication of a Church, p 969.

Lismore   24 July
SAINT DECLAN, Bishop

Optional Memoria

A native of the Deisi in county Waterford, he evangelized his native
territory and was consecrated bishop. His principal church was at Ard-
more.

From the Common of Pastors, p 1040.

Achonry   9 August
SAINT NATHY, Bishop

Principal Patron   *Feast*

He lived in the sixth century. He was head of a monastery and evangelized
the surrounding districts.

From the Common of Pastors, p 1040.

Kilmore   9 August
SAINT FELIM, Bishop
Principal Patron   *Feast*

Felim lived probably in the sixth century. His church was at Kilmore.
Pope Clement XII sanctioned his cult as patron of the diocese.

From the Common of Pastors, p 1040.

Achonry   12 August
SAINT ATTRACTA, Virgin
Secondary Patron   *Memoria*

Attracta received the virgin's veil from St Patrick. She was widely famed
for her sanctity and works of charity.

From the Common of Women Saints: Religious, p 1072.

Limerick   12 August
SAINT LELIA, Virgin
Optional Memoria

Lelia lived probably in the sixth century. Her name is preserved in the
church-site of Killeely, now within the city of Limerick.

From the Common of Women Saints: Religious, p 1072.

Killala   12 August
SAINT MUREDACH, Bishop
Principal Patron   *Feast*

Muredach was a disciple of St Patrick, and by him set as bishop over the
church of Killala.

From the Common of Pastors, p 1040.

Cloyne   12 August
DEDICATION OF THE
CATHEDRAL
Solemnity in the cathedral   *Feast in the diocese*

From the Common of the Dedication of a Church, p 967.

Ross
14 August
SAINT FACHANAN, Bishop
Principal Patron   *Feast*

He was founder of the church of Ross and evangelized its neighbourhood.
He died at the end of the sixth century.

From the Common of Pastors, p 1040.

Galway, Kilfenora & Kilmacduagh
15 August
ASSUMPTION OF THE
BLESSED VIRGIN MARY*
Principal Patron of Galway, Dedication of the Cathedral
Solemnity

All as in the Proper of Saints, p 853.

Derry
23 August
SAINT EUGENE, Bishop
Principal Patron   *Feast*

His principal church, at Ardstraw or Ard Sratha, was once the cathedral
church of a diocese, but is now included in the diocese of Derry, which for
many centuries have venerated Eugene as its patron. He died in the year
618.

From the Common of Pastors, p 1040.

Kerry
26 August
DEDICATION OF THE
CATHEDRAL
Solemnity in the cathedral   *Feast in the diocese*

From the Common of the Dedication of a Church, p 967.

Ossory
30 August
SAINT FAICRE, Monk
Optional Memoria

He left Ireland to preach the gospel, and settled at Meaux, where he became renowned for miracles of healing. He died at the end of the seventh century.

From the Common of Men Saints: Religious, p 1064.

Meath   30 August
DEDICATION OF THE CATHEDRAL
Solemnity in the cathedral   *Feast in the diocese*

From the Common of the Dedication of a Church, p 967.

Connor   4 September
SAINT MAC NISSI, Bishop
Principal Patron   *Feast*

Mac Nissi or Macanisius was a disciple of St Patrick and first bishop of the diocese of Connor. He died in the year 514.

From the Common of Pastors, p 1040.

Ardagh & Clonmacnois   9 September
SAINT CIARAN, Abbot
Principal Patron of Clonmacnois   *Feast*

Ciaran was the founder of Clonmacnois, one of the most famous monasteries of Ireland. He died in the year 549.

From the Common of Men Saints: Religious, p 1064.

Cashel & Emly   12 September
SAINT AILBE, Bishop
Principal Patron   *Feast*

Ailbe was bishop of Emly and one of the apostles of the faith in Munster. Emly remained the church of the Munster kings of Cashel until Cashel itself became an ecclesiastical centre and the seat of an archbishopric. The dioceses of Cashel and Emly were united in the year 1718.

From the Common of Pastors, p 1040.

Kilmore   12 September
DEDICATION OF THE
CATHEDRAL
Solemnity in the cathedral   *Feast in the diocese*

From the Common of the Dedication of a Church, p 967.

Clogher   22 September
DEDICATION OF THE
CATHEDRAL
Solemnity in the cathedral   *Feast in the diocese*

From the Common of the Dedication of a Church, p 967.

Raphoe   23 September
SAINT EUNAN (ADOMNAN)
Abbot
Principal Patron   *Feast*

Adomnan, the ninth abbot of Iona, was author of a biography of its
founder, Columba, and several other works. He was also prominent in
civil and ecclesiastical affairs in Ireland. He died in the year 704.

From the Common of Men Saints: Religious, p 1064.

Cork   25 September
SAINT FINBARR, Bishop
Principal Patron   *Feast*

A native of Connacht, he retired to Gougane Barra in county Cork to live
the contemplative life. Later he founded the church of Cork and evangelized
its people. He died at the beginning of the seventh century.

From the Common of Pastors, p 1040, or of Men Saints: Religious,
p 1064.

Ossory   8 October
DEDICATION OF THE
CATHEDRAL

Solemnity in the cathedral   *Feast in the diocese*

From the Common of the Dedication of a Church, p 967.

Ossory,
City of Kilkenny   11 October
SAINT CANICE, Abbot

Ossory: *Optional Memoria*
Principal Patron of Kilkenny City: *Solemnity in City*

A native of Ulster, he was the friend and disciple of St Columba. Later he settled at Aghaboe in the diocese of Ossory. He also founded the church of Kilkenny, which bears his name. He died in the year 600.

From the Common of Men Saints: Religious, p 1064.

Down & Connor   16 October
SAINT GALL, Abbot

Optional Memoria

He was a monk of Bangor and with St Columbanus set out to preach the gospel in France. When Columbanus went to Italy Gall remained in what is now Switzerland, where the town and canton of St Gallen bear his name. He died in the year 624.

From the Common of Men Saints: Religious, p 1064.

All consecrated churches (except cathedrals)
23 October
DEDICATION OF THE
CHURCH

Solemnity

From the Common of the Dedication of a Church, p 967.

Waterford
& Lismore   25 October
# DEDICATION OF THE
# CATHEDRAL

Solemnity in the cathedral   *Feast in the diocese*

From the Common of the Dedication of a Church, p 967.

Cork, Cloyne, Ross   25 October
BLESSED
THADDEUS Mac CARTHY, Bishop
Memoria

He was appointed bishop of Ross, but was expelled from his see. Later he became bishop of the united dioceses of Cork and Cloyne, but met with opposition, in consequence of which he decided to appeal to the Holy See. On his return journey he died at Ivrea in the year 1497, where his cult began immediately after his death.

From the Common of Pastors, p 1040.

Waterford   27 October
SAINT OTTERAN, Monk
Principal Patron   *Feast*

Otteran was one of St Columba's companions and went with him to Iona in the year 563. The island cemetery where he was buried became known as 'the cemetery of Otteran'. Later many Norse kings and nobles were buried there, and when the Norse of Waterford became Christian they chose Otteran as their patron.

From the Common of Men Saints: Religious, p 1064.

Kilmacduagh   29 October
SAINT COLMAN, Bishop
Principal Patron   *Feast*

Colman, 'mac Duach', is patron of the diocese which bears his name, Kilmacduagh. He died about the year 632.

From the Common of Pastors, p 1040.

Armagh,
Down & Connor   3 November
SAINT MALACHY, Bishop
Principal Patron   *Feast*

A native of Armagh, Malachy first became bishop of Connor and later
archbishop of Armagh, from which he led the reform of the Irish church.
Later he retired to the bishopric of Down. He died at Clairvaux in the year
1148 while on a mission to the Pope. He was buried there in front of the
high altar, and five years later St Bernard was buried in the same grave.

From the Common of Pastors, p 1040.

All dioceses   6 November
ALL SAINTS OF IRELAND
                                          Feast

This feast was established by indult of Pope Benedict XV.

*As on the Solemnity of All Saints, 1 November, p 920, except for
the following:*

MORNING PRAYER

Scripture Reading   *Rev 7:14-15*
These are they who have come out of the great tribulation; they
have washed their robes and made them white in the blood of the
Lamb. Therefore are they before the throne of God, and serve him
day and night within his temple; and he who sits upon the throne will
shelter them with his presence.

Short Responsory
R̸ The just will live for ever; they are numbered among the sons
of God. *Repeat* R̸
V̸ Their lot is among the saints. R̸ Glory be. R̸

Benedictus ant: All the saints of heaven praise you; with one voice
all proclaim your glory, blessed Trinity, one God.

Concluding Prayer
Lord,
grant us your grace more abundantly

as we keep the festival of all the saints of our land:
we rejoice to be their countrymen on earth,
may we merit to be their fellow-citizens in heaven.
(We make our prayer) through our Lord.

EVENING PRAYER

Scripture Reading   *Rev 7:16-17*
They shall hunger no more, neither thirst any more; the sun shall
not strike them, nor any scorching heat. For the Lamb in the midst
of the throne will be their shepherd, and he will guide them to
springs of living water; and God will wipe away every tear from their
eyes.

Short Responsory
R/ Come, you blessed of my Father, inherit the Kingdom prepared
for you. *Repeat* R/
V/ Where I am there shall my servants be also. R/ Glory be. R/

Magnificat ant: Great is the reward of the saints with God: they
have died for Christ and so they live for ever.

The concluding prayer as at Morning Prayer, p 1207.

Dublin   14 November
SAINT LAURENCE O'TOOLE
Bishop
Principal Patron   *Feast*

Laurence became a monk at Glendalough and later archbishop of Dublin.
During the troubles of the Norman invasion he worked to ensure the
continued success of the reform movement in the Irish church. In the year
1180 he died at Eu in Normandy while on a mission to King Henry II.

*From the Common of Pastors, p 1040, or of Men Saints: Religious,
p 1064.*

All dioceses   23 November
SAINT COLUMBANUS, Abbot*

Feast

From the Proper of Saints, p 1040, and the Common of Men Saints: Religious, p 1064.

Cloyne   24 November
SAINT COLMAN, Bishop
Principal Patron   *Feast*

Colman was the founder and first bishop of the church of Cloyne. He died in the year 604.

From the Common of Pastors, p 1040.

Ossory   27 November
SAINT FERGAL, Bishop
Optional Memoria

Fergal or Virgil, abbot of Aghaboe, set out to preach the gospel in Europe. He was appointed bishop of Salzburg, where he died in the year 784.

From the Common of Pastors, p 1040.

Kildare & Leighlin   29 November
DEDICATION OF THE CATHEDRAL
Solemnity in the cathedral   *Feast in the diocese*

From the Common of the Dedication of a Church, p 967.

Galway   6 December
SAINT NICHOLAS, Bishop*
Secondary Patron of the Diocese   *Memoria*
Principal Patron of City   *Solemnity in Galway city*

Nicholas of Myra, patron saint of mariners, is venerated as principal patron of the city of Galway.

From the Proper of Saints, p 947, and the Common of Pastors, p 1040.

Meath

12 December
SAINT FINNIAN, Bishop
Principal Patron
Feast

Finnian was famed in his time as 'teacher of the saints of Ireland'. His church was at Clonard in Meath. He died in the year 549.

From the Common of Pastors, p 1040.

Killaloe

18 December
SAINT FLANNAN, Bishop
Principal Patron
Feast

Flannan was of the royal line of Thomond. Famed for his hospitality and his austerity, he died about the year 750.

From the Common of Pastors, p 1040.

Kilfenora

20 December
SAINT FACHANAN, Bishop
Principal Patron
Feast

Bishop Fachanan is venerated on this day as the principal patron of the diocese of Kilfenora.

From the Common of Pastors, p 1040.

SCOTLAND

13 January
SAINT KENTIGERN, Bishop
Memoria

Kentigern, also called Mungo, was a missionary to the Britons in Strathclyde and was consecrated their bishop. Driven out by persecution, he preached in north-west England and in Wales, but eventually returned to Scotland. He died in 603 and was buried in Glasgow.

From the Common of Pastors, p 1040, except:

Concluding Prayer
Lord our God,
you chose Saint Kentigern as bishop
to spread the light of faith
by the preaching of your Word:
grant our prayer
that we who celebrate his memory
may be always true to his teaching
and so grow daily in faith and holiness.
(We make our prayer) through our Lord.

10 March
BLESSED JOHN OGILVIE
Priest and Martyr

Feast

John Ogilvie was born in 1580 at Drum, near Keith. Educated a Calvinist, he was received into the Catholic Church by Father Cornelius a Lapide. He became a Jesuit, was ordained priest in 1613 and landed in Scotland that year. In Edinburgh and Glasgow he reconciled many to the ancient faith, but was betrayed, imprisoned and tortured, and finally hanged in Glasgow in 1615.

From the Common of Martyrs: One Martyr, p 1029, except for the following:

Concluding Prayer
Almighty and eternal God,
you gave to Blessed John
wisdom in defending the Catholic faith
and courage in facing a martyr's death:
listen to our prayers,
and send us an ever greater harvest
of faith, hope and love.
(We make our prayer) through our Lord.

17 March
SAINT PATRICK, Bishop*

Feast

From the Proper of Saints, p 747, and the Common of Pastors, p 1040.
Hymn as on p 1193.

9 June
SAINT COLUMBA, Abbot

Memoria

Columba was born of royal blood in Gartan, county Donegal. In the year 563 he left Ireland for Iona where he founded a monastery from which the faith was preached in the Highlands and Islands of Scotland. He died in 597 and was buried at Iona.

As given in the Proper for Ireland, p 1198.

26 August
SAINT NINIAN, Bishop

Memoria

Ninian was born in Cumbria about the year 360 and was ordained bishop in 394 at Rome, probably by Pope Siricius. He landed at Whithorn in 397 and built a church called 'Candida Casa' (White House). This church was a centre from which he and his disciples preached the gospel in Scotland, south-east of the Highland line. He died about 432 and was buried at Whithorn.

From the Common of Pastors, p 1040.

Concluding Prayer
Lord our God,
you brought the Picts and Britons
to a knowledge of the faith
through the teaching of Saint Ninian, the bishop:
in your goodness listen to our prayers:
grant that we who have received from him
the light of your truth
may remain strong in faith

and active in works of charity.
(We make our prayer) through our Lord.

16 November
SAINT MARGARET OF SCOTLAND*
Secondary Patron   *Feast*

From the Proper of Saints, p 1072, and the Common as there indicated.

30 November
SAINT ANDREW, Apostle*
Principal Patron of Scotland   *Solemnity*

From the Proper of Saints, p 942, except:

Hymn

When Christ our Lord to Andrew cried:
'Come, thou, and follow me,'
The fisher left his net beside
The Sea of Galilee.
To teach the truth his Master taught,
To tread the path he trod
Was all his will, and thus he brought
Unnumbered souls to God.

When Andrew's hour had come, and he
Was doomed like Christ to die,
He kissed his cross exultingly.
And this his loving cry:
'O noble Cross! O precious wood!
I long have yearned for thee;
Uplift me to my only good
Who died on thee for me.'

The faith that Andrew taught once shone
O'er all this kingdom fair;
The cross that Jesus died upon
Was honoured everywhere.

But evil men that faith beat down,
Reviling Andrew's name;
The cross, though set in kingly crown,
Became a sign of shame.

Saint Andrew, now in bliss above,
Thy fervent prayers renew
That Scotland yet again may love
The faith, entire and true;
That I the cross allotted me
May bear with patient love!
'Twill lift me, as it lifted thee,
To reign with Christ above.

The Benedictus

Blessed be the Lord, the God of Israel!*
He has visited his people and redeemed them.

He has raised up for us a mighty saviour*
in the house of David his servant,
as he promised by the lips of holy men,*
those who were his prophets from of old.

A saviour who would free us from our foes,*
from the hands of all who hate us.
So his love for our fathers is fulfilled*
and his holy covenant remembered.

He swore to Abraham our father to grant us,*
that free from fear,
   and saved from the hands of our foes,
we might serve him in holiness and justice*
all the days of our life in his presence.

As for you, little child,*
you shall be called a prophet of God,
   the Most High.
You shall go ahead of the Lord*
to prepare his ways before him,

To make known to his people their salvation*
through forgiveness of all their sins,
the loving-kindness of the heart of our God*
who visits us like the dawn from on high.

He will give light to those in darkness,†
those who dwell in the shadow of death,*
and guide us into the way of peace.